THE COMPLETE
MEXICAN
SOUTH AMERICAN & CARIBBEAN COOKBOOK

THE COMPLETE

MEXICAN

SOUTH AMERICAN & CARIBBEAN COOKBOOK

A vibrant and fascinating guide to ingredients, cooking techniques
and culinary traditions with over 350 delicious step-by-step recipes

JANE MILTON, JENNI FLEETWOOD, AND MARINA FILIPPELLI

METRO BOOKS
NEW YORK

This 2007 edition published by Metro Books,
by arrangement with Anness Publishing Ltd

Publisher: Joanna Lorenz
Editorial Director: Judith Simons
Editors: Jennifer Mussett, Joanne Rippin, Clare Gooden
Photographers: Nicki Dowey, Will Heap, Patrick McLeavey, Simon Smith and Janine Hosegood
Home Economists: Caroline Barty, Fergal Connolly, Joanne Craig, Annabel Ford, Tonia George and Lucy McKelvie
Stylist: Helen Trent
Designer: Nigel Partridge
Cover Design: Jonathan Davison
Additional recipes: Rosamund Grant, Elisabeth Lambert Ortiz, Maggie Mayhew, Kate Whiteman

Metro Books
122 Fifth Avenue
New York, NY 10011

ISBN-13: 978-0-7607-8712-0
ISBN-10: 0-7607-8712-3

10 9 8 7 6 5 4 3 2

Printed and bound in China

NOTES

Standard spoon and cup measures are level.

Large eggs are used unless otherwise stated.

Electric oven temperatures in this book are for conventional ovens. When using a fan oven, the temperature will probably need to be reduced by about 20–40°F. Since ovens vary, you should check with your manufacturer's instruction book for guidance.

Main front cover image shows Cassava Chips – for recipe, see page 84

ACKNOWLEDGMENTS

Jane Milton would like to thank her mother for typing the recipes and her father for proof-reading them. She would also like to thank Tom Estes from Cafe Pacifico for sharing his knowledge of tequila and much more.

Jenni Fleetwood would like to pay tribute to Elisabeth Lambert Ortiz, Elisabeth Luard and Judy Bastyra, experts on the food and drink of Latin America and the Caribbean. She would also like to thank Jane Raphaely, and the 107ers for decades of support.

Marina Filippelli would like to thank her friends and family who were always present with suggestions, advice and a healthy appetite, especially Lizzie and Nick. Special mention also goes to her parents who instilled in her a love for the food and culture of Brazil.

Additional picture material provided by South American Pictures: pages 7–31.

CONTENTS

INTRODUCTION: A BRIEF HISTORY

Latin America and the Caribbean is a vast area comprising a large number of individual countries, each with diverse ways of preparing and serving food. The only thing they have in common is that they have all been subject to a Spanish or Portuguese influence, even if only, as is the case with some Caribbean islands, by way of exposure to their neighbors.

The events that led to the domination of the continent by two European powers began when Christopher Columbus petitioned for support for a voyage of discovery across the Atlantic in search of a sea route to India. At first he was turned down, but King Ferdinand and Queen Isabella of Spain eventually agreed to his request, largely out of a desire to find a new source for the spices the people of southern Spain had learned to love when under the control of the recently expelled Moors.

Columbus set sail on August 3, 1492, and in October of that year he reached Watling Island in the Caribbean. Convinced he had reached the Indies, he continued to Cuba and Hispaniola (now Haiti and the Dominican Republic). In 1500, the Portuguese explorer Pedro Cabral landed on the coast of Brazil,

and two years later Columbus reached the South American mainland. The early explorers were not interested in conquest, but individuals such as Hernán Cortés and Francisco Pizarro were dedicated to it. During the 16th century, they invaded Mexico and Peru respectively, while other parts of Latin America fell to other conquistadors. In the process, great civilizations were overthrown and the stage was set for the total takeover of the continent by Spain and Portugal.

It was Napoleon III, the 19th-century French emperor, who coined the term "Latin America" and applied it to those countries on the American continent where Spanish and Portuguese were spoken, including the Spanish-speaking Caribbean islands and Mexico. The term is now used to include all the islands.

The term "Latin America" suggests that nothing of value existed before the conquest, and it does not acknowledge the indigenous peoples nor the great civilizations—Maya, Aztec, and Inca—they spawned. However, the term has value, if only as shorthand, in giving some indication as to the major cultural and culinary influences in this part of the world in the post-Columbian era.

NEW SETTLERS

When the first conquistadors landed in Latin America, they found many foreign ingredients. The most important of these was corn, which the indigenous peoples called *maïs*. Like wheat, corn could be used to make bread, but it was more versatile. The husks could be used as wrappers; the stalks for training beans; and the silks as ties. The cobs could be eaten fresh or stored for the winter.

Where corn and beans grew, so did squash. This remarkable food also kept well and yielded delicious seeds. Tomatoes were another important find, as were chiles. When Columbus first tasted a dish made using these fiery red and green pods, he assumed its heat came from black pepper and named the pods peppers.

The ships that brought the invaders sailed back to Spain laden with produce, then returned with settlers who brought their own bounty—cattle, pigs, sheep, wheat, sugarcane, and nuts.

Below: The Caribbean islands and Central America have a vast coastline, and fish and shellfish play an enormous part in their cuisines.

Priests came to Latin America too. Their aim was to convert the native population, but they also had valuable horticultural skills to pass on. The South American winemaking industries were started by priests who needed a ready supply of communion wine.

Lands were settled and crops were planted, but such activities required labor. At first the native population gave their assistance, but they soon rebelled. The situation grew worse with the *encomienda* system, which gave Spanish individuals land rights. The indigenous peoples were forced to work for no payment other than Spanish lessons and religious instruction. They were shockingly exploited and the work was hard, especially for those already weakened by disease. They died in their thousands.

SLAVES AND SETTLERS

The colonists responded by importing African slaves to work the burgeoning sugar plantations. The Africans made a huge contribution to the regional cuisines, especially in Brazil. The climate was similar to their homeland, so the many vegetables and fruits they brought with them flourished.

Above: Although the cuisines of Latin America differ from country to country, there are some common ingredients.

Below: Native South American ingredients are sold daily at a busy traditional vegetable market in Peru.

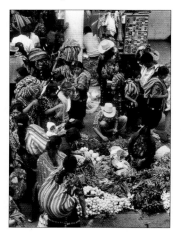

The Spanish and Portuguese settlers intermarried freely with indigenous and African women and, as a result, the *mestizo* ("mixed") population grew.

The food became *mestizo* too. Many of the cooks were either indigenous or African women, and they prepared a mixture of their own recipes plus the dishes their employers wanted. Spanish ingredients—such as onions, garlic, and rice—were incorporated, and Spanish dishes were adapted to include chiles, tomatoes, and even cocoa. This two-way trade led to a vibrant Latino cuisine, bursting with color and flavor.

Other nations made a valuable contribution too. Indentured laborers from India, Southeast Asia, and the Far East have all contributed their own styles of cooking, and some Caribbean islands are, in culinary terms, forever England, France, Denmark, or Holland, depending on their settlers.

Latin America is a turbulent part of the globe where the only certain thing is change; this is as true of the cuisine as anything else. Immigrants continue to introduce new dishes, and tourists take away memories of delicious meals they hope to recreate at home. This time the trade is between Latin America and the world. While pizza becomes commonplace in Brazil, ceviche is enjoyed in Canada, and Californian chefs hanker for *huitlacoche* (corn truffles).

Latin America still has secrets to divulge. In the jungles and hidden Andean valleys, there are undoubtedly new ingredients waiting to be discovered. These will add another layer to a cuisine that is as exciting as it is extraordinary, and keeps on evolving.

MEXICO

Food is a very important aspect of the Mexican way of life. Producing and purchasing the raw materials, preparing food, and eating it account for a large part of each day, and wonderful dishes are created to mark special occasions and celebrations.

SOME HISTORICAL INFLUENCES ON THE MEXICAN DIET

In pre-Columbian Mexico, there was already an established pattern of agriculture. Foods such as corn (maize), beans, chiles, and peppers were widely cultivated, along with avocados, tomatoes, sweet potatoes, guavas, and pineapples. Vegetables such as *jicama, chayote,* and *sapote* were also grown.

During the Mayan era, the priests, who were the ruling class, allocated land for the growing of crops. They also arranged for the storage of seed and the distribution of surplus food. The warlike Aztecs, who came to power in the 15th century, were less inclined to share. Their rulers appropriated food for themselves, including chocolate, which was made into a frothy drink, believed to be an aphrodisiac.

The Aztecs inherited a rich culinary tradition. The central market in Tenochtitlan was famous for its fabulous array of foods, and it is reported that

Montezuma often required of his servants that they prepare more than two dozen dishes daily for his delectation. The emperor would then stroll among the groaning tables, discussing the ingredients with his chefs, before making his selection. During the subsequent meal, young women, chosen for their beauty, would bring him hot tortillas and gold cups filled with frothy chocolate.

COLUMBUS COMES TO MEXICO

When the Spaniards first arrived in Mexico in 1492, they had few cooks with them, and so local people were hired to prepare food. Dishes made with corn, chiles, beans, tomatoes, and chocolate were prepared, and the Spaniards became particularly fond of chiles, chocolate, and vanilla. With the Spanish came livestock, which was warmly welcomed. Until this time, the native turkeys and the occasional wild boar were the only source of meat.

The introduction of the domestic pig was significant not merely for its meat, but also for the lard, which was used for frying and became a staple ingredient in Mexican kitchens. Frying had not been possible before, due to the absence of

Below: A modern mural by Diego Rivera showing pre-Columbian corn sellers.

Above: Corn cultivation in Mexico's pre-Columbian era. Mural by Diego Rivera.

animal fats and oils. The Spaniards began to adapt their own recipes to the local ingredients, and the local people, in turn, adapted their cooking to include meat, which had been such a rarity in the past. The fusion began.

In 1519 the Spanish adventurer Hernando Cortés landed near the site of present day Veracruz. Within three years he had conquered Mexico, and the country was ruled as a viceroyalty of Spain for the next three hundred years. Cortés portrayed himself as the liberator of the tribes oppressed by the Aztecs and used his fanatical missionary zeal to justify his own exploitation of the Mexicans. Monks and nuns were sent from Spain to convert the pagan Mexicans to Catholicism. When they reached the New World, these religious missionaries had more than missals in their luggage; they also brought seeds, and soon citrus fruit, wheat, rice, and onions augmented the supplies that served the Mexican kitchen.

TEXAS IS LOST TO THE U.S.A.

Mexican independence from Spain was finally gained in 1821, after a lengthy war. Three years later, on the death of General Iturbide, a new republic was established. At that time Mexico possessed large tracts of land in what is

Above: Hernando Cortés, the Spanish conqueror of Mexico.

now the United States, including Texas. In 1836, Texas formed an independent republic, joining the U.S.A. some nine years later. This triggered the Mexican Civil War, as a result of which Mexico ceded to the United States all territories north of the Rio Grande. From a culinary perspective, this is significant, as it helps to explain the historic links between Mexico and the "Lone Star" State, and the origin of the Tex-Mex style of cooking. It also accounts for the popularity of the Mexican style of cooking in California and New Mexico.

FRENCH OCCUPATION OF MEXICO

The Civil War proved costly in financial terms, and put the country greatly in debt to France, England, and Spain. When they could no longer repay the debt to France, that country seized the opportunity to take control of Mexico. Austrian-born Maximilian Hapsburg, a relative of Napoleon, was put in charge of the French occupation. The French met with considerable resistance, and the *Cinco de Mayo* (May 5th) holiday commemorates a famous Mexican victory over their forces. However, this success was short-lived, and France installed Maximilian as Emperor of Mexico in 1864. The French occupation lasted only three years, but left a lasting

legacy in the beautiful breads and pastries for which Mexican cooking is now renowned. Following Maximilian's execution in 1867, Mexico experienced another period of unrest, but since 1920 has been more stable.

OTHER INFLUENCES

The Mexican culture is often described as "*mestizo*." The word means "a mixture" and was originally applied only to the offspring of ethnic peoples and Spanish invaders. Today it reflects many culinary influences from beyond its borders, such as the introduction of brewing by German settlers. The Germans also introduced a cheese, now called *queso de Chihuahua* after the town in northern Mexico where the settlers lived. The presence of many sweet-and-sour

Below: Maya Indians in traditional dress perform the dance of the mestizos.

dishes in the Mexican cuisine reflects an Oriental influence, as does the Mexican classification of foods as "hot" or "cold." This has nothing to do with the temperature at which these foods are served, but relates instead to the effect they have on the body. "Hot" foods are considered to be easily digested and warming, whereas foods designated as "cold" are held to be difficult to digest and likely to lower body heat. Examples of hot foods are coffee, honey, and rice, while fish, limes, and boiled eggs would all be regarded as cold. A proper balance between hot and cold foods is believed to be vital for good health.

Mexican cuisine is sure to continue to evolve, adapt, and embrace foreign influences. It is also likely to become more homogenous as regional recipes are absorbed in the national repertoire. Like its language, the food and eating habits of a country are never static.

REGIONAL COOKING IN MEXICO

Mexico has not one single cuisine, but many. It is a vast country, the third largest in Latin America, with a wide diversity of landscapes, from snow-capped mountains to citrus groves, and a distinct range of climatic zones. These geographical factors have helped to shape a variety of different styles of cooking within the same country. The extremely mountainous nature of the landscape led in the days before the Spanish Conquest to the development of a large number of isolated and completely distinct Indian communities, each with its own style of cooking. When the Spanish invaded, they certainly had a considerable impact on the cuisine in the areas where they were most active, but parts of the country remained impervious to their influence, and the people there continued to cook in much the same

Above: Bananas and mangoes on sale in a street market in Chihuahua.

way as their parents and grandparents had done before them.

Even today, when tourism has introduced new ingredients and ideas, there remain pockets of Mexico where contact with the outside world is limited, and where old dishes, some of which hark back to Aztec times, are preserved.

The altitude, rather than the latitude, determines the climate in Mexico. The coastal region below 3000 feet is *tierra caliente*—the hot zone. Here the climate is sub-tropical, and mangoes, pineapples, and avocados flourish. Next comes *tierra templada*, the temperate zone, which rises to 6000 feet.

CULINARY REGIONS

Even in present-day Mexico, regional foods are still very apparent. This is due in some measure to the different climates, which mean certain things cannot grow in every area, or to favorable geographic locations: in Vera Cruz, a coastal area, fish dishes are prevalent. In the coming years, this is likely to be eroded more as improved transportation allows products from the different regions to be transported more easily and quickly between areas.

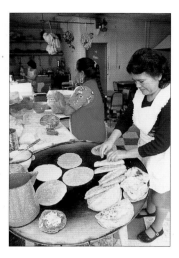

Above: Cooking tortillas in a Mexican street-cafe.

Many familiar vegetables and fruits are grown in Mexico, including green beans, bell peppers, tomatoes, cabbages, cauliflowers, onions, eggplant, and zucchini. At the greatest altitude lies the cold zone (*tierra fria*).

These areas of Mexico are all very different from each other, and when it is considered that the rainfall varies from as little as 2 inches a year in the north-west to over 120 inches in parts of the southwest, it is easy to comprehend how so many diverse styles of cooking came to evolve. Better infrastructure may mean that the regionality of the cuisine will be eroded in time, but at the moment each region has a strong individual identity.

THE NORTH

The northern area of Mexico, stretching from Sonora, near the Gulf of California, to Monterrey in Nuevo León, has some striking contrasts. The mountain areas are sparsely populated, and life here is very tough. Sonora and Chihuahua are the cattle, rearing parts of Mexico. Good grazing encouraged the Spanish to establish herds of their hardy longhorns here, and specialties of the region include a beef stew called *Caldiddo* and the famous dried beef, or *carne seca.* This is produced by first salting the beef, then drying it and finally treating it with lemon juice and pepper.

The ubiquitous beans are as popular in the north as they are elsewhere. A favorite dish of the local *charros* or cowboys is *frijoles* (beans), cooked with scraps of meat, chiles, herbs, and spices over an open fire. So well loved is the dish that it is often served in homes and restaurants.

Monterrey is the industrial heart of the region. Brewing employs a large percentage of the population, and this is the home of *frijoles borrachos,* a dish that consists of beans cooked in beer with onion, spices, and garlic. The flavor of the beer permeates the beans, earning them their name, which translates as "drunken beans."

The north of Mexico is also the main cheese-producing region. Cheese was introduced by monks who traveled with the Spanish conquerors. Chihuahua is known for *chiles con queso*—melted cheese with chile strips.The greatest treasure of the north is the soft flour tortilla, produced here because this is the only part of Mexico where wheat is grown. Burritos, portable parcels of meat, beans, and rice wrapped in wheat flour tortillas, are typical of this region.

Baja California is a peninsula in the northwestern corner of the country, bordering the Pacific and the Gulf of California. It is the oldest continuously producing wine-making region of Mexico. In recent years the region's wines, particularly the whites, have won international acclaim.

THE COASTAL REGIONS

The northern Pacific coast has some magnificent beaches. The sea is well stocked with fish, especially bass, tuna, and swordfish. *Ceviche*, that delicious dish made of raw fish "cooked" by the action of lime juice, is very popular in the region. It is often made from shrimp or other local shellfish.

This area generally has good soil, and grains of various types are widely cultivated, as well as chiles and other vegetables. So famous are the tomatoes produced in this region that the state basketball team is called *Tomateros* (the tomato growers). There are a number of coconut plantations along the coast, and dishes such as coconut soup are popular. Further south is the state of Jalisco, the home of tequila. Red snapper are caught on this part of the coast and cooked over open fires.

Below: Maguey, *growing here in the Oaxaca valley, is used in tequila.*

Above: Strings of chiles drying in the sun on the Pacific coast of Mexico.

Inland is the colonial town of Guadalajara, famous for *pozole,* a pork stew thickened with hominy—yellow or white corn which has been dried and has had the husk and germ removed, and which has been eaten by the Indians in Mexico for centuries. Another specialty is *birria,* a stew made from lamb or kid.

Down the coast is Acapulco, a very cosmopolitan city with Latin, Asian, and indigenous Indian influences. The cuisine of this area—Oaxaca—has strong Spanish influences, but is also home to some of the most traditional Mexican dishes, such as the *moles*— gloriously rich meat stews that incorporate nuts and chocolate. This is orange country, too, and citrus fruit features strongly in the recipes of the region. *Asadero,* a supple cheese similar to the Italian cheese *Provolone,* originated in Oaxaca.

Chiapas, the southernmost state bordering Guatemala, exhibits some influences from that country. Chiles are commonly served alongside dishes, as accompaniments, rather than as integral ingredients.

The eastern seaboard, lapped by the Caribbean Sea, is known as the Gulf Coast. The climate here is tropical, and this is reflected in the food. Bananas, vanilla, avocados, coffee, and coconuts grow on the coast, mangoes and pineapples in the south, and to the north are orchards of apples and pears.

The Gulf Coast has abundant fish stocks. The southern state of Tabasco, on the isthmus of Tehuantepec, is

Below: A palm tree in Chetumal with coconuts ready for harvesting.

Above: Prickly pear cactus growing at Santa Bulalia.

particularly famous for its fish. The catch includes sea bass, striped bass, crabs, lobsters, and shrimp. The port of Veracruz has a famous fish market, with red snapper the local specialty. The cuisine in this area is rich, and many of the towns have lent their names to dishes or ingredients.

In this part of Mexico, *tamales* (little filled parcels) are rolled in banana leaves, rather than the corn husks that are used elsewhere. Another local specialty is *jicama,* a crisp vegetable, which is served raw with a sprinkling of lime juice and ground chiles.

THE BAJIO, CENTRAL MEXICO, AND MEXICO CITY

To the north of Mexico City is the Bajio, a fertile area bordered by mountains. This is sometimes referred to as Colonial Mexico, and many of the local specialties are distinctly Spanish in origin, such as stuffed tongue and rich beef stews. Traditional Mexican foods are to be found here too, especially *nopales* (cactus paddles) and prickly pears (cactus fruit). *Pulque*—the drink made from the juice of the agave (or century) plant—is popular in this area. Pork is the favorite meat, often served as *Carnitas.* These are pieces of pork that are cooked in lard flavored with orange, until the outside of each piece is crisp, while the inside is beautifully tender and succulent.

Central Mexico, a land-locked area, lies to the south of Mexico City, and includes the towns of Puebla and Tlaxcala. Puebla is the home of the classic dish, *Chiles en Nogada,* which consists of stuffed chiles dipped in batter, then fried and served with a walnut sauce. Puebla is also associated with the famous *Mole Poblano*, which was said to have been invented by nuns in a local convent. *Mole Poblano* is a wonderfully complex dish in which turkey or chicken is cooked in a paste made by mixing crushed dried chiles, cinnamon, and cloves, with sesame seeds and ground nuts, as well as onion, garlic, and sometimes tomatillos.

Tlaxcala, which means "the place of many tortillas," is a town renowned for its food. Chicken stuffed with fruit and nuts is one popular dish, while another consists of lamb cooked in agave leaves. Both are usually washed down with the local *pulque*.

Vast, sprawling and vibrant, Mexico City is one of the most cosmopolitan places on earth, a fact that is reflected in its food. It is often said that Mexicans love to eat and would eat all day if they could, and in Mexico City there is nothing to stop them. The streets are filled with vendors selling all sorts of snacks. Some offer tortas and tortillas filled with various meats (including the chorizo for which nearby Toluca is famous), cheeses, beans, and chiles. Others sell *tamales, sopes,* and tacos to the commuters who rush past on their way to work. Another item available on

Above: Dried chiles and other fruit for sale on the streets of Mexico City.

Below: Thick tortillas are served here with cooked meats, chiles, and beans.

market stalls is *cuitlacoche*, a corn fungus that tastes like a flavorful mushroom. This has been regarded as a delicacy since pre-Columban times. *Cuitlacoche* is cooked and used to fill *crepas* (crêpes), which the Mexicans adopted into their cuisine after the French occupation in the 19th century.

THE SOUTH

Although there are differences between all the regions of Mexico, it is in the Yucatán that these are most marked. This is partly due to the isolation of the area, which was for centuries cut off from the rest of the country by dense

rainforest and swampland. The Maya lived here before the conquistadors came to Mexico, and their influence on the cooking can still be seen, particularly in *pibil*-style dishes, which got their name from the *pib* or pit in which they were steamed in Mayan times.

Although the poor soil does not readily support agriculture, corn is grown in areas where the vegetation has been cut and burned, and is ground to make meal, *masa harina*, which is used for corn tortillas and a host of other Mexican dishes. The pungent herb *epazote* is used in the cooking of this region, imparting a distinctive flavor.

Good fish, squid, and shellfish, including the large shrimp for which the area is well known, are available all along the coast. *Ceviche* is a popular dish, and is made from several different types of fish and shellfish, either singly or in combination.

Huevos Motuleños, comprised of eggs with refried beans and tomato sauce, is a well known Yucatec dish. Also typical of the area are dry spice pastes, called *recados*. These are mixtures of dried spices and vinegar or citrus juice, which are rubbed onto meat before it is cooked. *Recados* are made throughout the country, but they are particularly popular in the Yucatán. Some include ground achiote seed (annatto powder), which is valued for the earthy flavor and bright yellow color it imparts. Another hallmark of Yucatec cooking is the habañero, a fiery chile that is grown exclusively in the region.

Below: A field of corn on the cob drying on the plants.

MEXICAN MEAL PATTERNS

Many of the traditional Mexican dishes are very labor-intensive, reflecting the old society where the women worked all day long collecting the food required and then preparing it. Today, despite industrialization, the traditional meal patterns are still observed, especially in rural areas. Most Mexicans still eat their main meal in the middle of the day, and follow it by a siesta. Even in the cities, where meals are beginning to conform to the international pattern of breakfast, lunch, and dinner, the biggest meal of the day is still eaten at lunchtime.

DESAYUNO

This is a light meal eaten first thing in the morning, soon after waking. It usually consists of a cup of coffee and a bread or pastry—perhaps *churros* or *pan dulce* (sweetened bread).

ALMUERZO

Having started work very early in the morning, most Mexicans are ready for something fairly substantial by about 11 AM. Almuerzo is more brunch than

Above: Prickly chayote, *used in Mexican salads and vegetable dishes.*

Below: Green chiles for sale in a Mexican market.

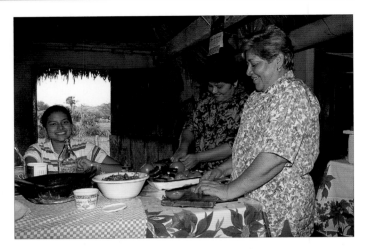

breakfast, and usually includes an egg dish such as *Huevos Rancheros* or scrambled eggs with salsa and cheese. Tortillas are served, and coffee, milk, or fruit juice washes everything down.

COMIDA

This is the main meal of the day, generally eaten at a leisurely pace from about 3 PM. The meal is made up of several courses. Soup is almost always served, and this is followed by a rice or pasta dish. The aptly named *platillo fuerte*—the phrase means "heavy dish"—is the main attraction. This dish is accompanied by tortillas, salad, and pot beans or refried beans. The clay pot used to cook the pot beans—*Frijoles de Olla*—adds flavor to them. Garlic, cilantro, onion, and stock with chiles are additional ingredients, and cream or cheese is stirred in just before serving. The meal closes with *postre* (dessert) and an after-dinner coffee.

MERIENDA

A light supper, this is often made up from the leftovers of the lunchtime *comida* dishes, which are wrapped in a tortilla to make a burrito. If a more substantial meal is required, a stew or *mole* might be served, with *Cafe con Leche* or hot chocolate to follow the food. *Merienda* is usually eaten between 8 and 9 PM.

Above: Women prepare the main family meal in a rural Mexican kitchen.

CENA

This more elaborate meal—dinner—is served when entertaining guests in the evening or on special occasions. It replaces the *merienda* and is made up of two or three courses served any time between 8 PM and midnight.

THE MAIN EVENT

Comida—the main meal of the day—provides the perfect opportunity for relaxing with family or friends. Here are some suggestions of suitable dishes to serve at this time:

SOPA

A hearty soup would not be appropriate, as this is the prelude to a large meal. *Thalpeno*, a thin soup with chicken and avocado, would be ideal, as would a cold coconut soup.

SOPA SECA

Translating as "dry soup," this is actually a rice or pasta dish, served after the conventional soup and before the main course. Rice or vermicelli is cooked in a little oil and then simmered in a broth with onions, garlic, tomatoes, and other vegetables. Most of the liquid used is absorbed by the rice or pasta, hence the name. The rice dishes vary—peas are sometimes added to the basic recipe, and cilantro and chiles are used to make the popular "Green Rice." In another variation, yellow rice is flavored and colored with achiote (annatto), a golden coloring made from the ground seeds of a flowering tree.

PESCADO Y LEGUMBRES

Sometimes a fish course is served before the main dish. Typically this would be *Ceviche*—raw fish "cooked" by the action of lime juice. Alternatively, a vegetable dish might be offered; perhaps a native vegetable such as *jicama*, served as a salad with a chili and lime dressing. Plantains are also popular, and either these or zucchini might be fried along with cheese and green chiles.

PLATILLO FUERTE

The "heavy dish" is typically a stew, served with corn tortillas and a salad. Meatballs in a tomato and chili sauce is one option; pork with green cactus sauce another. A fisherman's stew of mussels, scallops, shrimp, and cod would also be suitable. For the accompaniment, a cactus or *chayote* salad would be ideal, or a fresh-tasting salsa of *rajas con limon*—strips of chile and lime.

Above: A family eating their main meal in an open-air restaurant in Mexico City.

FRIJOLES

Cooked dried beans are an inevitable—and important—part of the main meal. Traditionally, they formed a very big part of the staple diet of the indigenous people, so the number and variety of bean dishes is exhaustive. Most people, if asked to name a Mexican bean dish, suggest Refried Beans, which is all too often a flavorless mush of badly seasoned pinto beans. The home-cooked equivalent couldn't be more different: tender beans deliciously flavored with bay leaves, garlic, and chiles. Equally delicious are pot beans, *Frijoles de Olla*—dry pinto beans put into a pot and cooked very slowly with water and a little lard until they are tender. These are traditionally served with Guacamole, salsa, sour cream, and crumbled cheese.

POSTRE Y CAFE

After such a heavy meal, the dessert often consists of a fruit platter or a simple, refreshing *Flan*—similar to a crème caramel. A cake made from ground pecans and honey is another favorite. *Comida* traditionally concludes with a drink of coarsely ground coffee sweetened with *piloncillo* (the unrefined

dark brown cane sugar typical of Mexico) and stirred with a cinnamon stick. A delicious alternative, which packs more punch, is coffee with a shot of Kahlúa or tequila.

SNACK FOODS

Mexicans love to snack. Street food is very popular throughout the country. In towns, stalls equipped with steamers sell *tamales*—little corn husk parcels filled with spiced meat or cheese—from first thing in the morning, so that shift workers can still have their *almuerzo* even if they cannot get home. Later in the day, the stalls sell corn soup or *menudo*, a soup made with tripe. Still more stalls are set up at lunchtime by women who serve homemade food to the workforce. The food is very similar to what would be eaten at home: soup, rice, or pasta dishes, stews with tortillas or bread, and desserts. In the evening, the stalls sell *quesadillas*, enchiladas, and *antojitos* ("little whims"). On the coast, traders sell shrimp on skewers, *Ceviche* (marinated raw fish) threaded on sticks, or *elotes*—tender ears of cooked corn dipped in cream and sprinkled generously with well-flavored crumbly cheese.

Below: Corn on the cob is cooked and sold as a snack at street stalls.

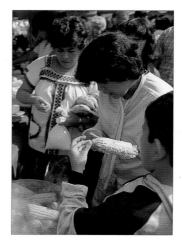

MEXICAN FEASTS AND FESTIVALS

Long before Christianity came to Mexico, the indigenous peoples worshipped gods whom they believed provided their food. The Aztecs were convinced that the world would come to an end unless the gods were constantly propitiated with prayers, sacrifices, and rituals. Corn was regarded as a divine gift—a miraculous staple food which grew in all climates and soils.

Feast days, when people cooked particular dishes or brought specific foods as offerings to the gods, were frequent events. When Christianity spread through Mexico, many of these days were appropriated by the Church and either assigned as saints' days or linked to celebrations marking important days in the religious calendar.

JANUARY 6TH – *DÍA DE LOS SANTOS REYES*

As the culmination of two weeks of Christmas festivities, January 6th marks the meeting between the Magi—the Three Kings—and the infant Jesus. Mexicans commemorate that exchange of gifts with ceremonies of their own, and this is the day on which Christmas presents are given and received. Central to the celebration is King's Day Bread, a yeasted sweet bread ring filled with crystallized fruit, covered with icing and decorated with candied fruit jewels.

Right: Mayas in traditional dress perform a bottle dance.

Below: A Mexican dancer wearing a Spanish-influenced traditional dress.

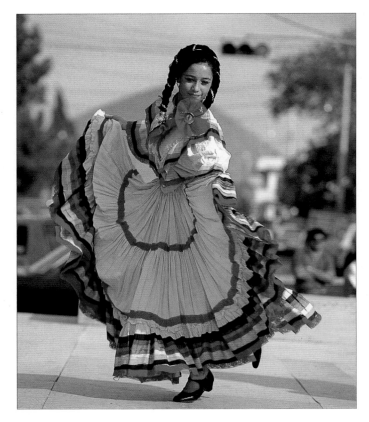

FEBRUARY – CARNIVAL

The weekend before the beginning of Lent sees the beginning of a five-day carnival, a final fling before the period of self-denial. Processions of brightly colored floats, dancing in the street, and feasting are all characteristic of this celebration.

APRIL – *SEMANA SANTA*

Holy week—the period leading up to Easter Day—is an important time in the Mexican calendar, particularly for the many Catholics in the country. One custom peculiar to Mexico is the breaking of confetti-filled eggs over the heads of friends and family.

MAY 5TH – *CINCO DE MAYO*

This day commemorates the defeat of the French army at the Battle of Puebla in 1862. After the defeat Napoleon sent 30,000 soldiers into the country, and after a year the French had taken power. *Cinco de Mayo* is of particular importance in the state of Puebla, but is celebrated in other parts of the country, and in some American states with large Mexican populations, such as southern central California and Texas. Nowadays the holiday is a celebration of Mexican culture, drink, and music.

Above: Sugar skulls on sale for the celebration of one of Mexico's most important festivals, The Day of the Dead.

SEPTEMBER 16TH – MEXICAN INDEPENDENCE DAY

A holiday to mark the day in 1810 when the revolt against Spanish rule began. Outside Mexico, the festival is often promoted by commercial outlets, such as Mexican restaurants and bars.

NOVEMBER 1 & 2 – *LOS DÍAS DE LOS MUERTES*

Commonly called The Day of the Dead, this is in fact a two-day festival that combines in one both the ancient Aztec tradition of worship of the dead and the Christian festival of All Saints' Day.

The festival originally came about because of a widely held belief that the souls of the dead are permitted to spend a brief period on earth every year—like a vacation—to give their families a chance to spend time with them. Family members gather at the graveside, bringing the favorite foods of the deceased person, as well as other symbolic dishes that are traditionally eaten on this day. The foods include a sweet pumpkin dessert and *tamales*. At the grave candles are lit, incense is burned, special prayers are said, and the food and drink are eaten in a party atmosphere. Although the festival commemorates the dead, it is seen by everyone as a joyous occasion. The Mexican attitude is that life is to be lived to the full, and death is simply a part of the cycle.

DECEMBER 25TH – *NAVIDAD*

For 12 days before Christmas Day, the festival is heralded by processions—called "*posadas*"—depicting Joseph, with Mary on the donkey, searching for a room at an inn. Christmas Day sees

Below: A shop window advertises "bread of the dead" for the festival.

the start of a two-week family holiday for most Mexicans. On the afternoon of the day itself, families share a special meal. This traditionally starts with the sharing of the *rosca*—a sweet ring-shaped loaf with a small ceramic doll representing the infant Jesus baked inside it. Whoever finds the doll in their slice of cake must host a party on February 2nd, *Día de Candelaria* (Candlemas). The high point of the Christmas feast is the main course, when *Mole Poblano*, a rich turkey dish made with chiles, nuts, tomatoes, garlic, cinnamon, and chocolate is served. It is accompanied by *tamales blancos*—corn husk parcels filled with a flavored mixture that is based on white cornmeal.

MEXICAN WEDDINGS

These almost always take place in church. It is traditional for the bride and groom to be united during the ceremony with a *lazo*—a large rosary that is wrapped around them both. Gold or silver coins, a Bible, and a rosary are given to the couple during the service by the "*padrinos*," a man and woman especially chosen by the bride and groom for this task. The coins symbolize prosperity. Mexican wedding cookies are served at the subsequent feast. Made from almonds and butter, baked and then sprinkled with confectioners' sugar, these have a shortbread-like texture.

THE CARIBBEAN

A culinary cruise around the Caribbean is richly rewarding, enjoying the ubiquitous fresh fish. Having feasted your eyes on sparkling turquoise seas, palm-fringed beaches, green velvet mountains, and exquisite gardens, you can dine on dishes that are as diverse as the islands themselves. These islands offer some of the best seafood in the world, plus fragrant stews, spicy side dishes, unusual salads, and sweet treats such as coconut ice cream and luxurious Caribbean fruit and rum cake.

EARLY HISTORY

The earliest inhabitants of the Caribbean islands were the Ciboney, hunter-gatherers who had themselves migrated from northern South America. They were supplanted by the Taino, Arawak-speaking fishermen and farmers, who in turn were harried by the warlike

Below: The Caribbean islands are very beautiful, lush, and fertile.

Caribs in a pattern that would be repeated again and again down the centuries as nation after nation fought for control of the islands.

The Taino were peace-loving people who lived in small communities and grew cassava, corn, squash, bell peppers, beans, sweet potatoes, and yams—crops that remain the mainstay of the Latin American diet. Those who lived on the coast caught fish, which they often ate raw, and their diet was supplemented with ducks, turtles, snakes, and small rodents.

The arrival of Christopher Columbus in 1492 spelled the beginning of the end for the Taino. Many of them succumbed to diseases, such as measles and smallpox, never before seen on the islands. Others died in the service of Spanish settlers who worked them cruelly on the land and digging for gold. The Caribs fared a little better. Most of them were now confined to the more eastern islands, and their fierce

reputation and remote location acted as a deterrent to would-be settlers. However, by the end of the 16th century, only a handful of the former inhabitants of the islands remained.

In their place came Spanish, English, French, and Dutch settlers, the latter occupying the islands that Christopher Columbus had overlooked: Aruba, Curaçao, and Bonaire. These islands, which would eventually become part of the Dutch Antilles, were "discovered" in 1499 by Alonso de Ojeda, one of Amerigo Vespucci's henchmen, and settled first by the Spanish, and then by Dutch traders in the first half of the 17th century. The British and French, meanwhile, were becoming solidly entrenched in the Caribbean. Having already taken St Christopher (St Kitts) in 1623, the British quickly set up colonies on the islands of Nevis, Barbados, Antigua, and Montserrat, while the French settled in Guadeloupe, Martinique, and St Lucia.

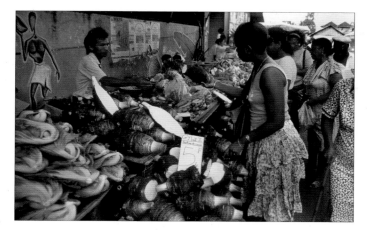

Above: *A local woman inspects the produce at a Caribbean street market.*

SPANISH POSSESSIONS

The Spanish continued to dominate the most strategically important islands of Cuba, Jamaica, Puerto Rico, and Hispaniola (modern-day Haiti and the Dominican Republic).

During the next 200 years, the islands of the Caribbean became pawns in the hands of the European powers. They sometimes changed hands so frequently that would-be settlers set sail from home in the belief that they would be ruled by their compatriots, only to discover on reaching their destination that it was now under the control of someone else. The island of St Martin, for instance, was tossed between Holland, Great Britain, and France more than a dozen times, the shortest period of occupation being just 10 days. The island is still half Dutch and half French, which explains why it is today known by two separate names: Sint Maarten and Saint Martin.

Today most of the islands have achieved autonomy from their European conquerors and have banded together to form Caricom, the Caribbean Community and Common Market.

Creole cooking

This term is used to describe many traditional Caribbean recipes. It generally refers to dishes that have their roots in both Europe and Africa, and is also used in Louisiana and some other southern states of the U.S.A. There, Creole cooking has French, Spanish, and African influences, whereas in the Caribbean, the Spanish and African influences are dominant. The expression *cocina criolla* is loosely applied throughout Latin America as a catch-all term for the native cuisine.

FOOD AND DRINK

The turmoil of the early years meant that recipes tended to do the rounds. The Spanish dish *pescado en escabeche* became known as eschovished fish, caveached fish, or *escovitch. Callaloo*, a soup made from the leaves of a plant similar to spinach, is another successful migrant, being known variously as *le calalou, callilu, callau,* and *calaloo.*

The French brought *bouillabaisse* to the islands, even though the fish used in the Caribbean version are very different from those found off the coast of Brittany. On Dominica and Montserrat, they found frogs so large that their local name—mountain chicken—does not seem inappropriate. These French settlers wasted no time in teaching local cooks how to prepare frog's legs.

The Danes contributed recipes such as herring gundy, a dish of salt herring with potatoes, peppers, and onion, and *croustadas*, which resemble savory waffles. From the Dutch came *erwensoep*—a hearty pea soup—and the utterly delicious stew cooked within a whole cheese, *keshy yena.*

Made from fermented sugarcane, some of the world's best rums are still produced in the Caribbean, and rum cocktails are always a popular choice.

Below: *Hard-working Caribbean fishermen bring the daily catch ashore, ready to be sold at market.*

Above: Sugarcane is a major export for the region; the annual harvest in Cuba is exhausting but rewarding work.

NEW CROPS

It is widely believed that Columbus planted the first sugarcane on the Caribbean islands. By the start of the 17th century, the crop's huge potential was being fully appreciated, and large sugarcane plantations had been established, together with plantations of other crops new to the islands, such as bananas, plantains, coffee, coconuts, and oranges.

Growing all of these new crops required a large amount of labor, and since the indigenous population had been largely wiped out, this led to the importation of slaves on a massive scale. They arrived in their thousands, enduring dreadful journeys by sea and harsh lives after reaching their destination. The slaves often had to subsist on dried fish or meat alone, since they were forbidden from raising cattle and denied the opportunity to catch fresh fish. The many traditional Caribbean dishes based on salt cod, such as Jamaican salt fish and ackee, originated during this period.

The slaves, who came mainly from West Africa, introduced ingredients such as yams and okra, which were quickly incorporated into the Caribbean cuisine. They improved their bland diet even further by the imaginative use of spices, laying the foundation for the hot pepper sauces that would become synonymous with the islands in years to come.

When slavery was eventually abolished in the 1830s, indentured laborers from the Middle East, India, and the Far East were brought to the islands; these laborers introduced yet more ingredients to the melange that is Caribbean cooking. Spicy curries and dishes such as lamb pelau entered the repertoire, along with *roti* and *dhal puri*, large flat breads filled with curried meat, fish, or potatoes.

Today it is mainly tourism that drives the economy of the Caribbean islands. Although this has had some negative effects on the local cuisine, mainly due to the introduction of the "international menu" that some travelers demand, it has also stimulated interest in regional specialities. The more dynamic Caribbean chefs are reveling in the wonderful ingredients that are at their disposal, especially the superb seafood on offer all year round. New and exciting dishes continue to emerge alongside old favorites.

STREET FOOD AND SNACKS

Snacking is a popular pastime on the Caribbean islands, which goes some way toward explaining the abundance of food available from roadside stalls and bars, or beach vendors. In fact, street food accounts for 20–30 percent of urban household expenditure on the islands. Whatever the time of day, wherever you are, tasty morsels can be found to satisfy your hunger pangs.

Among the items traditionally offered by street vendors are deliciously light fritters, made from conch, salt cod, or perhaps split peas, with scallions or chiles for extra flavor. Barbecued jerk chicken is another favorite, and for easy eating and instant gratification you cannot beat a bowl of crispy plantain and sweet potato chips or lightly cooked coconut jumbo shrimp, served with a glass of ice cold beer or one of the rum cocktails for which the islands are famous.

The quintessential Caribbean fast food, enjoyed by locals and tourists alike, is *roti*, a large flat bread with a tasty curried filling such as conch, goat, or a selection of vegetables. Plantain dumplings are also a popular choice.

Below: In Havana, Cuba, a street vendor prepares sausages, delicious stuffed pastries, and fried potatoes.

Above: The "Day of Kings" festival, which celebrates African gods, is a time for partying on the streets of Cuba.

FEASTS AND FESTIVALS

Carnival is the highlight of the year on the Caribbean islands. The build-up begins with the calypso season, which starts in January, then as Ash Wednesday approaches, signaling a period of sobriety and self-control, the streets ring to the sound of steel bands. In Aruba and Trinidad and Tobago, Carnival is a particularly extravagant affair. Local festivals are also held throughout the year. Puerto Rico commemorates the island's African-American heritage every June, and Jamaica has a popular reggae festival in July. Saints' days are always a good excuse for a celebration too, and they inevitably offer the opportunity to sample local food.

Special occasions are often marked by the roasting of a suckling pig. Slow roasting and regular basting ensures that the meat is beautifully tender, but the best part for many diners is the stuffing. This varies from island to island and from cook to cook, often being made to a recipe that is a closely guarded secret. It may be hot and spicy, fresh and fruity, or made from offal, with the heart, liver, and kidneys of the pig mixed with sausage, onions, and herbs. Rum or brandy is often added to give an extra kick.

No festival would be complete without food, and traditional Caribbean festival fare, available from street vendors, includes fish cakes, Jamaican saltfish fritters ("stamp and go"), and rice and peas. More adventurous regional delicacies include *griot* (hot Haitian fried pork), jerked chicken, and curried goat. Street-side food vendors can often be seen serving up more exotic foods, including fresh catfish and red snapper, Thai noodles, or Mexican empanadas. In addition, hot dogs, candy, fresh fruit smoothies, soft drinks, ice-cold beer, and rum cocktails are always popular.

The rum tradition
Not much goes on in the Caribbean that doesn't involve rum. It was developed in the 16th century by colonists who distilled molasses to trade for slaves in Africa. From here it was sent north to European markets, where a Spanish wine merchant, Facundo Bacardi, developed a process of charcoal filtering, to make rum taste better. Bacardi is now the leading brand of white rum and the best-selling spirit worldwide. Aged rum is darker, taking on the color of the barrel in which it ages. It has a mellower taste that makes it perfect for sipping. Not all dark rums are aged, however—some have color and flavor additives. There are dozens of rum cocktails available throughout the Caribbean. Three favorites are the daiquiri, the mojito, and the pina colada.

BRAZIL

Whether it is because it is the largest country in South America or because of its rich cultural and racial diversity, Brazil is a place that celebrates excess. The Brazilian people love to eat, love to drink, and love to dance. A trip to this, the only Portuguese-speaking country in South America, is a glorious assault on of the senses, and never more so than during Carnival, when the streets throb with the sounds of samba music and the vibrant colors of the costumes fizz like the fireworks that explode overhead. The food is just as exciting. Sample delicious seafood in Rio de Janeiro, unusual pork dishes in Minas Gerais, tender beef in Rio Grande, or the spicy

Below: The Amazon river and rainforest cover much of Brazil and are home to many unusual species and crops.

specialities of Bahia, where Africa meets South America in an explosion of unusual and fiery spices.

EARLY HISTORY

Some 50,000 years ago primitive peoples crossed from Asia to America by way of the Bering Strait land bridge and began the long trek south. Nobody knows for certain quite when they reached South America, but hunter-gatherers were certainly enjoying the fruits of the Amazon basin by 8000BC. Fish, manatees, turtles, game animals, and birds were plentiful, and they supplemented their diet with cassava (*manioc*), nuts, and fruits that grew in the area. Some migrated to the coast and survived mainly on shellfish, as is evident from the huge shell mounds that they left behind.

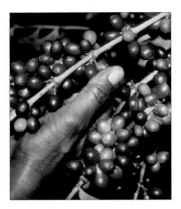

Above: Coffee berries are picked by hand when ripe, then exported around the globe in huge quantities.

Brazil did not have the great civilizations that evolved in Central America and the west of the continent. Instead, as the indigenous people abandoned their nomadic lifestyle for farming, settled communities or chiefdoms were established. As well as cassava, they grow corn, sweet potatoes, and squash, often on the shell mounds left by their predecessors. The existence of these early settlers was not as peaceful as it sounds, however. At least one of the tribes, the Tupinambá, were cannibals who not only ate their enemies, but fattened them up first.

PEDRO CABRAL

In 1500, the Portuguese explorer, Pedro Cabral, claimed Brazil for Portugal, but he only stayed long enough to erect a cross, say a few prayers, and take on board his ship some unusual wood that yielded a red dye—*pao Brasil*. His compatriots at home were not very excited about this new territory, but Portuguese merchants considered that the wood might be worth exploiting, and a few expeditions were mounted to cut down the trees. Trading stations were gradually set up along the coast to the north and south of Salvador de Bahia, and the country came to be known by the same name as the wood, Brazil.

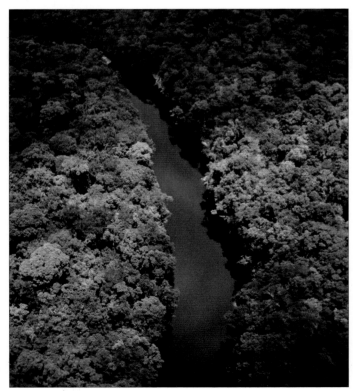

In the beginning, these Portuguese settlers and the indigenous peoples co-existed amicably enough, but when what had been a minor timber operation began to escalate into a mass export operation, the natives began to withdraw their labor. They were even less enthusiastic about working on the many sugar plantations that had been established from the middle of the 16th century onward. The Portuguese settlers tried to force the native South Americans by enslaving them, but so many died from exhaustion or disease that the plantation owners began to import African slaves instead.

SUGAR AND THE SLAVE TRADE

By the time slavery was finally abolished in Brazil toward the end of the 19th century, around four million African slaves had made the terrible journey from their native land to Brazil. Many did not even survive the long crossing, and many others died shortly after their arrival on the plantations (*engenhos*) where sugar was grown and processed.

A few successfully escaped to form their own secret communities, known as *quilombos*, while others survived their bondage by focusing on keeping alive their music, culture, and religion, and cooking food similar to that which they enjoyed at home. It was the Africans who originally introduced ingredients such as black-eyed peas, okra, and yams to Latin America, and these

thrived in a climate that was quite similar to that of West Africa. Food was used for purposes of ritual as well as sustenance, and some of the recipes cooked throughout Brazil today evolved from the foods prepared by African priestesses to offer to their gods.

GOLD RUSH

In the late 17th century, Brazilian explorers, known as *bandeirantes*, began to find gold in the mountain streams to the north of Rio de Janeiro. The ensuing gold rush led to a boom time in Brazil. Despite the relative inaccessibility of the main goldfields, new towns quickly began to spring up in the area that would later come to be known as Minas Gerais (which translates as "general mines").

Prospectors traveled to this area from all over Europe, hoping to make their fortune. Many of the country's sugar-cane planters also joined the gold rush, taking their slaves with them.

Above: In more cosmopolitan cities such as Rio, every imaginable cuisine from around the world is available.

Several years later, around 1720, diamonds were also discovered in the region, and for about a century, Brazil became the world's major supplier of both gold and diamonds. To this day, Minas Gerais remains one of the richest areas in the country.

THE ROYAL COURT

In 1808, after the occupation of Portugal by the French, the Portuguese royal court decamped to Rio de Janeiro, making the city the new capital of their empire. When King Dom João VI finally returned to Spain in 1821, he left his son Dom Pedro I behind to rule Brazil. Dom Pedro I was subsequently recalled to Portugal, but he defied his father and the Portuguese government and declared Brazil's independence in 1822, with himself as emperor.

Dendê oil

African slaves transported to Brazil initially missed one of their favorite ingredients, dendê oil, which comes from the fruit of the African oil palm and is valued for its rich orange-red color. Fortunately, they soon discovered that a similar color could be obtained by adding crushed annatto (achiote) seeds to ordinary oil. Dendê oil is now widely used in Brazilian cooking, especially in Bahia, where the African influence is strongest.

GERMAN FARMERS

Dom Pedro's wife, Empress Dona Leopoldina, conceived the idea of peopling the vast area of southern Brazil with European farmers to work the land. Thousands of German colonists arrived and settled in the state of Rio Grande do Sul. In places such as Novo Hamburgo and Blumenau, their culinary contribution is evident and remains today, with sauerkraut, sausages, spätzle, and delicious sweet pastries.

COFFEE – THE NEW CROP

In the century following independence, coffee replaced sugar as Brazil's premier export product. Further foreign immigration was encouraged for the purpose of having enough labor to work on the coffee plantations. Immigrants, especially Italians, quickly followed by Japanese, Spanish, and Portuguese, flocked to cities such as Sao Paulo. Coffee was the major source of income for Brazil in the 1870s and the 1880s, and in 1889 the powerful coffee producers helped to bring about a military coup, after which Brazil became a republic.

Below: Large freshwater catfish are displayed for sale at the busy Ver o Peso *market in the Amazon.*

FOOD AND DRINK

There is a wide variety of food on offer throughout Brazil. In the coastal belt, where the majority of the population lives, cosmopolitan cities such as Rio de Janeiro, Salvador, and Sao Paulo have every type of restaurant imaginable to choose from, including those that specialize in regional cuisine.

Among the specialities is *feijoada completa*, not so much a dish as a lavish feast. A huge platter of fresh and smoked meats, including pig's tongue, is flanked by black beans, rice, spring greens, farofa (flavored toasted cassava flour), orange slices, and several sauces, all washed down with *caipirinha*, which is a mixture of *cachaça*, sugar, and lime. Although they have a burgeoning wine industry in the temperate south, Brazilians prefer to drink iced beer or *cachaça*, which is often mixed with fruit juice or milk.

Rice is grown in Brazil and is the most widely used accompaniment, along with the ubiquitous farofa. In coastal areas, fine seafood is on offer.

REGIONAL CUISINES

There are four main regional cuisines in Brazil, plus the cooking of the Amazon region, where roasted game, exotic freshwater fish, and unusual fruits can be encountered.

Above: The traditional Brazilian Saturday lunch is feijoada completa, *a meal of meats, rice, beans, greens, and farofa.*

Comida Mineira is the cuisine of Minas Gerais. For over a century, Minas Gerais was the wealthiest part of Brazil, and it is still rich in minerals. Farming is also important there. Crops include corn, beans, coffee, and fruit, and there are large herds of beef and dairy cattle. Pork is the favorite meat, especially *lombo*, pork tenderloin. Bean dishes are also typical of the region, a favorite being *tutu*, which consists of black beans cooked with cubes of bacon and cassava flour and served with meat. Minas Gerais is also well known for its cheeses.

> **The well-traveled chile**
> When African slaves introduced the malagueta chile to Brazil, few people realized it was a returning immigrant. It originated in Central America, was taken to the northern hemisphere by the Spanish and eventually found its way to West Africa, finally returning to the continent of its birth in the baggage of slaves bound for Brazil.

Comida Baiana is perhaps the best known style of cooking in Brazil, celebrating that province's connection with Africa. Popular ingredients here include okra, dendê oil, dried shrimp, cilantro, coconut milk, and lots of fresh seafood. A popular snack is *acarajés*, tasty bean patties or fritters, split and filled with various sauces. *Moqueca* is an aromatic dish of seafood, tomatoes, bell peppers, fresh cilantro, and dendê oil, invariably served with farofa to soak up the delicious coconut sauce. Brazilians like to finish a meal with fresh fruit. Desserts tend to be very sweet and are often based on custards in the Portuguese style. Avocado is often served as a mousse or ice cream.

Comida do Sertão is the cuisine of the vast plateau in the northeast of Brazil and can be sampled in the country's capital, the purpose-built city of Brasília. Dried salted meat—*carne seca* —comes from this region, and beans are used in hearty meat dishes. Pumpkins, peppers, and corn also feature, along with exotic fruits such as guavas, mangoes, and carambolas. Favorite sweetmeats of the region include candied orange peel and candied figs.

Below: A Bahiana street vendor prepares local delicacies for passers-by, including acarajés, delicious fried bean fritters.

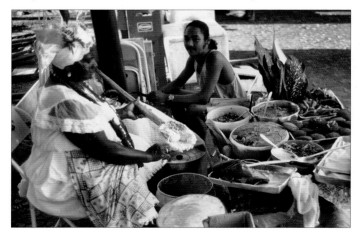

Comida Gaúcha means meat, and plenty of it. This describes the cooking style of the vast Brazilian cattle country down south. Big features of this area are the popular *churrascarias*—restaurants where you can sample almost every cut of meat imaginable, including all types of offal and a wide variety of delicious sausages.

Above: Brazil is renowned for its spectacular Mardi Gras carnival, when everyone takes to the streets to party.

STREET FOOD AND SNACKS

Brazilians like to be able to eat wherever and whenever the whim takes them, so street food is always on offer. This ranges from simple hot dogs, hamburgers, and toasted cheese sandwiches to the filled bean or cheese patties known as *acarajés*. Pastries on offer include *pastels*, *esfihas*, and *empadinhas*, which are baby empanadas stuffed with a variety of delectable fillings, such as fresh palm hearts in a tasty savory sauce.

FEASTS AND FESTIVALS

The main celebration of the year throughout Brazil is *Carnaval*. Rio de Janeiro is the city usually associated with this extravaganza, but Brazilians often prefer to celebrate by taking part in the less touristy but equally electric spectacles in cities such as Salvador, Recife, and Olinda. The build-up to *Carnaval* begins soon after Christmas and reaches its peak as Lent begins.

ARGENTINA, URUGUAY, AND PARAGUAY

The cuisines of these three countries have one major ingredient in common—beef. Argentines eat a great deal of it, and Uruguayans eat even more. It is less popular in Paraguay, but even there you will often find barbecues piled high with tender steaks, ribs, and parts of animals that you never knew existed. Few ethnic dishes survive in these countries, except in Paraguay, where the indigenous Guaraní once lived. Their traditional crops—cassava, corn, and sweet potatoes—are still staples.

EARLY HISTORY

Although this part of South America was claimed by Spain in the early part of the 16th century, there was no rush to colonize the territory. The first of the explorers to come ashore, Juan Días de Solís, was attacked by hostile natives and—according to some records—eaten. This was a powerful deterrent, although it did not prevent one of the survivors of the expedition from pressing on to Paraguay and then Bolivia. Here he acquired some silver, which was discovered after his death on

Below: Gauchos on an Argentine cattle ranch demonstrate their riding skills for Dia de la Tradicion.

the return journey. This sparked a rumor that Spain's recent acquisition might hold riches. The country was christened Argentina, meaning "place of silver," but when reality failed to match rumor the Spanish lost interest. In any event, by 1531 they were preoccupied with Peru, where gold and silver was being "liberated" from the Inca Empire by Francisco Pizarro.

The first permanent settlements in Argentina were in the Andean valleys close to the border. Santiago del Estero, Tucumán, and Córdoba were established in 1535. A year later, Pedro de Mendoza set up camp close to the Rio de la Plata, on a site that would one day become Buenos Aires. His hopes of founding a city were dashed, however, when natives attacked and he was forced to decamp to Uruguay.

Until the arrival of the Spanish, this part of South America was peopled by various tribes of hunter-gatherers turned farmers, growing crops such as corn, cassava, sweet potatoes, beans, and peppers. Coastal peoples supplemented their diet with food from the sea—fish, shellfish, and even seals. There were no great civilizations in this area, like those that existed in Peru or Central America. Pottery, stone carvings,

Above: The different varieties of corn display many striking colors—here they have been left to dry in the sun.

and rock paintings survive, but few of the inhabitants themselves withstood the arrival of the Europeans. War and disease quickly decimated their numbers, and by the end of the 19th century, very few of the early people remained.

THE PAMPAS

In 1581, the Spanish made a second attempt to establish a settlement on the banks of the Rio de la Plata in Argentina, and this time they succeeded. The extensive plains, or pampas, surrounding the place they called Buenos Aires proved to be incredibly fertile, and agriculture was rapidly established.

Cattle and horses that had escaped the original settlement had bred freely, and vast herds of animals now roamed across the pampas. This unexpected bounty was exploited by gauchos, or cowboys, who broke the horses and corralled the cattle. At first the animals were mainly killed for their hides, but when large salting plants were established in the early 19th century, the beef industry burgeoned. The pampas were fenced off, and huge estates, or *estancias*, were quickly established. Only the very rich could afford to buy these estates, and soon the landed class became the most powerful people in Argentina.

In 1816, the country, for the first time, became independent. During the second half of the 19th century, demand for cheap food in Europe led to further expansion of the beef industry, and immigrants poured in. Meat processing factories, including the famous Fray Bentos plant just across the river in Uruguay, were built. At the same time, sheep farming was becoming established in Patagonia, and by the early part of the 20th century, Argentina was a major exporter of beef and lamb, wheat and wool. These remain important today, although now much of the pampas is given over to grain and oil-seed farming.

AN ARGENTINE ASADO

The traditional way of cooking meat in Argentina is *al asador*—on the spit. The meat is impaled on metal rods, which are stuck into the ground at an angle to prevent the meat juices from dripping onto the fire. Whole carcasses or sections of carcasses are cooked this way, and the meat is sliced off and served after guests have enjoyed the traditional appetizers—kidneys, morcilla and chorizo sausages, livers, and *chinchulin* (loops of stuffed intestine).

Below: The herbal tea drink, yerba maté, is drunk throughout Argentina, and is often served in a dried, decorated gourd.

FOOD AND DRINK

With so much good quality beef at their disposal, it is not surprising that meals revolve mainly around meat, which is usually served with a piquant sauce, *chimichurri*. Fish is not as popular as meat, despite being in plentiful supply, and vegetables are not much in evidence either. Meat consumption is lower in Paraguay, which, along with northern Argentina, is the only area where ethnic cuisine is still widely served. Cornmeal is used to make delicious spoonbreads and puddings. Cassava, which Paraguayans call *mandioca*, is baked with cheese and eggs or transformed into flat breads that resemble tortillas. The influence of indigenous cooks is also evident in Argentine dishes such as *carbonada criolla*, a stew served in a pumpkin; and *humitas*, a pureed corn mixture which is often steamed in corn husks.

Immigrants have exerted considerable influence on the food of Argentina and Uruguay. The pasta and pizzas in Buenos Aires and Montevideo are said to be as good as any in Italy, and the Italians also inspired an Argentine dish in which pork is baked in milk. The Spanish influence remains strong, but Middle Eastern, Chinese, Japanese, and Korean settlers have also made their

Above: In Buenos Aires, Argentina, a chef prepares large pieces of meat to be broiled at a traditional asado.

mark. In the beautiful Lake District, where the Andes provide a towering backdrop to towns that look more European than South American, visitors can sample delicious fondues, sweet pastries, or the local chocolate.

Yerba maté, a type of herbal tea, is the drink of choice in Argentina, Uruguay, and Paraguay, along with wine, beer, and *caña,* a cane spirit.

STREET FOOD AND SNACKS

Empanadas with various fillings are popular, as are tiny cheese and ham sandwiches. Pastries are often very sweet, especially the ones that incorporate *dulce de leche* (caramelized milk). Churros, the Spanish answer to doughnuts, are enjoyed with hot drinks.

FEASTS AND FESTIVALS

The most interesting festivals in this area are those that focus on the gaucho tradition. These include demonstrations of riding skills and the opportunity to sample a traditional *asado*. In Montevideo, the summer Carnaval is famous for the African drumming that accompanies *candombe* dance troupes.

PERU, BOLIVIA, AND ECUADOR

Many of the world's most popular foods come from the arable Andean highlands of Peru, Bolivia, and Ecuador. Potatoes originated in this region, as did tomatoes, squashes, pine nuts, quinoa, tamarillos, sweet potatoes, and several types of bean. All of these foods were cultivated by some of the most fascinating civilizations the world has ever seen.

EARLY HISTORY

Unlike Brazil and Argentina, where no major civilizations were based, this part of South America has been home to a succession of highly developed cultures. Among these were the Nasca of Southern Peru, who etched the soil with elaborate geoglyphs so large that their shapes— patterns, birds, and animals—can only be fully appreciated from the air. In the north of the country, the Mochica people built impressive pyramids, while the Tiahuanuco established an empire that ruled Peru, Bolivia, Chile, and Argentina for over 1,000 years. Shortly after their collapse toward the end of

Below: Corn grows in abundance on the Incan agricultural terraces in the Peruvian highlands.

the 12th century, a Quechua tribe, one of many in the mountains, began to establish a power base in the area around Cuzco. Their leader, known as the Inca, was Manco Capac. Within 300 years, the Inca empire stretched from Colombia to northern Chile and ruled over more than 15 million subjects. Aside from their military might, skilled governance, and prodigious building skills, the Incas also improved farming by introducing terracing and irrigation, cultivating new crops such as cassava and peanuts, and elevating the already high status of corn by declaring that only the Supreme Inca himself could plant the first seed of the new season.

The Inca civilization endured until 1533, when Cuzco fell to the Spanish conquistador Francisco Pizarro. Along with Ecuador and Bolivia, Peru (which at that time included the northern part of present-day Chile) became part of the Viceroyalty of Peru, administered first from Lima and then from Quito. A period of Spanish colonial rule followed, coming to an end when Peru declared its independence in 1821. Ecuador did the same thing a year later, and Bolivia followed in 1825.

FOOD AND DRINK

Their shared history, first as part of the great Inca empire and later under Spain, means that the countries of Peru, Ecuador, and Bolivia share similar cuisines, though each country has its own specialities. The Spanish influence is most noticeable on the coast, while in the high Andes, Quechua people fought to preserve their customs, eschewing Spanish ingredients and cooking methods. Away from the big cities, it is still possible to come across dishes that have changed little for centuries.

Potatoes are eaten extensively throughout this region. Cooks are fortunate in having a wide variety of potatoes to choose from, and they take great care in selecting the right type for the dish. The yellow Papa Amarilla, for instance, tastes great in *causa*, a Peruvian specialty, which has an infinite number of variations. One way of preparing it is to layer cooked potatoes with flaked fish, chopped tomatoes, and avocado; another variation tops the potato with an onion sauce before garnishing it with hard-boiled eggs, lettuce, peppers, and olives. Equally delicious is *ocopa arequipena*, in which cooked potatoes are covered in a spicy cheese and walnut sauce.

A typical Peruvian dish is *carapulcra*. Dried potatoes, a throwback to Inca days when potatoes were freeze-dried on top of the high mountains, then squeezed dry and placed in the sun until hard, are traditionally used for this dish, although fresh potatoes can be substituted if the dried variety are unavailable. Potato and cheese rissoles are extremely popular in Ecuador, while in Bolivia potatoes are often simply mashed with a little oil and lemon juice, then served with chopped cassava, locally known as *yuca*, and corn, both of which are staple foods.

One of the most fascinating Peruvian ingredients is quinoa, known as the "mother grain" by the Incas. The tiny grains have a mild, slightly bitter taste and firm texture, and should be cooked in the same way as rice. Quinoa is an excellent source of protein and can be added to stews, bakes, or salads.

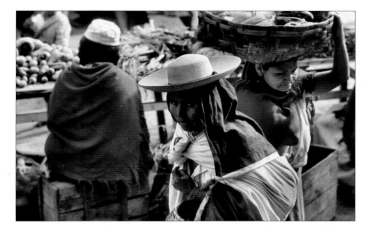

Above: At an Ecuadorian market in Otavalo, women in traditional costume buy fresh fruit and vegetables.

FISH AND MEAT

Bolivia is one of only two landlocked countries in Latin America. As a result, the inhabitants do not eat as much sea fish as their neighbors, but fresh fish in the form of trout from Lake Titicaca is very popular. Peruvians enjoy a wide variety of fish and are especially fond of corvina or striped bass. They also have access to excellent seafood. The Pacific seaboard is noted for its delicious ceviche, the dish famous for "cooking" the fish by marinating it in fresh citrus juices. Lime juice is usually used in ceviche, but in Ecuador the juice of bitter oranges is preferred.

Although Peruvians produce beef and pork and enjoy both, they are particularly partial to duck and chicken and also like to eat *cuyes* (guinea pigs). These vegetarian animals are raised in much the same way as rabbits or hens, and smallholders will often let them range freely around their homes. *Cuyes* are also raised commercially, on farms. Popular ways of cooking *cuyes* include stewing in a rich sauce and broiling over an open fire. Other exotic meats can be sampled in the jungles of Ecuador, where animals such as wild boars and monkeys are often eaten.

Because mountain-bred animals are often tough, their meat is usually chopped into very small pieces, then stewed with corn and the rocoto or mirasol chiles that are widely used in this part of Latin America. This helps to tenderize the meat.

Many fruits are grown in this region, including pineapples, cherimoyas, mangoes, guavas, and passion fruit. Bananas and plantains are also widely cultivated, especially in Ecuador. Other important ingredients are walnuts, pine nuts, and peanuts, which are often ground to make rich sauces.

A favorite drink is *pisco*, a grape brandy that is common to Peru and Chile. *Chicha*, a type of beer made from fermented corn, is also drunk.

STREET FOOD AND SNACKS

A popular snack is *anticuchos* (ox heart kebabs). The meat is trimmed, marinated in spiced vinegar, and speared on lengths of sugarcane before being broiled with a spicy basting sauce. Other street foods include empanadas or *pastelos* (pastries stuffed with a variety of tasty fillings) and *humitas* (fresh corn dough with a savory or sweet filling, steamed in a corn husk parcel). Crisp plantain chips are an Ecuadorian specialty, while Bolivians like to snack on caramel-coated popcorn called *pasacaya*.

FEASTS AND FESTIVALS

Easter is celebrated in style in all three countries. The best-known Quechua festival is Inti Raymi (the festival of the sun), which celebrates the winter solstice on June 24th each year. This huge celebration often continues for days. In Ecuador, the self-proclaimed banana capital of the world, there is a banana festival every September.

Below: In La Paz, Bolivia, a market trader displays just some of the many varieties of potato grown in the region.

CHILE

A slender ribbon of a country, Chile is dominated by the Andes mountain range and measures some 3,000 miles from north to south, but is never much more than 100 miles wide. In the north is the strangely beautiful Atacama Desert; in the south, beyond the Continental ice field, lies a rugged land of glaciers and fjords. Between these extremes is a temperate, fertile zone where fruits and vegetables grow abundantly. The waters off the coast of Chile provide superb seafood.

EARLY HISTORY

The north of Chile was once ruled by the Incas, but before they came to prominence in the early 13th century, the land played host to a succession of tribal groups. The first of these is believed to have settled in the south of the country as early as 14,000 years ago. More recent inhabitants were the

Below: Chile's ice fields, such as Torres del Paine, Patagonia, lie to the south of a more temperate, fertile area.

Aymara, who cultivated corn and potatoes in the far north, trading these foods for guano, a rich fertilizer gathered by coastal tribes. Also occupying the northern region were the Atacameño, whose descendants still uphold some of their tribal traditions. Another important group, the Mapuche, were fierce warriors who successfully kept the Inca and Spanish invaders at bay for centuries.

The Spanish finally gained a foothold in Chile in 1541, when Pedro de Valdivia founded Santiago. The town was almost lost six months later when natives attacked, but the community survived, and less than 20 years later the Spanish were firmly entrenched.

The colonists quickly began to establish large estates or haciendas over much of the country. These were initially worked by native South Americans who were little more than slaves, but when the spread of European diseases virtually annihilated the native population, tenant farmers of mixed blood (*mestizos*) took their place.

Until the 18th century, Chile remained a largely agrarian country. As the Audiencia de Chile, linked for administrative purposes to the Vice-royalty of Peru, it was ruled from Lima, and was only permitted to trade with the mother country. All goods destined for Spain therefore had to go via Lima.

Chile was ripe for change when Napoleon's invasion of Spain in the early 19th century signaled the beginning of the end of that country's dominance in Latin America. When Napoleon placed his brother on the Spanish throne, the citizens of Santiago who were loyal to the deposed King Ferdinand VII refused to acknowledge the usurper, and declared on September 18, 1810 that they would rule Chile themselves until the French were ousted from Spain. This independence was short-lived, however, as troops from Peru soon reestablished control. Independence would only be formally declared in 1818, after José de San Martin's liberation army had crossed from Argentina into Chile.

Above: Garlands of dried shellfish hang from market stalls in Puerto Montt, Chile, a town known for its seafood.

After initial turmoil, the country became relatively stable. Agriculture and mining prospered, and were bolstered by the arrival of settlers from Ireland, England, Germany, France, Italy, Croatia, and the Middle East. All of these immigrants had an influence on the Chilean cuisine, but the national diet still has strong links with its origins, and traditional ingredients such as corn, squash, beans, and potatoes are widely used.

FOOD AND DRINK

Any discussion about food in Chile inevitably centers on the extent, excellence, and variety of seafood available. The plankton-rich Humboldt current is responsible for the largesse, which includes crabs, clams, mussels, abalone, razor clams, sea urchins, squid, octopus, scallops, and lobsters. Some or all of these types of seafood, plus less identifiable specialties such as *picorocco* (giant barnacles), are likely to be among the treats on offer at that most Chilean of feasts, the *curanto*, a massive cookout that involves a carefully constructed pit, hot rocks, and leaves to seal in the steam.

Fish is equally abundant. Popular varieties include congrio, a slender fish that resembles an eel; corvina, a type of bass; swordfish, and the Patagonian toothfish. Chile is also one of the world's biggest exporters of salmon.

Corn features widely in many recipes, from soups and breads to the delicious *pastel de choclo*, which is a traditional stew topped with a corn crust. Meat is not as central to the diet as it is in neighboring Argentina, but Chile produces some fine beef, pork, and lamb nevertheless.

Chilean desserts are similar to those served elsewhere on the continent, mainly taking their inspiration from Spain and making great use of the thick, sweet caramelized milk called *dulce de leche*. The central valleys produce excellent fresh fruit throughout the year, and deliciously sweet cakes and pastries are also available, courtesy of German settlers.

Chileans enjoy a good bottle of wine and are extremely proud of their vineyards, which are rapidly gaining worldwide recognition. Also popular is draft beer, known locally as *schop*, and the delicious grape brandy, *pisco*.

A curanto on Chiloé
The beautiful archipelago of Chiloé, situated off Puerto Montt, is famous for its fine seafood, wooden churches and laid-back atmosphere. This is a great place to sample the *curanto*— a full-scale Chilean seafood feast.

STREET FOOD AND SNACKS

For munching on the move, Chileans have meat, seafood, empanadas, *humitas,* and sandwiches, from steak with all the trimmings to *ave-palta* (chicken and avocado).

FEASTS AND FESTIVALS

Independence Day on September 18th is celebrated with music, dancing, eating, and drinking, and marks the start of summer. The rodeo season also starts in September, with the major event, the National Rodeo, taking place in March. Ngillatun is an ancient Mapuche festival celebrating harvest and fertility.

Below: An impressive array of fresh fruit and vegetables are on offer at a market in Valdivia in Chile's Lake District.

COLOMBIA AND VENEZUELA

At the upper end of South America lie two countries that are as mysterious as they are magnificent. Colombia and Venezuela have some of the most rugged terrain on the continent. From the tropical rainforest of the coast, the land rises to range after range of high mountains, the cordilleras of the Andes. Ravines, mighty rivers, and dense vegetation make exploration difficult, and communities have historically been isolated. Until the first settlers arrived there was, therefore, no universal style of eating, and the Spanish were able to establish theirs as the core cuisine in both countries.

EARLY HISTORY

Columbus discovered the mouth of the Orinoco River in 1498. The first Spanish settlement in Venezuela was established in 1521 and in Colombia four years later. In the early 19th century both countries united with Ecuador and Panama to form the union of Gran Colombia, after their independence was won by Simon Bolivar. Venezuela left the union to become a separate state in 1830, as did Ecuador, and Panama eventually left the union in 1903.

FOOD AND DRINK

Both Colombia and Venezuela have lowland plains, temperate zones above 3,000 feet and highlands leading to alpine-style meadows. At sea level, sugar, cacao, coconuts, bananas, and rice are cultivated. Higher up are the coffee plantations and corn fields, and above these cereal crops, potatoes, and temperate fruits are all grown. This huge diversity of landscape means that both countries have a wide range of foods available to them, from the traditional ingredients such as cassava, squash, beans, and corn to a dazzling array of fruits.

Favorite Venezuelan dishes include delicacies such as *mondongo* (tripe with vegetables, corn and potatoes), *sancocho* (fish stew), and *parrillado* (barbecued meats), while Colombian specialities include rabbit in coconut milk, chicken hotpot with three different types of potato, and a delicious

pineapple custard. Colombia has the benefit of a coastline on both the Caribbean Sea and the Pacific Ocean, so it has a wonderful selection of fish and seafood readily available. *Arepas* (flat corn breads) are a very popular snack. Both countries produce lots of coffee, and it is one of their major exports; Colombian coffee is reckoned to be among the finest in the world.

Above: Roadside vendors are a common sight in Colombia, selling fruits such as bananas, melons, and pineapples.

A seasonal speciality and a great delicacy in the lowland regions are flying ants, which are toasted and served like peanuts. In Venezuela a delicious spicy sauce, *katara*, is made from the heads of leaf-cutter ants.

The lure of El Dorado

The rumor of a land where gold was so plentiful that people powdered themselves with gold dust lured many 16th-century adventurers to the countries now known as Guyana, Surinam, and French Guiana. The glut of gold never materialized but the Spanish, Dutch, English, and French all thought that the land was worth fighting for.

The English eventually triumphed in Guyana, but only after many years of Dutch settlement. Surinam went to the Dutch and French Guiana became first a French penal colony and then an overseas department of France. Still heavily subsidized by France, French Guiana has a distinctly Gallic atmosphere, with pavement cafes and food with a distinctly French flavor. In Guyana and Surinam, where African slaves and indentured laborers from India, China, and the East Indies were imported to work the sugar plantations, the cooking is more eclectic. Javanese noodle dishes and Chinese stir-fries are sold alongside native South American dishes like pepperpot—a stew with meat tenderized by cassareep (cassava extract). Seafood is popular, especially shrimp, and plantains, bananas, cassava, beans, peanuts, and squash are also widely used. The area is famous for its superb fruit, and for unusual vegetables like *pom*, a large yellow root that closely resembles cassava.

CENTRAL AMERICA

The land that connects Mexico with the rest of South America consists of seven countries: Guatemala, Belize, El Salvador, Honduras, Nicaragua, Costa Rica, and Panama. Beans and rice are the staple foods in all these countries, but there are also fine fish to be had, thanks to the proximity of the Pacific Ocean and the Caribbean Sea.

EARLY HISTORY

The empire of the Maya extended to Honduras. When they disappeared from Central America around AD900 they not only left behind ruined cities like Tikal in Guatemala, but also new foods and sophisticated farming techniques, some of which were adopted by natives.

Columbus reached the shores of Honduras and then Costa Rica in 1502, but the area was not settled until some 20 years later, after troops led by Pedro de Alvarado came south from Mexico. Alvarado took Guatemala, Honduras and El Salvador. By 1530 there were Spanish colonists in most of Central America. Government was a haphazard affair, but in 1535 Guatemala, Honduras, El Salvador, Nicaragua, and Costa Rica were incorporated into the Viceroyalty of New Spain, headquartered in Mexico City.

Below: Corn fields flourish alongside impressive mountains at the southeast tip of Lake Atitlan in Guatemala.

In 1821, the quintet opted out and two years later formed a federal republic, known as the United Provinces of Central America. The states were all autonomous, however. Belize became British, largely by default. Although the area was technically Spanish, British buccaneers established bases there and were later joined by British soldiers from Jamaica. In 1798 the British connection was formalized, and the link was only broken in 1981 when Belize became independent. Panama, meanwhile, looked to the south and was part of the Union of Gran Colombia until 1903. The building of the Panama Canal brought affluence to the area, and Panama is still one of the wealthier countries in Central America.

FOOD AND DRINK

The food of Central America is not as exciting as the surroundings, but competing against orchid-clad forests, volcanoes, waterfalls, barrier reefs, and beautiful beaches would be a tall order. Dishes based on rice and beans are everywhere, but there are plenty of alternatives. Fish is universally popular. Varieties include tuna, mackerel, snapper, pompano, swordfish, and mahi-mahi. The fish is often cooked simply and served whole, but there are also plenty of rich fish soups and stews. Lobsters, clams, shrimp, and other types of seafood are also widely

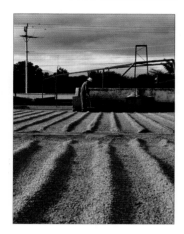

Above: In Costa Rica, a worker spreads out coffee beans to dry in the sun.

available. Chicken is always on the menu, alongside specialities such as *mondongo* (tripe stew) and *cecina* (beef marinated in citrus juices). There is a strong Mexican influence in Guatemala and Belize; Panama takes inspiration from Colombia; and Creole dishes are found on the Caribbean coast. Coffee is grown in Costa Rica, El Salvador, and Guatemala and is enjoyed by everyone, from the very young to the very old.

Fabulous fruits

Central America is blessed with bountiful fruit. Markets throughout the region are filled with bananas, cherimoyas, mangoes, papayas, pineapples, and guavas, plus many more varieties that are local to each country. Delicious fruit drinks are a popular choice. *Refrescos* or *frescos* are milk- or water-based, while *batidas* sometimes contain rum or a similar spirit. Also refreshing are *pipas*, large green coconuts that stallholders cut open on request so that thirsty purchasers can sip the cool liquid inside.

THE MEXICAN, SOUTH AMERICAN, AND CARIBBEAN KITCHEN

Mexican, South American, and Caribbean cuisine is founded on simple ingredients of excellent quality. Fresh seafood, quality cuts of meat, and locally grown fruits and vegetables are abundant. Each country has developed its own specialties, with common flavorings and techniques.

EQUIPMENT

Latin American cooks are endlessly inventive, not only in the way they cook, but also in their approach to kitchen equipment. While the items featured here could give your cooking a more authentic touch, few are essential. If you intend making your own tortillas, a press and *comal* will be extremely useful, but for most purposes, it is perfectly possible to improvise.

METATE

Made from a sloping piece of volcanic rock and looking rather like a three-legged stone stool, this grinding stone is used to make *masa* dough from skinned, cooked corn kernels. It can also be used to grind cocoa and *piloncillo* (unrefined cane sugar). The grinding is done with the aid of a stone roller, a *muller*, which is made from the same stone as the *metate*. Before a new *metate* can be used, it must be tempered. A mixture of dry rice and salt is placed on the grinding surface, and the *muller* is rocked back and forth to press the mixture into the surface and remove any loose pieces of sand or grit. These are fairly difficult to obtain outside South America, but they are available by mail order.

Below: A metate *is a traditional grinding stone made from volcanic rock. The design has not changed for many centuries.*

MOLCAJETE AND TEJOLOTE

The Mexican mortar, the *molcajete*, is traditionally made from volcanic rock and must be tempered in the same way as the *metate*. The short, stubby pestle used to grind ingredients is called a *tejolote*. The best *molcajetes* are heavy and not too porous. Before purchasing, grind the *molcajete* briefly with the *tejolote*. If the stone seems soft and a lot of dust is formed, it is probably too porous. Similar to the Thai equivalent, which it closely resembles, it is ideal for grinding herbs, garlic, chiles, and other spices such as achiote (annatto), as well as nuts and seeds for making *mole poblano*, for example. Fresh salsas, such as guacamole, are often made with a *molcajete* and *tejolote*. The flavors of the ingredients are crushed out, which gives a rustic texture and flavor. However, grinding spices or pounding chiles with a *molcajete* and *tejolote* is hard work, so many Mexican cooks use a food processor or a blender instead.

Above: A mortar and pestle, or molcajete e tejolote, *is an essential tool for grinding spices and chiles.*

TORTILLA PRESS

In Mexico and other parts of Latin America where tortillas and similar griddle cakes are made, the *masa* dough was traditionally shaped by hand. Skilled women were able to make an astonishing number of perfectly shaped tortillas in a very short time, but this is something of a dying art. Today most people use tortilla presses, and in tortilla bakeries or *tortillerias* the whole process is mechanized. The most effective tortilla presses are made from cast iron, but because these must be oiled before use, and carefully maintained, many people prefer steel presses. Tortilla presses consist of two round metal plates, hinged together. They come in various sizes and are heavy, in order to limit the leverage needed to work them. The dough is placed between the plates, which are then squeezed together with the aid of a lever. Placing thin sheets of plastic on the plates or covering them with plastic bags before making the tortillas will ensure that they are easy to remove once they are pressed. Tortilla presses are sold in good speciality kitchen shops and are also widely available by mail order.

*Below:
Perfect tortillas
can be easily
pressed with a heavy
steel or cast-iron tortilla
press.*

CUSCUZEIRO

This looks a bit like a metal colander supported on a frame, and it is used as a mold for the popular Brazilian dish *cuscuz paulista*. The *cuscuzeiro* is lined with a variety of foods that will look

EARTHENWARE DISHES

The Spanish influence on the region's cuisine is clearly visible in the clay pots (*ollas*) that are traditionally used for cooking stews and sauces throughout Latin America. Often beautifully hand-painted and decorated, they give food a unique earthy flavor, but are seldom found outside the region, as their fragility means that they do not travel well and are rarely exported. Sadly, modern materials and designs have made them relatively rare in Latin America itself. Flat earthenware dishes decorated around the edge are more easily found, and these are often used as serving dishes. Traditional Spanish *cazuelas* (shallow terracotta dishes) and casseroles also make excellent alternatives.

COMAL

This is a thin circular griddle, traditionally used over an open fire to cook tortillas. They were placed among the hot coals and pulled out with long sticks. Clay *comals* take longer to heat up, but they do not require oiling before use, unlike metal ones. If you cannot find a *comal*, a cast-iron griddle or large frying pan will do the job equally well.

FARINHERRA

This is a traditional shaker used mainly in Brazil for sprinkling *farinha de mandioca* (cassava flour) over meat or fish dishes, such as *feijoada*, to mop up the sauce and juices.

decorative when the dish is turned out, for example, slices of tomato, hard-boiled eggs, or slices of pepper, with perhaps a few fresh shrimp. A moist cornmeal mixture is then packed on top of these ingredients. More layers are added until the container is full, and it is then covered and steamed. When turned out, the layers of the *cuscuz* look pretty and it tastes delicious. The name suggests that *cuscuz* evolved from couscous, and the method of preparation certainly calls to mind the North African dish.

Above: For slow-cooking rich stews and sauces, Latin American cooks often use ollas, *traditional hand-decorated Spanish clay pots, which give an authentic flavor.*

Left: Available as metal or clay varieties, a comal *is the traditional griddle pan used for cooking tortillas.*

CORN

The Aztecs called it "first mother and father, the source of life." Corn was equally highly revered in Peru, first by the indigenous South Americans, who worshipped the corn goddess, and then by the Incas, who decreed that corn could only be planted after the Supreme Inca had turned the first sod with a golden plough reserved for this purpose.

Corn was a sacred food, of huge significance. Not only was it a vital source of sustenance, but it also provided shelter, fencing, and even clothing. Every part of the plant was used, even the silks surrounding the kernels, which became ties for tamales. When corn was cooked, whoever added it to the pot had first to breathe on it to rid it of its fear of dying and accustom it to the heat.

Some corn was eaten fresh, but most was dried and stored, then processed to make a type of porridge called *atole*. This was a lengthy chore, made easier by the discovery that the skins came off much more easily if the kernels were heated in a lime solution. When boiled in fresh water, the skinned kernels made a mash (*pozole*), versions of which were eaten by the indigenous peoples of Central and South America.

The cooked skinned kernels were also the basis for *masa*, a dough made by crushing the corn. The dough was then transformed into tortillas or similar flat breads, using techniques that are much the same today.

Corn is a valuable carbohydrate food, but it is deficient in the amino acids lysine and tryptophan. If corn is the sole food source, as in some parts of Africa, diseases such as kwashiorkor and pellagra result. The problem has not arisen in South America or the Caribbean, however, because the basic diet also includes beans and squash, which compensate for the nutritional deficiencies of corn.

History

Corn evolved in Central America, but its precise origin is not known. No wild forms have ever been found, and its ancestor may have been a type of grass with tiny kernels, each embedded in a cob no bigger than a navy bean. How the grass evolved into the much larger plant with rows of kernels growing side by side on a substantial cob is not known, but the indigenous farmers were highly efficient plant breeders.

Corn was already widely grown throughout South America when Columbus first encountered it on the island of Cuba. The tall, leafy plant was called *maïs*, and

Above: White Andean corn is ground and used to make masa *dough.*

Below: South American corn comes in many colors, including vibrant red.

in many parts of the globe it is still known as maize. The alternative name arose because Columbus and his crew saw it as a staple food equivalent to the corn they grew back home, and dubbed it native corn.

Varieties

There are five main varieties of corn. Dent corn is the most widely grown globally, and is mainly used for animal feeds and oil. Other varieties are popcorn, flint corn, flour corn, and sweet corn, which is the type used in cooking. Baby sweet corn cobs are often picked before they are mature, then cooked and eaten whole. Yellow corn kernels are the most common, but the corn grown in South America comes in other colors too, including red, blue, purple, and the pale white that is typical of the Andean region. There are even variegated types available, which have sweet white, red, and purple kernels on the same cob. For flavor, one of the most highly prized varieties is Peru's purple corn, *maiz morado*, which has a subtle citrus flavor and is used to make *mazamorra*, a delicious pudding, or the unusual drink, *chicha morrada*.

Buying and storing

If possible, corn should be cooked within 24 hours of being picked. This is because the sugar in the kernels starts to turn into starch as soon as the cobs are cut. Look for husks that are clean, shiny, and well filled. If you are not sure whether the corn is ripe or not, take a look at the tassels, which should be golden brown. Unless you are planning to cook the corn the minute you get home, do not part the green husks to check out the contents; once the kernels have been exposed to the air, they will quickly begin to dry out.

Preparing corn

Corn can be cooked in many different ways, but when served as an accompaniment it is usually simply boiled.

1 Strip off the green husks surrounding the cobs.

2 If only the kernels are required, lift the cob slightly and slice downwards using a sharp knife to remove a few rows at a time.

3 Whether using whole cobs, slices, or just the kernels, plunge the corn into lightly salted boiling water for 4–5 minutes, until tender. Drain and serve with a pat of butter.

Huitlacoche
During times of drought, corn kernels are sometimes infected by a fungus, which turns them grey and causes them to swell to many times their original size. Far from being a disaster, this is seen as a boon, because the "corn truffles" as they are sometimes known, have a delicious, earthy flavor when cooked and are regarded as a delicacy around the world.

Cooking

Corn remains a staple ingredient in modern Latin America. Young, tender corn cobs are first stripped of their husks and then either steamed or cooked whole on a brazier or barbecue as a delicious fast-food snack. The pureed kernels also make an excellent soup. In Argentina, corn is often added to stews, such as the popular meat stew, *carbonada criolla*, while in Ecuador the kernels are mixed with salt cod and other vegetables to make the traditional dish *fanesca*.

CORNMEAL

Also known as maize flour, cornmeal remains slightly gritty when cooked, giving a characteristic texture to the flat breads for which it is most often used. The product known cornstarch is a pure starch extracted from the grain. When mixed with regular wheat flour in a cake, it produces a lighter result. *Masa harina* is sometimes known as tortilla flour, which indicates its purpose. Although Latin cooks will often make *masa* (tortilla dough) from cooked corn kernels, the flour is an easier option. It comes in various grades, depending on what sort of corn it is made from. *Masarepa* is a similar product, used for making *arepas*, the flat griddle cakes that are popular in Venezuela and Colombia.

Right: Wet corn is ground to make masa harina, *which can then be used to make corn tortillas.*

Above: Dried corn husks should be soaked in cold water before use.

DRIED CORN HUSKS

These make handy wrappers for Mexican tamales and Peruvian *humitas*. They are fairly brittle, so should be soaked in water for about 30 minutes before being used to wrap ingredients. Dried corn husks are not always easy to obtain outside Latin America, so baking parchment can be used instead.

CORN TORTILLAS

Have ready a tortilla press and two
clean plastic bags, slit if necessary so
that they will lie flat. Tortillas are more
traditionally cooked on a special griddle
called a *comal*, but a cast-iron griddle
or large heavy frying pan will work just
as well.

MAKES 12 × 6-INCH TORTILLAS

INGREDIENTS
    2 cups *masa harina*
    pinch of salt
    1 cup warm water

1 Place the *masa harina*, salt, and water
in a large bowl and combine using a
wooden spoon until it forms a dough.

2 Turn out the dough onto a lightly
floured surface and knead well for
3–4 minutes, until firm, smooth, and no
longer sticky. Cover the bowl with
plastic wrap and let the dough stand at
room temperature for 1 hour.

3 Pinch off 12 pieces of dough of equal
size and roll each piece into a ball.
Work with one piece of dough at a time,
keeping the rest of the pieces of dough
covered with plastic wrap so that they
do not dry out.

4 Open the tortilla press and place a
plastic bag on the bottom. Put a dough
ball on top and press with the palm of
your hand to flatten slightly.

5 Lay a second plastic bag on top of the
round of dough and close the press.
Press down firmly several times to
flatten the dough into a thin round.

6 Place a large frying pan or griddle
over medium heat. Open the press and
lift out the tortilla, keeping it
sandwiched between the plastic bags.
Carefully peel off the first bag, then
gently turn the tortilla over onto the
palm of your hand. Carefully peel off
the second plastic bag. It can help if
you peel the plastic off smoothly with a
firm, yet not too forceful, hand. Pull
back toward your wrist.

7 Flip the tortilla onto the hot frying pan
or griddle and cook for about 1 minute
or until the lower surface is blistered
and is just beginning to turn golden
brown. Turn over using a spatula and
keep warm until ready to serve.

8 Place a clean dish towel in a large
ovenproof dish. Transfer the cooked
tortilla to the dish, wrap the dish towel
over the top, and cover with a lid. Keep
warm while you cook the remaining
tortillas in the same way.

COOK'S TIP

If you do not have a tortilla press, you
can improvise by placing the dough
between two clean plastic bags and
rolling it out with a rolling pin.

Basic *Masa*

Traditionally, tortillas are made
with *masa*. *Masa* is made by
mixing dried white corn with food-
grade calcium oxide, although this
is difficult to locate in small
quantities. For making tortillas,
most cooks, even in Mexico, find it
easier to use *masa harina*, which
is the flour made when *masa* is
dried and ground. *Masa harina*
should not be confused with
cornmeal or polenta, which are
made from corn that has not been
soaked or cooked with lime. The
taste of tortillas made with *masa
harina* is slightly different from that
of tortillas made from fresh *masa*,
but the flour is much easier to
cook with and eliminates the need
for a *metate*.

Flour Tortillas

Flour tortillas are more common than corn tortillas in the north of Mexico, especially in the areas around Sonora and Chihuahua, where wheat is grown. Flour tortillas differ from corn tortillas in that they include shortening, which gives them more pliability and elasticity. For best results, make sure you use good quality all-purpose flour.

MAKES ABOUT 12 x 10-INCH TORTILLAS

INGREDIENTS
    5 cups all-purpose flour,
      sifted
    ½ teaspoon baking powder
    pinch of salt
    scant ½ cup shortening
    ½ cup warm water

1 Mix the flour, baking powder, and salt in a large bowl. Rub in the shortening, then gradually add enough water to draw the flour together into a stiff dough.

2 Turn out the dough onto a lightly floured work surface and knead it for 10–15 minutes, until it is elastic. Use the heel of your hand, using your other hand to steady the dough, preventing it from shifting position on the board.

3 Divide the dough into 12 even-size pieces and roll into balls using the palms of your hand. Cover the pieces with plastic wrap while you are working, to keep them from drying out.

4 Roll out each ball on a lightly floured surface. Give the dough a quarter turn after each roll to keep the round even. Keep rolling until the round is about 12 inches.

5 Warm a large, heavy frying pan or griddle over medium heat. Cook one tortilla at a time, placing each one in the ungreased pan or on the griddle and cooking it for 45 seconds–1 minute or until the lower surface begins to blister and brown. Turn over and cook the other side for about 1 minute.

6 Wrap the cooked tortillas in a clean, dry dish towel to keep them soft and warm while you make the rest.

COOK'S TIPS
• If the corn tortillas crack when they are pressed, remove the dough from the press, return it to the bowl, and add a little extra water.
• To reheat cold tortillas, sprinkle them with a few drops of water, wrap them in foil, and place in an oven preheated to 275°F for 10 minutes. Alternatively, wrap them in plastic wrap and microwave on maximum power for about 20 seconds.

Quick and easy tortilla fillings
• Cut a skinned chicken breast into thin slices and stir-fry with slices of red and yellow pepper. When the chicken is cooked add the juice of a lime and some fresh oregano, add salt and pepper to taste, then use the mixture to fill freshly warmed tortillas. Add some grated cheese if you wish and a spoonful of sour cream.
• If you have some rice and refried beans left from the previous day, mix them together and reheat in a frying pan with a little oil. When the mixture is thoroughly heated, spoon into the tortillas with some grated cheese, slices of tomato, and scallions.
• Stir-fry some mushrooms with plenty of black pepper. Add a dash of soy sauce and a little heavy cream, season to taste, then spoon into the tortillas.

FOLDING AND COOKING TORTILLAS

Many Mexican dishes are made with tortillas. The difference lies in the filling, folding, and cooking.

BURRITOS

These are flour tortilla envelopes enclosing various fillings and then folded into the classic shape and the edges sealed with flour and water.

CHIMICHANGAS

A chimichanga is a burrito that has been folded, chilled to allow the edges to seal, and then deep-fried in hot oil until crisp and golden.

CHALUPAS

Chalupas are pieces of *masa* shaped to resemble canoes or boats and fried until opaque and golden. They are topped with beans, salsa, and cheese.

ENCHILADAS

These can be made from either corn or wheat tortillas. A little filling is laid down the center of a tortilla, which is then rolled to make a tube, much like cannelloni. Filled tortillas are laid side by side in a baking dish before being topped with a sauce and baked or finished under the broiler.

FAJITAS

These are ideal for informal dinner parties, as various fillings are placed on the table with the hot tortillas, and guests fill and roll their own. The tortilla is then folded to form a pocket around the filling.

FLAUTAS

Corn tortillas are filled with a pork or chicken mixture, rolled tightly into flute shapes, then fried until crisp.

QUESADILLAS

These tasty treats are made by placing a corn or flour tortilla in a warm frying pan and spreading one half lightly with salsa. A little chicken or a few shrimp are sometimes added, and fresh cheese is sprinkled on top. The other half of the tortilla is then folded over, and the quesadilla is cooked for 1–2 minutes, during which time it is turned once.

TACOS

The crisp tortilla shells that are often sold in supermarkets as tacos are in fact a Tex-Mex invention. True Mexican tacos are corn tortillas that have been filled and folded in half; they still remain soft. *Taquitos* are miniature tacos—ideal for picnics or parties.

TOSTADAS

These are individual corn tortillas fried until crisp and then topped with shredded meat, refried beans, salsa, Guacamole, sour cream, and a little fresh cheese. The finger-food versions are called *tostaditas*.

TOTOPOS

Triangles of corn tortilla, fried until crisp, are called *totopos*. Serve them with salsa—they are delicious served while still warm.

READY-MADE TORTILLAS

Making Mexican meals is much easier than it once was, thanks to the availability of ready-made tortillas and tortilla chips.

CORN TORTILLAS

Many supermarkets stock 6-inch fresh corn tortillas. Look for them in the bread section. They are ideal for making tacos, tostadas, *totopos,* and enchiladas. They do not have a very long shelf life, but they do freeze well. Follow the manufacturer's instructions for warming them, as methods vary.

FLOUR TORTILLAS

These are available in 6-inch, 8-inch, and 10-inch rounds, and the packaging is usually marked in inches rather than centimeters. The smallest ones are perfect for fajitas or flour tortilla quesadillas, while the 8-inch tortillas are a good size for large quesadillas (to share). Use the largest tortillas for burritos and chimichangas, as they allow more room for the filling. Like corn tortillas, fresh flour tortillas are sold in the bread section of supermarkets or in vacuum packages in the ethnic food section. The longer-life products tend to be a bit drier and less pliable than the fresh variety, which can be frozen. Flour tortillas sold in stores often contain lard, which makes them softer than the ones that use vegetable oil or fat.

TACO SHELLS

A Tex-Mex invention, these are so awkward to eat that they are responsible for turning many people off Mexican food. They are, however, an excellent substitute for *chalupas,* if making your own is too difficult. Fill them with salsa, beans, and fresh, crumbly cheese.

TORTILLA CHIPS

The quality and authenticity of these vary greatly. The best are often to be found in the ethnic food sections of supermarkets rather than with the chips and snacks. Many of the ones sold in the snack food section have added flavorings, some of which are not remotely Mexican. Plain, lightly salted chips are best for dipping with salsa. Many specialty food stores and health food stores sell organic corn chips and naturally colored red and blue corn chips (made from colored corn kernels). These look especially good mixed with yellow corn chips in a dish. Warm them in a low oven or microwave before serving.

Above: Blue and yellow tortilla chips. Plain, lightly salted chips are best for dipping in salsa.

Below: Taco shells are difficult to eat but do have their uses.

Above: Corn tortillas

Below: Wheat-flour tortillas

RICE

After its introduction to Latin America and the Caribbean by the Spanish in the 16th century, rice rapidly became a staple food crop. Large tracts of wetlands are given over to rice production, especially in Brazil, which grows as much rice as Japan. Rice is an important source of protein and carbohydrates for the poorest sector of the population, especially in urban areas where individuals spend 15 percent of their income on white rice.

In Brazil, rice is an essential accompaniment to almost all main meals, particularly the national dish, *feijoada*, and is often layered in a mold with many other ingredients. Rice is also an extremely important ingredient in Caribbean cooking. In Peru, Colombia, and Ecuador, where cooked rice is served quite dry, its granular texture earns it the name *arroz graneado*. Rice is also used to make drinks, such as the Mexican *horchata* and Ecuador's fermented rice drink, *arroz fermentado*.

Varieties

White long-grain rice is the variety grown throughout the region, although the influence of immigrants means that other varieties are imported. White rice has been fully milled to remove the outer husk from the inner kernel, leaving a white grain with a delicate fragrance and slightly nutty flavor.

Left: White long-grain rice is served as an accompaniment throughout Latin America and the Caribbean.

Buying and storing

Buy good quality rice in packages and store it in a cool, dry place. Rice keeps well, but once opened, it should be transferred to an airtight container. If cooked rice is cooled quickly, it can be stored for up to 24 hours in the refrigerator. Make sure it is piping hot before it is served next time. Don't reheat rice more than once, and never keep it warm for long periods, because there is a risk of food poisoning.

Preparing rice

White long-grain rice is fluffy and absorbent when cooked, and makes the perfect accompaniment to soups, stews, and sauces. It may also be cooked with other ingredients to make a composite dish. If serving rice as an accompaniment:

1 Add 1 tablespoon oil to a pan, heat gently, then add 1 clove of crushed garlic.

2 Add the rice to the pan and roast the grains for a few minutes until they begin to turn golden.

3 Transfer the rice to a pan full of lightly salted water. Bring to the boil, then add a tight-fitting lid and simmer gently until all of the liquid has been absorbed.

If the rice is to be mixed with other ingredients, for example in the Mexican dish, *sopa seca*, try the following method. It encourages the rice to absorb other flavors and reduces the final cooking time.

Quinoa

Indigenous to Peru, quinoa is a complete protein, possessing all eight essential amino acids. Low in saturated fat and high in fiber, it is a good source of calcium, potassium, zinc, iron, magnesium, and B vitamins. Cooked like rice, the grain becomes soft and creamy, but the germ stays crunchy.

1 In a pan or heatproof bowl, soak the rice in freshly boiled water for 10 minutes.

2 Drain thoroughly before adding the other ingredients.

This fairly unusual method of cooking rice is very popular throughout the region, especially in Colombia, and is particularly delicious served with seafood.

1 Add ¼ cup coconut milk to a pan with a pinch of brown sugar.

2 Add the rice, bring to the boil, and simmer gently for 10–15 minutes, or until tender.

POTATOES

The potato is native to South America and was discovered by pre-Inca peoples in the foothills of the Andes. Archaeological digs in Peru and Bolivia have uncovered evidence that it was used as a food as long ago as 400BC. In Peru, the potato had religious significance, and the potato goddess was depicted with a potato plant in either hand. Potato designs were found in Nazca and Chimu pottery. One of the ways the native South Americans had of measuring time was to gauge how long it took to cook potatoes to certain consistencies. The Incas perfected the art of freeze-drying potatoes 2,000 years ago by leaving them out on lofty mountain tops to produce the early convenience food *chuno*. In an entirely natural process, the night air froze the potatoes and the sun completed the lengthy dehydration process.

When the Inca empire was invaded by Francisco Pizarro in the 16th century, potatoes were among the plunder that the Conquistadors took back to Spain with them. Cultivation quickly spread throughout Europe via explorers such as Sir Francis Drake. Today there are up to 4,000 varieties worldwide. The potato is the staple food for two-thirds of the world's population and our third most important food crop.

Under the skin

Most of the nutrients in potatoes are either in or just beneath the skin, so it is best to avoid peeling potatoes if at all possible.

If you need to peel them, use a potato peeler that removes only the very top surface.

Potatoes are one of the best all-round sources of nutrition known to man. A valuable carbohydrate food, they also contain fairly high levels of protein. They are a very good source of vitamin C, a fact that was of huge value to early seafarers, who discovered that feeding potatoes to their crews helped to prevent scurvy. Potatoes also contain potassium, iron, and vitamin B.

Varieties

In the UK, only about 15 varieties of potato are on general sale, but in Peruvian markets it is claimed that you can buy up to 100 different types, ranging in size from tiny potatoes to large ovals. Worldwide there are thought to be around 4,000 varieties. The colors are equally diverse, including red, black, yellow, brown and purple. Most are known only by their local names, but some are beginning to reach markets in the northern hemisphere. Look out for the Purple Peruvian, with its earthy, slightly nutty-tasting lavender flesh. Also prized, particularly for mashing, is the buttery Papa Amarilla, or yellow potato. Among the varieties with dark skins and dazzling white flesh are the Yanaimilla and the Compis. Potatoes will grow anywhere from sea level to 14,000 feet, so it is not surprising that so many different varieties continue to be cultivated in their place of origin.

Buying and storing

When buying potatoes, it is important to choose a variety that will give you the right results for the cooking method you intend to use. Check the labels or ask for advice from the seller. Store potatoes in a dark, cool, dry place. Paper bags are better than plastic ones, which create humid conditions and hasten deterioration.

Above: Grown in Uruguay and Venezuela, the Red Pontiac has dark red skin and white waxy flesh.

Preparing and cooking

In Latin America, potatoes are usually either boiled in the minimum of water, as in the Peruvian speciality *ocopa arequipena*, or diced and fried, which is a popular method in Mexico. Chiles are frequently added. Purple Peruvian potatoes are excellent in salads, and they require less cooking than white or yellow potatoes.

Below: With striking dark skin and white flesh, Compis potatoes are grown by farmers in the Andean highlands.

BEANS

Along with corn and rice, beans are an extremely important food throughout the Caribbean and Latin America. The inhabitants of Mexico and Central America eat around six times as many beans as are consumed in Great Britain every year, and in Chile, where meat can be relatively scarce, they are a vital source of protein. Beans are served, in one form or another, at most meals.

Several varieties of bean are indigenous to this part of the world. They were traditionally planted with corn and squash, the idea being that the corn stalks would support the growing beans, while the squash plants spread out to suffocate encroaching weeds. This ancient method of cultivation also ensured that the beans enriched the soil depleted by the corn. The beans were served fresh in season, but vast amounts were dried to furnish versatile and nutritious dishes all year round. In the Caribbean, beans are often referred to as "peas."

Beans are a good source of protein and carbohydrate and supply vitamins A, B_1, and B_2. They also contribute valuable amounts of minerals such as potassium and iron to the diet.

Below: Black beans are an essential ingredient in the extravagant Brazilian national dish, feijoada.

Varieties

Black beans These small, shiny, kidney-shaped beans, sometimes known as black turtle beans, are particularly popular in Mexico, the Caribbean, and Brazil. They are highly valued for their creamy white flesh and delicate earthy , flavor reminiscent of mushrooms. Their skins remain bright and shiny after cooking, so they look dramatic when combined with rice or other ingredients. Black beans are often used in salsas and soups, and are eaten as an accompaniment to Brazil's national dish, *feijoada*. In Costa Rica they are often fried with white rice to make the traditional breakfast dish, *gallo pinto*.

White beans A type of navy bean, these vary in size but are always the same plump oval shape. When cooked, they have an earthy, rather floury flavor, and a fairly soft texture, but they retain their shape well. White beans are an extremely versatile ingredient and can be substituted for most other varieties when a recipe calls for dried beans.

Pinto beans A smaller, paler version of the borlotti bean, the pinto has an attractive orange-pink skin speckled

Above: Versatile white beans, a type of navy bean, are plump and soft with a delicious floury texture.

with rust-colored flecks. One of the many relatives of the kidney bean, pinto beans are native to Latin America. They feature extensively in Mexican cooking as well as in the cuisines of most other Spanish-speaking countries. The skins soften on cooking, which makes them easy to mash, so they are the perfect ingredient for the popular Mexican dish, *frijoles refritos* (refried beans).

Red kidney beans The shiny, dark red skin of these beans hides a

pale interior. They retain their shape
and color when cooked and have a
soft, mealy texture. Red kidney beans
are particularly popular in Brazil,
Mexico and some parts of the
Caribbean, where they are used to
make a delicious red bean chili and
the Jamaican specialty, rice and peas.
They can also be used instead of
the traditional pinto beans to make
a variation on refried beans.
Lima beans These beans originated in
Peru and are named after that country's
capital city. Cream-colored and tender,
with soft flesh, these hold their shape
well when cooked. Lima beans have
a delicate flavor, similar to that of
walnuts. Fresh lima beans are delicious.
One variety of lima bean is the large
white butter bean, which is familiar
throughout Europe. Be careful not to
overcook lima beans, as they become
pulpy and mushy in texture.
Black-eyed peas Small and white, with a
distinctive black mark, these beans
were introduced to the Caribbean from
West Africa. They need not be soaked
before use because they rapidly
become tender when cooked. They
taste slightly sweet and readily absorb
other flavors, especially in stews and
curries. Add black-eyed peas to soups
and salads for extra flavor.
Gungo peas Also known as pigeon peas,
these are approximately the size of a
garden pea. They have a sweetish,
slightly acrid flavor, and are used fresh,
canned, or dried.
Chickpeas Also known as garbanzo
beans, robust and hearty chickpeas
resemble shelled hazelnuts and have
a delicious nutty flavor and creamy
texture, although they require lengthy
cooking. Spanish migrants first
introduced chickpeas to Latin America,
and although they have never been
as important or popular as native beans,
they are now naturalized throughout
the region. When fresh, they can be
eaten raw or cooked, but they are
more commonly available dried.
The skin on chickpeas can be tough
and you may like to remove it. Do this
once the chickpeas are fully cooked
and cooled.

*Above: Chickpeas were first introduced
to Latin America by Spanish settlers and
quickly became a popular ingredient.*

Buying and storing

When buying fresh beans, buy young
ones with bright, firm skins, because
the pods of older beans are likely to
be slightly tough. Be sure to use fresh
beans as soon as possible after
purchase, because they do not store
well. Most fresh beans need little
preparation other than trimming the
ends, but older beans may need stringing.
When buying dried beans, look for
plump, shiny beans with smooth,
unbroken skins. Beans toughen with age
and will take longer to cook the older
they are, so although they will keep for
up to a year in a cool, dark place, it is
best to buy them in small quantities
from a store with a regular turnover of
stock. Avoid beans that look dusty or
dirty, and store them in an airtight
container in a cool, dark, dry place.
Canned beans are a useful standby
as they require no soaking or lengthy
cooking. Choose canned beans that
do not have any added sugar or salt,
and be sure to drain and rinse well
before use. Canned beans still contain
a reasonable amount of nutrients.

Preparing dried beans
Dried beans must be soaked
before cooking.

1 Tip the beans into a colander or
strainer and pick them over to
remove any grit or damaged beans.

2 Rinse the beans under cold
running water and then drain.

3 Soak in cold water overnight,
changing the water once.

4 Drain the soaked beans, rinse
them, then place in a large pan
with plenty of cold water.

5 Bring to the boil and boil
vigorously for 10 minutes to
remove natural toxins (this is
particularly important with lima
beans or red kidney beans).

6 Reduce the heat and simmer
until the beans are tender.

COOK'S TIP
If you don't have time to soak dried
beans overnight, put them in a pan
with water to cover, bring them to
the boil, then remove from the heat
and leave to soak for about 1 hour.

CHILES AND SWEET PEPPERS

Chiles and their mild-mannered cousins, the bell peppers, are without doubt Latin America's greatest contribution to the global kitchen. Full of flavor, colorful, nutritious, and versatile, they are now so widely used in many different cuisines that it is difficult to imagine a world without them.

FRESH CHILES

The first chiles were tiny wild berries that grew in the South American jungle thousands of years ago. The plants gradually spread northward from central South America through Central America and the Caribbean to southwestern North America, evolving over the centuries into the wide range of shapes and sizes encountered today.

It was Christopher Columbus who introduced chiles to the rest of the world. When he tasted a highly spiced dish on San Salvador, he assumed that its heat came from black pepper. He named the plant *pimiento* (pepper), and this name endured long after he realized his mistake. Columbus took chile plants back with him when he returned to Europe, and by the 16th century they were widely distributed. Today the chile is the most extensively cultivated and most commonly used spice in the world.

There are as many as 200 different varieties of chile, varying enormously in shape, size, color, flavor, and, most of all, in the amount of heat they deliver.

Below: Poblanas, popular in Mexico, are often roasted to intensify their flavor.

Above: Scotch bonnet chiles are popular throughout the Caribbean and are used to make hot pepper sauce.

The fiery sensation from chiles is caused by capsaicin, an alkaloid that not only causes a burning sensation in the mouth, but also triggers the brain to release endorphins, natural painkillers that promote a sense of wellbeing and stimulation; this is why eating chiles can become quite addictive. Capsaicin is concentrated in the seeds and membrane of the pods, so removing these parts before eating will reduce the fieriness of a chile considerably. Chiles are an excellent source of vitamin C and also yield valuable quantities of beta-carotene, folate, potassium, and vitamin E. They stimulate the appetite, help improve circulation, and can also be used as a powerful decongestant.

Varieties

Of the vast range of chiles grown in Latin America and the Caribbean, the following are the most popular. They have been rated on a scale of one to ten for heat and are listed in order of potency, mildest first. Be careful: the heat can vary widely, even with chiles from the same plant, so use these ratings as a guide only.

Left: Jalapeños and the smaller serrano chiles are either bright green or red, depending on ripeness.

Poblano These mild to medium-hot chiles (heat scale 3) are very popular in Mexico. Big and beautiful, poblanos are about 3 inches long, with thick flesh and a rich, earthy flavor. They start off dark green with a purple-black tinge and ripen to dark red. Green poblanos are always used cooked, and roasting gives them a more intense flavor. They are perfect for stuffed dishes such as *chiles rellenos* and taste good in traditional mole sauces. Dried poblanos are called anchos.

Jalapeño Well known and widely used the world over, jalapeños are medium-hot (heat scale 4–7). Plump and glossy, they are used in stews, salsas, breads, sauces, and dips. Green jalapeños have a fresh, grassy flavor; red ones are slightly sweeter. Smoke-dried jalapeños are known as chipotle chiles.

Fresno Plump and cylindrical, these chiles are usually sold when red. They have thick flesh and a hot, sweet flavor (heat scale 5). Fresnos are excellent in salsas, ceviche, stuffings, bread, and pickles. Roasting brings out their delicious sweetness.

Serrano Thin-skinned and quite slender, serranos are the classic Mexican green chile (*chiles verdes*) and are always used in guacamole. Although they are quite fiery (heat scale 7), they have a clean, biting heat, matched by a high acidity. Both red and green serranos are frequently added to cooked dishes. They can also be pickled.

Left: Sweet, juicy fresnos are perfect for fresh salsas or pickles.

Aji mirasol Extensively used in Peruvian cooking, these chiles are narrow and tapered, with a tropical fruit flavor, yet they are decidedly hot (heat scale 6–7). Fresh yellow ones are particularly prized for salsas and ceviche. They are also used in cooked dishes, such as soups or stews, and are sometimes made into a paste, which is mixed with oil to make a hot dipping sauce.

Brazilian malagueta These very hot chiles (heat scale 8) are believed to be a wild form of tabasco. Very small, only about ¾ inch long, they have thin flesh and a fresh yet fiery taste. Malaguetas are often added to marinades and vinegars.

Jamaican hot, Scotch bonnet, and habañero These chiles are closely related and are all intensely fiery (heat scale 10). The Jamaican hot is bright red and has a sweet hot flavor. It goes well with tropical fruits and is also used in fresh salsas, Caribbean fish stews, curries, and spicy chutneys. The Scotch bonnet is an essential ingredient in many Caribbean dishes, especially curries and jerk sauce, and is used to make Jamaican hot pepper sauce.

Below: Chili powder is a good alternative when fresh chiles are not available.

Measuring the heat

The heat level of a chile is often measured in Scoville units on a scale where 0 is the rating for a bell pepper and 557,000 relates to the hottest chile grown in Latin America, the habañero. The simpler system used in this book rates the chiles on a scale of one to ten, with one indicating the mildest and ten the hottest.

Preparing Fresh Chiles

Take great care when handling chiles, as the capsaicin they contain is an extremely powerful irritant. Wear rubber gloves while preparing chiles or wash your hands in soapy water afterward. If you touch your skin by mistake, splash the affected area with cold water. Avoid scratching or rubbing inflamed skin, because this could aggravate the problem.

1 Cut the chile in half lengthwise, cut off the stalk, and carefully scrape out the seeds (unless you wish to leave them in for extra heat).

2 Remove the remaining core and any white membrane.

3 Finely slice or chop each piece, depending on use.

BELL PEPPERS

Sometimes known as capsicums, bell peppers are native to Mexico and Central America and were widely grown there in pre-Columbian times. Pepper seeds were carried to Spain in 1493 and from there spread rapidly throughout Europe. They also spread rapidly throughout South America and were a staple food of the Incas in Peru. They contribute color and flavor to a huge variety of dishes, including salsas, stews, and spicy meat fillings, as well as fish dishes, vegetable accompaniments, and salads. Bell peppers come in many unusual shapes and sizes, from chile-size rounds to slender drops, bells, and even hearts. Colors range from bright green, through yellow and orange to vibrant red, and

Above: Delicious either cooked or raw, bell peppers should look glossy, feel firm, and have a crisp, juicy bite. Avoid those that are wrinkled.

there is even a dark purple variety (but this does turn green when cooked). Mild and sweet in flavor, with crisp, juicy flesh when ripe, they can be eaten either raw in salads or cooked. A popular way of serving peppers is to stuff and bake them.

Buying and storing

Whether you are buying hot chiles or mild bell peppers, look for firm, shiny specimens with unblemished skins. Avoid peppers that are limp, that wrinkle when touched or that have "blistered" areas on the skin. Green peppers should be purchased before they change color, but should not be too dark as this indicates immaturity and lack of flavor. Avoid red peppers with dark patches on the skin, as this could be a sign that they have begun to rot inside. Store peppers in the vegetable crisper in the refrigerator. Sweet peppers will keep well for up to a week and chiles up to three weeks.

Preparing bell peppers

Depending on use, the core and seeds should usually be removed before cooking bell peppers.

1 Halve or quarter the peppers, then, using a small, sharp knife, carefully cut out the core, any white membrane, and the seeds.

2 If the peppers are being used whole, for example to be stuffed, cut around the stem and pull out the seeds like a plug.

Roasting peppers and chiles

To really bring out the delicious, sweet flavor of fresh peppers and chiles, try roasting them.

1 Place them under a hot broiler and turn occasionally until the skins blister and char.

2 Alternatively, dry-fry them in a frying pan or griddle until the skins are scorched.

3 Place them in a strong plastic bag and tie the top tightly, or place them in a bowl and cover with plastic wrap.

4 After approximately 20 minutes, remove the skins, then slit each pepper or chile. Remove the seeds and membrane, and tear or slice the flesh into pieces.

DRIED CHILES

Travel through Latin America and you will frequently see bunches of colorful chiles dangling from hooks on the walls of houses. In the bright sunshine they soon dehydrate and can be packed away until needed. When rehydrated, the chiles will not taste the same as before. In many cases they will have acquired a new intensity and richness of flavor, which is one of the reasons why Mexicans really value dried chiles and view them as distinct from the fresh, often giving them completely different names. Each variety has unique characteristics, and cooks will often blend several types to get exactly the results they require.

Varieties

The following are the most widely used varieties of dried chile.

Ancho These dried red poblanos have a rich deep color and mild fruity flavor (heat scale 3). Anchos can be stuffed and are often used in mole sauces.

Mulato Related to the ancho and with the same level of heat, mulatos taste smoky rather than fruity.

Guajillo These large dried chiles, orange-red in color, have a slightly acidic flavor (heat scale 3–4).

Right: Habañeros are used for chili sauces.

Below: Anchos are delicious stuffed or added to stews.

Left: Cascabels have a delicious, slightly nutty flavor.

Pasada Roasted, peeled, and dried, these chiles have a toasty flavor (heat scale 3–4), with apple, licorice, and cherry notes.

Cascabel The name means "little rattle" and refers to the sound the seeds make when the chiles are shaken. Thick-skinned and smooth, cascabels have a rich, woody flavor (heat scale 4).

Pasilla Long, slender, and very dark, the flavor of pasillas is rich with hints of berries and licorice (heat scale 4).

Chipotle Smoke-dried jalapeños, these have wrinkled dark red skin and thick flesh. Chipotles need long, slow cooking to soften them and bring out their full, smoky taste (heat scale 6–10).

Aji mirasol The dried version of Peru's favorite chile is deep yellowish red with a berry-like fruit flavor (heat scale 6–7).

Pequin These small chiles are pale orange-red in color, with a light, sweet, smoky flavor suggestive of corn and nuts (heat scale 8–9). They are excellent in sauces, salsas, and soups and can be crushed over food as a condiment.

Habañero Used in moderation, these have a wonderful tropical fruit flavor (heat scale 10). Like dried Scotch bonnets, they are often used to make classic hot pepper sauces, particularly in the Caribbean, and are also good when added to fish stews and salsas.

Above: Pasadas are often used in sauces for meat or fish, or in rich spicy stews.

Buying and storing

Dried chiles should be flexible. Avoid any that smell musty or have powdery skins, as this could indicate insect infestation. Store for up to 1 year in an airtight container in a cool, dry place.

Preparing dried chiles

To appreciate their full flavor, dried chiles should be soaked before use. Toasting dried chiles before soaking will give a lovely smoky flavor. If the chiles are to be used in a slow-cooked stew, soaking is not necessary.

1 Lightly dry-fry or toast the dried chiles in a frying pan or griddle for a couple of minutes.

2 Seed large chiles and tear into pieces, then soak in warm water until soft. Soak smaller chiles before cutting into pieces.

Caribbean hot sauces

Most islands have their own recipe for hot chili sauce. Based on the fiery habañero or Scotch bonnet chile pepper, they should be used sparingly by the uninitiated.

OTHER VEGETABLES

A visit to a market in any Latin American country is a real feast for the eyes. Fruit and vegetables are laid on mats or heaped high on tables, strings of chiles hang overhead, and everywhere there are people bustling or bargaining. The colors are glorious, the aromas are unfamiliar, and there will usually be several local specialties on sale.

CHAYOTES

Also known as christophenes or chokos, these pale green gourds are particularly popular in the Caribbean, where they are used in soups, salads, and stews. Raw chayote is crisp and clean-tasting, rather like water chestnut. The cooked vegetable has a rather bland flavor, so needs plenty of seasoning. Cholesterol-free and low in calories, chayotes are a good source of fiber and vitamin C.

Buying and storing

Choose smooth, unwrinkled chayotes and store in the refrigerator. They keep well but are best used as soon as possible after purchase.

SQUASH

Cultivated in Latin America long before Columbus sailed, squash is an important food. Many different types are eaten in Latin America, from zucchini to huge hard-skinned pumpkins. Squash are eaten in both savory and

Below: Halved chayotes can be baked for a simple yet delicious side dish.

Preparing chayotes

Chayotes can be peeled, chopped and cooked in soups or stews, or cut in half and baked.

1 Preheat the oven to 375°F Cut the chayotes in half, place them skin side down on a shallow baking tray and brush with a little olive oil.

2 Bake for approximately 25 minutes or until tender.

---

sweet dishes, often with brown sugar. Pumpkin and shrimp is an unusual but delicious combination. A hollowed-out pumpkin makes a good container for cooking and serving, as in the Argentine stew, *carbonada criolla*. A good source of fiber and carbohydrate, pumpkins are low in calories. Varieties with bright flesh are high in vitamin A.

Buying and storing

If buying zucchini or other summer squash, the general rule is that the smaller the specimen, the better the flavor. Store zucchini in the refrigerator and use as soon as possible. Due to their hard skins, unbruised pumpkins and other winter squash keep well. Cut pumpkin should be covered in plastic wrap and stored in the refrigerator.

Roasting squash

Instead of roasting, pieces of squash could be lightly boiled or steamed and added to stews.

1 Preheat the oven to 375°F. Cut the squash into wedges, remove the skin and seeds.

2 Place the wedges in a large roasting pan with a little olive oil and roast for approximately 45 minutes or until tender.

Below: Pumpkins can be easily stored over the long winter months, making them a popular ingredient all year round in many Latin American countries.

Above: Thin slices of sweet potato are fried to make chips, a popular street snack throughout Latin America.

SWEET POTATOES AND YAMS

These root vegetables are not related, although the American habit of calling red sweet potatoes yams can lead to confusion, and the two are sometimes mixed up. Sweet potatoes have been grown in South America for centuries. In pre-Inca times, sun-dried sweet potato slices were a popular treat, and Mayan cooks also used the vegetable to provide a sweet note in many savory meat and fish dishes. Yams were brought to South America by African slaves and are widely used throughout the Caribbean and Brazil. Both of these vegetables provide some vitamin C, while orange-fleshed sweet potatoes also contain beta-carotene.

Varieties

There are hundreds of varieties of both sweet potatoes and yams. In Latin American cooking, the red-skinned sweet potato with white flesh is best known. The most commonly used yam is brown, with moist cream-colored flesh that becomes dry when cooked.

Buying and storing

Buy vegetables that are firm and dry, with no soft areas. Store loose or in a brown paper bag in a cool, dry place, but do not put them in the refrigerator.

Preparing and cooking

Like regular potatoes, sweet potatoes can be scrubbed and baked in their skins, or peeled and sliced, then boiled or fried. They are delicious mashed or creamed, and make very good chips. Yams must be thickly peeled and should be washed well before and after slicing; this helps to remove any toxins that may be present in the raw tuber. Always cook yams very thoroughly.

CASSAVA

Also known as *manioc, mandioc,* or *yuca* (in Peru), this starchy tuber looks like a long, fat sausage with dark, rough outer skin. Native to Brazil, it is also a popular ingredient in West Indian cooking. It is important to distinguish between sweet and bitter cassava: the root and leaves of the former can safely be eaten, but bitter cassava contains cyanide. Although bitter cassava is used for making beer, tapioca, and cassava flour—*farinha de mandioca*—it must be detoxified first. Sweet cassava is a carbohydrate food with a high fiber

Below: Sweet cassava is a native root vegetable high in fiber and nutrients.

content, and the leaves are a valuable source of protein. *Cassareep* is a delicious syrup made from cassava and flavored with cinnamon and cloves. It is an essential ingredient in the traditional Jamaican pepperpot stew. Cassava is fairly bland, so it is best served with a sauce or dressing such as the traditional Cuban *mojo*, which is a mixture of oil, citrus juices, and garlic.

Buying and storing

Most cassava that is exported around the world is first coated in a layer of wax to keep it fresh. When buying sweet cassava, look for roots that are fairly firm, dry, and odor-free.

Preparing cassava

An extremely versatile vegetable, sweet cassava can be cooked in a number of ways.

1 Scrub the root, peel, then cut into fairly large pieces, removing the fibrous core.

2 Drop the pieces into a bowl of acidulated water to prevent discoloration.

3 Boil, steam, bake, or fry the cassava pieces until tender.

PALM HEARTS

The terminal bud of the Acai, or cabbage palm, has long been considered a regional delicacy. Native to South America, this fast-growing palm is now widely cultivated in vast plantations, mainly in Brazil and Costa Rica. Fresh palm hearts make very good eating, but are rarely available outside the country of origin. Canned palm hearts have a slightly different texture from fresh, but are still delicious and make a good alternative. Low in saturated fat and cholesterol, palm hearts are a valuable source of vitamin C.

Buying and storing

Fresh palm hearts should be pale, moist, and evenly colored. To enjoy them at their best, use as soon as possible after purchase. Canned hearts are much more readily available.

Preparing and cooking

To prepare fresh palm hearts, simply strip off the outer layers. Eat them raw or roast or steam in the same way as asparagus. Canned palm hearts are delicious in soups, salads, and pies.

Below: Canned palm hearts make a good alternative if fresh ones are unavailable.

Above: Look for okra pods that are firm, plump, and smooth, but not too big.

OKRA

Also known as ladies' fingers, these pods ooze a sticky liquid when cut, which acts as a thickener in sauces. Okra was introduced to Latin America by African slaves and is an important ingredient in Brazilian and Caribbean cooking. A source of vitamin C, fiber-rich okra also contains folate, thiamin, and calcium.

Buying and storing

Okra should be a fresh, pale green color. Buy smaller pods and avoid any that are flabby, shriveled, or bruised. Store in the refrigerator and use as soon as possible after purchase.

Preparing and cooking

If cooking whole, trim the top of each pod. If destined for a composite dish, where the viscous liquid will act as a thickener, cut the pods into slices. Otherwise, leave whole. Okra can be steamed, boiled, or fried. Try it Brazilian-style, with chicken and chiles. The Barbadian speciality, Cou-cou, combines okra with cornmeal.

LEAFY GREEN VEGETABLES

A number of leafy green vegetables are on sale in Latin American markets, and many are available only in certain areas. The young tops of cassava and sweet potatoes are regularly eaten, as is amaranth, a chard-like vegetable esteemed by the Aztecs. *Callaloo* is the name given to the leaves of two related tubers that are used for a popular Caribbean soup. *Nopales* are the edible leaves of the prickly pear cactus, while bottled *nopales*, commonly known as *nopalitos*, can be found in specialist food stores.

Unusual tubers

Jicama is indigenous to Mexico but has achieved widespread popularity thanks to its crisp, juicy flesh. Also known as yam bean or Chinese turnip, it can be eaten raw with orange juice and chii powder, or cooked, and is especially good in salsas.
Oca looks like a short, fat wrinkled carrot. There are several varieties available, including white, yellow, red, and purple. Its sharp taste is moderated by sun-drying the tubers before cooking.
Yacón, related to the Jerusalem artichoke, is highly valued in Peru and Bolivia for its sweet, crunchy flesh. It can be eaten either raw or cooked.

Añu is a white or yellow tuber from a nasturtium-like plant with edible leaves and flowers. It is an important crop in Ecuador, Peru, Bolivia, Colombia, and Venezuela.

Jicama has crisp, juicy flesh, similar to green apples or water chestnuts.

FRUIT VEGETABLES

Neither savory nor sweet, these are popular throughout Latin America.

TOMATOES

Along with chiles and corn, tomatoes are one of Latin America's most important contributions to the global cooking pot. Although they originated in the lands to the west of the Andes, both the Mayas and the Aztecs grew the little cherry-sized fruit vegetables, and the Spanish introduced them to Europe. Largely composed of water, tomatoes, are a good source of vitamins A and C. Raw ones contain useful amounts of vitamin E. Tomatoes also contribute the powerful antioxidant, lycopene, which may help to lower the risk of cancer.

Varieties

There are hundreds of varieties ot tomato. Cherry tomatoes, the closest in size to their Peruvian ancestors, are delicious in salads, juicy plum tomatoes make excellent sauces, and beefsteak tomatoes are great for stuffing. Tomatillos (literally translated as "little tomatoes") are covered in brown papery husks. The fruit itself is green, with a clean, slightly acidic flavor.

Buying and storing

For the best flavor, buy tomatoes straight from the grower and store them at room temperature. Chilling tomatoes dulls their taste. Fresh tomatillos are difficult to obtain outside Latin America, but canned ones make a perfectly acceptable substitute.

Below: Fresh tomatillos are a tasty addition to spicy Mexican salsas.

Above: Tomatoes were enjoyed by the Mayas and Aztecs in ancient times.

Preparing and cooking

When adding to salsas and sauces, tomatoes should ideally have the skin removed. To skin tomatoes, cut a cross on the base, put them in a heatproof bowl, and pour over boiling water. Leave for 30–60 seconds, then remove the remaining skin with a sharp knife. In Mexico, tomatillos are used fresh and raw, mostly in salsas, but they also taste great cooked.

AVOCADOS

The most nutritious of all the fruit vegetables, the avocado is native to Mexico, where it is called *acuacate*. In Brazil it is known as *abacate*, and in the US, as the alligator pear.

Nutrition

Despite the hefty calorie content— half an avocado delivers around 143kcals—the fat they contain is mostly mono-unsaturated and is a valuable source of energy. Avocados are protein-rich and also contain vitamins E, C, and B6, plus copper and iron.

Varieties

Among the many varieties, some with soft, smooth skins, others encased in dark, wrinkled shells, the avocado with the best flavor is the hass, a dark avocado with buttery, golden yellow flesh.

Buying and storing

Obtaining the perfect avocado can be a tricky business. Some supermarkets package the fruits with a "ready to eat" label, which is helpful if the avocados are hard-skinned. To test if a soft-skinned avocado is ripe, press the top end gently—it should just give. Ripe avocados can be stored in the refrigerator; unripe ones should be put in a paper bag with a banana to soften.

Preparation and cooking

Avocados soon discolor when cut, but sprinkling the cut surface with lemon juice will help prevent this. To halve an avocado, run a knife lengthwise around the fruit, cutting in to the pit, then ease the halves apart. Remove the pit and peel the halves before chopping the flesh. The most common use for avocados is in guacamole, but they also taste wonderful in soups and mousses. Avocados are seldom cooked, but in Latin America slices are often added to soups or stews just before serving. In Brazil, avocado is served as a creamy dessert, *creme de abacate*.

Below: Although high in calories, avocados contain healthy fats and plenty of vitamins and minerals.

GUACAMOLE

Guacamole originated in Mexico, but has become one of the world's most popular dishes. Mashed avocado is the main ingredient, but other items, such as onion, garlic, diced tomato, chopped chiles, lime or lemon juice, as well as seasonings, are added. The smooth, buttery taste of the avocado gives this dip a creamy texture, yet it contains no saturated fat. Guacamole is often served with tortilla chips as a simple dip. It is an essential accompaniment to fajitas, is used in *tortas*, and is served alongside meat and fish dishes.

Simple Guacamole

1 Cut two avocados in half. Remove the pits and scoop the flesh out of the shells. Place it in a blender and process until almost smooth. Transfer into a bowl and add the juice of half a lime.

2 Add one-quarter of a small onion, chopped finely, a crushed garlic clove, and a handful of cilantro, also chopped finely.

3 Add salt and other seasoning to taste and serve immediately, with tortilla chips for dipping. The Guacamole will keep in the refrigerator for 2–3 days if it is kept in an airtight container.

VARIATION

Try adding chopped fresh tomatoes and fresh chile to give your guacamole added flavor, texture, and fire.

Preparing avocado

1 If a recipe calls for avocado halves or mashed avocado, run a small, sharp knife all the way around the fruit, starting at the top and cutting right in until the knife touches the pit.

2 Gently prise the two halves apart with the knife.

3 Push the knife blade into the pit, then lift it away. If any of the brown skin from the pit remains on the avocado flesh, remove it. The avocado halves can be served with vinaigrette, filled with shrimp or topped with thin slices of ham. Alternatively, the flesh can be scooped into a bowl and mashed.

1 For avocado slices, cut the fruit in half, remove the pit, then nick the skin at the top of each half and ease it away until you can peel off the skin completely; if the avocado is ripe, it will come off cleanly and easily.

2 Cut the peeled avocado halves into slices, leaving them attached at one end if you want to fan them on the plate. Sprinkle them with lemon or lime juice to stop them from discoloring too quickly.

1 For cubes of avocado, score the half of avocado and then, with the tip of the knife, gently lift each cube out one by one.

Left: Tomatillos with husks

TOMATILLOS/TOMATE VERDE

Despite the name by which we know them—and the fact that they are sometimes referred to as Mexican green tomatoes—tomatillos are not members of the tomato family. Instead, they are related to physalis, those pretty little orange fruits surrounded by papery lanterns, which are so popular as garnishes. They have been grown in Mexico since Aztec times, when they were known as *miltomatl*. Mexicans seldom use the term "tomatillo, preferring to call these fruits by one of their many local names, which include *fresadilla* and *tomate milpero*.

Description

Ranging in color from yellowish green to lime, tomatillos are firm and round, about the size of a small tomato but lighter in weight, as they are not juicy. Fresh ones usually have the brown papery husk attached to them at the stem end. The flavor resembles that of tart apples with a hint of lemon, and is enhanced by cooking, although a *salsa cruda* of raw tomatillos has a very pleasant, clean taste.

Buying and Storing

Fresh tomatillos are difficult to find outside Mexico, but some specialist stores sell them, and they are also available by mail order in season. They can also be grown from seed, a most worthwhile enterprise for anyone who loves their clean, slightly acidic flavor. If you do locate a supply of fresh tomatillos, look for firm fruit with tight-fitting husks, and store them in the refrigerator for up to one week.

In the same way that canned carrots bear little resemblance to fresh ones, canned tomatillos are softer and not as tasty as fresh, but they are more readily available and preferable to missing out on this great flavor completely. When buying canned tomatillos, be sure to take account of the loss of weight when the liquid is drained off—it can be as much as a third of the total.

Main Uses and Cooking Tips

Tomatillos are used in table salsas and in the sauce (*tomate verde salsa*) which is poured over enchiladas before they are cooked. They can also be used instead of tomatoes in guacamole, giving a piquant flavor to the sauce. To cook fresh tomatillos, remove the husks and dry fry them in a heavy-based frying pan until the skins have begun to char and the flesh has softened. Alternatively, put them in a pan with water to cover, bring to the boil, then simmer them until they soften and begin to break down. If the dish in which they are used requires stock, use the cooking liquid.

Above: Canned tomatillos

Salsa cruda de tomatillo

1 To make a rough-textured salsa with tomatillos, process 1 pound raw tomatillos in a food processor or chop them finely, then mix with one chopped small onion and one crushed garlic clove. Add two seeded and chopped jalapeño chiles and salt to taste.

2 Finely chop a small bunch of fresh cilantro and add it to the tomatillo mixture.

3 Stir well, spoon into a clean bowl, and serve at once with freshly made corn tortilla chips.

FRUIT

Some of the world's most colorful, exotic, and intensely flavored fruits are to be found throughout Latin America and the Caribbean.

PINEAPPLES

The taste of a freshly picked ripe pineapple is incomparable. Their aroma is so intense that a single pineapple can perfume the entire house, and the flesh is so sweet that it is unnecessary to add sugar or any other sweetener. Cultivated in Central America and the Caribbean long before the arrival of Columbus, this majestic fruit has become popular the world over. Costa Rica and the Dominican Republic are the major producers. Pineapples are used in both sweet and savory dishes and make refreshing drinks. In Venezuela and Columbia, pineapple is a popular flavoring for sweet custard desserts. Rich in vitamin C and a valuable source of fiber, pineapples also contain bromelain, a protein-digesting enzyme that soothes digestive complaints.

Varieties

There are hundreds of varieties of pineapple, ranging in size from the small "baby pineapples" to specimens 12 inches long. Some turn a deep golden yellow as they ripen, while others remain a bronze-green color. The latest varieties to be cultivated are deliciously sweet and juicy.

Below: Papaya is a popular addition to Latin American fruit salads.

Above: Pineapples can be used to make a delicious refresco or fruit drink.

Buying and storing

Choose firm, ripe fruit with no bruising. The leaves should be glossy and fresh, and there should be a distinctive pineapple aroma. One test of ripeness is to gently pull a leaf from the bottom of the plume; if it comes away easily, the pineapple is ripe. Store whole pineapples in a cool place, but not the refrigerator, and use them as quickly as possible. Slices or cubes of pineapple should be stored in an airtight container and chilled in the refrigerator, where they will keep for up to three days.

PAPAYAS

These Latin American natives were slow to gain popularity in Europe. Before careful packaging techniques and speedy air travel ensured that the fruit reached its destination in good condition, the papayas on sale throughout Europe were far from their best

Preparing pineapple

The fruit is usually served fresh and raw, but cooking brings out the sweet flavor still more, and pineapple tastes particularly good in hot, spicy dishes. Avoid using fresh pineapple in gelatine-based desserts, as the bromelain will prevent it from setting.

1 To broil pineapple, cut the fruit into quarters, remove the core from each piece, then loosen the flesh by running a sharp knife between the flesh and the skin, as when preparing melon.

2 Douse liberally with rum, sprinkle with brown sugar, and place under a hot broiler until caramelized.

3 To cube pineapples, quarter the fruit, then remove the core and skin from each quarter, taking care to cut out the peppery "eyes." Cube the wedges or cut them into sticks.

—hard and unappetizing or soft and squashy. Today the situation has improved considerably, and more and more people are now beginning to appreciate the sweet, scented flesh of this delicious fruit. Papayas are extremely easy to digest, thanks to an enzyme called papain, which they contain. Papain is a natural tenderizer, a fact that was well known to the pre-Colombian Indians who often marinated their meat in papaya juice to improve the quality. Amply stocked with vitamins A and C, and calcium, papayas are also a valuable source of fiber.

Preparing mangoes

Ripe mangoes are juicy and can be messy to eat. For convenience, cut the fruit into cubes or strips.

1 Cut a broad slice from either side of the mango, removing the "cheeks" or plump sides.

2 For long pieces, peel the skin from each cheek, slice the flesh lengthwise, then cut off any flesh still sticking to the pit.

3 To dice mango, leave the flesh on the skin and use a sharp knife to mark it into neat squares.

4 Gently press the mango cheek back on itself so that the pieces stand proud. Either eat straight from the skin with a spoon or use a sharp knife to slice off the chunks.

Varieties

All papayas are pear-shaped, but the size varies considerably, with some weighing up to 11 pounds or more. The skin starts off green, before ripening to a bright yellow or red. The sweet, scented flesh can be either pink or yellow. A hybrid form of papaya is the *babaco* from Ecuador, a fruit that can be served fresh or cooked. Stewed *babaco* tastes particularly good with roast meats.

Buying and storing

Look for small, soft papayas with undamaged, yellow skins. Handle them gently and use them as soon as possible. Store ripe papayas in the refrigerator; unripe papayas will continue to ripen at room temperature.

Preparing and serving

Cut the fruit in half and scoop out the seeds. The flavor of papaya is often improved with a squirt of fresh lime juice. Papaya can be combined with coconut milk to make a soothing drink, while in the Caribbean, the unripe fruit is used in savory dishes.

MANGOES

While many exotic native fruits have been transported from Latin America to European countries, mangoes made the journey in the opposite direction. These delectable fruits originated in Asia, but were enthusiastically embraced by Caribbean and Central American farmers as soon as they were introduced. The meltingly tender flesh, with its unique fragrance and flavor, makes mangoes a

Below: A Caribbean native, Julie, one of more than 300 varieties of mango has sweet, tender flesh and an intense perfumed fragrance.

popular choice for drinks, desserts, and even some savory dishes. Ripe mangoes are a good source of fiber, and they contain generous amounts of vitamin C. The vibrant orange flesh also makes them a valuable source of beta-carotene.

Varieties

Over 300 varieties of mango are commercially cultivated, with many more being grown in tropical gardens. One of the most popular varieties imported into Europe from the Caribbean is Julie. This medium-sized mango, slightly flattened on one side, comes mainly from the islands of Jamaica and Trinidad and Tobago. It contains only a small amount of fiber and is particularly noted for its fine flavor. Two other favorites are the kidney-shaped Madame Francis, which originated in Haiti, and the Brazilian Itamarica. Of the fiberless varieties, the Jamaican Bombay Green is highly regarded, as is Brazil's Mango de Ubá.

Buying and storing

Not all mangoes turn yellow or become rosy-cheeked when ripe, so color is not necessarily a clear indication of ripeness. Avoid fruit with dark patches on the skin, as this is a sign that the fruit is past its best. A perfect mango will have an intense sweet aroma and will yield when lightly pressed. Unripe mangoes will quickly ripen if placed in a paper bag with a banana.

*Above: Guavas
are used to make the
delicious sweetmeat dulce de guayaba.*

GUAVAS

Native to Central and South America, guavas were introduced to Europe by the Conquistadors. Brazil remains a major producer of these highly perfumed fruits, known as *guayabas* in Mexico. Guavas are usually used in desserts, but their flavor is such that they are equally good in savory dishes, especially with fish. Guavas are an excellent source of vitamin C, better than most citrus fruits. They also contain vitamins A and B₆.

Varieties

The fruits can be oval or round, with shiny skin that turns pale yellow when ripe. Some varieties have creamy white flesh, while others have pink or even

*Below:
Grapefruits
are native to
Latin America.*

purple flesh. Guava flesh has a clean, sweet, slightly acidic flavor, and a rather musky scent, but this disappears when the fruit is cooked.

Buying and storing

Look for firm, fairly small fruit that has ripened to a uniform yellow. Avoid any that are bruised or pockmarked. Wrap them well to avoid contaminating other foods with their musky odour, and store them in the refrigerator.

Preparing and serving

If the guavas are young there is no need to peel them. Just wash the fruit, then slice it, removing the larger seeds. Older fruit will need to be skinned and seeded. Guavas can be eaten raw with a little sugar to bring out their flavor, or cooked. In Latin America, sweetened guava pulp is used to make *dulce de guayaba*, which is similar to *membrillo*, the Spanish quince "cheese."

CITRUS FRUITS

The only citrus fruit that originated in Latin America is the grapefruit. A descendant of the Polynesian pomelo or shaddock, it is said to have been cultivated on Barbados. Grapefruit is thought to be useful in helping to lower cholesterol. Oranges came from China and India, and were introduced to the Caribbean by early traders. Seville oranges are particularly popular in the islands—although too bitter to eat raw, they are widely used in poultry and meat dishes. Limes were also an early import, hugely valued because they helped to prevent scurvy. Limes grow well in Latin America, and their juice is widely used. Its most famous function is as a marinade for raw fish; the

---

Dulce de guayaba

This sweet guava paste, popular throughout Latin America, is delicious served with a hard cheese such as Manchego.

1 Peel 2¼ pounds guavas, then half each guava and scoop the seeds into a bowl. Add scant 1 cup water and set aside.

2 Chop the guavas and put them in a large, heavy pan. Pour over water to cover, bring to the boil, then cover and simmer, stirring frequently, for about 2 hours. Strain in the juice from the guava seeds and stir well.

3 Puree the mixture in a food processor, then press through a strainer into a bowl. Using a cup measure, scoop it into a heavy pan, noting the number of cups. Add an equal number of cups of sugar and stir in 2 tablespoons lime juice.

4 Stir over a low heat until the mixture reddens and becomes very thick. Pour into a shallow pan and smooth the surface. Dry out in a barely warm oven and serve in small squares.

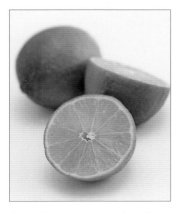

Above: Limes are a popular ingredient, especially in Mexican dishes.

action of the acid on the protein cooks the fish. Lemons are used in Latin American cooking, but are secondary to limes. All forms of citrus fruit are low in calories and are good sources of fiber and vitamin C.

Varieties

Grapefruit may be white, pink, or ruby. There is also a green-skinned variety with sweet flesh. Oranges are either sweet or bitter. There are many varieties of sweet oranges, including Valencias, which are juicy and seedless. Of the bitter oranges, Sevilles are the best known. In addition to being used in cooking, bitter oranges are the basis for several Caribbean liqueurs, including curaçao. There are three main types of lime—Tahitian, Mexican, and Key Limes. Mexican limes are fairly small but have a strong and aromatic flavor.

Buying and storing

The juiciest fruits are those that feel fairly heavy for their size. Choose those with firm skin, avoiding any that are damaged or wrinkled. This advice is especially

relevant to limes because they perish more quickly than other forms of citrus fruit. Choose bright green limes with shiny skins that are unmarked by brown patches. Grapefruit, lemons, and limes should be stored in a cool place or the refrigerator for up to 1 week; oranges have a slightly longer shelf-life and will keep well for up to 2 weeks at cool room temperature.

BANANAS

Introduced to South America from Portugal in the 16th century, bananas rapidly became naturalized and are today a very important food crop in the region. In some areas, such as the Windward Islands in the Caribbean, they are practically the only crop. A large proportion of the world's organic bananas come from this area, as well as from the Dominican Republic and Mexico. Bananas are convenient, nutritious, tasty, and so easy to digest that they can be eaten by everyone, old or young. With high levels of potassium, bananas also contribute vitamins C and B6. The carbohydrate they contain boosts flagging energy levels. Banana leaves are used as a wrapper for *pastelles*, the corn meal and meat parcels that are a specialty on Trinidad and Tobago, and similar wrapped dishes.

Varieties

There are hundreds of different varieties of banana, though few are identified by name. Most familiar in our stores are the common yellow curved bananas, but it is sometimes possible to buy the tiny Brazilian lady fingers or sugar bananas. Red bananas, which come from Ecuador, have orange flesh and taste particularly good when cooked.

Buying and storing

Bananas are harvested when they are still green. By the time they reach stores in the northern hemisphere they have begun to ripen, and most are at their peak after being allowed to ripen in a warm room for a day or two. The skin of the fruit will become progressively darker, and will acquire brown speckles, but even at this stage, the flesh will probably be perfectly good to eat. Do not throw away very soft bananas; they can be used to make banana bread.

Preparing and serving

There's nothing tricky about preparing a banana—simply peel back the skin and eat. If you want to eat half a banana, fold the skin back across the uneaten piece, wrap the fruit well and it will still be edible the next day. Bananas are delicious fresh but can also be cooked. A popular way of preparing them in the Caribbean is to bake them, or cook them on the barbecue, with plenty of brown sugar and a dash of rum to caramelize.

Above: Bananas are an important crop in Latin America and the Caribbean; much of the world's supply comes from plantations in these areas.

OTHER FRUITS

Latin America and the Caribbean are also home to some more unusual fruits, including the following.

Ackees The only part of this bright red fruit that is edible is the creamy-colored aril, which looks a bit like scrambled egg. Ackee has an interesting texture and a subtle flavour and is one of the key ingredients of the Jamaican dish salt fish and ackee. Canned ackees are available from Caribbean food stores.

Breadfruit This large green fruit has very starchy flesh. Although very ripe breadfruit can be eaten raw, they are more often roasted, as a Caribbean specialty, baked, boiled, or fried. They are available fresh or canned.

Cherimoyas Indigenous to the region, cherimoyas have delicious creamy flesh that tastes like a cross between banana and pineapple, with a texture similar to papaya. The skin and seeds should not be eaten. Varieties include custard apples and soursops.

Prickly pears These are the fruit of a Central American cactus. Beneath the prickly skin, the flesh is sweet-scented, with a taste similar to melon. Prickly pear flesh can be eaten raw with a squeeze of lime juice and a sprinkling of chili powder to bring out the flavor.

Right: Beneath the pink skin, the flesh of the prickly pear is vibrant red.

Above: Be sure to remove tamarillo skin before eating or cooking the tangy flesh.

Tamarillos Native to the west coast of South America, these shiny, bright red oval fruits are grown commercially in Argentina, Brazil, Colombia, and Venezuela. The skin is very bitter and must be removed before the tangy flesh can be enjoyed. A tamarillo dip is the traditional accompaniment for *arepas*, the flat corn breads that are popular in Venezuela and Colombia.

Passion fruits These fragrant fruits come from Central and South America, and the best-tasting variety is round and very dark-skinned. The greenish yellow pulp has an exquisite flavor, and the seeds are edible, although some people prefer to remove them. Large yellow passion fruits that look rather like light bulbs are granadillas. These have grayish pulp and are neither as flavoursome nor as highly scented as passion fruits.

Above: Choose passion fruits with extra-dark skin, as these are sweetest.

Plantains

These are a type of banana grown as a vegetable, but the name is also used for green sweet bananas. True plantains taste very bitter and must be cooked before being eaten. Treat them like potatoes—they are good when baked in their skins, or they can be boiled, mashed, baked, or fried as chips. A popular snack on Spanish-speaking Caribbean islands is *tostones de plátano*, long slices of plantain that are partially fried, squashed flat, and fried again until brown and crisp.

Below: Fresh plantains are prepared and cooked more like a vegetable than a fruit.

NUTS

Nutrient-rich nuts are a huge part of the Latin American diet, and they appear in various guises, most commonly as a thickening ingredient in both sweet and savory sauces.

Coconuts Latin American cuisine relies heavily on coconuts. The liquid they contain is used to flavor drinks and desserts, while the dense nutmeat is a valuable ingredient in almost everything, including soups, seafood and meat dishes, and desserts. It is used fresh, dried, or as coconut milk or cream, which can be bought canned.

Cashew nuts These are the fruit of an evergreen tree. Each nut grows out of the bottom of a fleshy bulge, which is called a cashew apple. Although not technically a fruit, it closely resembles one, rewarding the picker with crisp, juicy flesh. The nuts themselves are toxic and shelling is a tortuous business, but when released and detoxified, they make a tasty snack and are also used in drinks and sauces.

Pecan nuts These glossy red-skinned nuts are cultivated in northern Mexico, where they are often used in recipes, that hark back to the French occupation in the 19th century. Pecan nuts have a very high fat content so should be eaten sparingly.

Below: Many Latin American desserts are based on coconut or coconut milk.

Pine nuts The nuts of several native pine trees, including the Chilean araucaria and the Brazilian parana pine, are used in Latin American cooking. All are highly nutritious.

Almonds were introduced to Latin America by the Spanish, who cannily added the caveat that they could not be grown on a large scale, thus ensuring that the trade with their native country continued. They are still largely imported, so are fairly expensive and tend to be saved for more extravagant dishes or special occasions. Almonds are still used to make traditional Mexican chocolate, while almond paste is the basis of the luxurious sweetmeat, *turrón*.

Below: Cashew nuts are eaten as a snack with a cold beer or caipirinha.

Below: Almonds are mainly imported from Spain, while pecans and walnuts are native.

Below: Peanuts are a popular ingredient in savory dishes, particularly with poultry.

Walnuts are grown in the highlands of central Mexico. Their bitter-sweet flavor makes them a popular ingredient in savory dishes as well as desserts. They taste delicious when baked with potatoes and chiles.

Brazil nuts are the seeds of towering trees that grow wild in the Amazon rainforest. Inside the large husks are around 20 nuts, packed tightly together. Very high in oil, Brazil nuts go rancid quickly when shelled, so crack them at the last minute.

Peanuts These are actually pulses not nuts, and they grow just beneath the soil. They have been cultivated in Peru for centuries and are a valuable food crop, contributing protein and fat to the diet. Peanut brittle is a popular sweet treat, while savory dishes include pork and potatoes in peanut sauce. Peanut oil and peanut butter are also used, the latter being the basis for a popular punch, which is often served in Trinidad with a shot of rum.

HERBS, SPICES, AND FLAVORINGS

Many of the herbs and spices used in Latin American cooking will be familiar to the foreign visitor. Bunches of thyme, basil, oregano, mint, parsley, and cilantro scent the air in city markets, and spices such as nutmeg, allspice, and cinnamon add their warm aroma. Asian immigrants have introduced cumin, five-spice power, and curry powder, but it is perhaps thelocal specialities that are of most interest to the food tourist: *epazote, palillo, guascas,* and the fiery chili sauces developed by Caribbean cooks.

THYME

Widely used, especially in Mexico, Colombia, and the Caribbean, this robust herb lends its inimitable flavor to dishes such as rice and peas, okra fried rice, Colombian chicken hot-pot, and thyme and lime chicken. The dried herb is included in the dry rub that is used to flavor *carnitas*.

Pebre
This hot cilantro and chile salsa from Chile is delicious with meats.

1 Whisk 1 tablespoon red wine vinegar with 2 tablespoons olive oil.

2 Add 2–3 aji mirasol chiles, seeded and very finely chopped, 1 finely chopped small onion, 2 crushed garlic cloves and 5 tablespoons water.

3 Mix well, then stir in 6 tablespoons chopped fresh cilantro. Cover and set aside for 2–3 hours at room temperature to allow the flavors to blend.

Below: Thyme is a popular flavoring in many Colombian dishes.

CILANTRO

Native to Europe, cilantro is grown in South America too, and is hugely popular, especially in Mexico and the Bahian cuisine of Brazil. Fresh cilantro leaves go particularly well with fish. Chili clam soup and Cuban seafood rice both owe their distinctive flavoring to this popular herb. It also goes well with avocado and is used in both guacamole and avocado soup. Mexican green tomato dishes inevitably include cilantro.

Right: Use mint to make a refreshing mojito.

Below: Cilantro is an essential ingredient in the Mexican salsa, guacamole.

MINT

South America cooks delight in using herbs in innovative ways. Mint and seafood is not an obvious combination, but their use of this familiar flavoring in chunky shrimp chowder works extremely well. Mint is also used to flavor drinks and salads.

INDIGENOUS HERBS

Annatto/achiote The seeds of a tropical flowering tree, annatto has long been used as a flavoring and natural dye. The dried seeds have a mild flavor, with a hint of orange blossom. Annatto oil, pressed from the hard orange pulp that surrounds the seeds, is a popular flavoring and coloring for meat, fish, and vegetable dishes. In the Yucatán peninsula and nearby Cuba, annatto seeds are often ground with cumin and oregano to make an aromatic rub for meats, such as spiced roast leg of lamb.

Epazote
Also known as goose-foot, this herb is as commonplace in South America as oregano is on the islands of Greece. The dried leaves are crumbled and sold in jars. *Epazote* is widely used in central and southern Mexico, especially in bean dishes. The taste has been compared to anis.

Palillo This is an indigenous Peruvian herb. Dried and ground, it has little flavor and is mainly used to give food an attractive golden color. Turmeric can be substituted, but use only half the amount suggested, as the flavor of turmeric can be overwhelming.
Guascas In Colombia, this herb is so common that it is sometimes viewed as a weed. The essential flavoring of the national dish, *ajiaco*, a delicious chicken soup, it is fairly difficult to obtain outside the country, except in dried and ground form. There is no real substitute as the flavor is unique, although it has been suggested that fennel comes close.
Huacatay comes from a plant that is closely related to the marigold. Pungent, with a rather unpleasant flavor, it is very much an acquired taste.

Caribbean spice mixes
These seasoning mixes are so frequently used in Caribbean recipes that it is perhaps worth making up a large amount and storing for future use.

Herb seasoning Chop 4 scallions and put them in a mortar. Add 1 chopped garlic clove and 1 tablespoon each fresh cilantro, thyme, and basil. Pound until smooth.

Spice seasoning Put 1 tablespoon garlic granules in a bowl. Add 1½ teaspoon each of ground black pepper, paprika, celery salt, and curry powder. Stir in 1 teaspoon superfine sugar. Mix well and store in a tightly sealed container in a dry, cool place.

SPICES

The most popular spices in Caribbean and Latin American cooking are those with warm flavors, such as cinnamon, cloves, cumin, nutmeg, and paprika. Several of these flavors are combined in the aptly named allspice, which comes from a type of tree related to the myrtle. Allspice berries are dark brown. When dried they resemble peppercorns. Both the whole berries and the ground spice are used in Latin American cooking. Ground allspice is one of the main flavorings in the traditional Caribbean specialty salt fish and ackee, and also appears in the marinade for the popular jerk chicken.

Vanilla is another warm spice. The beans come from a climbing tree orchid, which grows in parts of Central America. Added whole to warm milk or chocolate, they impart a wonderfully sweet and fragrant flavor. If just the seeds are required, slit the bean lengthwise and carefully scrape them out with a sharp knife.

Left: (Anticlockwise from top) Warm spices, such as allspice, cinnamon sticks, ground cinnamon, and annatto (achiote) are popular throughout Latin America.

SWEET AND SOUR

Ever since sugar was introduced to Latin America in the 16th century, sweetmeats (*dulces*) have been enormously popular. Elaborately shaped and decorated, they are an everyday indulgence, as are caramel desserts, such as flan, which resembles a caramel custard, but sometimes contains pineapple or coconut. Many cooks use unrefined sugar to make treats like these, selecting either *piloncillo*, the dark-brown Mexican sugar, or *panela*, the Colombian version.

As a contrast to all this sweetness, bitter flavors are also highly valued. Angostura bitters, an infusion of gentian root and herbs on a rum base, is often used to add a tart note to fish and meat dishes as well as drinks.

Below: On the island of Barbados, fresh grapefruit is often served with a dash of herb-flavored Angostura bitters.

DAIRY PRODUCTS AND EGGS

Dairy products came to Latin America relatively late, and although milk, cheese, and eggs are important foodstuffs, they do not have as prominent a role as in Europe or North America.

CHEESE

Before the Spanish conquest in the 16th century, fresh milk was a rarity in Latin America. In Peru, indigenous llamas, vicuñas, and alpacas that had been domesticated were occasionally milked, but cheesemaking was unknown until the arrival of Spanish missionaries. Nor did their presence spell instant conversion to cheesemaking, since finding a ready supply of milk would remain problematic for some time. The native animals were deemed unsuitable, and goats failed to thrive in the humid lowlands. It was only when dairy cattle were established in more temperate zones that cheesemaking was attempted on anything but a minor scale, and the monks who traveled with the conquerors taught local people.

Cow's milk was used to make *queso blanco* (white cheese)—the simple soft cheese that is now a familiar sight in most Latin American countries. In the upland areas where goats were farmed, some cheese was made, but sheep's milk was not used until fairly recently, when farmers in Chile began producing a sheep's milk cheese similar to that produced in the Pyrenées.

There are plenty of cattle in Argentina and Brazil, but they are mainly beef animals. Most of the cheese eaten in Brazil is imported, as the high humidity makes cheese production difficult. A fresh cheese—Minas Frescal—is made in the Minas Gerais region, north of Rio de Janeiro, together with a stretched curd cheese called Minas Prensado.

The influx of immigrants proved to be a trigger for cheese production in many parts of South America. In 19th century Argentina, homesick Italians developed a cheese that closely resembled Parmesan, Treboligiano, as well as a mozzarella-type cheese called Moliterno. Cheese similar to Edam and Gouda satisfied the longing of Dutch settlers on Aruba for familiar flavors.

Below: Queso anejo *is a firm, dry cheese— use fresh Italian Parmesan if unavailable.*

In Mexico, the demand for more European cheeses led to local production of cheeses such as Gruyère, Camembert, and Port Salut, as well as a version of the Spanish cheese, Manchego. However, soft white cheeses remain the mainstay of the industry.

Queso blanco Made in most Latin American countries and eaten throughout the region, this white cow's milk cheese is traditionally produced from skimmed milk coagulated with lemon juice. Soft and crumbly, it is often used on enchiladas.

Queso fresco As the name, which means "fresh cheese" suggests, this is not a cheese for keeping. Young and unripened, it is usually eaten within a day or two of being made. It is mild and light, with a grainy, slightly crumbly texture. *Queso fresco* is actually the generic name for a number of cheeses, all of which share several common characteristics. It is often used for crumbling on top of finished dishes such as scrambled eggs, cooked *nopales,* or other vegetables or bean dishes as a tasty garnish. *Queso fresco* has a fairly clean, sharp taste and is a good melting cheese so it is often used in tacos and on other tortilla-based snacks. If you can't find it in your local supermarket, substitute a good quality mozzarella or ricotta.

Queso anejo Meaning "aged cheese," this is the dried version of a feta-like cheese. *Queso anejo* is a sharp, salty, and fairly firm grating cheese similar to Parmesan, which makes a good substitute. It is often used for sprinkling on top of enchiladas

Queso Chihuahua Similar to *queso anejo*, but less salty, this originally comes from northern Mexico. It resembles Cheddar, and medium Cheddar can be used as a substitute. Alternatively, use the popular American cheese Monterey Jack, which originated as *queso del pais* (country cheese) and was introduced to California by Spanish missionaries in the 18th century.

Asadero This slightly tart-tasting cheese is sometimes called *queso Oaxaca,* after the place in Mexico where it was originally made. The name *asadero* means "roasting cheese." It is a fairly stringy, supple cheese that is at its best when melted. It is ideal for stuffing fresh chiles, bell peppers, or other vegetables, or meats, as it is unlikely to leak out during cooking. If *asadero* is unavailable, the closest equivalent is Italian mozzarella

Above: Asadero *melts very well and is perfect for stuffing vegetables and meat.*

Above: When chickens were introduced to Latin America by the Spanish, hen's eggs quickly became popular and were added to many dishes.

MILK

As is the case in Spain, fresh milk is quite difficult to come by in this part of the world because of the heat and humidity. As a result, unsweetened condensed milk and sweetened condensed milk have become more popular. The use of these treated milks is simply a practical solution to the problem of keeping milk fresh in the heat, but several delicious dishes have evolved that make the most of them as ingredients. The most famous of these is *dulce de leche*, an incredibly sweet, caramel-flavored concoction that is so thick and creamy it can be spread on bread like butter or jam. *Dulce de leche* is enomously popular among Latin American children. A rich bread and butter pudding from Barbados also makes the most of evaporated milk as one of its main ingredients.

Milk and cream are also used throughout the region in a similar way to in Europe—they are often combined with fruit to make refreshing drinks, added to rich desserts, and used in many savory sauces, stews, and soups. Canned unsweetened condensed or sweetened condensed milk are nearly always used instead of fresh cream or milk in hot drinks, such as coffee and hot chocolate, adding a distinctive rich, thick sweetness.

EGGS

Until the Spanish arrived in Latin America, the only eggs eaten were those from game birds, ducks, wild geese, reptiles, and insects. The Aztecs farmed wild turkeys, but although there is evidence of turkey eggs being used in religious festivals, the birds appeared to have been prized more for their plumage and meat. When chickens arrived on the scene, however, hen's eggs rapidly became a valued food, and today it would be hard to imagine Mexico without *huevos rancheros*, a complete egg-based breakfast, and *rompope*, a cinnamon eggnog; Brazil without *quindao*; or anywhere in Latin America without the traditional flan. Throughout the region, eggs are used in both sweet and savory dishes. Hard-boiled eggs are often used as a garnish on top of stews or vegetable dishes.

Below: Milk and cream are often added to fresh fruit to make refreshing drinks.

Bajan bread and butter custard
This Caribbean variation of bread and butter pudding relies on unsweeted condensed milk for its rich flavor.

SERVES 4
3 thin slices buttered bread, crusts removed, plus extra butter
14-ounce can unsweetened condensed milk
⅔ cup fresh milk
½ teaspoon pumpkin pie spice
3 tablespoons brown sugar
2 eggs
½ cup golden raisins
2 tablespoons rum
nutmeg

1 Lightly grease a baking dish with butter. Quarter each slice of bread and layer the pieces in the dish.

2 Whisk the milks, spice, sugar, and eggs in a bowl. Pour over the bread and leave to stand for 30 minutes.

3 Meanwhile, soak the golden raisins in the rum. Preheat the oven to 350°F.

4 Sprinkle the raisins over the pudding, grate over a little nutmeg, and bake for 30–45 minutes.

FISH AND SHELLFISH

When it comes to fish and shellfish, citizens of Latin America and the Caribbean are spoiled for choice. Every country except Bolivia and Paraguay has a coastline. You might expect the widest selection of fish to be available to the island dwellers of the Caribbean, but the finest seafood actually comes from the coastlines of Chile and Peru, where plankton brought up from the Antarctic by the icy Humboldt current provides a rich diet for the abundant sea life. The rivers and lakes teem with fresh fish, and both trout and salmon are farmed. The following list introduces just some of the fish available in Latin America, chosen either because they are particularly abundant or make a significant culinary contribution.

FRESH FISH

Snapper Two varieties of red snapper are to be found in the tropical waters of Central and South America. The American red snapper, which has lean white flesh with a very good flavor, is bright red all over, even including the eyes and fins. Its relative, the Caribbean red snapper, tends to be slightly smaller and is distinguished by its yellow eyes and paler belly. All snappers are very good to eat, whether baked, broiled, poached, steamed, or pan-fried. The sweet, delicate flesh goes well with many types of fruit and fruit vegetables, such as mango or avocado. Caribbean snapper is often simply stuffed and baked, and sometimes wrapped in strips of bacon to keep the flesh juicy and tender.

Below: Found in the Caribbean seas, warm-water groupers have fairly firm flesh that can be cooked and served in many ways.

Mahi mahi/dolphinfish/dorade Of all the many names for this flavorsome fish, dolphinfish is perhaps the most unfortunate, since it leads people to imagine, quite wrongly, that it is related to the dolphin. The mahi mahi looks like no other fish. It has an unusual square head and a long, tapering body, which makes it look somewhat like a cricket bat. The firm white flesh of mahi mahi has a delicious sweet flavor.

Mackerel Several varieties of king mackerel are fished off the coast of Latin America, including the *cero*, which is fairly abundant in the Gulf of Mexico, and the *sierra*, which frequents Pacific waters. Mackerel are at their most delicious when eaten extremely fresh, and are a popular choice to be "cooked" with lime juice and eaten as *escabeche*. When cooking mackerel, team it with robust or sharp flavors, to offset the richness.

Left: A large Caribbean red snapper can be stuffed and simply baked or broiled for a delicious meal.

Sea bass These look rather like salmon, with elegant, slim bodies and silvery scales. Various species are found in the Caribbean Sea and the Pacific Ocean. Sea bass can be broiled, baked, braised, poached, fried, or steamed, and they taste particularly good when combined with spicy flavors. In Peru, where the striped bass or corvina is preferred, the fish is cooked with chiles, while in Argentina it is often stuffed and baked.

Grouper These rather glum-looking fish, with their characteristic pouty lips, are members of the sea bass family. The warm-water groupers, such as those that are found in the Caribbean Sea, tend to have firmer flesh than delicate sea bass, and are good for poaching as well as frying, baking, or cooking on the barbecue.

Patagonian toothfish This large fish is commonly known as the Chilean sea bass. It does come from Chilean waters, but the sea bass label is not accurate because it belongs to a separate species. Famed for its fine flavor, the Patagonian toothfish is popular in the U.S.A. and Asia. There have been concerns about overfishing in recent years.

Buying fish

When buying fish, make sure that it is as fresh as possible. This is particularly important if you are intending to serve it as ceviche. Here's what to look for:
• There should be no apparent odor, other than a pleasant, faint smell of the sea.
• The eyes should be clear, bright and slightly bulging.
• The flesh should be firm and elastic; if you press it lightly with your finger it should spring back.
• The gills should gape, revealing a red or rosy interior.
• The scales should be firmly attached, not flaking off.

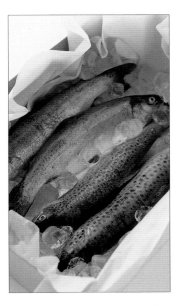

Swordfish are landed in the Gulf of Mexico and off the coast of Costa Rica from June to January and in Chile in late spring. The meaty flesh is low in fat and dries out quickly, so must be basted frequently if barbecued, or cooked in a sauce for the best results. Swordfish goes well with spicy flavors, and Latin American cooks like to cook it with chiles and tomatoes. When buying swordfish, which is usually sold as steaks, check that the flesh is slightly translucent. It should be creamy white or pale pink, with the darker areas shading to a reddish-brown color. Avoid steaks that look gray.

Pompano These are oily fish that taste similar to mackerel. They are available all year round, sometimes whole, but more often as fillets. There are several varieties in the warm seas off the coast of Central America, but the most common is the African

Left: Fresh trout are plentiful in Lake Titicaca, and are commonly eaten in the highlands of Peru and Bolivia.

pompano. This silvery, gray-finned fish has meaty flesh with a good, strong flavor. It is ideal for spicy dishes and goes well with chiles, cilantro, red bell peppers, and citrus fruit.

Congrio Found off the coasts of Chile and Peru, congrios resemble eels but are actually members of a distinctly separate species—*genypterus chilensis*. There are three types, all with firm, flavorsome flesh that flakes beautifully when cooked. This is one of the few fish to find its way into a poem. The Nobel prize-winning poet Pablo Neruda was so impressed with a bowl of congrio soup supped in his native Chile that he wrote an ode to the delicious fish.

Flying fish Also known as exocets, from which the name of the missile derives, these small fish really do look as if they are flying when you glimpse them leaping from the sea. Their propulsion comes from the tail and they stay in the air for several seconds, their large pectoral fins giving them lift. When freshly caught and pan-fried, flying fish taste delicious. Caribbean cooks like to rub them with a spicy mixture of garlic, herbs, and hot pepper sauce before coating them in seasoned flour and frying them.

Above: Fresh swordfish steaks are delicious barbecued with a lime and chile marinade.

Salt cod
Among the rations given to African slaves shipped over to work the sugar plantations was salt cod. They developed a taste for the rather unprepossessing looking food, and invented many recipes to make the most of its flavor. Some of these were based on those cooked by their Spanish or Portuguese masters, but they were often new. In Brazil, salt cod is served as a topping for baked eggs, while a Caribbean specialty is salt cod with scrambled eggs, spinach, and bacon.

Below: Salt cod is used in many traditional Caribbean dishes.

Trout There are plenty of trout in the cooler regions of Latin America. Rainbow, brown, and brook trout are found in the Patagonian lakes close to Bariloche, and the icy rivers that flow from the Andes to the sea in Peru are also a magnet for trout fishermen. Lake Titicaca, on the Andean highlands between Peru and Bolivia, also has a plentiful supply of trout. Trout has a fresh, clean flavor and, although it is often cooked very simply—either fried or broiled— more inventive chefs delight in introducing unusual flavor combinations. One particularly tasty Caribbean dish combines spiced trout fillets with a rich wine and plantain sauce. The rosy flesh also looks lovely and tastes delicious when paired with fresh shrimp.

SHELLFISH

Latin America is a great place for shellfish. In the markets you will not only come across familiar varieties, such as crabs and lobsters, but also rare and remarkable shellfish that look like algae-encrusted rocks, and sea urchins so large that their nickname—sea hedgehogs—seems entirely appropriate. In the Caribbean you can feast on conch, and in Brazil you can dine on some of the biggest shrimp you are ever likely to encounter.

Crabs Both sea and land crabs are a delicacy in Latin America. There are many different varieties, from the soft-shelled blue crabs of the Atlantic and Gulf coasts to the mighty Patagonian king crabs. In Brazil, mangrove crabs are a great favorite, while Mexicans are partial to the California or Dungeness crab. Sweet and succulent, crabmeat can be used in a wide variety of dishes. When carefully cooked, crab tastes good just as it is, but it also makes a great gumbo. Crab cakes are delicious.

In Trinidad and Tobago, a favorite dish is a mixture of onion and crabmeat in a rum sauce, served in crab shells.

Below: crabmeat is a Latin American delicacy, which can be added to soups or stews, alongside other seafood.

Above: Tender jumbo shrimp are often broiled with fresh coconut for a popular Brazilian street snack.

Shrimp Several different types of shrimp are found in the oceans surrounding the continent. The biggest and best are probably the Gulf shrimp, which are found in warm waters. Sometimes pinky gray in color, but more often brilliant scarlet, these are big and succulent. Shrimp are always included on a cold mixed fish and shellfish platter, but also feature in cooked dishes. They are often cooked with fresh coconut or coconut milk, an unusual combination but one that works extremely well.

Dried shrimp Tiny shrimp, tossed in dendê oil and dried in the sun until crunchy, are popular throughout Latin America, but particularly in Brazil's coastal Bahia region. They give flavor and texture to soups, stews, and salads, and are an essential ingredient in the Brazilian dipping sauce, *vatapá*. To prepare dried shrimp, rinse them under cold running water, then soak in hot water for about 35 minutes. They are often ground before being used.

Mussels On the west coast of the continent, where the sea is often turbulent, mussels cling tenaciously to the rocks until prised off by chefs or diners. They inevitably form part of the pit-cooked seafood extravaganza, the Chilean *curanto*, and are also used in a variety of soups and stews. Their sweet, tender flesh is nutritious, and they taste best when lightly steamed. Before cooking mussels, it is important to discard any that are not tightly closed, or which do not close when tapped. The opposite applies after cooking, when it is those mussels that have failed to open that must be discarded.

Clams Among the hundreds of different clams found in Latin America and the Caribbean, perhaps the most delicious are the *navajuelas* (razorshells) found off the coast of Chile and Peru. These clams have tubular brown shells. When packed in bundles, with bamboo sticks, with the soft creamy flesh of the animal protruding from one end. Razorshells are often served raw, but can be cooked. More familiar hard shell clams include quahogs and littlenecks, which are often used in *chupes* (chowders), and angelwing clams, which are harvested in Mexico, Cuba, Puerto Rico, and Chile.

Below: Fresh mussels are abundant in Chile, where seafood is plentiful.

Above: Razorshell clams, also known as navajuelas, can be cooked but are more often served raw.

Scallops Easily identified by their fan-shaped shells, scallops are a source of two delectable treats: the sweet, tender white meat and the bright orange roe or "coral." In Latin America, scallops are widely enjoyed, especially on the western seaboard. Black scallops, which are found off the coast of Ecuador, are especially sought after. Scallops are often eaten raw, with just a squeeze of lime, but they can be cooked. Keep the cooking time short, however—a couple of minutes at most.

A Chilean extravaganza
The ultimate South American seafood experience has to be the Chilean *curanto,* a sort of clambake but with a much wider selection of fish and shellfish, including squid, mussels, and scallops. A fire is made in a large stone-lined pit. When the stones are hot, the fish and shellfish are placed on top and covered with leaves. The pit is then sealed and only opened hours later when everything is cooked to perfection. One of the best places to sample a real *curanto* is on the island of Chiloe, otherwise, try the one-pot version called *curanto en olla.*

Right: Really fresh king scallops have the best flavor.

Conch Pronounced "konk", this is the animal that lives inside those big, beautiful pink-lined shells that many people display in their bath-rooms. A large relative of the whelk, conches are found in the warm, shallow waters of the Caribbean. The pink flesh is tasty and chewy and good to eat, whether raw or cooked, but it must be beaten to tenderize it first. The meat is often used in chowders, but is also good delicately fried. In Barbados, fresh conch fritters are a great favorite, and are often served as a quick bar snack, alongside an ice-cold beer.

Abalone Like the conch, this is a gastropod, a sea creature with a single large foot for locomotion. Abalone feed exclusively on seaweed. They thrive in the cold waters off southern Chile, which are close to the world's largest kelp forests. Abalone are extremely difficult to prise from the rocks that they cling to, which helps to explain why they are fairly expensive. They are highly prized not only for their flesh, but also for their beautiful shells, which are lined with iridescent mother-of-pearl. Abalone has a delicious flavor but must be carefully prepared. Like conch, it needs to be tenderized carefully. Cynics sometimes suggest that the only way to do this successfully is to run it over with a truck, but beating with a wooden mallet usually does the trick.

Sea urchins There are over 800 species of sea urchin found all over the world, but only a few are edible. The ones found in Chile—called *erizos*—are unusually large, up to 4 inches across. Regarded as a gourmet delicacy, they are generally eaten raw. A tasty vinaigrette dressing may be offered, but lovers of sea urchins generally prefer them completely unadorned.

Squid
This is a very popular ingredient, especially in Mexico, Central America, and the islands of the Caribbean. Squid has firm, lean, white flesh that can be tender and delicious when properly cooked. In Cuba, it forms part of a classic fish and shellfish rice dish, while in Chile it is combined with fresh chiles, potatoes, and tomatoes to make a rich, warming stew. Small pan-fried squid can be found for sale along the coasts of South America as a delicious beach snack.

Below: Squid is a popular ingredient in Latin American cooking, with squid casserole a common dish in many areas.

MEAT

Visit Argentina, and you could easily imagine that South America was some kind of monument to meat, yet it was not always so. Before the 16th century, cattle, sheep, and pigs were unknown on the continent, and the only meat that was consumed came from wild boar, game birds, including the wild turkey, cameloids, small mammals, iguanas, snakes, and some other reptiles.

BEEF

Fanning out from either side of the Rio de la Plata are the pampas, large grassy plains that are home to some of the finest beef cattle in the world. Stretching for thousands of miles, the pampas cover the temperate zones of Argentina and Uruguay.

It was the early colonists who introduced beef cattle to the region, along with the European grasses that soon supplanted native varieties. Those first cattle, with horses and other farm animals, were kept in compounds, but inevitably many escaped and, finding the pampas very much to their liking, multiplied to form the nucleus of what would eventually become vast wild herds. With both wild horses and cattle at large, it was only a matter of time before gauchos, the South American cowboys, tamed the one and set about capturing the other. Such private enterprise could not continue indefinitely, however. By the end of the 19th century, much of this cattle country was in

Below: Succulent thick rib joints are ideal for barbecuing.

the hands of private ranchers, and the gauchos had to work for them if they wanted to maintain their chosen way of life. Cattle farming became big business, and today much of the world's supply of beef comes not only from Argentina but also from Brazil, Peru, and Colombia. Large tracts of rainforest have been cleared to make way for new cattle stations; something that is of considerable and rising concern to environmentalists.

In Latin America, and especially in Argentina and Brazil, beef consumption is high. Argentines eat around one and a half times as much beef as Americans, with much of it cooked over coals, whether in restaurants or at outdoor *asados*. That the meat should be cooked to perfection is a matter of pride. Whole rib sections or flanks of beef are cooked vertically, speared on iron rods that are set at an angle to prevent the juices from dripping onto the fire. Smaller portions are laid out on barbecue grills, some of which are as big as table tennis tables.

A Brazilian specialty is the *churrasco*, or mixed grill, which includes excellent beef steaks. Variations on this traditional dish are a feature of special restaurants called *churrascarias* that also specialize in spit-roasts. Pot roasts are a popular choice too, and there are scores of different recipes for rich beef stews, often incorporating chiles, chorizo, or other sausages, fresh or dried fruit, or even fish and shellfish. Vegetables that

Above: Beef topside is a lean, tender joint of meat, often used for braising or pot-roasting.

cook down to a puree, like potatoes and pumpkin, are often used for thickening sauces, or the delicious juices are mopped up with farofa, a form of toasted cassava flour. Beef is also used to make meatballs or as a tasty and often spicy filling for empanadas, *humitas,* or tamales.

Dried meat

In the heat of Latin America, meat tends to go off fairly quickly, so before refrigeration was an option it was necessary to find ways of preserving it. Chief among these was drying, a method that remains popular to this day. To make *cecina*, beef or pork is salted and partially dried, then treated with fresh lemon juice before being briefly air-dried again. During the process the meat acquires a robust flavor, and when it is tenderized it makes extremely good eating. *Cecina* is used to add a rich flavor to stews or as fillings for tortillas and tamales. More thoroughly dehydrated meat is *charqui* or *jerky*, which is produced by air-drying strips of meat in the icy Andean winds. Also available is *carne seca*, the traditional sun-dried salt beef of Brazil, a version of which is also produced in Colombia.

Carnitas

These crisp morsels of marinated meat, usually pork, are a popular Mexican snack, especially in Bajio, to the north of Mexico City.

The meat is cooked in lard, with garlic and oranges, and has a delicious flavor. *Carnitas* are served with salsa as an appetizer or used as a delicious filling for tacos or burritos.

LAMB

The main sheep-farming areas of Latin America are Patagonia, the south of Argentina, and Uruguay. Sheep are also to be found on the Paramos, the high plateaux between the tree line and the snow line in Chile and Peru. Although lamb and mutton have historically been

Below: Lamb is becoming more popular in South America and is often rubbed with a mixture of spices.

less popular than beef in Argentina, lamb is now gaining ground. Mutton and lamb are popular in Mexico and the islands of the Caribbean, featuring in dishes such as lamb pelau, lamb and lentil soup and "seasoned-up" lamb in spinach sauce. A favorite way of cooking lamb is to marinate it in a mixture of garlic and warm spices, including ground annatto (achiote) seeds, then roast it with bell peppers and beans. The annatto gives the meat a rich red color.

PORK

When Spanish and Portuguese colonists introduced pigs to Mexico and other parts of Latin America, there was jubilation, not just because the meat tasted so good, but also because the lard was such a valuable ingredient for frying and baking. Pork hasn't got the high profile that beef enjoys, but it is a popular meat, especially in Mexico, the Caribbean, and Brazil, where pork ribs, smoked tongue, and pork sausage feature in the national dish, *feijoada*. A favorite Caribbean treatment is to roast pork with rum, while in Argentina and Peru, meat is cooked in milk. Pork cooked this way is very tender.

KID

In the upland areas where goats thrive, they are highly valued for their milk, meat, and hides. Kid— young goat— has a slighlty more gamey flavor than lamb, but the two types of meat are often used interchangeably. The famous Jamaican dish curry goat is frequently made using lamb

Above: The top end of a pork leg is excellent as a joint for roasting.

instead, although the title makes it obvious that this wasn't always the case. As well as a slightly stronger flavor, kid is a little tougher than lamb, and therefore needs a longer cooking time for the best results.

Offal

Latin American cooks don't just eat offal, they celebrate it. Intestines, hearts, kidneys, tripe, pigs' feet—in fact all the animal parts eschewed in many other places around the world—are elevated to gourmet status by careful cooking with herbs, spices, and sauces. Sausages of all types are also widely eaten, with chorizo being a particular favorite.

Below: Spanish-style chorizo and other dried sausages are often eaten in Latin America.

POULTRY

Although turkeys are native to Latin America and were first domesticated by the Aztecs, along with ducks, chickens were unknown until they were introduced by the Spanish and Portuguese colonists.

CHICKEN

As in many other places throughout the world, chickens can be found absolutely everywhere in Latin America: scratching in backyards, on sale at busy markets, and on the menu at home and in restaurants. In the Caribbean, where there is seldom enough land to raise large food animals, chickens are a practical source of protein. Chicken is often broiled; cut into strips and simmered in soups; roasted for traditional Sunday lunch; rubbed with jerk seasoning and cooked over the coals; or stewed in delicious hot-pots thickened with okra, squash, cassava, or peanut-based sauces. All over Latin America, and especially in Peru, you can find simple spit-roasted chickens—*pollos a la brasa*—on sale.

Below: Every part of Latin America and the Caribbean has its own favorite chicken recipe.

Jointing a duck
When preparing a duck, it is important to remember that there is not a great deal of meat on these birds. The simplest and fairest way of serving it is in four equal-size portions, so the duck must be jointed before cooking.

1 Place the whole bird, breast-up, on a chopping board. Remove the wing tips with poultry shears or a sharp knife and then cut the breast in half, working from the tail toward the neck.

2 Continue cutting the bird in half, along either side of the backbone.

3 Cut each piece of duck roughly in half, cutting diagonally.

DUCK

The wild ducks that wintered in Mexico were hunted for food long before the arrival of the Spanish, and muscovy duck was just one of the more than 300 dishes on the menu when the renowned Aztec emperor, Montezuma, sat down to dine. Duck is also extremely popular in Peru, where it is often cooked with fresh cilantro leaves. For lovers of duck, Latin America provides some delicious and unusual recipes, such as duck roasted with sweet potatoes and red wine, or cooked with rum.

TURKEY

Two types of turkey are native to Latin America, one emerging in Yucatán and Guatemala and the other in Mexico. Turkeys were introduced to Europe by the Spanish, and they soon became a popular choice in France, Italy, and Britain. The wild birds were fast runners and strong fliers, and their bright feathers were highly prized for ceremonial head-dresses and jewelry, and to provide flights for arrows. The Aztecs were the first to domesticate wild turkeys, which they called *huexolotlin*. Aside from being a valuable food source, turkeys also had a strong religious significance, and two festivals were held every year in their honor. Probably the most famous Latin American dish involving turkey is

Right: Duck is eaten throughout the region—a tasty Caribbean specialty is duck in rum.

Above: Quails are very small birds—for a main course, serve two per person.

the Mexican *poblano mole*. There are many versions of this, all of which involve the bird being cooked in a thick, rich sauce, which contains numerous fresh or dried chiles and several pieces of rich, bittersweet chocolate or cocoa powder. Turkey is often cooked with fresh fruit and tastes especially good with sweet, juicy mango in a traditional Caribbean dish.

GAME BIRDS

Wild birds were a vital part of the South American diet in the pre-Colombian era, and they are still hunted in many places today. Pheasant, partridge, quail, and pigeon are all regularly eaten, along with several types of jungle bird, including some breeds of parrot. Pheasant is particularly good for roasting or stewing, young partridge is best simply roasted and served in its own cooking juices, while pigeon is delicious braised or cooked in a pigeon pie. The *curassow*, a large black bird with a distinctive crest of curved

feathers, can be found from Mexico to Brazil. It is widely regarded as being the best game bird in Latin America, and is therefore in high demand, a fact that has led to over-hunting. Sadly, it has become an endangered species in some areas.

EXOTIC AND UNUSUAL MEATS

In Peru, guinea pigs (*cuyes*) have long been a favorite food. Domesticated in much the same way as chickens, roaming around backyards, they are cooked by similar methods. The vegetarian diet of *cuyes*, like rabbits, gives their meat a fairly light, delicate flavor. Roast *cuy* is sometimes on the menu at out-of-town restaurants and is readily available roasted at many Peruvian markets and on street stalls, but it is more often eaten at home.

Deer are hunted in forest regions, as are *moufflon*, a type of wild sheep, *peccaries*, which are similar to pigs, and wild goats. Llamas and other large cameloids were often cooked and eaten many centuries ago. In certain areas, they occasionally still are, but they tend to be more highly valued as pack animals. Subsistence hunters catch agoutis, tapirs, armadillos, capybara, monkeys, snakes, iguanas, and even tortoises. Turtles are also considered a delicacy and are occasionally eaten, although some countries have made their capture and trade illegal.

Above: Turkeys are native to Latin America and were bred by the Aztecs centuries ago.

Pheasant in green pipian sauce

This delicious recipe from the Yucatán peninsula can be used for almost any game bird.

SERVES 4

INGREDIENTS
2 tablespoons oil
2 oven-ready pheasants, halved lengthwise
1 onion, finely chopped
2 garlic cloves, crushed
10-ounce can tomatillos
generous 1 cup pepitas (pumpkin seeds), ground
1 tablespoon annatto (achiote) seeds, ground
2 cups chicken stock
salt and ground black pepper
fresh cilantro, to garnish

1 Heat the oil in a frying pan and sauté the pheasant halves until lightly browned. Place them in a large roasting pan.

2 Purée the onion, garlic and tomatillos, with their juice, in a food processor or blender. Scrape the purée into a pan and add the pepitas and annatto seeds.

3 Stir in the stock and cook gently for 10 minutes, taking care not to burn. Leave to cool.

4 Preheat the oven to 180°C/350°F/Gas 4. Pour the sauce over the pheasant and bake for about 40 minutes, basting occasionally. Garnish with fresh coriander (cilantro) and serve immediately.

DRINKS

There are some delightful ways of slaking your thirst in Latin America, from sipping cool coconut juice or a refreshing fruit drink to sampling local wines and spirits. If the latter makes you sleepy, there is always strong coffee to wake you up, or a cup of chocolate to help you relax.

ALCOHOL-FREE DRINKS

Fruit drinks These are something of a specialty in many parts of Latin America and the Caribbean. *Sugos* and *refrescos* or *frescas* are always worth sampling and are particularly popular with children. Made while you wait, from whatever local fruit is available, these fruit drinks tend to be on the sweet side. Ice helps to take the edge off, but they can be served without sugar if preferred. One unusual drink, which is very popular in Brazil, is *guaraná*. Made from the berries of a tree sacred to Amazonian tribes, the drink is sold in both still and carbonated forms and is credited with a vast range of health-giving properties. In the English-speaking islands of the Caribbean, ginger beer is a popular drink, especially around Christmas time, as is *agua de Jamaica*, a refreshing drink made from the bright red sepals of a tropical plant.

Below: Ginger beer is a popular drink in some parts of the Caribbean.

The perfect cup
In Latin America, any time is the right time for full-bodied coffee, and visitors are often staggered by the strength of the brew and the amount consumed. To make a perfect cup, follow these directions:
• Use fresh, cold water that has not been chemically softened.
• Use 4–5 tablespoons per 2½ cups.
• Boil the water, then let it cool slightly before pouring it onto the ground coffee.
• If you are using a jug or plunge pot, let the coffee stand for 3–4 minutes before pouring or plunging.
• Do not reheat coffee or keep it warm for long periods.

Coffee Two-thirds of the world's supply of coffee comes from Latin America and the Caribbean. Brazil is the leading grower and exporter, with Colombia second. Other important producers are Mexico, El Salvador, Guatemala, Costa Rica, Ecuador, and Peru. Coffee is not native to Latin America, however. It was introduced, so the story goes, by a young naval officer called Gabriel de Clieu, who carried a small sapling with him when he sailed to the Caribbean from Europe in 1723. On the voyage, the ship was becalmed, but De Clieu used part of his own water ration to keep the sapling alive until he could plant it on his estate in Martinique. It was clearly a robust specimen, however, because in fewer than 60 years there

Below: Coffee beans must first be roasted before they can be ground.

were 18 million coffee trees on Martinique and production had spread to Central and South America.

There are about 50 species of coffee, but the only ones that are commercially significant are *Coffea arabica* and *Coffea canephora (robusta)*. *Robusta* likes humid, tropical conditions and grows well below1,900 feet, while *arabica* prefers the heights and is cultivated between 1,900 and 6,500 feet. The young trees do best in well-drained volcanic soil. They need plenty of sun, but cannot tolerate excessively high temperatures, so shade trees are planted between the rows.

Coffee trees are beautiful. They bear jasmine-scented white flowers up to three times a year, and these are followed by the berry-like fruit. These start off green, but gradually ripen to red, when the cherries, as they are called, are harvested. After picking, which must be done by hand for coffee of the highest quality, the cherries go through lengthy processing to release the pair of beans hidden inside each. Before the beans can be ground to make coffee, they must be roasted. Coffee connoisseurs in Latin America like to roast and grind their own beans at home every day, but most of us buy our beans ready-roasted. In some countries, a light roast is preferred, while in others a dark roast is favored.

Discriminating drinkers demand specific types of coffee, such as Colombian Medellin, but most of what is exported has been blended, either to appeal to the majority or to persuade us to buy coffee tailored to a time of day: light for breakfast and full-bodied for after dinner, for instance.

Yerba maté
This herbal tea, made from the leaves of a plant that resembles holly, is popular in Argentina, Uruguay, Paraguay, and southern Brazil. It is traditionally sipped through a silver straw from a hollow gourd, the *maté*, from which it takes its name.

Above: Good quality chocolate is still produced in Bariloche, Patagonia.

Chocolate The cacao tree is indigenous to Latin America. One fifth of the world's production now comes from Brazil, with Ecuador only 2 percent behind. The Olmecs, who inhabited Central America around 1200BC, are credited with discovering that the cacao bean could be transformed into a delicious drink, but it was the Maya and later the Aztecs who perfected the art. For the emperor Montezuma, the perfect end to one of his legendary feasts was a gold cup full of the frothy beverage.

The Aztecs credited cocoa with medicinal powers, and used the drink to treat all sorts of ailments. In this they were ahead of their time, for cocoa has been proven to be high in antioxidants, the natural compounds that are widely believed to reduce cholesterol levels, fight cancer and heart disease, and delay signs of ageing. The drink the Aztecs enjoyed was not sweetened, but the natural bitterness of the chocolate was often offset by adding chiles and other warm spices, such as vanilla.

The Spanish first introduced chocolate to the rest of the world, and the beverage was soon being drunk in sophisticated resorts and cities all over

Above: Hot chocolate is the perfect end to a meal, according to Montezuma.

Europe. Although it is now as a form of confectionery that chocolate is best known and loved in Europe and the U.S.A., its main use in Latin America continues to be as a drink. Mexican chocolate is a delicate mixture of bittersweet chocolate, sugar, ground almonds, and cinnamon, and it tastes incredibly rich.

Swiss chocolate, Argentine-style
Although chocolate is more likely to be a drink than a sweet treat in Latin America, there is one place where bars of very good chocolate are regularly produced, and that is the beautiful Lake District of Patagonia. Descendants of Swiss, German, and northern Italian immigrants have established a thriving chocolate industry in Bariloche, with many locals hand-making their own chocolates. This Andean village is a visual delight, known for its mountains, its lakes, and the European look of its streets. The thriving chocolate industry helps to reinforce the town's decidedly Swiss character.

WINE

Much of South America is too hot for successful wine production. However, in Argentina and Chile, in the cool valleys on either side of the Andes, grapes flourish and wine is produced widely.

Argentina is the world's leading wine producer outside of Europe and the U.S.A., coming fifth in the global line-up. Until recently, Argentines drank most of the wine they produced themselves, but this is gradually changing. Despite producing less wine than Argentina, Chile has a bigger bite of the international market, and produces some highly regarded wines. Wine is also produced on a smaller scale in Uruguay, Brazil, and Mexico.

Argentina

The first vines were planted in Argentina in the middle of the 16th century by Jesuit priests eager to ensure a steady supply of communion wine. Gradually the vineyards became established, and the industry gained a useful boost in the 18th and 19th

Below: Parts of South America, particularly Chile and Argentina, are well known for both their red and white wines.

centuries with the arrival of European viticulturists. They introduced many of the varieties that continue to dominate: Merlot, Cabernet Sauvignon, Chardonnay, Chenin, and Pinot Noir.

Most of Argentina's wine comes from the western part of the country, in an area stretching from Rio Negro in the south to La Rioja and Salta in the north. By far the most productive region is Mendoza, which has well over a thousand wineries, despite having very low rainfall. This is because the whole area lies in the rain shadow of the Andes. Paradoxically, however, it is thanks to the Andes that the grapes flourish, as the vines are fed by irrigation from snow and ice-melt.

It is for red wines that Argentina is best known. These include Cabernet Sauvignon, Syrah, Merlot, Malbec, Bonarda, Pinot Noir, Tempranillo, and Sangiovese. Malbec is of particular interest. This black grape originated in France, but never fully realized its potential until it was introduced to South America. A wine with an intense, vibrant color, Malbec has been described as having distinctive berry flavors, with hints of damson, licorice and even chocolate.

Among the white wines produced are Chenin Blanc, Sauvignon Blanc, Chardonnay, and Semillon. From the northern provinces of Salta and La Rioja comes Torrontés, a varietal that is believed to have Spanish antecedents, but which is now strongly established in its adoptive country. Fresh, fruity, and deliciously dry, it is extremely popular.

Chile

Roughly one-third of the length of this slender ribbon of a country is given over to the growing of grapes. Although the northern part of the country is desert and the southern tip is too cold for wine production, the central temperate valleys have ideal conditions. The main wine-producing area stretches for just under 550 miles from north of Santiago to Concepción. This part of the country has a Mediterranean climate similar to that enjoyed in South Africa's Western Cape, and because the moisture-laden

Right: Red Stripe lager is one of Jamaica's most famous exports, and is popular throughout Europe and the U.S.A.

clouds that roll in from the ocean drop their rain in winter on the Chilean side of the Andes, irrigation is not the problem it is on the other side of the mountains in Argentina.

Wine production began with the introduction of the rustic Pais grape to Chile in 1548, and owes its present character to the introduction of French vines in the middle of the 19th century. Established varieties like Cabernet Sauvignon, Cabernet Franc, Merlot, Malbec, and Sauvignon Blanc soon flourished, and when European vineyards were devastated by a small insect—phylloxera —Chile was fortunately spared and made the most of this opportunity.

The Maipo Valley is the most famous wine-growing area of Chile and the site of some of the oldest established vineyards. It is well-known for producing excellent Cabernet Sauvignon. Also well known for reds are the Curicó and Colchagua Valleys, while some of the finest white wines come from the Aconcagua and Casablanca Valleys in the north. Mulchen, which is at the southern tip of the wine-producing region, is another white wine area, known especially for Sauvignon Blanc and Chardonnay wines.

Thanks to the huge north-south spread and a variety of microclimates, Chile has a wide range of both red and white wines, including several organic varieties. Aside from those varieties already mentioned, Merlot, Carmenère, Malbec, Syrah, Pinot Noir, and Viognier are also successfully produced.

BEER

Best known for light, thin lager drunk straight from the bottle with a wedge of lime, Central and South American beer actually has a much richer tradition than is widely appreciated. The Mayans were brewing beer from fermented corn stalks long before Spanish conquistadors invaded, while, in northern Mexico, the Aztecs enjoyed a fermented drink made with sprouted maize. The Spanish settlers set up small breweries from the 16th century onward, but beer came a poor second to distilled spirits, until German immigrants introduced lager to Mexico. Many of the brewing companies in existence today have German roots. Mexico remains the leading beer producer, followed by Brazil. Lager is the drink of choice and well-known brands include Corona Extra, Cuzco, Dos Equis, Sol, and Tecate. These lagers go well with spicy Latin American food. The Caribbean also has a strong beer culture and one of Jamaica's most famous exports is Red Stripe lager, now a familiar sight in the U.S.A. and the UK.

SPIRITS

Latin America has given the world some fine spirits, including rum and tequila.
Rum Legend has it that rum was discovered after sugar-cane mash was

Above: The best rum in the world is still produced in the Caribbean.

left to ferment in the Caribbean sun soon after the first sugar plantations were established on the islands in the 16th century. In the early 18th century, it became standard practice for the British Navy to issue sailors with a daily ration of rum, largely because the spirit endured extremes of weather so much better than beer. At the same time, rum was becoming popular in Britain. Over the centuries, the spirit has been refined, and aged rums now have the same sort of prestige as that accorded to single malt whiskies. Rum is still largely produced in the Caribbean, and some of the world's finest rums come from Jamaica, Cuba, the Dominican Republic, Martinique, Barbados, Haiti, and the British Virgin Islands. Rum is also produced in some parts of South America.
Cachaça Another cane spirit, *cachaça* is distilled from the first crush of the sugar cane.

Also called *pinga* or *aguardente*, it is the national drink of Brazil and is often mixed with freshly squeezed lime juice and sugar to make the delicious and popular *caipirinha* cocktail, which is often enjoyed with meals.
Pisco A grape brandy, the birthplace of *pisco* is in some doubt. It originated either in Peru or Chile, depending on which of those countries your informant favors. Its one-time reputation for rough fieriness does not apply to the top grades of *pisco*, which have a delicate, fruity flavor.

TEQUILA

Tequila is, without doubt, the Mexican spirit which is best known outside the country. A specific type of *mescal*, it is becoming steadily more popular, especially among younger drinkers and those seeking the notorious cocktails based on the Margarita.

Below: Mexico's finest exports include mescal (left) and tequila blanco (right).

Liqueurs

Some of the world's most popular liqueurs originated in parts of Central America and the islands of the Caribbean. Curaçao, the bitter orange liqueur invented by Dutch settlers on the island of the same name, was the forerunner of Grand Marnier and Cointreau. All are still made using Caribbean oranges. Tia Maria is a popular coffee liqueur from Jamaica. It is slightly sweeter than its Mexican rival, Kahlúa, while Toussaint, a coffee liqueur from Haiti, has a delectable strong espresso flavor that makes it extremely good for cooking as well as drinking.

The Spanish taught Mexicans the art of distilling, bringing about a new cultural era of alcohol and alcoholic spirit production. *Pulque*, the tasty national drink made from the cactus-type agave plant, was the perfect subject, and they began by distilling it to make *mescal*. This was then distilled a second time to produce tequila.

If *mescal* is brandy, then tequila is Cognac, and is subject to similar controls to those that are imposed by the French government on their famous spirit. There are also parallels with the production of Champagne, in that tequila production is tightly regulated and may only take place in specially designated areas. The producers have to be certified to use the name, and the certification process involves a large amount of checks, including the quality of the land on which the agave is grown, the blending of different types of the spirit, and the techniques used in preserving and aging.

It is thought that tequila takes its name from the plant from which it is sourced: *Agave tequilana*. However, it has also been suggested that the plant was named after the town in Jalisco where the drink was first made. The name means "volcano" in the local native dialect. Jalisco is also the home of *mariachi* music, which possibly explains how tequila gained its image.

Production

Tequila is made from the sap of the blue agave plant, which is not a cactus, as is commonly believed, but is related to the amaryllis. The leaves of each plant are cut off to leave the *piña*, which is then steam cooked. The juice is fermented, then distilled twice, the second time in a copper still, after which it is bottled or matured in casks. All aspects of the process are rigidly controlled and documented.

Flavor Variations

There are several different types of tequila, and innumerable brands of all of these. Each brand has a different flavor, determined by the soil and the climate where the agave was grown, the amount of sugar the agave contained and the finer details of the processing, including the cooking of the *piña* and the fermentation of the juice. Some tequilas are aged in casks, and the type of wood used, together with the duration of the aging process, will also influence the flavor of the finished product.

Not all tequilas are 100 percent agave spirit; some are blended with cane spirit, but by law tequila must contain at least 51 percent agave spirit. Blended tequilas are becoming less popular in foreign markets as consumers become more discriminating. At one time

Left: Mescal

Right: Tequila

Left: Tequila blanco

Below: Tequila and lime

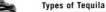

Right: A bottle of Tequila anejo

Types of Tequila

Joven or blanco tequila has been bottled immediately after distillation. It is usually clear, but can sometimes be golden in color. This classification also includes tequilas that have been aged for less than 60 days.

Reposada tequila is golden in color and has been aged in oak for 2–6 months. It has a more rounded flavor than joven tequila.

Anejo tequila has been aged in oak for a year or more and has a rich golden color.

Curados is the name given to blanco or joven tequila that has been naturally flavored. Cinnamon sticks, chiles, almonds, and vanilla beans are among the whole flavorings used, but extracts and syrups can also be used.

Developing a Taste for Tequila

The best way to become a discriminating tequila drinker is to try as many different brands and types as possible. Compare and contrast them in terms of their appearance, bouquet, viscosity, and flavor. Few tequilas taste of only one thing; most are a complex blend of flavors. They may taste sweet, earthy, woody, smooth, or even smoky. It is a good idea to taste a new tequila against a familiar brand to give a standard for comparison.

Tequila Drinking

Drinking a shot of tequila in the classic manner, with a lick of salt beforehand and a wedge of lime after, is one of the best ways to sample this drink. The method was originally adopted because the spirit was so crude that salt and lime were deemed necessary to make it palatable.

A natural progression from the tequila shot was the margarita. The rim of the glass is dipped in salt, the lime juice and tequila are combined,

and triple sec—orange liqueur—is added. A margarita may be served neat, as it comes out of the bottle, or over ice cubes, or "frozen" with crushed ice.

In Mexico, tequila is often sipped alternately with a glass of *sangrita*, a tomato juice flavored with chiles and other seasonings. When the tequila and tomato juice are combined, the drink becomes a Bloody Maria.

Below: Two types of Curados; bottles of blanco tequila that have had flavoring added. Here a few red chiles have been added to the bottle on the left, and three vanilla beans to the one on the right. The tequila will take on the flavor of the chile or vanilla in just a few days.

you could walk into a bar in Britain or Europe and find only one type of tequila—and that was primarily used for making margaritas. However, the increasing popularity of Mexican food has led to a gradual rise in the popularity of tequila and a greater appreciation of the various types, and in some places today there are even specialty tequila bars, which stock a vast range of different types and brands of this exciting spirit.

Left: Margarita

STREET FOOD AND SNACKS

Throughout the Caribbean and Latin America there is a tradition of street food. Market stalls, beach huts, bars, and snack houses all offer sweet or savory snacks, which make perfect accompaniments to fruit juice, cold beer, or cocktails.

CASSAVA FRIES

FOR A PERFECT SUNDOWNER, THERE'S NOTHING QUITE LIKE ENJOYING AN ICE-COLD BEER WITH SOME FRESHLY COOKED, GOLDEN CASSAVA FRIES. DON'T WORRY ABOUT CUTTING PERFECT-SIZED CHIPS; THEY SHOULD BE CHUNKY AND IRREGULAR, AND EXTRA CRISP.

SERVES FOUR

INGREDIENTS
1¾ pounds cassava
vegetable oil, for frying
salt

1 Peel the cassava and cut it lengthwise into 2-inch-wide pieces. Then cut these pieces into slices, about ¾-inch thick.

2 Place the slices in a large pan of salted water and bring to the boil. Lower the heat until the water simmers and cover the pan.

3 Cook the cassava for approximately 15 minutes or until the slices are tender and just beginning to break up. Drain the cassava thoroughly and pat dry with paper towels.

4 Pour vegetable oil to a depth of 2 inches in a deep, wide pan. Heat the oil, then add the cassava pieces. Fry for 3–4 minutes, turning occasionally, until the fries are golden and crisp all over. You may need to do this in batches.

5 Lift the fries from the pan with a slotted spoon and drain on paper towels. Season with salt and serve warm or at room temperature.

VARIATION
The fries are sometimes served with a sprinkling of grated Parmesan, in which case they will not need as much salt.

CHEESE TAMALES

CORNMEAL DUMPLINGS STEAMED IN CORN HUSKS ARE TO BE FOUND THROUGHOUT SOUTH AMERICA. THE RECIPE VARIES, WITH FRESH CORN KERNELS BEING USED INSTEAD OF CORNMEAL ON SOME OCCASIONS. THERE ARE MANY POSSIBLE FILLINGS; THIS RECIPE HAS ONE OF THE SIMPLEST.

MAKES TEN

INGREDIENTS
- 10 large dried corn husks or waxed paper
- 6 tablespoons vegetable shortening, at room temperature
- 2 cups *masa harina*
- 1 teaspoon salt
- 1 teaspoon baking powder
- 1–1¼ cups warm light vegetable stock
- 7 ounces fresh white cheese, such as feta, roughly chopped

1 Place the corn husks in a bowl and pour over boiling water to cover. Soak for 30 minutes, until the husks become soft and pliable. Remove from the water and pat dry with a clean dish towel.

2 Meanwhile put the vegetable shortening in a mixing bowl and beat with an electric whisk until light and fluffy. Test by dropping a small amount of the whipped shortening into a cup of water. If it floats, it is ready to use.

3 Combine the *masa harina*, salt, and baking powder in a separate bowl. Gradually add to the shortening, beating in 3 tablespoons at a time. As the mixture begins to thicken, start adding the stock, alternating the dry mixture and the stock until both have been used and the mixture is light and spreadable. If it feels tough, or dry to the touch, beat in a little more warm water, but don't add more stock, as the dough will already be flavorsome enough.

4 To assemble, lay the prepared corn husks on a board and spread about one-tenth of the *masa* mixture in the center of each, leaving a small border at either side, with a larger border at the top and bottom.

5 Place a piece of cheese in the center of the *masa* mixture. Fold one of the longer lengths of husk over, so that it covers the filling, then repeat with the opposite end. Close the package by folding over the two remaining sides, to make a neat parcel. Secure the tamales by tying each one with a piece of string or strip of corn husk.

6 Pile the tamales in a steamer basket placed over simmering water. Cover and steam for 1 hour. Check the level of the water occasionally, topping up if necessary. The tamales are ready when the dough comes away from the corn husk cleanly. Allow to stand for 10 minutes, then serve.

COOK'S TIP
Masa harina is a flour made with finely ground dried white corn kernels. It is most famously used to make corn tortillas, to which it imparts a nutty flavor. *Masa harina* can be found in Latin food stores and markets.

TORTILLA CHIPS

THESE ARE KNOWN AS TOTOPOS *IN* MEXICO, *AND THE TERM REFERS TO BOTH THE FRIED TORTILLA STRIPS USED TO GARNISH SOUPS AND THE TRIANGLES OF CORN TORTILLA USED FOR SCOOPING SALSA OR DIPS. USE TORTILLAS THAT ARE A FEW DAYS OLD; FRESH ONES WILL NOT CRISP UP AS WELL.*

SERVES FOUR

INGREDIENTS
  4–8 corn tortillas
  oil, for frying
  salt

1 Cut each tortilla into six triangular wedges. Pour oil into a large frying pan to a depth of ½ inch, place the pan over medium heat and heat until very hot (see Cook's Tip).

2 Fry the tortilla wedges in the hot oil in small batches until they turn golden and are crisp. This will only take a few moments. Remove with a slotted spoon and drain on paper towels. Sprinkle with salt.

VARIATION
When fried, flour tortillas do not crisp up as well as corn tortillas, but they make a delicious sweet treat when sprinkled with ground cinnamon and sugar. Serve them hot with cream.

COOK'S TIP
The oil needs to be very hot for cooking the tortillas—test it by carefully adding one of the wedges. It should float and begin to bubble in the oil immediately.

3 *Totopos* should be served warm. They can be cooled completely and stored in an airtight container for a few days, but will need to be reheated in a microwave or a warm oven before being served.

PEPITAS

THESE LITTLE SNACKS ARE ABSOLUTELY IRRESISTIBLE, ESPECIALLY IF YOU INCLUDE CHIPOTLE CHILES. THEIR SMOKY FLAVOR IS THE PERFECT FOIL FOR THE NUTTY TASTE OF THE PUMPKIN SEEDS AND THE SWEETNESS CONTRIBUTED BY THE SUGAR. SERVE THEM WITH PRE-DINNER DRINKS.

SERVES FOUR

INGREDIENTS
  1 cup pumpkin seeds
  4 garlic cloves, crushed
  ¼ teaspoon salt
  2 teaspoons crushed dried chiles
  1 teaspoon sugar
  a wedge of lime

COOK'S TIP
It is important to keep the pumpkin seeds moving as they cook. Watch them carefully and do not let them burn, or they will taste bitter.

1 Heat a small heavy frying pan, add the pumpkin seeds and dry-fry for a few minutes, stirring constantly as they swell.

2 When all the seeds have swollen, add the garlic and cook for a few more minutes, stirring constantly. Add the salt and the crushed chiles and stir to mix. Turn off the heat, but keep the pan on the stove. Sprinkle sugar on the seeds and shake the pan to ensure that they are all coated.

3 Transfer the *pepitas* to a bowl and serve with the wedge of lime for squeezing on the seeds. If the lime is omitted, the seeds can be cooled and stored in an airtight container for reheating later, but they are best served fresh.

TAMALES <u>DE</u> PICADILLO

IN ANCIENT TIMES THESE LITTLE PARCELS MADE FROM CORN HUSKS, POPULAR THROUGHOUT THE
WHOLE OF MEXICO, WERE COOKED IN THE HOT ASHES OF A CAMP FIRE.

<u>MAKES TWELVE</u>

INGREDIENTS

    12 dried corn husks
    ¼ cup vegetable shortening
    1 cup *masa harina*
    ½ teaspoon salt
    1 teaspoon baking powder
    ¾ cup chicken stock
For the picadillo
    1 tablespoon olive or corn oil
    1 pound ground beef
    ½ onion, finely chopped
    1 garlic clove, chopped
    1 eating apple
    ½ pound tomatoes, peeled, seeded,
      and chopped
    1 or 2 drained pickled jalapeño
      chiles, seeded and chopped
    1 ounce raisins
    ¼ teaspoon ground cinnamon
    ¼ teaspoon ground cumin
    salt and ground black pepper

1 Soak the corn husks in warm water for about 30 minutes until pliable.

2 Meanwhile, make the picadillo. Heat the oil in a frying pan. Add the beef, chopped onion, and garlic, and cook, stirring, until the beef is brown and the onion is tender.

3 Peel, core, and chop the apple. Add the pieces to the pan with all of the remaining picadillo ingredients. Cook, uncovered, for about 20–25 minutes, stirring occasionally to prevent sticking.

4 In a bowl, cream the shortening until it is light and fluffy. Mix the *masa harina* with the salt and baking powder, then gradually beat it into the shortening, taking care not to add too much at once.

5 Warm the chicken stock slowly. It should not be hot or it will melt the shortening.

6 Gradually beat enough of the chicken stock into the *masa* mixture to make a mushy dough. To see if the dough is ready, carefully place a small piece on top of a bowl of water. If it floats, the dough is ready; if it sinks, continue to beat the dough until the texture is light enough for it to float.

7 Drain a corn husk and lay it flat on a board. Spread about 2 tablespoons of the dough down the center part of the husk, leaving plenty of room all around for folding. Spoon 2 tablespoons of the picadillo onto the center of the dough.

8 Roll up the husk from one long side, so that the filling is completely enclosed, then fold the ends of the husks under. Make more tamales in the same way.

9 Prepare a steamer or use a metal colander and a deep pan into which the colander will fit with about 1 inch of space all around.

10 Put the tamales in the steamer, folded ends under. Alternatively, place them in the colander and pour boiling water into the pan to within 1 inch of the bottom of the colander. Steam the tamales for about 1 hour, or until the dough comes away from the husk. Top up the water as required to prevent the tamales from drying.

11 Serve the tamales immediately, in the husk, leaving guests to open them at the table to reveal the delicious picadillo filling inside.

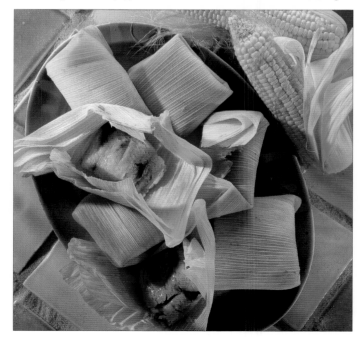

MIXED TOSTADAS

LIKE LITTLE EDIBLE PLATES, THESE TRADITIONAL MEXICAN FRIED TORTILLAS CAN SUPPORT ALMOST ANY INGREDIENTS YOU LIKE, SO LONG AS THEY ARE NOT TOO JUICY.

MAKES FOURTEEN

INGREDIENTS
    oil, for shallow frying
    14 freshly prepared unbaked
      corn tortillas
    1 cup mashed red kidney or pinto
      beans
    1 iceberg lettuce, shredded
    olive oil and vinegar dressing
      (optional)
    2 cooked chicken breast portions,
      skinned and thinly sliced
    8 ounces guacamole
    1 cup coarsely grated sharp Cheddar
      cheese
    pickled jalapeño chiles, seeded and
      sliced, to taste

1 Heat the oil in a shallow frying pan and fry the corn tortillas one by one, until golden brown on both sides and crisp but not hard.

2 Spread each tortilla with a layer of mashed pinto or kidney beans. Put a layer of shredded lettuce (which can either be left plain or lightly tossed with a little dressing) over the beans.

3 Arrange chicken slices on top of the lettuce. Carefully spread over a layer of the guacamole and finally sprinkle over the grated cheese.

4 Arrange the mixed tostadas on a large platter and serve immediately, while still warm. Use your hands to eat tostadas, as they are extremely messy.

VARIATIONS
• Instead of chicken, try using shredded pork, ground beef or turkey, or sliced chorizo.
• For a more authentic taste, use *queso fresco* or feta cheese instead of Cheddar.

CHILES RELLENOS

Stuffed chiles are popular all over Mexico. The type of chile used differs from region to region, but larger chiles are obviously easier to stuff than smaller ones. Poblanos and Anaheims are quite mild, but you can use hotter chiles if you prefer.

MAKES SIX

INGREDIENTS
  6 fresh poblano or Anaheim chiles
  2 potatoes, total weight about
    14 ounces
  scant 1 cup cream cheese
  1¾ cups grated aged
    Cheddar cheese
  1 teaspoon salt
  ½ teaspoon ground black pepper
  2 eggs, separated
  1 cup all-purpose flour
  ½ teaspoon white pepper
  oil, for frying
  chile flakes to garnish, optional

1 Make a neat slit down one side of each chile. Place them in a dry frying pan over medium heat, turning them frequently until the skins blister.

2 Place the chiles in a strong plastic bag and tie the top to keep the steam in. Set aside for 20 minutes, then carefully peel off the skins and remove the seeds through the slits, keeping the chiles whole. Dry the chiles with paper towels and set them aside.

COOK'S TIP
Take care when making the filling; mix gently, trying not to break up the potato pieces.

VARIATION
Whole ancho (dried poblano) chiles can be used instead of fresh chiles, but will need to be reconstituted in water before they can be seeded and stuffed.

3 Scrub or peel the potatoes and cut them into ½-inch dice. Bring a large pan of water to the boil, add the potatoes and let the water return to the boiling point. Lower the heat and simmer for 5 minutes or until the potatoes are just tender. Do not overcook. Drain them thoroughly.

4 Put the cream cheese in a bowl and stir in the grated cheese, with ½ teaspoon of the salt and the black pepper. Add the potato and mix gently.

5 Spoon some of the potato filling into each chile. Put them on a plate, cover with plastic wrap, and chill for 1 hour so that the filling becomes firm.

6 Put the egg whites in a clean, greasefree bowl and whisk them to firm peaks. In a separate bowl, beat the yolks until pale, then fold in the whites. Scrape the mixture onto a large, shallow dish. Spread out the flour in another shallow dish and season it with the remaining salt and the white pepper.

7 Heat the oil for deep frying to 375°F. Coat a few chiles first in flour and then in egg before adding carefully to the hot oil.

8 Fry the chiles in batches until golden and crisp. Drain on paper towels and serve hot, garnished with a sprinkle of chile flakes for extra heat, if desired.

TORTAS

THE MULTI-LAYERED FILLING OF TORTAS OFFERS LOTS OF DIFFERENT TASTES AND TEXTURES. TRADITIONALLY THEY ARE MADE USING ROLLS CALLED TELERAS.

<u>SERVES TWO</u>

INGREDIENTS
 2 fresh jalapeño chiles
 juice of ½ lime
 2 French bread rolls or 2 pieces
  of French bread
 ⅔ cup Refried Beans
 5 ounces roast pork
 2 small tomatoes, sliced
 4 ounces Cheddar cheese, sliced
 small bunch of cilantro
 2 tablespoons crème fraîche

VARIATIONS

The essential ingredients of a *torta* are refried beans and chiles. Everything else is subject to change. Ham, chicken, or turkey could all be used instead of pork, and lettuce is often added.

1 Cut the chiles in half, scrape out the seeds, then cut the flesh into thin strips. Put it in a bowl, pour in the lime juice and let stand.

2 If using rolls, slice them in half and remove some of the insides so that they are slightly hollowed. If using French bread, slice each piece in half lengthwise. Set the top of each piece of bread or roll aside and spread the bottom halves with the refried beans.

3 Cut the pork into thin shreds and put these on top of the refried beans. Top with the tomato slices. Drain the jalapeño strips and put them on top of the tomato slices. Add the cheese and sprinkle with cilantro leaves.

4 Turn the top halves of the bread or rolls over, so that the cut sides are facing up, and spread these with crème fraîche. Sandwich back together again and serve.

TAQUITOS WITH BEEF

MINIATURE *SOFT CORN TORTILLAS MOLDED AROUND A TASTY FILLING AND SERVED WARM. UNLESS YOU HAVE ACCESS TO MINIATURE FRESH CORN TORTILLAS, YOU WILL NEED A TORTILLA PRESS.*

SERVES TWELVE

INGREDIENTS
1¼ pounds rump steak, diced into
   ½-inch pieces
2 garlic cloves, peeled and left whole
3 cups beef stock
1 cup *masa harina*
pinch of salt
½ cup warm water
1½ teaspoons dried oregano
½ teaspoon ground cumin
2 tablespoons tomato paste
½ teaspoon sugar
salt and ground black pepper
shredded lettuce and Onion Relish,
   to serve

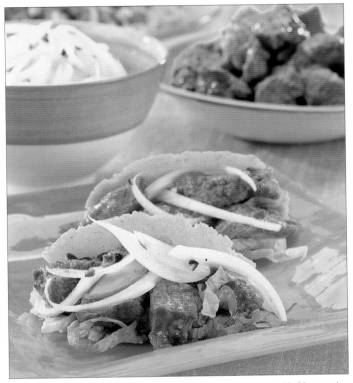

1 Put the beef and whole garlic cloves in a large pan and cover with the beef stock. Bring to a boil, lower the heat, and simmer for 10–15 minutes, until the meat is tender. Using a slotted spoon, transfer the meat to a clean pan and set it aside. Reserve the stock.

2 Mix the *masa harina* and salt in a large bowl. Add the warm water, a little at a time, to make a dough that can be worked into a ball. Knead this on a lightly floured surface for 3–4 minutes, until smooth, then wrap the dough in plastic wrap and let rest for 1 hour.

3 Divide the dough into 12 small balls. Open a tortilla press and line both sides with plastic (this can be cut from a new plastic sandwich bag).

4 Put a ball on the press and bring the top down to flatten it into a 2–2½-inch round. Flatten the remaining dough balls in the same way to make more tortillas. Carefully peel the plastic away from the tortilla and heat a griddle or frying pan until hot.

5 Cook each tortilla for 15–20 seconds on each side, and then for a further 15 minutes on the first side. Keep the tortillas warm and soft by folding them inside a slightly damp dish towel.

6 Add the oregano, cumin, tomato paste, and superfine sugar to the pan containing the reserved beef cubes, with a couple of tablespoons of the reserved beef stock, or just enough to keep the mixture moist. Cook gently for a few minutes to combine the flavors.

7 Place a little of the lettuce on a warm tortilla. Top with a little of the filling and a little onion relish, fold in half, and serve while still warm. Fill more tortillas in the same way.

PLANTAIN AND SWEET POTATO CHIPS

SALTY YET SWEET, THESE CRISP CHIPS ARE A CARIBBEAN SPECIALTY AND MAKE A DELICIOUS SNACK.

SERVES FOUR

INGREDIENTS
    2 green plantains
    1 small sweet potato
    oil, for deep-frying
    salt

VARIATIONS
For maximum crispness, it is important to use green plantains. If these are not available, substitute green bananas. Yams can be used instead of sweet potatoes. The vegetables must be soaked in cold salted water to prevent discoloration.

1 Using a small sharp knife, trim the plantains and cut them in half widthwise. Peel by slitting the skin with a knife, following the natural ridges, then lifting it off. Place the peeled plantains in a bowl of cold, salted water.

2 Peel the sweet potato under cold running water, and add it to the plantains in the bowl.

3 Heat the oil in a large pan or deep-fryer. Remove the vegetables from the salted water, pat dry on paper towels, and slice into thin rounds.

4 Fry the plantains and sweet potatoes in batches for about 2 minutes until crisp, then remove with a slotted spoon and drain on paper towels. Sprinkle with salt and serve when cool.

COCONUT JUMBO SHRIMP

POPULAR THROUGHOUT THE CARIBBEAN ISLANDS, THESE BUTTERFLIED SHRIMP LOOK VERY PRETTY, AND THEY TASTE WONDERFUL WHEN PARTNERED WITH A CRISP COCONUT AND CHIVE COATING.

SERVES FOUR

INGREDIENTS
    12 raw jumbo shrimp
    2 garlic cloves, crushed
    1 tablespoon lemon juice
    4 tablespoons dry unsweetened
      shredded coconut
    ⅔ cup chopped fresh chives
    ⅔ cup milk
    2 eggs, beaten
    salt and ground black pepper
    oil, for deep-frying
    lime or lemon wedges and fresh
      Italian parsley, to garnish

COOK'S TIP
If jumbo shrimp are difficult to obtain, substitute cooked shrimp. However, the raw shrimp will absorb more flavor from the marinade, so they are the ideal choice.

1 Peel and devein the shrimp, leaving the tails intact, then deepen the incision made when deveining the shrimp, cutting from the back almost to the belly so that they can be opened out. Rinse the shrimp under cold water and pat dry.

2 Mix the garlic and lemon juice with a little seasoning in a shallow dish, then add the shrimp. Toss to coat, cover, and marinate for about 1 hour.

3 Mix the coconut and chives in a separate shallow dish, and put the milk and eggs in two small bowls. Dip each shrimp into the milk, then into the beaten egg, and finally into the coconut and chive mixture.

4 Heat the oil in a large pan or deep-fryer and fry the shrimp for about 1 minute, until golden. Lift out and drain on paper towels. Serve hot, garnished with lime or lemon wedges and parsley.

BUTTERFLIED SHRIMP IN CHILI CHOCOLATE

ALTHOUGH THE COMBINATION OF HOT AND SWEET FLAVORS MAY SEEM ODD, THIS IS A DELICIOUS SNACK. THE USE OF BITTER CHOCOLATE ADDS RICHNESS WITHOUT INCREASING THE SWEETNESS.

2 Press the shrimp down firmly to flatten them out. Coat with the seasoned flour and set aside.

3 Gently heat the sherry and clementine or orange juice in a small pan. When warm, remove from the heat and stir in the chopped chocolate until melted.

SERVES FOUR

INGREDIENTS

8 large raw shrimp,
  in the shell
1 tablespoon seasoned flour
1 tablespoon dry sherry
juice of 4 clementines or
  1 large orange
½ ounce bittersweet chocolate,
  chopped
2 tablespoons olive oil
2 garlic cloves, finely chopped
1-inch piece fresh ginger, finely
  chopped
1 small red chile, seeded and
  chopped
salt and ground black pepper

1 Peel the shrimp, leaving just the tail sections intact. Make a shallow cut down the back of each shrimp and carefully pull out and discard the dark intestinal tract. Turn over the shrimp so that the undersides are uppermost, then carefully split them open from tail to top, using a small, sharp knife, cutting almost, but not quite, through to the back.

4 Heat the olive oil in a frying pan. Cook the garlic, ginger, and chile over a medium heat for 2 minutes, until golden. Remove with a slotted spoon and reserve. Add the shrimp, cut side down, to the pan; cook for 2–3 minutes, until golden brown with pink edges. Turn and cook for a further 2 minutes. Be sure not to overcook the shrimp, turning them only once to ensure that they are cooked through and yet retain succulence.

5 Return the garlic mixture to the pan and pour over the chocolate sauce. Cook for 1 minute, turning the shrimp to coat them in the glossy sauce. Season to taste and serve hot.

DESERT NACHOS

TORTILLA CHIPS ARE LIVENED UP WITH JALAPEÑOS IN THIS QUICK-AND-EASY SNACK. SERVED WITH A VARIETY OF SPICY MEXICAN DIPS, THIS ALWAYS PROVES TO BE A POPULAR DISH.

SERVES TWO

INGREDIENTS

1 pound blue corn tortilla chips
   or ordinary tortilla chips, according
   to taste
3 tablespoons chopped pickled
   jalapeño chiles, according to taste
12 black olives, sliced
2 cups grated Cheddar cheese

To serve
   guacamole
   salsa
   sour cream
   a sprinkling of chopped
      cilantro leaves
   lime wedges for squeezing

1 Preheat the oven to 350°F. Put the tortilla chips in a 9 x 13-inch ovenproof dish and spread them out evenly. Sprinkle the jalapeños, olives, and cheese evenly over the tortilla chips.

2 Place the prepared tortilla chips in the top of the oven and bake for 10–15 minutes, until the cheese melts. Serve the nachos immediately, with the guacamole, salsa, sour cream, cilantro, and lime.

EMPANADAS <u>WITH</u> ROPAS VIEJAS

THE FILLING FOR THESE EMPANADAS IS TRADITIONALLY MADE WITH MEAT THAT IS COOKED UNTIL IT IS SO TENDER THAT IT CAN BE TORN APART WITH FORKS. IT RESEMBLES TATTERED CLOTH, WHICH IS HOW IT CAME TO BE KNOWN AS ROPA VIEJA, WHICH MEANS "OLD CLOTHES."

SERVES SIX (TWELVE EMPANADAS)

INGREDIENTS
    1 cup *masa harina*
    2 tablespoons all-purpose flour
    ½ teaspoon salt
    ½–⅔ cup warm water
    1 tablespoon oil, plus extra,
       for frying
    9 ounces lean ground pork
    1 garlic clove, crushed
    3 tomatoes
    2 ancho chiles
    ½ small onion
    ½ teaspoon ground cumin
    ½ teaspoon salt

1 Mix the *masa harina*, flour, and salt in a bowl. Gradually add enough of the warm water to make a smooth, but not sticky, dough. Knead briefly, then shape into a ball, wrap in plastic wrap, and set aside.

2 Heat 1 tablespoon oil in a pan. Add the pork and cook, stirring frequently, until it has browned evenly. Stir in the garlic and cook for 2 more minutes. Remove from heat and set the pan aside.

3 Cut a cross in the bottom of each tomato, place them in a bowl, and pour over boiling water. After 3 minutes plunge the tomatoes into a bowl of cold water. Drain. The skins will peel back easily from the crosses. Remove the skins completely. Chop the tomato flesh and put in a bowl.

4 Slit the ancho chiles and scrape out the seeds. Chop the chiles finely and add them to the tomatoes. Chop the onion finely and add it to the tomato mixture, with the ground cumin.

5 Stir the tomato mixture into the pan containing the pork and cook over medium heat for 10 minutes, stirring occasionally. Season with salt to taste.

6 To make the tortillas, divide the empanada dough into 12 pieces and roll each piece into a ball. Open a tortilla press and line both sides with plastic (this can be cut from a new plastic sandwich bag). Put a ball of dough on the press and bring the top down to flatten it into a 3-inch round. Use the remaining dough balls to make more tortillas in the same way.

COOK'S TIP
If the empanada dough proves difficult to handle, a little oil or melted shortening can be kneaded into the dough to help make it more pliable.

7 Spoon a little of the meat mixture on one half of each tortilla, working quickly to keep the dough from drying out. Dampen the edges of the dough with a little water and fold, turnover-style, to make the empanadas.

8 Seal the edges on the empanadas by pinching them between the index finger and thumb of the left hand and the index finger of the right hand.

9 Heat a little oil in a large frying pan. When it is hot, fry the empanadas in batches until crisp and golden on both sides, turning at least once. Serve hot or cold.

CHEESY EGGS

THESE DELICIOUS CARIBBEAN STUFFED EGGS ARE SIMPLE TO MAKE AND IDEAL FOR LAST-MINUTE PARTY SNACKS. SERVE THEM WITH A CRISP SALAD GARNISH AND DHAL PURI.

SERVES SIX

INGREDIENTS

6 eggs
1 tablespoon mayonnaise
2 tablespoons grated Cheddar cheese
½ teaspoon ground white pepper
2 teaspoons chopped fresh chives
2 radishes, thinly sliced, to garnish
lettuce leaves, to serve

VARIATION

A variety of fillings can be used instead of Cheddar cheese. Canned sardines or tuna mayonnaise make a tasty alternative.

1 Cook the eggs in boiling water for about 10 minutes until hard-boiled. Lift out the eggs and place them in cold water. When cool, remove the shells.

2 Put the mayonnaise, Cheddar cheese, pepper, and chives into a small bowl. Cut the hard-boiled eggs in half lengthwise and carefully scoop out the yolks without breaking the whites. Add the yolks to the bowl.

3 Mash all the ingredients with a fork until well blended.

4 Fill each egg white with the egg yolk and cheese mixture, and arrange on a plate. Garnish with thinly sliced radishes and serve with crisp green lettuce leaves.

RED ENCHILADAS

THE METHOD OF FIRST DIPPING THE TORTILLAS IN SAUCE, THEN QUICKLY COOKING THEM IN OIL GIVES THE BEST FLAVOR, ALTHOUGH THEY CAN BE DIPPED AFTER BEING QUICKLY FRIED.

SERVES SIX

INGREDIENTS
    4 dried ancho chiles
    1 pound tomatoes, peeled, seeded,
    and chopped
    1 onion, finely chopped
    1 garlic clove, chopped
    1 tablespoon chopped fresh
    cilantro
    corn oil, for frying
    1 cup sour cream
    4 chorizo sausages, skinned
    and chopped
    18 freshly prepared unbaked
    corn tortillas
    2/3 cup freshly grated
    Parmesan cheese
    salt and ground black pepper

1 Roast the ancho chiles in a dry frying pan over a medium heat for 1–2 minutes, shaking the pan frequently. When cool, carefully slit the chiles, remove and discard the stems and seeds, and tear the pods into pieces. Put the pieces into a bowl, add warm water to just cover, and soak for 20 minutes.

2 Tip the chiles, with a little of the soaking water, into a food processor. Add the tomatoes, onion, garlic, and cilantro and process. Stop the processor halfway through blending, when the mixture is not yet smooth, to stir the ingredients and ensure that it becomes a smooth, unified puree.

3 Heat 1 tablespoon corn oil in a pan. Add the puree and cook gently over a medium heat, stirring, for 3–4 minutes. Season to taste with salt and pepper and then stir in the sour cream. Remove the pan from the heat and set it aside.

4 Heat a further 1 tablespoon corn oil in a small frying pan; sauté the chorizo for a few minutes until lightly browned. Moisten with a little of the sauce and set the pan aside.

5 Preheat the oven to 350°F. Heat 2 tablespoon corn oil in a frying pan. Dip a tortilla in the sauce and add to the pan. Cook for a few seconds, shaking the pan gently, turn over, and briefly fry the other side.

6 Slide the tortilla onto a plate, top with some of the sausage mixture, and roll up. Pack the prepared tortillas in a single layer in an ovenproof dish. Pour the sauce over, sprinkle with Parmesan, and bake for about 20 minutes.

TOSTADAS <u>WITH</u> TOMATO SALSA

A TOSTADA IS A CRISP, FRIED TORTILLA USED IN THIS RECIPE AS A BASE ON WHICH TO PILE THE TOPPING OF YOUR CHOICE. THIS VARIATION ON A SANDWICH MAKES A VERY TASTY SNACK.

SERVES SIX

INGREDIENTS

2 tablespoons oil, plus extra for frying
1 onion, chopped
2 garlic cloves, chopped
½ teaspoon chili powder
14-ounce can pinto beans, drained
⅔ cup chicken stock
1 tablespoon tomato paste
2 tablespoons fresh cilantro
6 wheat or corn tortillas
2 tablespoons sour cream
½ cup shredded
  Cheddar cheese
For the tomato salsa
1 small onion, chopped
1 garlic clove, crushed
2 fresh green chiles, seeded and
  finely chopped
1 pound tomatoes, chopped
2 tablespoons fresh cilantro

1 To make the salsa, put the onion and garlic in a serving bowl and stir in the chiles, tomatoes, and fresh cilantro. Season generously and mix well.

2 Heat 2 tablespoons oil in a heavy-based frying pan and fry the chopped onion for 3–5 minutes until softened. Add the garlic and chili powder, and fry for 1 minute, stirring constantly.

3 Add the beans. Pour in the stock and mix well. Mash the beans very roughly. Add the tomato paste, chopped cilantro, and seasoning to taste. Mix thoroughly and cook for a few minutes.

4 Fry 2 tortillas in hot oil for 1 minute, turning once, until crisp, then drain on paper towels. Fry the remaining tortillas in the same way.

5 Put a spoonful of the refried beans on each tostada, spoon over some tomato salsa, then some sour cream, sprinkle with grated Cheddar cheese, and garnish with cilantro.

COOK'S TIP
When you are in a hurry, you can use canned refried beans. Thin them with a little stock if necessary and cook them gently over a low heat for 5–10 minutes to ensure that they are properly heated through. Stir continuously to dissipate the heat and prevent burning.

ENCHILADAS <u>WITH</u> HOT TOMATO <u>AND</u> GREEN CHILI SAUCE

IN MEXICO, CHILES APPEAR IN ALMOST EVERY SAVORY DISH, EITHER AS CHILI POWDER OR CHOPPED, SLICED, OR WHOLE. BY MEXICAN STANDARDS, THIS IS A MILD VERSION OF THE POPULAR CHICKEN ENCHILADAS. IF YOU LIKE YOUR FOOD HOT, ADD EXTRA CHILES TO THE TOMATO SAUCE.

SERVES FOUR

INGREDIENTS

- 8 wheat tortillas
- 6 ounces Cheddar cheese, grated
- 1 onion, finely chopped
- 12 ounces cooked chicken, cut into small chunks
- 1¼ cups sour cream
- 1 avocado, sliced and tossed in lemon juice, to garnish

For the sauce

- 1–2 fresh green chiles
- 1 tablespoon vegetable oil
- 1 onion, chopped
- 1 garlic clove, crushed
- 14-ounce can chopped tomatoes
- 2 tablespoons tomato paste
- salt and ground black pepper

1 To make the sauce, cut the chiles in half lengthwise and carefully remove the cores and seeds. Slice the chiles very finely.

2 Heat the oil in a frying pan and fry the onion and garlic for about 3–4 minutes until softened. Stir in the tomatoes, tomato paste, and chiles. Simmer gently, uncovered, for 12–15 minutes, stirring frequently.

3 Pour the sauce into a food processor or blender, and process until smooth. Return to the heat and cook very gently, uncovered, for a further 15 minutes. Season to taste, then set aside.

4 Preheat the oven to 350°F. Butter a shallow ovenproof dish. Take one tortilla and sprinkle with some cheese and chopped onion, about 1½ ounces of chicken and 1 tablespoon of sauce. Pour over 1 tablespoon of sour cream, roll up, and place seam-side down in the dish.

5 Make 7 more enchiladas to fill the dish. Pour the remaining sauce over and sprinkle with the remaining cheese and onion. Bake for 25–30 minutes, until the top is golden. Serve with the remaining sour cream, either poured over or in a separate container, and garnish with the sliced avocado.

CHICKEN FLAUTAS

CRISP-FRIED MEXCIAN TORTILLAS WITH A CHICKEN AND CHEESE FILLING MAKE A DELICIOUS LIGHT MEAL, ESPECIALLY WHEN SERVED WITH A SPICY TOMATO SALSA. THE SECRET IS TO MAKE SURE THAT THE OIL IS SUFFICIENTLY HOT TO PREVENT THE FLUTES FROM ABSORBING TOO MUCH OF IT.

MAKES TWELVE

INGREDIENTS
    2 skinless, boneless chicken breasts
    1 onion
    2 garlic cloves
    1 tablespoon vegetable oil
    3½ ounces feta cheese, crumbled
    12 corn tortillas, freshly made or a
        few days old
    oil, for frying
    salt and ground black pepper
For the salsa
    3 tomatoes, peeled, seeded,
        and chopped
    juice of ½ lime
    small bunch of fresh cilantro,
        chopped
    ½ small onion, finely chopped
    3 fresh fresno chiles or similar
        fresh green chiles, seeded
        and chopped

1 Start by making the salsa. Mix the tomatoes, lime juice, cilantro, onion, and chiles in a bowl. Season with salt to taste and set aside.

COOK'S TIP
You might find it easier to keep the toothpicks in place until after the flutes have been fried, but do remove them before serving.

2 Put the chicken breasts in a large pan, add water to cover, and bring to the boil. Lower the heat and simmer for 15–20 minutes or until the chicken is cooked. Remove the chicken from the pan and let it cool a little. Using two forks, shred the chicken into small pieces. Set it aside.

3 Chop the onion finely and crush the garlic. Heat the oil in a frying pan, add the onion and garlic and fry over a low heat for about 5 minutes, or until the onion has softened but not colored. Add the shredded chicken, with salt and pepper to taste. Mix well, remove from the heat, and stir in the feta.

4 Before they can be rolled, soften the tortillas by steaming three or four at a time on a plate over boiling water for a few moments, until they are pliable. Alternatively, wrap them in microwave-safe film and then heat them in a microwave oven on full power for about 30 seconds.

5 Place a spoonful of the chicken filling on one of the tortillas and roll tightly to make a neat cylinder. Secure with a toothpick. Immediately cover the roll with plastic wrap to prevent the tortilla from drying out and splitting. Fill and roll the remaining tortillas in the same way.

6 Pour oil into a frying pan to a depth of 1 inch. Heat it until a small cube of bread, added to the oil, rises to the surface and bubbles at the edges before turning golden. Remove the toothpicks, then add the flutes to the pan, a few at a time.

7 Fry the flutes for 2–3 minutes until golden, turning frequently. Drain on paper towels and serve at once, with the salsa.

BLACK-EYED PEA AND SHRIMP FRITTERS

THIS BRAZILIAN SNACK, LOCALLY KNOWN AS ACARAJÉ, IS FROM BAHIA, A REGION HIGHLY INFLUENCED BY ITS AFRICAN SLAVE HERITAGE. WOMEN FRY THESE PATTIES TO ORDER. THEY ARE THEN CUT OPEN AND FILLED WITH VARIOUS SAUCES, ALL DELECTABLE BUT VERY MESSY TO EAT.

MAKES TEN

INGREDIENTS
  1¼ cups black-eyed peas
  ¼ cup dried shrimp
  1 onion, roughly chopped
  palm oil and vegetable oil, for frying
  salt
  chili oil, to serve
For the filling
  2 tablespoons palm oil
  ⅔ cup dried shrimp
  1 large onion, thinly sliced
  2 fresh hot red chiles, seeded and
    finely chopped

1 Put the black-eyed peas in a large bowl and cover with plenty of water. Soak overnight to loosen the skins. Drain, then soak for a further 30 minutes in hot (but not boiling) water.

2 Drain the peas and tip them onto a board. Rub them between your hands to separate them from their skins. The patties will be very dry if the skins are not removed.

3 Transfer the peas to a bowl and pour over cold water to cover. The loose skins will begin to rise to the surface. Remove them with a slotted spoon and throw them away. Stir the peas to encourage more skins to float to the surface, continuing until all the skins have been removed. You'll be able to chart your progress easily, as the peas lose their distinctive "eye" when peeled. Drain.

4 Blend the dried shrimp and onion in a food processor until smooth. Add the peas and blend to a thick puree. Season with salt.

5 Mix equal quantities of palm oil and vegetable oil to a depth of about 2 inches in a deep pan. Form the *acarajé* mixture into 10 oval shapes. Heat the oil and fry half of the fritters for 5 minutes or until golden. Lift out with a slotted spoon and drain on paper towels. Between batches, skim the oil to remove any burnt bits.

6 Make the filling. Heat the oil in a frying pan. When hot, add the dried shrimp and sauté for 2–3 minutes until golden. Lift out with a slotted spoon and drain on paper towels. Lower the heat and stir in the onion slices. Cook for 5 minutes until soft, then add the chile. Sauté for 1 minute and set aside.

7 Cut each fritter open lengthwise and fill with the onion mixture. Add a couple of dried shrimp and drizzle with chili oil.

BEEF EMPANADAS

You'll find these pastry turnovers throughout Latin America, with Colombia's being perhaps the most famous. They come with a variety of fillings, including beef, pork, vegetables, and cheese. What better way for using up leftovers?

MAKES TWENTY

INGREDIENTS
2 cups plain flour
½ teaspoon salt
scant ½ cup cold butter, cut into
   small chunks
juice of ½ lime
¼ cup lukewarm water
vegetable oil, for deep-frying
chili salsa, to serve (optional)
For the filling
1 pound beef shin or shank
4 tablespoons olive oil
¼ teaspoon ground cumin
1 garlic clove, crushed
2 teaspoons paprika
1 cup light beef stock
1 pound potatoes, peeled and cubed
2 tomatoes, finely chopped
3 scallions, finely chopped
salt and ground black pepper

3 Stir in the stock and bring to the boil. Cover and cook over a low heat for 30 minutes. Stir in the potatoes, tomatoes, and scallions. Cook for 15 minutes more, or until the beef and potatoes are tender. Season with salt and pepper to taste, then leave to cool.

4 Meanwhile, place the flour and salt in a food processor. Add the small chunks of butter and pulse until the mixture resembles fine bread crumbs. Combine the lime juice and water and slowly pour into the food processor, with the motor still running. As soon as the pastry comes together, tip it onto a a soft dough. Shape into a ball, cover in plastic wrap and chill for at least 20 minutes.

5 On a floured surface roll out the pastry until it is very thin. Cut out 2½-inch circles, using a cookie cutter.

6 Spoon about 1½ teaspoons of the filling into the center of a pastry circle, then brush the edges with water. Fold the pastry over to form a half-moon, then press around the edges to seal. Repeat with the rest of the pastry.

7 Pour vegetable oil to a depth of 2 inches into a deep frying pan. Heat the oil, then add five or six empanadas. Fry for 5 minutes until golden brown, turning halfway through cooking. Remove from the pan with a slotted spoon and drain. Repeat with the remaining empanadas. Serve with a little chili salsa, if using.

1 Make the filling. Cut the beef into large chunks and chop in a food processor until finely diced, but not ground. This will tenderize the meat, cutting the cooking time.

2 Heat 2 tablespoons of the olive oil in a wide, heavy pan over a high heat. Add the beef chunks and sauté until golden brown. Push the beef to the side and add the cumin, crushed garlic, and paprika to the pan. Reduce the heat and cook, stirring gently, for around 2 minutes, until the spices begin to release their delicious aroma.

SOPES WITH PICADILLO

THESE ARE SMALL, THICK TORTILLAS MADE WITH MASA HARINA *WITH CRIMPED EDGES, WHICH ARE FILLED LIKE TARTS. THEY ARE AN ACQUIRED TASTE AS THEY REMAIN "DOUGHY" WHEN COOKED, BUT THEY CAN BECOME QUITE ADDICTIVE. THE FILLING—PICADILLO—IS VERY POPULAR IN MEXICO AND IS USED IN MANY DIFFERENT RECIPES.*

SERVES SIX

INGREDIENTS

scant 2 cups *masa harina*
½ teaspoon salt
¼ cup chilled shortening
1¼ cups warm water
1 tablespoon vegetable oil
9 ounces lean ground beef
2 garlic cloves, crushed
1 red bell pepper, seeded and chopped
¼ cup dry sherry
1 tablespoon tomato paste
½ teaspoon ground cumin
1 teaspoon ground cinnamon
¼ teaspoon ground cloves
½ teaspoon ground black pepper
3 tablespoons raisins
¼ cup sliced almonds
fresh parsley sprigs, to garnish

1 Put the *masa harina* and salt in a large bowl. Grate the chilled shortening into the bowl and rub it into the dry ingredients until no visible pieces remain. Add the warm water, a little at a time, to make a dough that can be worked into a ball. Knead the dough on a lightly floured surface for 3–4 minutes, until smooth. Set aside.

2 Heat the oil in a large pan. Add the ground beef and cook over high heat, stirring until it has browned. Stir in the garlic and continue cooking for 2–3 minutes, stirring occasionally.

3 Stir in the red pepper, sherry, tomato puree, and spices. Cook for 5 more minutes, then add the raisins and the sliced almonds. Lower the heat and simmer for 10 minutes. The meat should be cooked through and the mixture moist, but not wet. Keep hot.

4 Divide the dough into six balls. Open a tortilla press and line both sides with plastic (this can be cut from a new plastic sandwich bag). Put a ball on the press and bring the top down to flatten it into a 4-inch round, thicker than the conventional tortilla. Use the remaining dough balls to make five more rounds.

5 Heat a griddle or frying pan until hot. Add one of the rounds and fry until the underside is beginning to brown and blister. Turn the round over and cook the other side briefly, until the color is just beginning to change. Slide onto a plate and crimp the rim to form a raised edge. Fill with the spicy beef and keep hot while cooking and filling the remaining tartlets. Garnish with parsley.

COOK'S TIP

Take care that the dough for the *sopes* does not become dry. Wrap it in plastic wrap while it is set aside.

PANUCHOS

THESE STUFFED TORTILLAS ARE A BIT DIFFICULT TO MAKE, BUT WELL WORTH THE EFFORT. THIS DISH IS PARTICULARLY POPULAR IN THE YUCATÁN.

SERVES SIX (TWELVE *PANUCHOS*)

INGREDIENTS
1 cup *masa harina*
pinch of salt
½ cup warm water
2 skinless, boneless chicken breasts
1 teaspoon dried oregano
about 1 cup *Frijoles de Olla*, blended
 to a smooth puree
2 hard-boiled eggs, sliced
oil, for shallow-frying
salt and ground black pepper
Onion Relish, to serve

1 Mix the *masa harina* and salt in a large bowl. Add the warm water, a little at a time, to make a dough that can be worked into a ball. Knead this on a lightly floured surface for 3–4 minutes, until smooth, then wrap the dough in plastic wrap and let rest for 1 hour.

2 Put the chicken in a pan, add the dried oregano, and pour in water to cover. Bring to a boil, then lower the heat and simmer for 10 minutes or until the chicken is cooked. Remove the chicken from the pan, discard the water, and let the chicken cool a little. Using two forks, shred the chicken into small pieces. Set it aside.

3 Divide the dough into 12 small pieces and roll into balls. Open a tortilla press and line both sides with plastic (this can be cut from a new plastic sandwich bag). Put a dough ball on the press and flatten it into a 2½-inch round. Use the remaining dough balls to make more tortillas in the same way.

4 Cook each tortilla in a hot frying pan for 15–20 seconds on each side. After another 15 seconds on one side, remove and wrap in a clean dish towel.

5 Cut a slit in each tortilla, about ½ inch deep around the rim. Put a spoonful of the bean puree and a slice of hard-boiled egg in each slit.

6 Heat the oil for shallow frying in a large frying pan. Fry the tortilla pockets until they are crisp and golden brown on all sides, turning at least once during cooking. Drain them on paper towels and place on six individual serving plates. Top with a little of the shredded chicken and some onion relish. Season to taste and serve immediately.

QUESADILLAS

THESE CHEESE-FILLED TORTILLAS ARE THE MEXICAN EQUIVALENT OF GRILLED CHEESE SANDWICHES.
SERVE THEM AS SOON AS THEY ARE COOKED, OR THEY WILL BECOME CHEWY. IF YOU ARE MAKING THEM
FOR A CROWD, FILL AND FOLD THE TORTILLAS AHEAD OF TIME, BUT ONLY COOK THEM TO ORDER.

SERVES FOUR

INGREDIENTS

   7 ounces mozzarella, Monterey Jack,
     or mild Cheddar cheese
   1 fresh fresno chile (optional)
   8 flour tortillas, about
     6-inches across
   Onion Relish or Classic Tomato Salsa,
     to serve

VARIATIONS
Try spreading a thin layer of your favorite
Mexican salsa on the tortilla before
adding the cheese, or adding a few
pieces of cooked chicken or shrimp
before folding the tortilla in half.

1 If using mozzarella cheese, it must be
drained thoroughly and then patted dry
and sliced into thin strips. Monterey
Jack and Cheddar cheese should both
be coarsely grated, as finely grated
cheese will melt and ooze out when
cooking. Set the cheese aside in a bowl.

2 If using the chile, spear it on a long-
handled metal skewer and roast it over
the flame of a gas burner until the skin
blisters and darkens. Do not let the
flesh burn. Alternatively, dry-fry it in a
griddle until the skin is scorched. Place
the roasted chile in a strong plastic bag
and tie the top to keep the steam in.
Set aside for 20 minutes.

3 Remove the chile from the bag and
peel off the skin. Cut off the stem, then
slit the chile and scrape out the seeds.
Cut the flesh into eight thin strips.

4 Warm a large frying pan or griddle.
Place one tortilla on the pan or griddle
at a time, sprinkle about an eighth of
the cheese on one half and add a strip
of chile, if using. Fold the tortilla over
the cheese and press the edges
together gently to seal. Cook the filled
tortilla for 1 minute, then turn over and
cook the other side for 1 minute.

5 Remove the filled tortilla from the pan
or griddle, cut it into three triangles or
four strips, and serve immediately, with
the onion relish or tomato salsa.

MEXICAN RICE

VERSIONS OF THIS DISH—A RELATIVE OF SPANISH RICE—ARE POPULAR ALL OVER SOUTH AMERICA. CLASSIFIED AS A SOPA SECA OR DRY SOUP, IT IS A DELICIOUS MEDLEY OF RICE, TOMATOES, AND AROMATIC FLAVORINGS. THE STOCK IN WHICH THE RICE IS COOKED IS LARGELY ABSORBED BY THE TIME THE DISH IS READY TO BE SERVED.

SERVES SIX

INGREDIENTS
  1 cup long-grain rice
  7-ounce can chopped tomatoes in
    tomato juice
  ½ onion, roughly chopped
  2 garlic cloves, roughly chopped
  2 tablespoons vegetable oil
  scant 2 cups chicken stock
  ½ teaspoon salt
  3 fresh fresno chiles or other fresh
    green chiles, trimmed
  1 cup frozen peas (optional)
  ground black pepper

1 Put the rice in a large heatproof bowl and pour in boiling water to cover. Stir once, then let stand for 10 minutes. Transfer to a strainer over the sink, rinse under cold water, then drain again. Set aside to dry slightly.

2 Meanwhile, pour the tomatoes and juice into a food processor or blender, add the onion and garlic and process until smooth.

3 Heat the oil in a large, heavy pan, add the rice, and cook over medium heat until it becomes a delicate golden brown. Stir occasionally to ensure that the rice does not stick to the bottom of the pan.

4 Add the tomato mixture and stir over a moderate heat until all the liquid has been absorbed. Stir in the stock, salt, whole chiles, and peas, if using. Continue to cook the mixture, stirring occasionally, until all the liquid has been absorbed and the rice is just tender.

5 Remove the pan from the heat, cover it with a tight-fitting lid, and let it stand in a warm place for 5–10 minutes. Remove the chiles, fluff up the rice lightly, and serve, sprinkled with black pepper. The chiles may be used as a garnish, if desired.

COOK'S TIP
Do not stir the rice too often after adding the stock or the grains will break down and the mixture will become starchy.

PAN-FRIED SQUID

VISIT A BEACH BAR ANYWHERE ALONG THE COAST OF SOUTH AMERICA AND THIS IS PRECISELY THE TYPE OF SNACK YOU ARE LIKELY TO FIND ON SALE.

SERVES FOUR

INGREDIENTS
2¼ pounds fresh small squid
2 tablespoons olive oil
2 garlic cloves, crushed
1 fresh red chile, seeded and
  finely chopped
3 tablespoons *cachaça*
juice of 1 lime
salt
chunks of bread, to serve

1 Clean the squid under cold water. Pull the tentacles away from the body. The squid's entrails will come out easily. Remove the piece of cartilage from inside the body cavity and discard it.

VARIATION
If you cannot find *cachaça*, replace it with white rum or vodka.

2 Wash the body and peel away the membrane that covers it. Cut between the tentacles and head, discarding the head and entrails. Leave the tentacles whole, but discard the hard beak in the middle. Cut the body into small pieces.

3 Heat the oil over a high heat. Add the garlic, chile, and squid. Season with salt and cook for 2–3 minutes, until the squid is opaque and lightly charred.

4 Pour in the *cachaça* and continue cooking the squid until most of the liquid has evaporated. Remove the pan from the heat and then stir in the lime juice.

5 Tip the squid onto a plate and serve with chunks of bread to soak up the delicious cooking juices. Offer toothpicks for picking up the pieces of squid.

FRIED WHITEBAIT WITH CAYENNE PEPPER

FOR THE PERFECT BEACH SNACK, TRY THESE CRISP, SPICY, BITESIZE FISH WITH A SQUEEZE OF LIME.

SERVES FOUR

INGREDIENTS
½ cup plain
  (all-purpose) flour
¼ teaspoon cayenne pepper
9 ounces whitebait
vegetable oil, for deep-frying
salt and ground black pepper
lime wedges, to serve

VARIATIONS
Small fresh anchovies are also delicious cooked whole in this way. Alternatively, make up a mixed platter using whitebait, squid and shrimp.

1 Sift the flour and cayenne pepper into a deep bowl or large shallow dish. Season with plenty of salt and ground black pepper.

2 Thoroughly coat the whitebait in the seasoned flour, then shake off any excess flour and make sure the whitebait are separate. Do this in batches, placing the coated fish on a plate ready for frying.

3 Pour oil to a depth of 2 inches into a deep, wide pan. Heat the oil until very hot, then add a batch of whitebait and fry for 2–3 minutes until golden. Remove from the pan with a slotted spoon and drain on paper towels. Repeat with the remaining whitebait.

4 Pile the fried whitebait on a plate, season with salt, and serve immediately with the lime wedges.

EGGS WITH CHORIZO

IN MEXICO, THERE ARE TWO TYPES OF CHORIZO SAUSAGE. THE FIRST IS FRESHLY MADE AND SOLD LOOSE; THE SECOND IS PACKED IN SAUSAGE SKINS AND AIR-DRIED, LIKE SPANISH CHORIZO. THIS IS A RECIPE FOR THE FORMER. FRESHLY MADE CHORIZO CAN BE USED IN A NUMBER OF SAVORY DISHES, BUT IS PARTICULARLY GOOD WITH SCRAMBLED EGGS, AS HERE.

SERVES FOUR

INGREDIENTS
2 tablespoons lard
1¼ pounds ground pork
3 garlic cloves, crushed
2 teaspoons dried oregano
1 teaspoon ground cinnamon
½ teaspoon ground cloves
½ teaspoon ground black pepper
2 tablespoons dry sherry
1 teaspoon caster sugar
1 teaspoon salt
6 eggs
2 tomatoes, peeled, seeded and
   finely diced
½ small onion, finely chopped
¼ cup milk or light cream
fresh oregano sprigs, to garnish
warm corn or flour tortillas,
   to serveπ

1 Melt the lard in a large frying pan over medium heat. Add the pork mince and cook until browned, stirring frequently. Stir in the garlic, dried oregano, cinnamon, cloves, and black pepper. Cook for 3–4 more minutes.

2 Add the sherry, sugar, and salt to the pork, stir well and cook for 3–4 minutes, until the flavors are blended. Remove from heat.

3 Put the eggs in a bowl. Beat lightly to mix, then stir in the finely diced tomatoes and chopped onion.

4 Return the chorizo mixture to the heat. Heat it through and pour in the egg mixture. Cook, stirring constantly, until the egg is almost firm.

5 Stir in the milk or cream and check the seasoning. Garnish with fresh oregano and serve with warm corn or flour tortillas.

CHILES IN CHEESE SAUCE

THIS MAKES AN EXCELLENT APPETIZER, LIGHT LUNCH OR DIP TO SERVE WITH DRINKS. THE CHILES AND TEQUILA GIVE IT QUITE A KICK.

SERVES FOUR TO SIX

INGREDIENTS
4 fresh fresno chiles or other fresh
   green chiles
1 tablespoon vegetable oil
½ red onion, finely chopped
5 cups grated Monterey Jack cheese
2 tablespoons crème fraîche
⅔ cup heavy cream
2 firm tomatoes, peeled
1 tablespoon reposada tequila
Tortilla Chips, to serve

COOK'S TIP
Cross-cut the bottom of a tomato and cover with boiling water. Plunge into cold water and the skin will peel off easily.

1 Place the chiles in a dry frying pan over medium heat, turning them frequently until the skin blisters and darkens. Place the chiles in a strong plastic bag and tie the top to keep the steam in. Set aside for 20 minutes, then carefully peel off the skins. Slit the chiles and scrape out the seeds, then cut the flesh into thin strips. Cut these in half lengthwise.

2 Heat the oil in a frying pan and sauté the onion over medium heat for 5 minutes, until it is beginning to soften. Add the cheese, crème fraîche and cream. Stir over low heat until the cheese melts and the mixture becomes a rich, creamy sauce. Stir in the thick chile strips.

3 Cut the tomatoes in half and scrape out the seeds. Cut the flesh into ½-inch pieces and stir these into the sauce.

4 Just before serving, stir in the tequila. Pour the sauce into a serving dish and serve warm, with the tortilla chips.

MOLETTES

*THIS IS THE MEXICAN VERSION OF BEANS ON TOAST. SOLD BY STREET TRADERS AROUND
MID-MORNING, THEY MAKE THE PERFECT SNACK FOR THOSE WHO HAVE MISSED BREAKFAST.*

<u>SERVES FOUR</u>

INGREDIENTS
  4 crusty rolls
  ¼ cup butter, softened
  1⅓ cups Refried Beans
  1¼ cups grated Cheddar cheese
  green salad leaves, to garnish
  ½ cup Classic Tomato Salsa,
    to serve

1 Cut the rolls in half, then take a
sliver off the bottom so that they lie
flat. Remove a little of the insides.
Spread them lightly with enough butter
to crisp.

2 Arrange them on a baking sheet and
broil for about 5 minutes or until they
are crisp and golden. Meanwhile, heat
the refried beans over low heat in a
small pan.

3 Scoop the beans into the rolls, then
sprinkle the grated cheese on top. Pop
back under the broiler until the cheese
melts. Serve with the tomato salsa and
garnish with salad leaves.

EGGS MOTULENOS

*A TASTY AND FILLING BREAKFAST OR MIDDAY SNACK, BLACK BEANS, WHICH ARE ALSO KNOWN AS
TURTLE BEANS, ARE TOPPED WITH EGGS AND CHILI SAUCE AND SURROUNDED BY PEAS AND HAM.*

<u>SERVES FOUR</u>

INGREDIENTS
  generous 1 cup black beans, soaked
    overnight in water
  1 small onion, finely chopped
  2 garlic cloves
  small bunch of cilantro, chopped
  1 cup frozen peas
  4 corn tortillas
  2 tablespoons oil
  4 eggs
  5 ounces cooked ham, diced
  4 tablespoons hot chili sauce
  3 ounces feta cheese, crumbled
  salt and ground black pepper
  Classic Tomato Salsa, to serve

2 Cook the peas in a small pan of
boiling water until they are just tender.
Drain and set aside. Wrap the tortillas in
aluminum foil and place them on a plate.
Stand the plate over a pan of boiling water
and steam them for about 5 minutes.
Alternatively, wrap them in microwave
plastic wrap and heat them in a microwave on full power for about 30 seconds.

4 Place the tortillas on warmed plates
and top each one with some beans.
Place an egg on each tortilla, spoon on
1 tablespoon hot chili sauce, then
surround each egg with some peas and
ham. Sprinkle feta on the peas and
serve immediately, with salsa on the side.

1 Drain the beans, rinse them under
cold water, and drain again. Put them in
a pan, add the onion and garlic and
water to cover. Bring to a boil, then
simmer for 40 minutes. Stir in the
cilantro, with salt and pepper to taste,
and keep the beans hot.

3 Heat the oil in a frying pan and fry the
eggs until the whites are set. Lift them
onto a plate and keep them warm while
you quickly heat the ham and peas in
the oil remaining in the pan.

EGGS RANCHEROS

THERE ARE MANY VARIATIONS ON THIS POPULAR DISH, WHICH IS GREAT FOR BREAKFAST OR BRUNCH.
THE COMBINATION OF CREAMY EGGS WITH ONION, CHILE, AND TOMATOES WORKS WONDERFULLY WELL.

SERVES FOUR FOR BREAKFAST

INGREDIENTS
  2 corn tortillas, several days old
  oil, for frying
  2 fresh green jalapeño chiles
  1 garlic clove
  4 scallions
  1 large tomato
  8 eggs, beaten
  ⅔ cup light cream
  small bunch of cilantro,
    finely chopped
  salt and ground black pepper

1 Cut the tortillas into long strips. Pour oil into a frying pan to a depth of ½ inch. Heat the oil until it is very hot, watching it closely.

2 Fry the tortilla strips in batches for a minute or two until they are crisp and golden, turning them occasionally, then drain on paper towels.

COOK'S TIP
When cooking the tortilla strips, it is important that the oil is the correct temperature. To test if the oil is ready to use, carefully add a strip of tortilla. If the strip floats and the oil immediately bubbles around its edges, the oil is ready.

3 Spear the chiles on a long-handled metal skewer and roast them over the flame of a gas burner until the skins blister and darken. Do not let the flesh burn. Alternatively, dry-fry them in a griddle until the skins are scorched. Place them in a strong plastic bag and tie the top to keep the steam in. Set aside for 20 minutes.

4 Meanwhile, crush the garlic and chop the scallions finely. Cut a cross in the bottom of the tomato. Place it in a heatproof bowl and pour on boiling water to cover. After 3 minutes, lift the tomato out using a slotted spoon and plunge it into a bowl of cold water. Let sit for a few minutes to cool.

5 Drain the tomato, remove the skin, and cut it into four pieces. Using a teaspoon, scoop out the seeds and the core, then dice the flesh finely.

6 Remove the chiles from the bag and peel off the skins. Cut off the stems, then slit the chiles and scrape out the seeds. Chop the flesh finely. Put the eggs in a bowl, season with salt and pepper, and beat lightly.

7 Heat 1 tablespoon oil in a large frying pan. Add the garlic and scallions and sauté gently for 2–3 minutes, until soft. Stir in the diced tomato and cook for 3–4 more minutes, then stir in the chiles and cook for 1 minute.

8 Pour the eggs into the pan and stir until they start to set. When only a small amount of uncooked egg remains visible, stir in the cream so that the cooking process is slowed down and the mixture cooks into a creamy mixture rather than a solid mass.

9 Stir the chopped cilantro into the scrambled eggs. Arrange the tortilla strips on four serving plates and spoon on the eggs. Serve immediately.

MEXICAN TORTILLA PARCELS

SEEDED GREEN CHILES ADD JUST A FLICKER OF FIRE TO THE SPICY TOMATO FILLING IN THESE PARCELS, WHICH ARE PERFECT AS A MAIN COURSE, APPETIZER, OR SNACK.

SERVES FOUR

INGREDIENTS

1½ pounds tomatoes
4 tablespoons sunflower-seed oil
1 large onion, finely sliced
1 garlic clove, crushed
2 teaspoons cumin seeds
2 fresh green chiles, seeded
  and chopped
2 tablespoons tomato paste
1 vegetable bouillon cube
7-ounce can corn, drained
1 tablespoon chopped fresh
  cilantro
1 cup grated Cheddar cheese
8 wheat tortillas
fresh cilantro, shredded lettuce, and
  sour cream, to serve

1 Peel the tomatoes: place them in a heatproof bowl, add boiling water to cover, and leave for 30 seconds. Lift out with a slotted spoon and plunge into a bowl of cold water. Leave for 1 minute, then drain. Slip the skins off the tomatoes and chop the flesh.

2 Heat half the oil in a frying pan and fry the onion with the garlic and cumin seeds for 5 minutes, until the onion softens. Add the chiles and tomatoes, then stir in the tomato paste. Crumble the bouillon cube over, stir well, and cook gently for 5 minutes, until the chile is soft but the tomato has not completely broken down. Stir in the corn and fresh cilantro and heat gently to warm through. Keep warm.

3 Sprinkle grated cheese in the middle of each tortilla. Spoon some tomato mixture over the cheese. Fold over one edge of the tortilla, then the sides, and finally the remaining edge, to enclose the filling completely.

4 Heat the remaining oil in a frying pan and fry the filled tortillas for 1–2 minutes on each side until golden and crisp. Lift them out carefully with tongs and drain on paper towels. Serve immediately, with cilantro, shredded lettuce, and sour cream.

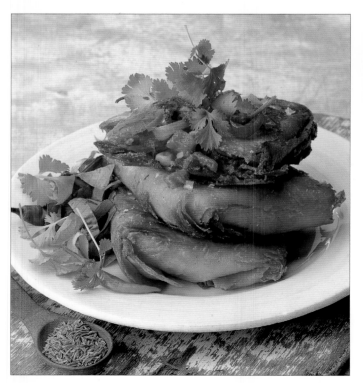

COOK'S TIP
Mexican wheat tortillas (sometimes described as wheatflour tortillas) are available in most supermarkets. They are handy to keep in the pantry as a wrapping for a variety of vegetable mixtures.

CARIBBEAN CRAB CAKES

CRABMEAT MAKES WONDERFUL FISH CAKES, AS EVIDENCED WITH THESE GUTSY MORSELS. SERVED WITH A RICH TOMATO DIP, THEY BECOME GREAT PARTY FOOD TOO, ON "STICKS."

MAKES ABOUT FIFTEEN

INGREDIENTS
    8 ounces white crabmeat (fresh,
        frozen, or canned)
    4 ounces cooked potatoes, mashed
    2 tablespoons fresh herb seasoning
    ½ teaspoon mild mustard
    ½ teaspoon ground black pepper
    ½ fresh hot chile pepper,
        finely chopped
    1 teaspoons fresh oregano
    1 egg, beaten
    all-purpose flour, for dredging
    vegetable oil, for frying
    lime wedges and cilantro sprigs, to
        garnish
    fresh whole chile peppers, to garnish
For the tomato dip
    1 tablespoon butter or margarine
    ½ onion, finely chopped
    2 canned plum tomatoes, chopped
    1 garlic clove, crushed
    ⅔ cup water
    1–2 teaspoons malt vinegar
    1 tablespoon chopped cilantro
    ½ hot fresh chile pepper, chopped

1 To make the crab cakes, mix together the crabmeat, potatoes, herb seasoning, mustard, peppers, oregano, and egg in a large bowl. Chill the mixture in the bowl for at least 30 minutes.

2 Meanwhile, make the tomato dip to accompany the crab cakes. Melt the butter or margarine in a small pan over a medium heat.

3 Add the onion, tomatoes, and garlic, and sauté for about 5 minutes until the onion is tender. Add the water, vinegar, cilantro, and hot chile pepper. Bring to the boil, then reduce the heat and simmer for 10 minutes.

4 Transfer the mixture to a food processor or blender, and blend to a smooth paste. Pour into a bowl. Keep warm or chill as wished.

5 Using a spoon, shape the crab into rounds, and dredge with flour, shaking off the excess. Heat a little oil in a frying pan and fry, a few at a time, for 2–3 minutes on each side. Drain on paper towels and keep warm in a low oven while cooking the remainder.

6 Serve with the tomato dip and garnish with lime wedges, cilantro sprigs, and whole chiles.

SPICED PLANTAIN CHIPS

PLANTAINS ARE MORE STARCHY THAN THE BANANAS TO WHICH THEY ARE RELATED, AND MUST BE COOKED BEFORE BEING EATEN. IN LATIN AMERICA THE FRUIT IS USED MUCH AS A POTATO WOULD BE. THIS SNACK HAS A LOVELY SWEET TASTE, WHICH IS BALANCED BY THE HEAT FROM THE CHILI POWDER AND SAUCE. COOK THE CHIPS JUST BEFORE YOU PLAN TO SERVE THEM.

SERVES FOUR AS AN APPETIZER OR SNACK

INGREDIENTS
    2 large plantains
    oil, for shallow-frying
    ½ teaspoon chili powder
    1 teaspoon ground cinnamon
    hot chili sauce, to serve

COOK'S TIP
Plantain skins are very dark, almost black, when the fruit is ready to eat. If they are green when you buy them, let them ripen at room temperature for a few days before use.

1 Peel the plaintains. Cut off and throw away the ends, then slice the fruit into rounds, cutting slightly on the diagonal to give larger, flatter slices.

2 Pour the oil for frying into a small frying pan, to a depth of about ½ inch. Heat the oil until it is very hot, watching it closely. Test by carefully adding a slice of plantain; it should float and the oil should immediately bubble up around it.

3 Fry the plantain slices in small batches or the temperature of the oil will drop. When they are golden brown, remove from the oil with a slotted spoon and drain on paper towels.

4 Mix the chili powder with the cinnamon. Put the plantain chips on a serving plate, sprinkle them with the chili and cinnamon mixture, and serve immediately, with a small bowl of hot chili sauce for dipping.

POPCORN WITH LIME AND CHILI

IF THE ONLY POPCORN YOU'VE HAD CAME OUT OF A CARTON AT THE MOVIES, TRY THIS MEXICAN SPECIALTY. THE LIME JUICE AND CHILI POWDER ARE INSPIRED ADDITIONS, AND THE SNACK IS QUITE A HEALTHY CHOICE TO SERVE WITH DRINKS.

MAKES ONE LARGE BOWL

INGREDIENTS
  2 tablespoons vegetable oil
  1¼ cups corn kernels
    for popcorn
  2 teaspoons chili powder
  juice of 2 limes

1 Heat the oil in a large, heavy frying pan until it is very hot. Add the popcorn and immediately cover the pan with a lid and reduce the heat.

2 After a few minutes the corn should start to pop. Resist the temptation to lift the lid to check. Shake the pan occasionally so that all of the corn will be cooked and browned.

3 When the sound of popping corn has stopped, quickly remove the pan from the heat and let cool slightly. Take off the lid and with a spoon, and lift out and discard any corn kernels that have not popped. The uncooked corn will have fallen to the bottom of the pan and is completely inedible.

4 Add the chili powder. Shake the pan again and again to make sure that all of the corn is covered with a colorful dusting of chili.

5 Transfer the popcorn to a large bowl and keep warm. Add a squeeze of lime juice immediately before serving.

SOUPS

The colonizers of Latin America and the Caribbean introduced soup
to the region, transforming their original recipes by using local ingredients.
Light soups, such as heart of palm soup, are ideal as an appetizer, while
heartier soups, such as chili clam broth, make excellent light meals.

VERMICELLI SOUP

THIS POPULAR MEXICAN SOUP, DELICIOUS AS AN APPETIZER, DRAWS INSPIRATION FROM TRADITIONAL ITALIAN CUISINE, USING INGREDIENTS SUCH AS VERMICELLI, GARLIC AND PARMESAN CHEESE.

SERVES FOUR

INGREDIENTS
  2 tablespoons olive or corn oil
  ⅓ cup vermicelli
  1 onion, roughly chopped
  1 garlic clove, chopped
  1 pound tomatoes, peeled, seeded,
    and roughly chopped
  4 cups chicken stock
  ¼ teaspoon sugar
  1 tablespoon finely chopped fresh
    cilantro
  salt and ground black pepper
  chopped fresh cilantro, to garnish
  ¼ cup freshly grated Parmesan
    cheese, to serve

COOK'S TIP
Vermicelli burns easily, so move it about in the frying pan and remove from the heat as soon as it is brown.

1 Heat the olive or corn oil in a shallow frying pan and gently sauté the vermicelli over a moderate heat until golden brown. Take care not to let the strands burn. Remove the vermicelli with a slotted spoon and drain thoroughly on paper towels.

2 Puree the chopped onion, garlic, and tomatoes in a food processor until smooth. Return the frying pan to the heat. When the oil is hot, add the puree.

3 Cook the tomato puree, stirring constantly, for about 5 minutes.

4 Transfer the puree to a pan. Add the vermicelli and pour in the stock. Season to taste. Stir in the cilantro, bring to the boil, then lower the heat, cover the pan, and simmer until the vermicelli is tender.

5 Serve sprinkled with chopped cilantro, with the Parmesan on the side.

TOMATO SOUP

THE TASTE OF FRESH CILANTRO ADDS A MEXICAN FLAVOR TO THIS CLASSIC TOMATO SOUP RECIPE. SPRINKLE GENEROUSLY WITH BLACK PEPPER AND SERVE WITH CRUSTY BREAD FOR A SATISFYING LUNCH.

SERVES FOUR

INGREDIENTS
  1 tablespoon corn or peanut oil
  1 onion, finely chopped
  2 pounds tomatoes, peeled, seeded,
    and chopped
  2 cups chicken stock
  2 large fresh cilantro sprigs
  salt and ground black pepper

1 Heat the oil in a pan and gently fry the finely chopped onion, stirring frequently, for about 5 minutes, or until it is soft and translucent but not brown.

2 Add the chopped tomatoes, chicken stock, and cilantro sprigs to the pan. Bring to the boil, then lower the heat, cover the pan, and simmer gently for about 15 minutes.

3 Remove and discard the cilantro. Press the soup through a strainer and return it to the clean pan. Season and heat through. Serve sprinkled with ground black pepper.

CREAMY HEART ᵒᶠ PALM SOUP

THIS DELICATE SOUP HAS A LUXURIOUS, CREAMY, ALMOST VELVETY TEXTURE. THE SUBTLE YET DISTINCTIVE FLAVOR OF THE PALM HEARTS IS LIKE NO OTHER, ALTHOUGH IT IS MILDLY REMINISCENT OF ARTICHOKES AND ASPARAGUS. SERVE WITH FRESH BREAD FOR A SATISFYING LUNCH.

SERVES FOUR

INGREDIENTS

2 tablespoons butter
2 teaspoons olive oil
1 onion, finely chopped
1 large leek, finely sliced
1 tablespoon all-purpose flour
4 cups well-flavored chicken stock
12 ounces potatoes, peeled
  and cubed
2 x 14-ounce cans hearts of palm,
  drained and sliced
1 cup heavy cream
salt and ground black pepper
cayenne pepper and chopped fresh
  chives, to garnish

1 Heat the butter and oil in a large pan over a low heat. Add the onion and leek, and stir well until coated in butter. Cover and cook for 5 minutes until softened and translucent.

2 Sprinkle over the flour. Cook, stirring, for 1 minute.

3 Pour in the stock and add the potatoes. Bring to the boil, then lower the heat and simmer for 10 minutes. Stir in the hearts of palm and the cream, and simmer gently for 10 minutes.

4 Process in a blender or food processor until smooth. Return the soup to the pan and heat gently, adding a little water if necessary. The consistency should be thick but not too heavy. Season with salt and ground black pepper.

5 Ladle the soup into heated bowls and garnish each with a pinch of cayenne pepper and a scattering of fresh chives. Serve immediately.

VARIATION
For a richer, buttery flavor, add the flesh of a ripe avocado when blending.

PEANUT AND POTATO SOUP WITH CILANTRO

PEANUT SOUP IS A FIRM FAVORITE THROUGHOUT CENTRAL AND SOUTH AMERICA, AND IS PARTICULARLY POPULAR IN BOLIVIA AND ECUADOR. AS IN MANY LATIN AMERICAN RECIPES, THE PEANUTS ARE USED AS A THICKENING AGENT, WITH UNEXPECTEDLY DELICIOUS RESULTS.

SERVES SIX

INGREDIENTS
- 4 tablespoons peanut oil
- 1 onion, finely chopped
- 2 garlic cloves, crushed
- 1 red bell pepper, seeded and chopped
- 9 ounces potatoes, peeled and diced
- 2 fresh red chiles, seeded and chopped
- 7 ounces canned chopped tomatoes
- 1¼ cups unsalted peanuts
- 6¼ cups beef stock
- salt and ground black pepper
- 2 tablespoons chopped fresh cilantro, to garnish

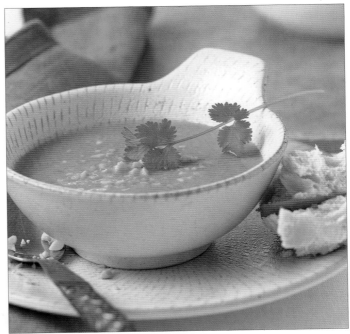

1 Heat the oil in a large, heavy pan over a low heat. Stir in the onion and cook for 5 minutes, until beginning to soften. Add the garlic, pepper, potatoes, chiles, and tomatoes. Stir well to coat the vegetables evenly in the oil, cover, and cook for 5 minutes, until softened.

2 Meanwhile, toast the peanuts by gently cooking them in a large dry frying pan over a medium heat. Keep a close eye on them, moving the peanuts around the pan until they are evenly golden. Take care not to burn them.

COOK'S TIP
Replace the unsalted peanuts with peanut butter if you like. Use equal quantities of chunky and smooth peanut butter for the ideal texture.

3 Set 2 tablespoons of the peanuts aside, to use as a garnish. Transfer the remaining peanuts to a food processor and process until finely ground. Add the vegetables and process again until smooth.

4 Return the mixture to the pan and stir in the beef stock. Bring to the boil, then lower the heat and simmer for 10 minutes.

5 Pour the soup into heated bowls. Garnish with a generous scattering of cilantro and the remaining peanuts.

TLALPEÑO-STYLE SOUP

THIS SIMPLE CHICKEN SOUP ORIGINATES FROM TLALPAN, A SUBURB OF MEXICO CITY. THE SOUP IS MADE MORE SUBSTANTIAL BY THE ADDITION OF CHEESE AND CHICKPEAS.

SERVES SIX

INGREDIENTS
6¼ cups chicken stock
½ chipotle chile, seeded
2 skinless, boneless chicken breasts
1 medium avocado
4 scallions, finely sliced
14-ounce can chickpeas, drained
salt and ground black pepper
¾ cup grated Cheddar cheese,
   to serve

1 Pour the stock into a large pan and add the dried chile. Bring to the boil, add the whole chicken breasts, then lower the heat and simmer for about 10 minutes or until the chicken is cooked. Remove the chicken from the pan and let it cool a little.

2 Using two forks, shred the chicken into small pieces. Set it aside. Pour the stock and chile into a blender or food processor and process until smooth. Return the stock to the pan.

COOK'S TIP
When buying the avocado for this soup choose one that is slightly underripe, which makes it easier to handle when peeling and slicing.

3 Cut the avocado in half, remove the skin and pit, then slice the flesh into ¾-inch pieces. Add it to the stock, with the scallions and chickpeas. Return the shredded chicken to the pan, with salt and pepper to taste, and heat gently.

4 Spoon the soup into heated bowls. Sprinkle grated cheese on top of each portion and serve immediately.

CORN SOUP

QUICK AND EASY TO PREPARE, THIS COLORFUL SOUP HAS A SWEET AND CREAMY FLAVOR. IT IS A FAVORITE ALL OVER MEXICO, ESPECIALLY FOR CHILDREN.

SERVES SIX

INGREDIENTS
2 red bell peppers
2 tablespoons vegetable oil
1 medium onion, finely chopped
3–4 cups corn niblets, thawed
   if frozen
3 cups chicken stock
⅔ cup light cream
salt and ground black pepper

1 Dry-fry the peppers in a griddle pan over a moderate heat, turning them frequently until the skins are blistered all over. Place them in a strong plastic bag and tie the top to keep the steam in. Set aside for 20 minutes, then remove the peppers from the bag and peel off the skin.

2 Cut the peppers in half and scoop out the seeds and cores. Set one aside. Cut the other into ½-inch dice.

3 Heat the oil in a large pan. Add the onion and fry over a low heat for about 10 minutes, until it is translucent and soft. Stir in the diced pepper and corn and fry for 5 minutes over a moderate heat.

4 Spoon the contents of the pan into a food processor, pour in the chicken stock, and process until almost smooth. This processing can be done in batches, if necessary.

5 Return the soup to the pan and reheat it. Stir in the cream, with salt and pepper to taste. Core, seed, and cut the reserved pepper into thin strips and add half of these to the pan. Serve the soup in heated bowls, garnished with the remaining pepper strips.

COOK'S TIP
Look out for roasted red peppers in jars. These come ready-skinned and are useful in all sorts of recipes. Used here, they make a quick soup even speedier.

CHILLED COCONUT SOUP

REFRESHING, COOLING, AND NOT TOO FILLING, THIS SOUP IS THE PERFECT ANTIDOTE TO HOT WEATHER. AT A FORMAL MEAL IN MEXICO IT WOULD BE SERVED AFTER AN APPETIZER, TO REFRESH THE PALATE BEFORE THE MAIN COURSE.

SERVES SIX

INGREDIENTS
    5 cups milk
    2⅔ cups dry unsweetened shredded
      coconut
    1⅔ cups coconut milk
    1⅔ cups chicken stock
    scant 1 cup heavy cream
    ½ teaspoon salt
    ½ teaspoon ground white pepper
    1 teaspoon superfine sugar
    small bunch of fresh cilantro

1 Pour the milk into a large pan. Bring it to the boil, stir in the coconut, lower the heat, and allow to simmer for 30 minutes. Spoon the mixture into a food processor and process until smooth. This may take a while—up to 5 minutes—so pause frequently and scrape down the sides of the bowl.

2 Rinse the pan to remove any coconut, pour in the processed mixture, and add the coconut milk. Stir in the chicken stock (homemade, if possible, which gives a better flavor than a bouillon cube), cream, salt, pepper, and sugar. Bring the mixture to the boil, stirring occasionally, then lower the heat and cook for 10 minutes.

3 Reserve a few cilantro leaves to garnish, then chop the rest finely and stir into the soup. Pour the soup into a large bowl, let it cool, then cover and put in the refrigerator until chilled. Just before serving, taste the soup and adjust the seasoning, as chilling will alter the taste. Serve in chilled bowls, garnished with the cilantro leaves.

AVOCADO SOUP

THIS DELICIOUS AND VERY PRETTY SOUP IS PERFECT FOR DINNER PARTIES AND HAS A FRESH, DELICATE FLAVOR. YOU MIGHT WANT TO ADD A DASH MORE LIME JUICE JUST BEFORE SERVING FOR ADDED ZEST.

SERVES FOUR

INGREDIENTS

2 large ripe avocados
1¼ cups crème fraîche
4 cups well-flavored chicken stock
1 teaspoon salt
juice of ½ lime
small bunch of cilantro
½ teaspoon freshly ground
   black pepper

COOK'S TIP
Because this soup contains avocados, it may discolor if left to stand, so make it just before serving.

1 Cut the avocados in half, remove the peel and lift out the pits. Chop the flesh coarsely and place it in a food processor with 3–4 tablespoons of the crème fraîche. Process until smooth.

2 Heat the chicken stock in a pan. When it is hot, but still below simmering point, stir in the rest of the crème fraîche, with the salt.

3 Add the lime juice to the avocado mixture, process briefly to mix, then gradually stir the mixture into the hot stock. Heat gently, but do not let the mixture approach the boiling point.

4 Chop the cilantro. Pour the soup into individual heated bowls and sprinkle each portion with cilantro and black pepper. Serve immediately.

FISH AND SWEET POTATO SOUP

THE SUBTLE SWEETNESS OF THE POTATO COMBINES WITH THE STRONGER FLAVORS OF FISH AND OREGANO TO MAKE THIS AN APPETIZING SOUP, POPULAR THROUGHOUT THE CARIBBEAN.

SERVES FOUR

INGREDIENTS
6 ounces white fish fillet, skinned
½ onion, chopped
1 sweet potato, about 6 ounces,
   peeled and diced
1 small carrot, about 2 ounces,
   chopped
1 teaspoon chopped fresh oregano or
   ½ teaspoon dried oregano
½ teaspoon ground cinnamon
5½ cups fish stock
5 tablespoons light cream
chopped fresh parsley, to garnish

1 Remove any bones from the fish and put it in a pan. Add the onion, sweet potato, carrot, oregano, cinnamon, and half of the stock. Bring to the boil, then simmer for 20 minutes or until the potatoes are cooked.

2 Leave to cool, then pour into a food processor and blend until smooth.

3 Return the soup to the pan, stir in the remaining fish stock, and gently bring to the boil. Reduce the heat.

4 Stir the cream into the soup, then gently heat it through without boiling. If the soup boils, the cream will curdle. Serve hot, garnished with the chopped parsley.

CARIBBEAN VEGETABLE SOUP

THIS HEARTY VEGETABLE SOUP IS FILLING ENOUGH TO BE SERVED ON ITS OWN FOR LUNCH, BUT STRIPS OF COOKED MEAT, POULTRY, OR FISH CAN ALSO BE ADDED.

SERVES FOUR

INGREDIENTS
2 tablespoons butter or margarine
1 onion, chopped
1 garlic clove, crushed
2 carrots, sliced
6¼ cups vegetable stock
2 bay leaves
2 fresh thyme sprigs
1 celery stick, finely chopped
2 green bananas, peeled
   and quartered
6 ounces white yam or eddoe,
   peeled and cubed
2 tablespoons red lentils
1 christophene, peeled
   and chopped
2 tablespoons macaroni (optional)
salt and ground black pepper
chopped scallion, to garnish

1 Melt the butter or margarine in a pan and fry the onion, garlic, and carrots for a few minutes, stirring occasionally. Add the stock, bay leaves, and thyme, and bring to the boil.

2 Add the celery, green bananas, white yam or eddoe, lentils, christophene, and macaroni, if using. Season with salt and ground black pepper, and simmer for 25 minutes or until the vegetables are cooked through. Serve garnished with chopped scallion.

VARIATION
Use other root vegetables, such as potatoes or sweet potatoes, if yam or eddoes are not available.

MEXICAN BEAN CHILI <u>WITH</u> NACHOS

STEAMING BOWLS OF BEEF CHILI SOUP, PACKED WITH BEANS, ARE DELICIOUS TOPPED WITH CRUSHED TORTILLAS AND CHEESE. POP THE BOWLS UNDER THE BROILER TO MELT THE CHEESE, IF YOU LIKE.

SERVES FOUR

INGREDIENTS
    3 tablespoons olive oil
    12 ounces round steak, cut into
        small cubes
    2 onions, chopped
    2 garlic cloves, crushed
    2 green chiles, seeded and chopped
    2 tablespoons mild chili powder
    1 teaspoon ground cumin
    2 bay leaves
    2 tablespoons tomato paste
    3¾ cups beef stock
    2 x 14-ounce cans mixed beans,
        drained and rinsed
    3 tablespoons chopped fresh
        cilantro
    salt and ground black pepper
For the topping
    bag of plain tortilla chips, lightly
        crushed
    2 cups Monterey Jack
        cheese, grated

3 Reduce the heat, cover, and simmer for about 45 minutes or until the meat is tender.

4 Put a quarter of the beans into a bowl, mash with a potato masher, and stir into the soup to thicken it. Add the remaining beans and simmer for 5 minutes. Season, and stir in the cilantro. Ladle into bowls and spoon tortilla chips on top. Pile grated cheese over the tortilla chips and serve.

VARIATION
Use Cheddar cheese instead of Monterey Jack, if you prefer.

1 Heat the oil in a large pan over a high heat and brown the meat all over. Use a draining spoon to remove it from the pan. Reduce the heat and add the onions, garlic, and chiles, then cook for 4–5 minutes, until softened.

2 Add the chili powder and ground cumin, and cook for a further 2 minutes. Return the meat to the pan, then stir in the bay leaves, tomato paste, and beef stock. Bring to the boil.

ROASTED PUMPKIN SOUP WITH PUMPKIN CRISPS

THE PUMPKIN IS ROASTED WHOLE, THEN SPLIT OPEN AND SCOOPED OUT TO MAKE THIS DELICIOUS SOUP; TOPPED WITH CRISP STRIPS OF FRIED PUMPKIN, IT IS A REAL TREAT.

SERVES SIX TO EIGHT

INGREDIENTS
   3–3½ pounds pumpkin
   6 tablespoons olive oil
   2 onions, chopped
   3 garlic cloves, chopped
   3-inch piece of fresh ginger root,
     grated
   1 teaspoon ground coriander
   ½ teaspoon ground turmeric
   pinch of cayenne pepper
   4 cups vegetable stock
   salt and ground black pepper
   1 tablespoon sesame seeds and
     fresh cilantro leaves,
     to garnish
For the pumpkin crisps
   wedge of fresh pumpkin, seeded
   ½ cup olive oil

1 Preheat the oven to 400°F. Prick the pumpkin around the top several times with a fork. Brush the pumpkin with plenty of the oil and bake for 45 minutes or until tender. Leave until cool enough to handle.

2 Take care when cutting the pumpkin, as there may still be a lot of hot steam inside. When cool enough to handle, scoop out and discard the seeds. Scoop out and chop the flesh.

3 Heat about 4 tablespoons of the remaining oil (you may not have to use all of it) in a large pan and add the onions, garlic, and ginger, then cook gently for 4–5 minutes. Add the coriander, turmeric, and cayenne, and cook for 2 minutes. Stir in the pumpkin flesh and stock. Bring to the boil, reduce the heat, and simmer for about 20 minutes, until tender.

4 Cool the soup slightly, then puree it in a food processor or blender until smooth. Return the soup to the rinsed-out pan and season well.

COOK'S TIP
If only very large pumpkins are available, simply cut off two or three large wedges weighing 3–3½ pounds in total. Brush them with oil and roast as above for 20–30 minutes or until tender.

5 Meanwhile, prepare the pumpkin crisps. Using a swivel-blade potato peeler, pare long thin strips off the wedge of pumpkin. Heat the oil in a small pan and fry the strips in batches for 2–3 minutes, until crisp. Drain on paper towels.

6 Reheat the soup and ladle it into bowls. Top with the pumpkin crisps and garnish each portion with sesame seeds and cilantro leaves.

SOUTH AMERICAN RED BEAN SOUP

THIS SOUP IS IN TEX-MEX STYLE, AND IT IS SERVED WITH A COOLING AVOCADO AND LIME SALSA.
IF YOU RELISH CHILES, ADD A LITTLE MORE CAYENNE FOR A TRULY FIERY EXPERIENCE.

SERVES SIX

INGREDIENTS
2 tablespoons olive oil
2 onions, chopped
2 garlic cloves, chopped
2 teaspoons ground cumin
¼ teaspoon cayenne pepper
1 tablespoon paprika
1 tablespoon tomato paste
½ teaspoon dried oregano
14-ounce can chopped tomatoes
2 x 14-ounce cans red kidney beans,
 drained and rinsed
3¾ cups water
salt and ground black pepper
Tabasco sauce, to serve

For the guacamole salsa
 2 avocados
 1 small red onion, finely chopped
 1 green chile, seeded and finely
  chopped
 1 tablespoon chopped fresh
  cilantro
 juice of 1 lime

1 Heat the oil in a large, heavy-based pan and add the onions and garlic. Cook for about 4–5 minutes, until softened. Add the cumin, cayenne, and paprika, and cook for 1 minute, stirring continuously.

2 Stir in the tomato paste and cook for a few seconds, then stir in the oregano. Add the chopped tomatoes, kidney beans, and water.

3 Bring the tomato and bean mixture to the boil and simmer for 15–20 minutes. Cool the soup slightly, then puree it in a food processor or blender until smooth. Return to the rinsed-out pan and add seasoning to taste.

4 To make the guacamole salsa, halve, pit, and peel the avocados, then dice them finely. Place in a small bowl and gently, but thoroughly, mix with the finely chopped red onion and chile, and the cilantro and lime juice.

5 Reheat the soup and ladle into bowls. Spoon a little guacamole salsa into the middle of each bowl and serve, offering Tabasco sauce for those who want to spice up their soup.

CORN AND RED CHILE CHOWDER

CORN AND CHILES MAKE GOOD BEDFELLOWS, AND HERE THE COOL COMBINATION OF CREAMED CORN AND MILK IS THE PERFECT FOIL FOR THE RAGING HEAT OF THE CHILES.

SERVES SIX

INGREDIENTS
- 2 tomatoes, skinned
- 1 onion, roughly chopped
- 13-ounce can creamed corn
- 2 red bell peppers, halved and seeded
- 1 tablespoon olive oil, plus extra for brushing
- 3 red chiles, seeded and chopped
- 2 garlic cloves, chopped
- 1 teaspoon ground cumin
- 1 teaspoon ground coriander
- 2½ cups milk
- 1½ cups chicken stock
- 3 corn cobs, kernels removed
- 1 pounds potatoes, finely diced
- 4 tablespoons heavy cream
- 4 tablespoons chopped fresh parsley
- salt and ground black pepper

1 Process the tomatoes and onion in a blender until smooth. Add the corn and process again, then set aside. Preheat the broiler to high.

2 Put the peppers and chiles, skin-sides up, on a broiler rack and brush with oil. Broil for 8–10 minutes, until the skins blister. Transfer to a bowl and cover with plastic wrap, then leave to cool. Peel and dice.

3 Heat the oil in a large pan and add the chopped chiles and garlic. Cook, stirring, for 2–3 minutes, until softened.

4 Add the ground cumin and coriander, and cook for a further 1 minute. Stir in the corn puree and cook for about 8 minutes, stirring occasionally.

5 Pour in the milk and stock, then stir in the corn kernels, potatoes, red bell pepper, and seasoning to taste. Cook for 15–20 minutes, until the corn and potatoes are tender.

6 Pour into deep bowls and add the cream, then scatter over the chopped parsley and serve at once.

TORTILLA SOUP

THERE ARE SEVERAL TORTILLA SOUPS. THIS ONE IS AN AGUADA—OR LIQUID—VERSION, AND IS INTENDED FOR SERVING AS AN APPETIZER OR LIGHT MEAL. IT IS VERY EASY AND QUICK TO PREPARE. YOU CAN ALSO MAKE IT IN ADVANCE AND FRY THE TORTILLA STRIPS AS IT REHEATS. THE CRISP TORTILLA PIECES ADD AN UNUSUAL TEXTURE.

SERVES FOUR

INGREDIENTS
  4 corn tortillas, freshly made or a few
    days old
  1 tablespoon vegetable oil, plus
    extra, for frying
  1 small onion, finely chopped
  2 garlic cloves, crushed
  14-ounce can plum tomatoes, drained
  4 cups chicken stock
  small bunch of cilantro
  salt and ground black pepper

1 Using a sharp knife, cut each tortilla into four or five strips, each measuring about ¾ inch wide.

2 Pour vegetable oil to a depth of ¾ inch into a heavy frying pan. Heat until a small piece of tortilla, added to the oil, floats on the top and bubbles at the edges.

3 Add a few tortilla strips to the hot oil and fry for a few minutes, until crisp and golden brown all over, turning them occasionally. Remove with a slotted spoon and drain on a double layer of paper towels. Cook the remaining tortilla strips in the same way.

4 Heat the 1 tablespoon vegetable oil in a large heavy pan. Add the chopped onion and garlic and cook over medium heat for 2–3 minutes, stirring constantly with a wooden spatula, until the onion is soft and translucent. Do not let the garlic turn brown or it will give the soup a bitter taste.

5 Chop the tomatoes using a large sharp knife and add them to the onion mixture in the pan. Pour in the chicken stock and stir well. Bring to a boil, then lower the heat and let simmer for about 10 minutes, until the liquid has reduced slightly.

6 Chop the cilantro. Add to the soup, reserving a little to use as a garnish. Season to taste.

7 Place a few of the crisp tortilla pieces in the bottom of four warmed soup bowls. Ladle the soup on top. Sprinkle each portion with the reserved chopped cilantro and serve.

COOK'S TIP
An easy way to chop the cilantro is to put the cilantro leaves in a mug and snip with a pair of scissors. Hold the scissors vertically in both hands and work the blades back and forth until the cilantro is finely chopped.

Jamaican Rice and Pea Soup with Salt Cod

BASED ON THE CLASSIC CARIBBEAN DISH OF RICE AND PEAS, THIS RECIPE IS MADE WITH BLACK-EYE PEAS, BUT KIDNEY BEANS OR, MORE TRADITIONALLY, PIGEON PEAS CAN BE USED INSTEAD.

1 Heat the oil and 2 tablespoons of the butter in a large, heavy-based pan. Add the bacon lardons and cook for 3–4 minutes, until golden. Stir in the onion, garlic, and chile and cook for a further 4–5 minutes.

2 Add the rice, stir well, and cook for 1–2 minutes, until the grains are translucent. Stir in the thyme, cinnamon stick, and black-eyed peas and cook for 1–2 minutes. Pour in the water and bring to the boil. Reduce the heat to low and cook for 25–30 minutes.

3 Meanwhile, wash the soaked salt cod under cold running water. Pat dry with paper towels and remove the skin. Cut into generous bitesize pieces and toss in the flour until evenly coated. Shake off the excess flour.

4 Melt the remaining butter in a large, heavy-based frying pan. Add the cod, in batches if necessary, and cook for 4–5 minutes, until tender and golden. Remove the cod and set aside.

5 Stir the coconut milk into the cooked rice and peas. Remove the cinnamon stick and cook the soup for 2–3 minutes. Stir in the spinach and cook for a further 2–3 minutes.

6 Add the cod and chopped parsley, season to taste with salt and pepper, and heat through. Ladle the soup into bowls and serve.

SERVES SIX

INGREDIENTS
1 tablespoon sunflower-seed oil
6 tablespoons butter
4 ounces thick rindless bacon strips, cut into lardons
1 onion, chopped
2 garlic cloves, chopped
1 red chile, seeded and chopped
generous 1 cup long grain rice
2 fresh thyme sprigs
1 cinnamon stick
14-ounces can black-eyed peas, drained and rinsed
3¾ cups water
12 ounces salt cod, soaked for 24 hours, changing the water several times
all-purpose flour, for dusting
14-ounce can coconut milk
6 ounces baby spinach leaves
2 tablespoons chopped fresh parsley
salt and ground black pepper

COOK'S TIP
Lardons are neat strips of fatty meat, such as belly of pork or fatty bacon. They are thicker and slightly longer than matchsticks. Cut them from very thick bacon strips or from a joint of bacon or gammon.

AVOCADO AND LIME SOUP

INSPIRED BY GUACAMOLE, THE POPULAR AVOCADO DIP, THIS CREAMY SOUP RELIES ON GOOD QUALITY
RIPE AVOCADOS FOR ITS FLAVOR AND COLOR.

SERVES FOUR

INGREDIENTS
3 ripe avocados
juice of 1½ limes
1 garlic clove, crushed
handful of ice cubes
1⅔ cups vegetable stock, chilled
1⅔ cups milk, chilled
⅔ cup sour cream, chilled
few drops of Tabasco sauce
salt and ground black pepper
fresh cilantro leaves,
   to garnish
extra virgin olive oil, to serve
For the salsa
4 tomatoes, peeled, seeded and
   finely diced
2 scallions, trimmed and chopped
1 fresh green chile, seeded and
   chopped
1 tablespoon chopped fresh
   cilantro
juice of ½ lime

1 Prepare the salsa first. Mix all the
ingredients and season well. Chill in the
refrigerator until required.

2 Halve and pit the avocados. Scoop
the flesh out of the avocado skins
and place in a food processor or
blender. Add the lime juice, garlic,
ice cubes, and ⅔ cup of the
vegetable stock.

3 Process the soup until smooth.
Pour into a large bowl and stir in the
remaining stock, the milk, sour cream,
Tabasco sauce, and seasoning.

4 Ladle the soup into bowls or glasses
and spoon a little salsa on top. Add a
splash of olive oil to each portion and
garnish with fresh cilantro leaves.
Serve at once.

COOK'S TIPS
• It is easy to remove the pit from an
avocado. Halve the avocado and simply
tap the pit firmly with the blade of a
large knife. Twist the knife gently and
the pit will pop out.
• This soup may discolor if it is left
standing for too long, but the flavor will
not be spoiled. Give it a quick whisk just
before serving.

CRAB, COCONUT, AND CILANTRO SOUP

QUICK AND EASY TO PREPARE, THIS SOUP HAS ALL THE FLAVORS ASSOCIATED WITH THE BAHIA REGION OF BRAZIL: CREAMY COCONUT, PALM OIL, FRAGRANT CILANTRO, AND, OF COURSE, CHILE.

SERVES FOUR

INGREDIENTS

   2 tablespoons olive oil
   1 onion, finely chopped
   1 celery stick, finely chopped
   2 garlic cloves, crushed
   1 fresh red chile, seeded and
     chopped
   1 large tomato, peeled and chopped
   3 tablespoons chopped fresh
     cilantro
   4 cups fresh crab or fish stock
   1¼ pounds crabmeat
   1 cup coconut milk
   2 tablespoons palm oil
   juice of 1 lime
   salt
   hot chili oil and lime wedges,
     to serve

1 Heat the olive oil in a pan over a low heat. Stir in the onion and celery, and sauté gently for 5 minutes, until softened and translucent. Stir in the garlic and chile and cook for a further 2 minutes.

2 Add the tomato and half the cilantro, and increase the heat. Cook, stirring, for 3 minutes, then add the stock. Bring to the boil, then simmer for 5 minutes.

3 Stir the crab, coconut milk, and palm oil into the pan, and simmer over a very low heat for a further 5 minutes. The consistency should be thick, but not stew-like, so add some water if needed.

4 Stir in the lime juice and remaining cilantro, then season with salt to taste. Serve in heated bowls with the chili oil and lime wedges on the side.

CHILI CLAM BROTH

THIS SOUP OF SUCCULENT CLAMS IN A TASTY STOCK COULD NOT BE EASIER TO PREPARE. POPULAR IN COASTAL AREAS OF COLOMBIA, IT MAKES THE PERFECT LUNCH ON A HOT SUMMER'S DAY.

SERVES SIX

INGREDIENTS

2 tablespoons olive oil
1 onion, finely chopped
3 garlic cloves, crushed
2 fresh red chiles, seeded and
finely chopped
1 cup dry white wine
14-ounce can plum tomatoes,
drained
1 large potato, about 9 ounces,
peeled and diced
1⅔ cups fish stock
3 pounds fresh clams
1 tablespoon chopped fresh
cilantro
1 tablespoon chopped fresh
Italian parsley
salt
lime wedges, to garnish

1 Heat the oil in a pan. Add the onion and sauté for 5 minutes over a low heat. Stir in the garlic and chiles, and cook for a further 2 minutes. Pour in the wine and bring to the boil, then simmer for 2 minutes.

2 Add the tomatoes, diced potato, and stock. Bring to the boil, cover, and lower the heat so that the soup simmers.

3 Season with salt and cook for 15 minutes, until the potatoes are beginning to break up and the tomatoes have made a rich sauce.

4 Meanwhile, wash the clams thoroughly under cold running water. Gently tap any that are open, and discard them if they do not close.

5 Add the clams to the soup, cover the pan, and cook for about 3–4 minutes, or until the clams have opened, then stir in the chopped herbs. Season with salt to taste.

6 Check over the clams and throw away any that have failed to open. Ladle the soup into warmed bowls. Offer the lime wedges separately, to be squeezed over the soup just before eating.

CHUNKY SHRIMP CHUPE

CHOWDERS, KNOWN AS CHUPES IN SOUTH AMERICA, ARE A MEAL IN THEMSELVES. POTATOES ARE ALWAYS INCLUDED, BUT THE OTHER INGREDIENTS VARY. THIS IS A SEAFOOD VERSION.

SERVES SIX

INGREDIENTS

1¼ pounds raw jumbo shrimp
3 cups fish stock
1 carrot, finely chopped
2 celery sticks, thinly sliced
3 tablespoons annatto (achiote) oil
1 large onion, finely chopped
1 red bell pepper, seeded and diced
2 garlic cloves, crushed
2 fresh red chiles, seeded
  and chopped
1 teaspoon turmeric
1 large tomato, peeled and chopped
1½ pounds potatoes, peeled and cut
  into 1-inch cubes
1 cup fresh or frozen peas
1 tablespoon chopped fresh mint
1 tablespoon chopped fresh cilantro
salt

1 Peel the shrimp and set them aside. Place the shells in a large pan with the fish stock, carrot, and celery. Bring to the boil, then simmer over a low heat for 20 minutes. Strain into a bowl or pitcher and set the stock aside.

VARIATION
Traditionally this soup would be made using *huacatay*, a pungent Peruvian herb that tastes like a cross between mint and cilantro.

2 Heat the oil in a large pan over a low heat. Stir in the onion and red bell pepper, and sauté for 5 minutes. Stir in the garlic, chiles, and turmeric, and cook for a further 2 minutes.

3 Add the chopped tomato and potatoes to the pan, season to taste with salt, and cook for about 10 minutes, allowing the tomato to break down slightly and the potatoes to absorb the flavors of the other ingredients.

4 Pour in the strained stock and bring to the boil. Lower the heat and simmer for 15 minutes, or until the potatoes are cooked through.

5 Stir the shrimp and peas into the soup and simmer for 4–5 minutes or until the shrimp become opaque. Finally, stir in the mint and cilantro, and serve in warmed bowls.

CARIBBEAN SALT COD WITH CREAMED YAM

INSPIRED BY THE INGREDIENTS OF THE CARIBBEAN, THIS COLORFUL CHUNKY SOUP IS SERVED IN DEEP BOWLS AROUND A CHIVE-FLAVORED SWEET YAM MASH.

SERVES SIX

INGREDIENTS

7 ounces salt cod, soaked for
24 hours, changing the water
several times
1 tablespoon olive oil
1 garlic clove, chopped
1 onion, chopped
1 green chile, seeded and chopped
6 plum tomatoes, peeled
and chopped
1 cup white wine
2 bay leaves
3¾ cups water
8 ounces okra
8 ounces callaloo or spinach
2 tablespoons chopped fresh parsley
salt and ground black pepper
For the creamed yam
1½ pounds yam
juice of 1 lemon
¼ cup butter
2 tablespoons heavy cream
1 tablespoon chopped fresh chives

1 Drain and skin the salt cod, then rinse it under cold running water. Cut the flesh into bitesize pieces, removing any bones, and set aside.

2 Heat the oil in a heavy pan. Add the garlic, onion, and chile, and cook for 4–5 minutes, until softened and the onions are transparent.

3 Add the salt cod and cook for 3–4 minutes. Stir in the tomatoes, wine, and bay leaves, and bring to the boil. Pour in the water, bring to the boil, then simmer for 10 minutes.

4 Meanwhile, trim the stalk ends off the okra and cut the pods into chunks. Add to the soup, and cook for 10 minutes. Stir in the callaloo or spinach and cook for 5 minutes, until the okra is tender.

5 Meanwhile, prepare the creamed yam. Peel the yam and cut it into large dice, then place in a pan with the lemon juice and add cold water to cover. Bring to the boil and cook for 15–20 minutes, until tender. Drain well, then return the yam to the pan and dry it out over the heat for a few seconds. Mash with the butter and cream, and season well. Stir in the chives.

6 Season the soup and stir in the chopped parsley. Spoon portions of creamed yam into the centers of six soup bowls and ladle over the soup.

SPICED LAMB SOUP

THE COMBINATION OF LAMB WITH PUMPKIN AND GREEN BANANAS, AND PLENTY OF SPICES, MAKES THIS UNUSUAL SOUP FULL OF FLAVOR. IT IS SUBSTANTIAL ENOUGH TO MAKE A COMPLETE MEAL.

SERVES FOUR

INGREDIENTS

⅔ cup split black-eyed peas, soaked
   overnight
1½ pounds shoulder of lamb, cut
   into medium chunks
1 teaspoon chopped fresh thyme
2 bay leaves
5 cups water
1 onion, sliced
8 ounces pumpkin, diced
2 black cardamom pods
1½ teaspoons ground turmeric
1 tablespoon chopped cilantro
½ teaspoon caraway seeds
1 green chile, seeded and chopped
2 green bananas
1 carrot
salt and ground black pepper

1 Drain the black-eyed peas, place them in a large pan, and cover with fresh cold water.

2 Bring the peas to the boil, boil rapidly for 10 minutes, and then reduce the heat and simmer, covered for 40–50 minutes, until tender, adding more water if necessary. Remove from the heat and set aside to cool.

3 Meanwhile, put the lamb in a large pan, add the thyme, bay leaves, and water and bring to the boil. Cover and simmer for 1 hour, until tender.

4 Add the onion, pumpkin, cardamoms, turmeric, cilantro, caraway, chile, and seasoning and stir. Bring back to a simmer and then cook, uncovered, for 15 minutes, until the pumpkin is tender.

5 When the peas are cool, spoon into a blender or food processor with their liquid and blend to a smooth puree.

6 Cut the bananas into medium slices and the carrot into thin slices. Stir into the soup with the peas and cook for 10–12 minutes. Season and serve.

PLANTAIN SOUP <u>WITH</u> CORN <u>AND</u> CHILE

THIS COLORFUL SOUP IS IDEAL FOR VEGETARIANS IF MADE WITH VEGETABLE RATHER THAN CHICKEN STOCK. THE PINCH OF NUTMEG ADDS A UNIQUE FLAVOR.

<u>SERVES FOUR</u>

INGREDIENTS
  2 tablespoons butter or margarine
  1 onion, finely chopped
  1 garlic clove, crushed
  10 ounces yellow plantains, peeled
    and sliced
  1 large tomato, peeled and chopped
  1 cup corn kernels
  1 teaspoon dried tarragon, crushed
  3¾ cups vegetable or chicken stock
  1 green chile, seeded and chopped
  pinch of grated nutmeg
  salt and ground black pepper

1 Melt the butter or margarine in a pan over a medium heat, add the onion and garlic and cook for a few minutes until soft. Add the plantain, tomato, and corn, and cook for 5 minutes.

2 Add the tarragon, vegetable stock, chile, and salt and pepper, and simmer for about 10 minutes, or until the plantain is tender. Stir in the nutmeg and serve immediately.

KALE, CHORIZO, AND POTATO SOUP

THIS HEARTY WINTER SOUP HAS A SPICY KICK TO IT, WHICH COMES FROM THE CHORIZO SAUSAGE. THE SOUP BECOMES MORE POTENT IF CHILLED OVERNIGHT, AND IT IS WORTH BUYING THE BEST POSSIBLE CHORIZO SAUSAGE TO IMPROVE THE FLAVOR.

SERVES SIX TO EIGHT

INGREDIENTS
    8 ounces kale, stems removed
    8 ounces chorizo sausage
    1½ pounds red potatoes
    7½ cups vegetable stock
    1 teaspoon ground black pepper
    pinch cayenne pepper (optional)
    12 slices French bread, broiled
    salt and ground black pepper

1 Place the kale in a food processor and process for a few seconds to chop it finely.

2 Prick the sausages and place in a pan with enough water to cover. Simmer for 15 minutes. Drain and cut into thin slices.

3 Boil the potatoes for about 15 minutes, or until tender. Drain and place in a bowl, then mash, adding a little of the cooking liquid to form a thick paste.

4 Bring the stock to the boil and add the kale. Add the chorizo and simmer for 5 minutes. Add the potato paste gradually, and simmer for 20 minutes. Season with black pepper and cayenne.

5 Place bread slices in each bowl, and pour the soup over. Serve sprinkled with pepper.

CORN AND SWEET POTATO SOUP

THE COMBINATION OF CORN AND SWEET POTATO GIVES THIS SOUP A REAL DEPTH OF FLAVOR AS WELL AS MAKING IT LOOK VERY COLORFUL. IT MAKES A HEARTY APPETIZER OR CAN BE A MEAL IN ITSELF WITH A CHUNK OF BREAD OR SOME TORTILLA CHIPS AND SALSA ON THE SIDE.

SERVES SIX

INGREDIENTS

- 1 tablespoon olive oil
- 1 onion, finely chopped
- 2 garlic cloves, crushed
- 1 small red chile, seeded and finely chopped
- 7½ cups vegetable stock
- 2 teaspoons ground cumin
- 1 medium sweet potato, diced
- ½ red bell pepper, finely chopped
- 1 pound corn kernels
- salt and ground black pepper
- lime wedges, to serve

1 Heat the oil in a heavy pan and fry the onion for 5 minutes until softened. Add the garlic and chile, and fry for a further 2 minutes.

2 Add 1¼ cups of the vegetable stock, and simmer for about 10 minutes.

3 Mix the cumin with a little stock to form a paste and then stir into the soup. Add the diced sweet potato, stir, and simmer for 10 minutes. Season and stir again.

4 Add the pepper, corn, and remaining stock, and simmer for 10 minutes. Process half of the soup until smooth, and then stir into the chunky soup. Season and serve with lime wedges for squeezing over.

BEEF <u>AND</u> CASSAVA SOUP

THIS SIMPLE, TASTY SOUP IS ALMOST A STEW. SUCH SOUPS, MADE IN ONE POT, ARE EVERYDAY FARE IN LATIN AMERICA. THE ADDITION OF WINE IS NOT TRADITIONAL, BUT IT ENHANCES THE FLAVOR.

<u>SERVES FOUR</u>

INGREDIENTS
1 pound stewing beef, cubed
5 cups beef stock
1¼ cups white wine
1 tablespoon soft brown sugar
1 onion, finely chopped
1 bay leaf
1 bouquet garni
1 fresh thyme sprig
1 tablespoon tomato paste
1 large carrot, sliced
10 ounces cassava or yam, peeled and cubed
2 ounces fresh spinach, chopped
a little hot pepper sauce, to taste
salt and ground black pepper

1 Mix the cubed beef, stock, white wine, sugar, chopped onion, bay leaf, bouquet garni, thyme, and tomato paste in a large pan. Bring to the boil, then cover and simmer very gently for about 1¼ hours. If you want very tender meat, allow about 2–2¼ hours.

2 Add the sliced carrot, cubed cassava or yam, spinach, and a few drops of hot pepper sauce. Season with salt and ground black pepper to taste, and simmer for a further 15 minutes, until the meat and vegetables are both tender. Serve in heated bowls.

LAMB AND LENTIL SOUP

LENTILS ARE POPULAR ON CARIBBEAN ISLANDS, SUCH AS TRINIDAD AND TOBAGO, WHERE THEY WERE INTRODUCED BY SOUTHEAST ASIAN LABORERS RECRUITED TO WORK THE SUGARCANE PLANTATIONS.

SERVES FOUR

INGREDIENTS
6¼–7½ cups water or stock
2 pounds neck of lamb,
  cut into pieces
½ onion, chopped
1 garlic clove, crushed
1 bay leaf
1 clove
2 fresh thyme sprigs
8 ounces potatoes
¾ cup red lentils
2½ cups water
salt and ground black pepper
chopped fresh parsley

1 Pour 16¼ cups of the water or stock into a large pan and add the lamb, chopped onion, crushed garlic, bay leaf, clove, and thyme sprigs. Bring to the boil, then lower the heat and simmer gently for about 1 hour, until the lamb is tender.

2 Peel the potatoes and cut them into rough 1-inch cubes. Add them to the soup in the pan and cook for a further 5 minutes.

3 Add the red lentils to the pan, stirring them gently into the stock, then season the soup to taste with a little salt and plenty of ground black pepper. Add approximately 1¼ cups of warm water to completely cover the meat and vegetables.

4 Bring the soup back to the boil, then lower the heat, cover, and simmer for 25 minutes or until the lentils are cooked, stirring occasionally. Add a little more water during cooking if the soup becomes too thick. Just before serving, stir in the chopped parsley.

FISH

Fish plays an important part in Latin-American cuisine, and the most popular recipes rely on the freshest fish cooked simply. In parts of Brazil and the Caribbean, where the local cuisine has been shaped by the culinary traditions of African slaves, richly flavored fish stews are more popular.

BAKED SEA BASS <u>WITH</u> COCONUT

THIS ELEGANT COLOMBIAN DISH IS IDEAL FOR A DINNER PARTY. THE BAY LEAVES GIVE A DEPTH OF FLAVOR TO THE CHILI AND COCONUT SAUCE.

<u>SERVES FOUR</u>

INGREDIENTS
   1 whole large sea bass, about 2
     pounds, cleaned
   2 fresh red chiles, seeded and finely
     chopped
   1 onion, finely sliced
   2 garlic cloves, crushed
   juice of 1 lime
   1 tablespoon olive oil
   2 bay leaves
   scant 1 cup coconut milk
   salt

VARIATION
For a complete meal, cook some
vegetables in the roasting pan with the
sea bass. Sliced carrots, fennel, and/or
zucchini would all go well with the
coconut sauce.

1 Preheat the oven to 350°F. Thoroughly
rinse the fish inside and out, then pat
dry with paper towels. Place in a large
roasting pan and season all over
with salt.

2 Generously sprinkle the chopped
chiles, onion, garlic, lime juice, and
olive oil over the fish. Add the bay
leaves to the pan and bake the fish in
the oven for about 15 minutes.

3 Pour the coconut milk over the fish
and return it to the oven for a further
10 minutes, or until the flesh flakes
easily when tested with the tip of a
sharp knife.

4 Cut along the back of the fish. This
will release the flesh from the bones,
making it easy to divide into portions.
Serve with the sauce. A rice dish would
make a good accompaniment.

PAN-FRIED SEA BREAM <u>WITH</u> LIME <u>AND</u> TOMATO SALSA

THE MOST POPULAR WAY OF COOKING A FRESH PIECE OF FISH IS TO PAN-FRY IT OR BROIL IT. IN THIS RECIPE A SIMPLE SALSA IS FLASHED IN THE PAN AT THE END OF COOKING, TO MAKE A LIGHT SAUCE.

<u>SERVES FOUR</u>

INGREDIENTS
   4 sea bream fillets
   juice of 2 limes
   2 tablespoons chopped cilantro
   1 fresh red chile, seeded and
     finely chopped
   2 scallions, sliced
   3 tablespoons olive oil, plus extra
     to serve
   2 large tomatoes, diced
   salt
   cooked white rice, to serve

1 Place the fish fillets in a shallow china
or glass dish large enough to hold them
all in a single layer.

2 Mix the lime juice, cilantro, chile,
and scallions in a pitcher. Stir in half
the oil, then pour this marinade over the
fish. Cover and marinate for around
15–20 minutes. Do not be tempted to
marinate the fish for longer than this or
the acid in the marinade will start to
"cook" it.

3 Heat the remaining oil in a large,
heavy frying pan over a high heat. Lift
each piece of fish from the marinade
and pat dry with paper towels.

4 Season the fish with salt and place in
the hot pan, skin-side down. Cook for
2 minutes, then turn and cook for a
further 2 minutes, until the flesh is
opaque all the way through.

5 Add the marinade and the chopped
tomatoes to the pan. Bring the sauce to
the boil and cook for about 1 minute,
until the tomatoes are lightly cooked
but still retain their shape. Drizzle a
little olive oil over the fish and serve on
individual warm plates, with white rice
and the tomato salsa.

HALIBUT <u>WITH</u> PEPPERS <u>AND</u> COCONUT MILK

THIS AROMATIC DISH, KNOWN LOCALLY AS MOQUECA, *COMES FROM THE STATE OF BAHIA, ON THE EAST COAST OF BRAZIL. COOKED AND SERVED IN AN EARTHENWARE DISH, IT IS USUALLY ACCOMPANIED BY WHITE RICE AND FLAVORED CASSAVA FLOUR TO SOAK UP THE DELICIOUS SAUCE.*

SERVES SIX

INGREDIENTS
   6 halibut, cod, haddock, or monkfish
     fillets, each about 4 ounces
   juice of 2 limes
   8 fresh cilantro sprigs
   2 fresh red chiles, seeded
     and chopped
   3 tomatoes, sliced into thin rounds
   1 red bell pepper, seeded and sliced
     into thin rounds
   1 green bell pepper, seeded and
     sliced into thin rounds
   1 small onion, sliced into thin rounds
   scant 1 cup coconut milk
   4 tablespoons palm oil
   salt
   cooked white rice, to serve
For the flavored cassava flour
   2 tablespoons palm oil
   1 medium onion, thinly sliced
   2¼ cups cassava flour

1 Place the fish fillets in a large, shallow dish and pour over water to cover. Pour in the lime juice and set aside for 30 minutes. Drain the fish thoroughly and pat dry with paper towels. Arrange the fish in a single layer in a heavy pan which has a tight-fitting lid.

2 Sprinkle the cilantro and chiles over the fish, then top with a layer each of tomatoes, peppers, and onion. Pour the coconut milk over, cover, and leave to stand for 15 minutes before cooking.

3 Season with salt, then place the pan over a high heat and cook until the coconut milk comes to the boil. Lower the heat and simmer for 5 minutes. Remove the lid, pour in the palm oil, cover again, and simmer for 10 minutes.

4 Meanwhile make the flavored cassava flour. Heat the oil in a large frying pan over a very low heat. Stir in the onion slices and cook for 8–10 minutes, until soft and golden. Stir in the cassava flour and cook, stirring constantly, for 1–2 minutes, until lightly toasted and evenly colored by the oil. Season with salt.

5 Serve the *moqueca* with the rice and flavored cassava flour.

CARIBBEAN FISH STEAKS

WEST INDIAN COOKS LOVE SPICES, AND USE THEM TO GOOD EFFECT. THIS QUICK AND EASY RECIPE IS A TYPICAL EXAMPLE OF HOW CHILES, CAYENNE, AND ALLSPICE CAN BE USED WITH LIME TO ADD AN EXOTIC ACCENT TO A TOMATO SAUCE FOR FISH.

SERVES FOUR

INGREDIENTS

3 tablespoons sunflower-seed oil
6 shallots
1 garlic clove
1 fresh green chile, seeded and finely chopped
14-ounce can chopped tomatoes
2 bay leaves
¼ tsp cayenne pepper
1 teaspoon ground allspice
juice of 2 limes
4 cod steaks
1 teaspoon molasses sugar
2 teaspoons angostura bitters
salt

VARIATION
This unusual and exotic sauce is also good over broiled pork chops.

1 Slowly heat the oil in a frying pan. Finely chop the shallots and add them to the frying pan. Cook for 5 minutes until soft. Crush a peeled garlic clove into the frying pan and add the chile. Cook for a further 2 minutes, then stir in the tomatoes, bay leaves, cayenne pepper, allspice, and lime juice, with a little salt to taste.

2 Cook gently for 15 minutes, then add the cod steaks and baste with the tomato sauce. Cover and cook for 10 minutes. Transfer the steaks to a warmed dish and keep hot while you prepare the sauce. Stir the sugar and angostura bitters into the sauce, simmer for 2 minutes, then pour over the fish.

SALMON IN MANGO AND GINGER SAUCE

MANGO AND SALMON MAY SEEM UNLIKELY PARTNERS, BUT THE FLAVORS COMPLEMENT EACH OTHER VERY WELL, ESPECIALLY WHEN THE DISTINCT FLAVOR OF TARRAGON IS ADDED TO THE EQUATION.

SERVES TWO

INGREDIENTS

2 salmon steaks, each about
  10 ounces
a little lemon juice
1–2 garlic cloves, crushed
1 teaspoon dried tarragon, crushed
2 shallots, roughly chopped
1 tomato, roughly chopped
1 large, ripe mango, peeled, pitted
  and chopped
⅔ cup fish stock or water
1 tablespoon syrup from a jar of
  crystallized ginger
2 tablespoons butter
salt and ground black pepper

1 Place the salmon steaks in a single layer in a shallow dish and sprinkle with the lemon juice, garlic, tarragon, and salt and pepper. Cover and set aside in the refrigerator for at least 1 hour.

2 Meanwhile, place the shallots, tomato, and mango in a blender or food processor and blend until smooth. Add the fish stock or water and the ginger syrup, blend again, and set aside.

3 Melt the butter in a frying pan and cook the salmon steaks for about 3 minutes on each side.

4 Add the mango puree, cover, and simmer for a further 5 minutes, until the salmon is cooked and flakes easily.

5 Transfer the salmon to plates. Heat the sauce, adjust the seasoning, and pour over the salmon. Serve hot.

FRIED SNAPPER WITH AVOCADO

THE COMBINATION OF CRISP FRIED FISH AND SILKY SMOOTH AVOCADO WORKS EXTREMELY WELL IN THIS RECIPE. ON THE ISLANDS OF THE CARIBBEAN, WHERE THIS RECIPE ORIGINATED, THE FISH IS OFTEN SERVED WITH FRIED DUMPLINGS OR HARD-DOUGH BREAD.

SERVES FOUR

INGREDIENTS

1 lemon
4 red snappers, each about 8 ounces,
  prepared
2 teaspoons spice seasoning
flour, for dusting
oil, for frying
2 avocados and cooked corn, sliced
  widthwise, to serve
chopped fresh parsley and lime
  slices, to garnish

1 Squeeze the lemon juice both inside and outside the fish, and sprinkle with the spice seasoning. Place the fish in a shallow dish, cover, and set aside in a cool place to marinate for a few hours.

2 Lift the marinated fish out of the dish and dust thoroughly with the flour, shaking off any excess.

3 Heat the oil in a large non-stick frying pan over a medium heat. Add the fish and fry gently for about 10 minutes on each side.

4 Meanwhile, cut the avocados in half, remove the pits, and cut in half again. Peel away the skin and cut the flesh into thin strips.

5 When the fish are cooked through and the skin is crisp and brown, transfer them to warmed serving plates. Add the avocado and corn slices. Garnish with the chopped parsley and lime slices, and serve immediately.

COOK'S TIP
Using two frying pans will allow you to cook all four fish simultaneously. Alternatively, cook two and keep them hot in a covered dish in a warm oven while cooking the remaining pair.

SALT COD FOR CHRISTMAS EVE

THIS MEXICAN DISH IS MILDER THAN THE SIMILAR SPANISH DISH, BACALDO A LA VIZCAINA. IT IS EATEN ON CHRISTMAS EVE THROUGHOUT MEXICO.

SERVES SIX

INGREDIENTS

1 pound dried salt cod
7 tablespoons extra virgin olive oil
1 onion, halved and thinly sliced
4 garlic cloves, crushed
2 x 14-ounce cans chopped tomatoes
  in tomato juice
¾ cup sliced almonds
½ cup pickled jalapeño
  chile slices
1 cup green olives stuffed
  with pimiento
small bunch of fresh parsley,
  finely chopped
salt and ground black pepper
fresh Italian parsley, to garnish
crusty bread, to serve

1 Put the cod in a large bowl and pour in enough cold water to cover. Soak for 24 hours, changing the water at least five times during this period.

2 Drain the cod and remove the skin using a large sharp knife. Shred the flesh finely using two forks, and put it into a bowl. Set it aside.

3 Heat half the oil in a large frying pan. Add the onion slices and sauté over medium heat until the onion has softened and is translucent.

4 Remove the onion from the pan and set aside. Make sure you transfer the oil with the onion, as it is an important flavoring in this dish and mustn't be discarded. In the same pan add the remaining olive oil. When the oil is hot but not smoking, add the crushed garlic and sauté gently for 2 minutes.

5 Add the canned tomatoes and their juice to the pan with the garlic. Cook over medium-high heat for about 20 minutes, stirring occasionally, until the mixture has reduced and thickened.

COOK'S TIPS

• Salt cod is available at specialty fish dealers, Spanish delicatessens, and West Indian stores.
• Any leftovers can be used to fill burritos or empanadas.

6 Meanwhile, spread out the sliced almonds in a single layer in a large heavy frying pan. Toast them over medium heat for a few minutes, shaking the pan lightly throughout the process so that they turn golden brown all over. Do not let them burn.

7 Add the jalapeño chile slices and stuffed olives to the toasted almonds.

8 Stir in the shredded fish, mixing it in thoroughly, and cook for 20 more minutes, stirring occasionally, until the mixture is almost dry.

9 Season to taste, add the parsley, and cook for another 2–3 minutes. Garnish with parsley leaves and serve in heated bowls, with crusty bread.

CEVICHE <u>WITH</u> RED ONION, AVOCADO, <u>AND</u> SWEET POTATO

CEVICHE IS A SOUTH AMERICAN DISH OF FISH MARINATED IN CITRUS JUICE AND ONION, WHICH HAS A SIMILAR EFFECT TO COOKING, MAKING THE FISH OPAQUE AND FIRM IN TEXTURE.

SERVES SIX AS A STARTER

INGREDIENTS
    1¼–1½ pounds white fish
        fillets, skinned
    1 red onion, thinly sliced
    pinch of dried red chili flakes
    grated rind of 1 small lime and
        juice of 5 limes
    1–1¼ pounds sweet potatoes
    5 tablespoons mild olive oil
    3–5 teaspoons rice vinegar
    ½–1 teaspoons superfine sugar
    ½ teaspoon ground toasted
        cumin seeds
    ½–1 fresh red or green chile,
        seeded and finely chopped
    1 large or 2 small avocados,
        peeled, pitted, and sliced
    8 ounces peeled cooked shrimp
    3 tablespoons chopped fresh cilantro
    2 tablespoons roasted peanuts,
        chopped
    salt and ground black pepper

3 Place the oil in a bowl and whisk in the rice vinegar and sugar to taste, then add the cumin, season, and whisk in the fresh chile and grated lime rind.

4 In a glass bowl, toss together the fish, sweet potatoes, avocado slices, shrimp, and most of the cilantro, and the dressing.

5 Toss in the remaining half of the sliced red onion. Sprinkle with the remaining cilantro and the peanuts, and serve at once.

COOK'S TIP
Choose orange-fleshed sweet potatoes, if you can, for this dish.

1 Cut the fish into strips or chunks. Sprinkle half the onion in a glass dish and lay the fish on top. Add the chili flakes and pour in the lime juice. Cover and chill for 2–3 hours, spooning the lime juice over the fish once or twice. Drain, and discard the onion.

2 Steam or boil the sweet potatoes for 20–25 minutes, or until just tender. Peel and slice, or cut into wedges.

SEARED TUNA STEAKS
WITH RED ONION SALSA

RED ONIONS ARE IDEAL FOR THIS SALSA, NOT ONLY FOR THEIR MILD AND SWEET FLAVOR, BUT ALSO BECAUSE THEY LOOK SO APPETIZING. SALAD, RICE, OR BREAD ARE GOOD ACCOMPANIMENTS.

SERVES FOUR

INGREDIENTS

4 tuna loin steaks, each weighing
  about 6–7 ounces
1 teaspoon cumin seeds, toasted
  and crushed
pinch of dried red chili flakes
grated rind and juice of 1 lime
2–4 tablespoons extra virgin
  olive oil
salt and ground black pepper
lime wedges and fresh cilantro sprigs,
  to garnish
For the salsa
  1 small red onion, finely chopped
  7 ounces red or yellow cherry
    tomatoes, roughly chopped
  1 avocado, peeled, pitted,
    and chopped
  2 kiwi fruits, peeled and chopped
  1 fresh red chile, seeded and
    finely chopped
  ½ ounce fresh cilantro, chopped
  6 fresh mint sprigs, leaves
    only, chopped
  1–2 teaspoons Thai fish sauce
    (*nam pla*)
  1 teaspoon molasses sugar

1 Wash the tuna steaks and pat dry. Sprinkle with half the cumin, the dried chili, salt, pepper, and half the lime rind. Rub in 2 tablespoons of the oil and set aside in a glass or china dish for about 30 minutes.

2 Meanwhile, make the salsa. Mix the onion, tomatoes, avocado, kiwi fruits, fresh chile, chopped cilantro, and mint. Add the remaining cumin, the rest of the lime rind, and half the lime juice. Add Thai fish sauce and sugar to taste. Set aside for 15–20 minutes, then add more Thai fish sauce, lime juice, and olive oil if required.

3 Heat a ridged cast-iron grill pan. Cook the tuna, allowing about 2 minutes on each side for rare tuna or a little longer for a medium result.

4 Serve the tuna steaks garnished with lime wedges and cilantro sprigs. Serve the salsa separately or spoon onto the plates with the tuna.

RED SNAPPER WITH CILANTRO AND ALMONDS

THIS SIMPLE TREATMENT IS PERFECT FOR RED SNAPPER, A FISH THAT IS VERY POPULAR IN MEXICO, WHERE FRESH RED SNAPPER CAN BE PICKED UP FROM MARKET STALLS ON THE COAST.

SERVES FOUR

INGREDIENTS
¾ cup all-purpose flour
4 red snapper fillets
salt and ground black pepper
6 tablespoons butter
1 tablespoon vegetable oil
¾ cup sliced almonds
grated zest and juice of 1 lime
small bunch of cilantro,
  finely chopped
warm flour tortillas, to serve

COOK'S TIP
Warm the tortillas by wrapping them in foil and steaming them on a plate over boiling water for a few minutes. Alternatively, wrap them in microwave-safe plastic wrap and heat them in a microwave on full power for about 30 seconds.

1 Preheat the oven to 275°F. Spread out the flour in a shallow dish and add seasoning. Dry the fish fillets with paper towels, then coat each fillet in the seasoned flour.

2 Heat the butter and oil in a frying pan. Add the snapper fillets, in batches if necessary, and cook for 2 minutes. Turn the fillets over carefully and cook the other side until golden.

3 Using a spatula, carefully transfer the fillets to a shallow dish and keep them warm in the oven. Add the almonds to the fat remaining and fry them for 3–4 minutes, until golden.

4 Add the lime zest, juice, and cilantro to the almonds in the frying pan and stir well. Heat through for 1–2 minutes, then pour the mixture onto the fish. Serve with warm flour tortillas.

VERACRUZ-STYLE RED SNAPPER

THIS IS A CLASSIC MEXICAN DISH THAT BORROWS BAY LEAVES AND OLIVES FROM SPAIN TO GO WITH THE NATIVE CHILES.

SERVES FOUR

INGREDIENTS
4 whole red snapper, cleaned
juice of 2 limes
4 garlic cloves, crushed
1 teaspoon dried oregano
½ teaspoon salt
drained bottled capers, to garnish
lime wedges, to serve (optional)
For the sauce
½ cup olive oil
2 bay leaves
2 garlic cloves, sliced
4 fresh jalapeño chiles, seeded and
cut in strips
1 onion, thinly sliced
8 fresh tomatoes
½ cup pickled jalapeño
chile slices
1 tablespoon soft dark brown sugar
½ teaspoon ground cloves
½ teaspoon ground cinnamon
1¼ cups green olives stuffed
with pimiento

1 Preheat the oven to 350°F. Rinse the fish inside and out, then pat dry with paper towels. Place in a large roasting pan in a single layer.

2 Mix the lime juice, garlic, oregano, and salt in a small bowl. Pour the mixture onto the fish. Bake for about 30 minutes or until the flesh flakes easily when tested with the tip of a sharp knife.

3 Meanwhile, make the sauce. Heat the olive oil in a pan, add the bay leaves, garlic, and chile strips; fry over low heat for 3–4 minutes.

4 Add the onion slices to the oil in the pan and cook for 3–4 more minutes, until all the onion is softened and translucent.

5 Cut a cross in the bottom of each tomato. Place them in a heatproof bowl and pour in boiling water to cover. After 3 minutes, lift the tomatoes out on a slotted spoon and plunge them into a bowl of cold water. Drain. The skins will have begun to peel back from the crosses.

6 Skin the tomatoes completely, then cut them in half and squeeze out the seeds. Chop the flesh finely and add it to the onion mixture. Cook for 3–4 minutes, until the tomato is starting to soften.

7 Add the pickled jalapeños, brown sugar, ground cloves, and cinnamon to the sauce. Cook for 10 minutes, stirring frequently, then stir the olives into the sauce and pour a little onto each fish. Garnish with the capers and serve with lime wedges, if desired. A rice dish would make a good accompaniment.

PICKLED FISH

THIS DELICIOUS DISH HAS A LOVELY ROUNDED FLAVOR AS THE SWEETNESS OF THE VEGETABLES BALANCES OUT THE SHARPNESS OF THE PICKLED FISH. ADD A GARNISH OF CAPERS AND CHILE STRIPS.

SERVES FOUR

INGREDIENTS
- 2 pounds white fish fillets
- 4 tablespoons freshly squeezed lime or lemon juice
- 1¼ cups olive or corn oil
- 2 whole cloves
- 6 peppercorns
- 2 garlic cloves
- ½ teaspoon ground cumin
- ½ teaspoon dried oregano
- 2 bay leaves
- 1 cup white wine vinegar
- 1 drained canned jalapeño chile, seeded, and cut into strips
- 1 onion, thinly sliced
- 1 cup olive or corn oil
- salt

For the garnish
- sprigs of fresh herbs such as oregano, cilantro, or parsley

3 Combine the cloves, peppercorns, garlic, cumin, oregano, bay leaves, and vinegar in a pan. Bring to the boil, add the jalapeño chile and onion, then simmer for 3–4 minutes.

4 Add the remaining oil, and bring to a simmer. Pour over the fish. Cool, cover, and chill for 24 hours. To serve, lift out the fillets with a spatula and arrange on a serving dish. Garnish with fresh herbs.

1 Cut the fish fillets into eight equal size pieces and arrange them in a single layer in a shallow dish. Drizzle with the lime or lemon juice. Cover and leave to marinate for 15 minutes, turning the fillets once.

2 Lift out the fillets with a spatula, pat them dry with paper towels, and season with salt. Heat 4 tablespoons of the oil in a frying pan and sauté the fish until lightly golden brown. Transfer to a platter and set aside.

CITRUS FISH <u>WITH</u> CHILES

LEMON IS THE NATURAL FLAVORING FOR WHITE FISH, AND IN THIS DISH THE BAKED LEMONY FLAVORS INFUSE THE FISH WITH A WONDERFUL TANGY RICHNESS.

SERVES FOUR

INGREDIENTS
4 halibut or cod steaks
juice of 1 lemon
1 teaspoon garlic granules
1 teaspoon paprika
1 teaspoon ground cumin
¾ teaspoon dried tarragon
about 4 tablespoons olive oil
flour, for dusting
1¼ cups fish stock
2 red chiles, seeded and
  finely chopped
2 tablespoons chopped fresh
  cilantro
1 red onion, cut into rings
salt and ground black pepper

1 Place the fish in a shallow bowl and mix together the lemon juice, garlic, paprika, cumin, tarragon, and a little salt and pepper. Spoon over the lemon mixture, cover loosely with plastic wrap, and marinate for a few hours or overnight in the refrigerator.

3 Pour the fish stock around the fish and simmer, covered, for about 5 minutes, until the fish is thoroughly cooked through.

5 Transfer the fish and sauce to a serving plate and keep warm.

2 Heat the oil in a frying pan, dust the fish with flour, and fry for a few minutes each side, until golden brown all over.

4 Add the chopped red chiles and 1 tablespoon of the cilantro to the pan. Simmer for 5 minutes.

6 Wipe the pan with paper towels, heat some olive oil, and stir-fry the onion rings until speckled brown. Sprinkle over the fish with the remaining chopped cilantro and serve.

MEXICAN SPICY FISH

IN MEXICO FISH IS OFTEN MARINATED IN A SPICY MIXTURE BEFORE COOKING. HERE THE FISH IS FLAVORED WITH CUMIN, CINNAMON, AND ANNATO, A TRADITIONAL MEXICAN SPICE.

SERVES SIX

INGREDIENTS
    3–3½ pounds striped bass or
      any non-oily white fish, cut into
      6 steaks
    ½ cup corn oil
    1 large onion, thinly sliced
    2 garlic cloves, chopped
    12 ounces tomatoes, sliced
    2 drained canned jalapeño chiles,
      rinsed and sliced
For the marinade
    4 garlic cloves, crushed
    1 teaspoon black peppercorns
    1 teaspoon dried oregano
    ½ teaspoon ground cumin
    1 tsp ground annatto
    ½ teaspoon ground cinnamon
    ½ cup mild white vinegar
    salt
    Italian parsley, to garnish

1 Arrange the fish steaks in a single layer in a shallow dish. Make the marinade. Using a pestle, grind the garlic and black peppercorns in a mortar. Add the dried oregano, cumin, annatto, and cinnamon, and mix to a paste with the vinegar. Add salt to taste and spread the marinade on both sides of each of the fish steaks. Cover and leave in a cool place for 1 hour.

2 Select a flameproof dish large enough to hold the fish in a single layer and pour in enough of the oil to coat the base. Arrange the fish in the dish with any remaining marinade.

3 Top the fish with the onion, garlic, tomatoes, and chiles, and pour the rest of the oil over the top.

4 Cover the dish and cook over a low heat on top of the stove for 15–20 minutes, or until the fish is no longer translucent. Serve immediately, garnished with Italian parsley.

Salt Cod ⁱⁿ Mild Chili Sauce

Dried salt cod is a great favorite throughout Latin America. This preparation originated in Spain and Portugal, where it remains popular today.

SERVES SIX

INGREDIENTS
    2 pounds dried salt cod
    1 onion, chopped
    2 garlic cloves, chopped
For the sauce
    6 dried ancho chiles
    1 onion, chopped
    ½ teaspoon dried oregano
    ½ teaspoon ground coriander
    1 serrano chile, seeded and
      chopped
    3 tablespoons corn oil
    3 cups fish or chicken stock
    salt
For the garnish
    1 fresh green chile, sliced

1 Soak the cod in cold water for several hours, depending on how hard and salty it is. Change the water once or twice during soaking.

2 Drain the fish and transfer it to a pan. Pour in enough water to cover. Bring to a gentle simmer and cook for about 15 minutes, until the fish is tender. Drain, reserving the stock. Remove any skin or bones from the fish and cut it into 1½-inch pieces.

3 Make the sauce. Remove the stems and shake out the seeds from the ancho chiles. Tear the pods into pieces, put in a bowl of warm water, and soak until they are soft. Drain and put into a food processor with the onion, oregano, cilantro, and serrano chile. Process to a puree.

4 Heat the oil in a frying pan and cook the puree, stirring, for about 5 minutes. Stir in the fish or chicken stock and simmer for 3–4 minutes. Add the prepared cod and simmer for a few minutes longer to heat the fish through and blend the flavors. Serve garnished with the sliced chile.

RED SNAPPER BURRITOS

FISH MAKES A GREAT FILLING FOR A TORTILLA, ESPECIALLY WHEN IT IS SUCCULENT RED SNAPPER MIXED WITH RICE, CHILE, AND TOMATOES.

<u>SERVES SIX</u>

INGREDIENTS

3 red snapper fillets
½ cup long-grain white rice
2 tablespoons vegetable oil
1 small onion, finely chopped
1 teaspoon ground achiote seed
   (annatto powder)
1 pasilla or similar dried chile,
   seeded and ground
¾ cup sliced almonds
7-ounce can chopped tomatoes in
   tomato juice
1¼ cups grated Monterey Jack or
   mild Cheddar cheese
8 x 8-inch flour tortillas
fresh Italian parsley to garnish
lime wedges (optional)

1 Preheat the broiler. Broil the fish on an oiled rack for about 5 minutes, turning once. When cool, remove the skin and flake the fish into a bowl. Set it aside.

2 Meanwhile, put the rice in a pan, cover with cold water, cover, and bring to a boil. Drain, rinse, and drain again.

3 Heat the oil in a pan and sauté the onion until soft and translucent. Stir in the ground achiote (annatto powder) and the chile and cook for 5 minutes.

4 Add the rice, stir well, then stir in the fish and almonds. Add the tomatoes, with their juice. Cook over medium heat until the juice is absorbed and the rice is tender. Stir in the cheese and remove from the heat. Warm the tortillas.

5 Divide the filling among the tortillas and fold them as shown, to make neat parcels. Garnish with fresh parsley and serve with lime wedges, if desired. A green salad makes a good accompaniment.

SEA BASS WITH ORANGE CHILI SALSA

THE CITRUS SALSA HAS A FRESHNESS THAT PROVIDES THE PERFECT CONTRAST TO THE WONDERFUL
FLAVOR OF FRESH SEA BASS.

SERVES FOUR

INGREDIENTS
    4 sea bass fillets
    salt and ground black pepper
    cilantro, to garnish
For the salsa
    2 fresh green chiles
    2 oranges or pink grapefruit
    1 small onion

1 Make the salsa. Roast the chiles in a dry griddle until the skins are blistered, being careful not to let the flesh burn. Put them in a strong plastic bag and tie the top to keep the steam in. Set aside for 20 minutes.

COOK'S TIP
If the fish has not been scaled, do this by running the back of a small filleting knife against the grain of the scales. They should come off cleanly. Rinse and pat dry with paper towels.

2 Slice the top and bottom off each orange or grapefruit and cut off all the peel and pith. Cut between the membranes and put each segment in a bowl.

3 Remove the chiles from the bag and peel off the skins. Cut off the stalks, then slit the chiles and scrape out the seeds. Chop the flesh finely. Cut the onion in half and slice it thinly. Add the onion and chiles to the orange pieces and mix lightly. Season and chill.

4 Season the sea bass fillets. Line a steamer with waxed paper, letting extra hang over the sides to enable the fish to be lifted out after cooking. Place the empty steamer over a pan of water and bring to a boil.

5 Place the fish in a single layer in the steamer. Cover with a lid and steam for about 8 minutes or until just cooked. Garnish with cilantro and serve with the salsa and a vegetable side dish of your choice.

FRIED SOLE WITH LIME

SIMPLE FISH DISHES LIKE THIS ONE CAPITALIZE ON THE DELICIOUS FLAVOR OF GOOD FRESH FISH.

<u>SERVES FOUR</u>

INGREDIENTS

¾ cup all-purpose flour
2 teaspoons garlic salt
1 teaspoon ground black pepper
4 sole fillets
oil, for frying
juice of 2 limes
small bunch of fresh parsley,
    chopped, plus extra sprigs,
    to garnish
fresh salsa, to serve

COOK'S TIP
Make sure the oil is hot enough when
you add the fish, or it will be absorbed
by the fish and the dish will be
too greasy.

1 Combine the flour, garlic salt, and
pepper. Spread out the seasoned flour
mixture in a shallow dish. Pat the sole
fillets dry with paper towels, then turn
them in the seasoned flour until they
are evenly coated.

2 Pour oil into a wide frying pan to a
depth of ½ inch. Heat it until a cube
of bread added to the oil rises to the
surface and browns in 45–60 seconds.

3 Add the fish, in batches if necessary,
and fry for 3–4 minutes. Lift each fillet
out and drain it on paper towels.
Transfer to a heated serving dish.

4 Squeeze the juice of half a lime onto
each piece of fish and sprinkle with the
chopped parsley. Serve immediately,
with a fresh salsa to complement the
fish. Garnish with parsley sprigs. New
potatoes would also go well.

BAKED SALMON WITH GUAVA SAUCE

*GUAVAS HAVE A CREAMY FLESH WITH A SLIGHT CITRUS TANG, WHICH MAKES THEM THE PERFECT FRUIT
FOR A SAUCE TO SERVE WITH SALMON. THE SAUCE WORKS WELL WITH OTHER FISH AND IS ALSO GOOD
WITH CHICKEN OR TURKEY.*

<u>SERVES FOUR</u>

INGREDIENTS

6 ripe guavas
3 tablespoons vegetable oil
1 small onion, finely chopped
½ cup well-flavored chicken stock
2 teaspoons hot pepper sauce
4 salmon steaks
salt and ground black pepper
strips of red bell pepper to garnish

COOK'S TIP
Ripe guavas have yellow skin and
succulent flesh that ranges in color from
white to deep pink or salmon red. They
are exceptionally rich in vitamin C. Ripe
fruit will keep in the refrigerator for a
few days; green guavas will need to be
placed in a warm spot until they ripen.

1 Cut each guava in half. Scoop the
seeded soft flesh into a sieve placed
over a bowl. Press it through the sieve,
discard the seeds and skin and set the
pulp aside.

2 Heat 2 tablespoons of the oil in a
frying pan. Sauté the chopped onion for
about 4 minutes over medium heat until
softened and turned translucent.

3 Stir in the guava pulp, with the
chicken stock and hot pepper sauce.
Cook, stirring constantly, until the sauce
thickens. Keep it warm until needed.

4 Brush the salmon steaks on one side
with a little of the remaining oil. Season
them with salt and pepper. Heat a
griddle or ridged pan until very hot and
add the salmon steaks, oiled side down.
Cook for 2–3 minutes, until the
underside is golden, then brush the
surface with oil, turn each salmon steak
over and cook the other side until the
fish is cooked and flakes easily when
tested with the tip of a sharp knife.

5 Transfer each steak to a warmed
plate. Serve, garnished with strips of red
pepper on a pool of sauce. A fresh
green salad is a good accompaniment.

TROUT IN WINE SAUCE WITH PLANTAIN

EXOTIC FISH FROM THE WARM CARIBBEAN WATERS, SUCH AS MAHI MAHI OR GROUPER, WOULD ADD A DISTINCTIVE FLAVOR TO THIS TASTY DISH, WHICH IS EATEN THROUGHOUT THE REGION. IF YOU CANNOT FIND EXOTIC FISH, HOWEVER, TROUT IS IDEAL, OR YOU CAN USE ANY FILLETED WHITE FISH.

SERVES FOUR

INGREDIENTS
4 trout fillets
spice seasoning, for dusting
2 tablespoons butter or margarine
1–2 garlic cloves
⅔ cup white wine
⅔ cup fish stock
2 teaspoons clear honey
1–2 tablespoons chopped
  fresh parsley
1 yellow plantain
salt and ground black pepper
oil, for frying
green salad, to serve

1 Season the trout fillets by coating them in the spice seasoning. Place in a shallow dish, cover with plastic wrap, and marinate in a cool place for at least 1 hour.

2 Melt the butter or margarine in a large frying pan and heat gently for 1 minute. Add the fish fillets. Sauté for about 5 minutes, until cooked through, turning carefully once. Transfer to a plate and keep hot.

3 Add the garlic, white wine, fish stock, and honey to the pan and bring to the boil, stirring. Lower the heat and simmer to reduce slightly. Return the fish to the pan and spoon over the sauce. Sprinkle with the parsley and simmer gently for 2–3 minutes.

4 Meanwhile, peel the plantain, and cut it into rounds. Heat a little oil in a small frying pan and fry the plantain slices for 2–3 minutes, until golden, turning once. Transfer the fish to warmed serving plates. Stir the sauce, season, and pour over the fish. Serve with the fried plantain and a green salad.

COOK'S TIP
Plantains belong to the banana family and can be green, yellow, or brown, depending on how ripe they are. Unlike bananas, they must be cooked.

ESCHOVISHED FISH

THIS PICKLED FISH DISH IS OF SPANISH ORIGIN AND IS VERY POPULAR THROUGHOUT THE CARIBBEAN ISLANDS. IT GOES BY VARIOUS NAMES, INCLUDING ESCOVITCH AND CAVÉACHED FISH, BUT NO MATTER WHAT THE NAME, IT INEVITABLY TASTES DELICIOUS.

SERVES SIX

INGREDIENTS
    2 pounds cod fillet
    ½ lemon
    1 tablespoon spice seasoning
    flour, for dusting
    oil, for frying
    lemon wedges, to garnish
For the sauce
    2 tablespoons vegetable oil
    1 onion, sliced
    ½ red bell pepper, sliced
    ½ christophene, peeled, seeded, and
      cut into small pieces
    2 garlic cloves, crushed
    ½ cup malt vinegar
    5 tablespoons water
    ½ teaspoon ground allspice
    1 bay leaf
    1 small fresh Scotch bonnet or
      Habañero chile, chopped
    1 tablespoon soft brown sugar
    salt and ground black pepper

1 Place the fish in a shallow dish, squeeze over the lemon juice, then sprinkle with the spice seasoning. Pat the seasoning into the fish using your hands, then cover and leave to marinate in a cool place for at least 1 hour.

VARIATION
Cod fillets are very expensive so, if they are available, try using whole red snapper or red mullet, which are often used for this dish in the Caribbean.

2 Cut the cod fillet across into 3-inch pieces. Dust the pieces of fish with a little flour, shaking off any excess.

3 Heat the oil in a heavy frying pan and fry the fish pieces for 2–3 minutes, turning occasionally, until they are golden brown and crisp. Using a metal spatula or slotted spoon, lift the cooked fish pieces out of the pan and place in a serving dish. Keep hot.

4 Make the sauce. Heat the oil in a frying pan and fry the onion for 4–5 minutes. Add the pepper, christophene, and garlic, and stir-fry for 2 minutes.

5 Pour in the vinegar, then add the water, allspice, bay leaf, chile, and sugar. Simmer for 5 minutes, then season. Leave to stand for 10 minutes, then pour the sauce over the fish. Serve hot, garnished with the lemon wedges.

CHARGRILLED TUNA <u>WITH</u> FIERY PEPPER PUREE

TUNA IS AN OILY FISH THAT BARBECUES WELL AND IS MEATY ENOUGH TO COMBINE SUCCESSFULLY WITH STRONG FLAVORS—EVEN HOT CHILES, AS IN THIS RED PEPPER PUREE, WHICH IS EXCELLENT SERVED WITH CRUSTY BREAD OR TORTILLAS.

SERVES FOUR

INGREDIENTS
   4 tuna steaks, about 6 ounces each
   finely grated rind and juice of 1 lime
   2 tablespoons olive oil
   salt and freshly ground black pepper
   lime wedges, to serve
For the pepper puree
   2 red bell peppers, halved
   3 tablespoons olive oil, plus extra for
     brushing
   1 small onion
   2 garlic cloves, crushed
   2 red chiles
   1 slice white bread, crusts removed,
     diced
   salt

1 Trim any skin from the tuna and place the steaks in a single layer in a wide dish. Sprinkle over the lime rind and juice, olive oil, salt, and black pepper. Cover with plastic wrap and chill in the refrigerator until required.

2 To make the pepper puree, brush the pepper halves with a little olive oil and cook them, skin side down, on a hot barbecue, until the skin is charred and blackened. Place the onion in its skin on the barbecue and cook until browned, turning it occasionally.

COOK'S TIP
The pepper puree can be made in advance, cooking the peppers and onion under a hot broiler; keep it in the refrigerator until you cook the fish.

3 Leave the peppers and onion until cool enough to handle, then remove the skins, using a sharp kitchen knife.

4 Place the cooked peppers and onion with the garlic, chiles, bread, and olive oil in a food processor. Process until smooth. Add salt to taste.

5 Drain the tuna steaks from the marinade and cook them on a hot barbecue for 8–10 minutes, turning once, until golden brown. Serve the steaks with the pepper puree and lime wedges, with crusty bread if you like.

MACKEREL ESCABECHE

THIS TRADITIONAL WAY OF PRESERVING FISH IN VINEGAR, WAS BROUGHT TO LATIN AMERICA BY THE SPANISH AND PORTUGUESE. OILY FISH, SUCH AS MACKEREL AND SARDINES, LEND THEMSELVES PARTICULARLY WELL TO THIS TREATMENT. IT TAKES AT LEAST A DAY, SO ALLOW PLENTY OF TIME.

SERVES SIX

INGREDIENTS
    12 small mackerel fillets
    juice of 2 limes
    6 tablespoons olive oil
    2 red onions, thinly sliced
    2 garlic cloves, thinly sliced
    2 bay leaves
    6 black peppercorns
    ½ cup red wine vinegar
    ½ cup all-purpose flour
    salt and ground black pepper

1 Place the mackerel fillets side by side in a large, shallow glass or china dish. Pour over the lime juice. Season with salt and pepper, and cover. Marinate in the refrigerator for 20–30 minutes, but no longer.

2 Meanwhile, heat half the oil in a frying pan. Add the onions and cook over a low heat for 10 minutes, until softened but not colored. Stir in the garlic and cook for 2 minutes.

3 Add the bay leaves, peppercorns, and vinegar to the pan and simmer over a very low heat for 5 minutes.

COOK'S TIP
If you are planning to keep the fish for more than one day, make sure it is completely immersed in the vinegar, then top with a thin layer of olive oil. Cover tightly. It will keep in the refrigerator for up to 1 month.

4 Pat the mackerel fillets dry and coat them in the flour. Heat the remaining oil in a large frying pan and fry the fish, in batches, for 2 minutes on each side.

5 Return the fish to the dish in which they were originally marinated. Pour the vinegar marinade over the fish. Leave to marinate for 24 hours before serving.

SALMON WITH TEQUILA CREAM SAUCE

USE REPOSADA TEQUILA, WHICH IS LIGHTLY AGED, FOR THIS SAUCE. IT HAS A SMOOTHER, MORE
ROUNDED FLAVOR, WHICH GOES WELL WITH THE CREAM.

<u>SERVES FOUR</u>

INGREDIENTS
3 fresh jalapeño chiles
3 tablespoons olive oil
1 small onion, finely chopped
⅔ cup fish stock
grated rind and juice of 1 lime
½ cup light cream
2 tablespoons reposada tequila
1 firm avocado
4 salmon fillets
salt and ground white pepper
strips of green bell pepper and fresh
   Italian parsley to garnish

1 Roast the chiles in a frying pan until the skins are blistered, being careful not to let the flesh burn. Put them in a strong plastic bag and tie the top to keep the steam in. Set aside for 20 minutes.

2 Heat 1 tablespoon of the oil in a pan. Add the onion and sauté for 3–4 minutes, then add the stock, lime rind and juice. Cook for 10 minutes, until the stock starts to reduce. Remove the chiles from the bag and peel off the skins, slit, and scrape out the seeds.

3 Stir the cream into the onion and stock mixture. Slice the chile flesh into strips and add to the pan. Cook over low heat, stirring constantly, for 2–3 minutes. Season to taste with salt and white pepper.

4 Stir the tequila into the onion and chile mixture. Leave the pan over very low heat. Peel the avocado, remove the pit, and slice the flesh. Brush the salmon fillets on one side with a little of the remaining oil.

5 Heat a frying pan or ridged pan until very hot and add the salmon, oiled side down. Cook for 2–3 minutes, until the underside is golden, then brush the top with oil, turn each fillet over, and cook the other side until the fish is cooked and flakes easily when tested with the tip of a sharp knife.

6 Serve on a pool of sauce, with the avocado slices. Garnish with strips of green pepper and fresh parsley. This is good with Fried Potatoes.

YUCATAN-STYLE SHARK STEAK

A FIRM-FLESHED FISH, SHARK IS WIDELY AVAILABLE, EITHER FRESH OR FROZEN. IT NEEDS CAREFUL WATCHING, AS OVERCOOKING WILL MAKE IT DRY AND TOUGH, BUT THE FLAVOR IS EXCELLENT.

SERVES FOUR

INGREDIENTS
grated zest and juice of 1 orange
juice of 1 small lime
3 tablespoons white wine
2 tablespoons olive oil
2 garlic cloves, crushed
2 teaspoons ground achiote seed
(annatto powder)
½ teaspoon cayenne pepper
½ teaspoon dried marjoram
1 teaspoon salt
4 shark steaks
fresh oregano leaves, to garnish
4 flour tortillas and any suitable
salsa, to serve

COOK'S TIP
Shark freezes successfully, with little or no loss of flavor on thawing, so use frozen steaks if you can't find fresh.

1 Put the orange zest and juice in a shallow nonmetallic dish which is large enough to hold all the shark steaks in a single layer. Add the lime juice, white wine, olive oil, garlic, ground achiote (annatto powder), cayenne, marjoram, and salt. Mix well.

2 Add the shark steaks to the dish and spoon the marinade on them. Cover and set aside for 1 hour, turning once.

3 Heat a griddle until very hot and cook the marinated shark steaks for 2–3 minutes on each side. Alternatively, they are very good cooked on the barbecue, as long as they are cooked after the coals have lost their fierce initial heat. Do not overcook.

4 Garnish the shark steaks with oregano and serve with the tortillas and salsa. A green vegetable would also go well.

SWORDFISH TACOS

IT IS IMPORTANT NOT TO OVERCOOK SWORDFISH, OR IT CAN BE TOUGH AND DRY. COOKED CORRECTLY, HOWEVER, IT IS ABSOLUTELY DELICIOUS AND MAKES A GREAT CHANGE FROM BEEF OR CHICKEN AS A TACO FILLING.

<u>SERVES SIX</u>

INGREDIENTS
  3 swordfish steaks
  2 tablespoons vegetable oil
  2 garlic cloves, crushed
  1 small onion, chopped
  3 fresh green chiles, seeded
    and chopped
  3 tomatoes
  small bunch cilantro, chopped
  6 fresh corn tortillas
  ½ iceberg lettuce, shredded
  salt and ground black pepper
  lemon wedges, to serve (optional)

1 Preheat the broiler. Put the swordfish on an oiled rack over a broiler pan and broil for 2–3 minutes on each side. When cool enough to handle, remove the skin and flake the fish into a bowl.

2 Heat the oil in a pan. Add the garlic, onion, and chiles, and sauté for 5 minutes or until the onion is soft and translucent.

3 Cut a cross in the bottom of each tomato and pour in boiling water. After 3 minutes plunge into cold water. Remove the skins and seeds, and chop the flesh into ½-inch dice.

4 Add the tomatoes and swordfish to the onion mixture. Cook for 5 minutes over low heat. Add the cilantro and cook for 1–2 minutes. Season to taste.

5 Wrap the tortillas in foil and steam on a plate over boiling water until pliable. Place some shredded lettuce and fish mixture on each tortilla. Fold in half and serve with lemon wedges, if desired.

BROILED SWORDFISH <u>WITH</u> CHILI <u>AND</u> LIME SAUCE

SWORDFISH IS A PRIME CANDIDATE FOR THE BROILER, AS LONG AS IT IS NOT OVERCOOKED. IT TASTES WONDERFUL WITH A SPICY SAUCE WHOSE FIRE IS TEMPERED WITH CRÈME FRAÎCHE.

<u>SERVES FOUR</u>

INGREDIENTS
  2 fresh serrano chiles
  4 tomatoes
  3 tablespoons olive oil
  grated zest and juice of 1 lime
  4 swordfish steaks
  ½ teaspoon salt
  ½ teaspoon ground black pepper
  ¾ cup crème fraîche
  fresh Italian parsley to garnish

1 Roast the chiles in a dry griddle until the skins are blistered. Put in a strong plastic bag and tie the top. Set aside for 20 minutes, then peel off the skins. Cut off the stalks, then slit the chiles, scrape out the seeds and slice the flesh.

2 Cut a cross in the bottom of each tomato. Place them in a heatproof bowl and pour in boiling water to cover. After 3 minutes, lift the tomatoes out on a slotted spoon and plunge them into a bowl of cold water. Drain. The skins will have begun to peel back from the crosses. Remove all the skin from the tomatoes, then cut them in half and squeeze out the seeds. Chop the flesh into ½-inch pieces.

3 Heat 1 tablespoon of the oil in a small pan and add the strips of chile, with the lime zest and juice. Cook for 2–3 minutes, then stir in the tomatoes. Cook for 10 minutes, stirring the mixture occasionally, until the tomato is pulpy.

4 Brush the swordfish steaks with olive oil and season. Broil for 3–4 minutes or until just cooked, turning once. Meanwhile, stir the crème fraîche into the sauce, heat it through, and pour onto the swordfish steaks. Serve garnished with fresh parsley. Broil some vegetables as well.

MARINATED RED MULLET

THIS POPULAR LATIN AMERICAN RECIPE IS BASED ON A SPANISH WAY OF COOKING FISH EN ESCABECHE BY FIRST FRYING IT, THEN MARINATING IT. IF YOU ARE UNABLE TO FIND FRESH MULLET, SNAPPER, SEA BREAM, OR TILAPIA ARE ALL GOOD ALTERNATIVES.

SERVES SIX

INGREDIENTS
1½ teaspoons mild Spanish paprika,
    preferably Spanish smoked
    pimentón
3 tablespoons all-purpose flour
½ cup olive oil
6 red mullet, each weighing about
    11 ounces, filleted
2 eggplants, sliced or cut into long
    wedges
2 red or yellow bell peppers, seeded
    and thickly sliced
1 large red onion, thinly sliced
2 garlic cloves, sliced
1 tablespoon sherry vinegar
juice of 1 lemon
brown sugar, to taste
1 tablespoon chopped fresh oregano
18–24 black olives
3 tablespoons chopped fresh Italian
    parsley
salt and ground black pepper

1 Mix 1 teaspoon of the paprika with the flour and season well with salt and black pepper. Heat half the oil in a large frying pan. Dip the fish into the flour, turning to coat both sides, and fry for 4–5 minutes, until browned on each side. Place the fish in a glass or china dish suitable for marinating it.

2 Add 2 tablespoons of the remaining oil to the pan and fry the eggplant wedges until softened and browned. Drain thoroughly on a paper towel to remove excess oil, then add the eggplant to the fish.

3 Add another 2 tablespoons oil to the pan and cook the peppers and onion gently for 6–8 minutes, until softened but not browned. Add the garlic and remaining paprika, then cook for a further 2 minutes. Stir in the sherry vinegar and lemon juice with 2 tablespoons water and heat until simmering. Season to taste with sugar.

4 Stir in the oregano and olives, then spoon over the fish. Set aside to cool, then cover and marinate in the refrigerator for several hours or overnight.

5 About 30 minutes before serving, bring the fish and vegetables back to room temperature. Stir in the parsley just before serving.

COD CARAMBA

THIS COLORFUL MEXICAN DISH, WITH ITS CONTRASTING CRUNCHY TOPPING AND TENDER FISH FILLING, CAN BE MADE WITH ANY ECONOMICAL WHITE FISH SUCH AS COLEY OR HADDOCK. SERVE WITH A TASTY GREEN SALAD FOR A HEARTY MIDWEEK SUPPER.

SERVES SIX

INGREDIENTS
    1 pound cod fillets
    8 ounces smoked cod fillets
    1¼ cups fish stock
    ¼ cup butter
    1 onion, sliced
    2 garlic cloves, crushed
    1 green and 1 red bell pepper,
      seeded and diced
    2 zucchini, diced
    ⅔ cup drained canned or thawed
      frozen corn kernels
    2 tomatoes, peeled and chopped
    juice of 1 lime
    Tabasco sauce
    salt, ground black pepper, and
      cayenne pepper
For the topping
    3 ounces tortilla chips
    ½ cup grated Cheddar cheese
    cilantro sprigs, to garnish
    lime wedges, to serve

3 Stir in the corn and tomatoes, then add lime juice and Tabasco to taste. Season with salt, black pepper, and cayenne. Cook for 2 minutes to heat the corn and tomatoes, then stir in the fish and transfer to a dish that can safely be used under the broiler.

4 Preheat the broiler. Make the topping by crushing the tortilla chips, then mixing in the grated cheese. Add cayenne pepper to taste and sprinkle over the fish. Place the dish under the broiler until the topping is crisp and brown. Garnish with cilantro sprigs and lime wedges.

1 Lay the fish in a shallow pan and pour over the fish stock. Bring to the boil, lower the heat, cover, and poach for about 8 minutes, until the flesh flakes easily. Leave to cool slightly, then remove the skin and separate the flesh into large flakes. Keep hot.

2 Melt the butter in a pan, add the onion and garlic, and cook gently over a low heat until soft and translucent. Add the peppers, stir, and cook for about 2 minutes. Stir in the zucchini and cook for 3 minutes more, until all the vegetables are tender.

CREOLE FISH STEW

THIS IS A SIMPLE DISH THAT LOOKS AS GOOD AS IT TASTES. IT IS A GOOD CHOICE FOR A DINNER PARTY, BUT REMEMBER TO ALLOW TIME FOR MARINATING THE FISH.

SERVES SIX

INGREDIENTS
  2 whole red bream, porgy, or large
    snapper, prepared and cut into
    1-inch pieces
  2 tablespoons spice seasoning
  2 tablespoons malt vinegar
  flour, for dusting
  oil, for frying
For the sauce
  2 tablespoons vegetable oil
  1 tablespoon butter or margarine
  1 onion, finely chopped
  10 ounces fresh tomatoes, peeled
    and finely chopped
  2 garlic cloves, crushed
  2 fresh thyme sprigs
  2½ cups fish stock or water
  ½ teaspoon ground cinnamon
  1 fresh hot chile, chopped
  1 red and 1 green bell pepper,
    seeded and finely chopped
  salt
  fresh oregano sprigs, to garnish

1 Toss the pieces of fish with the spice seasoning and vinegar in a bowl. Cover and set aside to marinate for at least 2 hours at cool room temperature or overnight in the refrigerator.

COOK'S TIP
Take care when preparing the chile, as the capsaicin it contains is a powerful irritant and will burn the skin. Wear gloves if possible and avoid touching your face until you have removed them. Leave the chile seeds in, or remove them for a slightly milder result.

2 When ready to cook, place a little flour in a large, shallow bowl and use to coat the fish pieces, shaking off any excess flour.

3 Heat a little oil in a large frying pan. Add the fish pieces and fry for about 5 minutes, turning the pieces carefully, until golden brown, then set aside. Do not worry if the fish is not quite cooked through; it will finish cooking in the sauce.

4 To make the sauce, heat the oil and butter or margarine in a frying pan and stir-fry the onion for 5 minutes. Add the tomatoes, garlic, and thyme and simmer for a further 5 minutes. Stir in the stock or water, cinnamon, and chile.

5 Add the fish pieces and the chopped peppers. Simmer until the fish is cooked and the stock has reduced to a thick sauce. Season with salt. Serve hot, garnished with the oregano.

SALT FISH <u>AND</u> ACKEE

*THIS IS A CLASSIC JAMAICAN DISH, THAT IS ALSO POPULAR THROUGHOUT THE CARIBBEAN. IT IS
OFTEN SERVED WITH BOILED GREEN BANANAS AS WELL AS FRIED DUMPLINGS.*

SERVES FOUR

INGREDIENTS
  1 pound salt cod
  2 tablespoons butter or margarine
  2 tablespoons vegetable oil
  1 onion, chopped
  2 garlic cloves, crushed
  8 ounces tomatoes, chopped
  ½ hot chile, chopped (optional)
  ½ teaspoon ground black pepper
  ½ teaspoon dried thyme
  ½ teaspoon ground allspice
  2 tablespoons chopped scallion
  1 pound, 6-ounce can ackees,
    drained
  fried dumplings, to serve

1 Place the salt cod in a bowl and pour
in enough cold water to cover. Leave to
soak for at least 24 hours, changing the
water about five times. Drain and rinse
in fresh cold water.

2 Put the salt cod in a large pan of cold
water. Bring the water to the boil, then
remove the fish and leave it to cool on
a plate. Carefully remove and discard
the skin and bones, then flake the fish
and set it aside.

3 Heat the butter or margarine and oil
in a large, heavy frying pan over a
medium heat. Add the onion and garlic
and sauté for 5 minutes. Stir in the
tomatoes, with the chile, if using, and
cook gently for a further 5 minutes.

4 Add the salt cod, black pepper,
thyme, allspice, and scallion, stir to mix,
then stir in the ackees, taking care not
to crush them. If you prefer a more
moist dish, add a little water or stock.
Serve hot with fried dumplings.

ESCABECHE

A CLASSIC DISH THAT THE MEXICANS INHERITED FROM THE SPANISH, ESCABECHE IS OFTEN CONFUSED WITH CEVICHE, WHICH CONSISTS OF MARINATED RAW FISH. IN ESCABECHE, THE RAW FISH IS INITIALLY MARINATED IN LIME JUICE, BUT IS THEN COOKED BEFORE BEING PICKLED.

SERVES FOUR

INGREDIENTS
    2 pounds whole fish fillets
    juice of 2 limes
    1¼ cups olive oil
    6 peppercorns
    3 garlic cloves, sliced
    ½ teaspoon ground cumin
    ½ teaspoon dried oregano
    2 bay leaves
    ⅓ cup pickled jalapeño chile
      slices, chopped
    1 onion, thinly sliced
    1 cup white wine vinegar
    1¼ cups green olives stuffed with
      pimiento, to garnish

1 Place the fish fillets in a single layer in a shallow nonmetallic dish. Pour on the lime juice, turn the fillets over once to ensure that they are completely coated, then cover the dish and let marinate for 15 minutes.

2 Drain the fish in a colander, then pat the fillets dry with paper towels. Heat 4 tablespoons of the oil in a large frying pan, add the fish fillets and sauté for 5–6 minutes, turning once, until they are golden brown. Use a spatula to transfer them to a shallow dish that will hold them in a single layer.

3 Heat 2 tablespoons of the remaining oil in a frying pan. Add the peppercorns, garlic, ground cumin, oregano, bay leaves and jalapeños, and cook over low heat for 2 minutes, then increase the heat, add the onion slices and vinegar and bring to a boil. Lower the heat and simmer for 4 minutes.

4 Remove the pan from heat and carefully add the remaining oil. Stir well, then pour the mixture onto the fish. Let cool, then cover the dish and marinate for 24 hours in the refrigerator.

5 When you are ready to serve, drain off the liquid and garnish the pickled fish with the stuffed olives. Salad leaves would make a good accompaniment.

COOK'S TIP
Use the largest frying pan you have when cooking the fish. If your pan is too small, it may be necessary to cook them in batches. Do not overcrowd the pan, as they will cook unevenly.

CHILEAN SQUID CASSEROLE

*THIS HEARTY STEW IS IDEAL ON A COLD EVENING. THE POTATOES DISINTEGRATE TO THICKEN AND
ENRICH THE SAUCE, MAKING A WARMING, COMFORTING MAIN COURSE.*

<u>SERVES SIX</u>

INGREDIENTS

1¾ pounds squid
3 tablespoons olive oil
5 garlic cloves, crushed
4 fresh jalapeño chiles, seeded and
  finely chopped
2 celery sticks, diced
1¼ pounds small new potatoes or
  baby salad potatoes, scrubbed,
  scraped, or peeled and quartered
1⅔ cups dry white wine
1⅔ cups fish stock
4 tomatoes, diced
2 tablespoons chopped fresh Italian
  parsley
salt
white rice or *arepas* (corn breads),
  to serve

1 Clean the squid under cold water.
Pull the tentacles away from the body.
The squid's entrails will come out easily.
Remove the cartilage from inside the
body cavity and discard it. Wash
the body thoroughly.

2 Pull away the membrane that covers
the body. Cut between the tentacles and
head, discarding the head and entrails.
Leave the tentacles whole but discard
the hard beak in the middle. Cut the
body into thin rounds.

COOK'S TIP
Adding the tomatoes and parsley at the
end gives a real freshness to the sauce.
If you'd prefer an even heartier dish, add
these ingredients to the pan with the
potatoes. Replace the white wine with a
Chilean cabernet sauvignon.

3 Heat the oil, add the garlic, chiles,
and celery, and cook for 5 minutes.
Stir in the potatoes, then add the wine
and stock. Bring to the boil, then
simmer, covered, for 25 minutes.

4 Remove from the heat and stir in the
squid, tomatoes, and parsley. Cover the
pan and leave to stand until the squid is
cooked. Serve immediately.

JAMAICAN FISH CURRY

THIS RECIPE USES SOME OF THE MOST COMMON SPICES IN CARIBBEAN CUISINE, WHERE THE INFLUENCE OF INDIA IS CLEARLY VISIBLE. THE TASTE IS FOR STRONG, PUNGENT FLAVORS RATHER THAN FIERY HEAT, AND THE RICE IS AN INTEGRAL PART OF THE DISH.

SERVES FOUR

INGREDIENTS

   2 halibut steaks, total weight about
     1¼–1½ pounds
   2 tablespoons peanut oil
   2 cardamom pods
   1 cinnamon stick
   6 allspice berries
   4 cloves
   1 large onion, chopped
   3 garlic cloves, crushed
   2–3 teaspoons grated fresh
     ginger root
   2 teaspoons ground cumin
   1 teaspoon ground coriander
   ½ teaspoon cayenne pepper,
     or to taste
   4 tomatoes, peeled, seeded,
     and chopped
   1 sweet potato, about 8 ounces,
     cut into ¾-inch cubes
   2 cups fish stock
     or water
   4-ounce piece of creamed coconut
   1 bay leaf
   generous 1 cup white
     long grain rice
   salt

1 Rub the halibut steaks well with salt and set aside.

2 Heat the oil in a flameproof casserole dish and stir-fry the cardamom pods, cinnamon stick, allspice berries and cloves for about 3 minutes to release the delicate aromas.

3 Add the chopped onion, crushed garlic, and grated ginger. Continue cooking for about 4–5 minutes over a gentle heat, stirring frequently, until the onion is soft.

4 Add the ground cumin, cilantro, and cayenne pepper, and cook briefly, stirring all the time.

VARIATION
Other types of fish can be used, although the strong taste of the sauce makes it a good recipe for white fish with hearty flavors. Try cod and haddock, or more meaty fish and shellfish such as swordfish, monkfish, or shrimp.

5 Stir in the tomatoes, sweet potato, fish stock or water, creamed coconut, and bay leaf. Season well with salt. Bring to the boil, then lower the heat, cover, and simmer for about 15–18 minutes, until the sweet potato is tender.

6 Cook the rice according to your preferred method. Meanwhile, add the halibut steaks to the pan of curry sauce and spoon the sauce over to cover them completely. Cover the pan with a tight-fitting lid and simmer gently for about 10 minutes, until the fish is just tender and flakes easily.

7 Spoon the rice into a warmed serving dish, spoon over the curry sauce, and arrange the halibut steaks on top. Garnish with chopped cilantro, if you like, and serve immediately.

COOK'S TIP
Sweet potato discolors very quickly when cut. If preparing ingredients in advance, put the cubes of potato into a bowl of cold water with 2–3 tablespoons lemon juice until ready to use.

PUEBLO BAKED FISH

THE LIME JUICE IS A PERFECT PARTNER FOR THE TROUT, WHICH IS AN OILY FISH. MARINATING MEANS THAT THE FISH IS BEAUTIFULLY TENDER WHEN COOKED.

SERVES FOUR

INGREDIENTS
2 fresh pasilla chiles
4 rainbow trout, cleaned
4 garlic cloves
2 teaspoons dried oregano
juice of 2 limes
½ cup sliced almonds
salt and ground black pepper

1 Roast the chiles in a dry frying pan or griddle until the skins are blistered, being careful not to let the flesh burn. Put them in a strong plastic bag and tie the top to keep the steam in. Set aside for 20 minutes.

2 Meanwhile, rub a little salt into the cavities in the trout, to ensure that they are completely clean, then rinse them under cold running water. Drain and pat dry with paper towels.

COOK'S TIP
Cooking fish in a paper parcel means that it stays very moist. Trout cooks perfectly by this method, but you could use other fish; try tuna steaks, small mackerel or salmon fillets.

3 Remove the chiles from the bag and peel off the skins. Cut off the stems, then slit the chiles and scrape out the seeds. Chop the flesh roughly and put it in a mortar. Crush with a pestle until the mixture forms a paste.

4 Place the chili paste in a shallow dish that will hold all the trout in a single layer. Slice the garlic lengthwise and add to the dish.

5 Add the oregano and 2 teaspoons salt, then stir in the lime juice and pepper to taste. Add the trout, turning to coat them in the mixture. Cover the dish and set aside for at least 30 minutes, turning the trout again halfway through.

6 Preheat the oven to 400°F. Have ready four pieces of aluminum foil, each large enough to wrap a trout. Top each sheet with a piece of wax paper of the same size.

7 Place one of the trout on one of the pieces of paper, moisten with the marinade, then sprinkle about a quarter of the almonds on the top.

8 Bring up the sides of the paper and fold over to seal in the fish, then fold the foil over to make a neat parcel. Make three more parcels in the same way, then place them side by side in a large roasting pan.

9 Transfer the parcels to the oven and bake for 25 minutes. Put each parcel on an individual plate, or open them in the kitchen and serve unwrapped if you prefer. This dish goes well with new potatoes and cooked fresh vegetables.

SHELLFISH

Surrounded on all sides by the sea, it is not surprising that Mexico and the Caribbean produce so many wonderful dishes based on shellfish, many barbecued or broiled with light flavoring and spices. Whether served as a snack, a main meal, or in a salad, freshness is the vital attribute.

CHILEAN SEAFOOD PLATTER

*FRESHNESS IS IMPORTANT FOR THIS RAW SEAFOOD APPETIZER, SO CHILEAN COOKS USE THE PRIME
CATCH OF THE DAY, INCLUDING EXOTIC SHELLFISH. YOU CAN USE WHATEVER IS AVAILABLE LOCALLY.*

SERVES SIX

INGREDIENTS
  1 pound raw jumbo shrimp
  12 clams
  12 mussels
  6 scallops
  6 oysters
  12 razor clams
  lime wedges, to serve
For the salsa
  4 tablespoons chopped fresh
    cilantro
  1 tablespoon chopped fresh
    Italian parsley
  2 shallots, finely chopped
  1 fresh green chile, seeded and
    finely chopped
  juice of 2 limes
  2 tablespoons olive oil
  salt

3 Use an oyster knife to open the raw
shellfish. Push the point of the knife
into the hinge, then twist to loosen.
Push the knife along the edge of the
whole shell so it can be opened.

4 Use the knife to loosen the fish from
their shells and carefully remove the
black "string" that runs along the edge
of the scallop.

5 Arrange the seafood, in the shells,
on a platter and serve with the fresh
cilantro and chile salsa, and lime
wedges, if you like. Eat immediately.

1 Combine the salsa ingredients in
a bowl and season to taste. Make
the salsa a few hours in advance, if
possible, so that the delicate flavors
have time to develop.

2 Bring a pan of salted water to the
boil. Plunge the shrimp into the water
and remove from the pan as soon as
they turn pink. Refresh the shirmp in a
bowl of cold water, drain, and set aside.

COOK'S TIP
If you prefer to cook the shellfish, it
could be steamed quickly and then
refreshed in cold water before being
served. Do not overcook the shellfish,
or it will become tough.

CEVICHE

*THIS FAMOUS DISH IS PARTICULARLY POPULAR ALONG MEXICO'S WESTERN SEABOARD, IN PLACES SUCH
AS ACAPULCO. IT CONSISTS OF VERY FRESH RAW FISH, "COOKED" BY THE ACTION OF LIME JUICE.*

SERVES SIX

INGREDIENTS
    7 ounces raw peeled shrimp
    7 ounces shelled scallops
    7 ounces squid, cleaned and cut
      into serving pieces
    7 limes
    3 tomatoes
    1 small onion
    1 ripe avocado
    ¼ cup chopped fresh oregano, or
      2 teaspoons dried
    1 teaspoon salt
    ground black pepper
    fresh oregano sprigs, to garnish
    crusty bread and lime wedges,
      to serve (optional)

1 Spread out the shrimp, scallops and
squid in a non-metallic bowl. Squeeze
six of the limes and pour the juice on
the mixed seafood to cover it completely.
Cover the dish with plastic wrap and set
aside for 8 hours or overnight.

2 Drain the seafood in a colander to
remove the excess lime juice, then pat
it dry with paper towels. Place the
shrimp, scallops, and squid in a bowl.

3 Cut the tomatoes in half, squeeze out
the seeds, then dice the flesh. Cut the
onion in half, then slice it thinly. Cut
the avocado in half lengthwise, remove the
pit and peel, then cut the flesh into
½-inch dice.

4 Add the tomatoes, onion, and
avocado to the seafood with the oregano
and seasoning. Squeeze the remaining
lime and pour on the juice. Garnish with
oregano and serve, with crusty bread
and lime wedges, if desired.

SHRIMP WITH ALMOND SAUCE

GROUND ALMONDS ADD AN INTERESTING TEXTURE TO THE CREAMY, PIQUANT SAUCE THAT ACCOMPANIES THESE SHRIMP.

SERVES SIX

INGREDIENTS

1 ancho or similar dried chile
2 tablespoons vegetable oil
1 onion, chopped
3 garlic cloves, roughly chopped
8 tomatoes
1 teaspoon ground cumin
½ cup chicken stock
generous 1 cup
 ground almonds
¾ cup crème fraîche
½ lime
2 pounds cooked peeled shrimp
salt
cilantro and scallion strips,
 to garnish
cooked rice and warm tortillas,
 to serve

1 Place the dried chile in a heatproof bowl and pour in boiling water to cover. Let soak for 30 minutes until softened. Drain, remove the stem, then slit the chile and scrape out the seeds with a small sharp knife. Chop the flesh roughly and set it aside.

2 Heat the oil in a frying pan and sauté the onion and garlic until soft.

VARIATIONS
Try this sauce with other types of fish, too. Adding just a few shrimp and serving it over steamed sole would make a very luxurious dish. The sauce is also very good with chicken.

3 Cut a cross in the bottom of each tomato. Place them in a heatproof bowl and pour in boiling water to cover. After 3 minutes, lift the tomatoes out on a slotted spoon and plunge them into a bowl of cold water. Drain. The skins will have begun to peel off.

4 Skin the tomatoes completely, then cut them in half and scoop out the seeds. Chop the flesh into ½-inch cubes and add it to the onion mixture, with the chopped chile. Stir in the ground cumin and cook for 10 minutes, stirring occasionally.

5 Put the mixture in a food processor or blender. Add the stock and process on high speed until smooth.

6 Pour the mixture into a large pan, add the ground almonds, and stir over low heat for 2–3 minutes. Stir in the crème fraîche until it has been incorporated completely.

7 Squeeze the juice from the lime and stir it into the sauce. Season with salt to taste, then increase the heat and bring the sauce to the simmering point.

8 Add the shrimp and heat for 2–3 minutes, depending on size, until warmed through. Serve on a bed of rice and pass warm tortillas separately.

SHRIMP <u>IN</u> GARLIC BUTTER

THIS QUICK AND EASY DISH IS PERFECT FOR SERVING TO FRIENDS WHO DON'T MIND GETTING THEIR HANDS DIRTY. PROVIDE A PLATE FOR THE SHRIMP SHELLS AND PASS WARM TORTILLAS FOR MOPPING UP THE DELECTABLE JUICES.

SERVES SIX

INGREDIENTS
2 pounds large jumbo shrimp, in
   their shells, thawed if frozen
½ cup butter
1 tablespoon vegetable oil
6 garlic cloves, crushed
grated zest and juice of 2 limes
small bunch of cilantro, chopped
warm tortillas, to serve
lemon slices, for the finger bowls

1 Rinse the shrimp in a colander, remove their heads, and let them drain. Heat the butter and oil in a large frying pan, add the garlic, and sauté over low heat for 2–3 minutes.

2 Add the lime zest and juice. Cook, stirring constantly, for 1 more minute.

COOK'S TIP
Cook the shrimp in a large frying pan or cast-iron flameproof dish that can be taken directly to the table, so that they retain their heat until they are served.

3 Add the shrimp and cook them for 2–3 minutes, until they turn pink. Remove from heat, sprinkle with cilantro, and serve with the warm tortillas. Give each guest a finger bowl filled with water, and a slice of lemon, for cleaning their fingers after shelling the shrimp, and provide paper napkins.

SHRIMP SALAD

IN MEXICO, THIS SALAD WOULD FORM THE FISH COURSE IN A FORMAL MEAL, BUT IT IS SO GOOD THAT YOU'LL WANT TO SERVE IT ON ALL SORTS OF OCCASIONS. IT IS PERFECT FOR A BUFFET LUNCH.

SERVES FOUR

INGREDIENTS

1 pound cooked peeled shrimp
juice of 1 lime
3 tomatoes
1 ripe but firm avocado
2 tablespoons hot chili sauce
1 teaspoon sugar
⅔ cup sour cream
2 Boston lettuces, separated
  into leaves
salt and ground black pepper
fresh basil leaves and strips of green
  bell pepper to garnish

1 Put the shrimp in a large bowl, add the lime juice and salt and pepper. Toss lightly, then leave to marinate.

2 Cut a cross in the bottom of each tomato. Place them in a heatproof bowl and pour in boiling water to cover.

3 After 3 minutes, lift the tomatoes out on a slotted spoon and plunge them into a bowl of cold water. Drain. The skins will have begun to peel back easily from the crosses.

4 Skin the tomatoes completely, then cut them in half and squeeze out the seeds. Chop the flesh into ½-inch cubes and add it to the shrimp.

5 Cut the avocado in half, remove the skin and pit, then slice the flesh into ½-inch chunks. Add it to the shrimp and tomato mixture.

6 Mix the hot chili sauce, sugar, and sour cream in a bowl. Fold into the shrimp mixture. Line a bowl with the lettuce leaves, then top with the shrimp mixture. Cover and chill for at least 1 hour, then garnish with fresh basil and strips of green pepper. Crusty bread makes a perfect accompaniment.

CRAB WITH GREEN RICE

THIS IS A POPULAR DISH IN THE WESTERN COASTAL AREAS OF MEXICO. SHRIMP CAN BE USED INSTEAD OF CRABMEAT IF YOU PREFER, AND THE DISH ALSO WORKS WELL WITH WARM CORN TORTILLAS.

SERVES FOUR

INGREDIENTS
  generous 1 cup long-grain
    white rice
  3⅓ cups drained
    canned tomatillos
  large bunch of cilantro
  1 onion, roughly chopped
  3 poblano or other fresh green
    chiles, seeded and chopped
  3 garlic cloves
  3 tablespoons olive oil
  1¼ pounds crabmeat
  1¼ cups fish stock
  ¼ cup dry white wine
  salt
  sliced scallions, to garnish

1 Put the rice in a heatproof bowl, pour in boiling water to cover and let stand for 20 minutes. Drain thoroughly.

2 Put the tomatillos in a food processor or blender and process until smooth. Chop half the cilantro and add to the tomatillo puree, with the onion, chiles, and garlic. Process again until smooth.

3 Heat the oil in a large pan. Add the rice and fry over medium heat for 5 minutes, until all the oil has been absorbed. Stir occasionally to prevent the rice from sticking.

4 Stir in the tomatillo mixture, with the crabmeat, stock, and wine. Cover and cook over low heat for about 20 minutes or until all the liquid has been absorbed. Stir occasionally and add a little more liquid if the rice starts to stick to the pan. Add salt as required, then spoon into a dish and garnish with the remaining cilantro and the sliced scallions. Green salad and lime wedges make good accompaniments.

SCALLOPS WITH GARLIC AND CILANTRO

SHELLFISH IS OFTEN COOKED VERY SIMPLY IN MEXICO, HOT CHILI SAUCE AND LIME BEING POPULAR INGREDIENTS IN MANY FISH RECIPES.

SERVES FOUR

INGREDIENTS
20 scallops
2 zucchini
6 tablespoons butter
1 tablespoon vegetable oil
4 garlic cloves, chopped
2 tablespoons hot chili sauce
juice of 1 lime
small bunch of cilantro,
    finely chopped

COOK'S TIP
Oil can withstand higher temperatures than butter, but butter gives fried food added flavor. Using a mixture, as here, is the perfect compromise.

1 If you have bought scallops in their shells, open them. Hold a scallop shell in the palm of your hand, with the flat side facing up. Insert the blade of a knife close to the hinge that joins the shells and prise them apart. Run the blade of the knife across the inside of the flat shell to cut off the scallop. Only the white adductor muscle and the orange coral are eaten, so pull off and discard all other parts. Rinse the scallops under cold running water.

2 Cut the zucchini in half, then into four pieces. Melt the butter in the oil in a large frying pan. Add the zucchini and cook until soft. Remove from the pan. Add the garlic and fry until golden. Stir in the hot chili sauce.

3 Add the scallops to the sauce. Cook, stirring constantly, for 1–2 minutes only. Stir in the lime juice, chopped cilantro, and the zucchini pieces. Serve immediately on heated plates.

JUMBO SHRIMP IN A COCONUT AND NUT CREAM

FOR THIS BRAZILIAN RECIPE, COCONUT MILK IS USED TO MAKE VATAPÁ, *A LUXURIOUS SAUCE THICKENED WITH CASHEWS, PEANUTS, AND BREAD CRUMBS, THEN USED TO COOK SHRIMP.*

4 Grind the peanuts and cashew nuts in a food processor until they become a fine powder. Stir into the pan and cook for about 1 minute more.

SERVES SIX

INGREDIENTS
 2¼ cups fresh white bread crumbs
 7 tablespoons coconut milk
 30 raw jumbo shrimp, about
   2 pounds
 1⅔ cups fish stock
 2 large tomatoes, roughly chopped
 1 onion, quartered
 2 fresh red chiles, seeded and
   roughly chopped
 4½ ounces dried shrimp
 3 tablespoons palm oil
 2 garlic cloves, crushed
 1 ounce fresh ginger root, grated
 ¾ cup roasted peanuts
 ½ cup cashew nuts
 4 tablespoons coconut cream
 juice of 1 lime
 salt and ground black pepper
 chopped fresh cilantro and hot chili
   oil, to serve

1 Place the bread crumbs in a bowl and stir in the coconut milk. Leave to soak for at least 30 minutes. Puree, in a blender or food processor, then scrape into a bowl and set aside.

2 Meanwhile, peel the fresh shrimp and set them aside in a cool place. Place the shells in a pan and add the fish stock and tomatoes. Bring to the boil, then simmer over a low heat for 30 minutes. Strain into a bowl, pressing the shrimp shells against the sides of the strainer with a wooden spoon to extract as much flavor as possible. Reserve the shrimp stock but discard the shells.

3 Put the onion, chiles, and dried shrimp in a blender or food processor and blend to a puree. Scrape into a large pan and stir in the palm oil. Cook over a very low heat for 5 minutes. Add the garlic and ginger and cook for a further 2 minutes.

5 Stir in the bread-crumb puree and shrimp stock and bring to the boil. Reduce the heat and continue to cook, stirring constantly, for 6–8 minutes, until thick and smooth.

6 Add the coconut cream, lime juice, and shrimp. Stir over the heat for 3 minutes until the shrimp are cooked through and the *vatapá* resembles a thin porridge. If necessary, stir in a little water. Season with salt and black pepper.

7 Serve immediately, adding a scattering of chopped cilantro and a couple of drops of chili oil to each portion. Cooked white rice makes a good accompaniment.

VARIATIONS
• Instead of shrimp, try using white fish.
• For chicken *vatapá*, replace the shrimp with chicken pieces, seasoned and pan-fried in a little olive oil until tender. Use chicken stock rather than fish stock.

STUFFED CRAB

SERVE THIS SIMPLE DISH AS AN APPETIZER AT A DINNER PARTY. A TRADITIONAL BRAZILIAN RECIPE, IT IS USUALLY SERVED EITHER IN CRAB SHELLS OR SMALL EARTHENWARE DISHES.

SERVES SIX

INGREDIENTS
14 ounces crabmeat
juice of 1 lime
1 cup fresh bread crumbs
7 tablespoons whole milk
2 tablespoons butter
1 onion, finely chopped
2 garlic cloves, crushed
2 tomatoes, finely chopped
1 tablespoon chopped fresh
   Italian parsley
2 egg yolks, plus extra for glazing
1 tablespoon dried bread crumbs
1 tablespoon grated Parmesan cheese
salt
lemon wedges, to serve

1 Place the crabmeat in a large glass bowl and squeeze over the lime juice. Marinate for about 20 minutes. Meanwhile, put the bread crumbs in a separate bowl with the milk and leave to soak for 10 minutes.

2 Melt the butter in a pan over a low heat. Add the chopped onion and cook gently for 10 minutes until softened. Stir in the crushed garlic and cook for 1 minute more. Drain the crabmeat and squeeze out all of the excess liquid from the bread crumbs.

COOK'S TIP
The crab mixture can be prepared in advance. Spoon it into the individual crab shells or bowls and cover. Keep refrigerated until needed, then add the topping and bake in a preheated oven at 400°F for 10–15 minutes.

3 Add the crabmeat, tomatoes, and bread crumbs to the pan and stir well to combine. Return to a medium heat and cook, stirring, for 4–5 minutes. Stir in the chopped parsley and season to taste with salt and ground pepper—the mixture should actually taste over-seasoned at this stage.

4 Lower the heat and add the egg yolks, stirring vigorously for 1 minute. Do not allow the mixture to boil.

5 Preheat the broiler. Transfer the mixture to six empty crab shells, or small ovenproof dishes and brush with beaten egg yolk. Combine the dried bread crumbs and Parmesan, and sprinkle a thin coating over the crab meat. Broil for 3–4 minutes, until golden. Serve with the lemon wedges.

CRAB AND CORN GUMBO

A TYPICALLY CREOLE DISH, THIS IS THICKENED WITH A CLASSIC NUT-BROWN ROUX. IT IS POPULAR ON THE CARIBBEAN ISLANDS OF MARTINIQUE AND ST BARTS.

SERVES FOUR

INGREDIENTS

2 tablespoons butter or margarine
¼ cup all-purpose flour
1 tablespoon vegetable oil
1 onion, finely chopped
4 ounces okra, trimmed and chopped
2 garlic cloves, crushed
1 tablespoon finely chopped celery
2½ cups fish stock
⅔ cup sherry
1 tablespoon tomato ketchup
½ teaspoon dried oregano
¼ teaspoon ground pumpkin
   pie spice
2 teaspoons Worcestershire sauce
dash of hot pepper sauce
2 fresh corn cobs, sliced
1 pound crab claws
fresh cilantro, to garnish

1 Melt the butter or margarine in a large, heavy pan over a low heat. Add the flour and stir together to make a roux.

2 Cook for about 10 minutes, stirring constantly to prevent the mixture from burning. The roux will turn golden brown and then darken. As soon as it becomes a rich nut brown, turn the roux onto a plate, scraping it all out of the pan, and set aside.

3 Heat the oil in the same pan over a medium heat, add the chopped onion, the okra, garlic, and celery, and stir well. Cook for about 2–3 minutes, then add the fish stock, sherry, tomato ketchup, dried oregano, mixed spice, Worcestershire sauce, and a dash of hot pepper sauce.

4 Bring to the boil, then lower the heat, and simmer gently for about 10 minutes, or until all the vegetables are tender. Add the roux, stirring it thoroughly into the sauce, and cook for about 3–4 minutes, until thickened.

5 Add the corn cobs and crab claws and continue to simmer gently over a low heat for about 10 minutes, until both are cooked through.

6 Spoon onto warmed serving plates and garnish with a few sprigs of fresh cilantro. Serve immediately.

COOK'S TIP
The roux must not be allowed to burn. Stir it constantly over a low heat. If dark specks appear in the roux, it must be discarded and a fresh roux made.

SHRIMP AND POTATO OMELET

MORE LIKE A SPANISH TORTILLA THAN A FRENCH OMELET, THIS DISH MAKES A DELICIOUS LUNCH WHEN SERVED WITH A FRESH LEAFY GREEN SALAD. THE SWEET SHRIMP ARE COOKED GENTLY INSIDE THE OMELET, STAYING TENDER AND SUCCULENT.

SERVES SIX

INGREDIENTS

    7 ounces potatoes, peeled and diced
    2 tablespoons olive oil
    1 onion, finely sliced
    ½ teaspoon paprika
    2 large tomatoes, peeled, seeded,
      and chopped
    7 ounces peeled raw shrimp
    6 eggs
    ½ teaspoon baking powder
    salt

1 Cook the potatoes in a pan of salted boiling water for about 10 minutes, or until tender.

2 Meanwhile, pour the oil into a 9-inch frying pan that can safely be used under the broiler. Place over a medium heat. Add the onion slices and stir well to coat evenly in the oil. Cook for 5 minutes until the onions begin to soften. Sprinkle over the paprika and cook for 1 minute more.

3 Stir in the tomatoes. Drain the cooked potatoes thoroughly and add them to the pan. Stir gently to mix. Increase the heat and cook for 10 minutes, or until the mixture has thickened and the potatoes have absorbed the flavor of the tomatoes. Remove from the heat and stir in the shrimp.

4 Preheat the broiler. Beat the eggs, stir in the baking powder and salt. Pour into the pan and mix thoroughly. Cover and cook for 8–10 minutes, until the omelet has almost set, then finish under the broiler.

CUBAN SEAFOOD RICE

THIS IS THE PERFECT DISH FOR A LARGE GATHERING. THE MORE PEOPLE YOU MAKE IT FOR, THE MORE TYPES OF SEAFOOD YOU CAN ADD, AND THE TASTIER IT WILL BECOME.

SERVES EIGHT

INGREDIENTS

1 pound raw shrimp
4 cups fish stock
1 pound squid
16 clams
16 mussels
4 tablespoons olive oil
1 onion, finely chopped
1 fresh red chile, seeded and
  finely chopped
2 garlic cloves, crushed
1⅔ cups long-grain rice
3 tablespoons chopped fresh
  cilantro
juice of 2 limes
salt and ground black pepper

1 Peel the shrimp and set them aside. Place the shells in a pan and add the fish stock. Bring to the boil, then simmer for 15 minutes. Strain into a bowl, discarding the shells.

2 Clean the squid under cold running water. Pull the tentacles away from the body. The squid's entrails will come out easily. Remove the clear piece of cartilage from inside the body cavity and discard it. Wash the body thoroughly.

3 Pull away the purplish-gray membrane that covers the body. Now cut between the tentacles and head, discarding the head and entrails. Leave the tentacles whole but discard the hard beak in the middle. Cut the body into thin rounds.

4 Scrub the clams and mussels under cold running water. Pull away the "beard" from the mussels and discard any open shells that fail to close when tapped. Place the shellfish in a bowl, cover with a wet paper towel, and put in the refrigerator until needed.

COOK'S TIP
Live shellfish are best kept in a cool, moist environment. Place them in a bowl covered with wet paper towels and store them in the refrigerator.

5 Pour half the olive oil into a pan with a tight fitting lid. Place over a high heat. When the oil is very hot, add the squid and season well. Stir-fry for 2–3 minutes, until the squid curls and begins to brown. Remove the pieces from the pan with a slotted spoon and set aside.

6 Add the shrimp to the pan and cook for 2 minutes. The moment they turn pink, remove them from the heat.

7 Pour the remaining oil into the pan. Stir in the onion and sauté over a low heat for 5 minutes. Add the chile and garlic, and cook for 2 minutes. Tip in the rice, and cook, stirring, for 1 minute, until lightly toasted but not colored.

8 Add the shrimp stock and bring to the boil. Cover, lower the heat, and simmer, for 15–18 minutes.

9 Add the clams and mussels and cover the pan. Cook for 3–4 minutes, until their shells open. Remove from the heat and discard any that have remained closed. Stir the cooked squid, shrimp, cilantro, and lime juice into the rice. Season and serve immediately.

PUMPKIN <u>AND</u> SHRIMP

THIS CARIBBEAN RECIPE IS AN EXCELLENT WAY OF MAKING A SMALL AMOUNT OF SEAFOOD GO A LONG WAY. THE DRIED SHRIMP AND COOKED SHRIMP ARE DELICIOUS WITH THE SPICED PUMPKIN.

SERVES FOUR

INGREDIENTS
⅓ cup dried shrimp
2 tablespoons vegetable oil
2 tablespoons butter or margarine
1 red onion, chopped
1¾ pounds pumpkin, peeled
   and chopped
8 ounces peeled cooked
   shrimp
½ teaspoon ground cinnamon
½ teaspoon five-spice powder
2 garlic cloves, chopped
2 tomatoes, chopped
chopped fresh parsley and lime
   wedges, to garnish

1 Rinse the dried shrimp under cold water and put them in a bowl. Pour in enough hot water to cover, then leave them to soak for about 35 minutes.

2 Meanwhile, heat the oil and butter or margarine in a large frying pan. Add the onion and sauté over a medium heat for 5 minutes, until soft.

3 Add the pumpkin and cook for about 5–6 minutes, until it starts to soften. Tip in the peeled shrimp and the dried shrimp with their soaking water. Stir in the cinnamon, five-spice powder, and chopped garlic.

4 Add the tomatoes and cook over a gentle heat, stirring occasionally, until the pumpkin is soft.

5 Spoon onto a warmed serving plate and serve hot, garnished with the chopped parsley and lime wedges.

SPICY SHRIMP WITH CORNMEAL

THESE CRISPY FRIED SHRIMP WITH A CORNMEAL COATING AND A CHEESE TOPPING ARE TRULY DELICIOUS WHEN SERVED WITH A SPICY TOMATO SALSA AND LIME WEDGES TO EASE THE HEAT.

SERVES FOUR

INGREDIENTS

1¾ cup cornmeal
1–2 teaspoons cayenne pepper
½ teaspoons ground cumin
1 teaspoon salt
2 tablespoons chopped fresh
  cilantro
2 pounds large raw shrimp, peeled
  and deveined
flour, for dredging
¼ cup vegetable oil
1 cup grated
  Cheddar cheese
To serve
  lime wedges
  salsa

1 Preheat the broiler to hot. In a large mixing bowl, combine the cornmeal, cayenne, cumin, salt, and chopped cilantro.

2 Coat the shrimp lightly in flour, then dip them in water and roll them in the cornmeal mixture to coat.

3 Heat the oil in a non-stick frying pan. When hot, add the shrimp, in several batches if necessary. Cook them until they are opaque throughout, for about 2–3 minutes on each side. Drain on paper towels.

4 Place the shrimp in a large ovenproof dish, or in individual dishes. Sprinkle the cheese evenly over the top. Broil about 3 inches from the heat until the cheese melts and is lightly browned, for about 2–3 minutes.

5 Serve immediately, with lime wedges and tomato salsa.

VARIATIONS
Chopped fresh Italian parsley may be substituted for cilantro. Grated Monterey Jack cheese may be used in place of Cheddar.

FISHERMAN'S STEW

THIS IS JUST THE SORT OF ONE-POT MEAL YOU CAN IMAGINE FISHERMEN COOKING FOR THEMSELVES, USING FRESHLY CAUGHT FISH AND A FEW VEGETABLES.

SERVES SIX

INGREDIENTS
1¼ pounds mussels
3 onions
2 garlic cloves, sliced
1¼ cups fish stock
12 scallops
1 pound cod fillet
2 tablespoons olive oil
1 large potato, about 7 ounces
few sprigs of fresh thyme, chopped
1 red and 1 green bell pepper
½ cup dry white wine
1 cup crème fraîche
10 ounces peeled shrimp
¾ cup grated aged
  Cheddar cheese
salt and ground black pepper
fresh thyme sprigs, to garnish

1 Clean the mussel shells, removing any beards. Discard any that stay open when tapped. Rinse in cold water.

2 Pour water to a depth of 1 inch into a large, deep frying pan. Chop one onion and add it to the pan, with the sliced garlic. Bring to a boil, then add the mussels and cover the pan tightly.

3 Cook the mussels for 5–6 minutes, shaking the pan occasionally. Remove them as they open, discarding any that remain shut. Remove the mussels from their shells and set them aside.

4 Strain the cooking liquid from the mussels through a muslin-lined sieve to remove any remaining sand. Make up the liquid with fish stock to 1¼ cups.

5 If you have bought scallops in their shells, open them: hold a scallop shell in the palm of your hand, with the flat side facing up. Insert the blade of a knife close to the hinge that joins the shells and prise apart. Run the blade of the knife across the inside of the flat shell to cut off the scallop. Only the white adductor muscle and the orange coral are eaten, so pull off and discard all other parts. Rinse the scallops under cold running water to remove any grit or sand, then put them in a bowl and set them aside.

6 Cut the cod into large cubes and put it in a bowl. Season with salt and pepper and set aside.

7 Cut the remaining onions into small wedges. Heat the olive oil in a large pan and fry the onion wedges for 2–3 minutes. Slice the potato about ½-inch thick and add to the pan, with the fresh chopped thyme. Cover and cook for about 15 minutes, until the potato has softened.

8 Core the peppers, remove the cores and seeds, then dice the flesh. Add to the onion and potato mixture, and cook for a few minutes. Stir in the mixed mussel and fish stock, with the wine and crème fraîche.

9 Bring to just below the boiling point, then add the cod and scallops. Lower the heat and simmer for 5 minutes, then add the shrimp. Simmer for another 3–4 minutes, until all the seafood is cooked. Stir in the mussels and warm through for 1–2 minutes. Season the sauce if necessary. Spoon into bowls, garnish with the thyme sprigs, and sprinkle on the cheese. Crusty bread would be an ideal accompaniment.

MEAT

The gaucho nations of Argentina, Paraguay, and Uruguay are real meat-eaters, and large cuts of beef, lamb, and pork are cooked whole at their famous barbecues. Richly flavored stews and pot roasts are also popular, made with herbs, spices, and fruits, or as a combination of mixed meats, as in the Brazilian national dish Feijoada.

THE GAUCHO BARBECUE

THERE IS NO BETTER WAY OF ENJOYING THE PRESTIGIOUS PAMPAS BEEF THAN WITH A TRADITIONAL BARBECUE. THE MEAT IS COOKED SIMPLY, WITH NO NEED FOR RUBS OR MARINADES, THEN ENJOYED WITH A DELICIOUS SELECTION OF SALADS AND SALSAS.

SERVES SIX

INGREDIENTS
¼ cup coarse sea salt
scant 1 cup warm water
6 pork sausages
2¼ pounds beef short ribs
2¼ pounds round steak, in
  one piece
salads, salsas, and breads, to serve

COOK'S TIP
Regularly basting the meat in salted water keeps it moist and succulent.

1 Dissolve the sea salt in the warm water in a bowl. Leave to cool.

2 Prepare the barbecue. If you are using a charcoal grill, light the coals about 40 minutes before you want to start cooking. Wait until the coals are no longer red but are covered in white ash. Occasionally add coals to the barbecue to maintain this temperature.

3 Start by cooking the sausages, which should take 15–20 minutes depending on the size. Once cooked on all sides, slice the sausages thickly and arrange on a plate. Let guests help themselves while you cook the remaining meats.

4 The short ribs should be placed bony side down on the grill. Cook for 15 minutes, turn, brush the cooked side of each rib with brine, and grill for a further 25–30 minutes. Slice and transfer to a plate for guests to help themselves.

5 Place the whole rump steak on the grill and cook for 5 minutes, then turn over and baste the browned side with brine. Continue turning and basting in this way for 20–25 minutes in total, until the meat is cooked to your liking. Allow the meat to rest for 5 minutes, then slice thinly and serve with salads, salsa, and bread.

VARIATION
A selection of meat cuts can be used, from sirloin to flank steak or chuck steak. Sweetbreads, skewered chicken hearts, and kidneys are popular additions to the Gaucho barbecue, as well as chicken, lamb, and pork. The star of the show, however, will always be the beef.

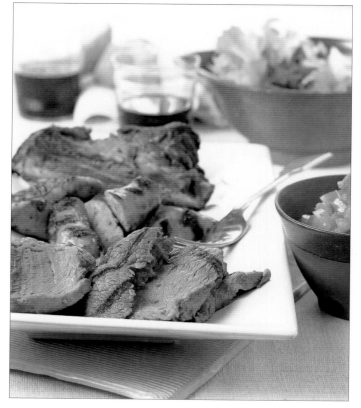

BEEF STUFFED WITH EGGS AND SPINACH

THIS TRADITIONAL ARGENTINIAN DISH MAKES A GREAT LUNCH WHEN SERVED COLD WITH A SALAD, BUT CAN ALSO BE SERVED HOT FOR DINNER WITH SOME BOILED POTATOES. ITS NAME, MATAMBRE ("KILL HUNGER") IS SOMEWHAT UNFAIR; FOR ALTHOUGH FILLING, IT IS NOT A HEAVY DISH.

SERVES SIX

INGREDIENTS
    4 tablespoons olive oil
    1 small carrot, finely chopped
    1 celery stick, finely chopped
    1 onion, finely chopped
    2 eggs
    1½ pounds flank steak
    9 ounces spinach, trimmed
    ½ teaspoon cayenne pepper
    6¼ cups beef stock
    salt and ground black pepper
    boiled potatoes or salad, to serve

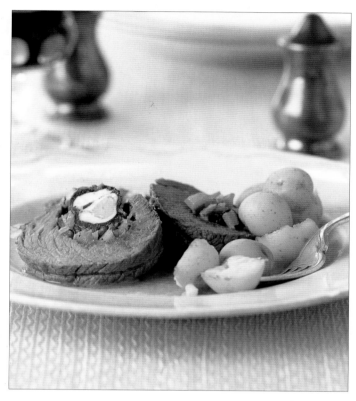

1 Heat half the olive oil in a frying pan over a medium heat. Add the carrot, celery, and onion, and sauté for 5 minutes, until soft and beginning to color.

2 Meanwhile, hard-boil the eggs. Place them in a pan with cold water to cover. Bring to the boil, then lower the heat to a simmer. Cook for 10 minutes, then lift out and cool in a bowl of cold water. Shell the eggs, then slice them thinly.

3 Season the steak generously with salt and ground black pepper. Spread the cooked onion mixture over the beef, leaving a ½-inch border round the edge. Arrange the spinach over the onion, then top with the egg. Season with extra salt and cayenne pepper.

COOK'S TIP
Flank steak is ideal for slow cooking, becoming so tender you can almost cut it with a fork. If you cannot get flank, skirt steak is very similar.

4 Roll the meat up tightly, being careful not to lose any of the stuffing. Tie with string four or five times along the length of the roll.

5 Heat the remaining oil in a pan. Add the beef roll to the pan and cook on all sides until golden brown. Pour in the stock, then bring to the boil. Lower the heat, cover, and simmer gently for 1½–2 hours, until very tender.

6 Remove the beef from the stock and slice it as thinly as possible. Serve hot with boiled potatoes or as part of a buffet or picnic.

CARBONADA CRIOLLA

MEAT AND FRUIT ARE OFTEN COMBINED IN ARGENTINIAN COOKING, AND THIS COLORFUL STEW IS A PRIME EXAMPLE. THE TENDER BEEF COOKED IN RED WINE BALANCES THE SWEETNESS OF THE PEACHES, POTATOES, AND PUMPKIN. MAKE SURE THE PUMPKIN FITS IN YOUR OVEN.

SERVES EIGHT

INGREDIENTS
    1 large pumpkin, about 11 pounds
    4 tablespoons olive oil
    2¼ pounds braising steak, cut into
        1-inch cubes
    1 large onion, finely chopped
    3 fresh red chiles, seeded
        and chopped
    2 garlic cloves, crushed
    1 large tomato, roughly chopped
    2 fresh bay leaves
    2½ cups beef stock
    1½ cups red wine
    1¼ pounds potatoes, peeled and cut
        into ¾-inch cubes
    1¼ pounds sweet potatoes, peeled
        and cut into ¾-inch cubes
    1 corn cob, cut widthwise into
        6 slices
    3 peaches, peeled, pitted, and cut
        into thick wedges
    salt and ground black pepper

1 Wash the outside of the pumpkin. Using a sharp knife, carefully cut a slice off the top 2½ inches from the stem, to make a lid. Using a spoon, scoop out the seeds and stringy fibers, and discard. Scoop out some of the flesh, leaving a shell about ¾-inch thick inside of the pumpkin. Cut the flesh you have removed into ½-inch pieces.

COOK'S TIP
Calabaza is a large West Indian pumpkin, with a greenish orange skin, that is often used for *carbonada criolla*. Look for it in Caribbean markets.

2 Brush the inside of the pumpkin and the flesh side of the lid with a little olive oil. Season with salt and ground black pepper. Place both pumpkin and lid on a baking sheet, flesh side up. Set aside.

3 Preheat the oven to 400°F. Heat half the remaining oil in a large, heavy pan over a high heat. Add the beef, season and sauté for 8–10 minutes, until golden brown, then remove with a slotted spoon—you may need to do this in batches. Avoid adding too much beef to the pan or it will steam rather than brown.

4 Lower the heat and add the remaining oil to the pan. Stir in the onion and chiles, and sauté for 5 minutes. Scrape the base of the pan with a wooden spoon, to loosen any sediment. Add the garlic and tomato, and cook for 2 minutes more.

5 Return the meat to the pan and add the bay leaves, stock, and red wine. Bring to the boil, then lower the heat to a gentle simmer. Cook for 1 hour or until the meat is tender.

6 Place the baking sheet containing the pumpkin and its lid in the oven and bake for 30 minutes.

7 Add the potatoes, sweet potatoes, pieces of pumpkin, and corn to the stew. Pour in more liquid if needed and bring to the boil. Reduce the heat to a simmer, cover, and cook for 15 minutes.

8 Finally add the peach wedges and season with salt and black pepper to taste. Spoon the stew into the partially cooked pumpkin, cover with the pumpkin lid, and bake for 15 minutes, or until the pumpkin is tender.

9 Carefully lift the filled pumpkin onto a large, strong platter and take it to the table. Ladle the stew onto plates, then cut the empty pumpkin into six to eight wedges, depending on the number of people to be served.

GARLIC AND CHILI MARINATED BEEF WITH CORN-CRUSTED ONION RINGS

FRUITY, SMOKY, AND MILD MEXICAN CHILES COMBINE WELL WITH GARLIC IN THIS MARINADE FOR BROILED STEAK. POLENTA MAKES A CRISP COATING FOR THE ACCOMPANYING FRIED ONION RINGS.

SERVES FOUR

INGREDIENTS
   ¾ ounce large mild dried red chiles
   (such as *mulato* or *pasilla*)
   2 garlic cloves, plain or smoked,
   finely chopped
   1 teaspoon ground toasted
   cumin seeds
   1 teaspoon dried oregano
   4 tablespoons olive oil
   4 × 6–8-ounce beef steaks (rump,
   round, or rib-eye)
   salt and ground black pepper
For the onion rings
   2 onions, sliced into rings
   1 cup milk
   ¾ cup coarse cornmeal or polenta
   ½ teaspoon dried red chili flakes
   1 teaspoon ground toasted
   cumin seeds
   1 teaspoon dried oregano
   vegetable oil, for deep-frying

3 Wash and dry the steaks, rub the chili paste all over them, and leave to marinate for up to 12 hours.

4 For the onion rings, soak the onions in the milk for 30 minutes. Mix the cornmeal, chili, cumin, and oregano, and season with salt and pepper.

5 Heat the oil for deep-frying to 325–350°F, or until a cube of day-old bread turns brown in about a minute.

6 Drain the onion rings and dip each one into the cornmeal mixture, coating it thoroughly. Fry for 2–4 minutes, until browned and crisp. Do not overcrowd the pan, but cook in batches. Lift the onion rings out of the pan with a slotted spoon and drain on paper towels.

7 Heat a barbecue or cast-iron broiler pan. Season the steaks with salt and broil for about 4 minutes on each side for a medium result; reduce or increase this time according to how rare or well done you like steak. Serve the steaks with the onion rings.

1 Cut the stalks from the chiles and discard the seeds. Toast the chiles in a dry frying pan for 2–4 minutes, until they give off their aroma. Place the chiles in a bowl, cover with warm water, and leave to soak for 20–30 minutes. Drain and reserve the water.

2 Process the chiles to a paste with the garlic, cumin, oregano, and oil in a food processor. Add a little soaking water, if needed. Season with pepper.

MEXICAN SPICY BEEF TORTILLA

THIS DISH IS NOT UNLIKE A LASAGNE, EXCEPT THAT THE SPICY MEAT IS MIXED WITH RICE AND IS LAYERED BETWEEN MEXICAN TORTILLAS, WITH A HOT SALSA SAUCE FOR AN EXTRA KICK.

SERVES FOUR

INGREDIENTS
1 onion, chopped
2 garlic cloves, crushed
1 fresh red chile, seeded and
  thinly sliced
12-ounce round steak, cut into
  small cubes
1 tablespoon oil
2 cups cooked long-grain rice
beef stock, to moisten
3 large wheat tortillas
For the salsa picante
2 x 14-ounce cans chopped tomatoes
2 garlic cloves, halved
1 onion, quartered
1–2 fresh red chiles, seeded and
  roughly chopped
1 teaspoon ground cumin
1 teaspoon cayenne pepper
1 teaspoon fresh oregano or
  ½ teaspoon dried oregano
tomato juice or water, if required
For the cheese sauce
4 tablespoons butter
½ cup all-purpose flour
2½ cups milk
1 cup grated Cheddar cheese
salt and ground black pepper

1 Preheat the oven to 350°F. Make the salsa picante. Place the tomatoes, garlic, onion, and chiles in a blender or food processor and process until smooth. Pour into a small pan, add the spices and oregano, and season with salt.

2 Gradually bring the mixture to the boil, stirring occasionally. Boil for 1–2 minutes, then lower the heat, cover with a lid, and simmer gently for about 15 minutes. The sauce should be thick, but of a pouring consistency. If it is too thick, dilute it with a little fresh tomato juice or water.

3 Make the cheese sauce. Melt the butter in a pan and stir in the flour. Cook for 1 minute. Add the milk, stirring all the time until the sauce boils and thickens. Stir in all but 2 tablespoons of cheese and season to taste. Cover the pan with a lid and set aside.

4 Mix the onion, garlic, and chile in a bowl. Add the steak cubes and mix well.

5 Heat the oil in a frying pan and stir-fry the meat mixture for about 10 minutes, until the meat cubes have browned and the onion is soft. Stir in the rice and enough beef stock to moisten. Season to taste with salt and freshly ground black pepper.

6 Pour about a quarter of the cheese sauce into the bottom of a round ovenproof dish. Add a tortilla and then spread over half the salsa, followed by half the meat mixture.

7 Repeat these layers, then add half the remaining cheese sauce and the final tortilla. Pour over the remaining cheese sauce and sprinkle the reserved grated cheese on top. Bake in the preheated oven for about 15–20 minutes, or until golden on top.

TACOS <u>WITH</u> SHREDDED BEEF

IN MEXICO TACOS ARE MOST OFTEN MADE WITH SOFT CORN TORTILLAS, WHICH ARE FILLED AND FOLDED IN HALF. IT IS UNUSUAL TO SEE THE CRISP SHELLS OF CORN THAT ARE SO WIDELY USED IN TEX-MEX COOKING. TACOS ARE ALWAYS EATEN IN THE HAND.

SERVES SIX

INGREDIENTS
    1 pound rump steak, diced
    1 cup *masa harina*
    ½ teaspoon salt
    ½ cup warm water
    2 teaspoons dried oregano
    1 teaspoon ground cumin
    2 tablespoons oil
    1 onion, thinly sliced
    2 garlic cloves, crushed
    fresh cilantro, to garnish
    shredded lettuce, lime wedges, and
        salsa, to serve

1 Put the steak in a deep frying pan and pour over water to cover. Bring to the boil, then lower the heat and simmer for 1–1½ hours.

2 Meanwhile, make the tortilla dough. Mix the *masa harina* and salt in a large mixing bowl. Add the warm water, a little at a time, to make a dough that can be worked into a ball. Knead the dough on a lightly floured surface for 3–4 minutes, until smooth, then wrap the dough in plastic wrap and leave to rest for 1 hour.

3 Put the meat on a board, let it cool slightly, then shred it, using two forks. Put the meat in a bowl. Divide the tortilla dough into six equal balls.

4 Open a tortilla press and line both sides with plastic (this can be cut from a new plastic sandwich bag). Put each ball on the press and flatten it into a 6–8-inch round.

5 Heat a griddle or frying pan until hot. Cook each tortilla for 15–20 seconds on each side, and then for a further 15 seconds on the first side. Keep the tortillas warm and soft by folding them inside a slightly damp dish towel.

6 Add the oregano and cumin to the shredded meat and mix well. Heat the oil in a frying pan and fry the onion and garlic for 3–4 minutes, until softened. Add the spiced meat mixture and toss over the heat until heated through.

7 Place some shredded lettuce on a tortilla, top with shredded beef and salsa, fold in half, and serve with lime wedges. Garnish with fresh cilantro.

BEEF ENCHILADAS <u>WITH</u> RED SAUCE

ENCHILADAS ARE USUALLY MADE WITH CORN TORTILLAS, ALTHOUGH IN PARTS OF NORTHERN MEXICO FLOUR TORTILLAS ARE SOMETIMES USED.

SERVES THREE TO FOUR

INGREDIENTS
1¼-pound rump steak, cut into
   2-inch cubes
2 ancho chiles, seeded
2 pasilla chiles, seeded
2 garlic cloves, crushed
2 teaspoons dried oregano
½ teaspoon ground cumin
2 tablespoons vegetable oil
7 fresh corn tortillas
shredded onion and Italian parsley, to
   garnish
mango salsa, to serve

1 Put the steak in a deep frying pan and cover with water. Bring to the boil, then lower the heat and simmer for 1–1½ hours, or until very tender.

2 Meanwhile, put the dried chiles in a bowl and pour over the hot water. Leave to soak for 30 minutes, then tip the contents of the bowl into a blender and whizz to a smooth paste.

3 Drain the steak and let it cool, reserving 1 cup of the cooking liquid. Meanwhile, fry the garlic, oregano, and cumin in the oil for 2 minutes.

4 Stir in the chili paste and the reserved cooking liquid from the beef. Tear one of the tortillas into small pieces and add it to the mixture. Bring to the boil, then lower the heat. Simmer for 10 minutes, stirring occasionally, until the sauce has thickened. Shred the steak, using two forks, and stir into the sauce. Heat through for a few minutes.

5 Spoon some of the meat mixture onto each tortilla and roll it up to make an enchilada. Keep the enchiladas in a warmed dish until you have rolled them all. Garnish with shreds of onion and fresh Italian parsley and then serve immediately with the mango salsa.

VARIATION
For a richer version place the rolled enchiladas side by side in a gratin dish. Pour over 1¼ cups sour cream and ¾ cup grated Cheddar cheese. Place under a preheated broiler for 5 minutes, or until the cheese melts and the sauce bubbles. Serve at once, with the salsa.

BLACK BEAN CHILI CON CARNE

FRESH GREEN AND DRIED RED CHILES ADD PLENTY OF FIRE TO THIS CLASSIC TEX-MEX DISH OF TENDER BEEF COOKED IN A RICH AND SPICY TOMATO SAUCE.

SERVES SIX

INGREDIENTS
1¼ cups dried black beans
1¼-pound braising steak
2 tablespoons vegetable oil
2 onions, chopped
1 garlic clove, crushed
1 fresh green chile, seeded and
  finely chopped
1 tablespoon paprika
2 teaspoons ground cumin
2 teaspoons ground coriander
14-ounce can chopped tomatoes
1¼ cups beef stock
1 dried red chile, crumbled
1 teaspoon hot pepper sauce
1 fresh red bell pepper, seeded and
  chopped
salt
fresh cilantro, to garnish
boiled rice, to serve

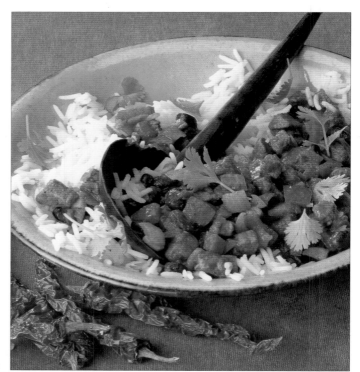

1 Put the beans in a large pan. Cover with cold water, bring to the boil, and boil vigorously for about 10 minutes. Drain, tip into a bowl, cover with cold water, and leave to soak overnight.

2 Preheat the oven to 300°F. Cut the steak into small dice. Heat the oil in a large, flameproof casserole. Add the onion, garlic, and green chile, and cook gently for 5 minutes until soft. Transfer the mixture to a plate.

3 Increase the heat to high, add the meat to the casserole, and brown on all sides, then stir in the paprika, ground cumin, and ground coriander.

4 Add the tomatoes, beef stock, dried chile, and hot pepper sauce. Drain the beans and add them to the casserole, with enough water to cover. Bring to simmering point, cover, and cook in the oven for about 2 hours. Stir occasionally and add extra water, if necessary, to prevent the casserole from drying out.

5 Season the casserole with salt and add the chopped red bell pepper. Replace the lid, return the casserole to the oven, and cook for about 30 minutes more, or until the meat and beans are tender. Sprinkle over the fresh cilantro and serve with boiled rice.

VARIATION
Use ground beef in place of the braising steak.

COOK'S TIP
Red kidney beans are traditionally used in chili con carne, but in this recipe black beans are used instead. They are the same shape and size as red kidney beans but have a shiny black skin.

SPICY MEATBALLS <u>WITH</u> TOMATO SAUCE

WHEREVER YOU GO IN LATIN AMERICA, YOU'LL FIND A DIFFERENT INTERPRETATION OF THIS HEARTY FAMILY DISH. SPANISH IN ORIGIN, THE MEATBALLS ARE OFTEN MADE WITH PORK OR VEAL, OR A MIXTURE OF MEATS, AND KNOWN AS ALBONDIGAS.

SERVES FOUR

INGREDIENTS
1¼ pounds ground beef
3 garlic cloves, crushed
1 small onion, finely chopped
1 cup fresh bread crumbs
½ teaspoon ground cumin
1 egg, beaten
½ cup all-purpose flour
4 tablespoons olive oil
salt
cooked white rice, to serve
For the sauce
2 tablespoons olive oil
1 small onion, thinly sliced
2 red bell peppers, seeded
and diced
2 fresh red chiles, seeded
and chopped
2 garlic cloves, crushed
⅔ cup canned chopped tomatoes
1⅔ cups light beef stock
ground black pepper

1 Place all the meatball ingredients, except the flour and oil, in a large bowl. Using your hands, mix until thoroughly combined. Season with salt and shape the mixture into even-size balls. Wet your hands to prevent the mixture from sticking. Dust lightly with flour.

2 Heat the oil in a large frying pan and cook the meatballs, in batches, for 6–8 minutes, or until golden. When all the meatballs have been browned, wipe the pan clean with paper towels.

3 Pour the olive oil into the pan and cook the onion and peppers over a low heat for 10 minutes, until soft. Add the chiles and garlic, and cook for a further 2 minutes. Pour in the tomatoes and stock, and bring to the boil. Lower the heat, cover the pan, and simmer for 15 minutes. Season to taste.

4 Add the meatballs to the pan and spoon the sauce over them. Bring back to the boil, then cover and simmer for 10 minutes. Serve with rice.

COOK'S TIP
An electric frying pan is ideal for cooking the meatballs, as its large surface area will allow you to fry them in one or two batches, and there is plenty of room for reheating them in the sauce.

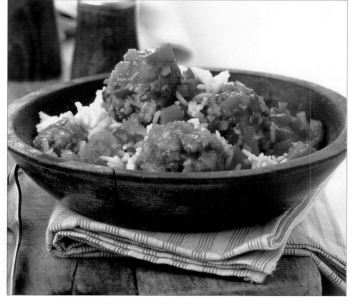

FEIJOADA

THIS MIXED MEAT AND BLACK BEAN STEW IS INDISPUTABLY THE NATIONAL DISH OF BRAZIL AND IS TRADITIONALLY SERVED FOR SATURDAY LUNCH. IT'S IMPOSSIBLE TO MAKE A GOOD FEIJOADA FOR FEWER THAN TEN PEOPLE, SINCE THERE ARE SO MANY DIFFERENT TYPES OF MEAT INVOLVED. THE MEATS CAN VARY, BUT THE BEANS HAVE TO BE VERY SMALL AND BLACK.

SERVES 12

INGREDIENTS
    5½ cups black turtle beans
    1 smoked pig's tongue, optional
    1¼-pound *carne seca* or beef jerky
    9 ounces salted pork ribs
    12 ounces smoked fatty bacon, in
        one piece
    1¼ pounds smoked pork ribs
    11 ounces pork sausages
    11 ounces smoked chorizo
    2 fresh bay leaves
    4 tablespoons vegetable oil
    5 garlic cloves, crushed
    salt
    fresh orange slices, peeled, to serve
    cooked white rice
    toasted cassava flour
    stir-fried kale
    chili oil

1 Wash the beans in running water, then place in a bowl with cold water to cover. Soak overnight. Rinse the tongue, *carne seca* or beef jerky, and salted pork ribs in cold running water and place in a separate bowl. Pour over water to cover and soak for 8 hours, or overnight, changing the soaking water three or four times.

2 Drain the beans and place them in a very large heavy pan. Pour in enough water to cover, and bring to the boil over a high heat. Skim the surface, then lower the heat. Cover the pan and simmer for 1 hour.

3 Meanwhile, drain the soaked meats, rinse them again under cold running water, and transfer to a second large heavy pan. Add the fatty bacon and smoked pork ribs, then cover with water. Bring to the boil over a high heat, skim the surface, then cover the pan. Lower the heat and simmer for 1 hour.

4 Transfer the cooked meats, with their cooking liquid, to the pan with the beans. Add the pork sausages, chorizo, and bay leaves. If necessary, add more water to cover. Bring to the boil, skim the surface, cover, and continue simmering for about 30 minutes.

5 Heat the oil in a large frying pan over a low heat. Add the crushed garlic cloves and cook, stirring, for about 2 minutes, being careful not to let it burn.

6 Ladle some beans from the large pan into the frying pan and fry, mashing the beans with a wooden spoon. Return the mashed beans to the meat mixture and lower the heat for 5 minutes. Taste the stew and add some salt if needed.

7 Lift the meats from the pan and cut them into even-size pieces. Arrange on a platter, keeping each type of meat separate. Spoon a ladleful of beans over the meats. Pour the remaining beans into a large serving bowl.

8 Take the beans and meats to the table with a platter of peeled, sliced oranges, cooked white rice, toasted cassava flour, stir-fried kale, and chili oil.

COOK'S TIPS
• *Carne seca*, a Brazilian beef jerky, can be bought in Brazilian or Portuguese food stores. You can make a *feijoada* without it, but it won't be as rich.
• Toasted cassava flour is sold in Latin American or Portuguese food stores. Here it is served from the package, but it can be flavored with palm oil or eggs.

STUFFED BEEF WITH CHEESE AND CHILI SAUCE

THIS RECIPE HAS ITS ORIGINS IN NORTHERN MEXICO, WHICH IS BEEF COUNTRY. IT IS A GOOD WAY TO COOK STEAKS, EITHER UNDER THE BROILER OR ON THE GRILL.

SERVES FOUR

INGREDIENTS
    4 fresh serrano chiles
    ½ cup full-fat soft cheese
    2 tablespoons reposada tequila
    2 tablespoons oil
    1 onion
    2 garlic cloves
    1 teaspoon dried oregano
    ½ teaspoon salt
    ½ teaspoon ground black pepper
    1½ cups grated Cheddar cheese
    4 fillet steaks, at least
        1-inch thick

3 Put the cream cheese in a small heavy pan and stir over low heat until it has melted. Add the chile strips and the tequila, and stir to make a smooth sauce. Keep warm over very low heat.

6 Cut each steak almost but not quite in half across its width, so that it can be opened out, butterfly-style. Preheat the broiler to its highest setting.

1 Dry-roast the chiles in a griddle over medium heat, turning them frequently, until the skins are blistered but not burnt. Put them in a strong plastic bag and tie the top to keep the steam in. Set aside for 20 minutes.

4 Heat the oil in a frying pan and sauté the onion, garlic, and oregano for about 5 minutes over medium heat, stirring frequently, until the onion has browned. Season with the salt and pepper.

7 Spoon a quarter of the cheese and onion filling on one side of each steak and close the other side over it. Place the steaks in a broiler pan and broil for 3–5 minutes on each side, depending on how you like your steak. Serve on heated plates with the vegetables of your choice, and with the cheese and chili sauce poured on top.

2 Remove the chilies from the bag, slit them, and scrape out the seeds with a sharp knife. Cut the flesh into long narrow strips, then cut each strip into several shorter strips.

5 Remove the pan from heat and stir in the grated cheese so that it melts into the onion mixture.

COOK'S TIP
One of the easiest ways of testing whether a steak is cooked is by touch. A steak that is very rare or "blue" will feel soft to the touch; the meat will be relaxed. A rare steak will feel like a sponge, and will spring back when lightly pressed. A medium-rare steak offers more resistance, while a well-cooked steak will feel very firm.

HEARTY BEEF STEW

BROWN ALE ENRICHES THIS CARIBBEAN BEEF STEW AND GIVES IT A REAL KICK. VARY THE AMOUNT TO SUIT YOUR TASTE, BUT DON'T OVERDO IT OR YOU WILL OVERWHELM THE TASTE OF THE PAPRIKA.

2 Simmer the peas for 30 minutes, or until tender but still quite firm. Drain the peas, reserving the cooking liquid.

3 Melt the butter or margarine in a large pan and sauté the onion for a few minutes. Add the beef, paprika, garlic, cinnamon, and sugar, and fry for about 5 minutes, stirring frequently.

4 Pour in the beef stock and brown ale, cover, and cook gently for 1½ hours, until the beef is almost cooked.

SERVES FOUR

INGREDIENTS
⅓ cup black-eyed peas
2 tablespoons butter or margarine
1 onion, chopped
1½ pounds stewing beef, cubed
1 teaspoon paprika
2 garlic cloves, crushed
2 teaspoons ground cinnamon
2 teaspoons sugar
2½ cups beef stock
⅔ cup brown ale
3 tablespoons unsweetened
  condensed milk
salt and ground black pepper
steamed baby patty-pan squash

1 Put the black-eyed peas in a bowl and pour over water to cover. Leave to soak overnight, then drain, tip into a large pan, cover with water, and bring to the boil. Boil rapidly for 3–4 minutes, then reduce the heat.

5 Add the evaporated milk and peas. Season with salt and pepper, and continue cooking until the beans and beef are tender. Serve with steamed baby patty-pan squash.

OXTAIL <u>AND</u> LIMA BEANS

THIS IS A TRADITIONAL CARIBBEAN STEW—OLD-FASHIONED, ECONOMICAL, AND FULL OF GOODNESS. IT REQUIRES PATIENCE BECAUSE OF THE LONG COOKING TIME. THERE IS NOT MUCH MEAT ON THE OXTAIL, SO IT IS NECESSARY TO BUY A LARGE AMOUNT.

<u>SERVES FOUR</u>

INGREDIENTS

13½ pounds oxtail, chopped into
   pieces
1 onion, finely chopped
3 bay leaves
4 fresh thyme sprigs
3 whole cloves
½ cup water
scant 1 cup dried lima beans,
   soaked overnight
2 garlic cloves, crushed
1 tablespoon tomato paste
14-ounce can chopped tomatoes
1 teaspoon ground allspice
1 fresh hot chile
salt and ground black pepper

1 Put the pieces of oxtail in a large heavy pan, add the chopped onion, bay leaves, thyme, and cloves, and cover with water. Bring to the boil.

2 Reduce the heat, cover the pan, and simmer gently for at least 2½ hours, or until the meat is very tender. If the meat looks like it might dry out, add a little extra water, being careful not to add too much at one time.

3 Meanwhile, drain the lima beans and tip them into a large pan. Pour in water to cover. Bring to the boil, lower the heat, and simmer for about 1–1¼ hours, or until just tender. Drain and set aside until ready to use.

COOK'S TIP
Unless you are confident using a meat cleaver to chop the oxtail into short lengths, ask your butcher to do it for you.

VARIATION
Navy beans can be used in the same way as lima beans in the recipe.

4 When the oxtail is cooked, add the garlic, tomato puree, tomatoes, allspice, and chile, and season. Add the beans, simmer for 20 minutes, then serve.

"SEASONED-UP" LAMB IN SPINACH SAUCE

IN THE CARIBBEAN, ESPECIALLY ON THE ENGLISH-SPEAKING ISLANDS, YOU WILL OFTEN HEAR DISHES DESCRIBED AS "SEASONED UP." THIS REFERS TO THE USE OF A SPICY RUB OR MARINADE, A TECHNIQUE THAT WORKS WELL WITH CHEAPER CUTS OF MEAT.

SERVES FOUR

INGREDIENTS

    1½ pounds boneless lamb, cubed
    ½ teaspoon ground ginger
    ½ teaspon dried thyme
    2 tablespoons olive oil
    1 onion, chopped
    2 garlic cloves, crushed
    1 tablespoon tomato paste
    ½ fresh hot chile, chopped (optional)
    2½ cups lamb stock or water
    4 ounces fresh spinach, finely
      chopped
    salt and ground black pepper

1 Put the lamb cubes in a dish. Sprinkle over the ginger and thyme, season, and mix well to coat. Cover and marinate for at least 2 hours or overnight in the refrigerator.

2 Heat the olive oil in a heavy pan, add the onion and garlic, and fry gently for 5 minutes or until the onion is soft.

3 Add the lamb with the tomato paste and chile, if using. Fry over a medium heat for about 5 minutes, stirring frequently, then add the lamb stock or water. Cover and simmer for about 30 minutes, until the lamb is tender.

4 Stir in the spinach and simmer for around 8 minutes. Serve hot.

LAMB PELAU

INDIAN IMMIGRANTS INTRODUCED THE PILAU TO THE CARIBBEAN. THE NAME HAS CHANGED SLIGHTLY, BUT RICE DISHES LIKE THIS ONE REMAIN TRUE TO THEIR ORIGINS.

SERVES FOUR

INGREDIENTS

    1 pound stewing lamb
    1 tablespoon curry powder
    1 onion, finely chopped
    2 garlic cloves, crushed
    ½ teaspoon dried thyme
    ½ teaspoon dried oregano
    1 fresh or dried chile
    2 tablespoons butter or margarine,
      plus extra for serving
    2½ cups beef stock, chicken stock,
      or coconut milk
    1 teaspoon ground black pepper
    2 tomatoes, chopped
    2 teaspoons sugar
    2 tablespoons chopped scallion
    2½ cups basmati rice
    scallion strips, to garnish

1 Cut the lamb into cubes and place in a dish. Add the curry powder, onion, garlic, herbs, and chile, and stir well. Cover with plastic wrap and leave to marinate for 1 hour.

2 Melt the butter or margarine in a pan and fry the lamb for 5–10 minutes. Pour in the stock or coconut milk, bring to the boil, then lower the heat and simmer for 35 minutes or until tender.

3 Add the black pepper, tomatoes, sugar, chopped scallion, and rice. Stir well and reduce the heat. Make sure that the rice is covered by 1 inch of liquid; add a little water if necessary. Cover the pan; simmer the pelau for 25 minutes, or until the rice has absorbed the liquid and is cooked. Spoon into a serving bowl and stir in a little extra butter or margarine. Garnish with scallion strips and serve.

LAMB STEW ᵂᴵᵀᴴ CHILI SAUCE

THE CHILES IN THIS STEW ADD DEPTH AND RICHNESS TO THE SAUCE, WHILE THE POTATO SLICES
ENSURE THAT IT IS SUBSTANTIAL ENOUGH TO SERVE ON ITS OWN.

SERVES SIX

INGREDIENTS
  6 guajillo chiles, seeded
  2 pasilla chiles, seeded
  1 cup hot water
  3 garlic cloves, peeled
  1 teaspoon ground cinnamon
  ½ teaspoon ground cloves
  ½ teaspoon ground black pepper
  1 tablespoon vegetable oil
  2¼ pounds lean boneless lamb
    shoulder, cut into ¾-inch cubes
  14 ounces potatoes, scrubbed and
    cut into ½-inch thick slices
  salt
  strips of red bell pepper and fresh
    oregano to garnish

COOK'S TIP
When frying the lamb, don't be tempted
to cook too many cubes at one time, as
the meat will steam rather than fry.

1 Snap or tear the dried chiles into
large pieces, put them in a bowl, and
pour in the hot water. Let soak for
30 minutes, then transfer the contents
of the bowl to a food processor or
blender. Add the garlic and spices.
Process until smooth.

2 Heat the oil in a large pan. Add the
lamb cubes, in batches, and stir-fry
over high heat until the cubes are
browned on all sides.

3 Return all the lamb cubes to the pan,
spread them out, then cover them with
a layer of potato slices. Add salt to
taste. Put a lid on the pan and cook
over medium heat for 10 minutes.

4 Pour over the chili mixture and mix
well. Replace the lid and simmer over a
low heat for about 1 hour or until the
meat and the potato are tender. Serve
with a rice dish, and garnish with strips
of red bell pepper and fresh oregano.

ALBONDIGAS

DON'T BE DAUNTED BY THE LENGTH OF THE INGREDIENT LIST. THESE MEATBALLS ARE ABSOLUTELY DELICIOUS, AND THE CHIPOTLE CHILE GIVES THE SAUCE A DISTINCTIVE, SLIGHTLY SMOKY FLAVOR.

SERVES FOUR

INGREDIENTS
    8 ounces ground pork
    8 ounces lean ground beef
    1 onion, finely chopped
    1 cup fresh white bread crumbs
    1 teaspoon dried oregano
    ½ teaspoon ground cumin
    ½ teaspoon salt
    ½ teaspoon ground black pepper
    1 egg, beaten
    oil, for frying
    fresh oregano sprigs, to garnish
For the sauce
    1 chipotle chile, seeded
    1 tablespoon vegetable oil
    1 onion, finely chopped
    2 garlic cloves, crushed
    ¾ cup beef stock
    14-ounce can chopped tomatoes
      in tomato juice
    7 tablespoons bottled strained
      tomatoes

1 Mix the ground pork and beef in a bowl. Add the onion, bread crumbs, oregano, cumin, salt, and pepper. Mix with clean hands until all the ingredients are well combined.

2 Stir in the egg, mix well, then roll into 1½-inch balls. Put these on a baking sheet and chill while you prepare the sauce.

3 Soak the dried chile in hot water to cover for 15 minutes. Heat the oil in a pan and sauté the onion and garlic for 3–4 minutes, until softened.

4 Drain the chile, reserving the soaking water, then chop it and add it to the onion mixture. Fry for 1 minute, then stir in the beef stock, tomatoes, and soaking water, with salt and pepper to taste. Bring to a boil, lower the heat, and simmer, stirring occasionally, while you cook the meatballs.

5 Heat the oil for frying in a frying pan and fry the meatballs in batches for about 5 minutes, turning them occasionally, until browned.

6 Drain off the oil and transfer all the meatballs to a shallow casserole. Pour on the sauce and simmer for 10 minutes, stirring gently from time to time so that the meatballs are coated but do not disintegrate. Garnish with the oregano and serve. Plain white rice makes a good accompaniment.

COOK'S TIP
Dampen your hands before shaping the meatballs, and the mixture will be less likely to stick.

SPICED ROAST LEG OF LAMB

PEPPERS AND BLACK-EYED PEAS ARE DELICIOUS COOKED WITH THIS SPICED LAMB—THE BEANS SOAK
UP THE MEAT JUICES AND COMBINE WITH RED BELL PEPPERS TO MAKE A SUCCULENT ONE-POT MEAL.

SERVES SIX

INGREDIENTS
    1 leg of lamb, about 4 pounds
    4 garlic cloves, crushed
    1 teaspoon ground cumin
    2 teaspoons ground annatto
      (achiote) seeds
    2 tablespoons sweet paprika
    1 teaspoon dried oregano
    3 tablespoons olive oil
    3 red bell peppers, cored, seeded,
      and thickly sliced
    2 x 14-ounce can black-eyed peas,
      drained
    7 tablespoons dry white wine
    salt and ground black pepper
    cooked white rice or polenta, to serve

COOK'S TIP
Look for ground annatto in South
American or Caribbean markets, or
replace with saffron or turmeric.

1 Weigh the lamb and calculate the
cooking time. For medium-cooked
lamb, allow 20 minutes per 1 pound,
plus 20 minutes. Allow either 5 minutes
more or less per 1 pound for rare and
well-done meat.

2 Mix the garlic, cumin, annatto,
paprika, and oregano in a bowl. Stir in
half the olive oil. Using a spoon, rub the
paste all over the lamb. Cover and
marinate in a cool place for 2–3 hours.

3 Preheat the oven to 350°F. Place the
lamb in a roasting pan with the peppers
and black-eyed peas. Pour in the wine
and drizzle with the remaining oil.
Season, then roast for the calculated
time. Check occasionally, adding water
if the vegetables begin to dry out.

4 When the lamb is cooked, remove
from the oven and cover the meat
loosely with foil. Leave to rest for 15
minutes, then serve with rice or polenta.

RABBIT <u>IN</u> COCONUT MILK

THIS UNUSUAL DISH COMES FROM COLOMBIA. THE RABBIT IS STEWED IN A LIGHTLY SPICED TOMATO SAUCE, AND WHEN IT IS ALMOST READY, COCONUT MILK IS STIRRED IN TO ENRICH THE SAUCE.

SERVES FOUR

INGREDIENTS

1 rabbit, cut into 8 pieces (ask your butcher to do this for you)
3 garlic cloves, crushed
¼ teaspoon paprika
¼ teaspoon ground cumin
3 tablespoons olive oil
1 large onion, thinly sliced
1 bay leaf
14-ounce can plum tomatoes, drained and roughly chopped
⅔ cup chicken stock
1 cup coconut milk
salt and ground black pepper
white rice or boiled potatoes, to serve

3 Add the rabbit to the oil remaining in the pan, season, and cook until golden. Do this over a very low heat to avoid burning the spices.

4 Return the onion slices to the pan and add the bay leaf. Stir in the tomatoes and stock, and bring to the boil. Lower the heat, cover, and simmer for 45 minutes.

VARIATION
This dish is often made with chicken rather than rabbit. The ingredients remain the same, but the cooking time should be reduced by 15 minutes.

5 Stir in the coconut milk. Continue to simmer, uncovered, for a further 15 minutes, until the rabbit is tender and the sauce has thickened. Serve immediately with white rice or boiled potatoes.

1 Wash the rabbit under cold water, then pat the pieces dry with paper towels. Combine the garlic, paprika, and cumin in a bowl, and rub the mixture all over the rabbit. Cover with plastic wrap and leave to marinate for 1 hour, or overnight in the refrigerator.

2 Heat the oil in a pan, add the onion slices, and cook for 5 minutes, until tender. Remove the onion with a slotted spoon and set aside.

CARIBBEAN LAMB CURRY

THIS JAMAICAN DISH IS POPULARLY KNOWN AS CURRIED GOAT OR CURRY GOAT, ALTHOUGH KID, LAMB, OR MUTTON ARE EQUALLY LIKELY TO BE USED TO MAKE IT.

SERVES SIX

INGREDIENTS

2 pounds boned leg of mutton
  or lamb
4 tablespoons curry powder
3 garlic cloves, crushed
1 large onion, chopped
leaves from 4 fresh thyme sprigs,
  or 1 teaspoon dried thyme
3 bay leaves
1 teaspoon ground allspice
2 tablespoons vegetable oil
¼ cup butter or margarine
3¾ cups lamb stock or water
1 fresh hot chile, chopped
fresh cilantro sprigs,
  to garnish
cooked rice, to serve

3 Melt the butter or margarine in a large heavy pan. Add the seasoned mutton or lamb and fry over a medium heat for about 10 minutes, turning the meat frequently.

4 Stir in the stock or water and chile, and bring to the boil. Lower the heat, cover, and simmer for 1½ hours or until the meat is tender. Garnish with cilantro and serve with rice.

1 Cut the meat into 2-inch cubes, discarding excess fat and any gristle. Place it in a large bowl.

2 Add the curry powder, garlic, onion, thyme, bay leaves, allspice, and oil. Mix well, then cover the bowl and place in the refrigerator. Marinate for at least 3 hours or overnight.

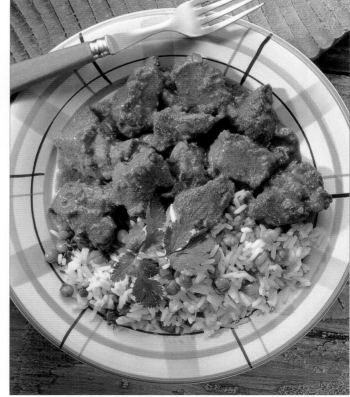

PORK WITH PINEAPPLE

*THIS UNUSUAL DISH FROM MEXICO COMBINES THE SWEET, JUICY TASTE OF FRESH PINEAPPLE WITH
FIERY HOT CHILES, AND THE REFRESHING TANG OF COOL MINT.*

SERVES SIX

INGREDIENTS

2 tablespoons corn oil
2 pounds boneless pork shoulder or
  loin, cut into 2-inch cubes
1 onion, finely chopped
1 large red bell pepper, seeded and
  finely chopped
1 or more jalapeño chiles, seeded
  and finely chopped
1 pound fresh pineapple chunks
8 fresh mint leaves, chopped
1 cup chicken stock
salt and ground black pepper
fresh mint sprigs, to garnish
boiled rice, to serve

3 Add the mint leaves, then cover the
casserole with a tight-fitting lid.

4 Simmer gently for about 2 hours or
until the pork is tender.

5 Season to taste, garnish the casserole
with fresh sprigs of mint, and serve with
plain boiled rice. Serve immediately,
while still hot.

COOK'S TIP
If fresh pineapple is not available, use
pineapple chunks from a can. Make sure
it is canned in its own juice, however,
and not in syrup or other fruit juice.

1 Heat the oil in a large frying pan and
sauté the pork in batches until the
cubes are lightly colored. Transfer the
pork to a flameproof casserole, leaving
the oil behind in the pan.

2 Add the chopped onion, red pepper,
and the chiles to the oil remaining in
the pan. Sauté until the onion is tender,
then add to the casserole with the
pineapple. Stir to mix.

STUFFED LOIN OF PORK

PORK FEATURES TWICE IN THIS DELICIOUS AND LUXURIOUS DISH, WHICH CONSISTS OF A ROAST LOIN STUFFED WITH A RICH GROUND PORK MIXTURE. THE PERFECT CENTERPIECE FOR A SPECIAL-OCCASION DINNER, IT IS SERVED IN MEXICO AT WEDDINGS AND SIMILAR CELEBRATIONS.

SERVES SIX

INGREDIENTS
 3–3½ pounds boneless pork loin,
   butterflied and ready for stuffing
For the stuffing
 ⅓ cup raisins
 ½ cup dry white wine
 1 tablespoon vegetable oil
 1 onion, diced
 2 garlic cloves, crushed
 ½ teaspoon ground cloves
 1 teaspoon ground cinnamon
 1¼ pounds ground pork
 ⅔ cup vegetable stock
 2 tomatoes
 ½ cup chopped almonds
 ½ teaspoon each salt and ground
   black pepper

1 Make the stuffing. Put the raisins and wine in a bowl. Set aside. Heat the oil in a large pan, add the onion and garlic, and cook for 5 minutes over low heat.

2 Add the cloves and cinnamon, then the pork. Cook, stirring, until the pork has browned. Add the stock. Simmer, stirring frequently, for 20 minutes.

3 While the pork is simmering, peel the tomatoes. Cut a cross in the bottom of each tomato, then put them both in a heatproof bowl. Pour in boiling water to cover. Leave the tomatoes in the water for 3 minutes, then lift them out on a slotted spoon and plunge them into a bowl of cold water. Drain. The skins will have begun to peel back from the crosses.

4 Remove the skins completely, then chop the flesh.

5 Stir the tomatoes and almonds into the pork mixture, add the raisins and wine. Cook until the mixture is reduced to a thick sauce. Let cool.

6 Preheat the oven to 350°F. Open out the pork loin and trim it neatly. Season the pork stuffing with salt and pepper to taste. Spread on the surface of the meat in a neat layer, taking it right to the edges and keeping it as even as possible.

7 Roll up the pork loin carefully and tie it at intervals with kitchen string. Weigh the pork and calculate the cooking time at 30 minutes per pound, plus another 30 minutes.

8 Put the stuffed pork joint in a roasting pan, season with salt and pepper, and roast for the calculated time. When the joint is cooked, transfer it to a meat platter, place a tent of aluminum foil over it, and let it stand for 10 minutes before carving and serving with the roast vegetables of your choice.

COOK'S TIP
Your butcher will prepare the pork loin for you, if you give plenty of notice.

ENCHILADAS WITH PORK AND GREEN SAUCE

THE GREEN TOMATILLO SAUCE PROVIDES A TART CONTRAST TO THE PORK FILLING IN THIS POPULAR DISH. CASCABELS ARE DRIED CHILES THAT RATTLE WHEN SHAKEN.

SERVES THREE TO FOUR

INGREDIENTS
1¼ pounds pork shoulder, diced
1 cascabel chile
2 tablespoons oil
2 garlic cloves, crushed
1 onion, finely chopped
scant 2 cups drained
  canned tomatillos
6 fresh corn tortillas
¾ cup grated Monterey Jack or
  mild Cheddar cheese

1 Put the diced pork in a pan and pour in water to cover. Bring to a boil, lower the heat, and simmer for 40 minutes.

2 Meanwhile, soak the dried chile in hot water for 30 minutes until softened. Drain, remove the stem, then slit the chile and scrape out the seeds.

3 Drain the pork and let it cool slightly, then shred it, using two forks. Put the pork in a bowl and set it aside.

4 Heat the oil in a frying pan and sauté the garlic and onion for 3–4 minutes, until translucent. Chop and add the chile with the tomatillos. Cook, stirring constantly, until the tomatillos start to break up. Lower the heat and simmer the sauce for 10 more minutes. Cool slightly, then puree in a blender.

5 Preheat the oven to 350°F. Soften the tortillas by wrapping them in foil and steaming on a plate over boiling water for a few minutes, until they are pliable. Alternatively, wrap them in microwave-safe plastic wrap and heat in a microwave on full power for about 30 seconds.

6 Spoon one-sixth of the shredded pork onto the center of a tortilla and roll it up to make an enchilada. Place it in a shallow baking dish that is large enough to hold all the enchiladas in a single layer. Fill and roll the remaining tortillas and add them to the dish.

7 Pour the sauce onto the enchiladas to cover completely. Sprinkle evenly with cheese. Bake for 25–30 minutes or until the cheese bubbles. Serve immediately. Tomato salad makes a good accompaniment for this dish.

PORK ᴵᴺ GREEN SAUCE ᵂᴵᵀᴴ CACTUS

CHILE VERDE IS A CLASSIC SAUCE. THE INCLUSION OF CACTUS PIECES—A POPULAR INGREDIENT IN MEXICAN COOKING—GIVES THIS DISH AN INTRIGUING FLAVOR THAT WILL DOUBTLESS PROVE A GOOD CONVERSATION STARTER AT THE DINNER TABLE.

SERVES FOUR

INGREDIENTS
2 tablespoons vegetable oil
1¼ pounds pork shoulder, cut in
  1-inch cubes
1 onion, finely chopped
2 garlic cloves, crushed
1 teaspoon dried oregano
3 fresh jalapeño chiles, seeded
  and chopped
scant 2 cups drained
  canned tomatillos
⅔ cup vegetable stock
11-ounce jar *nopalitos*, drained
salt and ground black pepper
warm fresh corn tortillas, to serve

COOK'S TIP
Nopalitos are cactus paddles that have been cut into strips and pickled in vinegar or packed in brine. Look for them at specialty food stores.

1 Heat the oil in a large pan. Add the pork cubes and cook over high heat, turning several times, until browned all over. Add the onion and garlic, and sauté gently until soft, then stir in the oregano and chopped jalapeños. Cook for 2 more minutes.

2 Transfer the canned tomatillos to a blender, add the stock and process until smooth. Add to the pork mixture, cover, and cook for 30 minutes.

3 Meanwhile, soak the *nopalitos* in cold water for 10 minutes. Drain, then add to the pork and continue cooking for about 10 minutes or until the pork is cooked through and tender.

4 Season the mixture with salt and plenty of ground black pepper. Serve with warm corn tortillas.

TAMALES FILLED WITH SPICED PORK

THESE TAMALES ARE AMONG THE MOST ANCIENT OF MEXICAN FOODS. AT ONE TIME THE NEAT LITTLE CORN HUSK PARCELS FILLED WITH PLAIN, SAVORY, OR SWEET MASA DOUGH WERE COOKED IN THE ASHES OF A WOOD FIRE. TODAY THEY ARE MORE LIKELY TO BE STEAMED, BUT THE THRILL OF UNWRAPPING THEM REMAINS THE SAME.

SERVES SIX

INGREDIENTS
1¼ pounds lean pork, cut into
  2-inch cubes
3 cups chicken stock
4½ cups *masa harina*
2 cups shortening, softened
2 tablespoons salt
12 large or 24 small dried corn husks
2 ancho chiles, seeded
1 tablespoon vegetable oil
½ onion, finely chopped
2–3 garlic cloves, crushed
½ teaspoon allspice berries
2 dried bay leaves
½ teaspoon ground cumin
lime wedges, to serve (optional)

1 Put the pork cubes in a large pan. Pour in water to cover. Bring to a boil, lower the heat, and simmer for 40 minutes.

2 Meanwhile, heat the chicken stock in a separate pan. Put the *masa harina* in a large bowl and add the hot stock, a little at a time, to make a stiff dough.

3 Put the shortening in another bowl and beat with an electric whisk until light and fluffy, as when beating butter for a cake. Test by dropping a small amount of the whipped shortening into a cup of water. If it floats, it is ready for use.

4 Continue to beat the shortening, gradually adding the *masa* dough. When all of it has been added and the mixture is light and spreadable, beat in the salt. Cover closely with plastic wrap to prevent the mixture from drying out.

5 Put the corn husks in a bowl and pour in boiling water to cover. Let soak for 30 minutes. Soak the seeded chiles in a separate bowl of hot water for the same amount of time. Drain the pork, reserving 7 tablespoons of the cooking liquid, and chop the meat finely.

6 Heat the oil in a large pan and fry the onion and garlic over medium heat for 2–3 minutes. Drain the chiles, chop them finely, and add them to the pan. Put the allspice berries and bay leaves in a mortar, grind them with a pestle, then work in the ground cumin. Add to the onion mixture and stir well. Cook for 2–3 more minutes. Add the chopped pork and reserved cooking liquid, and continue cooking over medium heat until all the liquid is absorbed. Let cool slightly.

7 Drain the corn husks and pat them dry in a clean dish towel. Place one large corn husk (or overlap two smaller ones) on a board. Spoon about one-twelfth of the *masa* mixture onto the center of the husk wrapping and spread it almost to the sides.

8 Place a spoonful of the meat mixture on top of the *masa*. Fold the two long sides of the corn husk over the filling, then bring up each of the two shorter sides in turn, to make a neat parcel. Slide one of the two short sides inside the other, if possible, to prevent the parcel from unraveling, or tie with string or strips of the corn husk.

9 Place the *tamales* in a steamer basket over a pan of steadily simmering water and steam for 1 hour, adding water as needed. To test if the *tamales* are ready, unwrap one. The filling should separate from the husk cleanly. Pile the *tamales* on a plate, let stand for 10 minutes, then serve with lime wedges, if desired. Guests unwrap their own *tamales* at the table.

PORK ROASTED <u>WITH</u> HERBS, SPICES, <u>AND</u> RUM

IN THE CARIBBEAN, THIS SPICY ROAST PORK IS A FAVORITE DISH THAT IS USUALLY COOKED ON A BARBECUE AND SERVED ON SPECIAL OCCASIONS AS PART OF A BUFFET.

SERVES EIGHT

INGREDIENTS

 2 garlic cloves, crushed
 3 tablespoons soy sauce
 1 tablespoon malt vinegar
 1 tablespoon finely chopped celery
 2 tablespoons chopped scallion
 1½ teaspoons dried thyme
 1 teaspoon dried sage
 ½ teaspoon pumpkin pie spice
 2 teaspoons curry powder
 ½ cup rum
 1 tablespoon raw sugar
 3½ pounds boned loin of pork
 salt and ground black pepper
 scallion curls, to garnish
 creamed sweet potato, to serve
For the sauce
 2 tablespoons butter or
   margarine, diced
 1 tablespoon tomato paste
 1¼ cups chicken or pork stock
 1 tablespoon chopped fresh parsley
 1 tablespoon raw sugar
 hot pepper sauce, to taste

1 In a bowl, mix the garlic, soy sauce, vinegar, celery, scallion, thyme, sage, spice, curry powder, rum, and sugar. Add a little salt and pepper.

2 Open out the pork and slash the meat, without cutting through it completely. Place it in a shallow dish. Spread most of the spice mixture all over the pork, pressing it well into the slashes. Rub the outside of the joint with the remaining mixture, cover the dish with plastic wrap, and chill in the refrigerator overnight.

COOK'S TIP

In the Caribbean, pork is baked until it is very well done, so reduce the cooking time if you prefer meat slightly more moist. To get the full flavor from the marinade, start preparation the day before.

3 Preheat the oven to 375°F. Roll the meat up, then tie it tightly in several places with strong cotton string to hold it together.

4 Spread a large piece of foil across a roasting pan and place the marinated pork loin in the center. Baste the pork with a few spoonfuls of the marinade and wrap the foil around the meat.

5 Roast the pork in the oven for 1¾ hours, then slide the foil out from under the meat and discard it. Baste the pork with any remaining marinade and cook for a further 1 hour. Check occasionally that the meat is not drying out and baste with the pan juices.

6 Meanwhile, make the sauce. Transfer the pork to a warmed serving dish, cover with foil, and leave to stand in a warm place for 15 minutes. Pour the meat juices into a pan. Add the butter or margarine, tomato puree, stock, parsley, and sugar, with hot pepper sauce, and salt to taste. Simmer until reduced.

7 Serve the pork sliced, with the creamed sweet potato. Garnish with the scallion curls and serve the sauce separately.

TOSTADAS WITH SHREDDED PORK AND SPICES

CRISP FRIED TORTILLAS TOPPED WITH REFRIED BEANS AND SPICED SHREDDED PORK MAKE A DELECTABLE TREAT AND ARE OFTEN SOLD AT STALLS IN MEXICAN CITY STREETS.

SERVES SIX

INGREDIENTS

6 corn tortillas, freshly made or a few
   days old
oil, for frying
For the topping
   1¼ pounds pork shoulder, cut into
     1-inch cubes
   ½ teaspoon salt
   1 tablespoon oil
   1 small onion, halved and sliced
   1 garlic clove, crushed
   1 pasilla chile, seeded and ground
   1 teaspoon ground cinnamon
   ½ teaspoon ground cloves
   1 cup Refried Beans
   6 tablespoons sour cream
   2 tomatoes, seeded and diced
   4 ounces feta cheese, crumbled
   fresh oregano sprigs, to garnish

COOK'S TIP

In Mexico, the local fresh goat or cow's milk cheese—*queso fresco*—would be used; feta is the nearest equivalent.

1 Make the topping. Place the pork cubes in a pan, pour in water to cover, and bring to a boil. Lower the heat, cover, and simmer for 40 minutes. Drain, discarding the cooking liquid. Shred the pork, using two forks. Put it in a bowl and season with the salt.

2 Heat the oil in a large frying pan. Add the onion, garlic, chile, and spices. Stir over the heat for 2–3 minutes, then add the shredded meat and cook until the meat is thoroughly heated and has absorbed the flavorings. Heat the refried beans in a separate, small pan.

3 Meanwhile, cook the tortillas. Pour oil into a large frying pan to a depth of ¾ inch. Heat the oil and fry one tortilla at a time, pressing down with a spatula or a pair of tongs to keep it flat. As soon as a tortilla is crisp, lift it out and drain it on paper towels.

4 Place each tortilla on a plate. Top with refried beans. Add a little of the meat mixture, then spoon 1 tablespoon of the sour cream on each. Divide the chopped tomato among the tostadas and top with the crumbled feta. Serve immediately, garnished with fresh oregano.

PORK <u>IN</u> MILK

ITALIAN IMMIGRANTS FIRST TOOK THIS TUSCAN RECIPE TO ARGENTINA. IN PERU, RAISINS AND SEVERAL SWEET SPICES ARE ADDED, BUT FOR THIS VERSION ONLY CLOVES ARE USED, GIVING A SUBTLE FLAVOR.

SERVES SIX

INGREDIENTS

2¼ pounds pork loin, on the bone
2 tablespoons butter
1 tablespoon olive oil
4 cups whole milk
3 whole cloves
4 garlic cloves, peeled but left whole
1 bay leaf
juice of 2 lemons
salt and ground black pepper
boiled potatoes, to serve

COOK'S TIP
The milk will curdle because of the addition of lemon juice. Don't be tempted to strain it, or you'll lose half the flavor. When you blend it, it will become perfectly smooth again.

1 Preheat the oven to 350°F. Season the pork and select a roasting pan that will hold it snugly. Heat the butter and oil in the roasting pan over a medium heat. When the butter has melted, add the pork and baste it all over. Cook for 10–15 minutes, turning, until golden brown all over.

2 Pour in the milk and add the cloves, garlic, bay leaf, and lemon juice. Cook in the oven for 1¾–2 hours.

3 Remove the roasting pan from the oven and transfer the pork loin to a serving platter to rest for 5 minutes. Skim the fat from the cooking liquid and, using a teaspoon, remove the cloves and bay leaf. Place the pan on the stovetop and boil over a high heat until the sauce is reduced by half.

4 Process the sauce in a food processor until smooth. Carve the pork and serve it with the sauce and boiled potatoes.

BAKED HAM <u>WITH</u> ORANGE <u>AND</u> LIME

THE DELICIOUS CITRUS GLAZE ON THIS HAM CONTRASTS BEAUTIFULLY WITH THE SWEETNESS OF THE MEAT FOR THIS PERFECT SUNDAY LUNCH DISH. PLAIN RICE AND BLACK BEANS, THOSE FAVORITE LATIN AMERICAN SIDE DISHES, ARE THE OBVIOUS ACCOMPANIMENT.

SERVES EIGHT

INGREDIENTS

1 green unsmoked cured ham, about 4½ pounds
grated rind of 1 orange
grated rind of 1 lime
1 bay leaf
3 fresh parsley stalks
6 black peppercorns
5 garlic cloves, crushed
1 tablespoon dried oregano
2 fresh red chiles, seeded and finely chopped
juice of 1 orange
juice of 2 limes
2 tablespoons soft brown sugar
ground black pepper

1 Put the gammon in a large pan and pour in cold water to cover. Add the orange and lime rind, the bay leaf, parsley, and peppercorns. Bring to the boil over a high heat, cover, and lower the heat so that the water is bubbling at a gentle simmer. Cook the gammon for about 2 hours.

2 Preheat the oven to 425°F. When the gammon is cooked, remove the pan from the heat. Leave until the gammon is cool enough to handle, then transfer it to a chopping board. Carefully pull away the skin, leaving the fat on the meat.

3 Mix the crushed garlic, oregano, chopped chiles, orange and lime juice, and sugar in a bowl, and stir well to combine. Add a generous amount of ground black pepper. Rub the mixture all over the gammon, coating it evenly. Transfer to a roasting pan and bake for 20–25 minutes or until golden.

4 Slice the ham and serve. Alternatively, enjoy as part of a buffet or picnic.

CARNITAS

SUCCULENT LITTLE PIECES OF MEAT (USUALLY PORK), CARNITAS, LITERALLY "LITTLE MEATS," CAN BE EATEN AS PART OF A MAIN DISH OR USED TO FILL TACOS OR BURRITOS. THEY ARE ALSO SERVED WITH SALSA AS SNACKS OR ANTOJITOS (NIBBLES).

SERVES EIGHT AS AN APPETIZER,
SIX AS A MAIN COURSE

INGREDIENTS
  2 dried bay leaves
  2 teaspoons dried thyme
  1 teaspoon dried marjoram
  3–3½ pounds mixed boneless pork
    (loin and leg)
  3 garlic cloves
  ½ teaspoon salt
  scant 1 cup shortening
  1 orange, cut into 8 wedges
  1 small onion, thickly sliced
  warm flour tortillas, to serve
For the salsa
  small bunch of cilantro
  1 white onion
  8–10 pickled jalapeño chile slices
  3 tablespoons freshly squeezed
    orange juice

1 Crumble the bay leaves into a mortar. Add the dried thyme and dried marjoram, and grind the mixture with a pestle to a fine powder.

COOK'S TIP
If the *carnitas* are to be served in tacos or burritos, shred or chop them. Make the chunks about half the given size if serving them as *antojitos*. Reduce the cooking time accordingly.

2 Cut the pork into 2-inch cubes and place it in a nonmetallic bowl. Add the herbs and salt. Using your fingers, rub the spice mixture into the meat. Cover and marinate for at least 2 hours, preferably overnight.

3 To make the salsa, remove the stems from the cilantro and chop the leaves roughly. Cut the onion in half, then slice each half thinly. Finely chop the jalapeño chile slices.

4 Mix all the salsa ingredients in a bowl, pour in the freshly squeezed orange juice and toss gently to mix. Cover and chill until needed.

5 Heat the shortening in a flameproof casserole. Add the pork mixture, with the oranges, garlic cloves, and onion. Brown the pork cubes on all sides.

6 Using a slotted spoon, lift out the onion and garlic, and discard. Cover the casserole and continue to cook over low heat for about 1½ hours.

7 Remove the lid and lift out and discard the orange wedges. Continue to cook the mixture, uncovered, until all the meat juices have been absorbed and the pork cubes are crisp on the outside and tender and moist inside. Serve with warm tortillas and the salsa.

PORK CASSEROLE <u>WITH</u> ONIONS, CHILE, <u>AND</u> DRIED FRUIT

INSPIRED BY SOUTH AMERICAN COOKING, A MOLE—PASTE—OF CHILE, SHALLOTS, AND NUTS IS ADDED TO THIS CASSEROLE OF PORK AND ONIONS. PART OF THE MOLE IS ADDED AT THE END OF COOKING TO RETAIN ITS FRESH FLAVOR. SERVE WITH RICE AND A GREEN SALAD.

SERVES SIX

INGREDIENTS
    1½ tablespoons all-purpose flour
    2¼ pounds shoulder or leg of pork,
      cut into 2-inch cubes
    3–4 tablespoons olive oil
    2 large onions, chopped
    2 garlic cloves, finely chopped
    2½ cups fruity white wine
    7 tablespoons water
    4 ounces ready-to-eat prunes
    4 ounces ready-to-eat dried apricots
    grated rind and juice of
      1 small orange
    pinch of molasses sugar (optional)
    2 tablespoons chopped fresh parsley
    ½–1 fresh green chile, seeded and
      finely chopped (optional)
    salt and ground black pepper
For the mole
    3 *ancho* chiles and 2 *pasilla* chiles
      (or other varieties of large, medium-
      hot dried red chiles)
    2 tablespoons olive oil
    2 shallots, chopped
    2 garlic cloves, chopped
    1 fresh green chile, seeded
      and chopped
    2 teaspoons ground cilantro
    1 teaspoon mild Spanish paprika
      or *pimentón*
    ½ cup blanched almonds,
      toasted
    1 tablespoon chopped fresh oregano
      or ½ teaspoon dried oregano

1 Make the mole paste first. Toast the dried chiles in a dry frying pan over a low heat for 1–2 minutes, until they are aromatic, then soak them in warm water for 30 minutes.

2 Drain the chiles, reserving the soaking water, and discard their stalks and seeds. Preheat the oven to 325°F.

3 Heat the oil in a small frying pan and fry the shallots, garlic, fresh green chile, and ground coriander over a very low heat for 5 minutes.

4 Transfer the shallot mixture to a food processor or blender and add the drained chiles, paprika or *pimentón*, almonds, and oregano. Process the mixture, adding 3–4 tablespoons of the chile soaking liquid to make a workable paste.

5 Season the flour with salt and black pepper, then use to coat the pork. Heat 3 tablespoons of the olive oil in a large, heavy-based frying pan and fry the pork, stirring frequently, until sealed on all sides. Transfer the pork cubes to a flameproof casserole.

6 If necessary, add the remaining oil to the frying pan and cook the onions and garlic gently for 8–10 minutes, stirring occasionally.

7 Add the wine and water to the frying pan. Cook for 2 minutes. Stir in half the mole paste, bring back to the boil, and bubble for a few seconds before pouring over the pork.

8 Season lightly with salt and pepper, and stir to mix, then cover and cook in the oven for 1½ hours.

9 Increase the oven temperature to 350°F. Stir in the prunes, apricots, and orange juice. Test the seasoning, adding the muscovado sugar if necessary, cover, and cook for another 30–45 minutes.

10 Place the casserole over a direct heat and stir in the remaining mole paste. Simmer, stirring once or twice, for 5 minutes. Serve sprinkled with the orange rind, chopped parsley, and fresh chile, if using.

TORTILLA PIE WITH CHORIZO

THIS IS A POPULAR MEXICAN BREAKFAST DISH, KNOWN AS CHILAQUILES. *THE FRIED TORTILLA STRIPS STAY CRISP IN THE TOMATILLO, CREAM, AND CHEESE SAUCE.*

SERVES SIX

INGREDIENTS
  2 tablespoons lard or 2 tablespoons
    vegetable oil
  1¼ pounds ground pork
  3 garlic cloves, crushed
  2 teaspoons dried oregano
  1 teaspoon ground cinnamon
  ½ teaspoon ground cloves
  ½ teaspoon ground black pepper
  2 tablespoons dry sherry
  1 teaspoon superfine sugar
  1 teaspoon salt
  12 corn tortillas, freshly made or a
    few days old
  oil, for frying
  3 cups grated Monterey Jack or mild
    Cheddar cheese
  1¼ cups crème fraîche
For the tomatillo sauce
  scant 2 cups drained canned
    tomatillos
  4 tablespoons stock or water
  2 fresh serrano chiles, seeded and
    roughly chopped
  2 garlic cloves
  small bunch of cilantro
  ½ cup sour cream

1 Preheat the oven to 350°F. Heat the shortening or oil in a large pan. Add the pork and crushed garlic. Stir over medium heat until the meat has browned, then stir in the oregano, cinnamon, cloves, and pepper. Cook for 3–4 more minutes, stirring constantly, then add the sherry, sugar, and salt. Stir for 3–4 minutes, until all the flavors are blended, then remove the pan from heat.

2 Cut the tortillas into ¾-inch strips. Pour oil into a frying pan to a depth of ¾ inch and heat to 375°F. Fry the tortilla strips in batches until crisp and golden brown all over.

3 Spread half the pork mixture in a baking dish. Top with half the tortilla strips and grated cheese, then add dollops of crème fraîche. Repeat the layers. Bake for 20–25 minutes or until bubbling.

4 To make the sauce, put all the ingredients except the sour cream in a food processor or blender. Reserve a little cilantro for sprinkling. Process until smooth. Scrape into a pan, bring to a boil, then lower the heat and simmer for 5 minutes.

5 Stir the sour cream into the sauce, with salt and pepper to taste. Pour the mixture on top and serve immediately, sprinkled with cilantro.

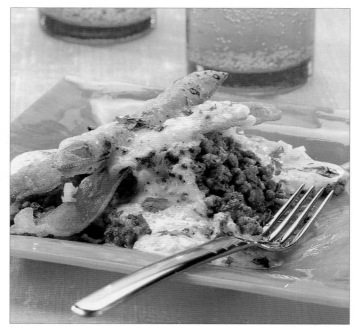

SCRAMBLED EGGS <u>WITH</u> CHORIZO

THIS POPULAR MEXICAN DISH IS OFTEN EATEN FOR BREAKFAST. DRIED, SPANISH-STYLE CHORIZO GIVES THE EGGS A RICH GOLDEN COLOR AND DELICIOUS SMOKY FLAVOR. BUY THE SAUSAGE IN ONE PIECE AND SLICE IT JUST BEFORE COOKING.

SERVES FOUR

INGREDIENTS
    1 tablespoon olive oil
    5 ounces dried chorizo, cut into
      ½-inch slices
    ½ teaspoon paprika
    8 eggs, lightly beaten
    salt
    country bread and green salad,
      to serve

VARIATION
For extra fire and spice, add a dash of a hot pepper sauce, such as Tabasco, to the beaten egg mixture.

1 Heat the oil in a large frying pan over a medium heat and pan-fry the chorizo slices for 1–2 minutes, until browned and crisp.

COOK'S TIP
The chorizo will brown very quickly, so do not leave it to cook unattended or it may burn.

2 Add the paprika, stir for 30 seconds, then pour in the beaten eggs. Season lightly with salt. As the eggs start to set, break them up with a fork.

3 Remove the pan from the heat when the mixture is still quite moist; it will continue cooking off the heat. Serve with the bread and a green salad.

POULTRY

Chicken is the meat most frequently eaten in the Caribbean and Latin America. The Caribbean Sunday roast is extremely popular, but for delicious weekday meals try thyme and lime chicken, or chicken with okra. Colombian chicken hot-pot and carapulcra, a chicken and pork dish from Peru, are both national dishes. Turkey and duck are also popular throughout the region.

CUBAN CHICKEN PIE

THIS IS A GREAT FAMILY MEAL, PERFECT FOR A SUNDAY LUNCH. THE FILLING, WHICH INCLUDES CAPERS, OLIVES, AND RAISINS, PROVIDES A FLAVORSOME CONTRAST TO THE CRISP CORN TOPPING.

SERVES SIX

INGREDIENTS

    1 chicken, about 3½ pounds
    6 peppercorns
    1 bay leaf
    3 fresh parsley sprigs
    2 tablespoons olive oil
    1 large onion, finely chopped
    2 hard-boiled eggs, chopped
    2 tomatoes, roughly chopped
    ½ cup pitted green olives,
      roughly chopped
    1 tablespoon drained bottled capers
    scant ½ cup raisins
    salt and ground black pepper
For the topping
    3⅓ cups drained canned or thawed
      frozen corn kernels
    3½ ounces butter
    2 teaspoons superfine sugar
    3 eggs, lightly beaten
    salt

1 Put the chicken in a large, heavy pan and add enough water to cover. Add the peppercorns, bay leaf, and parsley, and bring to the boil over a high heat. Lower the heat, cover, and simmer gently for 1 hour or until cooked through.

2 Allow the chicken to cool in the cooking liquid. When cold enough to handle, lift the chicken out of the pan and, using two forks, shred the flesh roughly. Discard the skin and bones.

3 Make the topping. Tip the corn kernels into a blender or food processor and puree until smooth. Melt the butter in a pan over a low heat. Stir in the pureed corn and sugar. Season generously with salt and cook, stirring, for 10 minutes, until the mixture thickens and comes away from the sides of the pan.

4 Remove from the heat and leave to cool for 10 minutes, then slowly stir in the beaten eggs, a little at a time. Set the topping mixture aside.

5 Preheat the oven to 350°F. Heat the oil in a large frying pan and stir in the chopped onion. Cook gently for 5 minutes, until soft and translucent, and season with salt and black pepper to taste.

6 Stir in the chopped hard-boiled eggs, chopped tomatoes, olives, capers, and raisins. Fold in the shredded chicken, making sure that it is well distributed throughout the mixture.

7 Spoon the pie filling into a 10 x 8-inch baking dish. Using a spoon, spread the corn topping evenly over the top of the chicken filling and bake for 45 minutes, until golden brown. Leave to stand for about 10 minutes before serving on warm plates.

VARIATION
Shortcrust pastry can be used instead of the corn topping.

CHICKEN WITH OKRA

SERVE THIS CLASSIC BRAZILIAN DISH FOR A FAMILY SUPPER. IT IS TOTALLY FUSS-FREE, TAKING VERY LITTLE TIME AND EFFORT TO PREPARE.

SERVES FOUR

INGREDIENTS
  1 tablespoon olive oil
  4 chicken thighs
  1 large onion, finely chopped
  2 garlic cloves, finely crushed
  2 fresh red chiles, seeded and
    finely chopped
  ½ cup water
  12 ounces okra
  2 large tomatoes, finely chopped
  salt
  boiled white rice or polenta, to serve
  hot chili oil (optional)

COOK'S TIP
As okra cooks, the pods release a sticky juice, which coats and flavors the chicken. If you don't like this sticky texture, however, cook the pods whole, simply trimming off the tops but not cutting into the pods themselves.

1 Heat the oil in a wide pan over a low heat. Season the chicken thighs with salt and add them to the pan, skin-side down. Cook until golden brown, turn them over, and add the chopped onion.

2 Sauté for 5 minutes, until the onion has softened; then add the garlic and chopped chiles. Cook for a further 2 minutes. Add half the water to the pan and bring to the boil. Lower the heat, cover, and cook for 30 minutes.

3 Trim the okra and slice into thin rounds. Add to the pan with the tomatoes. Season with salt and pour in the remaining water. Cover and simmer gently for about 10–15 minutes, or until the chicken pieces are tender and fully cooked. The chicken is ready when the flesh can be pulled off the bone easily.

4 Serve immediately with boiled white rice or polenta, and offer some hot chili oil on the side.

BURRITOS WITH CHICKEN AND RICE

IN MEXICO, BURRITOS ARE A POPULAR STREET FOOD, EATEN ON THE RUN. THE SECRET OF A SUCCESSFUL BURRITO IS TO HAVE ALL THE FILLING NEATLY PACKAGED INSIDE THE TORTILLA FOR EASY EATING, SO THESE SNACKS ARE SELDOM SERVED WITH A POUR-ON SAUCE.

SERVES FOUR

INGREDIENTS
½ cup long-grain rice
1 tablespoon vegetable oil
1 onion, chopped
½ teaspoon ground cloves
1 teaspoon dried or fresh oregano
7-ounce can chopped tomatoes in
  tomato juice
2 skinless, boneless chicken breasts
1¼ cups grated Monterey Jack or
  mild Cheddar cheese
4 tablespoons sour cream
  (optional)
8 x 8–10-inch fresh flour tortillas
salt
fresh oregano, to garnish (optional)

1 Bring a pan of lightly salted water to a boil. Add the rice and cook for 8 minutes. Drain, rinse, and then drain again.

2 Heat the oil in a large pan. Add the onion, with the ground cloves and oregano, and fry for 2–3 minutes. Stir in the rice and tomatoes and cook over low heat until all the tomato juice has been absorbed. Set the pan aside.

3 Put the chicken breasts in a large pan, pour in enough water to cover, and bring to a boil. Lower the heat and simmer for about 10 minutes, or until the chicken is cooked through. Lift the chicken out of the pan, put on a plate, and cool slightly.

4 Preheat the oven to 325°F. Shred the chicken by pulling the flesh apart with two forks, then add the chicken to the rice mixture, with the grated cheese. Stir in the sour cream, if using.

COOK'S TIP
If you use very fresh tortillas, you may be able to dispense with the toothpicks. Secure the tortilla parcels by damping the final fold with a little water. When you lay the burritos in the dish, place them with the folded surfaces down.

5 Wrap the tortillas in aluminum foil and place them on a plate. Stand the plate over boiling water for about 5 minutes. Alternatively, wrap in microwave-safe plastic wrap and heat in a microwave on full power for 1 minute.

6 Spoon one-eighth of the filling into the center of a tortilla and fold in both sides. Fold the bottom up and the top down to form a parcel. Secure with a toothpick.

7 Put the filled burrito in a shallow dish or casserole, cover with foil, and keep warm in the oven while you make seven more. Remove the toothpicks before serving, sprinkled with fresh oregano.

CHICKEN AND TOMATILLO CHIMICHANGAS

THESE FRIED BURRITOS ARE A COMMON SIGHT ON STREET STALLS AND IN CAFÉS ALONG THE MEXICAN BORDER WITH TEXAS, BUT ARE NOT SO WELL KNOWN FURTHER SOUTH.

SERVES FOUR

INGREDIENTS

2 skinless, boneless chicken breasts
1 chipotle chile, seeded
1 tablespoon vegetable oil
2 onions, finely chopped
4 garlic cloves, crushed
½ teaspoon ground cumin
½ teaspoon ground coriander
½ teaspoon ground cinnamon
½ teaspoon ground cloves
scant 2 cups drained canned
   tomatillos
2⅓ cups cooked pinto beans
8 x 8–10-inch fresh flour
   tortillas
oil, for frying
salt and ground black pepper

1 Put the chicken breasts in a large pan, pour in water to cover, and add the chile. Bring to a boil, lower the heat, and simmer for 10 minutes, or until the chicken is cooked through and the chile has softened. Remove the chile and chop it finely. Lift the chicken breasts out of the pan and put them on a plate. Let cool slightly, then shred with two forks.

2 Heat the oil in a frying pan. Sauté the onions until translucent, then add the garlic and ground spices, and cook for 3 more minutes. Add the tomatillos and pinto beans. Cook over medium heat for 5 minutes, stirring constantly to break up the tomatillos and some of the beans. Simmer gently for 5 more minutes. Add the chicken and seasoning.

3 Wrap the tortillas in aluminum foil and place them on a plate. Stand the plate over boiling water for about 5 minutes until they become pliable. Alternatively, wrap them in microwave-safe plastic wrap and heat them in a microwave on full power for 1 minute.

4 Spoon one-eighth of the bean filling into the center of a tortilla, fold in both sides, then fold the bottom of the tortilla up and the top down to form a neat parcel. Secure with a toothpick.

5 Heat the oil in a large frying pan and fry the chimichangas in batches until crisp, turning once. Remove them from the oil with a slotted spoon and drain on paper towels. Serve hot.

COOK'S TIP

The word "pinto" means speckled, which aptly describes these attractive dried beans. If you prepare them yourself, they will need to be soaked overnight in water, then cooked in unsalted boiling water for 1–1¼ hours, until tender.

DRUNKEN CHICKEN

TEQUILA IS THIS CHICKEN'S MAGIC INGREDIENT, AND THE DISH HAS A DELICIOUS SWEET-AND-SOUR FLAVOR. SERVE IT WITH GREEN OR YELLOW RICE AND FLOUR TORTILLAS TO MOP UP THE SAUCE.

2 Heat the remaining vegetable oil in a large, deep frying pan. Add the onion slices and crushed garlic and cook for 2–3 minutes. Meanwhile, peel, core, and dice the apples.

3 Add the diced apple to the onion mixture with the almonds and plantain slices. Cook, stirring occasionally, for 3–4 minutes, then add the soaked raisins, with any remaining sherry. Add the chicken pieces to the pan.

4 Pour the stock and tequila over the chicken mixture. Cover the pan with a lid and cook for 15 minutes, then take off the lid and cook for 10 more minutes or until the sauce has reduced by about half.

SERVES FOUR

INGREDIENTS
scant 1 cup raisins
½ cup sherry
1 cup all-purpose flour
½ teaspoon salt
½ teaspoon ground black pepper
3 tablespoons vegetable oil
8 skinless chicken thighs, bone-in
1 onion, halved and thinly sliced
3 garlic cloves, crushed
2 tart apples, such as
  Granny Smith
1 cup sliced almonds
1 ripe plantain, peeled and sliced
1½ cups well-flavored chicken stock
1 cup tequila
fresh herbs, chopped, to garnish
  (optional)

1 Put the raisins in a bowl and pour in the sherry. Set aside to plump up. Season the flour with the salt and pepper and spread it out on a large, flat dish or soup plate. Heat 2 tablespoons of the oil in a large frying pan. Dip each chicken thigh in turn in the seasoned flour, then fry in the hot oil until browned, turning occasionally. Drain on paper towels.

5 Check that the chicken thighs are cooked by lifting one out of the pan and piercing it in the thickest part with a sharp knife or skewer. Any juices that come out should be clear. If necessary, cook the chicken for a little longer before serving, sprinkled with chopped fresh herbs, if desired.

COLOMBIAN CHICKEN HOT-POT

COLOMBIANS ARE JUSTIFIABLY PROUD OF THIS NATIONAL DISH. TRADITIONALLY, THREE NATIVE VARIETIES OF POTATOES ARE USED, EACH WITH A DIFFERENT TEXTURE, TO CREATE A TASTY THICK BROTH. THE ADDITION OF CILANTRO AND CORN PROVIDES A COMPLEMENTARY SWEETNESS.

SERVES EIGHT

INGREDIENTS
  3½ pounds chicken
  3 scallions
  2 bay leaves
  6 fresh cilantro sprigs
  6 whole black peppercorns
  1½ pounds floury potatoes, peeled
    and cut into ½-inch chunks
  1½ pounds waxy potatoes, peeled
    and cut into ½-inch chunks
  1½ pounds baby new potatoes or
    salad potatoes
  2 corn cobs, each cut into 4 pieces
  salt
  capers and sour cream, to serve
For the avocado salsa
  1 hard-boiled egg
  1 large ripe avocado
  1 scallion, finely chopped
  1 tablespoon chopped fresh
    cilantro
  1 fresh green chile, seeded and finely
    chopped
  salt

1 Put the chicken in a large pan or flameproof casserole and cover with water. Add the scallions, bay leaves, cilantro sprigs, and peppercorns. Season, bring to the boil, and skim the surface of the liquid.

2 Reduce the heat to a gentle simmer, cover, and cook for 1 hour or until the chicken is tender and fully cooked. Remove from the heat and allow the chicken to cool in the cooking liquid.

3 Drain the chicken, reserving the cooking liquid to use as stock. Place the chicken on a board and cut it into 8 pieces. It should be so tender that the legs are easy to pull off.

4 Separate the thighs from the drumsticks. Use a knife to cut between the two breasts, then gently ease the meat off the bone. Cut the breasts in half, set the chicken pieces aside on a plate, and discard the rest of the carcass.

5 Skim the fat from the top of the cooking liquid, then strain it into a clean pan. Bring to the boil. Add the floury and waxy potatoes and simmer for 15 minutes. Stir in the new potatoes or salad potatoes and corn and simmer for a further 20 minutes.

6 By this time, the floury potatoes will have broken up, and they will have helped to thicken the liquid. The waxy potatoes should be soft and partly broken. The new or salad potatoes should be tender but still whole. Return the chicken pieces to the pan and reheat gently but thoroughly.

7 Meanwhile, make the fresh avocado salsa. Peel and roughly chop the hard-boiled egg. Using a fork, mash it in a small bowl.

8 Just before serving, cut the avocado in half lengthwise and, using a teaspoon, scoop the flesh into a separate bowl. Mash well with a fork, then stir in the chopped hard-boiled egg until thoroughly combined. Add the scallions, fresh cilantro, and chile, mix well, then season to taste with salt.

9 Serve the chicken mixture in a heated casserole or earthenware dish, with bowls of hot tomato salsa, capers, and sour cream on the side, if you like.

COOK'S TIP
The quality and flavor of the chicken stock in this dish will depend entirely on what kind of chicken you use. It is worth spending a bit more and buying the best bird you can find, preferably free-range, corn-fed, or organic. You will really taste the difference.

CHICKEN WITH CHIPOTLE SAUCE

IT IS IMPORTANT TO USE CHIPOTLE CHILES IN THIS RECIPE, AS THEY IMPART A WONDERFULLY RICH AND SMOKY FLAVOR TO THE CHICKEN BREASTS. THE PUREE CAN BE MADE AHEAD OF TIME, MAKING THIS A VERY EASY RECIPE FOR ENTERTAINING.

SERVES SIX

INGREDIENTS
  6 chipotle chiles
  scant 1 cup water
  chicken stock (see method)
  3 onions
  6 boneless chicken breasts
  3 tablespoons vegetable oil
  salt and ground black pepper
  fresh oregano to garnish

1 Put the dried chiles in a bowl and pour in hot water to cover. Let stand for about 30 minutes, until very soft. Drain, reserving the soaking water in a measuring cup. Cut off the stem from each chile, then slit them lengthwise and scrape out the seeds with a small sharp knife.

2 Preheat the oven to 350°F. Chop the flesh of the chiles roughly and put it in a food processor or blender. Add enough chicken stock to the soaking water to make 1⅔ cups. Pour it into the processor or blender and process at maximum power until smooth.

3 Peel the onions. Using a sharp knife, cut them in half, then slice them thinly. Separate the slices.

4 Remove the skin from the chicken breasts and trim off any stray pieces of fat or membrane.

5 Heat the oil in a large frying pan, add the onions, and cook over low to medium heat for about 5 minutes, or until they have softened but not colored, stirring occasionally.

6 Using a slotted spoon, transfer the onion slices to a casserole that is large enough to hold all the chicken breasts in a single layer. Sprinkle the onion slices with a little salt and ground black pepper.

COOK'S TIP
If you are a lover of chipotle chiles, you may wish to use more than six.

7 Arrange the chicken breasts on top of the onion slices. Sprinkle with a little salt and several grindings of black pepper.

8 Pour the chipotle puree onto the chicken breasts, making sure that each piece is evenly coated.

9 Place the casserole in the preheated oven and bake for 45 minutes–1 hour or until the chicken is cooked through but is still moist and tender. Garnish with fresh oregano and serve with boiled white rice, and Frijoles de Olla.

SPINACH AND POTATO STUFFED CHICKEN BREASTS

THIS DISH CONSISTS OF LARGE CHICKEN BREASTS FILLED WITH A HERBED SPINACH MIXTURE, TOPPED WITH BUTTER AND BAKED UNTIL MOUTH-WATERINGLY TENDER.

2 Stir the spinach into the potato with the egg and cilantro. Season with salt and pepper to taste.

3 Cut almost all the way through the chicken breasts and open out to form a pocket in each. Spoon the filling into the center and fold the chicken back over again. Secure with toothpicks and place in a roasting pan.

4 Dot with butter and cover with foil. Bake for 25 minutes. Remove the foil and cook for a further 10 minutes until the chicken is golden.

5 Meanwhile, to make the sauce, heat the tomatoes, garlic, and stock in a pan. Boil rapidly for 10 minutes. Season and stir in the cilantro. Remove the chicken from the oven and serve with the sauce and fried mushrooms.

SERVES SIX

INGREDIENTS
　4 ounces floury potatoes, diced
　4 ounces spinach leaves,
　　finely chopped
　1 egg, beaten
　2 tablespoons chopped fresh
　　cilantro
　4 large chicken breasts
　4 tablespoons butter
For the sauce
　14-ounce can chopped tomatoes
　1 garlic clove, crushed
　⅔ cup hot chicken stock
　2 tablespoons chopped fresh cilantro
　salt and ground black pepper
　fried mushrooms, to serve

1 Preheat the oven to 350°F. Boil the potatoes in a large pan of lightly salted boiling water for 15 minutes or until tender. Drain the potatoes, place them in a large bowl, and roughly mash with a fork.

COOK'S TIP
Young spinach leaves have a sweeter flavor and are ideal for this dish.

MOLE POBLANO ^{DE} GUAJOLOTE

MOLE POBLANO DE GUAJOLOTE IS THE GREAT FESTIVE DISH OF MEXICO. IT IS SERVED AT ANY SPECIAL OCCASION, BE IT A BIRTHDAY, WEDDING, OR FAMILY GET-TOGETHER. RICE, BEANS, TORTILLAS, AND GUACAMOLE ARE THE TRADITIONAL ACCOMPANIMENTS.

SERVES SIX–EIGHT

INGREDIENTS
6–8 pounds turkey, cut into
   serving pieces
1 onion, chopped
1 garlic clove, chopped
6 tablespoons shortening or corn oil
salt
fresh cilantro and 2 tablespoons
   toasted sesame seeds, to garnish
For the sauce
6 dried ancho chiles
4 dried pasilla chiles
4 dried mulato chiles
1 drained canned chipotle chiles,
   seeded and chopped (optional)
2 onions, chopped
2 garlic cloves, chopped
1 pound tomatoes, peeled and chopped
1 stale tortilla, torn into pieces
⅓ cup seedless raisins
1 cup ground almonds
3 tablespoons sesame seeds, ground
½ teaspoon coriander seeds, ground
1 teaspoon ground cinnamon
½ teaspoon ground anise
¼ teaspoon ground black
   peppercorns
4 tablespoons vegetable shortening or
   corn oil
1½ ounces bitter chocolate, broken
   into squares
1 tablespoon sugar
salt and ground pepper

1 Put the turkey pieces in a pan or flameproof casserole large enough to hold them in one layer. Add the onion and garlic, and enough cold water to cover. Season with salt, bring to a simmer, cover, and cook for about 1 hour, or until the turkey pieces are thoroughly cooked.

2 Meanwhile, put the ancho, pasilla, and mulato chiles in a dry frying pan over a low heat and roast them for a few minutes, shaking the pan frequently.

3 Remove the stems and shake out the seeds. Tear the pods into pieces and put these into a small bowl. Add sufficient warm water to just cover, and soak, turning occasionally, for 30 minutes, until soft.

4 Lift out the turkey pieces and pat them dry with paper towels. Reserve the stock in a measuring pitcher. Heat the shortening or oil in a large frying pan and sauté the turkey pieces until lightly browned all over. Transfer to a plate and set aside. Reserve the oil that is left in the frying pan.

5 Tip the chiles, with the water in which they have been soaked, into a food processor. Add the chipotle chile, if using, with the onions, garlic, tomatoes, tortilla, raisins, ground almonds, and spices. Process to a puree. Do this in batches if necessary.

6 Add the oil to the frying pan used for sautéing the turkey. Heat the mixture, then add the chile and spice paste. Cook, stirring, for 5 minutes. Transfer the mixture to the pan or casserole in which the turkey was originally cooked. Stir in 2 cups of the turkey stock.

7 Add the chocolate, and season with salt and pepper. Cook over a low heat until the chocolate has melted. Stir in the sugar. Add the turkey, cover, and simmer gently for 30 minutes.

PEANUT CHICKEN

THE RICH SAUCE FOR THIS POPULAR CARIBBEAN DISH IS BEST MADE WITH SMOOTH PEANUT BUTTER,
ALTHOUGH IT CAN ALSO BE MADE WITH GROUND PEANUTS.

SERVES FOUR

INGREDIENTS
2 pounds boneless chicken
   breast portions, skinned and
   cut into cubes
2 garlic cloves, crushed
½ teaspoon dried thyme
½ teaspoon ground black pepper
1 tablespoon curry powder
1 tablespoon lemon juice
2 tablespoons butter or margarine
1 onion, chopped
3 tablespoons chopped tomatoes
1 fresh hot chile, seeded
   and chopped
2 tablespoons smooth peanut butter
scant 2 cups warm water
salt
fresh cilantro sprigs,
   to garnish
fried plantain, to serve
okra, to serve

1 Put the chicken in a large bowl and stir in the garlic, thyme, black pepper, curry powder, lemon juice, and a little salt. Cover and marinate in a cool place for 3–4 hours.

2 Melt the butter or margarine in a large pan. Add the onion, sauté gently for 5 minutes, then add the seasoned chicken. Fry over a medium heat for 10 minutes, turning frequently, and then stir in the tomatoes and chile.

3 In a small bowl, blend the peanut butter to a smooth paste with a little of the warm water and stir this paste into the chicken mixture.

4 Gradually stir in the remaining water, then simmer gently for about 30 minutes or until the chicken is fully cooked. Add a little more water if the sauce begins to dry out. Garnish with sprigs of fresh cilantro and serve hot with slices of fried plantain and okra.

BREAST OF TURKEY WITH MANGO AND WINE

FRESH TROPICAL MANGO AND WARM CINNAMON COMBINE TO GIVE A REAL TASTE OF THE CARIBBEAN.

SERVES FOUR

INGREDIENTS
4 turkey breast fillets
1 small ripe mango
1 garlic clove, crushed
¼ teaspoon ground cinnamon
1 tablespoon finely chopped
   fresh parsley
1 tablespoon crushed oyster crackers
3 tablespoons butter or margarine
1 garlic clove, crushed
6 shallots, sliced
⅔ cup white wine
salt and ground black pepper
diced fresh mango and chopped fresh
   parsley, to garnish

1 Cut a slit horizontally into each turkey fillet to make a pocket. Using a sharp knife, peel the mango and cut the flesh off the pit. Finely chop enough of the flesh to make 2 tablespoons and roughly dice the remainder.

2 Mix the garlic, cinnamon, parsley, cracker crumbs, and finely chopped mango in a bowl. Add 1 tablespoon of the butter or margarine with salt and pepper to taste and mash together.

3 Spoon a little of the mango mixture into each of the pockets in the turkey breast fillets and close, securing with a wooden toothpick if necessary. Season with a little extra ground black pepper.

4 Melt the remaining butter in a frying pan and sauté the crushed garlic and sliced shallots for about 5 minutes. Add the turkey fillets and cook for 15 minutes, turning once. Add the wine, cover, and simmer for 5–10 minutes, until the turkey is cooked. Add the mango, heat, and serve garnished with parsley.

CHICKEN FAJITAS

THE PERFECT DISH FOR CASUAL ENTERTAINING, FAJITAS ARE FLOUR TORTILLAS THAT ARE BROUGHT TO THE TABLE FRESHLY COOKED. GUESTS ADD THEIR OWN FILLINGS BEFORE FOLDING UP THE TORTILLAS.

SERVES SIX

INGREDIENTS
   3 skinless, boneless chicken breasts
   finely grated zest and juice of
     2 limes
   2 tablespoons sugar
   2 teaspoons dried oregano
   ½ teaspoon cayenne pepper
   1 teaspoon ground cinnamon
   2 onions
   3 bell peppers (1 red, 1 yellow or
     orange, and 1 green)
   3 tablespoons vegetable oil
   guacamole, salsa, and sour cream,
     to serve
For the tortillas
   2¼ cups all-purpose flour, sifted
   ¼ teaspoon baking powder
   pinch of salt
   ¼ cup shortening
   ¼ cup warm water

1 Slice the chicken breasts into ¾-inch wide strips and place these in a large bowl. Add the lime zest and juice, sugar, oregano, cayenne, and cinnamon. Mix thoroughly. Set aside to marinate for at least 30 minutes.

COOK'S TIP
Tortilla dough can be very difficult to roll out thinly. If the dough is breaking up, try placing each ball between two sheets of clean plastic wrap (this can be cut from a new sandwich bag). Roll out, turning over, still inside the plastic, until the tortilla is the right size.

2 Meanwhile, make the tortillas. Mix the flour, baking powder, and salt in a large bowl. Rub in the shortening, then add the warm water, a little at a time, to make a stiff dough. Knead this on a lightly floured surface for 10–15 minutes, until it is smooth and elastic.

3 Divide the dough into 12 small balls, then roll each ball into a 6-inch round. Cover the rounds with plastic wrap to keep them from drying out while you prepare the vegetables.

4 Cut the onions in half and slice them thinly. Cut the peppers in half, remove the cores and seeds, then slice the flesh into ½-inch wide strips.

5 Heat a large frying pan or griddle and cook each tortilla in turn for about 1 minute on each side or until the surface colors and begins to blister. Keep the cooked tortillas warm and pliable by wrapping them in a clean, dry dish towel.

6 Heat the oil in a large frying pan. Stir-fry the marinated chicken for 5–6 minutes, then add the bell peppers and onions, and cook for 3–4 more minutes more, until the chicken strips are cooked through and the vegetables are soft and tender, but still juicy.

7 Spoon the chicken mixture into a serving bowl and take it to the table with the cooked tortillas, guacamole, salsa, and sour cream. Keep the tortillas wrapped and warm.

8 To serve, each guest takes a warm tortilla, spreads it with a little salsa, adds a spoonful of guacamole, and piles some of the chicken mixture in the center. The final touch is to add a small dollop of sour cream. The tortilla is then folded over the filling and eaten.

BARBECUED JERK CHICKEN

JERK SEASONING IS A BLEND OF HERBS AND SPICES THAT IS RUBBED INTO MEAT BEFORE IT IS COOKED OVER CHARCOAL SPRINKLED WITH PIMIENTO BERRIES. IN JAMAICA, JERK SEASONING WAS ORIGINALLY USED ONLY FOR PORK, BUT JERKED CHICKEN TASTES JUST AS GOOD.

2 Make several lengthwise slits in the flesh on the chicken pieces. Place the chicken pieces in a dish and spoon the jerk seasoning over them. Use your hands to rub the seasoning into the chicken, especially into the slits.

3 Cover with plastic wrap and marinate for at least 4–6 hours or overnight in the refrigerator.

SERVES FOUR

INGREDIENTS
   8 chicken pieces
   oil, for brushing
   salad leaves, to serve
For the jerk seasoning
   1 teaspoon ground allspice
   1 teaspoon ground cinnamon
   1 teaspoon dried thyme
   ¼ teaspoon freshly grated nutmeg
   2 teaspoons raw sugar
   2 garlic cloves, crushed
   1 tablespoon finely chopped onion
   1 tablespoon chopped scallion
   1 tablespoon vinegar
   2 tablespoons oil
   1 tablespoon lime juice
   1 fresh hot chile pepper, chopped
   salt and ground black pepper

1 Make the jerk seasoning. Combine the ground allspice, cinnamon, thyme, grated nutmeg, sugar, garlic, both types of onion, vinegar, oil, lime juice, and chile pepper in a small bowl. Use a fork to mash them together until a thick paste is formed. Season to taste with a little salt and plenty of ground black pepper.

4 Preheat the broiler or prepare the barbecue. Shake off any excess seasoning from the chicken and brush the pieces with oil. Either place on a baking sheet and broil for 45 minutes, or cook on the barbecue for about 30 minutes. Whichever method you choose, it is important to turn the chicken pieces frequently. Serve hot with salad leaves.

COOK'S TIP
The flavor is best if you marinate the chicken overnight. If cooking on the barbecue, sprinkle the charcoal with aromatic herbs, such as rosemary or bay leaves, for even more flavor.

THYME AND LIME CHICKEN

LIMES GROWN IN LATIN AMERICA TEND TO BE PALER THAN THE ONES IN OUR SUPERMARKETS, BUT THEY ARE JUICY AND FULL OF FLAVOR. THIS CARIBBEAN RECIPE, WHICH COMBINES THEM WITH FRAGRANT THYME, IS A GREAT VEHICLE FOR THEM.

SERVES FOUR

INGREDIENTS
8 chicken thighs
2 tablespoons chopped scallion
2 teaspoons chopped fresh thyme or
1 teaspoon dried thyme
2 garlic cloves, crushed
juice of 2 limes or 1 lemon
6 tablespoons butter, melted
salt and ground black pepper
cooked rice, to serve
To garnish
lime slices
fresh cilantro sprigs

3 Spoon the remaining butter evenly over the top of the chicken pieces. Cover the dish tightly with plastic wrap and leave to marinate for at least 3–4 hours in the refrigerator. For the best flavor, prepare the chicken the day before and leave to marinate overnight.

4 Preheat the oven to 375°F. Remove the plastic wrap and cover the chicken with foil. Bake for about 1 hour, then remove the foil and cook for a further 5–10 minutes, until the chicken turns golden brown. Garnish with lime slices and fresh cilantro and serve with rice.

1 Put the chicken thighs skin-side down in a baking dish or roasting pan. Using a sharp knife, make a lengthwise slit along the thighbone of each. Mix the scallion with a little salt and pepper and press the mixture into the slits.

2 Mix the thyme, garlic, and lime or lemon juice in a small bowl. Add 4 tablespoons of the butter and mix well, then spoon a little of the mixture over each chicken thigh, spreading evenly.

CHICKEN, PORK, AND POTATOES IN PEANUT SAUCE

THIS TRADITIONAL PERUVIAN DISH, KNOWN AS CARAPULCRA, IS MADE WITH PAPASECA (DRIED POTATOES), WHICH BREAK UP WHEN COOKED, TO THICKEN THE SAUCE. THE SAME EFFECT IS ACHIEVED HERE BY USING FLOURY POTATOES, THE KIND THAT DISINTEGRATE WHEN COOKED FOR A LONG TIME.

SERVES SIX

INGREDIENTS

- ¾ cup unsalted peanuts
- 4 tablespoons olive oil
- 3 chicken breast portions, halved
- 1¼ pounds boneless pork loin, cut into ¾-inch pieces
- 1 large onion, chopped
- 2–3 tablespoons water
- 3 garlic cloves, crushed
- 1 teaspoon paprika
- 1 teaspoon ground cumin
- 1¼ pounds floury potatoes, peeled and thickly sliced
- scant 2½ cups vegetable stock
- salt and ground black pepper
- cooked rice, to serve

To garnish

- 2 hard-boiled eggs, sliced
- ½ cup pitted black olives chopped fresh Italian parsley

1 Place the peanuts in a large dry frying pan over a low heat. Toast for about 2–3 minutes, until golden all over. Watch them closely, shaking the pan frequently, as they have a tendency to burn. Leave to cool, then process in a food processor until finely ground.

2 Heat half the olive oil in a heavy pan. Add the chicken pieces, season with salt and ground black pepper, and cook for 10 minutes, until golden brown all over. Transfer the pieces of chicken to a plate, using a slotted spoon.

3 Heat the remaining oil in the pan. When it is very hot, add the pork. Season and sauté for 3–4 minutes, until golden brown. Transfer to the plate containing the chicken pieces.

4 Lower the heat and stir the onion into the oil in the pan. Cook for 5 minutes, adding the water if it begins to stick. Stir in the garlic, paprika, and cumin, and cook for 1 minute more.

5 Add the potatoes, stir, and cover the pan. Cook for 3 minutes. Add the peanuts and stock. Bring to the boil, and simmer gently for 20–30 minutes.

6 Return the chicken and pork to the pan and bring to the boil. Lower the heat, replace the lid, and simmer for 6–8 minutes, until the meat is fully cooked. Avoid overcooking the meat or it will become tough and stringy.

7 Garnish the stew with the egg slices, black olives, and chopped parsley. Serve with the rice.

COOK'S TIP

If you cannot locate unsalted peanuts, buy a pack of salted ready-roasted peanuts, wash them under cold running water, then pat dry and grind.

SPICY FRIED CHICKEN

THIS TRADITIONAL CARIBBEAN CRISPY CHICKEN DISH IS SUPERB EATEN HOT OR COLD. SERVED WITH A SALAD OR VEGETABLES, IT MAKES A DELICIOUS LUNCH AND IS ALSO IDEAL FOR PICNICS OR SNACKS.

SERVES FOUR

INGREDIENTS
    4 chicken drumsticks
    4 chicken thighs
    2 teaspoons curry powder
    ½ teaspoon garlic granules or
        1 garlic clove, crushed
    ½ teaspoon ground black pepper
    ½ teaspoon paprika
    about 1¼ cups milk
    oil, for deep frying
    ½ cup all-purpose flour
    salt
    dressed salad leaves, to serve

1 Sprinkle the chicken pieces with curry powder, garlic, pepper, paprika, and a little salt. Rub into the chicken, then cover and marinate for at least 2 hours, or overnight in the refrigerator.

2 Preheat the oven to 350°F. Cover the chicken with milk and leave to stand for a further 15 minutes.

3 Heat the oil in a large pan or deep-fryer and tip the flour onto a plate. Dip the chicken pieces in flour and add to the oil, taking care not to overcrowd the pan. Fry until golden but not fully cooked.

4 Remove the chicken pieces with a slotted spoon and place on a baking sheet. Continue until all the chicken pieces have been fried.

5 Place the baking sheet in the oven and bake the chicken for around 30 minutes. Serve hot or cold with dressed salad leaves.

SUNDAY ROAST CHICKEN

MUCH OF THE PREPARATION FOR THIS DISH IS DONE THE NIGHT BEFORE, MAKING IT IDEAL FOR A FAMILY LUNCH. THE CHICKEN IS SUCCULENT AND FULL OF FLAVOR, WITH A RICH GRAVY.

SERVES SIX

INGREDIENTS

3½ pounds chicken
1 teaspoon paprika
1 teaspoon dried thyme
½ teaspoon dried tarragon
1 teaspoon garlic granules or
  1 garlic clove, crushed
1 tablespoon lemon juice
2 tablespoons clear honey
3 tablespoons dark rum
melted butter, for basting
1¼ cups chicken stock
lime quarters, to garnish

1 Place the chicken in a roasting pan and sprinkle with paprika, thyme, tarragon, garlic, and salt and pepper. Rub the mixture all over the chicken, including underneath the skin. Cover with plastic wrap and leave to marinate for at least 2 hours or overnight in the refrigerator.

2 Preheat the oven to 375°. Mix the lemon, honey, and rum in a bowl. Stir well, then pour over and under the chicken skin, rubbing it in well to ensure the flavors are absorbed.

3 Spoon melted butter all over the chicken, then transfer to the oven and roast for 1½–2 hours, until fully cooked.

VARIATION
Extra herbs and rum can be used to make a richer, tastier gravy.

4 Transfer the chicken to a serving dish while you make the gravy. Pour the pan juices into a small pan. Add the chicken stock. Simmer for 10 minutes or until the gravy has reduced and thickened slightly. Adjust the seasoning and pour into a serving pitcher. Garnish the chicken with the lime and serve.

TURKEY MOLE

A MOLE IS A RICH STEW, TRADITIONALLY SERVED ON A FESTIVE OCCASION. THE WORD COMES FROM THE AZTEC "MOLLI," MEANING A CHILI-FLAVORED SAUCE. THERE ARE MANY DIFFERENT TYPES, INCLUDING THE FAMOUS MOLE POBLANO DE GUAJALOTE. TOASTED NUTS, FRUIT, AND CHOCOLATE ARE AMONG THE CLASSIC INGREDIENTS; THIS VERSION INCLUDES COCOA POWDER.

SERVES FOUR

INGREDIENTS
    1 ancho chile, seeded
    1 guajillo chile, seeded
    ¾ cup sesame seeds
    ½ cup whole blanched almonds
    ½ cup shelled unsalted
        peanuts, skinned
    1 small onion
    2 garlic cloves
    ¼ cup shortening or 4 tablespoons
        vegetable oil
    ⅓ cup canned tomatoes in
        tomato juice
    1 ripe plantain
    ⅓ cup raisins
    ½ cup ready-to-eat prunes, pitted
    1 teaspoon dried oregano
    ½ teaspoon ground cloves
    ½ teaspoon crushed
        allspice berries
    1 teaspoon ground cinnamon
    ¼ cup unsweetened cocoa powder
    4 turkey breasts
    fresh oregano, to garnish
        (optional)

1 Soak both types of dried chile in a bowl of hot water for 30 minutes, then lift them out and chop them roughly. Reserve 1 cup of the soaking liquid.

COOK'S TIP
It is important to use good quality cocoa powder, which is unsweetened.

2 Spread out the sesame seeds in a heavy frying pan. Toast them over medium heat, shaking the pan lightly so that they turn golden all over. Do not let them burn, or the sauce will taste bitter. Set aside 3 tablespoons of the toasted seeds for the garnish and put the rest in a bowl. Toast the almonds and peanuts in the same way and add them to the bowl.

3 Chop the onion and garlic finely. Heat half the shortening or oil in a frying pan, cook the chopped onion and garlic for 2–3 minutes, then add the chiles and tomatoes. Cook gently for 10 minutes.

4 Peel the plantain and slice it into short diagonal slices. Add it to the onion mixture with the raisins, prunes, dried oregano, spices, and cocoa. Stir in the 1 cup of the reserved water in which the chiles were soaked. Bring to a boil, stirring, then add the toasted sesame seeds, almonds, and peanuts. Cook for 10 minutes, stirring frequently, then remove from heat and let cool slightly.

5 Blend the sauce in batches in a food processor or blender until smooth. The sauce should be fairly thick, but a little water may be added if necessary.

6 Heat the remaining shortening or oil in a flameproof casserole. Add the turkey and brown over medium heat.

7 Pour the sauce onto the steaks and cover the casserole with aluminum foil and a tight-fitting lid. Cook over low heat for 20–25 minutes, or until the turkey is cooked and the sauce has thickened. Sprinkle with sesame seeds and chopped oregano, and serve with a rice dish and warm tortillas.

PERUVIAN DUCK WITH RICE

DUCK IS VERY POPULAR IN PERU. IN THIS RECIPE, THE RICE IS COOKED IN THE SAME LIQUID AS THE DUCK, SO IT ABSORBS THE AROMATIC FLAVORS OF THE HERBS AND SPICES.

SERVES SIX

INGREDIENTS
2 fresh red chiles, seeded
4 garlic cloves, roughly chopped
5 fresh cilantro stalks
1 teaspoon ground cumin
3 duck legs
salt and ground black pepper
1 large onion, finely chopped
2½ cups chicken stock
1 cup red wine
1¾ cups long-grain rice
1 cup frozen peas, thawed
1 tablespoon chopped fresh cilantro,
to garnish

VARIATION
If you find duck too fatty for your tastes, try making this dish with chicken legs or rabbit. It will be just as delicious.

1 Put the fresh chiles, garlic cloves, cilantro stalks, and ground cumin in a blender or food processor and process to a thick paste.

2 Cut the duck legs in half to separate the thigh from the drumstick. Place in a large, heavy pan with a tight-fitting lid. Place over a low heat. Season the duck with salt and ground black pepper. Cook until golden brown on all sides, set the duck aside, and pour away most of the fat, leaving about 2 tablespoons.

3 Add the onion to the pan and cook gently for 5 minutes. Stir in the chile and cilantro paste and cook for a further 2 minutes. Return the duck to the pan, pour in the stock and wine, and bring to the boil. Cover, reduce the heat, and simmer for 45 minutes.

4 Stir the rice into the pan, replace the lid, and cook for 18–20 minutes. Stir in the peas and remove from the heat. Leave to stand for 5 minutes and serve with a sprinkling of chopped cilantro.

DRUNKEN DUCK

THIS IS A LOVELY DISH FOR A DINNER PARTY. THE DUCK AND SWEET POTATOES COOK IN THE RED WINE AND WARM SPICES, CREATING A RICH, ALMOST CHOCOLATE-LIKE SAUCE.

SERVES FOUR

INGREDIENTS
1 duck, about 5 pounds
1 large onion, thinly sliced
½ teaspoon crushed dried chiles
2 garlic cloves, crushed
¼ teaspoon ground cloves
¼ teaspoon ground allspice
½ teaspoon ground cinnamon
1¾ pounds sweet potatoes, peeled
and cut into thick wedges
1 cup red wine
1 cup chicken stock
salt and ground black pepper
polenta or cooked rice, to serve

1 Preheat the oven to 400°F. Season the inside and outside of the duck. Place the duck in a large flameproof casserole over a low heat and cook, turning occasionally, until the skin has released some of its fat and turned a rich golden brown. Transfer the duck to a plate.

2 Pour away most of the duck fat from the pan, leaving about 2 tablespoons. Return the casserole to the heat, add the onion and crushed chiles, and stir well to coat in the fat, incorporating any sediment on the bottom of the pan.

3 Cook for 5 minutes until the onion is soft and translucent. Stir in the garlic and spices, and cook for 1 minute more.

4 Return the duck to the casserole, arrange the sweet potatoes around it, and pour in the wine and stock. Bring to the boil and cover. Move the dish to the oven and cook for 1¼–1½ hours.

5 Skim the fat from the top of the sauce and serve with soft polenta or plain rice.

VEGETARIAN DISHES AND SALADS

Although vegetarianism is not widespread in the Caribbean and Latin America, root vegetables, corn, and what might be considered exotic fruit and vegetables, such as heart of palm and okra, are used extensively. The salads in this chapter can either be enjoyed as a light lunch, as an appetizer, or as side dishes.

CORN SOUFFLÉ

LATIN AMERICAN SOUFFLÉS ARE QUITE DIFFERENT FROM THEIR FRENCH COUNTERPARTS. FOR EXAMPLE, THIS ONE WILL RISE ONLY SLIGHTLY, YET THE TEXTURE WILL STILL BE LIGHT AND AIRY.

SERVES SIX

INGREDIENTS
6 tablespoons butter
11 ounces sweet potato, peeled
  and cubed
11 ounces pumpkin, peeled
  and cubed
scant 2 cups frozen corn kernels,
  thawed
3 scallions, roughly chopped
5 ounces Cheddar cheese, grated
5 eggs
salt and ground black pepper

1 Preheat the oven to 350°F. Using 1 tablespoon of the butter, grease an 11 x 7-inch baking dish. Cook the sweet potato and pumpkin in a pan of lightly salted boiling water for 10 minutes, until tender. Drain and set aside.

2 Put 1½ cups of corn kernels into a food processor. Add the chopped scallions and process until smooth. Melt the remaining butter in a pan and stir in the corn and onion mixture. Cook, stirring, over a low heat, for about 1–2 minutes.

3 Add the cheese, stirring until it has melted. Season generously with salt and pepper. Remove from the heat.

4 Separate three of the eggs and add the remaining whole eggs to the bowl containing the yolks. Mix lightly, then stir the yolk mixture into the pan. Add the sweet potato, pumpkin, and remaining corn. Whisk the egg whites until stiff, then fold them into the soufflé mixture.

5 Transfer the mixture to the prepared dish and place the dish in a roasting pan. Pour in hot water to come halfway up the side of the dish and bake for 35–40 minutes, until golden. If the soufflé still wobbles when shaken gently, cook for a further 5–10 minutes. Leave to cool, then serve.

COOK'S TIP
For the best results, whisk the egg whites with a pinch of salt in a clean glass or metal bowl. When they are very stiff and no longer slide around the bowl when it is moved, they are ready for use.

LAYERED POTATO BAKE <u>WITH</u> CHEESE

INSPIRED BY THE PERUVIAN SIDE DISH, OCOPA AREQUIPENA, THIS FAMILY-SIZED POTATO CAKE IN A SPICY CHEESE AND WALNUT SAUCE IS SUBSTANTIAL ENOUGH FOR A MAIN COURSE.

4 Add the potatoes to a pan of salted water and cover. Bring to the boil, then simmer for 10 minutes. Drain and refresh under cold water. Drain again and cut into ½-inch slices. Shell the eggs and cut them into slices.

5 Preheat the oven to 350°F. Grease an 11 x 7-inch baking dish with butter. Arrange a layer of potatoes in the dish and generously spread with the prepared paste. Top with egg slices and a sprinkling of olives and pimiento strips. Continue layering until all the ingredients have been used, finishing with olives and pimientos.

6 Bake for 30 minutes, until the potatoes are very tender. Leave to cool for 5 minutes before serving.

SERVES SIX

INGREDIENTS

7 tablespoons olive oil
1 large onion, chopped
2 garlic cloves, crushed
1 teaspoons crushed dried chili
generous 1 cup walnut halves
generous ½ cup fresh cheese,
  such as ricotta
7 tablespoons warm water
3 eggs
1 pound large potatoes, peeled
butter, for greasing
scant ¾ cup pitted black olives
4 pimientos, cut into strips
salt

1 Heat 2 tablespoons of the oil in a small pan over a low heat. Add the chopped onion and sauté gently for 5 minutes, until softened. Stir in the garlic and crushed dried chili and cook for a further 2 minutes.

2 Put the walnuts in a blender or food processor. Blend until smooth, then add the cooked onion mixture, with the cheese and remaining olive oil. Season generously with salt and pour in the warm water. Blend to make a smooth paste. Set aside.

3 Put the eggs in a small pan of cold water. Bring to the boil, then lower the heat to a simmer. Cook for 10 minutes, then cool in a bowl of cold water.

FRIJOLES

In the Yucatán peninsula, where these spicy beans are very popular, black navy beans are cooked with the Mexican herb epazote.

SERVES SIX TO EIGHT

INGREDIENTS

1¾ cups dried red kidney, pinto, or
    black navy beans, picked over and
    rinsed
2 onions, finely chopped
2 garlic cloves, chopped
1 bay leaf
1 or more serrano chiles
    (small fresh green chiles)
2 tablespoons corn oil
2 tomatoes, peeled, seeded
    and chopped
salt
sprigs of fresh bay leaves,
    to garnish

1 Put the beans into a pan and add cold water to cover by 1 inch. Add half the onion, half the garlic, the bay leaf and chile(s). Bring to the boil, and boil vigorously for 10 minutes. Put the beans and liquid into an earthenware pot or large pan, cover, and cook over a low heat for 30 minutes. Add boiling water if the mixture becomes dry.

2 When the beans begin to wrinkle, add 1 tablespoon of the corn oil and cook for a further 30 minutes, or until the beans are tender. Add salt to taste and cook for 30 minutes more.

3 Remove the beans from the heat. Heat the remaining oil in a small frying pan and sauté the remaining onion and garlic until the onion is soft. Add the tomatoes and cook for 2–3 minutes.

5 Spoon 3 tablespoons of the beans into the tomato mixture. Mash to a paste. Stir this into the beans to thicken the liquid. Cook for just long enough to heat through, if necessary. Serve the beans in small bowls and garnish with sprigs of fresh bay leaves.

BLACK BEAN BURRITOS

BURRITOS—STUFFED TORTILLAS—ARE ONE OF THE MOST POPULAR SNACK FOODS IN MEXICO. IN THIS RECIPE THEY ARE STUFFED WITH SPICY BEANS AND TOPPED WITH A CHEESE SAUCE.

SERVES FOUR

INGREDIENTS

1 cup dried black beans,
   soaked overnight and drained
1 bay leaf
3 tablespoons sea salt
1 small red onion, chopped
2 cups grated cheese
3 tablespoons chopped pickled jalapeños
1 tablespoon chopped cilantro
3 cups tomato salsa
8 flour tortillas
diced avocado, to serve

1 Place the beans in a pan. Add water to cover and the bay leaf. Bring to the boil, cover, and simmer for 30 minutes. Add the salt and continue simmering for about 30 minutes, until tender. Drain and cool slightly. Discard the bay leaf.

2 Preheat the oven to 350ºF. Grease an ovenproof dish.

3 Combine the beans, onion, half the cheese, the jalapeños, cilantro, and one-third of the salsa. Stir and season.

4 Place one tortilla on a clean work surface. Spread a large spoonful of the filling down the middle, then roll it up to enclose the filling completely. Place the burrito in the prepared dish, seam-side down. Repeat this process with the remaining tortillas until the dish is full.

5 Sprinkle the remaining cheese over the burritos, in an even line right down the middle. Bake in the oven for about 15 minutes, or until the cheese melts completely and starts to bubble and brown. Do not overheat, as the edges of the tortilla will become dry and crisp.

6 Serve the bean burritos immediately, garnished with diced avocado and the remaining salsa. To make a more hearty meal, serve with a side salad, a potato salad, or a mixed bean salad.

CHILI CHEESE TORTILLA <u>WITH</u> FRESH TOMATO SALSA

GOOD WARM OR COLD, THIS IS LIKE A SLICED POTATO QUICHE WITHOUT THE PASTRY BASE, WELL SPIKED WITH CHILES. THE SALSA CAN BE MADE WITHOUT THE CHILES IF YOU PREFER.

SERVES FOUR

INGREDIENTS

3 tablespoons sunflower-seed or olive oil
1 small onion, thinly sliced
2–3 fresh green jalapeño chiles,
   seeded and sliced
7 ounces cold cooked potato,
   thinly sliced
generous 1 cup cheese, grated (use a
   firm but not hard cheese, such as
   Monterey Jack or Manchego)
6 eggs, beaten
salt and ground black pepper
fresh herbs, to garnish
For the salsa
1¼ pounds tomatoes, peeled, seeded,
   and finely chopped
1 fresh mild green chile, seeded and
   finely chopped
2 garlic cloves, crushed
3 tablespoons chopped fresh
   cilantro
juice of 1 lime
½ teaspoon salt

3 Using a slotted spoon, transfer the vegetables to a warm plate. Wipe the pan with paper towels, then add the remaining oil and heat until really hot. Return the vegetables to the pan. Scatter the cheese over the top. Season.

4 Pour in the beaten eggs, making sure that they seep under the vegetables. Cook the tortilla over a low heat, without stirring, until set. Serve hot or cold, cut into wedges, garnished with fresh herbs and with the salsa on the side.

1 To make the salsa, put the tomatoes in a bowl and add the chopped chiles, garlic, cilantro, lime juice, and salt. Mix well and set aside.

2 Heat 1 tablespoon of the oil in a large omelet pan and gently fry the onion and jalapeños for 5 minutes, stirring until softened. Add the potato and cook for 5 minutes until lightly browned, keeping the slices whole.

POTATO AND ONION TORTILLA

*THIS DEEP-SET TORTILLA WITH SLICED POTATOES AND ONIONS IS A STAPLE SNACK OR DISH
ORIGINATING FROM SPAIN AND POPULAR THROUGHOUT LATIN AMERICA. ADD CHEESE, HERBS, AND
OTHER VEGETABLES TO MAKE THIS INTO A MORE HEARTY MEAL.*

SERVES THREE TO FOUR

INGREDIENTS
  1¾ pounds medium potatoes
  scant ½ cup extra virgin olive oil
  2 onions, thinly sliced
  6 eggs
  sprigs of cilantro or parsley, to
    garnish

1 Peel and thinly slice the potatoes and
onions. Set the onions to one side.

2 Heat 5 tablespoons of the oil in a
frying pan and cook the potatoes,
turning frequently, for 10 minutes.

3 Add the onions and seasoning,
turning occasionally. Continue to cook
gently for a further 10 minutes, until the
onions are transparent and golden and
the potatoes are tender.

4 Meanwhile, break the eggs into a bowl
and beat them. Add a little seasoning.
Add the potatoes and onions, and mix
gently. Leave to stand for 10 minutes.

5 Wipe out the pan with paper towels
and heat the remaining oil in it. Pour
the egg, potato, and onion mixture into
the pan and spread it out in an even
layer. Cover and cook over a very gentle
heat for 20 minutes, until the eggs are
just set. Serve cut into wedges.

HEART OF PALM PIE

THE DELICATE CREAMY FILLING IN THIS PIE CONTRASTS BEAUTIFULLY WITH THE CRUMBLY PASTRY.
THIS RECIPE CAN ALSO BE USED TO MAKE SMALL BRAZILIAN EMPADINHAS—BABY SAVORY PIES—NOT TO
BE CONFUSED WITH EMPANADAS, THE LITTLE TURNOVERS.

SERVES EIGHT

INGREDIENTS
    5 cups all-purpose flour
    1 teaspoon salt
    ¾ cup butter
    6 tablespoons vegetable shortening
    1 egg yolk
    3 tablespoons cold water
For the filling
    2 tablespoons butter
    1 large onion, finely chopped
    4 garlic cloves, crushed
    1 tablespoon all-purpose flour
    scant 1 cup whole milk
    2 hard-boiled eggs, roughly chopped
    1 large tomato, peeled, seeded
        and cubed
    1 fresh red chile, seeded and
        finely chopped
    2 x 14-ounce cans heart of palm,
        drained and cut into ¾-inch slices
    1 tablespoon chopped fresh
        Italian parsley
    salt and ground black pepper
To glaze
    1 egg yolk
    1 tablespoon water

1 Place the flour, salt, butter, and vegetable shortening in a food processor and process until the mixture resembles fine bread crumbs. With the motor still running, add the egg yolk and the cold water. As soon as the mixture comes together, transfer to a floured surface. Knead it lightly until smooth. Divide the pastry into two rounds, one slightly larger than the other, wrap both in plastic wrap, and place in the refrigerator while you make the filling.

2 Melt the butter in a frying pan over a low heat. Stir in the chopped onion and cook for 5 minutes until soft. Add the garlic and cook for a further 2 minutes.

3 Stir the flour into the pan and cook, stirring, for 1 minute. Remove from the heat and slowly pour in the milk, a little at a time, stirring to prevent any lumps from forming.

4 Return to the heat and cook, stirring constantly, for 2 minutes to make a thin white sauce. Remove from the heat and stir in the chopped hard-boiled eggs, cubed tomato, chile, palm hearts, and parsley. Season with salt and pepper.

5 Preheat the oven to 375°F. Place a large baking sheet on the central shelf so that it heats up.

6 On a floured surface, roll out the larger piece of pastry and line the base and sides of a 9-inch round loose-based quiche pan. The pastry will be very crumbly, so it may tear in a few places. Should this happen, use your fingers to push the pastry together again. There should be no gaps.

7 Add the filling, then roll out the remaining pastry and use to top the pie. Do not worry about any small gaps in the pastry, as they add to the rustic character of the dish.

8 Make the glaze by mixing the egg yolk with the water. Using a pastry brush, glaze the pastry, then place the quiche pan on the heated baking sheet and bake the pie for 45 minutes, until the pastry is golden.

9 Leave the pie to cool for 5 minutes on a wire rack before removing it from the pan and putting it onto a large plate. Serve warm or at room temperature.

COOK'S TIP
Cooking the pie on a heated baking sheet ensures that the pastry cooks thoroughly, avoiding a soggy base.

MACARONI CHEESE PIE

MACARONI CHEESE IS A FAVORITE DISH ON THE ISLAND OF BARBADOS, WHERE IT IS OFTEN SERVED AS AN ACCOMPANIMENT, INSTEAD OF A STARCHY VEGETABLE SUCH AS POTATO. THIS TREATMENT MAKES AN EXCELLENT VEGETARIAN MAIN COURSE.

SERVES FOUR

INGREDIENTS

2 cups macaroni
3 tablespoons butter or margarine
3 tablespoons all-purpose flour
scant 2 cups milk
1 teaspoon mild mustard
½ teaspoon ground cinnamon
6 ounces sharp Cheddar cheese,
  grated
1 egg, beaten
1 tablespoon butter or margarine
2 tablespoons chopped scallion
3 tablespoons canned
  chopped tomatoes
⅔ cup corn kernels
salt and ground black pepper
chopped fresh parsley, to garnish

1 Heat the oven to 350°F. Cook the macaroni in a pan of salted boiling water for 10 minutes. Drain, rinse under cold water, and drain again.

2 Melt 2 tablespoons of the butter in a pan and add the flour. Cook for 1 minute, then add the milk, whisking constantly. Heat until the mixture boils, then simmer gently for 5–10 minutes.

3 Stir in the mustard and cinnamon, with two-thirds of the cheese. Season to taste. Cook gently, stirring frequently, until the cheese has melted, then remove from the heat and whisk in the egg. Cover closely and set aside.

4 Heat the remaining butter or margarine in a small frying pan and cook the scallion, chopped tomatoes, and corn over a gentle heat for 5–10 minutes.

5 Tip half the cooked macaroni into a greased ovenproof dish. Pour over half the cheese sauce and mix well, then spoon the tomato and corn mixture evenly over the mixture.

6 Tip the remaining macaroni into the pan containing the cheese sauce, stir well, and then spread carefully over the tomato and corn mixture.

7 Top with the remaining grated cheese. Bake for about 45 minutes, or until the top is golden and bubbly. If possible, leave to stand for 30 minutes before serving, garnished with parsley.

RED BEAN CHILI

SATISFYING, SPICY AND SIMPLE TO PREPARE, THIS VEGETARIAN CARIBBEAN VERSION OF THE CLASSIC MEXICAN CHILI IS COMFORT FOOD AT ITS BEST. EXPERIMENT WITH DIFFERENT TYPES OF CHILE PEPPERS, INCLUDING DRIED VARIETIES LIKE THE MEXICAN CHIPOTLES.

SERVES FOUR

INGREDIENTS

   2 tablespoons vegetable oil
   1 onion, chopped
   14-ounce can chopped tomatoes
   2 garlic cloves, crushed
   1¼ cups white wine
   about 1¼ cups vegetable stock
   1 cup red lentils
   2 fresh thyme sprigs or 1 teaspoon
     dried thyme
   2 teaspoons ground cumin
   3 tablespoons dark soy sauce
   ½ fresh hot chile, seeded and
     finely chopped
   1 teaspoon pumpkin pie spice
   1 tablespoon oyster sauce (optional)
   8-ounce can red kidney
     beans, drained
   2 teaspoons sugar
   salt
   boiled white rice with corn,
     to serve

1 Heat the oil in a pan and fry the onion for 2–3 minutes, until slightly softened.

2 Add the tomatoes and garlic, cook for about 10 minutes, then stir in the white wine and vegetable stock.

VARIATION
This vegetarian chili can be adapted to accommodate meat-eaters by substituting either ground beef or lamb for the lentils.

3 Stir in the lentils, thyme, cumin, soy sauce, chile, spice, and oyster sauce, if using.

COOK'S TIP
Fiery chiles can irritate the skin, so always wash your hands thoroughly after handling them and avoid touching your eyes.

4 Cover and simmer for 40 minutes or until the lentils are cooked, stirring occasionally and adding more water if the lentils begin to dry out.

5 Stir in the kidney beans and sugar and cook for 10 minutes more. Season to taste and serve with boiled white rice and corn.

PEPPERS STUFFED <u>WITH</u> BEANS

STUFFED PEPPERS ARE A POPULAR MEXICAN DISH. A SPECIAL VERSION—CHILES EN NOGADA—IS SERVED ON 28 AUGUST TO MARK INDEPENDENCE DAY. THE GREEN PEPPERS ARE SERVED WITH A FRESH WALNUT SAUCE AND POMEGRANATE SEEDS TO REPRESENT THE COLORS OF THE MEXICAN FLAG.

SERVES SIX

INGREDIENTS
- 6 large green bell peppers
- 2 eggs, separated
- ½ teaspoon salt
- corn oil, for frying
- all-purpose flour, for dusting
- ½ cup whipping cream
- 1 cup grated Cheddar cheese
- fresh cilantro sprigs,
  to garnish

For the beans
- 1¼ cups dried red kidney, pinto, or
  black navy beans
- 2 onions, finely chopped
- 2 garlic cloves, finely chopped
- 1 bay leaf
- 1 or more serrano chiles
- 8–10 tablespoons corn oil
- 2 tomatoes, peeled and chopped

1 Put the beans into a pan and add cold water to cover. Add half the chopped onion, half the garlic, the bay leaf, and the chiles. Boil vigorously for about 10 minutes. Transfer the beans and liquid into a large flameproof casserole or pan, then cover and cook over a low heat for 30 minutes.

2 Add 1 tablespoon of the corn oil to the beans and cook for a further, 30 minutes or until the beans are tender. Add salt to taste and cook for 30 minutes more.

3 Remove the beans from the heat. Heat the remaining oil in a small frying pan and sauté the remaining onion and garlic until soft. Add the tomatoes and cook for a few minutes more. Add the tomato and onion mixture to the beans.

4 Roast the peppers over a gas flame or under a medium broiler, turning occasionally, until the skins have blackened and blistered. Transfer the peppers to a plastic bag, secure the top and leave for 15 minutes.

5 Meanwhile, heat 2 tablespoons of the oil in a large frying pan. Add about 3 tablespoons of the beans. Mash them with a wooden spoon or potato masher, gradually adding more beans and oil until they have formed a heavy paste.

6 Preheat the oven to 350°. Remove the peppers from the bag. Hold each pepper in turn under cold running water and rub off the skins. Slit the peppers down one side and remove the seeds and ribs. Stuff with the beans.

7 Beat the egg whites in a bowl until they stand in firm peaks. In another bowl, beat the yolks together with the salt. Fold gently into the whites.

8 Pour the corn oil into a large frying pan to a depth of about 1 inch and heat. Spread out the flour in a shallow bowl or dish.

9 Dip the filled peppers in the flour and then in the egg mix. Fry in batches until golden brown all over. Arrange the peppers in an ovenproof dish. Pour over the cream and sprinkle with the cheese. Bake for 30 minutes or until the topping is golden brown and the peppers are hot. Serve garnished with fresh cilantro.

BLACK-EYED PEA STEW <u>WITH</u> SPICY PUMPKIN

THIS WONDERFULLY WARM AND TASTY DISH IS A HEARTY WINTER FAVORITE IN CENTRAL AMERICA AND THE CARIBBEAN, ALTHOUGH IT CAN ALSO BE FOUND THROUGHOUT MEXICO. THE PUMPKIN ADDS A SWEETNESS, MAKING THIS DELICIOUS COMFORT DISH.

SERVES THREE TO FOUR

INGREDIENTS
   1¼ cups black-eyed peas, soaked
     overnight
   1 onion, chopped
   1 green or red bell pepper, seeded
     and chopped
   2 garlic cloves, chopped
   1 vegetable bouillon cube
   1 thyme sprig or 1 teaspoon
     dried thyme
   1 teaspoon paprika
   ½ teaspoon apple pie spice
   2 carrots, sliced
   1–2 tablespoons palm oil
   salt and hot pepper sauce
For the spicy pumpkin
   1½ pounds pumpkin
   1 onion
   2 tablespoons butter or margarine
   2 garlic cloves, crushed
   3 tomatoes, peeled and chopped
   ½ teaspoon ground cinnamon
   2 teaspoons curry powder
   pinch of grated nutmeg
   ⅔ cup water
   salt, hot pepper sauce, and
     ground black pepper

1 Drain the peas, place in a pan, and cover with water. Bring to the boil.

2 Add the onion, green or red pepper, garlic, bouillon cube, herbs, and spices. Simmer for 45 minutes, or until the beans are just tender. Season to taste with salt and a little hot pepper sauce.

3 Add the carrots and palm oil and continue cooking for 10–12 minutes, until the carrots are cooked, adding a little more water if necessary. Remove from the heat and set aside.

4 To make the spicy pumpkin, cut the pumpkin into cubes and finely chop the onion.

5 Melt the butter or margarine in a large pan and add the pumpkin, onion garlic, tomatoes, spices, and water. Stir well to combine and simmer until the pumpkin is soft.

6 Season to taste with salt, hot pepper sauce, and black pepper. Serve with the black-eyed peas.

SPICY VEGETABLE CHOW MEIN

CHOW MEIN IS POPULAR IN GUYANA, WHERE IT IS USUALLY MADE WITH SHREDDED CHICKEN OR SHRIMP. THIS VEGETARIAN VERSION CAN BE ADAPTED TO SUIT ALL TASTES.

SERVES THREE

INGREDIENTS

8 ounces egg noodles
¾ cup fine green beans
2–3 tablespoons vegetable oil
2 garlic cloves, crushed
1 onion, chopped
1 small red bell pepper, chopped
1 small green bell pepper, chopped
2 celery sticks, finely chopped
½ teaspoon five-spice powder
1 vegetable bouillon cube
½ teaspoon ground black pepper
1 tablespoon soy sauce (optional)
salt

COOK'S TIP
Shredded omelet or sliced hard-boiled eggs are popular garnishes for chow mein.

1 Cook the noodles in a large pan of salted boiling water for 10 minutes or according to the instructions on the package. Drain and cool. Blanch the beans.

2 Heat the oil in a wok or large frying pan and stir-fry the garlic, onion, red and green peppers, beans, and celery, tossing them together to mix.

3 Add the five-spice powder, vegetable bouillon cube, and ground black pepper, stir well, and cook for 5 minutes, until the vegetables are just tender but still slightly crunchy.

4 Stir in the noodles and soy sauce, if using. Taste the chow mein and season with salt if required. Serve immediately.

EGGPLANTS STUFFED WITH SWEET POTATO

SLICES OF EGGPLANT ROLLED AROUND A SWEET POTATO AND CHEESE FILLING MAKE AN UNUSUAL CARIBBEAN SUPPER DISH, OR TRY THEM AS AN APPETIZER FOR A VEGETARIAN MEAL.

SERVES FOUR

INGREDIENTS

I cup sweet potatoes, peeled and
   quartered
½ teaspoon chopped fresh thyme
¾ cup Cheddar cheese, diced
2 tablespoons chopped scallion
1 tablespoon each chopped red and
   green bell pepper
1 garlic clove, crushed
2 large eggplants
2 tablespoons all-purpose flour
1 tablespoon spice seasoning
olive oil, for frying
butter, for greasing
2 tomatoes, sliced
salt and ground black pepper
chopped fresh parsley,
   to garnish

1 Preheat the oven to 350°F. Cook the sweet potatoes in a pan of boiling water for 15–20 minutes, until tender, then drain and mash.

2 Add the thyme, cheese, scallion, peppers, and garlic. Mix well and season.

3 Cut each eggplant lengthwise into four slices. Mix the flour and spice seasoning on a plate and dust over each eggplant slice.

4 Heat a little oil in a large frying pan and fry each eggplant slice until browned, but not fully cooked. Drain and cool. Spoon a little of the potato mixture into the middle of each eggplant slice and roll up.

5 Butter two large pieces of foil and cover with the slices of tomato. Place four rolls on each piece of foil. Wrap up the parcels and bake for 20 minutes. Serve hot, garnished with the parsley.

TOMATO RICE AND BEANS WITH AVOCADO SALSA

MEXICAN-STYLE RICE AND BEANS MAKE A DELICIOUS SUPPER DISH. SPOON ONTO TORTILLAS AND SERVE WITH A TANGY SALSA. ALTERNATIVELY, SERVE AS AN ACCOMPANIMENT TO A SPICY STEW.

SERVES FOUR

INGREDIENTS

¼ cup dried or ½ cup canned kidney beans, rinsed and drained
8 tomatoes, halved and seeded
2 garlic cloves, chopped
1 onion, sliced
3 tablespoons olive oil
generous 1 cup long-grain brown rice, rinsed
2½ cups vegetable stock
2 carrots, diced
¾ cup green beans
salt and ground black pepper
4 wheat-flour tortillas and sour cream, to serve

For the avocado salsa
1 avocado
juice of 1 lime
1 small red onion, diced
1 small fresh red chile, seeded and chopped
1 tablespoon chopped fresh cilantro

1 If using dried kidney beans, place in a bowl, cover with cold water, and leave to soak overnight, then drain and rinse well. Place in a pan with enough water to cover and bring to the boil. Boil rapidly for 10 minutes, then reduce the heat. Simmer for 40–50 minutes until tender; drain and set aside.

2 Make the avocado salsa. Halve and pit the avocado. Peel and dice the flesh, then toss it in the lime juice. Add the onion, chile, and cilantro. Mix well.

3 Preheat the broiler to high. Place the tomatoes, garlic, and onion on a baking tray. Pour over 1 tablespoon of the oil and toss to coat. Broil for 10 minutes or until the tomatoes and onions are softened, turning once. Set aside to cool. Heat the remaining oil in a pan, add the rice, and cook for 2 minutes, stirring, until light golden.

4 Puree the cooled tomatoes and onion in a food processor or blender, then add the mixture to the rice and cook for a further 2 minutes, stirring frequently. Pour in the vegetable stock, then cover, and cook gently for 20 minutes, stirring occasionally.

5 Stir 2 tablespoons of the kidney beans into the salsa. Add the rest to the rice mixture with the carrots and green beans, and cook for 10 minutes, until the vegetables are tender. Season well. Remove the pan from the heat and leave to stand, covered, for 15 minutes.

6 Warm the tortillas and place one on each serving plate. Spoon the hot rice and bean mixture on top. Serve immediately, with the avocado salsa and a bowl of sour cream.

LEEK, SQUASH, AND TOMATO GRATIN

COLORFUL AND SUCCULENT, YOU CAN USE VIRTUALLY ANY KIND OF SQUASH FOR THIS AUTUMN GRATIN, FROM PATTY PANS AND ACORN SQUASH TO PUMPKINS.

SERVES FOUR TO SIX

INGREDIENTS

1 pound peeled and seeded squash, cut into ½-inch slices
4 tablespoons olive oil
1 pound leeks, cut into thick, diagonal slices
1½ pounds tomatoes, peeled and thickly sliced
½ teaspoon ground toasted cumin seeds
1¼ cups light cream
1 fresh red chile, seeded and sliced
1 garlic clove, finely chopped
1 tablespoon chopped fresh mint
2 tablespoons chopped fresh parsley
4 tablespoons fine white bread crumbs
salt and ground black pepper

VARIATION
For a curried version of this dish, use ground coriander as well as cumin, and coconut milk instead of cream. Use fresh cilantro instead of the mint and parsley.

1 Steam the squash over boiling salted water for 10 minutes.

2 Heat half the oil in a frying pan and cook the leeks gently for 5–6 minutes until lightly colored. Try to keep the slices intact. Preheat the oven to 375°F.

3 Layer all the squash, leeks, and tomatoes in an 8-cup gratin dish, arranging them in rows. Season with salt, pepper, and cumin.

4 Pour the cream into a small pan and add the sliced chile and chopped garlic. Bring to the boil over a low heat, then stir in the mint. Pour the mixture evenly over the layered vegetables, using a rubber spatula to scrape all the sauce out of the pan.

5 Cook for 50–55 minutes, or until the gratin is bubbling and tinged brown. Sprinkle the parsley and bread crumbs on top and drizzle over the remaining oil. Bake for another 15–20 minutes, until the bread crumbs are browned and crisp. Serve immediately.

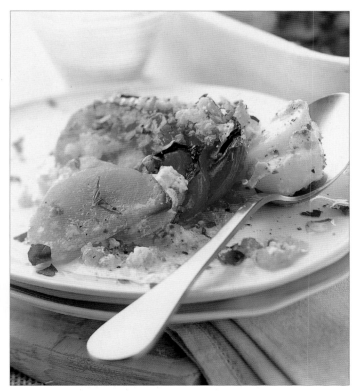

BEAN AND TOMATO CASSEROLE

JUICY TOMATOES AND FILLING CANNELLINI BEANS BAKED—A GREAT DISH FOR A COLD DAY.

SERVES FOUR

INGREDIENTS
   3 tablespoons extra virgin olive oil or
     sunflower-seed oil
   3 tablespoons chopped fresh Italian
     parsley
   14-ounce can cannellini beans,
     rinsed and drained
   2¼ pounds firm ripe tomatoes
   1 teaspoon superfine sugar
   scant 1 cup day-old bread crumbs
   ½ teaspoon chili powder or paprika
   salt
   chopped fresh parsley, to garnish
   rye bread, to serve

1 Preheat the oven to 400°F. Brush a large ovenproof dish with 1 tablespoon of the oil.

2 Sprinkle the chopped Italian parsley over the base of the dish and cover with the beans. Cut the tomatoes into even slices, discarding the two end slices of each. Arrange the slices of tomato in the dish over the beans so that they overlap slightly. Sprinkle them with a little salt and the sugar.

3 In a mixing bowl, stir together the bread crumbs, the remaining olive or sunflower-seed oil and chili powder or paprika, whichever you are using.

4 Sprinkle the crumb mixture over the tomatoes, and bake in the oven for 50 minutes. Serve hot or cold, garnished with chopped parsley and accompanied by rye bread.

MIXED VEGETABLE CASSEROLE

THE VEGETABLES IN THIS RICH TOMATO SAUCE CAN BE VARIED ACCORDING TO SEASON.

SERVES FOUR

INGREDIENTS
   1 eggplant, diced into 1-inch pieces
   ½ cup okra, halved lengthwise
   1 cup frozen or fresh peas or baby
     peas
   ¾ cup green beans, cut into 1-inch
     pieces
   14-ounce can small cannellini beans,
     rinsed and drained
   4 zucchini, cut into ½-inch pieces
   2 onions, finely chopped
   1 pound potatoes, diced into
     1-inch pieces
   1 red bell pepper, seeded and sliced
   14-ounce can chopped tomatoes
   ⅔ cup vegetable stock
   4 tablespoons olive oil
   5 tablespoons chopped fresh parsley
   1 teaspoon paprika
   salt
   crusty bread, to serve
For the topping
   6 tomatoes, sliced
   1 zucchini, sliced

1 Slice the tomatoes and zucchini for the topping.

2 Put all the other ingredients in an ovenproof dish, combine them well.

3 Preheat the oven to 375°F. Arrange alternate slices of tomato and zucchini attractively on the top of the other vegetables.

4 Put the lid on or cover the casserole tightly with foil. Bake in the oven for 60–70 minutes, until all the vegetables are tender. Remove the lid or foil for the last 15 minutes to brown the topping slightly, if you like. Serve either hot or cold with wedges of crusty bread.

COOK'S TIP
For the finest flavor, use extra virgin olive oil in the bake and vine-ripened or home-grown tomatoes for the topping.

SPINACH PLANTAIN ROUNDS

THIS DELECTABLE WAY OF SERVING PLANTAINS IS POPULAR THROUGHOUT THE CARIBBEAN ISLANDS.
THE PLANTAINS MUST BE FAIRLY RIPE, BUT STILL FIRM. THE ROUNDS CAN BE SERVED EITHER HOT OR
COLD, WITH A SALAD, OR AS A VEGETABLE ACCOMPANIMENT.

SERVES FOUR

INGREDIENTS
   2 large ripe plantains
   oil, for frying
   2 tablespoons butter or margarine
   2 tablespoons finely chopped onion
   2 garlic cloves, crushed
   1 pound fresh spinach, chopped
   pinch of freshly grated nutmeg
   1 egg, beaten
   whole-wheat flour,
      for dusting
   salt and ground black pepper

1 Using a small sharp knife, carefully cut each plantain lengthwise into four pieces.

2 Heat a little oil in a large frying pan and fry the pieces of plantain on both sides until golden brown but not fully cooked. Lift out and drain on paper. towels. Reserve the oil in the pan.

3 Melt the butter or margarine in a separate pan and sauté the onion and garlic for 2–3 minutes, until the onion is soft. Add the spinach and nutmeg, with salt and pepper to taste. Cover and cook for about 5 minutes, until the spinach has wilted. Cool, then tip into a strainer and press out any excess moisture.

4 Curl the plantain pieces into rings and secure each ring with half a wooden toothpick. Pack each ring with a little of the spinach mixture.

5 Place the egg and flour in two separate shallow dishes. Add a little more oil to the frying pan, if necessary, and heat until medium hot. Dip the plantain rings in the egg and then in the flour and fry on both sides for 1–2 minutes, until golden brown. Drain on paper towels and serve.

PEPPERY BEAN SALAD

THIS PRETTY CARIBBEAN SALAD USES CANNED BEANS FOR SPEED AND CONVENIENCE. THE CONTRAST BETWEEN THE CRISP RADISHES AND PEPPERS AND THE SOFTER TEXTURE OF THE BEANS IS ONE REASON WHY IT WORKS SO WELL. THE TASTY DRESSING PLAYS A PART, TOO.

SERVES SIX

INGREDIENTS
   15-ounce can kidney beans, drained
   15-ounce can black-eyed peas,
   drained
   15-ounce can chickpeas, drained
   ¼ red bell pepper
   ¼ green bell pepper
   6 radishes
   1 tablespoon chopped scallion
   sliced scallion, to garnish
For the dressing
   1 teaspoon ground cumin
   1 tablespoon tomato ketchup
   2 tablespoons olive oil
   1 tablespoon white wine vinegar
   1 garlic clove, crushed
   ½ teaspoon hot pepper sauce
   salt

1 Drain the canned beans and chickpeas into a colander and rinse them thoroughly under cold running water. Shake off the excess water and tip them into a large salad bowl.

2 Core, seed, and roughly chop the peppers. Trim the radishes and slice them thinly. Add to the beans with the chopped pepper and scallion.

COOK'S TIP
For maximum flavor, it is best to allow the ingredients to marinate for at least 3–4 hours.

3 In a small bowl, mix the ground cumin, ketchup, olive oil, white wine vinegar, and garlic. Add the hot pepper sauce and a little salt to taste, and stir again until thoroughly mixed.

4 Pour the dressing over the salad and mix thoroughly with a fork. Cover with plastic wrap and chill for at least 1 hour before serving, garnished with sliced scallion.

AVOCADO AND GRAPEFRUIT SALAD

THIS IS A LIGHT, REFRESHING LUNCHTIME SALAD. THE BUTTERY TEXTURE OF THE AVOCADOS, COMBINES WITH THE TANGINESS OF THE GRAPEFRUIT TO MAKE THE PERFECT SUMMER DISH. SERVE IT AS A LIGHT MAIN COURSE OR AS AN ACCOMPANIMENT TO BARBECUED MEATS.

SERVES FOUR

INGREDIENTS
  6 tablespoons olive oil
  2 tablespoons white wine vinegar
  1 pink grapefruit
  2 large ripe avocados
  1 romaine lettuce, separated into
    leaves
  salt and ground black pepper

1 Using a balloon whisk or a fork, whisk the olive oil and white wine vinegar together in a large bowl, season to taste with salt and ground black pepper, and vigorously whisk again.

VARIATIONS
Try other fruit combinations. Mango and strawberries go well together, as do papaya and limes.

2 Slice the top and bottom off the grapefruit. Peel the fruit by running a small knife all around it, between the peel and flesh. Make sure all the bitter pith is removed. Hold the grapefruit over the bowl containing the dressing and cut carefully between the membranes, so that all the segments fall into the bowl. Squeeze the remaining pulp over the bowl to extract all the juice.

3 Run a knife around the length of the avocados. Twist the sides in opposite directions to separate the halves. Use a large spoon to remove the pit, then peel the halves. Slice the flesh and cover these with the dressing, to stop them from discoloring.

4 Tear the lettuce into pieces and add to the bowl. Toss to coat. Adjust the seasoning to taste and serve.

QUINOA SALAD WITH CITRUS DRESSING

QUINOA IS A TYPE OF GRAIN GROWN IN THE ANDES. A STAPLE FOOD OF THE REGION, IT HAS BEEN CULTIVATED SINCE THE TIME OF THE INCAS AND AZTECS. QUINOA IS PACKED WITH PROTEIN AND IS ALSO GLUTEN FREE, SO IT IS IDEAL FOR VEGETARIANS AND THOSE WHO ARE GLUTEN INTOLERANT.

SERVES SIX

INGREDIENTS
1 cup quinoa
6 tablespoons olive oil
juice of 2 limes
juice of 1 large orange
2 fresh green chiles, seeded and
  finely chopped
2 garlic cloves, crushed
½ cucumber, peeled
1 large tomato, seeded and cubed
4 scallions, sliced
2 tablespoons chopped fresh mint
1 tablespoon chopped fresh
  Italian parsley
salt

COOK'S TIP
Quinoa can also be eaten plain as an accompaniment to meat or fish dishes.

1 Put the quinoa in a strainer, rinse thoroughly under cold water, then tip into a large pan. Pour in cold water to cover and bring to the boil. Lower the heat and simmer for 10–12 minutes, until tender. Drain and leave to cool.

2 Make a dressing by whisking the oil with the citrus juices. Stir in the chiles and garlic, and season with salt.

3 Cut the cucumber in half lengthwise and, using a teaspoon, scoop out and discard the seeds. Cut into ¼-inch slices and add to the cooled quinoa with the tomato, scallions, and herbs. Toss well to combine.

4 Pour the dressing over the salad and toss again until well mixed. Check the seasoning and serve.

OKRA AND TOMATO SALAD

FOR THIS SALAD THE OKRA IS COOKED AS LITTLE AS POSSIBLE, KEEPING IT CRUNCHY. SERVE AS A SIDE SALAD, OR STIR IN SOME BABY SPINACH FOR A MEMORABLE MAIN COURSE.

<u>SERVES FOUR</u>

INGREDIENTS
    4 tablespoons olive oil
    1 tablespoon red wine vinegar
    1 red onion, very thinly sliced
    3 tomatoes, peeled and seeded
    14 ounces okra
    salt and ground black pepper

1 In a large bowl, whisk together the olive oil and red wine vinegar. Season with salt and ground black pepper. Toss the slices of red onion into the dressing and leave to marinate while you prepare and cook the okra.

2 Trim the tough stalks from the okra, but avoid cutting into the pods, otherwise you will release a sticky liquid. Cook the okra in a pan of lightly salted boiling water for 4–5 minutes, until just tender. Drain and dry on paper towels. Leave the small okra whole, but cut any larger ones diagonally in half.

3 Stir the cooked okra into the dressing, mix thoroughly, and leave to marinate for about 20–25 minutes.

4 Cut the tomatoes into thin wedges and add them to the bowl. Gently toss them together with the okra. Season to taste with salt and ground black pepper and serve immediately.

TOMATO, HEART OF PALM, AND ONION SALAD

THIS SIMPLE SALAD CAN BE ASSEMBLED IN MINUTES. IT IS AN EXCELLENT DISH FOR INTRODUCING ANYONE TO THE DELICATE FLAVOR OF PALM HEARTS.

<u>SERVES FOUR</u>

INGREDIENTS
    4 beefsteak tomatoes
    1 small onion, thinly sliced
    14-ounce can hearts of palm
For the dressing
    juice of 1 lime
    2 teaspoons Dijon mustard
    4 tablespoons olive oil
    salt and ground black pepper

1 Cut the tomatoes into ½-inch slices and arrange on a large serving platter. Sprinkle the thin onion slices over the tomatoes and season to taste with salt and ground black pepper.

3 Make the dressing by whisking the lime juice, mustard, and oil in a bowl. Season with salt and ground pepper. Drizzle over the salad and serve.

COOK'S TIP
If the tomatoes are not perfectly ripe, sprinkle the slices with a large pinch of superfine sugar, to help bring out their sweetness.

2 Drain the canned hearts of palm thoroughly, cut them into ½-inch slices, and sprinkle the slices over the tomatoes and onions.

VARIATION
If you cannot get hearts of palm, this salad will be just as delicious using artichoke hearts instead.

CHAYOTES WITH CORN AND CHILES

SHAPED LIKE PEARS OR AVOCADOS, CHAYOTES ARE MEMBERS OF THE SQUASH FAMILY AND HAVE A RATHER BLAND TASTE. HOWEVER, THEY MARRY EXTREMELY WELL WITH OTHER INGREDIENTS, SUCH AS THE CORN AND ROASTED JALAPEÑOS IN THIS MEXICAN MEDLEY.

SERVES SIX

INGREDIENTS
  4 fresh jalapeño chillies
  3 chayotes
  oil, for frying
  1 red onion, finely chopped
  3 garlic cloves, crushed
  1⅓ cups corn kernels, thawed
    if frozen
  ⅔ cup cream cheese
  1 teaspoon salt (optional)
  ⅓ cup freshly grated Parmesan
    cheese

1 Dry-roast the fresh jalapeño chiles in a griddle pan, turning them frequently so that the skins blacken but do not burn. Place them in a plastic bag, tie the top securely, and set them aside for 20 minutes.

2 Meanwhile, peel the chayotes, cut them in half, and remove the seed from each of them. Cut the flesh into ½-inch cubes.

COOK'S TIP
Chayotes go by several names, including christophene and choko. Store them in a plastic bag in the refrigerator and they will keep for up to 1 month.

3 Heat the oil in a frying pan. Add the onion, garlic, chayote cubes, and corn. Fry over a moderate heat for 10 minutes, stirring occasionally.

4 Remove the jalapeños from the bag, peel off the skins, and remove any stems. Cut them in half, scrape out the seeds, then cut the flesh into strips.

5 Add the chiles and cream cheese to the pan, stirring gently, until the cheese melts. Place in a serving dish.

6 Stir in salt, if needed, then spoon into a warmed dish. Sprinkle with Parmesan cheese and serve. This makes a good accompaniment for cold roast meats.

SPINACH SALAD

YOUNG SPINACH LEAVES MAKE A WELCOME CHANGE FROM LETTUCE AND ARE EXCELLENT IN THIS MEXICAN SALAD. THE ROASTED GARLIC IS AN INSPIRED ADDITION TO THE DRESSING.

SERVES SIX

INGREDIENTS

    1¼ pounds baby spinach leaves
    ⅓ cup sesame seeds
    ¼ cup butter
    2 tablespoons olive oil
    6 shallots, sliced
    8 fresh serrano chiles, seeded and
      cut into strips
    4 tomatoes, sliced
For the dressing
    6 roasted garlic cloves
    ½ cup white wine vinegar
    ½ teaspoon ground white pepper
    1 bay leaf
    ½ teaspoon ground allspice
    2 tablespoons chopped fresh thyme,
      plus extra sprigs, to garnish

COOK'S TIP
To roast individual garlic cloves simply place in a roasting tray in a moderate oven for about 15 minutes until soft.

1 Make the dressing. Remove the skins from the garlic when cool, then chop and combine with the vinegar, pepper, bay leaf, allspice, and chopped thyme in a jar with a screw-top lid. Close the lid tightly, shake well, then put the dressing in the refrigerator until needed.

2 Wash the spinach leaves and dry them in a salad spinner or clean dish towel. Put them in a plastic bag in the refrigerator.

3 Toast the sesame seeds in a dry frying pan, shaking frequently over a moderate heat until golden. Set aside.

4 Heat the butter and oil in a frying pan. Fry the shallots for 4–5 minutes, until softened, then stir in the chile strips and fry for 2–3 minutes more.

5 In a large bowl, layer the spinach with the shallot and chile mixture, and the tomato slices. Pour over the dressing. Sprinkle with sesame seeds and serve, garnished with thyme sprigs.

BAKED SWEET POTATO SALAD

THIS SALAD HAS A TRULY TROPICAL TASTE, BLENDING THE CREAMINESS OF THE NATURAL YOGURT WITH THE HEARTINESS OF THE SWEET POTATO. IT IS IDEAL SERVED WITH CARIBBEAN DISHES.

SERVES FOUR TO SIX

INGREDIENTS
2¼ pounds sweet potatoes
For the dressing
  3 tablespoons chopped fresh
    cilantro
  juice of 1 lime
  ⅔ cup plain yogurt
For the salad
  1 red bell pepper, seeded and
    finely diced
  3 celery sticks, finely diced
  ¼ red skinned onion, finely chopped
  1 red chile, finely chopped
  salt and ground black pepper
  cilantro leaves, to garnish

1 Preheat the oven to 400°F. Wash the potatoes, pierce them all over, and bake in the oven for 40 minutes or until tender.

2 Meanwhile, mix the dressing ingredients together in a bowl and season to taste. Chill while you prepare the remaining ingredients.

3 In a large bowl, mix the red bell pepper, celery, onion, and chile together.

4 Remove the potatoes from the oven and when cool enough to handle, peel them. Cut the potatoes into cubes and add them to the bowl. Drizzle the dressing over and toss carefully. Season again to taste and serve, garnished with fresh cilantro.

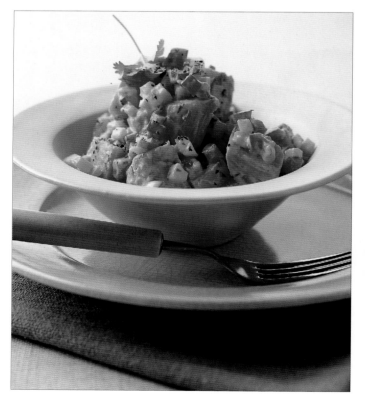

WARM HAZELNUT AND PISTACHIO SALAD

TWO KINDS OF CRUNCHY NUTS TURN ORDINARY POTATO SALAD INTO A REALLY SPECIAL ACCOMPANIMENT. SERVE WITH COLD SLICED MEAT OR ON ITS OWN AS A VEGETARIAN MEAL.

SERVES FOUR

INGREDIENTS
    2 pounds small new or salad potatoes
    2 tablespoons hazelnut or walnut oil
    4 tablespoons sunflower-seed oil
    juice of 1 lemon
    ¼ cup hazelnuts
    15 pistachio nuts
    salt and ground black pepper
    sprigs of Italian parsley,
        to garnish

VARIATION
Use chopped walnuts in place of the hazelnuts. Buy the broken pieces of nut, which are less expensive than walnut halves, but chop them smaller before adding to the salad.

1 Cook the potatoes in their skins in boiling salted water for about 10–15 minutes, until tender.

2 Drain the potatoes well and leave to cool slightly.

3 Meanwhile mix the hazelnut or walnut oil with the sunflower-seed oil and lemon juice. Season well.

4 Using a sharp knife, roughly chop the nuts.

5 Put the cooled potatoes into a large bowl and pour the dressing over. Toss to combine.

6 Sprinkle the salad with the chopped nuts. Serve immediately, garnished with Italian parsley.

JALAPEÑO <u>AND</u> SHRIMP SALAD

PICKLED JALAPEÑO CHILE GIVES A DISTINCTIVE SPICY FLAVOR TO THIS DELICIOUS SALAD.
IN MEXICO, IT IS QUITE USUAL TO SERVE SUCH A HEARTY SALAD AS A SEPARATE COURSE.

<u>SERVES FOUR</u>

INGREDIENTS

  1 iceberg lettuce or 2 Bibb lettuces
  4 tablespoons mayonnaise
  4 tablespoons sour cream
  3 cups cooked peeled shrimp,
    thawed if frozen
  ½ cup cooked green beans, chopped
  ½ cup cooked carrots, chopped
  ½ cucumber, chopped
  2 hard-boiled eggs, coarsely chopped
  1 drained pickled jalapeño chile,
    seeded and chopped
  salt

1 Line a large salad bowl or platter with the lettuce leaves. You can also chop the middle part of the lettuce up and combine it with the other ingredients.

2 Mix the mayonnaise and sour cream together in a small bowl and set aside.

3 Combine the shrimp, beans, carrot, cucumber, eggs, and chile in a separate bowl. Season with salt.

4 Fold the mayonnaise and sour cream mixture into the shrimp and pile into the lined salad bowl to serve.

Fava Bean, Mushroom, and Chorizo Salad

This salad can be served as a first course or as part of a buffet menu. Fresh fava beans are preferable for their taste, but frozen ones could be substituted.

SERVES FOUR

INGREDIENTS
    8 ounces shelled fava beans
    6 ounces chorizo sausage
    4 tablespoons extra virgin olive oil
    8 ounces cremini mushrooms, sliced
    handful of fresh chives
    salt and freshly ground black
        pepper

COOK'S TIP
This salad can be prepared a day in advance and stored in the refrigerator until needed, although it may not remain fresh and crisp for longer than a day, and the quality of the food will reduce if you keep it for longer periods. Remove from the refrigerator a few hours beforehand in order to allow the salad to reach room temperature before serving.

1 Cook the fava beans in a large pan of boiling, salted water until just tender. You can test them by breaking them in half and watching to see if they snap easily. If they begin to give between your fingers, they will be cooked sufficiently. Drain and refresh under cold running water.

2 If the beans are large, peel away the tough outer skins and discard them, setting aside the paler core.

3 Remove the skin from the chorizo sausage and cut it into small chunks. Heat the oil in a frying pan, add the chorizo, and cook for 2 minutes. Empty into a bowl with the mushrooms, mix well, and leave aside to cool.

4 Chop half the chives and stir the beans and chopped chives into the mushroom mixture. Season to taste. Serve the salad at room temperature, garnished with the remaining chives.

NOPALITOS SALAD

NOPALITOS—STRIPS OF PICKLED CACTUS PADDLES—ARE SOLD IN CANS OR JARS, AND ARE VERY USEFUL FOR MAKING QUICK AND EASY SALADS LIKE THIS ONE.

SERVES FOUR

INGREDIENTS
    scant 2 cups drained
        canned *nopalitos*
    1 red pepper
    2 tablespoons olive oil
    2 garlic cloves, sliced
    ½ red onion, thinly sliced
    ½ cup cider vinegar
    small bunch of cilantro, chopped
    salt

1 Preheat the broiler. Put the *nopalitos* in a bowl. Pour in water to cover and set aside for 30 minutes. Drain, replace with fresh water, and let soak for another 30 minutes.

2 Place the halves of the red pepper cut side down in a broiler. Broil the peppers until the skins blister and char, then put the pepper halves in a strong plastic bag, tie the top securely to keep the steam in, and set aside for 20 minutes.

3 Heat the oil in a small frying pan and fry the garlic over low heat until the slices start to turn golden. Using a slotted spoon, transfer them to a salad bowl. Pour the garlic-flavored oil into a pitcher and set it aside to cool.

4 Add the red onion slices to the salad bowl, then pour on the vinegar. Remove the red pepper from the bag, peel off the skins, then cut the flesh into thin strips. Add to the salad bowl.

5 Drain the *nopalitos* thoroughly and add them to the salad, with the cool garlic-flavored oil and a little salt, to taste. Toss lightly, then chill until needed. Sprinkle on the chopped cilantro just before serving. This is delicious served with crusty bread.

JICAMA, CHILE, AND LIME SALAD

A VERY TASTY, CRISP VEGETABLE, THE JICAMA *IS SOMETIMES CALLED THE MEXICAN POTATO. UNLIKE POTATO, HOWEVER, IT CAN BE EATEN RAW AS WELL AS COOKED. THIS MAKES A GOOD SALAD OR AN APPETIZER TO SERVE WITH DRINKS.*

SERVES FOUR

INGREDIENTS
- 1 *jicama*
- ½ teaspoon salt
- 2 fresh serrano chiles
- 2 limes

COOK'S TIP
Look for *jicama* at Asian supermarkets, as it is widely used in Chinese cooking. It goes by several names, and you may find it labeled as either yam bean or Chinese turnip.

1 Peel the *jicama* with a potato peeler or knife, then cut it into ¾-inch cubes. Put these in a large bowl, add the salt and toss well.

2 Cut the chiles in half, scrape out the seeds with a sharp knife, then cut the flesh into fine strips. Grate one of the limes thinly, removing only the colored part of the skin, then cut the lime in half and squeeze the juice.

3 Add the chiles, lime zest, and juice to the *jicama*, and mix thoroughly to ensure that all the *jicama* cubes are coated. Cut the other lime into wedges.

4 Cover and chill for at least 1 hour before serving with lime wedges. If the salad is to be served as an appetizer with drinks, transfer the *jicama* cubes to little bowls and pass them with toothpicks for spearing.

CHAYOTE SALAD

COOL AND REFRESHING, THIS SALAD IS IDEAL ON ITS OWN OR WITH FISH OR CHICKEN DISHES. THE SOFT FLESH OF THE CHAYOTES ABSORBS THE FLAVOR OF THE DRESSING BEAUTIFULLY.

SERVES FOUR

INGREDIENTS
  2 *chayotes*
  2 firm tomatoes
  1 small onion, finely chopped
  finely sliced strips of fresh red and
    green chile, to garnish
For the dressing
  ½ teaspoon Dijon mustard
  ½ teaspoon ground anise
  6 tablespoons white wine vinegar
  ¼ cup olive oil
  salt and ground black pepper

1 Bring a pan of water to a boil. Peel the *chayotes*, cut them in half, and remove the seeds. Add them to a boiling water. Lower the heat and simmer for 20 minutes, or until the *chayotes* are tender. Drain and set them aside to cool.

2 Meanwhile, peel the tomatoes. Cut a cross in the bottom of each tomato. Place them in a heatproof bowl and pour in boiling water to cover. After 3 minutes, lift the tomatoes out on a slotted spoon and plunge them into a bowl of cold water. Drain. The skins will have begun to peel back from the crosses. Remove the skins completely and cut the tomatoes into wedges.

3 Make the dressing by combining all the ingredients in a screw-top jar. Close the lid tightly and shake the jar vigorously.

4 Cut the *chayotes* into wedges and place in a bowl with the tomato and onion. Pour over the dressing and serve garnished with strips of fresh red and green chile.

CAESAR SALAD

ALTHOUGH THIS IS WIDELY REGARDED AS AN AMERICAN CLASSIC, CAESAR SALAD ACTUALLY ORIGINATED IN MEXICO, AND TAKES ITS NAME FROM THE CHEF, CAESAR CARDINI, WHO INVENTED IT IN HIS RESTAURANT IN TIJUANA IN 1924. PREGNANT WOMEN AND YOUNG CHILDREN ARE ADVISED TO AVOID EATING RAW EGGS.

SERVES FOUR

INGREDIENTS
   2 large garlic cloves, peeled and
   left whole
   ¼ cup extra virgin olive oil
   4 slices of bread, crusts
   removed, cubed
   1 romaine lettuce, separated into
   leaves
   6 drained canned anchovy fillets
   shavings of Parmesan cheese,
   to garnish
For the dressing
   1 egg
   2 teaspoons Dijon mustard
   generous dash of Worcestershire
   sauce
   2 tablespoons lemon juice
   2 tablespoons extra virgin olive oil
   salt and ground black pepper

1 Cut one garlic clove in half and rub it around the inside of a salad bowl. Put the remaining garlic in a large frying pan. Add the oil and heat gently for 5 minutes, then discard the garlic. Add the bread cubes to the hot oil, in batches if necessary, and fry them until they are crisp on all sides. Drain on paper towels.

2 Line the salad bowl with the romaine leaves. Carefully cut the anchovy fillets in half lengthwise and distribute them among the lettuce leaves. Toss the leaves to spread the flavor of the anchovies.

3 Crack the egg into a food processor or blender, with the Dijon mustard, Worcestershire sauce, and lemon juice. Season and process to blend briefly, then add the oil with the motor running.

4 Pour the dressing onto the salad in the bowl and toss lightly. Add the garlic croutons. Transfer to individual bowls or carry to the table in the salad bowl. Sprinkle on Parmesan shavings and serve.

GREEN BEAN AND CHILE PEPPER SALAD

THIS COLORFUL RED AND GREEN SALAD, GARNISHED WITH BEANS AND GREEN AND BLACK OLIVES, IS JUST THE THING FOR A LIGHT SUMMER LUNCH DISH OR AS PART OF A COLD BUFFET.

SERVES FOUR

INGREDIENTS
  2¼ cups cooked green beans,
    quartered
  2 red bell peppers, seeded and
    chopped
  2 scallions, chopped
  1 or more pickled serrano chiles,
    rinsed, seeded, and chopped
  1 iceberg lettuce, coarsely shredded,
    or mixed salad leaves
  olives, to garnish
For the dressing
  3 tablespoons red wine vinegar
  9 tablespoons olive oil
  salt and ground black pepper

1 Combine the cooked green beans, chopped peppers, chopped scallions, and chiles in a salad bowl.

2 Make the salad dressing. Pour the red wine vinegar into a bowl or pitcher. Add salt and ground black pepper to taste, then gradually whisk in the olive oil until well combined.

3 Pour the salad dressing over the prepared vegetables and toss lightly together to mix and coat thoroughly.

4 Line a large platter with the shredded lettuce leaves, and arrange the salad attractively on top. Garnish with the olives and serve.

MANGO, TOMATO, AND RED ONION SALAD

THIS SALAD MAKES A DELICIOUS APPETIZER AND IS OFTEN EATEN ON THE ISLANDS OF THE CARIBBEAN. UNDERRIPE MANGO CONTRIBUTES A SUBTLE SWEETNESS THAT GOES WELL WITH THE TOMATO.

SERVES FOUR

INGREDIENTS

1 firm underripe mango
2 large tomatoes or 1 beefsteak
  tomato, sliced
½ cucumber, peeled and
  thinly sliced
½ red onion, sliced into rings
1 garlic clove, crushed
2 tablespoons sunflower-seed or
  vegetable oil
1 tablespoon lemon juice
½ teaspoon hot pepper sauce
salt and ground black pepper
sugar, to taste
chopped chives, to garnish

1 Using a sharp knife, cut a thick slice or "cheek" from either side of the mango stone. Peel away the skin and slice the flesh into thin strips. Peel the remaining mango, remove the rest of the flesh, and slice it thinly.

2 Arrange a layer of tomato slices on a large serving plate or platter. Top with the cucumber slices, followed by the mango, and finish off with the thin slices of red onion.

3 Make the salad dressing. Crush the garlic clove into a small glass bowl. Add the oil, lemon juice, hot pepper sauce, salt, ground black pepper, and sugar, if you like. Using a balloon whisk or a fork, whisk these ingredients together until thoroughly mixed.

4 Drizzle the dressing evenly over the salad and garnish with chopped chives. Serve immediately.

COOK'S TIP
Choose the freshest, ripest tomatoes available for the best flavor.

PERUVIAN SALAD

THIS IS A SPECTACULAR-LOOKING SALAD THAT COULD BE SERVED AS A SIDE DISH OR A LIGHT LUNCH.
IN PERU, WHITE RICE WOULD BE USED, BUT BROWN RICE ADDS AN INTERESTING TEXTURE AND FLAVOR.

SERVES FOUR

INGREDIENTS

    2 cups cooked long-grain brown or
      white rice
    1 tablespoon chopped fresh parsley
    1 red bell pepper
    1 small onion, sliced into rings
    olive oil, for sprinkling
    4 ounces green beans, halved
    ½ cup baby corn
    4 quail eggs, hard-boiled and halved
    1–2 ounces Spanish ham, cut into
      thin slices (optional)
    1 small avocado
    lemon juice, for sprinkling
    3 ounces mixed salad leaves
    1 tablespoon capers
    about 10 stuffed olives, halved
For the dressing
    1 garlic clove, crushed
    4 tablespoons olive oil
    3 tablespoons sunflower-seed oil
    2 tablespoons lemon juice
    3 tablespoons plain yogurt
    ½ teaspoon mustard
    ½ teaspoon granulated sugar
    salt and ground black pepper

1 Make the dressing by placing all
the ingredients in a bowl and whisking
with a fork, or whisk until smooth.
Alternatively, place the ingredients in
an empty jam jar, screw the lid on
tightly, and shake well.

2 Put the cooked rice into a large,
glass salad bowl and spoon in half the
dressing. Add the chopped parsley,
stir well, and set aside.

3 Cut the pepper in half, remove the
seeds and pith, then place the halves
cut-side down in a small roasting pan.
Add the onion rings. Sprinkle the onion
with a little olive oil, place the pan under
a hot broiler, and cook for 5–6 minutes,
until the pepper blackens and blisters
and the onion turns golden. You may
need to stir the onion once or twice so
that it cooks evenly.

4 Stir the onion in with the rice. Put the
pepper in a plastic bag and knot the
top. When the steam has loosened the
skin on the pepper halves and they are
cool enough to handle, peel them and
cut the flesh into thin strips.

5 Cook the green beans in boiling water
for 2 minutes, then add the corn and
cook for 1–2 minutes more. Place in
a large mixing bowl and add the red
pepper strips, quail eggs, and ham.

6 Peel and dice the avocado. Put
the salad leaves in a separate mixing
bowl, add the avocado, and mix lightly.
Arrange the salad leaves and avocado
on top of the rice. In a separate bowl,
stir about 3 tablespoons of the dressing
into the green bean and pepper
mixture. Pile this on top of the salad.
Sprinkle the capers and stuffed olives
on top and serve the salad with the
remaining dressing.

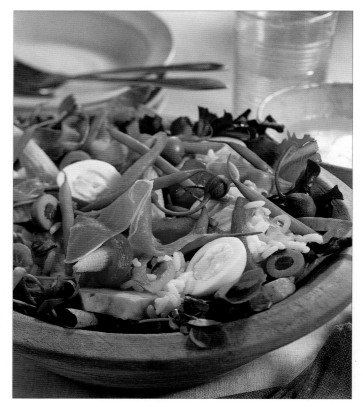

PUMPKIN SALAD

RED WINE VINEGAR BRINGS OUT THE SWEETNESS OF THE PUMPKIN. NO SALAD LEAVES ARE USED, JUST PLENTY OF FRESH PARSLEY. EATEN THROUGHOUT LATIN AMERICA, IT IS GREAT FOR A COLD BUFFET.

SERVES FOUR

INGREDIENTS
  1 large red onion, peeled and very
    thinly sliced
  scant 1 cup olive oil
  4 tablespoons red wine vinegar
  1½ pounds pumpkin, peeled and cut
    into 1½-inch pieces
  ¾ cup fresh Italian parsley leaves,
    chopped
  salt and ground black pepper

VARIATIONS
Try replacing the pumpkin with sweet
potatoes. Arugula or fresh cilantro
can be used instead of the parsley, if
you prefer.

1 Mix the onion, olive oil, and vinegar in
a large bowl. Stir well to combine.

2 Put the pumpkin in a large pan of
cold salted water. Bring to the boil, then
lower the heat, and simmer gently for
15–20 minutes. Drain.

3 Immediately add the drained pumpkin
to the bowl containing the dressing and
toss lightly with your hands. Leave to
cool. Stir in the chopped parsley,
cover with plastic wrap, and chill.
Allow the salad to come back to room
temperature before serving.

SIDE DISHES

Traditionally, Mexican, Caribbean, and Latin American meals consist of a meat, fish, or poultry dish accompanied by rice, beans, or potatoes, and a combination of side dishes, such as rice and peas or stir-fried kale. Each contributes its own unique flavor and character to a meal.

PLAIN RICE

RICE IS A STAPLE FOOD IN MANY PARTS OF LATIN AMERICA—IT IS EATEN AT MOST MEALS WITH ANYTHING AND EVERYTHING, AND IS OFTEN ACCOMPANIED BY BLACK BEANS.

<u>SERVES FOUR</u>

INGREDIENTS
    1 cup long-grain rice
    2 tablespoons vegetable oil
    2 garlic cloves, crushed
    scant 2 cups water
    salt

COOK'S TIP
If the rice is still tough after steaming, add a little water, cover, and return to the heat for a few minutes. If, instead, the rice is still sticky, return to the heat and cook over a very low heat with the lid off, until the excess moisture has evaporated.

1 Rinse the rice in a large bowl of cold water, then drain thoroughly in a fine strainer. Pour the oil into a heavy pan that has a tight-fitting lid. Heat gently, then add the garlic and cook, stirring, for 1 minute. Add the rice and stir for 2 minutes, until the grains are lightly toasted.

2 Pour in the water and season with salt. Bring to the boil, cover, and lower the heat again to a very gentle simmer. Cook for 18 minutes, without lifting the lid. Remove from the heat and leave the rice to rest, covered, for 5 minutes. Transfer to a serving bowl and fluff up with a fork before taking to the table.

BLACK BEANS

YOU'LL FIND BEANS ON MOST LATIN AMERICAN TABLES, WHATEVER THE DAY OF THE WEEK OR OCCASION. THE RECIPE WILL VARY SLIGHTLY, DEPENDING ON THE COUNTRY, THE AVAILABILITY OF ADDITIONAL INGREDIENTS, AND PERSONAL CHOICE. CHILES AND OTHER SPICES ARE OFTEN INCLUDED.

<u>SERVES SIX</u>

INGREDIENTS
    2½ cups black turtle beans, soaked
        overnight in water to cover
    4 ounces smoked fatty bacon, in
        one piece
    1 bay leaf
    2 tablespoons vegetable oil
    2 garlic cloves, crushed
    salt

COOK'S TIP
Do not season the beans until they are cooked, or they will become tough. As the sauce thickens, the beans have a tendency to stick, so stir frequently after returning the refried beans to the pan.

1 Drain the beans and put them in a large, heavy pan. Cover generously with cold water. Add the bacon and bay leaf, and bring to the boil. Skim the surface of the liquid, then lower the heat to a simmer. Cook for at least 1 hour or until the beans are tender, topping up the water if necessary.

2 Heat the oil in a pan over a medium heat. Cook the garlic for 2 minutes. Add two ladles of cooked beans and fry for 2–3 minutes, breaking up the beans.

3 Tip the refried beans back into the pan and season. Simmer over a very low heat for 10 minutes, then serve.

COCONUT RICE

DELICIOUSLY MOIST AND FULL OF FLAVOR, COCONUT RICE IS AN EXCELLENT ACCOMPANIMENT FOR ALL SORTS OF MAIN DISHES—THIS COLOMBIAN VERSION IS PARTICULARLY GOOD WITH FISH.

SERVES FOUR

INGREDIENTS
  3 x 14-fluid-ounce cans coconut
    milk
  1 teaspoon light brown sugar
  1 cup long-grain rice
  salt
  1 tablespoon butter

COOK'S TIP
Canned coconut milk is available sweetened as well as plain—be sure to buy the unsweetened, plain type for savory cooking.

  To make your own coconut milk, heat a coconut in the oven for 20 minutes, then crack it open and remove the flesh. Blend it in a food processor and then press it through cheesecloth.

1 Pour the coconut milk into a large pan that has a tight-fitting lid. Stir in the sugar. Bring to the boil and simmer until the liquid is reduced by half.

VARIATION
This tasty side dish is equally good when made with other varieties of rice. Depending on preference, try using short-grain, medium-grain, or basmati.

2 Add the rice to the pan, season with salt, and bring to the boil. Lower the heat to a simmer and cook, stirring often, for 5 minutes.

3 Stir the butter into the rice and cover the pan tightly. Simmer gently for a further 15 minutes, then remove from the heat. Leave covered for 5 minutes before transferring to a serving bowl.

TOASTED CASSAVA FLOUR <u>WITH</u> EGG <u>AND</u> BACON

BRAZILIAN COOKS MAKE GREAT USE OF FAROFA, FLAVORED TOASTED CASSAVA FLOUR, SPRINKLING IT OVER MEAT OR FISH DISHES TO MOP UP THE JUICES. TRY THIS VERSION WITH RICE AND BEANS.

SERVES SIX

INGREDIENTS
  1 tablespoon butter
  3½ ounces fatty bacon,
   in one piece
  2 eggs, lightly beaten
  1 tablespoon water
  2 cups toasted cassava flour
  1 tablespoon chopped fresh parsley
  salt

COOK'S TIP
Cassava flour resembles dried bread crumbs. Look for it in Latin American or Portuguese stores, where it will be labeled *farinha de mandioca*. It is sometimes called cassava meal.

1 Melt the butter in a pan over a low heat. Dice the bacon and add to the pan. Sauté for 5 minutes, until golden.

2 Mix the eggs with the water in a cup or small bowl. Tip the mixture into the pan and stir until it starts to set. The eggs should have the consistency of soft scrambled eggs—do not overcook them.

3 Add the cassava flour and stir vigorously over the heat for 1 minute, until thoroughly combined. Remove from the heat and stir in the chopped parsley. Season to taste with salt and transfer to a bowl to serve.

GREEN RICE

THIS RICE IS RARELY FEATURED ON MENUS IN MEXICAN RESTAURANTS, BUT IS OFTEN MADE IN THE HOME. EXTRA CHILES AND GREEN BELL PEPPER CAN BE DICED AND ADDED AT THE END, IF DESIRED.

SERVES FOUR

INGREDIENTS
2 fresh green chiles, preferably
    poblanos
1 small green bell pepper
1 cup long-grain white rice
1 garlic clove, roughly chopped
large bunch of cilantro
small bunch of fresh Italian parsley
2 cups chicken stock
2 tablespoons vegetable oil
1 small onion, finely chopped
salt

1 Dry roast the chiles and green pepper in a griddle pan, turning them frequently so that the skins blacken but the flesh does not burn. Place them in a strong plastic bag, tie the top securely, and set aside for 20 minutes.

2 Put the rice in a heatproof bowl, pour in boiling water to cover, and let stand for 20 minutes.

3 Drain the rice, rinse well under cold water, and drain again. Remove the chiles and peppers from the bag and peel off the skins. Remove any stems, then slit the vegetables and scrape out the seeds with a sharp knife.

4 Put the roasted vegetables in a food processor, with the garlic. Strip off the leaves from the cilantro and parsley stalks, reserve some for the garnish, and add the rest to the processor. Pour in half the chicken stock and process until smooth. Add the rest of the stock and process the puree again.

5 Heat the oil in a pan, add the onion and rice, and fry for 5 minutes over medium heat until the rice is golden and the onion translucent. Stir in the puree. Lower the heat, cover, and cook for 25–30 minutes or until all the liquid is absorbed and the rice is just tender. Add salt and garnish with the reserved herbs. Served with lime wedges, this rice goes extremely well with fish.

YELLOW RICE

THIS RICE DISH OWES ITS STRIKING COLOR AND DISTINCTIVE FLAVOR TO GROUND ACHIOTE SEED, WHICH IS DERIVED FROM ANNATTO.

SERVES SIX

INGREDIENTS
1 cup long-grain white rice
2 tablespoons vegetable oil
1 teaspoon ground achiote seed
    (annatto powder)
1 small onion, finely chopped
2 garlic cloves, crushed
2 cups chicken stock
⅓ cup drained pickled jalapeño chile
    slices, chopped
salt
cilantro leaves, to garnish

COOK'S TIP
Achiote, the seed of the annatto tree, is used as a food coloring and flavoring throughout Latin America. You can buy it at specialty spice shops and ethnic food stores. It is sometimes called annatto powder.

1 Put the rice in a heatproof bowl, pour in boiling water to cover, and let stand for 20 minutes. Drain, rinse under cold water, and drain again.

2 Heat the oil in a pan, add the ground achiote seed (annatto powder), and cook for 2–3 minutes. Add the onion and garlic, and cook for another 3–4 minutes, or until the onion is translucent. Stir in the rice and cook for 5 minutes.

3 Pour in the stock, mix well, and bring to a boil. Lower the heat, cover the pan with a tight-fitting lid, and simmer for 25–30 minutes, until all the liquid has been absorbed.

4 Add the chopped jalapeños to the pan and stir to distribute them evenly. Add salt to taste, then spoon into a heated serving dish and garnish with the cilantro leaves. Serve immediately.

RICE AND PEAS

IT MAY SEEM ODD THAT A DISH WITH KIDNEY BEANS AS A PRIMARY INGREDIENT IS CALLED RICE AND PEAS, BUT IN JAMAICA, WHERE IT ORIGINATED, FRESH PIGEON PEAS WERE ORIGINALLY USED. SINCE THE PEAS ARE SEASONAL, THE DISH IS MORE OFTEN MADE WITH DRIED KIDNEY BEANS.

2 Drain the beans and tip them into a large pan with a tight-fitting lid. Pour in enough water to cover the beans. Bring to the boil and boil for 10 minutes, then lower the heat and simmer for 1½ hours or until the beans are tender.

3 Add the thyme, creamed coconut or coconut cream, bay leaves, onion, garlic, allspice, and pepper. Season and stir in the measured water.

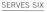

SERVES SIX

INGREDIENTS
    1 cup red kidney beans
    2 fresh thyme sprigs
    2-ounce piece of creamed coconut or
        ½ cup coconut cream
    2 bay leaves
    1 onion, finely chopped
    2 garlic cloves, crushed
    ½ teaspoon ground allspice
    1 red or green bell pepper, seeded
        and chopped
    2½ cups water
    2½ cups long-grain rice
    salt and ground black pepper

1 Put the red kidney beans in a large bowl. Pour in enough cold water to cover the beans generously. Cover the bowl and leave the beans to soak overnight.

4 Bring to the boil and add the rice. Stir well, reduce the heat, and cover the pan. Simmer for 25–30 minutes, until all the liquid has been absorbed. Serve as an accompaniment to fish, meat, or vegetarian dishes.

COU-COU

THIS TASTY OKRA AND MASHED CORNMEAL PUDDING IS A BAJAN NATIONAL DISH. TRADITIONALLY, IT IS SERVED WITH FRESH FLYING FISH COOKED IN A CARIBBEAN GRAVY, BUT IT CAN ALSO BE SERVED WITH ANY OTHER FISH, MEAT, OR VEGETABLE STEW.

SERVES FOUR

INGREDIENTS

4 ounces okra, trimmed and
   roughly chopped
1½ cups coarse cornmeal
2½ cups water or coconut milk
2 tablespoons butter
salt and ground black pepper

COOK'S TIP
Adding unsweetened coconut milk instead of water will give your cou-cou a special, rich flavor.

3 Cook on a very low heat, beating the mixture vigorously. Gradually add the measured water or coconut milk, beating after each addition to prevent the mixture from sticking to the pan and burning.

4 Cover and cook for about 20 minutes, beating occasionally. The cou-cou is cooked when the cornmeal granules are soft. Cover with foil and then a lid to keep the mixture moist and hot until required. Spread with butter before serving.

1 Bring a pan of water seasoned with a little salt and pepper to the boil. Add the chopped okra and cook for about 10 minutes. Remove the okra with a slotted spoon and set it aside.

2 Pour away half the liquid from the pan, then return the pan to the heat. Return the okra to the pan, then gradually beat in the cornmeal.

BUTTERED SPINACH AND RICE

THE LAYER OF FRESH COOKED SPINACH IN THIS POPULAR CARIBBEAN DISH IS SAID TO HAVE BEEN THE RESULT OF A HAPPY ACCIDENT. IT WAS INTENDED FOR A SEPARATE DISH, BUT THE COOK FORGOT TO ADD IT SO SIMPLY USED IT TO TOP THE RICE INSTEAD.

SERVES FOUR

INGREDIENTS

3 tablespoons butter or margarine
1 onion, finely chopped
2 fresh tomatoes, chopped
2½ cups basmati rice, rinsed
2 garlic cloves, crushed
2½ cups stock or water
12 ounces fresh spinach, shredded
salt and ground black pepper
2 tomatoes, sliced, to garnish

COOK'S TIP
If you are unable to get fresh spinach, use frozen leaf spinach instead. Thaw and drain approximately 8 ounces frozen spinach and cook on top of the rice for about 5 minutes. If you prefer, finely shredded collards make a delicious alternative to spinach.

1 Melt 2 tablespoons of butter or margarine in a large pan with a tight-fitting lid. Gently fry the onion for 3–4 minutes, until soft and translucent. Stir in the fresh chopped tomatoes.

2 Add the basmati rice and crushed garlic, gently cook for 5 minutes, then gradually add the stock or water, stirring constantly. Season to taste with plenty of salt and ground black pepper.

3 Cover and simmer gently for 10–15 minutes, until the rice is almost cooked, then reduce the heat to low.

4 Spread the spinach in a thick layer over the rice. Cover the pan and cook over a low heat for 5–8 minutes, until the spinach has wilted. Spoon into a serving dish, dot the remaining butter over the top and garnish with the sliced tomatoes. Serve immediately.

CREAMED SWEET POTATOES

SIMILAR TO TRADITIONAL MASHED POTATOES, THIS CARIBBEAN SPECIALTY USES WHITE SWEET POTATOES INSTEAD OF THE ORANGE VARIETY. THE GRATED NUTMEG ADDS AN EXTRA, IRRESISTIBLE SWEETNESS.

SERVES FOUR

INGREDIENTS

2 pounds sweet potatoes
¼ cup butter
3 tablespoons light cream
freshly grated nutmeg
1 tablespoon chopped fresh chives
salt and ground black pepper

COOK'S TIP
If you cannot get white sweet potatoes, white yams make a good substitute, especially poona (Ghanaian) yam.

1 Peel the sweet potatoes under cold running water and place in a bowl of salted water to prevent them from discoloring. Cut them into large chunks and place in a pan of cold water. Cook, covered, for 20–30, minutes until tender.

2 Drain the potatoes and return them to the dry pan. Add the butter, cream, nutmeg, chives, and seasoning. Mash with a potato masher and then fluff up with a fork. Serve warm as an accompaniment to a curry or stew.

COLOMBIAN CHEESY POTATOES

TENDER NEW POTATOES TOPPED WITH A CREAMY CHEESE AND TOMATO SAUCE MAKE A DELICIOUS SIDE DISH, WHICH IS GREAT SERVED WITH MEAT, POULTRY, OR FISH DISHES.

SERVES SIX

INGREDIENTS
 2¼ pounds new or salad potatoes
 2 tablespoons butter
 4 scallions, thinly sliced
 2 large tomatoes, peeled, seeded,
  and chopped
 scant 1 cup heavy cream
 1 cup grated mozzarella
 salt and ground black pepper

1 Place the potatoes in a large pan of salted cold water. Cover and bring to the boil. Lower the heat and simmer for 18–20 minutes, until tender.

2 Meanwhile, melt the butter in a frying pan over a low heat, add the scallions, and cook gently, stirring occasionally, for 5 minutes, until softened. Stir in the tomatoes and cook for a further 2–3 minutes, stirring occasionally, until the tomatoes break up.

3 Drain the potatoes and put them in a warmed serving bowl. Add the cream to the onion and tomato mixture, bring to the boil, then add the cheese, stirring until it melts. Season with salt and pepper to taste. Pour the hot sauce over the potatoes and serve immediately.

CARIBBEAN POTATO SALAD

COLORFUL VEGETABLES IN A CREAMY SMOOTH DRESSING MAKE THIS PIQUANT CARIBBEAN SALAD IDEAL TO SERVE ON ITS OWN OR WITH BROILED OR COLD MEATS.

SERVES SIX

INGREDIENTS
   2 pounds small waxy or salad
     potatoes, with the skins rubbed off
   2 red bell peppers, seeded
     and diced
   2 celery sticks, finely chopped
   1 shallot, finely chopped
   2 or 3 scallions, finely chopped
   1 mild fresh green chile, seeded and
     finely chopped
   1 garlic clove, crushed
   2 teaspoons finely chopped chives
   2 teaspoons finely chopped basil
   1 tablespoon finely chopped parsley
   1 tablespoon light cream
   2 tablespoons salad cream
   1 tablespoon mayonnaise
   1 teaspoon Dijon mustard
   1½ teaspoons sugar
   chopped chives, to garnish
   chopped red chile, to garnish

1 Cook the potatoes in a large pan of boiling water until tender but still firm. Drain and leave to one side. When cool enough to handle, cut the cooked potatoes into 1-inch cubes and place in a large salad bowl.

2 Add all the vegetables to the potatoes in the salad bowl, together with the chopped chile, crushed garlic, and all the chopped herbs.

3 Mix together the cream, salad cream, mayonnaise, mustard, and sugar in a small bowl. Stir well until the mixture is thoroughly combined and forms a smooth dressing.

4 Pour the dressing over the potato mixture and stir gently to coat evenly. Serve immediately, garnished with the chopped chives and chopped red chile.

VARIATIONS
Try adding other vegetables to this potato salad, such as tomatoes for flavor or lightly cooked green beans for a tasty crunch. Many traditional potato salads also include a coarsely chopped hard-boiled egg. This would work just as well in this Caribbean version.

POTATOES WITH CHORIZO AND GREEN CHILES

MEXICANS MAKE THEIR OWN CHORIZO SAUSAGE, SOMETIMES USING IT FRESH, BUT ALSO PUTTING IT INTO CASINGS TO DRY, WHEN IT RESEMBLES THE SPANISH VERSION THAT IS NOW POPULAR ALL OVER THE WORLD. THIS RECIPE MAKES A DELICIOUS BRUNCH DISH. TYPICAL OF PEASANT FOOD, IT IS BASED ON THE COMBINATION OF PLENTY OF POTATOES MIXED WITH STRONGLY FLAVORED MEAT TO HELP IT GO FURTHER.

SERVES FOUR TO SIX

INGREDIENTS
  2 pounds potatoes, peeled and diced
  2 tablespoons vegetable oil
  2 garlic cloves, crushed
  4 scallions, chopped
  2 fresh jalapeño chiles, seeded
    and diced
  11 ounces chorizo sausage, skinned
  1¼ cups grated Monterey Jack or
    Cheddar cheese
  salt (optional)

1 Bring a large pan of water to a boil and add the potatoes. When the water returns to a boil, lower the heat and simmer the potatoes for 5 minutes. Put the potatoes in a colander and drain thoroughly.

COOK'S TIP
Use firm-textured potatoes for this dish. Instead of Monterey Jack, you can also use Gouda or Cheddar.

2 Heat the oil in a large frying pan, add the garlic, scallions, and chiles and cook for 3–4 minutes. Add the diced potato and cook until the cubes begin to brown a little.

3 Cut the chorizo into small cubes and add these to the pan. Cook the mixture for 5 minutes more, until the sausage has heated through.

4 Season with salt if necessary, then add the cheese. Mix quickly and carefully, trying not to break up the cubes of potato. Serve immediately, while the cheese is still melting.

RED CAULIFLOWER

VEGETABLES ARE SELDOM SERVED PLAIN IN MEXICO. THE CAULIFLOWER HERE IS FLAVORED WITH A SIMPLE TOMATO SALSA AND FRESH CHEESE. THE SALSA COULD BE ANY TABLE SALSA; TOMATILLO IS PARTICULARLY GOOD. THE CONTRAST WITH THE TEXTURE AND MILD FLAVOR OF THE CAULIFLOWER MAKES FOR A TASTY DISH.

SERVES SIX

INGREDIENTS
    1 small onion
    1 lime
    1 medium cauliflower
    14-ounce can chopped tomatoes
    4 fresh serrano chiles, seeded and
      finely chopped
    ¼ teaspoon sugar
    3 ounces feta cheese, crumbled
    salt
    chopped fresh Italian parsley,
      to garnish

COOK'S TIP
Use a zester for the lime, if have you have one. This handy little tool enables you to pare off tiny strips of the zest, leaving the pith behind.

1 Chop the onion very finely and place in a bowl. With a zester, peel off the zest of the lime in thin strips. Add to the chopped onion.

2 Cut the lime in half and add the juice from both halves to the onion and lime zest mixture. Set aside so that the lime juice can soften the onion. Cut the cauliflower into florets.

3 Put the tomatoes in a pan and add the chiles and sugar. Heat gently. Meanwhile, place the cauliflower in a pan of boiling water and cook gently for 5–8 minutes, until tender.

4 Add the onions to the tomato salsa, with salt to taste, stir in, and heat through, then spoon about a third of the salsa into a serving dish.

5 Arrange the drained cauliflower florets on top of the salsa and spoon the remaining salsa on top.

6 Sprinkle with the feta, which should soften a little on contact. Serve immediately, sprinkled with chopped fresh Italian parsley.

GREEN LIMA BEANS IN SAUCE

MAKE THE MOST OF LIMA BEANS OR FAVA BEANS BY TEAMING THEM WITH TOMATOES AND FRESH CHILES IN THIS SIMPLE ACCOMPANIMENT.

SERVES FOUR

INGREDIENTS

 1 pound fresh lima beans or
  fava beans
 2 tablespoons olive oil
 1 onion, finely chopped
 2 garlic cloves, crushed
 14-ounce can plum tomatoes,
  drained and chopped
 about 3 tablespoons drained pickled
  jalapeño chile slices, chopped
 salt
 cilantro and lemon slices,
  to garnish

COOK'S TIP
Pickled chiles are often hotter than roasted chiles—taste one before adding to the recipe and adjust the quantity to suit your taste.

1 Bring a pan of lightly salted water to a boil. Add the lima beans or fava beans and cook for 15 minutes or until just tender.

2 Meanwhile, heat the olive oil in a frying pan, add the onion and garlic, and sauté until the onion is translucent. Add the tomatoes and continue to cook, stirring, until the mixture thickens.

3 Add the chile slices and cook for 1–2 minutes. Season with salt to taste.

4 Drain the beans and return them to the pan. Pour in the tomato mixture and stir over the heat for a few minutes. If the sauce thickens too quickly, add a little water. Spoon into a serving dish, garnish with the cilantro and lemon slices, and serve.

GREEN BEANS WITH EGGS

THIS IS AN UNUSUAL WAY OF COOKING GREEN BEANS, BUT TASTES DELICIOUS. TRY THIS DISH FOR A LIGHT SUPPER OR AS AN ACCOMPANIMENT TO A SIMPLE ROAST.

SERVES SIX

INGREDIENTS

 11 ounces string beans,
  trimmed and halved
 2 tablespoons vegetable oil
 1 onion, halved and
  thinly sliced
 3 eggs
 salt and ground black pepper
 ½ cup grated Monterey Jack or
  mild Cheddar cheese
 strips of lemon zest, to garnish

VARIATION
Freshly grated Parmesan can be used instead of the Monterey Jack or Cheddar cheese for a sharper flavor.

1 Bring a pan of water to a boil, add the beans, and cook for 5–6 minutes or until tender. Drain in a colander, rinse under cold water to preserve the bright color, then drain the beans once more.

2 Heat the oil in a frying pan and sauté the onion slices for 3–4 minutes, until soft and translucent. Break the eggs into a bowl and beat them with seasoning.

3 Add the egg mixture to the onion. Cook slowly over moderate heat, stirring constantly so that the egg is lightly scrambled. The egg should be moist throughout. Do not overcook.

4 Add the beans to the pan and cook for a few minutes until warmed through. Transfer the mixture to a heated serving dish, sprinkle on the grated cheese and lemon zest, and serve.

ZUCCHINI <u>WITH</u> CHEESE <u>AND</u> GREEN CHILES

THIS IS A VERY TASTY WAY TO SERVE ZUCCHINI, OFTEN A RATHER BLAND VEGETABLE, AND THE DISH LOOKS GOOD TOO. SERVE IT AS A VEGETARIAN MAIN DISH OR AN UNUSUAL SIDE DISH.

SERVES SIX AS AN ACCOMPANIMENT

INGREDIENTS

   2 tablespoons vegetable oil
   ½ onion, thinly sliced
   2 garlic cloves, crushed
   1 teaspoon dried oregano
   2 tomatoes
   ⅓ cup drained pickled jalapeño
     chili slices, chopped
   1¼ pounds zucchini
   ½ cup cream cheese, cubed
   salt and ground black pepper
   fresh oregano sprigs,
     to garnish

1 Heat the oil in a frying pan. Add the onion, garlic, and dried oregano. Sauté for 3–4 minutes, until the onion is soft and translucent.

2 Cut a cross in the bottom of each tomato. Place in a heatproof bowl and cover with boiling water. Leave in the water for 3 minutes, then lift out on a slotted spoon and plunge into a bowl of cold water. Drain. The skins will have begun to peel back from the crosses. Remove the skins and cut the tomatoes in half and squeeze out the seeds. Chop the flesh into strips.

3 Trim the zucchini, then cut them lengthwise into ½-inch wide strips. Slice the strips into matchsticks.

4 Stir the zucchini into the onion mixture and fry for 10 minutes, stirring occasionally, until just tender. Add the tomatoes and chopped jalapeños, and cook for 2–3 more minutes.

5 Add the cream cheese. Reduce the heat to the lowest setting. As the cheese melts, stir gently to coat the zucchini. Season with salt, pile into a heated dish, and serve, garnished with fresh oregano. If serving as a main dish, rustic bread makes a good accompaniment.

ZUCCHINI TORTE

THIS DISH LOOKS LIKE A SPANISH OMELET, WHICH IS TRADITIONALLY SERVED AT ROOM TEMPERATURE.
SERVE WARM OR PREPARE IT IN ADVANCE AND LET COOL, BUT DO NOT REFRIGERATE.

SERVES FOUR TO SIX

INGREDIENTS
    1¼ pounds zucchini
    ¼ cup vegetable oil
    1 small onion
    3 fresh jalapeño chiles, seeded
      and cut in strips
    3 large eggs
    ½ cup self-rising flour
    1 cup grated Monterey Jack or
      mild Cheddar cheese
    ½ teaspoon cayenne pepper
    1 tablespoon butter
    salt

1 Preheat the oven to 350°F. Top and tail the zucchini, then slice them thinly.

2 Heat the oil in a large frying pan. Add the zucchini and cook for a few minutes, turning them over at least once, until they are soft and beginning to brown. Using a slotted spoon, transfer them to a bowl. Slice the onion and add it to the oil remaining in the pan, with most of the jalapeño strips, reserving some for the garnish.

3 Sauté until the onions have softened and are golden. Using a slotted spoon, add the onions and jalapeños to the zucchini. Place them to one side and cover.

4 Beat the eggs in a large bowl. Add the self-rising flour, cheese, and cayenne. Mix well, then stir in the zucchini mixture, with salt to taste. Grease a 9-inch round, shallow ovenproof dish with the butter. Pour in the zucchini mixture and bake for 30 minutes, until risen, firm to the touch, and golden. Let cool.

5 Serve the zucchini torte in thick wedges, garnished with the remaining jalapeño strips. A tomato salad, sprinkled with chives, makes a colorful accompaniment.

PUMPKIN WITH SPICES

ROASTED PUMPKIN HAS A WONDERFUL, RICH FLAVOR. EAT IT STRAIGHT FROM THE SKIN, EAT THE
SKIN TOO, OR SCOOP OUT THE COOKED FLESH, ADD A SPOONFUL OF SALSA, AND WRAP IT IN A WARM
TORTILLA. IT ALSO MAKES FLAVORFUL SOUPS AND SAUCES.

SERVES SIX

INGREDIENTS
   2¼ pounds pumpkin
   ¼ cup butter, melted
   2 teaspoons hot chili sauce
   ½ teaspoon salt
   ½ teaspoon ground allspice
   1 teaspoon ground cinnamon
   chopped fresh herbs, to garnish
   Classic Tomato Salsa and crème
     fraîche, to serve

COOK'S TIP
Green, gray, or orange-skinned pumpkins
all roast well. The orange-fleshed
varieties are the most colorful when it
comes to cooking.

1 Preheat the oven to 425°F. Cut the
pumpkin into large pieces. Scoop out
and discard the fiber and seeds,
then put the pumpkin pieces in a
roasting pan.

2 Mix the melted butter and chili sauce
and drizzle the mixture evenly on the
pumpkin pieces.

3 Put the salt in a small bowl and add
the ground allspice and cinnamon.
Sprinkle the mixture on the pumpkin.

4 Roast for 25 minutes or until the
pumpkin flesh yields when pressed
gently. Serve on a heated platter and
pass the tomato salsa and crème
fraîche separately.

POTATO CAKES

QUICK AND EASY TO MAKE, THESE POTATO CAKES ARE DELICIOUS. SERVE THEM WITH SALSA AS A LIGHT MEAL, OR AS AN ACCOMPANIMENT TO ROAST OR PAN-FRIED MEATS.

MAKES TEN

INGREDIENTS

1 pound 6 ounces potatoes
1 cup grated Cheddar cheese
½ teaspoon salt
⅓ cup drained pickled jalapeño
  chile slices, finely chopped
  (optional)
1 egg, beaten
small bunch of cilantro,
  finely chopped
all-purpose flour, for shaping
oil, for shallow frying
fresh citrus salsa, to serve

3 When the dough is cool enough to handle, put it on a board. With floured hands, divide it into ten pieces of equal size. Shape each piece into a ball, then flatten to a cake.

4 Heat the oil in a large frying pan. Fry the potato cakes for 2–3 minutes over medium heat. Turn them over and cook until both sides are golden. Sprinkle with salt and chopped cilantro, and serve with salsa.

1 Peel the potatoes and halve them if large. Add them to a pan of cold water. Bring to a boil and cook for about 30 minutes, until tender. Drain, return to the pan, and mash. The mixture should not be smooth.

2 Scrape the potatoes into a bowl and stir in the grated cheese, with the salt and the chopped jalapeños, if using. Stir in the beaten egg and most of the chopped cilantro, and mix into a dough.

FRIED PLANTAINS

THESE ARE THE PERFECT ACCOMPANIMENT TO HIGHLY SPICED AND SEASONED FOODS. THEIR SWEET FLAVOR PROVIDES AN INTERESTING CONTRAST.

SERVES FOUR

INGREDIENTS
    4 ripe plantains
    6 tablespoons butter
    2 teaspoons vegetable oil
    strips of scallion and red bell pepper,
      to garnish

COOK'S TIP
Ripe plantains have dark, almost black skins. Do not use underripe plantains, which are very hard and do not soften on cooking.

1 Peel the plantains, cut them in half lengthwise, then cut them in half again. Melt the butter with the oil in a large frying pan.

2 Add the plantains to the pan in a single layer and fry for 8–10 minutes, turning halfway through. Spoon into a heated dish and serve, garnished with strips of scallion and red pepper.

FRIED POTATOES

THESE MAKE THE PERFECT ACCOMPANIMENT FOR CHORIZO, AND ALSO GO VERY WELL WITH EGGS AND BACON.

SERVES FOUR

INGREDIENTS
    6 fresh jalapeño chiles
    4 tablespoons vegetable oil
    1 onion, finely chopped
    1 pound waxy potatoes, scrubbed
      and cut into ½-inch cubes
    few sprigs of fresh oregano, chopped,
      plus extra sprigs, to garnish
    1 cup freshly grated Parmesan
      cheese (optional)

1 Dry-roast the jalapeños in a griddle pan, turning them frequently so that the skins blacken but do not burn. Place them in a strong plastic bag and tie the top to keep the steam in. Set aside for 20 minutes.

2 Remove the jalapeños from the bag, peel off the skins and remove any stems. Cut them in half, scrape out the seeds, then chop the flesh finely.

COOK'S TIP
If your frying pan does not have a lid, use aluminum foil instead.

3 Meanwhile, heat half the oil in a large, heavy frying pan that has a lid. Add the onion and sauté, stirring occasionally, for 3–4 minutes, until translucent, then add the potato cubes.

4 Stir to coat the potato cubes in oil, then cover the pan and cook over medium heat for 20–25 minutes, until the potatoes are tender. Shake the pan occasionally to stop them from sticking to the bottom.

5 When the potatoes are tender, push them to the side of the frying pan, then add the remaining oil.

6 When the oil is hot, spread out the potatoes again, and add the chopped jalapeños. Cook over high heat for 5–10 minutes, stirring carefully so that the potatoes turn golden brown all over but do not break up.

7 Add the chopped oregano, with the grated Parmesan, if using. Mix gently, spoon onto a heated serving dish and garnish with extra oregano sprigs. Serve as part of a cooked breakfast or brunch.

POTATO <u>AND</u> ONION TORTILLA
<u>WITH</u> FAVA BEANS

THE CLASSIC TORTILLA OR SPANISH OMELET INCLUDES NOTHING MORE THAN ONIONS, POTATOES, EGGS, AND OLIVE OIL. ADDING CHOPPED HERBS AND A FEW SKINNED FAVA BEANS MAKES THIS A VERY SUMMERY DISH TO ENJOY AT LUNCH, OR CUT IT INTO SMALL PIECES AND SERVE AS A SPANISH TAPAS.

SERVES TWO

INGREDIENTS
  3 tablespoons olive oil
  2 Bermuda onions, thinly sliced
  11 ounces waxy potatoes, cut into
    ½-inch dice
  1¾ cups shelled
    fava beans
  1 teaspoon chopped fresh thyme or
    summer savory
  6 large eggs
  3 tablespoons mixed chopped chives
    and chopped Italian parsley
  salt and ground black pepper

1 Heat 2 tablespoons of the oil in a 9-inch deep non-stick frying pan. Add the onions and potatoes, and stir to coat. Cover and cook gently, stirring frequently, for 20–25 minutes until the potatoes are cooked and the onions collapsed. Do not let the mixture brown.

2 Meanwhile, cook the beans in boiling salted water for 5 minutes. Drain well and set aside to cool.

3 When the beans are cool enough to handle, peel off the gray outer skins. Add the beans to the frying pan, together with the thyme or summer savory, and season with salt and pepper to taste. Stir well to mix and cook for a further 2–3 minutes.

4 Beat the eggs with salt and pepper to taste and the mixed herbs, then pour over the potatoes and onions and increase the heat slightly. Cook gently until the egg on the bottom sets and browns, gently pulling the omelet away from the sides of the pan and tilting it to allow the uncooked egg to run underneath.

5 Invert the tortilla onto a plate. Add the remaining oil to the pan and heat until hot. Slip the tortilla back into the pan, uncooked-side down, and cook for another 3–5 minutes to allow the underside to brown. Slide the tortilla out onto a plate. Divide as wished, and serve warm rather than piping hot.

BEAN FEAST WITH TOMATO AND AVOCADO SALSA

THIS IS A VERY QUICK AND EASY RECIPE USING CANNED BEANS, ALTHOUGH IT COULD BE MADE WITH DRIED BEANS. THEY WOULD NEED TO BE SOAKED OVERNIGHT, BOILED HARD FOR 10 MINUTES, THEN SIMMERED FOR 1–1½ HOURS UNTIL TENDER.

SERVES FOUR

INGREDIENTS

1 tablespoon olive oil
1 small onion, finely chopped
3 garlic cloves, finely chopped
1 fresh red Ancho chile, seeded and
   finely chopped
1 red bell pepper, seeded and
   coarsely chopped
2 plum tomatoes, chopped
2 bay leaves
2 teaspoons chopped fresh oregano
2 teaspoons ground cumin
1 teaspoon ground coriander
½ teaspoon ground cloves
1 tablespoon soft dark brown sugar
14-ounce can red kidney beans,
   rinsed and drained
14-ounce can small cannellini beans,
   rinsed and drained
14-ounce can borlotti beans, rinsed
   and drained
1¼ cups vegetable stock
salt and ground black pepper
fresh cilantro, to garnish
For the salsa
1 ripe, but firm, avocado
3 tablespoons fresh lime juice
1 small red onion
1 small fresh hot green chile
5 ripe plum tomatoes
3 tablespoons chopped fresh
   cilantro

1 Heat the oil and fry the onion for 3 minutes, until transparent. Add the garlic, chile, pepper, herbs, and spices.

2 Stir well and cook for a further 3 minutes, then add the sugar, beans, and stock, and cook for 8 minutes. Season with salt and plenty of ground black pepper.

3 To make the salsa, peel the avocado, cut it in half around the pit, then remove the pit by striking it with the blade of a large, sharp knife and lifting it out cleanly. Cut the flesh into ½-inch dice. Place in a mixing bowl with the lime juice and stir to mix.

4 Chop the red onion and slice the chile, discarding the seeds. Plunge the tomatoes into boiling water, leave for 30 seconds, and then peel away the skin. Chop the tomatoes.

5 Add the onion, chile, tomatoes, and cilantro to the avocado. Season with black pepper and stir to mix. Spoon the beans into a warmed serving dish or into 4 serving bowls. Serve with the tomato and avocado salsa, and garnish with sprigs of fresh cilantro.

CORN WITH CREAM

IN MEXICO, THIS WOULD BE MADE WITH HEAVY CREAM, BUT THE SAUCE HAS A BETTER CONSISTENCY WHEN MADE WITH CREAM CHEESE.

SERVES SIX AS A SIDE DISH

INGREDIENTS

4 ears of corn
¼ cup butter
1 small onion, finely chopped
⅔ cup drained pickled jalapeño
  chile slices
⅔ cup cream cheese
⅓ cup freshly grated Parmesan
  cheese, plus shavings,
  to garnish
salt and ground black pepper

1 Strip off the husks from the corn and pull off the silks. Place the ears in a bowl of water and use a vegetable brush to remove any remaining silks. Stand each ear in turn on a board and slice off the kernels, cutting as close to the cob as possible.

2 Melt the butter in a pan, add the chopped onion, and sauté for 4–5 minutes, stirring occasionally, until the onion has softened and is translucent.

3 Add the corn kernels and cook for 4–5 minutes, until they are just tender. Chop the jalapeños finely and stir them into the corn mixture.

4 Stir in the cream cheese and the grated Parmesan. Cook over low heat until both cheeses have melted and the corn kernels are coated in the mixture. Season to taste, transfer into a heated dish, and serve, topped with shredded Parmesan.

VARIATION
A simplified version of this dish is sold at street stalls in Mexico. Whole cooked ears of corn are dipped in cream, then sprinkled with crumbled fresh cheese. Next time you broil, try this as an appetizer. Alternatively, put whole ears of corn in a shallow baking dish and bake them in an oven preheated to 400°F for 30 minutes, until tender and golden. Pour in ½ cup sour cream or crème fraîche, then sprinkle the corn with 2 tablespoons freshly grated Parmesan cheese and serve. The corn can also be brushed with butter and broiled, but it must have plenty of room below the heat, or it will burn.

FRIJOLES DE OLLA

TRAVELERS OFTEN SAY THAT "BEANS IN A POT," AS IT IS TRANSLATED, TASTE DIFFERENT IN MEXICO FROM THOSE COOKED ANYWHERE ELSE. THE SECRET IS, QUITE LITERALLY, IN THE POT. TRADITIONALLY, CLAY POTS ARE USED, WHICH GIVE THE BEANS A WONDERFUL, SLIGHTLY EARTHY FLAVOR.

SERVES FOUR

INGREDIENTS
1¼ cups dried pinto beans, soaked
    overnight in water to cover
7½ cups water
2 onions
10 garlic cloves, peeled and
    left whole
small bunch of cilantro
salt
For the toppings
2 fresh red fresno chiles
1 tomato, peeled and chopped
2 scallions, finely chopped
4 tablespoons sour cream
2 ounces feta cheese

1 Drain the beans, rinse them under cold water, and drain again. Put the water in a large pan, bring to a boil, and add the beans.

2 Cut the onions in half and add them to the pan, with the whole garlic cloves. Bring to a boil again, then lower the heat and simmer for 1½ hours, until the beans are tender and there is only a little liquid remaining.

3 While the beans are cooking, prepare the toppings. Spear the chiles on a long-handled metal skewer and roast them over the flame of a gas burner until the skins blister and darken. Do not let the flesh burn.

4 Put the roasted chiles in a strong plastic bag and tie the top immediately to keep the steam in. Set aside for 20 minutes.

5 Remove the chiles from the bag and peel off the skins. If they do not easily come loose, they may not have been cooked enough and you should roast them further. Cut off the stalks, then slit the chiles and scrape out the seeds. Cut the flesh into thin strips and put it in a bowl. Spoon all the other toppings into separate bowls.

6 Ladle about 1 cup of the beans and liquid into a food processor or blender. Process to a smooth puree. If you prefer, simply mash the beans with a potato masher; try to achieve a smooth paste.

7 Return the puree to the pan, and stir in. Chop and add the cilantro, reserving some leaves to garnish, season with salt, and mix well. Ladle into warmed individual bowls and take them to the table with the toppings.

8 Serve the beans with the toppings and add cilantro to garnish. Crumble a little feta cheese over each portion.

POTATOES <u>WITH</u> RED CHILES

IF YOU LIKE CHILES, YOU'LL LOVE THESE POTATOES! IF YOU'RE NOT A FAN OF FIERY FLAVORS,
THEN SIMPLY LEAVE OUT ALL THE CHILE SEEDS AND USE THE FLESH BY ITSELF.

SERVES FOUR

INGREDIENTS
  12–14 small new or salad
    potatoes, halved
  2 tablespoons vegetable oil
  ½ teaspoon crushed dried
    red chiles
  ½ teaspoon white cumin seeds
  ½ teaspoon fennel seeds
  ½ teaspoon crushed coriander seeds
  1 teaspoon salt
  1 onion, sliced
  1–4 fresh red chiles, chopped
  1 tablespoon chopped fresh cilantro,
    plus extra, to garnish

COOK'S TIP
To prepare fresh chiles, slit down one
side and scrape out the seeds. Finely
slice or chop the flesh. Wear rubber
gloves if you have very sensitive skin.

1 Cook the potatoes in boiling salted
water until tender but still firm. Remove
from the heat and drain off the water.
Set aside until needed.

2 In a deep frying pan, heat the oil
over a medium-high heat, then reduce
the heat to medium. Add the crushed
chiles, cumin, fennel and coriander
seeds, and salt and fry, stirring, for
30–40 seconds.

3 Add the sliced onion and fry until
golden brown. Then add the potatoes,
red chiles, and cilantro, and stir well.

4 Reduce the heat to very low, then
cover and cook for 5–7 minutes. Serve
the potatoes hot, garnished with more
fresh cilantro.

CORN WITH A GARLIC BUTTER CRUST

WHETHER YOU ARE CATERING FOR VEGETARIANS OR SERVING THIS WITH MEAT DISHES, IT WILL DISAPPEAR IN A FLASH. THE CHARRED GARLIC BUTTER CRUST ADDS A NEW DIMENSION TO THE COBS.

SERVES SIX

INGREDIENTS
  6 ripe corn cobs
  1 cup butter
  2 tablespoons olive oil
  2 garlic cloves, crushed
  1 cup whole-wheat bread crumbs
  1 tablespoon chopped fresh
    parsley
  salt and freshly ground black
    pepper

1 Pull off the husks and silks and boil the corn cobs in a large pan of salted water until tender. Drain the corn cobs and leave to cool.

2 Melt the butter in a pan and add the olive oil, crushed garlic, salt, and freshly ground black pepper, and stir to blend. Pour the mixture into a shallow dish.

3 In another shallow dish, blend the bread crumbs and chopped fresh parsley. Roll the corn cobs in the melted butter mixture and then in the bread crumbs until they are well coated.

4 Cook the corn cobs on a hot barbecue for about 10 minutes, turning them frequently, until the bread crumbs are golden brown. Serve hot with skewers or forks to hold the cobs.

VEGETABLES IN PEANUT AND CHILI SAUCE

THIS DISH MAKES A WONDERFUL SLASH OF COLOR AND TASTE TO A MEAL. MAKE IT AS AN ACCOMPANIMENT FOR HEARTY PORK, LAMB, AND POULTRY DISHES.

SERVES FOUR

INGREDIENTS
1 tablespoon palm or vegetable oil
1 onion, chopped
2 garlic cloves, crushed
14-ounce can tomatoes, pureed
3 tablespoons smooth peanut butter
3²⁄₃ cups water
1 teaspoon dried thyme
1 green chile, seeded and chopped
1 vegetable bouillon cube
½ teaspoon ground allspice
2 carrots
4 ounces white cabbage
6 ounces okra
½ red bell pepper
²⁄₃ cup vegetable stock

1 Heat the oil in a large pan and cook the onion and garlic over a medium heat for 5 minutes, stirring frequently. When the onions are soft and transparent, add the tomatoes and peanut butter, and stir well.

2 Stir in the water, thyme, chile, bouillon cube, allspice, and a little salt. Bring to the boil, lower the heat, and simmer gently, uncovered, for about 35 minutes.

3 Cut the carrots into sticks, slice the cabbage, trim the okra, and seed and slice the red bell pepper.

4 Place the vegetables in a pan with the stock, bring to the boil, and cook until tender but still with a little "bite."

5 Drain the vegetables and place in a warmed serving dish. Pour the sauce over the top and serve.

CHILI ZUCCHINI

CALABACITAS IS AN EXTREMELY EASY RECIPE TO MAKE, AND IT IS ALSO DELICIOUS CHILLED. USE
YOUNG TENDER ZUCCHINI THAT REMAIN SWEET AND CRISP AFTER COOKING.

SERVES FOUR

INGREDIENTS

2 tablespoons corn oil
1 pound young zucchini, sliced
1 onion, finely chopped
2 garlic cloves, chopped
1 pound tomatoes, peeled, seeded
  and chopped
2 drained canned jalapeño chiles,
  rinsed, seeded, and chopped
1 tablespoon chopped fresh
  cilantro
salt
fresh cilantro, to garnish

1 Heat the oil in a flameproof casserole and fry the onions and garlic until soft. Add all the remaining ingredients, except the salt.

2 Cover with water and bring to simmering point. Cover and cook over a low heat for about 30 minutes, until the zucchini are tender, checking from time to time that the dish is not drying out. If it is, add a little tomato juice, stock, or water.

3 Season with salt to taste, and serve the Mexican way as a separate course in a bowl for each of your guests. Alternatively, serve as an accompaniment to any plainly cooked meat or poultry. Place it in a colorful serving dish and garnish with fresh cilantro.

REFRIED BEANS

THESE ARE NOT ACTUALLY FRIED TWICE, BUT THEY ARE COOKED TWICE, FIRST AS FRIJOLES DE OLLA
*AND THEN BY FRYING IN SHORTENING. IF THE ONLY REFRIED BEANS YOU'VE TRIED HAVE BEEN THE
CANNED ONES, YOU MAY HAVE FOUND THEM RATHER BLAND. THESE, HOWEVER, ARE SUPERB.*

SERVES FOUR

INGREDIENTS
    2 tablespoons shortening
    2 onions, finely chopped
    1 teaspoon ground cumin
    1 teaspoon ground coriander
    1 quantity Frijoles de Olla, without
      the toppings
    3 garlic cloves, crushed
    small bunch of fresh cilantro or
      4–5 dried avocado leaves
    2 ounces feta cheese
    salt

1 Melt the shortening in a large frying
pan. Add the onions, cumin, and
ground coriander. Cook gently over a
low heat for about 30 minutes or until
the onions caramelize and become soft.

2 Add a ladleful of the soft, cooked
beans. Fry them for only a few minutes,
simply to heat. Mash the beans into the
onions as they cook, using a fork or a
potato masher. Continue until all the
beans have been added, a little at a
time, then stir in the crushed garlic.

3 Lower the heat and cook the beans
to form a thick paste. Season with salt
and spoon into a warmed serving dish.
avocado leaves, and sprinkle most of
them over the beans. Crumble the feta
cheese over the top, then garnish with
the reserved sprigs or leaves.

FRIJOLES CHARROS

THESE "COWBOY BEANS" TASTE LIKE BOSTON BAKED BEANS, BUT WITH A BIT MORE PUNCH.
THE FLAVOR IMPROVES ON KEEPING, SO MAKE IT THE DAY BEFORE YOU INTEND TO SERVE IT.

SERVES SIX

INGREDIENTS
   2 x 14-ounce cans pinto beans
   ½ cup Mexican beer
   ⅔ cup drained pickled jalapeño chile
      slices
   2 tomatoes, peeled and chopped
   1 teaspoon ground cinnamon
   6 ounces bacon fat
   1 onion, chopped
   2 garlic cloves, crushed
   6 ounces rindless smoked lean
      bacon, diced
   3 tablespoons soft dark brown sugar
   wheat-flour tortillas, to serve

1 Put the drained pinto beans in a pan. Stir in the beer and cook over a high heat for 5 minutes, until some of the beer has been absorbed.

2 Lower the heat slightly and stir in the chopped jalapeño slices, then add the tomatoes and cinnamon. Continue to cook, stirring occasionally, for about 10 minutes.

3 Meanwhile, heat the bacon fat in a frying pan until it runs. The quantity suggested should yield about 3 tablespoons bacon fat.

4 Discard the bacon, then add the onion and garlic to the pan, and fry for about 5 minutes, until browned. Using a slotted spoon, lift out the garlic and onions and stir them into the beans.

5 Add the diced smoked bacon to the fat remaining in the frying pan and fry until crisp. Add the bacon and any remaining fat to the beans and mix well.

6 Stir in the sugar. Cook the bean and bacon mixture over a low heat, stirring constantly, until the sugar is dissolved. Serve immediately or spoon into a bowl, leave to cool, cover, then chill for reheating the next day. Serve with warmed wheat-flour tortillas.

OKRA FRIED RICE

OKRA WAS INTRODUCED TO MAINLAND SOUTH AMERICA AND THE ISLANDS OF THE CARIBBEAN BY THE AFRICAN SLAVES WHO WERE BROUGHT OVER TO WORK THE SUGAR PLANTATIONS. IT BECAME AN IMPORTANT AND MUCH-VALUED INGREDIENT.

SERVES FOUR

INGREDIENTS

1 tablespoon butter or margarine
2 tablespoons vegetable oil
1 garlic clove, crushed
½ red onion, finely chopped
4 ounces okra, trimmed
2 tablespoons diced green and red
  bell peppers
½ teaspoon dried thyme
2 fresh green chiles, finely chopped
½ teaspoon five-spice powder
1 vegetable bouillon cube
2 tablespoons soy sauce
1 tablespoon chopped fresh
  cilantro
2 cups cooked long-grain white rice
salt and ground black pepper
fresh cilantro, to garnish

1 Melt the butter or margarine in the oil in a frying pan or wok. Add the garlic and onion, and cook over a medium heat for 5 minutes, until the onion is soft but not browned.

2 Trim the okra, cutting off the stalks and points, then thinly slice the pods. Add to the pan or wok and cook gently for 6–7 minutes.

3 Add the green and red peppers, thyme, chiles, and five-spice powder. Cook for 3 minutes, then crumble in the bouillon cube.

4 Add the soy sauce, chopped cilantro, and rice, and heat through, stirring well. Season with salt and pepper. Spoon into a dish and serve hot, garnished with the cilantro sprigs.

EGGPLANTS <u>WITH</u> GARLIC <u>AND</u> SCALLIONS

THIS IS A SUPERB WAY OF SERVING EGGPLANT. IT CAN BE MADE EVEN MORE DELICIOUS BY ADDING LITTLE STRIPS OF SMOKED SALMON AT THE LAST MINUTE AND LETTING THEM JUST WARM THROUGH.

SERVES FOUR

INGREDIENTS

3 tablespoons vegetable oil
2 garlic cloves, crushed
3 tomatoes, peeled and chopped
2 pounds eggplants,
  cut into chunks
⅔ cup vegetable
  stock or water
2 tablespoons soy sauce
4 tablespoons chopped scallion
½ red bell pepper, seeded
  and chopped
1 fresh hot chile, seeded
  and chopped
2 tablespoons chopped fresh
  cilantro
salt and ground black pepper

1 Heat the oil in a wok or frying pan and fry the garlic and tomatoes for 3–4 minutes. Add the eggplants and toss with the garlic and tomatoes.

2 Pour in the stock or water and cover the pan. Simmer gently until the eggplants are very soft. Stir in the soy sauce and half of the scallion.

3 Add the red bell pepper and chile to the eggplant. Season with salt and pepper to taste. Mix well.

4 Stir in the cilantro and sprinkle with the remaining scallion. Spoon the eggplant mixture into a dish and serve at once. Alternatively, allow to cool until warm before serving.

CASSAVA <u>WITH A</u> CITRUS SALSA

THIS DISH CONSISTS OF DICED CASSAVA IN A CLASSIC CUBAN SAUCE CALLED MOJO. *WHEN THE COOKED CASSAVA IS COATED IN THE SHARP DRESSING, IT BECOMES IMBUED WITH THE DELICIOUS FLAVORS OF FRESH ORANGE, LIME, AND GARLIC.*

<u>SERVES FOUR</u>

INGREDIENTS
    1¾ pounds cassava, peeled and cut
        into chunks
    2 garlic cloves, crushed
    juice of 1 small orange
    juice of 1 lime
    3 tablespoons olive oil
    1 tablespoon chopped fresh
        Italian parsley
    salt

VARIATION
Mojo is also delicious with cooked
pumpkin and sweet potatoes.

1 Cook the cassava in a large pan of salted boiling water for 20–25 minutes, until it begins to break up. Drain in a colander and then transfer to a large serving plate.

2 Mix the garlic, orange juice, and lime juice in a bowl. Whisk in the oil, season with salt, and stir in the parsley. Drizzle the dressing over the cooked cassava and serve.

STIR-FRIED COLLARD GREENS

COLLARD GREENS ARE VERY POPULAR IN BRAZIL. THEY ARE EATEN WITH MEAT AND ARE THE TRADITIONAL ACCOMPANIMENT TO FEIJOADA. GARLIC ENHANCES THEIR SLIGHTLY BITTER FLAVOR, AND THEY TASTE EVEN BETTER WHEN COOKED WITH BACON AND CHILES.

SERVES SIX

INGREDIENTS
  1 pound collard greens
  1 tablespoon vegetable oil
  5 ounces smoked fatty bacon, in one piece
  2 garlic cloves, crushed
  ¼ teaspoon crushed dried chili
  salt

VARIATIONS
• If you cannot find collard greens, use curly kale or Savoy cabbage instead. These may not be as vibrant in color, but the taste will be very similar.
• Cubed pancetta can be used instead of the bacon.

1 Cut off the hard stalks from the collard greens. Lay the leaves flat on top of each other and roll into a tight cigar-shape. Slice very thinly, using a sharp knife.

2 Heat the oil in a large frying pan over a low heat. Cut the bacon into small cubes and sauté in the oil for 5 minutes, or until golden brown. Lift the cubes out of the pan with a slotted spoon and drain on paper towels.

3 Increase the heat, add the crushed garlic and dried chili to the oil remaining in the pan, and stir-fry for about 30 seconds.

4 Add the shredded collard greens and toss over the heat until just tender. Season to taste with salt, stir in the cooked bacon cubes, and serve immediately.

CORN STICKS

THIS TRADITIONAL CARIBBEAN RECIPE PRODUCES PERFECT CORN BREAD IN A LOAF PAN.
ALTERNATIVELY, IF YOU CAN FIND THE MOLDS, IT CAN BE USED TO MAKE ATTRACTIVE CORN STICKS.

MAKES FORTY

INGREDIENTS
    2 cups all-purpose flour
    2 cups fine cornmeal
    10 teaspoons baking soda
    ½ teaspoon salt
    4 tablespoons raw sugar
    scant 2 cups milk
    2 eggs
    4 tablespoons butter or margarine

COOK'S TIP
Because there is so much bicarbonate of
soda used in this recipe, the cornmeal
mixture begins to rise as soon as the
liquid is added, so make sure you bake
right away.

1 Preheat the oven to 375°F and grease
either corn-bread molds, if you can find
them, or a 2-pound loaf pan.

2 Sift together the flour, corn meal,
bicarbonate of soda, salt, and sugar into
a large bowl. In a separate bowl, whisk
the milk and eggs, then stir into the
flour mixture.

3 Melt the butter or margarine in a
small pan and stir gradually into the
cornmeal mixture.

4 Carefully spoon the thick mixture into
the molds or pan. Bake the corn sticks
for about 15 minutes. If using a loaf pan,
you will need to bake for around 30–35
minutes, until the corn bread is golden
and hollow-sounding when tapped.

MUSHROOMS <u>WITH</u> CHIPOTLE CHILES

THESE SPICY MUSHROOMS COULDN'T BE EASIER TO PREPARE. SERVE THEM AS AN APPETIZER, OR AS AN ACCOMPANIMENT TO MEAT AND POULTRY DISHES, WITH SOME BREAD TO SOAK UP THE JUICES.

SERVES SIX

INGREDIENTS
    4 cups white mushrooms
    4 tablespoons olive oil
    1 onion, finely chopped
    2 garlic cloves, chopped
    2 drained canned chipotle chiles,
      rinsed and sliced
    salt
    chopped fresh cilantro,
      to garnish

COOK'S TIP
Never wash mushrooms, as they
quickly absorb water and lose their
flavor. Wipe them with paper towels
or a clean, damp cloth.

1 Wipe the mushrooms gently and
carefully with paper towels. Heat the
olive oil in a large frying pan and add
the mushrooms, finely chopped onion,
chopped garlic, and sliced chiles. Stir to
coat in oil.

2 Cook the mixture over a medium heat
for 6–8 minutes, stirring occasionally,
until the onions and mushrooms are
tender. Season to taste with salt and
serve on small plates, sprinkled with a
little chopped fresh cilantro.

SALSAS

Mexican and Latin American cuisine is known for its salsas. Whether hot and spicy or cool and refreshing, these are served as a relish or stirred into dishes. There are delicious salsas to complement all kinds of foods, from shellfish or barbecued meat to tortillas and enchiladas.

ARGENTINIAN BARBECUE SALSA

THIS COMBINATION OF FINELY CHOPPED VEGETABLES AND TART DRESSING IS THE PERFECT PARTNER FOR ALL TYPES OF BROILED OR BARBECUED MEATS, SO IT IS NOT SURPRISING TO FIND BOWLS OF FRESH SALSA CREOLLA ON THE TABLE WHENEVER A BARBECUE OR ASADO IS BEING PEPARED. SIMILAR BARBECUE SALSAS CAN ALSO BE FOUND IN BRAZIL, URUGUAY, AND PARAGUAY.

SERVES SIX AS AN ACCOMPANIMENT

INGREDIENTS
2 fresh green chiles, seeded and very
finely chopped
1 garlic clove, crushed
1 onion, very finely chopped
1 large tomato, peeled, seeded, and
very finely chopped
1 tablespoon finely chopped fresh
Italian parsley
salt
7 tablespoons olive oil
2 tablespoons red wine vinegar

1 Combine the chopped chiles, crushed garlic, onion, and tomato in a bowl. Stir in the chopped parsley and season to taste with salt.

2 Pour in the oil and vinegar and stir well. Allow the flavors to mingle for at least 1 hour before serving with broiled or barbecued meats.

HOT CHILI SALSA

CONTRARY TO POPULAR BELIEF, LATIN FOOD IS NOT INTRINSICALLY SPICY. IT IS THE HOT CHILI OILS AND SALSAS, ADDED TO DISHES AT THE TABLE, THAT FAN THE FLAMES.

MAKES ONE SMALL JAR

INGREDIENTS
10 fresh red chiles, roughly chopped
1 large tomato, peeled and quartered
2 garlic cloves
juice of 1 lime
4 tablespoons olive oil
salt

COOK'S TIP
Treat this salsa with extreme caution. Just the oil is enough to add serious heat to a dish, especially if the salsa has had a chance to age. A couple of drops of the oil are enough for most people!

1 Place the chiles, tomato, and garlic in a food processor, then process the mixture until smooth.

2 Scrape the mixture into a small frying pan and place over a medium heat. Season with salt and cook, stirring, for 10 minutes, until the sauce is thick.

3 Remove from the heat and stir in the freshly squeezed lime juice. Transfer to a sterilized airtight jar and top with a thin film of olive oil before tightly screwing on the lid. As long as the sauce always has a film of oil on top, it will keep for ages at room temperature or in the refrigerator.

GREEN TOMATILLO SAUCE

This sauce, with its distinctive green color and sharp taste, is a popular choice for pouring over enchiladas. When the cream is added, it is perfect for poached fish or with chicken breasts. Fresh tomatillos are difficult to obtain outside Mexico, but the sauce can be made with canned tomatillos. Instructions for both versions are given here.

SERVES FOUR AS A SAUCE
FOR A MAIN COURSE

INGREDIENTS
    11 ounces fresh tomatillos, plus
        ½ cup stock or water **or** 11 ounces
        drained canned tomatillos, plus
        ¼ cup stock or water
    2 fresh serrano chiles
    4 garlic cloves, crushed
    1 tablespoon vegetable oil
    bunch of fresh cilantro
    ½ cup heavy cream (optional)
    salt

1 If using fresh tomatillos, remove the husks and cut the tomatillos into quarters. Place them in a pan and add the stock or water. Cook over a moderate heat for 8–10 minutes, until the flesh is soft and transparent.

2 Remove the stalks from the chiles, slit them and scrape out the seeds with a small knife. Chop the flesh roughly and place it in a food processor or blender with the garlic.

3 Add the tomatillos to the processor or blender with their cooking liquid and process for a few minutes until almost smooth. If using drained canned tomatillos, simply quarter and put in the blender or food processor with the smaller amount of stock or water and the chopped chiles and garlic. Process until almost smooth.

4 Heat the oil in a heavy-based frying pan and add the processed tomatillo puree. Reduce the heat and cook gently, stirring, for about 5 minutes until the sauce thickens. Be sure to keep stirring the sauce all the time, since it can easily catch and burn.

5 Chop the cilantro and add it to the sauce, with salt to taste. Cook for a few minutes, stirring occasionally.

6 Stir in the cream, if using, and warm the sauce through. Do not let it boil after adding the cream. Serve at once.

GUACAMOLE

ONE OF THE BEST-LOVED MEXICAN SALSAS, THIS BLEND OF CREAMY AVOCADO, TOMATOES, CHILES, CILANTRO, AND LIME NOW APPEARS ON TABLES THE WORLD OVER. BOUGHT GUACAMOLE USUALLY CONTAINS MAYONNAISE, WHICH HELPS TO PRESERVE THE AVOCADO, BUT THIS IS NOT AN INGREDIENT IN TRADITIONAL RECIPES.

SERVES EIGHT AS AN ACCOMPANIMENT

INGREDIENTS
4 medium tomatoes
4 ripe avocados, preferably fuerte
juice of 1 lime
½ small onion
2 garlic cloves
small bunch of fresh cilantro,
   chopped
3 fresh red fresno chiles
salt
tortilla chips, to serve

1 Cut a cross in the base of each tomato. Place the tomatoes in a heatproof bowl and pour over boiling water to cover.

2 Leave the tomatoes in the water for 3 minutes, then lift them out using a slotted spoon and plunge them into a bowl of cold water. Drain. The skins will have begun to peel back from the crosses. Remove the skins completely. Cut the tomatoes in half, remove the seeds with a teaspoon, then chop the flesh roughly and set it aside.

3 Cut the avocados in half, then remove the pits. Scoop the flesh out of the shells and place it in a food processor or blender. Process until almost smooth, then scrape into a bowl and stir in the lime juice.

4 Chop the onion finely, then crush the garlic. Add both to the avocado and mix well. Stir in the cilantro.

5 Remove the stalks from the chiles, slit them, and scrape out the seeds with a small sharp knife. Chop the chiles finely and add them to the avocado mixture, with the chopped tomatoes. Mix well.

6 Check the seasoning and add salt to taste. Cover with plastic wrap and chill for 1 hour before serving as a dip with tortilla chips. If it is well covered, guacamole will keep in the refrigerator for 2–3 days.

COOK'S TIP
Smooth-skinned fuerte avocados are native to Mexico, so would be ideal for this dip. If they are not available, use any avocados, but make sure they are ripe. To test, gently press the top of the avocado; it should give a little.

PINTO BEAN SALSA

THESE BEANS HAVE A PRETTY, SPECKLED APPEARANCE. THE SMOKY FLAVOR OF THE CHIPOTLE CHILES AND THE HERBY TASTE OF THE PASILLA CHILE CONTRAST WELL WITH THE TART TOMATILLOS. UNUSUALLY, THESE ARE NOT COOKED.

2 Soak the chipotle and pasilla chiles in hot water for about 10 minutes until softened. Drain, reserving the soaking water. Remove the stalks, then slit each chile and scrape out the seeds with a small sharp knife. Chop the flesh finely and mix it to a smooth paste with a little of the soaking water.

3 Roast the garlic in a dry frying pan over a moderate heat for a few minutes until the cloves start to turn golden. Crush them and add them to the beans.

SERVES FOUR AS AN ACCOMPANIMENT

INGREDIENTS
  generous ½ cup pinto beans, soaked
    overnight in water to cover
  2 chipotle chiles
  1 pasilla chile
  2 garlic cloves, peeled
  ½ onion
  7 ounces fresh tomatillos
  salt

1 Drain the beans and put them in a large pan. Pour in water to cover and place the lid on the pan. Bring to the boil, lower the heat slightly, and simmer the beans for 45–50 minutes or until tender. They should still have a little bite and should not have begun to disintegrate. Drain, rinse under cold water, then drain again and tip into a bowl. Leave the beans until cold.

COOK'S TIP
Canned tomatillos can be substituted, but to keep a clean, fresh flavor add a little lime juice.

4 Chop the onion and tomatillos and stir them into the beans. Add the chili paste and mix well. Add salt to taste, cover, and chill before serving.

BLACK BEAN SALSA

THIS SALSA HAS A VERY STRIKING APPEARANCE. IT IS RARE TO FIND A BLACK SAUCE, AND IT PROVIDES A WONDERFUL CONTRAST TO THE MORE COMMON REDS AND GREENS ON THE PLATE. THE PASADO CHILES ADD A SUBTLE CITRUS FLAVOR.

SERVES FOUR AS AN ACCOMPANIMENT

INGREDIENTS
  generous ½ cup black beans, soaked
    overnight in water
    to cover
  1 pasado chile
  2 fresh red fresno chiles
  1 red onion
  grated rind and juice of 1 lime
  2 tablespoons Mexican beer
    (optional)
  1 tablespoon olive oil
  small bunch of fresh cilantro,
    chopped
  salt

1 Drain the beans and put them in a large pan. Pour in water to cover and place the lid on the pan. Bring to the boil, lower the heat slightly, and simmer the beans for about 40 minutes or until tender. They should still have a little bite and should not have begun to disintegrate. Drain, rinse under cold water, then drain again and leave the beans until cold.

2 Soak the pasado chile in hot water for about 10 minutes until softened. Drain, remove the stalk, then slit the chile and scrape out the seeds with a small sharp knife. Chop the flesh finely.

COOK'S TIP
Mexican beer is a lager-type beer. Few brands are to be found in this country, but the most popular, *Dos Equis* (Double X), is readily available.

3 Spear the fresno chiles on a long-handled metal skewer and roast them over the flame of a gas burner until the skins blister and darken. Do not let the flesh burn. Alternatively, dry-fry them in a griddle pan until the skins are scorched. Then place the roasted chiles in a strong plastic bag and tie the top to keep the steam in. Set aside for 20 minutes.

4 Meanwhile, chop the red onion finely. Remove the chiles from the bag and peel off the skins. Slit them, remove the seeds, and chop them finely.

5 Tip the beans into a bowl and add the onion and both types of chile. Stir in the lime rind and juice, beer, oil, and cilantro. Season with salt and mix well. Chill before serving.

CHIPOTLE SAUCE

THE SMOKY FLAVOR OF THIS SAUCE MAKES IT IDEAL FOR BARBECUED FOOD, EITHER AS A MARINADE OR AS AN ACCOMPANIMENT. IT IS ALSO WONDERFUL STIRRED INTO CREAM CHEESE AS A SANDWICH FILLING WITH CHICKEN. CHIPOTLE CHILES ARE SMOKED DRIED JALAPEÑO CHILES.

SERVES SIX AS AN ACCOMPANIMENT

INGREDIENTS
   1¼ pounds tomatoes
   5 chipotle chiles
   3 garlic cloves, roughly chopped
   ⅔ cup red wine
   1 teaspoon dried oregano
   4 tablespoons clear honey
   1 teaspoon American mustard
   ½ teaspoon ground black pepper
   salt

1 Preheat the oven to 400°F. Cut the tomatoes into quarters and place them in a roasting pan. Roast for 45 minutes–1 hour, until they are charred and softened.

2 Meanwhile, soak the chiles in a bowl of cold water to cover for about 20 minutes or until soft. Remove the stalks, slit the chiles, and scrape out the seeds with a small sharp knife. Chop the flesh roughly.

3 Remove the tomatoes from the oven, let them cool slightly, then remove the skins. If you prefer a smooth sauce, remove the seeds. Chop the tomatoes and put them in a blender or food processor. Add the chopped chiles and garlic with the red wine. Process until smooth, then add the oregano, honey, mustard, and black pepper. Process briefly to mix, then taste and season with salt.

4 Scrape the mixture into a small pan. Place over a moderate heat and stir until the mixture boils. Lower the heat and simmer the sauce for about 10 minutes, stirring occasionally, until it has reduced and thickened. Spoon into a bowl and serve hot or cold.

GUAJILLO CHILI SAUCE

THIS SAUCE CAN BE SERVED OVER ENCHILADAS OR STEAMED VEGETABLES. IT IS ALSO GOOD WITH MEATS SUCH AS PORK, AND A LITTLE MAKES A FINE SEASONING FOR SOUPS OR STEWS. MADE FROM DRIED CHILI, IT HAS A WELL ROUNDED, FRUITY FLAVOR AND IS NOT TOO HOT.

SERVES FOUR AS AN ACCOMPANIMENT

INGREDIENTS
   2 tomatoes, total weight about
     7 ounces
   2 red bell peppers, cored, seeded,
     and quartered
   3 garlic cloves, in their skins
   2 ancho chiles
   2 guajillo chiles
   2 tablespoons tomato paste
   1 teaspoon dried oregano
   1 teaspoon soft dark brown sugar
   1¼ cups chicken stock

1 Preheat the oven to 400°F. Cut the tomatoes into quarters and place them in a roasting pan with the peppers and whole garlic cloves. Roast for 45 minutes–1 hour, until the tomatoes and peppers are slightly charred and the garlic has softened.

2 Put the peppers in a strong plastic bag and tie the top to keep the steam in. Set aside for 20 minutes. Remove the skin from the tomatoes. Meanwhile, soak the chiles in boiling water for 15 minutes until soft.

3 Remove the peppers from the bag and rub off the skins. Cut them in half, remove the cores and seeds, then chop the flesh roughly and put it in a food processor or blender. Drain the chiles, remove the stalks, then slit them and scrape out the seeds with a sharp knife. Chop the chiles roughly and add them to the peppers.

4 Add the roasted tomatoes to the food processor or blender. Squeeze the roasted garlic out of the skins and add to the tomato mixture, with the tomato puree, oregano, brown sugar, and stock. Process until smooth.

5 Pour the mixture into a pan, place over a moderate heat, and bring to the boil. Lower the heat and simmer for 10–15 minutes, until the sauce has reduced to about half. Transfer to a bowl and serve immediately or, if serving cold, cover, leave to cool, then chill until required. The sauce will keep in the refrigerator for up to a week.

ROASTED TOMATO SALSA

SLOW ROASTING THESE TOMATOES TO A SEMI-DRIED STATE RESULTS IN A VERY RICH, FULL-FLAVORED SWEET SAUCE. THE COSTENO AMARILLO CHILE IS MILD AND HAS A FRESH LIGHT FLAVOR, MAKING IT THE PERFECT PARTNER FOR THE RICH TOMATO TASTE. THIS SALSA IS GREAT WITH TUNA OR SEA BASS AND MAKES A MARVELOUS SANDWICH FILLING WHEN TEAMED WITH CREAMY CHEESE.

SERVES SIX AS AN ACCOMPANIMENT

INGREDIENTS
    1¼ pounds tomatoes
    8 small shallots
    5 garlic cloves
    sea salt
    1 fresh rosemary sprig
    2 costeno amarillo chiles
    grated rind and juice of ½ small
        lemon
    2 tablespoons extra virgin olive oil
    ¼ teaspoon soft dark brown sugar

1 Preheat the oven to 325ºF. Cut the tomatoes into quarters and place them on a baking tray.

2 Peel the shallots and garlic and add them to the roasting pan. Sprinkle with sea salt. Roast in the oven for 1¼ hours or until the tomatoes are beginning to dry. Do not let them burn or blacken, or they will have a bitter taste.

3 Leave the tomatoes to cool, then peel off the skins and chop the flesh finely. Place in a bowl. Remove the outer layer of skin from any shallots that have toughened.

4 Using a large, sharp knife, chop the shallots and garlic roughly, place them with the tomatoes in a bowl, and mix.

5 Strip the rosemary leaves from the woody stem and chop them finely. Add half to the tomato and shallot mixture and mix lightly.

6 Soak the chiles in hot water for about 10 minutes until soft. Drain, remove the stalks, slit them, and scrape out the seeds with a sharp knife. Chop the flesh finely and add it to the tomato mixture.

7 Stir in the lemon rind and juice, the olive oil, and the sugar. Mix well, taste, and add more salt if needed. Cover and chill for at least an hour before serving, sprinkled with the remaining rosemary. It will keep for up to a week in the refrigerator.

COOK'S TIP
Use plum tomatoes or vine tomatoes, which have more flavor than tomatoes that have been grown for their longevity rather than their flavor. Cherry tomatoes make delicious roast tomato salsa, and there is no need to peel them after roasting.

TAMARILLO SAUCE

THIS UNUSUAL PERUVIAN SAUCE MAKES A DELICIOUS DIP FOR SERVING WITH ArepAS—*THOSE IRRESISTIBLE CORNMEAL GRIDDLE CAKES THAT ARE FREQUENTLY FILLED WITH SOFT WHITE CHEESE. ALTERNATIVELY, ITS DELICIOUS HOT AND SPICY FLAVOR CONTRASTS BEAUTIFULLY WITH THE NATURAL SWEETNESS OF FRESH BROILED SEAFOOD.*

SERVES FOUR AS AN ACCOMPANIMENT

INGREDIENTS
- 1 pound fresh tamarillos
- ½ teaspoon ground ginger
- ¼ teaspoon ground cinnamon
- 1 fresh red chile, seeded and chopped
- 1 small onion, finely chopped
- 1 teaspoon light brown sugar
- 7 tablespoons water
- 2 tablepoons olive oil
- salt

COOK'S TIP
If tamarillos are heavier than they look, they will be ripe and juicy.

1 Place the whole fresh tamarillos in a large pan of boiling water for about 30 seconds. Drain, refresh in cold water, then carefully remove the peel with a sharp knife and discard it. Roughly chop the tamarillos.

2 Place the ginger and cinnamon in a small heavy pan over a low heat. Stir the mixture for 30 seconds, until the spices release their aroma. Add the chopped tamarillos, chile, onion, sugar, and water.

3 Bring to the boil, lower the heat, cover, and simmer for 20 minutes. Remove the lid and continue cooking until the sauce thickens. Stir in the oil and season with salt. Serve with broiled seafood.

AVOCADO SALSA

THERE ARE MANY VERSIONS OF AVOCADO SALSA, INCLUDING THE CLASSIC MEXICAN GUACAMOLE. HERE THE INGREDIENTS ARE CHOPPED AND DICED, RATHER THAN MASHED, WHICH ADDS TEXTURE AND ALLOWS ALL THE DELICIOUS FLAVORS TO REMAIN DISTINCT. PREPARE THIS SALSA AT THE LAST MINUTE TO PREVENT THE AVOCADOS FROM DISCOLORING.

SERVES FOUR AS AN ACCOMPANIMENT

INGREDIENTS
1 large ripe avocado
juice of 1 lime
1 tablespoon red wine vinegar
1 tomato, peeled, seeded
   and chopped
1 green bell pepper, seeded
   and diced
1 red onion, finely chopped
1 fresh red chile, seeded and
   finely chopped
3 tablespoons olive oil
salt

1 Prepare the avocado. Run a sharp knife around the whole length of the avocado, cutting right in until you touch the pit. Twist the two sides of the split avocado in opposite directions to separate the two halves.

2 Use a large spoon to remove the large pit, then peel both halves of the avocado. Dice the flesh and put it in a bowl with the lime juice.

3 Stir the vinegar, tomato, pepper, onion, and chile into the avocado and lime juice mixture. Gradually add the olive oil, mixing well.

COOK'S TIP
If there is any delay before serving this salsa, add the avocado pit to the mixture. This will prevent any discoloration. Remember to remove the pit before serving though.

4 Season to taste with salt and serve with tortilla chips, or as an accompaniment to meat, fish, or poultry.

JICAMA SALSA

The jicama is a round, brown root vegetable with a texture somewhere between that of a water chestnut and a crisp apple. It can be eaten raw or cooked, and is always peeled. Look for jicamas in ethnic food stores.

SERVES FOUR AS AN ACCOMPANIMENT

INGREDIENTS
  1 small red onion
  juice of 2 limes
  3 small oranges
  1 *jicama*, about 1 pound
  ½ cucumber
  1 fresh red fresno chile

1 Cut the onion in half, then slice each half finely. Place in a bowl, add the lime juice, and leave to soak while you prepare the remaining ingredients.

2 Slice the top and bottom off each orange. Stand an orange on a board, then carefully slice off all the peel and pith. Hold the orange over a bowl and cut carefully between the membranes so that the segments fall into the bowl. Having cut out all the segments, squeeze the pulp over the bowl to extract the remaining juice.

3 Peel the *jicama* and rinse it in cold water. Cut it into quarters, then slice finely. Add to the bowl of orange juice.

COOK'S TIP
The juices of citrus fruits are very useful in preserving color and freshness, and add more than flavoring to a recipe. For instance, lemon juice added to sliced apples keeps them white. Guacamole retains its color for two to three days if lime juice is added. In this recipe the lime juice will slightly soften the finely sliced onion.

4 Cut the cucumber in half lengthwise, then use a teaspoon to scoop out the seeds. Slice the cucumber and add to the bowl. Remove the stalk from the chile, slit it, and scrape out the seeds with a small sharp knife. Chop the flesh finely and add to the bowl.

5 Add the sliced onion to the bowl, with any remaining lime juice, and mix well. Cover and leave to stand at room temperature for at least 1 hour before serving. If not serving immediately, put the salsa in the refrigerator; it will keep for 2–3 days.

SWEET POTATO SALSA

VERY COLORFUL AND DELIGHTFULLY SWEET, THIS SALSA MAKES THE PERFECT ACCOMPANIMENT TO HOT, SPICY MEXICAN DISHES.

SERVES FOUR AS AN ACCOMPANIMENT

INGREDIENTS
  1½ pounds sweet potatoes
  juice of 1 small orange
  1 teaspoon crushed dried
    jalapeño chiles
  4 small scallions
  juice of 1 small lime (optional)
  salt

COOK'S TIP
This fresh and tasty salsa is also very good served with a simple broiled salmon fillet or other fish dishes, and makes a delicious accompaniment to veal escalopes or grilled chicken breasts.

1 Peel the sweet potatoes and dice the flesh finely. Bring a pan of water to the boil. Add the sweet potato and cook for 8–10 minutes, until just soft. Drain off the water, cover the pan, and put it back on the hob, having first turned off the heat. Leave the sweet potato to dry out for about 5 minutes, then tip into a bowl and set aside.

2 Mix the orange juice and crushed dried chiles in a bowl. Chop the scallions finely and add them to the juice and chiles.

3 When the sweet potatoes are cool, add the orange juice mixture and toss carefully until all the pieces are well coated. Cover the bowl and chill for at least 1 hour, then taste and season with salt. Stir in the lime juice if you prefer a fresher taste. The salsa will keep for 2–3 days in a covered bowl in the refrigerator.

NOPALES SALSA

NOPALES ARE THE TENDER, FLESHY LEAVES OR "PADDLES" OF AN EDIBLE CACTUS KNOWN VARIOUSLY AS THE CACTUS PEAR AND THE PRICKLY PEAR CACTUS. THIS GROWS WILD IN MEXICO BUT IS ALSO CULTIVATED. THE MOST FAMILIAR TYPE SOLD IN MEXICAN MARKETS HAS DARK GREEN OVALS WITH TINY THORNS. FRESH NOPALES ARE DIFFICULT TO TRACK DOWN OUTSIDE MEXICO, BUT IF YOU DO LOCATE A SUPPLY, LOOK FOR PADDLES THAT ARE FIRM AND SMOOTH SKINNED.

SERVES FOUR AS AN ACCOMPANIMENT

INGREDIENTS
   2 fresh red fresno chiles
   9 ounces *nopales* (cactus paddles)
   3 scallions
   3 garlic cloves, peeled
   ½ red onion
   3½ ounces fresh tomatillos
   ½ teaspoon salt
   ⅔ cup cider vinegar

1 Spear the chiles on a long-handled metal skewer and roast them over the flame of a gas burner until the skins blister and darken. Do not let the flesh burn. Alternatively, dry-fry them in a griddle pan until the skins are scorched. Place the roasted chiles in a strong plastic bag and tie the top to keep the steam in. Set aside for 20 minutes.

2 Remove the chiles from the bag and peel off the skins. Cut off the stalks, then slit the chiles and scrape out the seeds. Chop the chiles roughly and set them aside.

COOK'S TIP
Fresh *nopales* are sometimes available from specialist fruit and vegetable stores. Like okra, they yield a sticky gum, and are best boiled before being used. Fresh cactus will lose about half its weight during cooking. Look out for canned *nopales* (sometimes sold as *nopalitos*) packed in water or vinegar.

3 Carefully remove the thorns from the *nopales*. Wearing gloves or holding each cactus paddle in turn with kitchen tongs, cut off the bumps that contain the thorns with a sharp knife.

4 Cut off and discard the thick base from each cactus paddle. Rinse the paddles well and cut them into strips, then cut the strips into small pieces.

5 Bring a large pan of lightly salted water to the boil. Add the cactus paddle strips, scallions, and garlic. Boil for 10–15 minutes, until the paddle strips are just tender.

6 Drain the mixture in a colander, rinse under cold running water to remove any remaining stickiness, then drain again. Discard the scallions and garlic.

7 Chop the red onion and the tomatillos finely. Place in a bowl and add the cactus and chiles.

8 Spoon the mixture into a large preserving jar, add the salt, pour in the vinegar, and seal. Put the jar in the refrigerator for at least 1 day, turning the jar occasionally to ensure that the *nopales* are marinated. The salsa will keep in the refrigerator for up to 10 days.

CHILI BEAN DIP

THIS CREAMY AND SPICY DIP MADE FROM KIDNEY BEANS IS BEST SERVED WARM WITH TRIANGLES OF GOLDEN BROWN TOASTED PITTA BREAD OR A GENEROUS HELPING OF CRUNCHY TORTILLA CHIPS.

SERVES FOUR TO SIX AS AN
ACCOMPANIMENT

INGREDIENTS
2 garlic cloves
1 onion
2 fresh green chiles
2 tablespoons vegetable oil
1–2 teaspoons hot chili powder
14-ounce can kidney beans
¾ cup grated sharp Cheddar cheese
1 red chile, seeded
salt and freshly ground black
  pepper
freshly shaved strips of chile, to
  garnish

1 Finely chop the garlic and onion. Seed and finely chop the fresh green chiles.

2 Heat the oil in a frying pan and add the garlic, onion, green chiles, and chili powder. Cook gently for about 5 minutes, stirring frequently, until the onions have softened.

3 Drain the can of kidney beans, reserving the can juice. Blend all but 2 tablespoons of the beans to a puree in a food processor or blender.

4 Add the pureed beans to the pan with 2–3 tablespoons of the reserved can juice. Heat gently, stirring to mix well.

5 Stir in the whole kidney beans and the grated Cheddar cheese. Cook gently for about 2–3 minutes, stirring until all the cheese melts. Add salt and plenty of freshly ground black pepper to taste.

6 Cut the fresh red chile into tiny strips. Spoon the dip into four individual serving bowls and sprinkle the chile strips over the top of each one. Serve warm.

Cook's Tip
For a dip with a coarser texture, do not puree the kidney beans in a food processor or blender; instead, mash them with a potato masher.

PIQUANT PINEAPPLE RELISH

THIS FRUITY SWEET-AND-SOUR RELISH IS REALLY EXCELLENT WHEN IT IS SERVED WITH BROILED CHICKEN OR BACON SLICES.

SERVES FOUR TO SIX AS AN
ACCOMPANIMENT

INGREDIENTS
14-ounce can crushed pineapple in
   natural juice
2 tablespoons molasses sugar
2 tablespoons wine vinegar
1 garlic clove
4 scallions
2 red chiles
10 fresh basil leaves
salt and ground black pepper

1 Drain the crushed pineapple
pieces thoroughly and reserve about
4 tablespoons of the juice.

2 Place the juice in a small pan with the
molasses sugar and wine vinegar, then
heat gently, stirring, until the sugar
dissolves. Remove the pan from the
heat and add salt and pepper to taste.

3 Finely chop the garlic and scallions.
Halve the chiles, remove the seeds,
and finely chop the flesh. Finely shred
the basil.

4 Place the pineapple, garlic, scallions,
and chiles in a bowl. Mix well and pour
in the sauce. Leave to cool for 5
minutes, then stir in the basil.

Mango Salsa

This has a fresh, fruity taste and is perfect with fish or as a contrast to rich, creamy dishes. The bright colors make it an attractive addition to any table.

SERVES FOUR AS AN ACCOMPANIMENT

INGREDIENTS
    2 fresh red fresno chiles
    2 ripe mangoes
    ½ white onion
    bunch of fresh cilantro
    grated rind and juice of 1 lime

1 To peel the chiles, spear them on a long-handled metal skewer and roast them over the flame of a gas burner until the skins blister and darken. Do not let the flesh burn. Alternatively, dry-fry them in a griddle pan until the skins are scorched.

2 Place the roasted chiles in a strong plastic bag and tie the top to keep the steam in. Set aside for 20 minutes.

COOK'S TIP
Mangoes, in season, are readily available nowadays, but are usually sold unripe. Keep in a warm room for 24 hours or until they are just soft to the touch. Do not allow to ripen beyond this point.

3 Meanwhile, put one of the mangoes on a board and cut off a thick slice close to the flat side of the pit. Turn the mango around and repeat on the other side. Score the flesh on each thick slice with crisscross lines at ½-inch intervals, taking care not to cut through the skin. Repeat with the second mango.

4 Fold the mango halves inside out so that the mango flesh stands proud of the skin, in neat dice. Carefully slice these off the skin and into a bowl. Cut off the flesh adhering to each pit, dice it, and add it to the bowl.

5 Remove the roasted chiles from the bag and carefully peel off the skins. Cut off the stalks, then slit the chiles and scrape out the seeds.

6 Chop the white onion and the cilantro finely and add them to the diced mango. Chop the chile flesh finely and add it to the mixture in the bowl, together with the lime rind and juice. Stir well to mix, cover, and chill for at least 1 hour before serving. The salsa will keep for 2–3 days in the refrigerator.

Roasted Tomato and Cilantro Salsa

Roasting the tomatoes gives a greater depth to the flavor of this salsa, which also benefits from the warm, rounded flavor of roasted chiles.

SERVES SIX AS AN ACCOMPANIMENT

INGREDIENTS
    1¼ pounds tomatoes
    2 fresh serrano chiles
    1 onion
    juice of 1 lime
    bunch of fresh cilantro
    salt

1 Preheat the oven to 400°F. Cut the tomatoes into quarters and place them in a roasting pan. Add the chiles. Roast for 45 minutes–1 hour, until the tomatoes and chiles are charred and softened.

2 Place the roasted chiles in a strong plastic bag. Tie the top to keep the steam in and set aside for 20 minutes. Leave the tomatoes to cool slightly, then remove the skins and dice the flesh.

3 Chop the onion finely, then place in a bowl and add the lime juice and the chopped tomatoes.

4 Remove the chiles from the bag and peel off the skins. Cut off the stalks, then slit the chiles and scrape out the seeds with a sharp knife. Chop the chiles roughly and add them to the onion mixture. Mix well.

5 Chop the cilantro and add most to the salsa. Add salt, cover, and chill for at least 1 hour before serving, sprinkled with the remaining cilantro. This salsa will keep in the refrigerator for 1 week.

CHAYOTE SALSA

CHAYOTE—OR VEGETABLE PEAR, AS IT IS SOMETIMES CALLED—IS A GOURD-LIKE FRUIT, SHAPED LIKE A LARGE PEAR. SEVERAL VARIETIES GROW IN MEXICO, THE MOST COMMON BEING WHITE-FLESHED AND SMOOTH-SKINNED, WITH A TASTE REMINISCENT OF CUCUMBER. CHAYOTES SHOULD BE PEELED BEFORE BEING EATEN RAW OR COOKED. THE SEED, WHICH LOOKS A BIT LIKE A LARGE, FLAT ALMOND, IS EDIBLE. THE CONTRAST BETWEEN THE CRISP CHAYOTE, COOL MELON, AND HOT HABAÑERO SAUCE MAKES THIS A SPECTACULAR SALSA.

SERVES SIX AS AN ACCOMPANIMENT

INGREDIENTS
   1 chayote, about 7 ounces
   ½ small Galia or honeydew melon
   2 teaspoons habañero sauce or
      similar hot chili sauce
   juice of 1 lime
   ½ teaspoon salt
   ½ teaspoon sugar

COOK'S TIP
In some countries, chayotes are called christophenes or choko. They are also used in Chinese cooking, so will be found in Oriental stores.

1 Peel the *chayote*, then cut slices of flesh away from the pit. Cut the slices into thin strips. Cut the melon in half, scoop the seeds out, and cut each half into two pieces. Remove the skin and cut the flesh into small cubes. Place in a bowl with the *chayote* strips.

2 Mix the chili sauce, lime juice, salt, and sugar in a bowl or jug. Stir until all the sugar has dissolved. Pour over the melon and *chayote* mixture, and mix thoroughly. Chill for at least 1 hour before serving. The salsa will keep for up to 3 days in the refrigerator.

PUMPKIN SEED SAUCE

THE ANCESTORS OF MODERN-DAY MEXICANS DIDN'T BELIEVE IN WASTING FOOD, AS THIS TRADITIONAL RECIPE PROVES. IT IS BASED UPON PUMPKIN SEEDS, THE FLESH HAVING BEEN USED FOR ANOTHER DISH, AND HAS A DELICIOUS NUTTY FLAVOR. IT IS GREAT SERVED OVER STEAMED OR BOILED NOPALES (CACTUS PADDLES) AND IS ALSO DELICIOUS WITH COOKED CHICKEN OR RACK OF LAMB.

SERVES FOUR AS AN ACCOMPANIMENT

INGREDIENTS
    4½ ounces raw pumpkin seeds
    1¼ pounds tomatoes
    2 garlic cloves, crushed
    1¼ cups chicken stock, preferably
        freshly made
    1 tablespoon vegetable oil
    3 tablespoons red chili sauce
    salt (optional)

1 Preheat the oven to 400°F. Heat a heavy-based frying pan until very hot. Add the pumpkin seeds and dry-fry them, stirring constantly over the heat. The seeds will start to swell and pop, but they must not be allowed to scorch (see Cook's Tip). When all the seeds have popped, remove the pan from the heat.

2 Cut the tomatoes into quarters and place them on a baking tray. Roast in the hot oven for 45 minutes–1 hour, until charred and softened. Allow to cool slightly, then remove the skins using a small sharp knife.

3 Put the pumpkin seeds in a food processor and process until smooth. Add the tomatoes and process for a few minutes, then add the garlic and stock and process for 1 minute more.

COOK'S TIP
When dry-frying the pumpkin seeds, don't stop stirring for a moment or they may scorch, which would make the sauce bitter. It is a good idea to stand back a little, as some of the hot seeds may fly out of the pan.

4 Heat the oil in a large frying pan. Add the red chili sauce and cook, stirring constantly, for 2–3 minutes. Add the pumpkin seed mixture and bring to the boil, stirring all the time.

5 Simmer the sauce for 20 minutes, stirring frequently until the sauce has thickened and reduced by about half. Taste and add salt, if needed. Serve over meat or vegetables, or cool and chill. The sauce will keep for up to a week in the refrigerator.

FIERY CITRUS SALSA

THIS UNUSUAL SALSA MAKES A FANTASTIC MARINADE FOR SHELLFISH, SUCH AS BROILED OR BARBECUED SHRIMP. IT IS ALSO DELICIOUS DRIZZLED OVER BARBECUED MEAT.

<u>SERVES 4</u>

INGREDIENTS
1 orange
1 green apple
2 fresh red chiles
1 garlic clove
8 fresh mint leaves
juice of 1 lemon
salt and freshly ground black pepper

3 Halve the chiles and remove the seeds, then place them in a blender or food processor with the orange segments and juice, apple wedges, garlic, and mint.

4 Process until smooth. With the motor running, slowly pour in the lemon juice. Season to taste with salt and freshly ground black pepper and serve immediately.

1 Using a sharp knife, remove the peel and pith from the orange and, working over a bowl to catch the juices, cut out the segments. Squeeze any remaining juice into the bowl.

2 Use a sharp kitchen knife to peel the apple and slice it into thin wedges. Make sure that you remove and discard the whole apple core and any tough parts of the apple that may affect the crisp texture of the salsa.

BROILED CORN-ON-THE-COB SALSA

This is an unusual salsa and contains deliciously sweet vegetables. Use cherry tomatoes for an extra special flavor, and combine with the ripest and freshest corn on the cob.

SERVES FOUR

INGREDIENTS
  2 corn on the cob
  2 tablespoons melted butter
  4 tomatoes
  8 scallions
  1 garlic clove
  2 tablespoons fresh lemon juice
  2 tablespoons olive oil
  Tabasco sauce, to taste

1 Remove the husks and silky threads covering the corn on the cob. Brush the cobs with the melted butter and gently broil, or cook on the barbecue, for 20–30 minutes, turning occasionally, until tender and tinged brown.

2 To remove the kernels, stand each cob upright on a chopping board and use a large, heavy knife to slice down the length of the cob.

3 Plunge the tomatoes into boiling water for 30 seconds. Remove with a slotted spoon; cool in cold water. Slip off the skins and dice the tomato flesh.

4 Place 6 scallions on a chopping board and chop finely. Crush and chop the garlic and then mix together with the corn and tomato in a small bowl.

5 Stir the lemon juice and olive oil together, adding Tabasco sauce, salt and pepper to taste.

6 Pour this mixture over the salsa and stir well. Cover the salsa and leave to steep at room temperature for 1–2 hours before serving. Garnish with the remaining scallions.

COOK'S TIP
Make this salsa in the summer, when fresh cobs of corn are readily available.

ORANGE, TOMATO, AND CHIVE SALSA

FRESH CHIVES AND SWEET ORANGES PROVIDE A VERY CHEERFUL COMBINATION OF FLAVORS. THIS IS AN UNUSUAL SALSA THAT IS A VERY GOOD ACCOMPANIMENT TO SALADS.

SERVES FOUR AS AN ACCOMPANIMENT

INGREDIENTS
   2 large, sweet oranges
   1 beefsteak tomato, or 2 plum
      tomatoes if not available
   bunch of fresh chives
   1 garlic clove
   2 tablespoons extra virgin olive oil or
      grapeseed oil
   sea salt

1 Slice the base off 1 orange so that it will stand firmly on a chopping board. Using a large sharp knife, remove the peel by slicing from the top to the bottom of the orange. Repeat with the second orange.

2 Working over a bowl, segment each orange in turn. Slice toward the middle of the fruit, and slightly to one side of a segment, and then gently twist the knife to release the orange segment. Repeat. Squeeze any juice from the remaining membrane.

3 Roughly chop the orange segments and add them to the bowl with the collected orange juice. Halve the tomato and use a teaspoon to scoop the seeds into the bowl. With a sharp knife, finely dice the flesh and add to the oranges and juice in the bowl.

4 Hold the bunch of chives neatly together and use a pair of kitchen scissors to snip them into the bowl.

5 Thinly slice the garlic and stir it into the orange mixture. Pour over the olive oil, season with sea salt, and stir well to mix. Serve the salsa within 2 hours.

SOUR CREAM DIP

THIS COOLING TOMATO AND PEPPER DIP IS A PERFECT ACCOMPANIMENT TO HOT AND SPICY DISHES.
ALTERNATIVELY, SERVE IT AS A SNACK WITH THE FIERIEST TORTILLA CHIPS YOU CAN FIND.

SERVES TWO AS AN ACCOMPANIMENT

INGREDIENTS
1 small yellow bell pepper
2 tomatoes
2 tablespoons chopped fresh parsley
⅔ cup sour cream
shredded lemon rind,
  to garnish

VARIATIONS
• Vary the color combinations by using
yellow, orange, or red bell peppers with
red or yellow tomatoes. Green pepper
with yellow tomatoes looks good with the
chopped parsley.
• Use strained plain yogurt or crème
fraîche instead of sour cream.
• Use finely diced avocado or cucumber
in place of the pepper.

1 Halve the pepper lengthwise.
Remove the core and seeds, then cut
the flesh into tiny dice.

2 Halve the tomatoes, then scoop out
and discard the seeds and cut the flesh
into tiny dice.

3 Stir the pepper and tomato dice
and the chopped parsley into the sour
cream and mix well.

4 Spoon the dip into a small bowl and
chill. Garnish by sprinkling with
shredded lemon rind before serving.

CHILE STRIPS WITH LIME

THIS FRESH RELISH IS IDEAL FOR SERVING WITH STEWS, RICE DISHES, OR BEAN DISHES. THE OREGANO ADDS A SWEET NOTE AND THE ABSENCE OF SUGAR OR OIL MAKES THIS A VERY HEALTHY CHOICE.

2 Meanwhile, slice the onion very thinly and put it in a large bowl. Squeeze the limes and add the juice to the bowl, with any pulp that gathers in the strainer. The lime juice will soften the onion. Stir in the oregano.

3 Remove the chiles from the bag and peel off the skins. If the skins do not come off easily, you may need to griddle them for longer, placing them once again in a bag to cool. Slit them, scrape out the seeds with a small sharp knife, then cut the chiles into long strips, which are called "rajas."

4 Add the chile strips to the onion mixture, blend well, and season with salt to taste.

5 Cover the bowl and chill for at least 1 day before serving, to allow the flavors to blend. The salsa will keep for up to 2 weeks in a covered bowl in the refrigerator.

MAKES ABOUT 4 TABLESPOONS

INGREDIENTS
   10 fresh green chiles
   ½ white onion
   4 limes
   ½ teaspoon dried oregano
   salt

COOK'S TIP
This method of roasting chiles is ideal if you need more than one or two, or if you do not have a gas burner. To roast over a burner, spear the chiles, four or five at a time, on a long-handled metal skewer and hold them over the flame until the skins blister.

1 Roast the chiles in a griddle pan over a moderate heat until the skins are charred and blistered. The flesh should not be allowed to blacken, as this might make the salsa bitter. Place the roasted chiles in a strong plastic bag and tie the top to keep the steam in. Set aside for 20 minutes.

ONION RELISH

THIS POPULAR RELISH, KNOWN AS CEBOLLAS EN ESCABECHE, *IS TYPICAL OF THE* YUCATÁN *REGION OF* MEXICO *AND IS OFTEN SERVED WITH CHICKEN, FISH, OR TURKEY.*

MAKES ONE SMALL JAR

INGREDIENTS
  2 fresh red fresno chiles
  1 teaspoon allspice berries
  ½ teaspoon black peppercorns
  1 teaspoon dried oregano
  2 white onions
  2 garlic cloves, peeled
  ⅓ cup white wine vinegar
  scant 1 cup cider vinegar
  salt

3 Cut the onions in half and slice them thinly. Put them in a bowl. Dry-roast the garlic in a heavy-based frying pan until golden, then crush and add to the onions in the bowl.

4 Remove the chiles from the bag and peel off the skins. Slit the chiles, scrape out the seeds with a small sharp knife, then chop them.

COOK'S TIP
White onions have a pungent flavor and are good in this salsa; Spanish onions can also be used. Shallots also make an exellent pickle.

5 Add the ground spices to the onion mixture, followed by the chiles. Stir in both vinegars. Add salt to taste and mix thoroughly. Cover the bowl and chill for at least 1 day before use.

1 Spear the fresno chiles on a long-handled metal skewer and roast them over the flame of a gas burner until the skins blister. Do not let the flesh burn. Alternatively, dry-fry them in a griddle pan until the skins are scorched. Place the roasted chiles in a strong plastic bag and tie the top to keep the steam in. Set aside for 20 minutes.

2 Meanwhile, place the allspice, black peppercorns, and oregano in a mortar or food processor. Grind slowly by hand with a pestle, or process until coarsely ground.

HABAÑERO SALSA

THIS IS A VERY FIERY SALSA WITH AN INTENSE HEAT LEVEL. A DAB ON THE PLATE ALONGSIDE A MEAT OR FISH DISH ADDS A FRESH, CLEAN TASTE, BUT THIS IS NOT FOR THE FAINT-HEARTED. HABAÑERO CHILES, ALSO CALLED SCOTCH BONNETS, ARE VERY HOT. LANTERN-SHAPED, THEY RANGE IN COLOR FROM YELLOW TO A DEEP ORANGE-RED. COSTENO AMARILLO CHILES ARE YELLOW WHEN FRESH AND HAVE A SHARP CITRUS FLAVOR.

3 Put the chiles in a food processor and add a little of the soaking liquid. Puree to a fine paste. Do not lean over the processor—the fumes may burn your face. Remove the lid and scrape the mixture into a bowl.

4 Put the chopped scallions in another bowl and add the fruit juice, with the lime rind and juice. Roughly chop the cilantro.

SERVE SPARINGLY

INGREDIENTS
    5 dried roasted habañero chiles
    4 dried costeno amarillo chiles
    3 scallions, finely chopped
    juice of ½ large grapefruit or
      1 Seville orange
    grated rind and juice of 1 lime
    bunch of fresh cilantro
    salt

1 Soak the habañero and costeno amarillo chiles in hot water for about 10 minutes until softened. Drain, reserving the soaking water.

2 Wear rubber gloves to handle the habañeros. Remove the stalks from all chiles, then slit them and scrape out the seeds with a small sharp knife. Chop the chiles roughly.

5 Carefully add the cilantro to the chili mixture and mix very thoroughly. Add salt to taste. Cover and chill for at least 1 day before use. Serve the salsa very sparingly.

ADOBO SEASONING

ADOBO MEANS VINEGAR SAUCE, AND THIS ADOBO IS A CHILI VINEGAR PASTE USED FOR MARINATING PORK CHOPS OR STEAKS. ADOBOS ARE WIDELY USED IN THE COOKING OF THE YUCATÁN IN MEXICO.

MAKES ENOUGH TO MARINATE
SIX CHOPS OR STEAKS

INGREDIENTS
1 small head of garlic
5 ancho chiles
2 pasilla chiles
1 tablespoon dried oregano
1 teaspoon cumin seeds
6 cloves
1 teaspoon coriander seeds
4-inch piece of cinnamon stick
2 teaspoons salt
½ cup white wine vinegar

1 Preheat the oven to 350°F. Cut a thin slice off the top of the head of garlic, so that the inside of each clove is exposed. Wrap the head of garlic in foil. Roast for 45–60 minutes or until the garlic is soft.

2 Meanwhile, slit the chiles and scrape out the seeds. Put the chiles in a blender or a mortar. Add the oregano, cumin seeds, cloves, coriander seeds, cinnamon stick, and salt. Process or grind with a pestle to a fine powder.

3 Remove the garlic from the oven. When it is cool enough to handle, squeeze the garlic pulp out of each clove and grind into the spice mix.

4 Add the wine vinegar to the spice and garlic mixture and process or grind until a smooth paste forms. Spoon into a bowl and leave to stand for 1 hour, to allow the flavors to blend. Spread over pork chops or steaks as a marinade, before broiling or barbecuing.

RED RUB

THIS "RUB" OR DRY PASTE IS FREQUENTLY USED IN THE YUCATÁN REGION OF MEXICO FOR SEASONING MEAT. THE MIXTURE IS RUBBED ONTO THE SURFACE OF THE MEAT, WHICH IS THEN WRAPPED IN BANANA LEAVES AND COOKED SLOWLY IN A PIB, A HEATED STONE-LINED HOLE IN THE GROUND. MEAT COOKED THIS WAY IS REFERRED TO AS PIBIL-STYLE. TRY USING THE RUB ON PORK CHOPS OR CHICKEN PIECES BEFORE OVEN BAKING OR BARBECUING.

MAKES ENOUGH FOR ONE JOINT OF MEAT
OR FOUR CHICKEN BREASTS

INGREDIENTS
2 teaspoons achiote (annatto) seeds
1 teaspoon black peppercorns
1 teaspoon allspice berries
1 teaspoon dried oregano
½ teaspoon ground cumin
1 teaspoon freshly squeezed lime juice
1 small Seville orange or ½ grapefruit

1 Put the achiote (annatto) seeds in a mortar and grind them with a pestle to a fine powder. Alternatively, use a food processor. Add the peppercorns, grind again, then repeat the process with the allspice berries. Mix in the oregano and ground cumin.

2 Add the lime juice to the spice mixture. Squeeze the orange or grapefruit and add the juice to the spice mixture a teaspoonful at a time until a thick paste is produced. Don't be tempted to substitute a sweet orange if Seville oranges are out of season; the spice mixture must be tart.

3 Allow the paste to stand for at least 30 minutes so the spices absorb the juice. The correct consistency for the paste is slightly dry and crumbly. When ready to use, rub the paste onto the surface of the meat, then leave to marinate for at least 1 hour before cooking, preferably overnight. The rub will keep for up to 1 week in a covered bowl in the refrigerator, after which time some of the flavor will be lost.

COOK'S TIP
Achiote is the rusty red seed of the annatto, a tropical American tree. It is used in Mexico for flavoring and coloring cheeses, butter, and smoked fish. It is also used in Indian cooking and can be purchased from ethnic food stores.

RED SALSA

USE THIS AS A CONDIMENT WITH FISH OR MEAT DISHES, OR AS A DIPPING SAUCE FOR BAKED POTATO WEDGES. IT IS OFTEN ADDED TO RICE DISHES.

MAKES ABOUT 1 CUP

INGREDIENTS
3 large tomatoes
1 tablespoon olive oil
3 ancho chiles
2 pasilla chiles
2 garlic cloves, peeled and left whole
2 scallions
2 teaspoons soft dark brown sugar
½ teaspoon paprika
juice of 1 lime
½ teaspoon dried oregano
salt

1 Preheat the oven to 400°F. Quarter the tomatoes and place in a roasting pan. Drizzle over the oil. Roast for about 40 minutes until slightly charred, then remove the skin.

2 Soak the chiles in hot water for about 10 minutes. Drain, remove the stalks, slit, and then scrape out the seeds. Chop finely. Dry-roast the garlic in a heavy-based pan until golden.

3 Finely chop most of the scallions, retaining the top part of one for garnishing. Place the chopped onion in a bowl with the sugar, paprika, lime juice, and oregano. Slice the remaining scallions diagonally and set aside for the garnish.

4 Put the skinned tomatoes and chopped chiles in a food processor or blender and add the garlic cloves. Process until smooth.

5 Add the sugar, paprika, lime juice, scallions, and oregano to the blender. Process for a few seconds, then taste and add salt as required. Spoon into a pan and warm through before serving, or place in a bowl, cover, and chill until required. Garnish with the sliced scallions. The salsa will keep, covered, for up to 1 week in the refrigerator.

BREADS AND CAKES

European-style breads and cakes are available in most parts of the Caribbean and Latin America, but the recipes have evolved to reflect regional traditions, with cornmeal often being used instead of wheat flour. The breads make good accompaniments, while the cakes are often eaten for breakfast or as snacks.

CORN TORTILLAS

TO PREPARE THESE DELICIOUS MEXICAN SPECIALITIES, MAKE SURE YOU HAVE READY A TORTILLA PRESS AND A SMALL PLASTIC BAG, CUT OPEN AND HALVED CROSSWISE.

MAKES ABOUT 14

INGREDIENTS
   2½ cups *masa harina*
   1–1½ cups water

COOK'S TIP
Tortillas are very easy to make, but it is important to get the dough texture right. If it is too dry and crumbly, add a little water; if it is too wet, add more *masa harina*. If you misjudge the pressure needed for flattening the ball of dough to a neat circle on the tortilla press, just scrape it off, reroll it, and try again.

1 Put the *masa harina* into a bowl and stir in 1 cup of the water, mixing it to a soft dough that just holds together. If it is too dry, add a little more water. Cover the bowl with a cloth and set aside for 15 minutes.

2 Preheat the oven to 300°F. Open the tortilla press and line both sides with the prepared plastic sheets. Preheat a griddle until hot.

3 Knead the dough lightly and shape into 14 balls. Put a ball on the press and bring the top down firmly to flatten the dough out into a round shape.

4 Open the press. Peel off the top layer of plastic and, using the bottom layer, lift the tortilla out of the press. Peel off the bottom plastic and flip the tortilla onto the hot griddle.

5 Cook for 1 minute and turn over and cook for a minute more. Wrap in foil and keep warm. Repeat for the other tortillas.

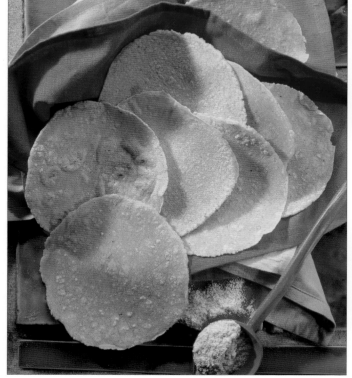

FLOUR TORTILLAS

THESE ARE MORE COMMON THAN CORN TORTILLAS IN THE NORTH OF MEXICO, FROM SONORA TO
CHIHUAHUA, WHERE WHEAT IS GROWN. FOR THE BEST RESULTS, USE A GOOD QUALITY ALL-PURPOSE FLOUR.

MAKES ABOUT 14

INGREDIENTS
2 cups all-purpose flour
1 teaspoon salt
1 tablespoon vegetable shortening
½ cup water

1 Sift the flour and salt into a large mixing bowl. Gradually rub in the vegetable shortening, using your fingertips, until the mixture resembles coarse bread crumbs.

2 Gradually add the water and mix to a soft dough. Knead lightly, form into a ball, cover with a cloth, and leave to rest for 15 minutes.

COOK'S TIP
Make flour tortillas whenever *masa harina* is difficult to find. To keep them soft and pliable, make sure they are kept warm until ready to serve, and eat as soon as possible.

3 Carefully divide the dough into about 14 portions and form these portions into small balls. One by one, roll out each ball of dough on a lightly floured wooden board to into a round shape measuring about 6 inches Trim these shapes if necessary.

4 Heat an ungreased griddle or frying pan over a moderate heat. Cook the tortillas for about 1½–2 minutes on each side. Turn over with a metal spatula when the bottom begins to brown. Wrap in foil and keep warm in the oven until ready to serve.

DHAL PURI

KNOWN AS ROTIS *IN THEIR NATIVE* INDIA, *THESE TASTY FLAT BREADS CAN ALSO BE MADE WITH WHITE FLOUR. A TRADITIONAL* CARIBBEAN *FAVORITE,* DHAL PURI *ARE DELICIOUS WITH MEAT, FISH, OR VEGETABLE DISHES AND ARE IDEAL FOR MOPPING UP LEFTOVER SAUCES.*

MAKES ABOUT 15

INGREDIENTS

4 cups self-rising flour
1 cup whole-wheat flour
1½ cups cold water
2 tablespoons oil, plus extra for
    frying
salt, to taste
For the filling
1½ cups yellow split peas
1 tablespoon ground cumin
2 garlic cloves, crushed

1 Sift the dry ingredients into a bowl, then tip in the grain remaining in the sieve. Add the water a little at a time, and knead gently until a soft dough forms. Continue kneading until supple, but do not overwork the dough.

2 Add the oil to the dough and continue to knead it until it is completely smooth. Put the dough in a plastic bag or plastic wrap. Place in a cool room or in the refrigerator and leave to rest for at least 30 minutes, or overnight if possible.

3 To make the filling, put the split peas in a large pan, pour over water to cover, and cook for about 10–15 minutes, until half cooked—they should be tender on the outside, but still firm in the middle. Allow the water to evaporate during cooking, until the pan is almost dry, but add a little extra water to prevent burning, if necessary.

4 Spread out the peas on a tray. When cool, grind to a paste, using a mortar and pestle or food processor. Mix with the cumin and garlic.

5 Divide the dough into about 15 balls, Slightly flatten each ball, put about 1 tablespoon of the split pea mixture into the center, and fold over the edges.

6 Dust a rolling pin and a board with flour and roll out the dhal puri, taking care not to overstretch the dough, until they are about 7 inches in diameter.

7 Heat a little oil in a frying pan. Cook the dhal puris for about 3 minutes on each side until light brown. Serve as soon as the last one is cooked.

FRIED DUMPLINS

IN THE CARIBBEAN AND GUYANA THESE FRIED DUMPLINS ARE SIMPLY CALLED "BAKES." THEY ARE USUALLY SERVED WITH SALT FISH OR FRIED FISH, BUT CAN BE EATEN QUITE SIMPLY WITH BUTTER AND JAM OR CHEESE, WHICH CHILDREN ESPECIALLY LOVE.

MAKES ABOUT TEN

INGREDIENTS
    4 cups self-rising flour
    2 teaspoons sugar
    ½ teaspoon salt
    1¼ cups milk
    oil, for frying

COOK'S TIP
Mix and knead the dough gently to avoid overworking it and making it tough. A quite light touch is all that is needed to make the dough smooth.

1 Sift the flour, sugar, and salt into a large bowl, add the milk and mix and knead until a smooth dough forms.

2 Divide the dough into ten balls, kneading each ball with floured hands. Press the balls gently to flatten them into 3-inch rounds.

3 Heat a little oil in a non-stick frying pan over medium heat. Place half the dumplins in the pan, reduce the heat to low, and fry for about 15 minutes, until they are golden brown, turning once.

4 Stand the dumplins on their sides for a few minutes to brown the edges, before removing them from the pan and draining thoroughly on paper towels. Serve immediately, while still warm.

CORN GRIDDLE CAKES

KNOWN AS AREPAS, THESE ARE A STAPLE BREAD IN SEVERAL LATIN AMERICAN COUNTRIES, PARTICULARLY COLOMBIA AND VENEZUELA. EAT THEM FILLED WITH SOFT WHITE CHEESE, AS HERE, OR PLAIN AS AN ACCOMPANIMENT. WITH THEIR CRISP CRUST AND CHEWY INTERIOR, AREPAS CAN BECOME STALE VERY QUICKLY, SO ARE BEST EATEN PIPING HOT.

MAKES 15

INGREDIENTS
    1¾ cups *masarepa* (or *masa harina*)
    ½ teaspoon salt
    1¼ cups water
    1 tablespoon oil
    7 ounces fresh white cheese, such
      as queso fresco or mozzarella,
      roughly chopped

1 Combine the *masarepa* or *masa harina* and salt in a bowl. Gradually stir in the water to make a soft dough, then set aside for about 20 minutes.

2 Divide the dough into 15 equal-sized balls, then, using your fingers, flatten each ball into a circle, approximately ½ inch thick.

3 Heat 1 teaspoon of the oil in a large, heavy frying pan over a medium heat. Using a paper towel, gently wipe the surface of the frying pan, leaving it just lightly greased.

4 Place five of the *arepas* in the frying pan. Cook for about 4 minutes, then flip over and cook for a further 4 minutes. The *arepas* should be lightly blistered on both sides.

5 Open the *arepas* and fill each with a few small pieces of fresh white cheese. Return to the pan to cook until the cheese begins to melt. Remove from the heat and keep warm.

6 Cook the remaining ten *arepas* in the same way, oiling the pan and wiping with a paper towel between batches, to ensure it is always lightly greased. Serve the *arepas* while still warm, so that the melted cheese is soft and runny.

COOK'S TIP
Masarepa is a flour made with the white corn grown in the Andes. Look for it in Latin American food stores. If not available, replace it with *masa harina*, the flour used to make tamales. The result will not be quite as delicate, but the *arepas* will be equally delicious.

VARIATION
Instead of cheese, try a delicious beef filling. Simply fry some ground beef in oil with ½ chopped onion, 1 small red chile, finely chopped, 1 crushed garlic clove, ground black pepper, and fresh thyme. When thoroughly cooked, stuff the mixture inside the *arepas*.

PARAGUAYAN CORN BREAD

THIS MOIST CORNMEAL BREAD IS SO RICH AND FLAVORSOME THAT IT CAN EASILY BE EATEN ON ITS OWN. IT TASTES BEST WHEN EATEN WARM, ESPECIALLY WHEN COVERED WITH MELTING BUTTER.

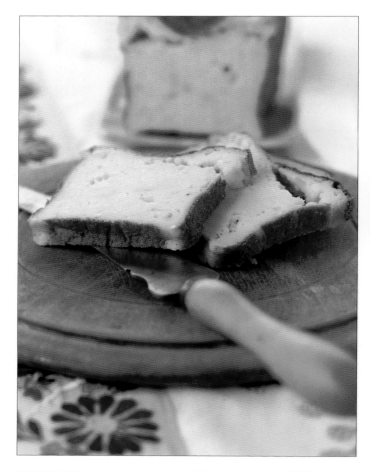

2 Pour in the milk and stir until heated, without allowing it to boil. Still stirring, add the cornmeal in a steady stream. Continue to stir until the mixture is smooth.

3 Remove from the heat and stir in the cheese and remaining butter. When both have melted, season with salt and ground pepper.

4 Whisk the egg whites in a bowl until they hold their shape. Stir the egg yolks into the cornmeal mixture, then gently fold in the egg whites.

5 Tip the mixture into the prepared loaf pan. Bake for 35–40 minutes, or until a skewer comes out clean when inserted in the bread. Turn out onto a wire rack to cool a little. Cut into slices and serve.

MAKES ONE LOAF

INGREDIENTS
  6 tablespoons butter
  1 large onion, finely chopped
  1⅔ cups whole milk
  2 cups cornmeal
  6 ounces mozzarella cheese,
    roughly grated
  2 large eggs, separated
  salt and ground black pepper

1 Preheat the oven to 400°F. Using 1 tablespoon of the butter, grease a loaf pan. Melt 2 tablespoons of the butter in a large pan over a low heat and fry the onions for 5 minutes until softened.

COOK'S TIP
If you can't get hold of cornmeal, use instant polenta instead.

MEXICAN "BREAD OF THE DEAD"

A CELEBRATORY LOAF MADE FOR ALL SOULS' DAY, WHEN MEXICANS PAY THEIR RESPECTS TO THE SOULS OF THE DEAD, IT IS TRADITIONALLY DECORATED WITH A DOUGH SKULL, BONES, AND TEARS.

MAKES ONE LARGE LOAF

INGREDIENTS
3 star anise
6 tablespoons cold water
6 cups unbleached white bread flour,
 plus extra for sprinkling
1 teaspoon salt
½ cup superfine sugar
1 ounce fresh yeast
¾ cup lukewarm water
3 eggs
4 tablespoons orange-flavored liqueur
½ cup butter, melted
grated rind of 1 orange
confectioners' sugar,
 for dusting

6 Shape the dough into a 10½-inch round and place in the prepared pan. Cover with lightly oiled clear plastic wrap and leave to rise, in a warm place, for 2–3 hours, or until doubled in bulk.

7 Meanwhile, preheat the oven to 375°F. Bake the loaf for 45–50 minutes, or until golden. Turn out onto a wire rack to cool. Dust with confectioners' sugar to serve.

VARIATION
Top the baked bread with orange-flavored frosting. Blend ½ cup confectioners' sugar and 1–2 tablespoons orange liqueur. Pour the frosting over the bread and let it dribble down the sides.

1 Grease a 10½-inch fluted round cake pan. Place the star anise in a small pan and add the cold water. Bring to the boil and boil for 3–4 minutes, or until the liquid has reduced to 3 tablespoons. Discard the star anise and leave the liquid to cool.

2 Sift the flour and salt together into a large bowl. Stir in the sugar and make a well in the center.

3 In a pitcher, dissolve the yeast in the lukewarm water. Pour into the center of the flour and mix in, using your fingers, until a smooth, thick batter forms. Sprinkle over a little more flour, cover with plastic wrap, and leave the batter in a warm place for 30 minutes, or until the mixture starts to bubble.

4 Beat the eggs, the reserved liquid flavored with star anise, orange liqueur, and melted butter together. Gradually incorporate into the flour mixture to form a smooth dough.

5 Turn out the dough onto a lightly floured surface and gently knead in the orange rind. Knead for 5–6 minutes until smooth and elastic.

MANGO QUICKBREAD

THIS FRUITY QUICKBREAD WITH A COCONUT TOPPING MAKES A DELICIOUS AFTERNOON TREAT.

<u>MAKES TWO LOAVES</u>

INGREDIENTS
2½ cups all-purpose flour
2 teaspoons baking soda
2 teaspoons ground cinnamon
½ teaspoon salt
½ cup margarine, at
  room temperature
3 eggs, at room temperature
1½ cups sugar
4 fluid ounces vegetable oil
1 large ripe mango, peeled and
  chopped
3¼ ounces dry unsweetened
  shredded coconut
2½ ounces raisins

1 Preheat the oven to 350°F. Line the bottom and sides of two 9 x 5-inch loaf pans with parchment paper and grease.

2 Sift together the flour, baking soda, cinnamon, and salt. Set aside.

3 With an electric mixer, cream the margarine until soft. Beat in the eggs and sugar until light and fluffy. Beat in the oil. Fold the dry ingredients into the creamed ingredients in three batches.

4 Fold in the mangoes, two-thirds of the coconut, and the raisins.

5 Spoon the batter into the pans.

6 Sprinkle over the remaining coconut. Bake until a skewer inserted in the center comes out clean, about 50–60 minutes. Let stand for 10 minutes before turning out onto a rack to cool completely.

ZUCCHINI QUICKBREAD

SERVE THIS UNUSUAL SAVORY QUICKBREAD SLICED, WITH PATS OF BUTTER FOR SPREADING.

<u>MAKES ONE LOAF</u>

INGREDIENTS
1¼ cups butter
3 eggs
8 fluid ounces vegetable oil
1½ cups sugar
2 medium unpeeled zucchini,
  grated
2½ cups all-purpose flour
2 teaspoons baking soda
1 teaspoon baking powder
1 teaspoon salt
1 teaspoon ground cinnamon
1 teaspoon grated nutmeg
¼ teaspoon ground cloves
1 cup walnuts, chopped

1 Preheat the oven to 350°F. Line the bottom and sides of a 9 x 5-inch loaf pan with parchment paper and grease.

2 In a small pan, melt the butter over low heat. Set aside.

3 With an electric mixer, beat the eggs and oil together until thick. Beat in the sugar. Stir in the melted butter and zucchini. Set aside.

4 Sift the dry ingredients and fold in the zucchini and walnuts. Pour into the pan and bake for 60–70 minutes. Let stand 10 minutes before turning out.

BUÑUELOS

THESE LOVELY LITTLE PUFFS LOOK LIKE MINIATURE DOUGHNUTS AND TASTE SO GOOD IT IS HARD NOT TO OVER-INDULGE. MAKE THEM FOR BRUNCH, OR SIMPLY SERVE THEM WITH A CUP OF CAFE CON LECHE OR CAFE DE OLLA.

MAKES 12

INGREDIENTS
  2 cups all-purpose flour
  pinch of salt
  1 teaspoon baking powder
  ½ teaspoon ground anise
  ½ cup superfine sugar
  1 extra large egg
  ½ cup milk
  ¼ cup butter
  oil, for deep frying
  2 teaspoons ground cinnamon
  cinnamon sticks, to decorate

1 Sift the flour, salt, baking powder, and ground anise into a mixing bowl. Add 2 tablespoons of the superfine sugar.

2 Place the egg and milk in a small jug and whisk well with a fork. Melt the butter in a small pan.

COOK'S TIP
Buñuelos are sometimes served with syrup for dunking, although they are perfectly delicious without. To make the syrup, mix ¾ cup soft dark brown sugar and scant 2 cups water in a small pan. Add a cinnamon stick and heat, stirring until the sugar has dissolved. Bring to the boil, then lower the heat and simmer for 15 minutes without stirring. Cool slightly before serving with the *buñuelos*.

3 Pour the egg mixture and milk gradually into the flour, stirring all the time, until well blended, then add the melted butter. Mix first with a wooden spoon and then with your hands to make a soft dough.

4 Lightly flour a work surface, tip the dough onto it, and knead for about 10 minutes, until smooth.

5 Divide the dough into 12 pieces and roll into balls. Slightly flatten each ball with your hand and then make a hole in the center with the floured handle of a wooden spoon.

6 Heat the oil for deep frying to a temperature of 375°F, or until a cube of dried bread, added to the oil, floats and then turns a golden color in 30–60 seconds. Fry the *buñuelos* in small batches until they are puffy and golden brown, turning them once or twice during cooking. As soon as they are golden, lift them out of the oil, using a slotted spoon, and lie them on a double layer of paper towels to drain.

7 Mix the remaining superfine sugar with the ground cinnamon in a small bowl. Add the *buñuelos*, one at a time, while they are still warm, toss them in the mixture until they are lightly coated, and either serve at once or leave to cool. Decorate with cinnamon sticks.

GARBANZO CAKE

THIS IS A MOIST CAKE, WITH A TEXTURE LIKE THAT OF CHRISTMAS PUDDING. IT IS FLAVORED WITH ORANGE AND CINNAMON AND TASTES WONDERFUL IN THIN SLICES, WITH FRESH MANGO OR PINEAPPLE AND A SPOONFUL OF NATURAL YOGURT.

<u>SERVES SIX</u>

INGREDIENTS

    2 x 10-ounce cans chickpeas,
       drained
    4 eggs, beaten
    1 cup superfine sugar
    1 teaspoon baking powder
    2 teaspoons ground cinnamon
    grated rind and juice of 1 orange
    cinnamon sugar (see Cook's Tip),
       for sprinkling

COOK'S TIP

To make cinnamon sugar, mix ¼ cup superfine sugar with 1 teaspoon ground cinnamon.

1 Preheat the oven to 350°F. Tip the chickpeas into a colander, drain them thoroughly, then rub them between the palms of your hands to loosen and remove the skins. Rinse any bits of skin away and put the chickpeas in a food processor and process until smooth.

2 Spoon the puree into a bowl and gently stir in the eggs, sugar, baking powder, cinnamon, orange rind, and orange juice. Grease and line a 1-pound loaf pan.

3 Pour the cake mixture into the loaf pan, level the surface, and bake for about 1½ hours or until a skewer inserted into the center comes out clean.

4 Remove the cake from the oven and leave to stand, in the pan, for about 10 minutes. Remove from the pan, place on a wire rack, and sprinkle with the cinnamon sugar. Leave to cool completely before serving. Try serving this with sliced fresh pineapple.

PECAN CAKE

THIS CAKE IS AN EXAMPLE OF THE FRENCH INFLUENCE ON MEXICAN COOKING. IT IS TRADITIONALLY SERVED WITH CAJETA—SWEETENED BOILED MILK—BUT WHIPPED CREAM OR CRÈME FRAÎCHE CAN BE USED INSTEAD. TRY SERVING THE CAKE WITH A FEW REDCURRANTS FOR A SPLASH OF COLOR.

SERVES EIGHT TO TEN

INGREDIENTS
 1 cup pecan nuts
 ½ cup butter, softened
 ½ cup soft light
  brown sugar
 1 teaspoon vanilla extract
 4 large eggs, separated
 ¾ cup all-purpose flour
 pinch of salt
 12 whole pecan nuts, to decorate
 cajeta, whipped cream, or crème
  fraîche, to serve
For drizzling
 ¼ cup butter
 scant ½ cup clear honey

1 Preheat the oven to 350°F. Grease an 8-inch round spring-form cake pan. Toast the pecan nuts in a dry frying pan for 5 minutes, shaking frequently. Grind in a blender or food processor. Place in a bowl.

2 Cream the butter with the sugar in a mixing bowl, then beat in the vanilla extract and egg yolks.

3 Add the flour to the ground nuts and mix well. Whisk the egg whites with the salt in a grease-free bowl until soft peaks form. Fold the whites into the butter mixture, then gently fold in the flour and nut mixture. Spoon the mixture into the prepared cake pan and bake for 30 minutes or until a skewer inserted in the center comes out clean.

4 Cool the cake in the pan for 5 minutes, then remove the sides of the pan. Stand the cake on a wire rack until cold.

5 Remove the cake from the base of the pan if necessary, then return it to the rack and arrange the pecans on top. Transfer to a plate. Melt the butter in a small pan, add the honey, and bring to the boil, stirring. Lower the heat and simmer for 3 minutes. Pour over the cake. Serve with *cajeta*, whipped cream, or crème fraîche.

CARIBBEAN FRUIT AND RUM CAKE

THIS POPULAR CAKE IS EATEN AT CHRISTMAS, WEDDINGS, AND OTHER SPECIAL OCCASIONS. IT IS KNOWN AS BLACK CAKE, BECAUSE THE TRADITIONAL RECIPE USES BURNT SUGAR.

MAKES ONE CAKE

INGREDIENTS
    2 cups currants
    3 cups raisins
    1 cup pitted prunes
    ⅔ cup candied peel
    1 teaspoon pumpkin pie spice
    6 tablespoons rum, plus more
        if needed
    1¼ cups sherry, plus more if needed
    1¾ cups soft dark brown sugar
    4 cups self-rising flour
    2 cups butter, softened
    10 eggs, beaten
    1 teaspoon natural vanilla
        extract

1 Wash the currants, raisins, prunes, and mixed peel, then drain and pat dry. Place in a food processor and process until roughly chopped. Transfer to a large bowl and add the the pumpkin pie spice, rum, and sherry. Stir in ½ cup of sugar. Mix well, then cover with a lid and set aside for anything from 2 weeks to 3 months—the longer it is left, the better the flavor will be.

2 Stir the fruit mixture occasionally, adding more alcohol, if you like, before replacing the cover and allowing it to infuse.

3 Preheat the oven to 325°F. Grease a 10-inch round cake pan and line it with a double layer of wax paper or parchment paper.

4 Sift the flour into a bowl, and set it aside. In a large mixing bowl, cream the butter with the remaining sugar. Beat in the eggs until the mixture is smooth and creamy, adding a little of the flour if the mixture starts to curdle.

5 Add the fruit mixture, then gradually stir in the remaining flour and the vanilla extract. Mix well, adding 1–2 tablespoons more sherry if the mixture is too stiff; it should just fall off the back of the spoon, but should not be too runny.

6 Spoon the mixture into the prepared pan, cover loosely with foil, and bake for about 2½ hours, until the cake is firm and springy. Leave to cool in the pan overnight. Unless serving immediately, sprinkle the cake with more rum and wrap in wax paper and in foil to keep it moist.

COOK'S TIP
Although it is usual to roughly chop the dried fruits, they can be marinated whole if you prefer. If there is no time to marinate the fruit, simmer it gently in the alcohol mixture for about 30 minutes, and leave overnight.

APPLE AND CINNAMON CRUMBLE CAKE

THIS SCRUMPTIOUS CAKE, POPULAR IN THE CARIBBEAN, HAS LAYERS OF SPICY FRUIT AND CRUMBLE AND IS QUITE DELICIOUS WHEN SERVED WARM WITH FRESH CREAM.

MAKES ONE CAKE

INGREDIENTS
   1 cup plus 2 tablespoons butter,
    softened
   1¼ cups superfine sugar
   4 eggs
   4 cups self-rising flour
   3 large cooking apples
   ½ teaspoon ground cinnamon
For the crumble topping
   ¾ cup raw sugar
   generous 1 cup all-purpose flour
   1 teaspoon ground cinnamon
   scant 1 cup dry unsweetened
    shredded coconut
   ½ cup butter

1 Preheat the oven to 350°F. Grease and base-line a 10-inch round cake pan. To make the crumble topping, mix the sugar, flour, cinnamon, and coconut in a bowl, then rub in the butter with your fingertips until the mixture resembles bread crumbs. Set aside.

2 Put the butter and sugar in a bowl and cream with an electric mixer until light and fluffy. Beat in the eggs, one at a time, beating well after each addition, and adding a little of the flour if the mixture starts to curdle.

3 Sift in half the remaining flour, mix well, then add the rest of the flour and stir until smooth.

4 Peel and core the apples, then grate them coarsely. Place the grated apples in a bowl, sprinkle with the cinnamon, and set aside.

5 Spread half the cake mixture evenly over the base of the prepared pan. Spoon the apples on top and sprinkle over half the crumble topping.

6 Spread the remaining cake mixture over the crumble and finally top with the remaining crumble topping.

7 Bake for 1 hour 10 minutes–1 hour 20 minutes, covering the cake with foil if it browns too quickly. Leave in the pan for about 5 minutes before turning out onto a wire rack. Serve when cool.

BANANA AND PECAN BREAD

BANANAS AND PECANS JUST SEEM TO BELONG TOGETHER. THIS IS A REALLY MOIST AND DELICIOUS QUICKBREAD. SPREAD IT WITH CREAM CHEESE OR JAM, OR SERVE AS A DESSERT WITH WHIPPED CREAM.

MAKES ONE LOAF

INGREDIENTS
- ½ cup butter, softened
- 1 cup molasses sugar
- 2 large eggs, beaten
- 3 ripe bananas
- ¾ cup pecan nuts, chopped
- 2 cups self-rising flour
- ½ teaspoon apple-pie spice

1 Preheat the oven to 350°F. Generously grease a 2-pound loaf pan and line it with non-stick parchment paper. Cream the butter and molasses sugar in a large mixing bowl until the mixture is light and fluffy. Gradually add the eggs, beating after each addition, until well combined.

2 Peel and then mash the bananas with a fork. Add them to the creamed mixture with the chopped pecan nuts. Beat until well combined.

COOK'S TIP
If the mixture shows signs of curdling when you add the eggs, stir in a little of the flour to stabilize it.

3 Sift the flour and mixed spice together and fold into the banana mixture. Spoon into the pan, level the surface, and bake for 1–1¼ hours or until a skewer inserted into the middle of the loaf comes out clean. Cool for 10 minutes in the pan, then invert the pan on a wire rack. Lift off the pan, peel off the lining paper, and cool completely.

PUMPKIN AND WALNUT BREAD

*PUMPKIN, NUTMEG, AND WALNUTS COMBINE TO YIELD A MOIST, TANGY, AND SLIGHTLY SWEET BREAD
WITH A GOOD FLAVOR. SERVE PARTNERED WITH MEATS OR CHEESE, OR SIMPLY LIGHTLY BUTTERED.*

MAKES ONE LOAF

INGREDIENTS
    1¼ pounds pumpkin, peeled,
      seeded, and cut into chunks
    6 tablespoons superfine sugar
    1 teaspoon grated nutmeg
    ¼ cup butter, melted
    3 eggs, lightly beaten
    3 cups unbleached white bread flour
    2 teaspoons baking powder
    ½ teaspoon salt
    ¾ cup walnuts,
      chopped

1 Grease and base line a loaf pan
measuring 8½ x 4½ inches. Preheat
the oven to 350°F.

2 Place the pumpkin in a pan, add
water to cover by about 2 inches, then
bring to the boil. Cover, lower the heat,
and simmer for 20 minutes, or until the
pumpkin is very tender. Drain well, then
puree in a food processor or blender.
Leave to cool.

COOK'S TIP
You may have slightly more pumpkin
puree than you actually need—use the
remainder in soup.

3 Place 1¼ cups of the puree in a large
bowl. Add the sugar, nutmeg, melted
butter, and eggs to the puree and mix
together. Sift the flour, baking powder,
and salt together into a large bowl, and
make a well in the center.

4 Add the pumpkin mixture to the
center of the flour and stir until smooth.
Mix in the walnuts. Transfer to the
prepared pan and bake for 1 hour or
until golden and starting to shrink from
the sides of the pan. Turn out onto a
wire rack to cool.

Nutty Chocolate Squares

PECANS AND CHOCOLATE ARE AN IRRESISTIBLE COMBINATION IN THESE NUTTY SQUARES.

MAKES 16

INGREDIENTS
2 eggs
12 teaspoons vanilla extract
pinch of salt
6 ounces pecan nuts, chopped
2 tablespoons all-purpose flour
2 ounces superfine sugar
4 fluid ounces light corn syrup
3 ounces semisweet chocolate,
  finely chopped
3 tablespoons butter
16 pecan halves, for decorating

1 Preheat an oven to 325°F. Line the bottom and sides of an 8-inch square baking pan with parchment paper and grease.

2 Whisk the eggs, vanilla, and salt.

3 In another bowl, mix together the pecans and flour. Set both aside.

4 In a pan, bring the sugar and golden syrup to a boil. Remove from the heat and stir in the chocolate and butter.

5 Mix in the beaten eggs, then fold in the pecan mixture.

6 Pour into the pan and bake until set, for about 35 minutes. Leave in the pan for 10 minutes before unmolding. Cut into 2-inch squares and press pecan halves into the tops while warm.

PECAN SQUARES

THESE AFTERNOON TREATS HAVE A SCRUMPTIOUS NUTTY TOPPING ON A PASTRY CRUST.

MAKES 36

INGREDIENTS
   2 cups all-purpose flour
   pinch of salt
   ½ cup granulated sugar
   1 cup cold butter or margarine,
     chopped
   1 egg
   finely grated rind of 1 lemon
For the topping
   ¾ cup butter
   3 ounces honey
   ¼ cup granulated sugar
   ½ cup dark brown sugar
   5 tablespoons whipping cream
   4 cups pecan halves

1 Preheat the oven to 375°F. Lightly grease a 15½ x 10½ x 1-inch jelly roll pan.

2 Sift the flour and salt into a large mixing bowl. Stir in the sugar. Cut and rub in the butter or margarine until the mixture resembles coarse bread crumbs. Add the egg and lemon rind, and blend with a fork until the mixture just holds together.

3 Spoon the mixture into the prepared pan. With floured fingertips, press into an even layer right up into the corners of the pan. Prick the pastry all over with a fork and chill in the refrigerator for 10 minutes.

4 Bake the pastry crust for 15 minutes. Remove the pan from the oven, but keep the oven on while making the topping.

5 To make the topping, melt the butter, honey, and both sugars. Bring to the boil. Boil, without stirring, for 2 minutes. Off the heat, stir in the cream and pecans. Pour over the crust, return to the oven, and bake for 25 minutes.

6 When cool, run a knife around the edge. Invert onto a baking sheet, place another sheet on top and invert again.

COOK'S TIP
To cut baked items neatly into squares or bars, use a sharp knife dipped into very hot water.

BARBADIAN COCONUT SWEET BREAD

OFTEN MADE AT CHRISTMAS TIME IN BARBADOS, THIS DELICIOUS COCONUT BREAD IS MOST ENJOYABLE WITH A CUP OF HOT CHOCOLATE OR A GLASS OF FRUIT PUNCH.

MAKES TWO SMALL LOAVES

INGREDIENTS
  ¾ cup butter or margarine
  ½ cup raw sugar
  2 cups self-rising flour
  scant 2 cups all-purpose flour
  4 ounces dry unsweetened shredded
    coconut
  1 teaspoon pumpkin pie spice
  2 teaspoons vanilla extract
  1 tablespoon rum (optional)
  2 eggs
  about ⅔ cup milk
  1 tablespoon superfine sugar,
    blended with 2 tablespoons water,
    to glaze

1 Preheat the oven to 350°F. Grease two 1-pound loaf pans or one 2-pound pan.

2 Place the butter or margarine and sugar in a large mixing bowl and sift in all of the flour. Rub the ingredients together with your fingertips until the mixture begins to resemble fine bread crumbs.

3 Add the coconut, mixed spice, vanilla extract, rum, if using, eggs, and milk. Mix together well with your hands. If the mixture is too dry, add more milk. Knead on a floured board until firm and pliable.

4 Halve the mixture and place in the loaf pans. Glaze with sugared water and bake for about 1 hour, or until a skewer inserted into the loaf comes out clean.

DUCKANOO

THIS TASTY CARIBBEAN CAKE, WHICH HAS ITS ORIGINS IN WEST AFRICA, IS STEAMED IN FOIL PARCELS TO RETAIN MOISTURE. IT CONSISTS MAINLY OF CORNMEAL AND COCONUT AND IS DELICIOUS WITH FRESH CREAM.

MAKES SIX

INGREDIENTS
3 cups fine cornmeal
12 ounces fresh coconut, chopped
2½ cups fresh milk
4 ounces currants or raisins
¼ cup butter or margarine, melted
½ cup raw sugar
4 tablespoons water
¼ teaspoon freshly grated nutmeg
½ teaspoon ground cinnamon
1 teaspoon vanilla extract

1 Place the cornmeal in a large bowl. Blend the coconut and the milk in a blender or food processor until smooth. Stir the coconut mixture into the cornmeal, then add all of the remaining ingredients and stir well.

2 Take 6 pieces of foil and fold into 5 x 6-inch pockets, leaving an opening on one short side. Fold over the edges of the remaining sides tightly to ensure that they are well sealed. This will prevent liquid from seeping in.

3 Put one or two spoonfuls of the cornmeal mixture into each foil pocket and fold over the final edge of foil to seal tightly.

4 Place the foil pockets in a large pan of boiling water. Cover and simmer for about 45–60 minutes. Lift the pockets out of the water and carefully remove the foil. Serve the duckanoo alone or with fresh cream.

CORNMEAL <u>AND</u> FENNEL SEED CAKE

BEING A STAPLE FOOD, CORNMEAL IS OFTEN USED IN BAKING. HERE IT MAKES A DELICIOUS TEA CAKE OR AFTER-SCHOOL SNACK CHILDREN.

MAKES ONE LOAF

INGREDIENTS
3 tablespoons sweet butter,
   softened
1 cup superfine sugar
1⅓ cups coarse cornmeal
1¾ cups all-purpose flour
1½ cups whole milk
2 teaspoons baking powder
1 teaspoon salt
4 eggs
1 teaspoon fennel seeds

1 Preheat the oven to 350°F. Grease a 9 x 5-inch loaf pan and line with parchment paper.

2 Cream the butter and sugar in a food processor until thoroughly combined. Add the remaining ingredients to the food processor and blend again to make a thin cake batter.

COOK'S TIP
The cake batter will seem very runny before baking. Don't let this worry you; the result will be a well-risen, moist cake.

VARIATION
A popular version of this cake is made with the addition of grated fresh white cheese. Stir 5 ounces into the cake batter before baking. The result will be much creamier and even more moist.

3 Pour the batter into the prepared loaf pan and bake for 40–45 minutes, or until a skewer inserted in the center of the cake comes out clean. Allow to cool slightly, then transfer to a wire rack. Serve at room temperature.

BANANA BREAD

THIS IS MORE OF A CAKE THAN A BREAD, AND IS DELICIOUS EATEN ON ITS OWN FOR BREAKFAST OR AS AN AFTERNOON SNACK. IT ALSO MAKES AN IMPRESSIVE INFORMAL DESSERT WHEN TOASTED, BUTTERED, AND SERVED WITH LASHINGS OF BRANDY CREAM.

MAKES ONE LOAF

INGREDIENTS
2 ripe bananas
½ cup butter, softened, plus extra
   for greasing
6 tablespoons light brown sugar
½ teaspoon ground cinnamon
½ teaspoon ground ginger
large pinch of ground cloves
2 eggs, lightly beaten
1½ cups self-rising flour
1 tablespoon milk (optional)
½ cup walnut pieces

1 Preheat the oven to 350°F. Grease a 9 x 5-inch loaf pan and line with parchment paper. Mash the bananas with a fork and set them aside.

2 Cream the butter with the sugar by hand or in a food processor until light and creamy. Add the spices, eggs, and flour, and blend again until thoroughly combined. The mixture should be thin enough to fall reluctantly off a spoon. If it is too thick, stir in the milk.

COOK'S TIP
Do not blend the banana in a food processor—it will become too runny.

3 Fold the mashed bananas and walnut pieces into the mixture, then tip it into the prepared loaf pan. Bake the banana bread for about 1 hour, or until a skewer inserted in the center comes out clean. Transfer to a wire rack to cool.

KINGS' DAY BREAD

ON TWELFTH NIGHT, JANUARY 6TH, MEXICAN CHILDREN RECEIVE GIFTS TO MARK THE DAY THE THREE KINGS BROUGHT GIFTS TO THE INFANT JESUS. THIS SWEETENED RICH BREAD, DECORATED WITH CANDIED FRUIT, IS AN IMPORTANT PART OF THE CELEBRATIONS. A DOLL AND A BEAN ARE HIDDEN INSIDE THE CAKE, AND THE PERSON WHO GETS THE DOLL HAS TO HOST A PARTY ON FEBRUARY 2ND, ANOTHER FEAST DAY. THE PERSON WHO FINDS THE BEAN BRINGS THE DRINKS.

SERVES EIGHT

INGREDIENTS
- ½ cup lukewarm water
- 6 eggs
- 2 teaspoons active dried yeast
- 2½ cups all-purpose flour
- ½ teaspoon salt
- ¼ cup granulated sugar
- ½ cup butter, plus 2 tablespoons melted butter, for glazing
- 1½ cups candied fruit and peel
- 1½ cups confectioners' sugar, plus extra, for dusting
- 2 tablespoons light cream
- candied fruit and cherries, to decorate

1 Pour the water into a small bowl, stir in the dried yeast, and leave in a warm place until frothy.

2 Crack four of the eggs and divide the yolks from the whites. Place the yolks in a small bowl and discard the whites.

3 Put 1¼ cups of the flour in a mixing bowl. Add the salt and sugar. Break the remaining two eggs into the bowl, then add the four egg yolks.

4 Add ½ cup of the butter to the bowl, together with the yeast and water mixture. Mix all the ingredients together well.

5 Put the candied fruit and peel into a separate bowl. Add ½ cup of the remaining flour and toss the fruit with the flour to coat it.

6 Add the floured fruit to the egg mixture, with the rest of the flour. Mix to a soft, non-sticky dough. Knead the dough on a lightly floured surface for about 10 minutes, until smooth.

7 Shape the dough into a ball. Using the floured handle of a wooden spoon, make a hole in the center, and enlarge.

8 Put the dough ring onto a greased baking sheet and cover with oiled plastic wrap. Leave in a warm place for 2 hours, until doubled in bulk.

9 Preheat the oven to 350°F. Brush the dough with the melted butter and bake for about 30 minutes or until it has risen well and is cooked through and springy.

10 Mix the confectioners' sugar and cream in a bowl. Drizzle the mixture over the bread when it is cool and decorate it with the candied fruit and cherries. Dust with confectioners' sugar.

PAN DULCE

THESE "SWEET BREADS" OF VARIOUS SHAPES ARE MADE THROUGHOUT MEXICO, AND ARE EATEN AS A SNACK OR WITH JAM OR MARMALADE FOR BREAKFAST.

MAKES 12

INGREDIENTS
½ cup lukewarm milk
2 teaspoons active dried yeast
4 cups strong bread flour
6 tablespoons superfine sugar
2 tablespoons butter, softened
4 extra large eggs, beaten
oil, for greasing
For the topping
6 tablespoons butter, softened
½ cup granulated sugar
1 egg yolk
1 teaspoon ground cinnamon
1 cup all-purpose flour

1 Pour the milk into a small bowl, stir in the dried yeast, and leave in a warm place until frothy.

2 Put the flour and sugar in a mixing bowl, add the butter and beaten eggs, and mix to a soft, sticky dough.

3 Place the dough on a lightly floured surface and dredge it with more flour. Using floured hands, turn the dough over and over until it is completely covered in a light coating of flour. Cover it with lightly oiled plastic wrap and leave to rest for 20 minutes.

4 Meanwhile, make the topping. Cream the butter and sugar in a bowl, then mix in the egg yolk, cinnamon, and flour. The mixture should have a slightly crumbly texture.

5 Divide the dough into 12 equal pieces and shape each of them into a round. Space well apart on greased baking sheets. Sprinkle the topping over the breads, dividing it more or less equally among them, then press it lightly into the surface.

6 Leave the rolls in a warm place to stand for about 30 minutes, until they are about one and a half times their previous size. Preheat the oven to 400°F and bake the breads for about 15 minutes. Allow to cool slightly before serving.

ALMOND COOKIES

*CONFECTIONERS' SUGAR AND BUTTER COMBINE TO GIVE THESE COOKIES A LIGHT, DELICATE TEXTURE.
THEY CAN BE MADE DAYS AHEAD, AND ARE DELICIOUS WITH DESSERTS OR COFFEE.*

MAKES ABOUT 24

INGREDIENTS

1 cup all-purpose flour
1½ cups confectioners' sugar
pinch of salt
½ cup chopped almonds
½ teaspoon almond extract
½ cup sweet butter, softened
confectioners' sugar, for dusting
halved almonds, to decorate

1 Preheat the oven to 350°F. Combine the flour, confectioners' sugar, salt, and chopped almonds in a bowl. Add the almond extract.

2 Put the softened butter in the center of the flour mixture and use a knife or your fingertips to draw the dry ingredients into the butter until a dough is formed. Shape the dough into a ball.

COOK'S TIPS
Use fancy or themed cutters for celebrations and special occasions.

3 Place the dough on a lightly floured surface and roll it out to a thickness of about ⅛ inch. Using a 3-inch cookie cutter, cut out about 24 rounds, re-rolling the dough as necessary. Place the rounds on baking sheets. Bake for 25–30 minutes until pale golden.

4 Leave for 10 minutes, then transfer to wire racks to cool. Dust thickly with confectioners' sugar before serving, decorated with halved almonds.

DESSERTS

*The abundant supply of sweet and juicy tropical fruit available in
Latin America and the Caribbean means that dessert usually consists of fresh
fruit. Otherwise, desserts tend to be rice dishes based on eggs and sugar and are
usually of Spanish or Portuguese origin, where rich custard tarts and
crème caramels have always been popular.*

FRUITS OF THE TROPICS SALAD

CANNED GUAVAS DO NOT HAVE QUITE THE SAME FLAVOR AS FRESH ONES, BUT ARE AN EXCELLENT INGREDIENT IN THEIR OWN RIGHT—DELICIOUS IN THIS CARIBBEAN FRUIT SALAD.

2 Chop the crystallized ginger and add it to the pineapple mixture.

3 Pour the ginger syrup into a blender or food processor. Add the remaining banana, the coconut milk, and the sugar. Pour in the reserved guava syrup and blend to a smooth creamy puree.

SERVES SIX

INGREDIENTS

1 medium pineapple
14 ounces can guava halves in syrup
2 bananas, sliced
1 large mango, peeled, pitted, and diced
4 ounces preserved crystallized ginger plus 2 tablespoons of the syrup from the jar
4 tablespoons thick coconut milk
2 teaspoons sugar
½ teaspoon freshly grated nutmeg
½ teaspoon ground cinnamon
strips of coconut, to decorate

1 Remove the leafy top of the pineapple, saving it to decorate the serving platter, if you like. Cut the pineapple lengthwise into quarters, then remove the peel and core from each piece. Cube the pineapple, and place in a serving bowl. Drain the guavas, reserving the syrup, and chop. Add the guavas to the bowl with half the bananas and all the mango.

4 Pour the banana and coconut dressing over the fruit, add a little grated nutmeg and a sprinkling of cinnamon. Cover and chill.

5 Serve the salad chilled, decorated with fresh strips of coconut. If you are serving the mixture on a large platter, the pineapple top can be placed in the center as a decoration.

COCONUT ICE CREAM

THIS HEAVENLY ICE CREAM, POPULAR THROUGHOUT THE CARIBBEAN, IS EASY TO MAKE AND USES PANTRY INGREDIENTS, SO IS PERFECT FOR EASY ENTERTAINING.

SERVES EIGHT

INGREDIENTS
    14-ounce can unsweetened
      condensed milk
    14-ounce can condensed milk
    14-ounce can coconut milk
    freshly grated nutmeg
    1 teaspoon almond extract
    fresh lemon balm sprigs, lime slices,
      and shredded coconut, to decorate

COOK'S TIP
If using an ice-cream maker, mix the ingredients in a pitcher, chill in the freezer for 30 minutes. Pour into the ice-cream maker and churn as directed.

3 Remove the bowl from the freezer and whisk the mixture vigorously until it is light and fluffy and has almost doubled in volume.

4 Pour into a freezer container, then cover and freeze. Soften slightly before serving, decorated with lemon balm, lime slices, and shredded coconut.

1 Mix the unsweetened condensed, condensed, and coconut milk in a large freezerproof bowl until well combined.

2 Stir in the grated nutmeg and almond extract. Place the bowl in the freezer and chill the mixture for about 1–2 hours or until semi-frozen.

MANGO SORBET

THIS FOOLPROOF RECIPE IS INCREDIBLY EASY TO MAKE WITHOUT AN ICE-CREAM MAKER. A SMOOTH TEXTURE AND FRUITY, CONCENTRATED FLAVOR IS GUARANTEED.

SERVES SIX

INGREDIENTS
  1 cup superfine sugar
  ⅔ cup water
  3 large ripe mangoes
  juice of 1 lime
  1 egg white

COOK'S TIP
Homemade sherbets tend to set more solidly than bought versions, so always transfer them to the refrigerator to thaw slightly before serving.

VARIATION
The sorbet can be made with ripe papayas instead of mangoes. Add the grated rind of the lime as well as the juice.

1 Dissolve the sugar in the water in a small pan over a low heat. Allow to cool.

2 Cut off a thick lengthwise slice from either side of each mango. Cut off any flesh, peel, and chop it roughly. Put the mango flesh in a food processor or blender and process until smooth.

3 Scrape into a freezerproof bowl and stir in the syrup and lime juice. Freeze for 2–4 hours, until almost solid.

4 Scoop into a food processor and blend until soft. Pour in the egg white and blend until combined. Return to the bowl, cover, and freeze until firm.

COLOMBIAN PINEAPPLE CUSTARD

THESE PINEAPPLE CRÈME CARAMELS ARE THE PERFECT DINNER PARTY DESSERT. THEY ARE VERY EASY TO MAKE, ESPECIALLY IF YOU BUY PREPARED FRESH PINEAPPLE FROM THE SUPERMARKET.

MAKES SIX

INGREDIENTS
    12 ounces peeled fresh
    pineapple, chopped
    ⅔ cup superfine sugar
    4 eggs, lightly beaten
For the caramel
    4 tablespoons granulated sugar
    juice of 1 lime

1 Put the pineapple in a blender or food processor and process until smooth. Scrape the puree into a pan and add the sugar. Cook for 5 minutes or until reduced by one-third. The mixture should be thick but not jam-like, so add a little water if it is too thick. Transfer to a bowl and leave to cool.

COOK'S TIP
Avoid over-whisking the eggs. Gently stir them into the pineapple mixture without incorporating air.

2 Meanwhile make the caramel. Place the granulated sugar in a heavy pan over a medium heat. As the sugar starts to caramelize around the edges, shake the pan to mix the sugar, but do not stir. Remove the pan from the heat as soon as all the sugar has dissolved and the caramel has become golden brown. Immediately stir in the lime juice, taking care not to burn yourself. The hot caramel will spit when the lime juice is added, but this will stop. Divide the caramel among six ramekins and turn them so that they are coated evenly.

3 Preheat the oven to 350°F. Stir the eggs into the cool pineapple mixture. Divide the mixture equally among the ramekins. Place the molds in a roasting pan and pour in warm water to come halfway up their sides. Cover with foil and bake for 45 minutes, until set. Allow to cool.

4 Just before serving, unmold the custards directly onto dessert plates. Loosen the edges with a knife, invert a dessert plate on top of each mold, and turn both over.

CHURROS

THESE DELECTABLE TREATS ARE TRADITIONALLY MADE BY FORCING DOUGH THROUGH A CHURRERA, WHICH IS A UTENSIL FITTED WITH A WOODEN PLUNGER. A FROSTING BAG FITTED WITH A LARGE STAR NOZZLE MAKES A GOOD SUBSTITUTE. CHURROS ARE USUALLY SERVED WITH CAFE DE OLLA OR MEXICAN HOT CHOCOLATE AND ARE PERFECT FOR DIPPING.

MAKES ABOUT 24

INGREDIENTS
3 cups all-purpose flour
1 teaspoon baking powder
2½ cups water
½ teaspoon salt
3 tablespoon soft dark brown sugar
2 egg yolks
oil, for deep frying
2 limes, cut in wedges
superfine sugar, for dusting

1 Sift the flour and baking powder into a bowl and set aside. Bring the measured water to the boil in a pan, add the salt and brown sugar, stirring all the time until both have dissolved. Remove from the heat, tip in all the flour and baking powder, and beat the mixture continuously until smooth.

2 Beat in the egg yolks, one at a time, until the mixture is smooth and glossy. Set the batter aside to cool. Have ready a frosting bag fitted with a large star nozzle which will give the *churros* their traditional shape.

3 Pour oil into a deep fryer or suitable pan to a depth of about 2 inches. Heat to 375°F, or until a cube of dried bread, added to the oil, floats, and turns golden after 1 minute.

4 Spoon the batter into the icing bag. Pipe five or six 4-inch lengths of the mixture into the hot oil, using a knife to slice off each length as it emerges from the nozzle. Fry for 3–4 minutes or until they are golden brown. Drain the *churros* on paper towels while cooking successive batches, then arrange on a plate with the lime wedges, dust them with superfine sugar, and serve warm.

SOPAIPILLAS

THESE GOLDEN PILLOWS OF PUFF PASTRY CAN BE SERVED AS A DESSERT, WITH HONEY, OR PLAIN WITH SOUPS. THEY ARE ALSO IDEAL FOR FINGER BUFFETS.

MAKES ABOUT 30

INGREDIENTS
2 cups all-purpose flour
1 teaspoon baking powder
1 teaspoon salt
2 tablespoons vegetable shortening
   or margarine
¾ cup warm water
oil, for deep frying
clear honey, for drizzling
ground cinnamon for sprinkling
crème fraîche or thick heavy cream,
   to serve

VARIATION
Instead of drizzling honey over the *sopaipillas*, use a mixture of ¼ cup superfine sugar and 2 teaspoons ground cinnamon.

1 Sift the flour, baking powder, and salt into a bowl. Rub in the shortening or margarine until the mixture resembles fine bread crumbs. Gradually add enough of the water to form a dough. Wrap the dough in plastic wrap and leave for 1 hour.

2 Working with half the dough at a time, roll it out to a square, keeping it as even and as thin as possible. Cut into 3-inch squares. When both pieces of the dough have been rolled and cut, set the squares aside.

3 Heat the oil for deep frying to 375°F, or until a cube of dried bread, added to the oil, floats and turns golden after 1 minute. Add a few pastry squares, using tongs to push them down into the oil. Cook in batches until golden on both sides, turning them once, and drain on paper towels.

4 When all the *sopaipillas* have been cooked, arrange on a large serving plate, drizzle with honey, and sprinkle with ground cinnamon. Serve warm, with crème fraîche or thick heavy cream.

COCONUT CREAM TART

THE ULTIMATE IN CARIBBEAN DESSERTS, THIS CREAMY PIE PROVIDES A WONDERFUL TREAT.

SERVES EIGHT

INGREDIENTS
- 6 ounces dry unsweetened shredded coconut
- 1 cup superfine sugar
- 4 tablespoons cornstarch
- ⅛ teaspoon salt
- 2½ cups milk
- 4 tablespoons whipping cream
- 2 egg yolks
- 2 tablespoons sweet butter
- 2 teaspoons vanilla extract

For the pastry
- 1¼ cups all-purpose flour
- ¼ teaspoon salt
- 3 tablespoons butter, chopped
- 2 tablespoons vegetable shortening
- 2–3 tablespoons iced water

1 For the pastry, sift the flour and salt into a bowl. Add the butter and shortening and cut in with a pastry blender until the mixture resembles coarse bread crumbs.

2 With a fork, stir in just enough water to bind the pastry. Gather into a ball, wrap in parchment paper, and refrigerate for 20 minutes.

3 Preheat the oven to 425°F. Roll out the pastry to ⅛-inch thick. Line a 9-inch pie dish. Trim and flute the edges. Prick the bottom. Line with parchment paper and fill with baking beans. Bake for 10 minutes. Remove the paper and beans, reduce the heat to 350°F, and bake until brown, 10–15 minutes.

4 Spread half the coconut on a baking sheet and toast in the oven for 6–8, minutes until golden, stirring often. Set aside.

5 Put the sugar, cornstarch and salt in a pan. In a bowl, whisk the milk, cream,

and egg yolks. Add to the pan.
6 Cook over a low heat, stirring, and bring to the boil. Boil for 1 minute, then remove from the heat. Add the butter, vanilla, and remaining coconut.

7 Pour into the pastry case. When cool, sprinkle over the toasted coconut.

LEMON COCONUT LAYER CAKE

LEMON JUICE GIVES THE COCONUT TOPPING A LOVELY TANGY FLAVOR, BALANCING THE SWEETNESS.

SERVES EIGHT TO TEN

INGREDIENTS

 1¼ cups all-purpose flour
 pinch of salt
 8 eggs
 3 cups superfine sugar
 1 tablespoon grated orange rind
 grated rind of 2 lemons
 juice of 1 lemon
 2½ ounces dry unsweetened
  shredded coconut
 2 tablespoons cornstarch
 1 cup water
 ⅓ cup butter
For the frosting
 ½ cup sweet butter
 1 cup confectioners' sugar
 grated rind of 1 lemon
 6–8 tablespoons lemon juice
 4 ounces dry unsweetened shredded
  coconut

1 Preheat the oven to 350°F oven. Line three 8-inch cake pans with parchment paper and grease. In a bowl, sift together the flour and salt, and set aside.

2 Place six of the eggs in a bowl set over hot water. With an electric mixer, beat until frothy. Beat in half the superfine sugar until the mixture doubles in volume and leaves a ribbon trail when the beaters are lifted, about 10 minutes.

3 Remove the bowl from the hot water. Fold in the orange rind, half the grated lemon rind, and 1 tablespoon lemon juice until blended. Fold in the coconut.

4 Sift over the flour mixture in three batches, folding in after each addition.

5 Divide the mixture between the prepared pans. Bake until the cakes pull away from the sides of the pans, 25–30 minutes. Let stand for 3–5 minutes, then turn out to cool on a rack.

6 In a bowl, blend the cornstarch with a little cold water to dissolve. Whisk in the remaining eggs just until blended.

7 In a pan, combine the remaining lemon rind and juice, the water, remaining sugar, and butter.

8 Over a moderate heat, bring the mixture to the boil. Whisk in the eggs and cornstarch mixture, and return to the boil. Whisk continuously until thick, about 5 minutes. Remove from the heat. Cover with plastic wrap to stop a skin forming, and set aside.

9 For the frosting, cream the butter and confectioners' sugar until smooth. Stir in the lemon rind and enough lemon juice to obtain a thick, spreadable consistency.

10 Sandwich the three cake layers with the lemon custard mixture. Spread the frosting over the top and sides. Cover the cake with the coconut, pressing it in gently.

CARAMEL CUSTARD

IF YOU ORDER "FLAN" FROM THE MENU IN MEXICO YOU MIGHT BE DISCONCERTED IF YOU WERE EXPECTING A SPONGE CASE FILLED WITH FRUIT. THIS HUGELY POPULAR PUDDING IS ACTUALLY A CARAMEL CUSTARD, AND HAS ITS ORIGINS IN SPAIN, WHERE THE SAME NAME IS USED. IT IS SIMILAR TO THE FRENCH CRÈME CARAMEL.

SERVES SIX

INGREDIENTS
  4 cups milk
  1 vanilla bean, split
  6 eggs
  ½ cup sugar
  1 teaspoon vanilla extract
For the caramel
  ¾ cup superfine sugar

1 Put six ramekins or dariole molds in a sink of hot water. Make the caramel. Spread out the superfine sugar evenly on the bottom of a large pan. Heat it slowly, without stirring, tilting the pan backwards and forward on the heat until the sugar melts.

2 Lift the heated ramekins or molds out of the water and dry them quickly. Watch the melted sugar closely, and when it turns a rich golden color, pour the mixture into the dishes and simply turn until they are coated, or brush the caramel over the insides of the dishes. Set them aside.

3 Preheat the oven to 350°F. Pour the milk into a pan, add the vanilla bean, and bring the milk to just below boiling point. Pour it into a pitcher and set it aside to cool.

4 Put the eggs in a bowl, beat them lightly, then gradually beat in the sugar. Remove the vanilla from the milk, then gradually mix the milk into the egg.

5 Strain the egg mixture into the caramel-lined ramekins or molds and stand them in a roasting pan. Pour boiling water into the roasting pan until it comes halfway up the sides of the dishes, then carefully put the pan in the oven.

6 Bake the caramel custards for about 40 minutes. The custards are done when a slender knife blade, inserted in one of them, comes out clean.

7 Lift the dishes out of the water, let them cool, then chill them for several hours in the refrigerator.

8 To serve, run a round-bladed knife around the edge of each custard, place a dessert plate upside down on top of the dish, and turn the dish and plate over together. Lift off the dish. Some of the caramel will settle in a puddle around the custard, so it is important not to choose dessert dishes that are too shallow. Try serving these custards with fresh fruit.

VARIATIONS
Flavor the custard with cinnamon, cocoa, or rum instead of vanilla. In the Tabasco region, where chestnuts grow, chestnut puree is sometimes added.

COLD MANGO SOUFFLÉS TOPPED WITH TOASTED COCONUT

FRAGRANT, FRESH MANGO IS ONE OF THE MOST DELICIOUS EXOTIC FRUITS AROUND, WHETHER IT IS SIMPLY SERVED IN SLICES OR USED AS THE BASIS FOR AN ICE CREAM OR SOUFFLÉ.

MAKES FOUR

INGREDIENTS

    4 small mangoes, peeled, pitted,
      and chopped
    2 tablespoons water
    1 tablespoon powdered gelatine
    2 egg yolks
    ½ cup superfine sugar
    ½ cup milk
    grated rind of 1 orange
    1¼ cups heavy cream
    toasted flaked or coarsely shredded
      coconut, to decorate

1 Place a few pieces of mango in the base of each of four ⅔-cup ramekins. Wrap a greased collar of non-stick parchment paper around the outside of each dish, extending well above the rim. Secure with adhesive tape, then tie tightly with string.

2 Pour the water into a small heatproof bowl and sprinkle the gelatine over the surface. Leave for 5 minutes or until spongy. Place the bowl in a pan of hot water, stirring occasionally, until the gelatine has dissolved.

3 Meanwhile, whisk the egg yolks with the superfine sugar and milk in another heatproof bowl. Place the bowl over a pan of simmering water and continue to whisk until the mixture is thick and frothy. Remove from the heat and continue whisking until the mixture cools. Whisk in the liquid gelatine.

4 Puree the remaining mango pieces in a food processor or blender, then fold the puree into the egg yolk mixture with the orange rind. Set the mixture aside until starting to thicken.

5 Whip the heavy cream to soft peaks. Reserve 4 tablespoons and fold the rest into the mango mixture. Spoon into the ramekins until the mixture is 1 inch above the rim of each dish. Chill for 3–4 hours or until set.

6 Carefully remove the paper collars from the soufflés. Spoon a little of the reserved cream on top of each soufflé and decorate with some toasted flaked or coarsely shredded coconut.

ALMOND PUDDING <u>WITH</u> CUSTARD

THIS DISH MAY WELL DATE FROM THE TIME OF THE FRENCH OCCUPATION OF MEXICO, FOR IT BEARS A CLOSE RESEMBLANCE TO ÎLE FLOTTANTE—FLOATING ISLANDS—ALTHOUGH IN THAT RECIPE THE MERINGUES ARE ACTUALLY POACHED IN THE CUSTARD. DELICIOUS AND VERY LIGHT, IT MAKES THE PERFECT DESSERT TO FOLLOW A SUBSTANTIAL MAIN COURSE.

SERVES SIX

INGREDIENTS
1 cup water
½ ounce sachet powdered gelatine
1¼ cups sugar
½ teaspoon almond extract
6 eggs, separated
pinch of salt
2 cups light cream
½ teaspoon vanilla extract
ground cinnamon, for dusting

1 Pour the water into a pan and sprinkle the gelatine over the surface. When it has softened, add 1 cup of the sugar and place the pan over a low heat. Stir until both the gelatine and the sugar have dissolved, then stir in the almond extract. Pour the mixture into a bowl and chill in the refrigerator until it starts to thicken.

2 Whisk the egg whites until they are stiff. Whisk the gelatine mixture until it is frothy, then fold in the egg whites carefully. Chill until firm.

3 Meanwhile, make the custard. Put the egg yolks, remaining sugar, and salt in a heavy pan. Stir in the cream and vanilla extract. Cook over a very low heat, stirring constantly until the custard thickens to a soft dropping consistency, enough to coat the back of a wooden spoon.

4 Pour the custard into dessert bowls. Cover each with a piece of dampened wax paper until ready to serve, to prevent the formation of a skin.

5 Serve each custard topped with a few spoonfuls of the meringue mixture and a sprinkle of ground cinnamon.

TAPIOCA PUDDING

THIS IS ONE OF THOSE DESSERTS THAT PROVOKES STRONG REACTIONS. MOST PEOPLE EITHER LOVE IT OR LOATHE IT, BUT IT IS VERY POPULAR THROUGHOUT LATIN AMERICA. FOR ITS MANY FANS, THERE IS NOTHING NICER THAN THIS CREAMY DESSERT STREWN WITH CRUNCHY CASHEWS.

SERVES SIX

INGREDIENTS
  generous ½ cup tapioca
  3 cups whole milk
  1 cinnamon stick, bruised
  3 tablespoons superfine sugar
  2 tablespoons chopped cashew nuts

1 Put the tapioca in a strainer and rinse under cold running water. Drain and tip into a heavy pan.

VARIATION
For coconut-flavored tapioca pudding, simply replace the milk with the same quantity of coconut milk.

2 Pour in the milk and soak for 30 minutes. Place the pan over a medium heat and bring to the boil. Add the bruised cinnamon stick, then lower the heat and simmer gently for 30 minutes, or until most of the milk has been absorbed. Stir occasionally to prevent the tapioca from sticking.

3 Stir in the sugar and gently simmer for a further 10 minutes. Carefully remove the cinnamon stick and spoon the pudding into individual dessert bowls. Lightly toast the cashew nuts in a dry frying pan, taking care not to burn them, and scatter over the puddings. Serve warm rather than hot or cold.

FRIED BANANAS WITH SUGAR AND RUM

CHILDREN LOVE FRIED BANANAS, BUT THIS CARIBBEAN VERSION WITH RUM DELIVERS AN EXTRA KICK AND IS STRICTLY FOR GROWN-UPS. FRIED BANANAS CAN BE INCREDIBLY SWEET, BUT THE LIME JUICE CUTS THROUGH THE SWEETNESS WITH DELICIOUS RESULTS.

SERVES FOUR

INGREDIENTS
 ¼ cup superfine sugar
 3 tablespoons rum
 5 tablespoons sweet butter
 grated rind and juice of
  1 lime
 4 bananas, peeled
 vanilla ice cream, to serve

1 Place the sugar, rum, butter, grated lime rind, and lime juice in a large heavy frying pan over a low heat. Cook for a few minutes, stirring occasionally, until the sugar has completely dissolved.

COOK'S TIP
Avoid using bananas that are too ripe, otherwise they may break apart in the pan before they get a chance to color.

2 Add the bananas to the pan, turning to coat them in the sauce. Cook over a medium heat for 5 minutes on each side, or until the bananas are golden.

3 Remove from the heat and cut the bananas in half. Serve two pieces of banana per person with a scoop of vanilla ice cream and a generous drizzle of the hot sauce.

COCONUT AND PUMPKIN COMPOTE

LATIN AMERICANS LOVE WHOLE PRESERVED FRUITS IN SYRUP. ALSO POPULAR ARE COMPOTES LIKE THIS ONE, TRADITIONALLY SERVED WITH FRESH CHEESE.

SERVES SIX

INGREDIENTS
    1¾ pounds pumpkin, peeled
      and seeded
    2¼ cups superfine sugar
    4 cloves
    1½ cups water
    1⅓ cups dry unsweetened shredded
      coconut
    ricotta cheese, to serve

1 Cut the pumpkin into even-size pieces and place in a heavy pan. Add the sugar, cloves, and water. Heat gently, without bringing to the boil, until the sugar has dissolved.

3 Stir in the coconut and simmer for a further 15 minutes. The mixture should be thick but still liquid, so add more water if necessary. Leave to cool, then transfer to an airtight container and store in the refrigerator for up to 2 weeks.

VARIATION

This preserve is more traditionally made without coconut. For pure pumpkin compote, leave out the coconut and double the quantity of pumpkin.

2 Increase the heat to medium. Simmer the mixture for 30–35 minutes, until the pumpkin is soft. Using a fork mash the cooked pumpkin until it is reduced to a rough puree.

4 Spoon the compote into a serving bowl and allow it to come to room temperature before serving with a fresh white cheese, such as ricotta.

DULCE DE LECHE

SPANISH IN ORIGIN, THIS TOFFEE-LIKE DESSERT IS A CHILDREN'S FAVORITE THROUGHOUT LATIN AMERICA. LITERALLY TRANSLATED AS "CARAMELIZED MILK," IT IS TRADITIONALLY MADE WITH MILK AND SUGAR, BUT THIS VERSION IS MUCH QUICKER AND JUST AS DELICIOUS.

SERVES SIX

INGREDIENTS
    14-ounce can condensed milk
    14-ounce can unsweetened
      condensed milk

VARIATION

A classic trick to making low-maintenance *dulce de leche* is to cook a whole, closed can of condensed milk in a pan of boiling water for 30 minutes, but this must be done with care as the can could explode if not continuously immersed in water. South American cooks often add a can of condensed milk to the pan when cooking beans, so side dish and dessert cook together.

1 Combine the condensed and evaporated milk in a heavy pan. Place over a medium heat and bring to the boil. Reduce the heat slightly and cook, stirring constantly, for 30–35 minutes until thickened and toffee-colored. Use a relatively large pan, as the milk has a tendency to boil over.

2 Pour into a sterilized jar and seal. *Dulce de leche* will keep for months, but with time, the texture will alter and won't be as smooth.

3 Serve with ice cream, as a filling for pancakes or cakes, or even with a white cheese, such as ricotta.

PUMPKIN IN BROWN SUGAR

RICH, STICKY, AND SWEET, THIS WARMING DESSERT LOOKS VERY ATTRACTIVE AND IS NOT AT ALL DIFFICULT TO PREPARE.

SERVES SIX

INGREDIENTS
  1 small pumpkin, about 800g/1¾lb
  350g/12oz/1½ cups soft dark
    brown sugar
  120ml/4fl oz/½ cup water
  5ml/1 tsp ground cloves
  12 cinnamon sticks, each about
    10cm/4in in length
  fresh mint sprigs, to decorate
  thick yogurt or crème fraîche, to serve

1 Halve the pumpkin, remove the seeds and fibres and cut into wedges. Arrange in a single layer in a shallow, flameproof casserole or heavy-based pan. Fill the hollows with the sugar.

2 Pour the water carefully into the pan, taking care not to wash all the sugar to the bottom. Make sure that some of the water trickles down to the bottom to prevent the pumpkin from burning. Sprinkle on the ground cloves and add two of the cinnamon sticks.

3 Cover the pan tightly and cook over a low heat for about 30 minutes, or until the pumpkin is tender and the sugar and water have formed a syrup. Check the casserole or pan occasionally to make sure that the pumpkin does not dry out or catch on the bottom.

4 Transfer the pumpkin to a platter and pour the hot syrup over. Decorate each portion with mint and cinnamon sticks and serve with thick yogurt or crème fraîche.

COOK'S TIP
Pumpkin cooked in this way can be used to fill sweet empanadas, so cook all of it and use the rest as filling.

COCONUT CUSTARD

LIGHT AND CREAMY, THIS IS THE PERFECT PUDDING FOR SERVING AFTER A SPICY MAIN COURSE.
CHILDREN LIKE IT, AND IT IS IDEAL FOR ENTERTAINING AS IT CAN BE MADE AHEAD OF TIME AND
KEPT IN THE REFRIGERATOR OVERNIGHT.

2 Add the coconut and cook over a low heat, stirring occasionally, for 5 minutes. Stir in the milk until the mixture has thickened slightly. Remove the cinnamon stick. Remove from the heat.

3 Whisk the eggs until light and fluffy. Gradually incorporate the coconut mixture, then scrape into a clean pan.

SERVES SIX

INGREDIENTS
225g/8oz/1 cup sugar
250ml/8fl oz/1 cup water
1 cinnamon stick, about 7.5cm/3in
   in length
175g/6oz/2 cups desiccated (dry
   unsweetened shredded) coconut
750ml/1¼ pints/3 cups milk
4 eggs
175ml/6fl oz/¾ cup whipping cream
50g/2oz/½ cup chopped almonds,
   toasted
strips of orange rind, to decorate

VARIATION
Use about 115g/4oz/1 cup fresh coconut, and grate it in a food processor.

1 To make the cinnamon syrup, place the sugar and water in a very large pan, add the cinnamon stick and bring to the boil. Lower the heat and simmer, uncovered, for 5 minutes.

4 Cook over a low heat, stirring constantly, until the mixture becomes a thick custard. Cool, then chill. Just before serving, whip the cream. Transfer to individual bowls, top with the cream, chopped almonds and orange rind and serve. Toasted sliced almonds also go well with this.

FRUIT PLATTER

MEXICANS LIKE TO EAT FRUIT WITH CHILE AND LIME AS AN APPETIZER OR HORS D'OEUVRE, BUT THE COMBINATION ALSO MAKES A REFRESHING END TO A MEAL. THE SELECTION OF FRUIT BELOW IS JUST A SUGGESTION; USE ANY FRUIT IN SEASON, BEARING IN MIND THAT THE AIM IS TO PRODUCE A COLORFUL PLATTER WITH PLENTY OF FLAVOR.

SERVES SIX

INGREDIENTS
½ small watermelon
2 mangoes
2 papayas
1 small pineapple
1 fresh coconut
1 *jicama*
juice of 2 limes, plus lime wedges,
  to serve
sea salt
mild red chili powder

1 Slice the watermelon thinly, then cut each slice into bite-size triangles, removing as many of the seeds as possible. Take a large slice off the pit on either side of each mango, then cross-hatch the mango flesh on each slice. Turn the slices inside out so that the cubes of mango flesh stand proud. Slice these off and put them in a bowl.

2 Cut the payayas in half, scoop out the seeds, then cut each half into wedges, leaving the skin on. Cut the leafy green top off the pineapple, then slice off the base. With a sharp knife, remove the skin, using a spiral action and cutting deeply enough to remove most of the "eyes." Use a small knife to take out any remaining "eyes." Cut the pineapple lengthwise in quarters and remove the core from the center of each piece. Slice each of the pieces into bitesize wedges.

3 Make a hole in two of the "eyes" at the top of the coconut, using a nail and hammer. Pour out the liquid. Tap the coconut with a hammer until it breaks into pieces. Remove the hard outer shell, then use a potato peeler to remove the thin brown layer. Cut the coconut into neat pieces.

4 Peel and slice the *jicama*. Arrange all the fruits on a platter, sprinkle them with lime juice, and serve with lime wedges and small bowls of sea salt and chili powder for sprinkling.

COOK'S TIP
Cut all the fruit into bitesize pieces, so that it can be speared on toothpicks and eaten.

ICE CREAM WITH MEXICAN CHOCOLATE

THIS RICH, CREAMY ICE CREAM HAS A WONDERFULLY COMPLEX FLAVOR, THANKS TO THE CINNAMON AND ALMONDS IN THE MEXICAN CHOCOLATE.

SERVES FOUR

INGREDIENTS
2 extra large eggs
½ cup superfine sugar
2 bars Mexican chocolate, total
  weight about 4 ounces
1⅔ cups heavy cream
scant 1 cup milk
chocolate curls, to decorate

1 Put the eggs in a bowl and whisk them with an electric whisk until they are thick, pale, and fluffy. Gradually whisk in the sugar.

2 Melt the chocolate in a heavy-based pan over a low heat, then add it to the egg mixture and mix thoroughly. Whisk in the cream, then stir in the milk, a little at a time. Cool the mixture, then chill. Pour the mixture into an ice-cream maker and churn until thick.

3 Alternatively, freeze it in a shallow plastic box in the fast-freeze section of the freezer for several hours, until ice crystals have begun to form around the edges. Process to break up the ice crystals, then freeze again. To serve, decorate with chocolate curls.

CAPIROTADA

MEXICAN COOKS BELIEVE IN MAKING GOOD USE OF EVERYTHING AVAILABLE TO THEM. THIS DESSERT WAS INVENTED AS A WAY OF USING UP FOOD BEFORE THE LENTEN FAST, BUT IS NOW EATEN AT OTHER TIMES TOO.

SERVES SIX

INGREDIENTS
1 small French stick, a few days old
⅓–½ cup butter, softened, plus extra
for greasing
scant 1 cup soft dark brown sugar
1 cinnamon stick, about 16 inches long
1⅔ cups water
3 tablespoons dry sherry
¾ cup sliced almonds, plus extra,
to decorate
1½ cup raisins
1 cup grated Monterey Jack or mild
Cheddar cheese
light cream, for pouring

1 Slice the bread into about 30 rounds, each ½-inch thick. Lightly butter on both sides. Cook in batches in a warm frying pan until browned, turning over once. Set the slices aside.

2 Place the sugar, cinnamon stick, and water in a pan. Heat gently, stirring all the time, until the sugar has dissolved. Bring to the boil, then lower the heat and simmer for 15 minutes without stirring. Remove the cinnamon stick, then stir in the sherry.

COOK'S TIP
This recipe works well with older bread that is quite dry. If you only have fresh bread, slice it and dry it out for a few minutes in a low oven.

3 Preheat the oven to 350°F. Grease an 8-inch square baking dish with butter. Layer the bread rounds, almonds, raisins, and cheese in the dish, pour the syrup over, letting it soak into the bread. Bake this dessert for about 30 minutes until golden brown.

4 Remove from the oven, leave to stand for 5 minutes, then cut into squares. Serve cold, with light cream poured over, decorated with the extra sliced almonds.

DRUNKEN PLANTAIN

UNTIL THEIR CUISINE WAS INFLUENCED BY THE SPANISH AND THE FRENCH, MEXICANS HAD NO PASTRIES OR CAKES, PREFERRING TO END THEIR MEALS WITH FRUIT, WHICH WAS ABUNDANT. THIS DESSERT IS QUICK AND EASY TO PREPARE, AND TASTES DELICIOUS.

SERVES SIX

INGREDIENTS
3 ripe plantains
¼ cup butter, diced
3 tablespoons rum
grated rind and juice of
1 small orange
1 teaspoon ground cinnamon
¼ cup soft dark brown sugar
½ cup whole almonds, in
their skins
fresh mint sprigs, to decorate
crème fraîche or thick heavy cream,
to serve

1 Preheat the oven to 350°F. Peel the plantains and cut them in half lengthwise. Put the pieces in a shallow baking dish, dot them all over with butter, then spoon over the rum and orange juice.

2 Mix the orange rind, cinnamon, and brown sugar in a bowl. Sprinkle the mixture over the plantains.

3 Bake for 25–30 minutes, until the plantains are soft and the sugar has melted into the rum and orange juice to form a sauce.

4 Meanwhile, slice the almonds and dry-fry them in a heavy-based frying pan until the cut sides are golden. Serve the plantains in individual bowls, with some of the sauce spooned over. Sprinkle the almonds on top, decorate with the fresh mint sprigs, and offer crème fraîche or heavy cream separately.

CARIBBEAN SPICED RICE PUDDING

SOME RECIPES FROM THE CARIBBEAN CAN BE EXTREMELY SWEET, PARTICULARLY DESSERTS. IF THIS RICE PUDDING IS A LITTLE TOO SWEET FOR YOUR TASTE, SIMPLY REDUCE THE SUGAR QUANTITY AND RELY UPON THE NATURAL SWEETNESS OF THE FRUIT.

SERVES SIX

INGREDIENTS

2 tablespoons butter
1 cinnamon stick
½ cup soft brown sugar
⅔ cup ground rice
5 cups milk
½ teaspoons allspice
⅓ cup golden raisins
3 ounces mandarin oranges, chopped
3 ounces pineapple, chopped

1 Melt the butter in a non-stick pan. Add the cinnamon stick and sugar. Heat over a medium heat until the sugar just begins to caramelize. Remove from the heat.

2 Carefully stir in the rice and three-quarters of the milk. Slowly bring to the boil, stirring all the time, being careful not to let the milk burn. Reduce the heat and simmer gently for about 10 minutes, or until the rice is cooked, stirring constantly.

3 Add the remaining milk, the allspice and the golden raisins. Leave to simmer for 5 minutes, stirring occasionally.

4 When the rice is thick and creamy, allow to cool slightly, then stir in the mandarin and pineapple pieces.

JAMAICAN FRUIT TRIFLE

THIS TRIFLE IS ACTUALLY BASED ON A CARIBBEAN FOOL THAT CONSISTS OF FRUIT STIRRED INTO THICK VANILLA-FLAVORED CREAM. THIS VERSION IS MUCH LESS RICH, REDRESSING THE BALANCE WITH PLENTY OF FRUIT, AND WITH CRÈME FRAÎCHE REPLACING SOME OF THE CREAM.

SERVES EIGHT

INGREDIENTS
1 large pineapple, peeled and cored
1¼ cups heavy cream
scant 1 cup crème fraîche
4 tablespoons confectioners' sugar, sifted
2 teaspoons pure vanilla extract
2 tablespoons white or coconut rum
3 papayas, peeled, seeded and chopped
3 mangoes, peeled, pitted, and chopped
thinly pared rind and juice of 1 lime
⅓ cup coarsely shredded or sliced coconut, toasted

1 Cut the pineapple into large chunks, place in a food processor or blender, and process briefly until chopped. Tip into a strainer placed over a bowl and leave for 5 minutes so that most of the juice drains from the fruit.

2 Whip the cream to soft peaks, then fold in the crème fraîche, sifted confectioners' sugar, vanilla extract, and rum.

3 Fold the drained chopped pineapple into the cream mixture. Place the chopped papayas and mangoes in a large bowl and pour over the lime juice. Gently stir the fruit mixture to combine. Shred the pared lime rind.

4 Divide the fruit mixture and the pineapple cream among eight dessert plates. Decorate with the lime shreds, toasted coconut and a few small pineapple leaves, if you like, and serve at once.

COOK'S TIP
It is important to let the pineapple puree drain thoroughly, otherwise, the pineapple cream will be watery. Don't throw away the drained pineapple juice—mix it with fizzy mineral water for a refreshing drink.

BRAZILIAN COCONUT FLAN

THIS IS A SOMEWHAT UNCONVENTIONAL BUT VERY SUCCESSFUL RECIPE FOR QUINDAO, A CLASSIC BRAZILIAN DESSERT MADE WITH NO FEWER THAN 18 EGG YOLKS. IT IS AVAILABLE AS A PACKAGED MIX THROUGHOUT LATIN AMERICA, BUT IT IS MUCH MORE DELICIOUS IF YOU MAKE YOUR OWN.

SERVES 12

INGREDIENTS
1⅔ cups dry unsweetened shredded
  coconut
scant 1 cup whole milk
3 tablespoons sweet butter, softened
2 cups superfine sugar, plus extra for
  dusting
18 egg yolks

1 Put the coconut in a bowl. Pour over the milk and leave to stand for about 15 minutes or until all the milk has been absorbed.

2 Meanwhile, grease a 9-inch ring mold with some of the butter and then lightly dust with a sprinkling of superfine sugar.

3 Put the remaining butter in a large bowl. Add the sugar and soaked coconut, and mix vigorously until thoroughly combined.

4 Using a wooden spoon, gently stir in the egg yolks, one at a time. When the ingredients are thoroughly combined, cover the bowl with a clean dish towel and leave the mixture to stand in a cool place for about 1 hour.

5 Tip the coconut mixture into the prepared ring mold and place this in the center of a large, deep roasting pan. Pour in enough warm water to come halfway up the outside of the mold. Place this bain marie and its pudding in a cold oven.

6 Heat the oven to 425°F and bake the flan for about 1 hour or until the surface is a dark golden, caramelized brown. Remove from the oven and leave to cool in the water in the roasting pan.

COOK'S TIP
You can use the extra egg whites to make a special fluffy tortilla or omlet. Whisk two or three of the whites up and fold them into the eggs before cooking.

7 When the flan is cold, loosen the edges carefully with a metal spatula. Cover with an upturned serving platter and turn the ring mold gently upside down. Gently lift off the ring mold, being careful not to let it touch the top of the flan. Serve cut in thick slices.

VARIATIONS
When available, use finely grated fresh coconut instead of dried. There is no need to soak the fresh coconut in the milk; just add both ingredients to the butter and sugar. For a more fragrant, even sweeter flan, try adding a whole vanilla pod to the egg and coconut mixture before it is left to stand. Make sure you remove it before cooking.

MEXICAN WEDDING COOKIES

ALMOST HIDDEN BENEATH THEIR VEIL OF CONFECTIONERS' SUGAR, THESE LITTLE SHORTBREAD COOKIES ARE TRADITIONALLY SERVED AT WEDDINGS, AND ARE ABSOLUTELY DELICIOUS. SERVE THEM AFTER DINNER WITH COFFEE AND PERHAPS A GLASS OF THE MEXICAN COFFEE LIQUEUR—KAHLÚA.

MAKES 30

INGREDIENTS
1 cup butter, softened
1½ cups confectioners' sugar
1 teaspoon vanilla extract
2¾ cups all-purpose flour
pinch of salt
1¼ cups pecan nuts, chopped

1 Preheat the oven to 375°F. Beat the butter until light and fluffy, then beat in 1 cup confectioners' sugar, with the vanilla extract.

2 Gradually add the flour and salt to the creamed mixture until it starts to form a dough. Add the finely chopped pecans with the remaining flour. Knead the dough lightly.

3 Divide the dough into 30 equal pieces and roll them into balls. Space about ¼ inch apart on baking sheets. Press each ball lightly with your thumb, to flatten it slightly.

4 Bake the cookies for 10–15 minutes, until they are starting to brown. Cool on the baking sheets for 10 minutes, then transfer to wire racks to cool completely.

5 Put the remaining confectioners' sugar in a bowl. Add a few cookies at a time, shaking them in the sugar until they are heavily coated. Serve right away or store in an airtight container.

ALMOND ORANGE COOKIES

THE COMBINATION OF VEGETABLE SHORTENING AND ALMONDS GIVES THESE COOKIES A LOVELY SHORT TEXTURE, SO THAT THEY MELT IN THE MOUTH. THEY ARE PERFECT WITH COFFEE OR HOT CHOCOLATE.

MAKES 36

INGREDIENTS
generous 1 cup vegetable shortening
generous ½ cup superfine sugar
2 eggs, beaten
grated rind and juice of
1 small orange
1¾ cups all-purpose flour, sifted with
1 teaspoon baking powder
1¾ cups ground almonds
For dusting
½ cup confectioners' sugar
1 teaspoon ground cinnamon

COOK'S TIP
If you can't be bothered to roll out the dough, just divide it into 36 pieces and roll each one into a ball. Place these on baking sheets and flatten each one into a cookie shape with a fork.

1 Preheat the oven to 400°F. Place the vegetable shortening in a large bowl and beat with an electric whisk until light and fluffy. Gradually beat in the superfine sugar.

2 Continue to whisk the mixture while you add the eggs, orange rind, and juice. Whisk for 3–4 minutes more, then stir in the flour mixture and ground almonds to form a dough.

3 Roll out the dough on a lightly floured surface until it is about ½ inch thick. Using cookie cutters, cut out 36 rounds, rerolling the dough if necessary. Gently lift the rounds onto baking sheets.

4 Bake for about 10 minutes, or until the cookies are golden. Leave to stand on the baking sheets for 10 minutes to cool and firm slightly.

5 Mix together the confectioners' sugar and cinnamon. Put the mixture in a small sieve or tea strainer and dust the cookies well. Leave to cool completely.

Rum <u>and</u> Banana Waffles

To save time, these scrumptious dessert waffles can be made in advance, wrapped tightly, frozen, and then warmed through in the oven just before serving.

<u>SERVES FOUR</u>

INGREDIENTS
    2 cups all-purpose flour
    2 teaspoons baking powder
    1 teaspoon baking soda
    1 tablespoon superfine sugar
    2 eggs
    ¼ cup butter, melted
    ¾ cup milk
    1¼ cups buttermilk
    1 teaspoon vanilla extract
    light cream, to serve
For the bananas
    6 bananas, thickly sliced
    1 cup chopped pecan nuts
    ⅓ cup raw sugar
    5 tablespoons maple syrup
    3 tablespoons dark rum

1 Sift the dry ingredients into a large mixing bowl. Make a well in the center. Add the eggs, melted butter, and milk. Whisk together, gradually incorporating the flour mixture, until smooth.

COOK'S TIP

If you don't own a waffle iron, prepare the batter as directed, but make small pancakes in a heavy-based frying pan. Alternatively, use ready-made waffles, which are available from large supermarkets, and reheat as directed on the packet before serving with the hot banana topping.

2 Add the buttermilk and vanilla to the batter and whisk well. Cover and leave to stand for 30 minutes. Preheat the oven to 300°F.

3 Heat a hand-held waffle iron over the heat. Stir the batter and add more milk if required (the consistency should be quite thick). Open the waffle iron and pour some batter over two thirds of the surface. Close it and wipe off any excess batter.

4 Cook for 3–4 minutes, carefully turning the waffle iron over once during cooking. If using an electric waffle-maker, follow the manufacturer's instructions for cooking.

VARIATIONS

Use other fruits for the waffle topping, if you like. Small chunks of fresh or drained, canned pineapple, thin wedges of peaches or nectarines, or even orange slices would be delicious alternatives to the banana.

5 When the batter stops steaming, open the iron and lift out the waffle with a fork. Put it on a heatproof plate and keep it hot in the oven. Repeat with the remaining batter to make eight waffles in all. Preheat the grill (broiler).

6 Cook the bananas: spread them out on a large shallow baking sheet and top with the nuts. Scatter over the raw sugar. Mix the maple syrup and rum together and spoon over.

7 Broil for 3–4 minutes or until the sugar begins to bubble. Serve on top of the waffles with light cream.

FRUIT-FILLED EMPANADAS

IMAGINE BITING THROUGH CRISP BUTTERY PASTRY TO DISCOVER A RICH FRUITY FILLING FLAVORED WITH ORANGES AND CINNAMON. THIS IS THE STUFF THAT DREAMS ARE MADE OF.

MAKES 12

INGREDIENTS
   2½ cups all-purpose flour
   2 tablespoons granulated sugar
   scant ½ cup chilled butter, cubed
   1 egg yolk
   iced water
   milk, to glaze
   superfine sugar, for sprinkling
   whole almonds and orange wedges
For the filling
   2 tablespoons butter
   3 ripe plantains, peeled and mashed
   ½ teaspoon ground cloves
   1 teaspoon ground cinnamon
   1⅓ cups raisins
   grated rind and juice of 2 oranges

1 Combine the flour and sugar in a mixing bowl. Rub in the chilled cubes of butter until the mixture resembles fine bread crumbs.

2 Beat the egg yolk and add to the flour mixture. Add iced water to make a smooth dough. Shape it into a ball.

3 Melt the butter for the filling in a pan. Add the plantains, cloves, and cinnamon and cook over a moderate heat for 2–3 minutes. Stir in the raisins, with the orange rind and juice. Lower the heat so that the mixture barely simmers. Cook for about 15 minutes, until the raisins are plump and the juice has evaporated. Set the mixture aside to cool.

4 Preheat the oven to 400°F. Roll out the pastry on a lightly floured surface. Cut it into 4-inch rounds. Place the rounds on a baking sheet and spoon on a little of the filling. Dampen the rim of the pastry rounds with water, fold the pastry over the filling, and crimp the edges to seal.

5 Brush the empanadas with milk. Bake them, in batches if necessary, for about 15 minutes or until they are golden. Allow to cool a little, sprinkle with superfine sugar, and serve warm, with whole almonds and orange wedges.

COOK'S TIP
Use a little of the leftover egg white instead of milk for glazing, if you like.

CHRISTMAS COOKIES <u>WITH</u> WALNUTS

AT CHRISTMAS TIME, THESE ARE INDIVIDUALLY WRAPPED IN SMALL SQUARES OF BRIGHTLY COLORED TISSUE PAPER AND ARRANGED IN LARGE BOWLS, OFTEN TRANSFORMED INTO GIFTS.

<u>MAKES 24</u>

INGREDIENTS
½ cup shortening, softened
¾ cup confectioners' sugar
1 teaspoon vanilla extract
1¼ cups unbleached all-purpose flour
¾ cup broken walnuts,
   finely chopped
½ cup confectioners' sugar, for
   dusting
2 teaspoons ground cinnamon

COOK'S TIP
Pecan nuts can be used instead of the walnuts, if you like.

1 Preheat the oven to 375°F. Place the lard in a large bowl and beat with an electric whisk until light and fluffy.

2 Gradually beat in ¼ cup of the confectioners' sugar, then add the vanilla extract and beat well.

3 Add the flour by hand, working it gently into the mixture. Do not be tempted to use a spoon, or the mixture will be too sticky. Add the walnuts and mix carefully.

4 Divide the dough evenly into 24 small pieces, roll each to a ball, and space well apart on baking sheets. Bake for 10–15 minutes, until golden, switching the baking sheets around halfway through, to ensure even baking. Cool the cookies on wire racks.

5 Put the remaining confectioners' sugar in a bowl and stir in the cinnamon. Add a few cookies at a time, shaking them in the sugar until they are heavily coated. Shake off the excess sugar. Serve wrapped in colored paper.

NUT BRITTLE

NUTS ARE VERY POPULAR IN SOUTH AMERICA AND VARIATIONS OF THIS SNACK ARE TO BE FOUND THROUGHOUT THE CONTINENT. IN BRAZIL IT'S CALLED PE-DE-MOLEQUE *(KID'S FEET)*.

MAKES ABOUT TEN

INGREDIENTS
vegetable oil, for greasing
2¼ cups unsalted peanuts
generous 1 cup granulated sugar

1 Using vegetable oil, grease a shallow 12 x 8-inch baking pan. Tip the sugar and peanuts into a heavy pan and place over a low heat.

3 When all the mixture has caramelized and has taken on a deep brown color, remove the pan from the heat and quickly pour the mixture into the prepared baking pan. Leave it to cool.

COOK'S TIP
Act quickly once the sugar has reached the ideal color, otherwise the caramel could burn and become bitter. Don't worry if the pieces of brittle don't snap evenly when cooled—they'll be just as delicious if irregular.

2 As the sugar begins to melt, start stirring the nuts with a wooden spoon, bringing the sugar that is beginning to caramelize around the edges of the pan into the center.

4 When the brittle has almost set, use a knife to mark it into regular squares or rectangles. This will make it easier to snap the cold brittle into pieces.

COCONUT CANDIES

THESE CHEWY CANDIES ARE A FAVORITE WITH CHILDREN. THEY CAN BE MADE PLAIN, BUT THE LIME JUICE AND CLOVES ADD AN INTERESTING TWIST THAT ADULTS CANNOT RESIST EITHER.

MAKES 25

INGREDIENTS
⅔ cup dry unsweetened shredded coconut
7 tablespoons water
¾ cup light brown sugar
large pinch ground cloves
juice of ½ lime

1 Line a baking tray with parchment paper. Place the coconut in a pan with the water and sugar. Heat gently until the sugar dissolves.

3 Drop spoonfuls of the mixture onto the lined tray, pressing the mixture down with the back of the spoon to flatten it lightly into chunky, irregular pieces. Leave to cool before eating.

COOK'S TIP
Store the coconut sweets in an airtight container in a cool place and they will last for a few weeks or more. If you use fresh ingredients, such as grated fresh coconut or pumpkin, they should be kept chilled and consumed within a week.

2 Stir in the ground cloves and lime juice and increase the heat. Cook, stirring with a wooden spoon, until the mixture has thickened and become dark golden brown.

VARIATION
Equal quantities of grated fresh coconut and grated raw pumpkin can be used instead of the dried hcoconut.

DRINKS

Nothing is more refreshing or nutritious than freshly squeezed fruit juice or coconut juice straight from the shell. Fruit bars serving these juices are found throughout the Caribbean and Latin America. The region is also famous for its cocktails, and every country has its favorite spirit—there's Brazilian cachaça, Peruvian pisco, Caribbean rum, and Mexican tequila.

MANGO SHAKE

CHILDREN LOVE FRESH FRUIT SHAKES, AND WITH THE VARIETY OF TROPICAL FRUIT AVAILABLE THROUGHOUT THE REGION, THEY ARE SPOILED FOR CHOICE.

MAKES 4 CUPS

INGREDIENTS
   2 large ripe mangoes
   3 cups whole milk
   juice of ½ lime
   superfine sugar, to taste

VARIATION
In Brazil, a similar drink is made with avocados. Simply use 2 ripe avocados in place of the mangoes. Until recently, Brazilians viewed avocados as fruit and would not have dreamed of eating them in savory dishes. Once you have tasted this unusual, delicious variation, you will understand why.

1 Place each mango in turn on a board with the narrow side down. Cut off a thick lengthwise slice, keeping as close to the pit as possible. Turn the mango around and repeat on the other side. Cut off the flesh that is still attached to the pit. Remove the peel and chop the flesh roughly.

2 Put the chopped mango in a blender or food processor and add the milk and lime juice. Process until smooth.

3 Pour the mango shake into a pitcher, stir in sugar to taste, and chill in the refrigerator. Serve in tall glasses with ice cubes.

PINEAPPLE AND MINT JUICE

THIS DRINK IS PERFECTLY REFRESHING ON A SUNNY DAY—THE MINT REALLY BRINGS OUT THE SWEETNESS OF THE FRUIT, AND ADDED SUGAR IS RARELY REQUIRED. IT IS A FAVORITE FOR ENJOYING ON THE BEACH OR RELAXING AT A STREET CAFE THROUGHOUT SOUTH AND CENTRAL AMERICA AND ACROSS THE CARIBBEAN, OFTEN WITH SMALL AMOUNTS OF OTHER FRUITS ADDED.

MAKES 4 CUPS

INGREDIENTS
   2¼ pounds pineapples
   10 fresh mint leaves
   crushed ice
   superfine sugar, to taste

VARIATION
To make a pineapple and mint granita, pour the juice into a shallow metal container and place in the freezer until almost firm. Break up the mixture using a fork and return it to the freezer. Repeat this procedure two or three times , until the mixture is semi-frozen, then serve.

1 Cut the top and base off each pineapple, then cut off the skin, being careful to remove all the "eyes." Discard the skin and cut the pineapple, including the core, into large chunks.

2 Blend the pineapple chunks with the mint leaves in a blender or food processor until smooth. Pour into a pitcher and stir in the crushed ice. Stir until the ice has dissolved slightly.

CASHEW NUT MILK

IN MAINLAND SPAIN AND MEXICO A SIMILAR DRINK—HORCHATA—IS MADE WITH ALMONDS, BUT THIS CUBAN VARIATION WITH CASHEWS IS EVEN MORE DELICIOUS. THE RESULT IS RICH AND CREAMY. IT IS GREAT FOR KIDS AND EVEN BETTER FOR ADULTS WHO NEED A HANGOVER CURE.

1 Finely grind the cashews in a food processor. Add the sugar and cinnamon, and grind the mixture again to make a smooth paste.

2 With the motor still running, gradually pour in 3¾ cups of boiling water, until the drink becomes smooth and frothy. Scrape down the mixture occasionally, if necessary.

MAKES 5 CUPS

INGREDIENTS
   3½ cups blanched cashews
   generous 1 cup superfine sugar
   ¼ teaspoon ground cinnamon

COOK'S TIP
For a smooth drink, make this the night before, allow it to stand in the refrigerator overnight, and strain before serving.

3 Pour the cashew nut milk into a pitcher. Cover and chill in the refrigerator. Stir well before serving in tall glasses. Float ice cubes in each glass. As the ice melts, it will dilute the drink, giving it a lighter texture.

PASSION FRUIT BATIDA

BRAZILIAN BATIDAS CAN BE MADE WITH A VARIETY OF JUICES, SUCH AS LIME OR COCONUT MILK.
DO NOT BE FOOLED BY THE FRUITY SWEETNESS: A SMALL GLASS OF BATIDA, SIPPED SLOWLY, IS MORE
THAN ENOUGH TO GET THE PARTY STARTED.

MAKES TWO

INGREDIENTS
  8 passion fruit
  scant 1 cup *cachaça*
  2 tablespoons superfine sugar
  3 ice cubes

2 Add the remaining ingredients, including the ice cubes, and shake vigorously or stir thoroughly.

3 Strain into two cocktail glasses and serve the *batida* immediately.

1 Cut the passion fruit in half and scoop the flesh and seeds into a cocktail shaker or mixing pitcher.

VARIATIONS
• Two other flavors of *batida* that are also very popular are lime and coconut. Simply replace the passion fruit with 4 tablespoons lime juice or coconut milk.
• If you are unable to find *cachaça*, replace with equal quantities of vodka.

CITRUS AGUA FRESCA

THESE REFRESHING FRUIT JUICES ARE SOLD FROM STREET STALLS IN TOWNS ALL OVER MEXICO.
THE VARIETIES OF FRUIT USED CHANGE WITH THE SEASONS.

SERVES FOUR

INGREDIENTS
   12 limes
   3 oranges
   2 grapefruit
   2½ cups water
   6 tablespoons superfine sugar
   extra fruit wedges, to decorate

1 Squeeze the juice from the limes, oranges, and grapefruit. Some fruit pulp may collect along with the juice. This should also be used, once any seeds have been discarded. Pour the mixture into a large pitcher.

2 Add the water and sugar, and stir until all the sugar has dissolved.

3 Chill for at least 1 hour before serving with ice and fruit wedges. The drink will keep for up to 1 week in a covered container in the refrigerator.

VARIATION
Use pink or ruby red grapefruit instead of white for a slightly sweeter drink with a deeper color.

TAMARIND AGUA FRESCA

TAMARIND, SOMETIMES REFERRED TO AS THE INDIAN DATE, IS NATIVE TO ASIA AND NORTH AFRICA. SEEDS CAME TO MEXICO VIA INDIA. IT IS USED MEDICINALLY AND AS AN ANTISEPTIC. THE FRUIT HAS A SWEET-SOUR TASTE AND MAKES A DRINK SIMILAR TO LEMONADE.

SERVES FOUR

INGREDIENTS
- 4 cups water
- 8 ounces tamarind pods
- 2 tablespoons superfine sugar

1 Pour the water into a pan and heat until warm. Remove from the heat and pour into a bowl. Peel the tamarind pods and add the pulp to the warm water. Soak for at least 4 hours.

2 Place a strainer over a clean bowl. Pour the tamarind pulp and water into the strainer, then press the pulp through the strainer with the back of a wooden spoon, leaving the black seeds behind. Discard the seeds.

3 Add the sugar to the tamarind mixture and stir well until dissolved. Allow to cool for a few minutes. Pour into a pitcher and chill thoroughly—the mixture will keep fresh if covered and chilled for at least one day. Serve in tumblers filled with ice.

COOK'S TIP
Jars of tamarind pulp or paste are sold at Indian food shops and Oriental stores. The dried pulp is also sold in solid blocks. All these products need soaking and straining, but you will be spared the time-consuming task of peeling the pods.

PINEAPPLE AND LIME AGUA FRESCA

THE VIVID COLORS OF THIS FRESH FRUIT DRINK GIVE SOME INDICATION OF ITS WONDERFUL FLAVOR. IT MAKES A DELICIOUS MIDDAY REFRESHER, MID-AFTERNOON BREAK, OR CHILLED PICK-ME-UP AT THE END OF A HARD DAY.

SERVES FOUR

INGREDIENTS
2 pineapples
juice of 2 limes
2 cups uncarbonated mineral water
¼ cup superfine sugar

COOK'S TIP
When peeling a pineapple cut off the top and bottom and remove the skin with a spiral action, cutting deeply enough to remove most of the "eyes." Any remaining "eyes" can be cut out using a small knife.

1 Peel the pineapples and chop the flesh, removing the core and "eyes." You should have about 1 pound of flesh. Put this in a food processor or blender and add the lime juice and half the mineral water. Puree to a smooth pulp. Stop the machine and scrape the mixture from the side of the goblet once or twice during processing.

2 Place a strainer over a large bowl. Tip the pineapple pulp into the strainer and press it through with a wooden spoon. Pour the strained mixture into a large pitcher, cover, and chill in the refrigerator for about 1 hour.

3 Stir in the remaining mineral water and sugar to taste. Serve with ice.

LIME AGUA FRESCA

This is the lime version of real English lemonade. Traditionally, lime peel would have been ground in a molcajete to extract the oil. Mexican limes—limones—are harder and more tart than the smooth-skinned varieties most often sold in Western supermarkets.

<u>SERVES SIX</u>

INGREDIENTS

7½ cups water
6 tablespoons superfine sugar
10 limes, plus slices, to decorate

1 Pour the water into a pitcher, add the sugar, and stir until all the sugar has dissolved. Chill for at least 1 hour.

2 Using a zester or grater, remove the rind from the limes, taking care to take only the colored zest, not the pith. Squeeze the juice from the limes and add this to the chilled sugar water, with the lime rind. Stir well and chill again until required. Serve with ice in tall glasses, decorated with lime slices.

COOK'S TIP
To extract the maximum amount of juice from the limes, roll firmly between your palms for a few moments, or pierce with a skewer, put in a bowl, and microwave on maximum power for 10–15 seconds before juicing. This works with all citrus fruits.

PISCO SOUR

THIS COCKTAIL, ENJOYED IN PERU, BOLIVIA, ECUADOR, AND CHILE, GETS ITS NAME FROM THE PERUVIAN BRANDY WITH WHICH IT IS MADE. GIVE THE COCKTAIL A GOOD SHAKE TO ENCOURAGE THE EGG WHITES TO FOAM UP, AND FINISH WITH THE BITTER, SPICY TASTE OF ANGOSTURA.

MAKES TWO

INGREDIENTS
    7 tablespoons *pisco*
    2 teaspoons egg white
    2 tablespoons superfine sugar
    juice of 1 lime
    6 ice cubes
    Angostura bitters

COOK'S TIPS
• Don't stir the cocktail after adding the Angostura bitters, so each sip tastes slightly different.
• If you prefer not to eat raw egg white, the drink can be made without it.

1 Chill two tumblers in the freezer for 10 minutes, until they are frosty white.

2 Combine all the ingredients, except for the Angostura bitters, in a cocktail shaker and shake vigorously for about 30 seconds.

3 Strain into the chilled glasses. If you like you can fill the tumblers with ice first, which will dilute the cocktail slightly. Shake 2–3 drops of the bitters on top, without stirring them into the cocktail. Serve immediately.

CAIPIRINHA

THIS BRAZILIAN DRINK CAN BE ENJOYED AT ANY TIME OF DAY—ON THE BEACH WHILE SNACKING ON SEAFOOD, AS AN APERITIF BEFORE A MEAL, AND EVEN WITH STEAK AT A BARBECUE. IT IS A VERY POPULAR DRINK IN THE CITIES, ESPECIALLY AT MARDI GRAS FESTIVITIES. AS ANY TOURIST TO BRAZIL WILL KNOW, ONCE YOU HAVE TASTED IT, YOU ARE HOOKED FOR LIFE!

MAKES TWO

INGREDIENTS
    2 limes
    2 tablespoons superfine sugar
    7 tablespoons *cachaça*
    crushed ice

1 Wash the limes thoroughly, scrubbing the rind to remove any artifical wax coating that may have been applied. You can buy limes that do not have this wax coating, which will make it easier to crush out the juice from the rind. Cut each scrubbed lime into eight large chunks.

2 Place the lime chunks in two tall glasses and divide the sugar equally between them. Pound the sugar and lime together with a pestle. The skill lies in being vigorous enough to extract the juice and oil from the rind, yet delicate enough not to break the glass.

3 Top with the crushed ice and divide the *cachaça* equally between the glasses. Stir vigorously and serve.

VARIATION
Use the same recipe to make *caipiroska*, with vodka replacing the *cachaça*.

You could also try making a *caipirissima*, using white rum instead of *cachaça*.

TEQUILA

THERE ARE SEVERAL DIFFERENT TYPES OF TEQUILA, MEXICO'S NATIONAL SPIRIT. EACH TYPE OF
TEQUILA IS AVAILABLE IN A NUMBER OF DIFFERENT BRANDS, EACH WITH A DISTINCTIVE FLAVOR
INFLUENCED BY THE SOIL TYPE, THE SUGAR CONTENT AND FLAVOR OF THE AGAVE PLANTS, THE
LOCAL CLIMATE, AND THE COOKING AND FERMENTING PROCESSES.

There are many different ways of serving tequila. Perhaps the best known of these is the slammer, when shots of chilled tequila are drunk with salt and lime. *Joven* (young) or *reposada* (rested) tequila is often served at room temperature in small shot glasses called *caballitos*, and sipped slowly so that all the flavors can be savored. *Anejo* (aged) tequila should be served in a small balloon glass (a large glass would allow too much of the aroma to escape). It can be diluted with a little water, but ice should not be added.

TEQUILA SLAMMERS
Mexicans have long enjoyed the taste of lime and salt with their food and drink. Beer is also taken with lime and salt.

INGREDIENTS
  chilled tequila
  salt
  wedges of lime

HOW TO SERVE TEQUILA
Pour a shot glass of tequila. Lick the space between the thumb and the index finger on your left hand, then sprinkle this area with salt. Taking care not to spill the salt, hold a lime wedge in the same hand. Pick up the shot glass in your right hand. Lick the salt, down the tequila in one, suck the lime, then slam down your empty glass. Some drinkers manage salt, lime, and tequila in the same hand, but this takes practice.

TEQUILA SUNRISE

THIS DRINK TAKES ITS NAME FROM THE WAY THE GRENADINE—A BRIGHT RED CORDIAL MADE FROM POMEGRANATE JUICE—FIRST SINKS IN THE GLASS OF ORANGE JUICE AND THEN RISES TO THE SURFACE. IT BECAME POPULAR IN THE TWENTIES AND THIRTIES WHEN COCKTAILS WERE ALL THE RAGE IN THE CARIBBEAN AND IN MEXICO.

SERVES ONE

INGREDIENTS

1½ tablespoons golden tequila
4 tablespoons freshly squeezed
   orange juice
juice of 1 lime
1 teaspoon grenadine

VARIATION
To make a Pink Cadillac, use Grand Marnier instead of orange juice. This will provide a lovely two-tone effect from the red grenadine on the bottom covered by a layer of deep orange-brown Grand Marnier. It has a delicious tangy orange flavor from the liqueur.

1 Half fill a cocktail glass with crushed ice. Pour in the tequila, then the orange and lime juices, which should be freshly squeezed. Don't be tempted to use concentrated orange juice from a carton or bottled lime juice, or the flavor of the finished drink will be spoiled.

2 Quickly add the grenadine, pouring it down the back of a teaspoon held in the glass so that it sinks to the bottom of the drink. This will give the drink its characteristic two-tone coloring. Serve immediately.

PINEAPPLE TEQUILA

FLAVORS SUCH AS ALMONDS OR QUINCE HAVE BEEN ADDED TO BLANCO OR REPOSADA TEQUILA FOR SOME TIME. MANY BARS HAVE DEVELOPED UNIQUE FLAVORS BY COMBINING INGREDIENTS SUCH AS CHILES WITH BLANCO TEQUILA AND LEAVING THEM FOR A PERIOD OF TIME. THE METHOD BELOW WILL MAKE A SMOOTH FRUITY DRINK.

SERVES SIX

INGREDIENTS
- 1 large pineapple
- 2 ounces soft dark brown sugar
- 1 litre blanco tequila
- 1 vanilla bean

1 Rinse a large (about 3½ pints) wide-necked bottle or demijohn and sterilize by placing it in an oven and then turning on the oven and setting it at 225°F. After 20 minutes remove the bottle from the oven with oven gloves and allow to cool.

2 Cut the top off the pineapple and then cut away the skin, being careful to get rid of all the scales. Cut in half, remove the hard center core, and discard it. Chop the rest of the pineapple into chunks, ensuring they are small enough to fit in the bottle neck.

3 When the bottle is completely cold, put the pineapple into the bottle. Mix the sugar and tequila together in a jug until the sugar dissolves and then pour into the bottle. Split the vanilla bean and add it to the rest of the ingredients.

4 Gently agitate the bottle a few times each day to stir the contents. Allow the tequila to stand for at least 1 week before drinking. When all the tequila has been drunk, the pineapple can be used in desserts such as ice cream, or warmed with butter and cinnamon and served with cream.

VARIATION
If you like, add a piece of fresh pineapple and some ice to each glass before serving.

MARGARITA

THE MOST RENOWNED TEQUILA COCKTAIL, THIS CAN BE SERVED OVER ICE CUBES OR "FROZEN"—
MIXED WITH CRUSHED ICE IN A COCKTAIL SHAKER TO CREATE A LIQUID SORBET EFFECT,
THEN POURED INTO THE GLASS. THE SHARP BITTERNESS OF THE TEQUILA IS OFFSET BY THE
TARTNESS OF THE LIME AND THE SALT ON THE LIP OF THE GLASS.

SERVES ONE

INGREDIENTS
3 tablespoons tequila
1½ tablespoons triple sec
1½ tablespoons freshly squeezed
lime juice
crushed ice or ice cubes
lime wedge and salt, for
frosting glass

COOK'S TIP
White tequila is the traditional spirit to
use, but today many people prefer to
make margaritas with reposada tequila,
which gives a more rounded flavor.

1 Frost a cocktail glass by rubbing the
outer rim with the wedge of lime. Dip
the glass in a saucer of salt so that it is
evenly coated. It is important that there
is no salt inside the glass, so take care
that lime juice is only applied to the
outer rim.

2 Combine the tequila, triple sec, and
lime juice in a cocktail shaker, add
crushed ice, if using, and shake to mix.
Carefully pour into the frosted glasses.
If crushed ice is not used, place ice
cubes in the glass and then pour the
mixture over.

MANGO AND PEACH MARGARITA

ADDING PUREED FRUIT TO THE CLASSIC TEQUILA MIXTURE ALTERS THE CONSISTENCY AND MAKES FOR A GLORIOUS DRINK THAT RESEMBLES A MILKSHAKE BUT PACKS CONSIDERABLY MORE PUNCH.

SERVES FOUR

INGREDIENTS

    2 mangoes, peeled and sliced
    3 peaches, peeled and sliced
    ½ cup tequila
    4 tablespoons triple sec
    4 tablespoons freshly squeezed
      lime juice
    10 ice cubes, crushed, if necessary
      (see Cook's Tip)
    mango slices, skin on, to decorate

COOK'S TIP

Check that your processor or blender can be used for crushing ice. If you are not sure, break ice cubes into smaller pieces by putting them in a strong plastic bag and pounding them with a meat hammer.

1 Place the mango and peach slices in a food processor or blender. Process or blend until all the fruit is finely chopped, scrape down the sides of the goblet, then blend again until the puree is perfectly smooth.

2 Add the tequila, triple sec, and lime juice, process or blend for a few seconds, then add the ice. Process or blend again until the drink has the consistency of a milkshake.

3 Pour into cocktail glasses, decorate with the mango slices, and serve.

LICUADO ᴰᴱ MELON

AMONG THE MOST REFRESHING DRINKS MEXICANS MAKE ARE FRUIT EXTRACTS MIXED WITH HONEY AND CHILLED WATER. PILE SOME ICE INTO A GLASS AND POUR OVER THE SUCCULENT LIQUID.

SERVES FOUR

INGREDIENTS
    1 watermelon
    4 cups chilled water
    juice of 2 limes
    honey

3 Tip the mixture into a large strainer set over a bowl. Using the back of a wooden spoon, press gently on the fruit to extract all the liquid.

4 Squeeze the limes by cutting each lime in half and pressing the flesh with a fork. Stir in the lime juice and sweeten to taste with honey.

1 Cut the watermelon flesh into chunks, cutting away the skin and discarding the shiny black seeds.

2 Place the chunks in a large bowl, pour over the chilled water, and leave to stand for 10 minutes.

COOK'S TIP
It can be hard to extract the juice from a lime; often they have little juice, and it is firmly compacted within their flesh. Pressing machines are excellent for juicing citrus fruits, although the small hand squeezers can make for hard work. Using a fork to crush the insides can be very useful if you are having trouble getting the last drips out—and you may get some juicy bits of flesh too.

MOJITO

A REFRESHING CUBAN COCKTAIL, THIS INCORPORATES RUM, MINT, AND LIME. TAKE YOUR TIME DRINKING IT, AND THE FLAVOR OF THE MINT WILL GRADUALLY INTENSIFY.

MAKES ONE

INGREDIENTS
  juice of 1 lime
  1 tablespoon superfine sugar
  4 fresh mint sprigs
  5 tablespoons white rum
  crushed ice
  6 tablespoons club soda

COOK'S TIPS
• If you don't have a refrigerator that delivers crushed ice or a blender with sufficiently tough blades, put the ice in a freezer bag, wrap it in a dish towel, and beat it with a rolling pin. Alternatively, process the ice in a blender or food processor briefly.
• Shaking the cocktail bruises the mint leaves, releasing their flavour. If you do not have a cocktail shaker, bruise the mint leaves by hand before adding them.

1 Mix the lime juice and sugar in a cocktail shaker and shake until the sugar has dissolved. If necessary, add a few drops of the soda water to provide a little more moisture.

VARIATION
If you like, use cane sugar syrup instead of the superfine sugar to provide a more authentic West Indian experience.

2 Add three of the mint sprigs, the rum, and some crushed ice, and shake vigorously. Pour into a tall glass, top with the soda water, and decorate with the remaining mint. You can make a larger quantity and keep it chilled in an airtight bottle, although you should drink it quickly, as it will only keep for a few hours.

CUBA LIBRE

THIS SIMPLE COCKTAIL HAS ALWAYS BEEN VERY POPULAR, THE HEADY CONCOCTION OF WHITE OR GOLDEN RUM AND COLA REFRESHED WITH ICE AND THE STING OF LIME MAKES IT A GREAT FAVORITE THROUGHOUT THE CARIBBEAN. HOWEVER, IN ITS CUBAN HOMELAND THE NAME HAS BECOME POLITICALLY INCORRECT SINCE CASTRO TOOK POWER IN 1959. CUBAN EXILES HAVE SARCASTICALLY RENAMED IT MENTIRITA, MEANING "LITTLE LIE."

MAKES ONE

INGREDIENTS
  crushed ice
  3 tablespoons white rum
  5 tablespoons cola
  1 lime wedge, optional

COOK'S TIPS
Rum is made by fermenting and distilling the thick brown liquid (molasses) that is left behind after extracting sugar from sugar cane.

1 Spoon the crushed ice into a tall glass and top with the white rum.

2 Pour in the cola and decorate with a wedge of lime. Serve immediately.

STRAWBERRY AND BANANA PREPARADO

SIMILAR TO A SMOOTHIE, THIS IS A THICK, CREAMY FRUIT DRINK. LEAVE OUT THE ALCOHOL FOR CHILDREN OR IF YOU WOULD PREFER A LONG, REFRESHING DAYTIME DRINK.

SERVES FOUR

INGREDIENTS
 2 cups strawberries, plus extra, to
  decorate
 2 bananas
 4-ounce block of creamed coconut
 ½ cup water
 ¾ cup white rum
 4 tablespoons grenadine
 10 ice cubes

1 Hull the strawberries and chop them in halves or quarters if they are large fruits. Peel the bananas and chop them into rough chunks.

2 Put the fruit in a food processor or blender, crumble in the coconut, and add the water. Process until smooth, scraping down the sides of the goblet as necessary.

3 Add the rum, grenadine, and ice cubes, crushing the ice first unless you have a heavy-duty processor. Blend until smooth and thick. Serve at once, decorated with the extra strawberries.

BLOODY MARIA

THIS SIMPLE COCKTAIL CONSISTS OF TEQUILA AND TOMATO JUICE MIXED TOGETHER AND SERVED IN THE SAME GLASS. THE TABASCO SAUCE PROVIDES A SPICY KICK.

SERVES TWO

INGREDIENTS
    1 cup tomato juice, chilled
    1 teaspoon Worcestershire sauce
    4 tablespoons tequila
    few drops of Tabasco sauce
    juice of ½ lemon
    pinch of celery salt
    salt and ground black pepper
    2 celery sticks, cut into sticks,
        to serve

1 Pour the chilled tomato juice into a large pitcher and stir in the tequila. Add the Worcestershire sauce and stir the mixture well.

2 Add a few drops of Tabasco sauce and the lemon juice. Taste and season with celery salt, salt, and pepper. Serve over ice cubes, with celery sticks.

SANGRITA

SIPPING SANGRITA AND TEQUILA ALTERNATELY IS A TASTE SENSATION NOT TO BE MISSED, THE WARM FLAVORS OF THE FIRST BALANCING THE HARSHNESS OF THE SECOND. THE DRINKS ARE OFTEN SERVED WITH ANTOJITOS (NIBBLES) AS AN APPETIZER.

SERVES EIGHT

INGREDIENTS
   1 pound ripe tomatoes
   1 small onion, finely chopped
   2 small fresh green fresno chiles,
     seeded and chopped
   ½ cup juice from freshly squeezed
     oranges
   juice of 3 limes
   ½ teaspoon superfine sugar
   pinch of salt
   1 small shot glass of golden or aged
     tequila per person

1 Cut a cross in the base of each tomato. Place the tomatoes in a heatproof bowl and pour over boiling water to cover. Leave for 3 minutes.

2 Lift the tomatoes out on a slotted spoon and plunge them into a second bowl of cold water. The skins will have begun to peel back from the crosses. Remove the skins, then cut the tomatoes in half and scoop out the seeds with a teaspoon.

3 Chop the tomato flesh and put in a food processor. Add the onion, chiles, orange juice, lime juice, sugar, and salt.

4 Process until all the mixture is very smooth, then pour into a pitcher and chill for at least 1 hour before serving. Offer each drinker a separate shot glass of tequila as well. The drinks are sipped alternately.

COOK'S TIP
This drink can be made with a 14-ounce can of chopped tomatoes and tastes almost as good as when made with fresh tomatoes.

SANGRIA

TESTAMENT TO THE SPANISH INFLUENCE ON MEXICAN COOKING, THIS POPULAR THIRST-QUENCHER IS OFTEN SERVED IN LARGE JUGS, WITH ICE AND CITRUS FRUIT SLICES FLOATING ON TOP.

SERVES SIX

INGREDIENTS
   3 cups dry red wine
   juice of 2 limes
   ½ cup freshly squeezed orange juice
   ½ cup brandy
   ¼ cup superfine sugar
   1 lime, sliced, to decorate

VARIATION
In some parts of Mexico a less potent but equally refreshing version of sangria is served. Fill tall glasses with ice. Fill each glass two-thirds full with fresh lime juice diluted with water and sweetened with sugar. Top up with red wine. Tequila is sometimes added to the lime mixture.

1 Combine the wine, lime juice, orange juice, and brandy in a large pitcher.

COOK'S TIP
If no superfine sugar is available, use sugar syrup. Heat ¼ cup granulated sugar in ¼ cup water. Boil for 3 minutes, chill, and store in a tightly sealed jar.

2 Stir in the sugar until it has dissolved completely.

3 Serve in tall glasses with ice. Decorate each glass with a slice of lime.

RAW SUGAR RUM PUNCH

THE INSPIRATION FOR THIS PUNCH CAME FROM THE RUM DISTILLERY AT PLANTATION DIAMOND ESTATE IN GUYANA, WHERE SOME OF THE FINEST RUM IN THE WORLD IS MADE, AND THE TANTALIZING AROMAS OF SUGAR CANE AND RUM PERVADE THE AIR.

SERVES FOUR

INGREDIENTS
⅔ cup orange juice
⅔ cup pineapple juice
⅔ cup mango juice
½ cup water
1 cup dark rum
a shake of angostura bitters
freshly grated nutmeg
2 tablespoons raw sugar
1 small banana
1 large orange

1 Pour the orange, pineapple, and mango juices into a large punch bowl. Stir in the water.

2 Add the rum, angostura bitters, nutmeg, and sugar. Stir gently for a few minutes until the sugar has dissolved.

3 Slice the banana thinly and stir the slices gently into the punch.

4 Slice the orange and add to the punch. Chill and serve in tumblers with ice.

VARIATIONS
You can use white rum instead of dark, if you prefer. To make a stronger punch, simply add more rum.

CARIBBEAN CREAM STOUT PUNCH

THIS FAIRLY UNUSUAL PUNCH, MADE USING STOUT, CONDENSED MILK, AND SHERRY, IS A WELL-KNOWN "PICK-ME-UP" THAT IS POPULAR ALL OVER THE CARIBBEAN. WITH A SWEET, HEADY AROMA OF VANILLA, IT SOOTHES AND REVIVES TIRED MINDS AND BODIES.

SERVES TWO

INGREDIENTS
    2 cups stout
    1¼ cups unsweetened condensed
      milk
    5 tablespoons condensed milk
    5 tablespoons sherry
    2 or 3 drops vanilla
      extract
    freshly grated nutmeg

1 Mix together the stout, evaporated and condensed milks, sherry, and vanilla extract in a blender or food processor, or whisk together in a large mixing bowl, until creamy.

2 Add a little grated nutmeg to the stout mixture and blend or whisk thoroughly again for a few minutes.

3 Chill for at least 45 minutes, or until really cold, before ladling into small glasses to serve.

CAFE ^{CON} LECHE

*MANY MEXICANS START THE DAY WITH THIS SPICED MILKY COFFEE, AND THOSE WHO HAVE
ENJOYED A HEARTY MIDDAY MEAL WILL OFTEN OPT FOR A CUP OF IT WITH A SWEET PASTRY AS THE
AFTERNOON MERIENDA. IT IS ALSO POPULAR THROUGHOUT THE CARIBBEAN AND CENTRAL AND
SOUTH AMERICA, WHERE IT IS SOMETIMES FLAVORED WITH COCOA OR CHOCOLATE EITHER WITH OR
INSTEAD OF THE TRADITIONAL CINNAMON STICKS.*

SERVES FOUR

INGREDIENTS
⅔ cup ground coffee
2 cups boiling water
2 cups milk
4 cinnamon sticks, each about
    4 inches long
sugar, to taste

1 Put the coffee in a press pot or
pitcher, pour on the boiling water, and
leave for a few minutes until the coffee
grounds settle at the bottom.

2 Push down the plunger of the press pot
or strain the pitcher of coffee to separate
the liquid from the grounds. Pour the
strained coffee into a clean pitcher.

3 Pour the milk into a heavy-based pan,
add the cinnamon sticks, and bring to
the boil, stirring occasionally.

4 Using a slotted spoon, lift out the
cinnamon sticks, and use a smaller
spoon to press down on them to release
any liquid they have absorbed. Set the
cinnamon sticks aside for serving.

5 Add the coffee to the hot milk, then
pour into cups. Add a cinnamon stick to
each cup. Drinkers should add sugar
to taste.

HORCHATA

*THIS DELICIOUS, AROMATIC RICE DRINK TASTES WONDERFULLY CREAMY, YET DOES NOT CONTAIN A
DROP OF MILK. MEXICANS SWEAR BY IT AS A MEANS OF SETTLING STOMACH UPSETS OR CURING
HANGOVERS, AND IT IS OFTEN SERVED AT BREAKFAST.*

SERVES FOUR

INGREDIENTS
2¼ cups long-grain rice
3 cups water
1¼ cups blanched whole almonds
2 teaspoons ground cinnamon
finely grated rind of 1 lime, plus
    strips of rind, to decorate
¼ cup sugar

1 Tip the rice into a strainer and rinse
thoroughly under cold running water.
Drain, tip into a large bowl, and pour
over the water. Cover and soak for at
least 2 hours, preferably overnight.

2 Drain the rice, reserving 2½ cups of
the soaking liquid. Spoon the rice into a
food processor or blender, and grind as
finely as possible.

3 Add the almonds to the processor or
blender and continue to grind in the
same way until finely ground.

4 Add the cinnamon, grated lime rind,
and sugar to the ground rice and
ground almonds. Add the reserved
soaking water from the rice and mix
until all the sugar has dissolved.

5 Serve in tall glasses with ice cubes.
Decorate with strips of lime rind.

CAFE ᴅᴇ OLLA

THIS IS ONE OF THE MOST POPULAR DRINKS IN MEXICO. THE NAME MEANS "OUT OF THE POT," WHICH REFERS TO THE CONTAINER IN WHICH THE COFFEE IS MADE. TRADITIONALLY, THE SWEETENER IS PILONCILLO, THE LOCAL UNREFINED BROWN SUGAR, BUT ANY SOFT DARK BROWN SUGAR CAN BE USED. THIS COFFEE IS ALWAYS DRUNK BLACK.

SERVES FOUR

INGREDIENTS
    4 cups water
    ½ cup *piloncillo* or soft dark
      brown sugar
    4 cinnamon sticks, each about
      6 inches long
    ⅔ cup freshly ground coffee, from
      dark-roast coffee beans

COOK'S TIP
If you do not have a fine strainer,
improvise with a regular one lined with
coffee filter paper. For a special occasion
serve the coffee with chocolate-dipped
cinnamon sticks which can be used to
stir with.

1 Place the water, sugar, and cinnamon sticks in a pan. Heat gently, stirring occasionally to make sure that the sugar dissolves, then bring to the boil. Boil rapidly for about 20 minutes until the syrup has reduced by a quarter.

2 Add the ground coffee to the syrup and stir well, then bring the liquid back to the boil. Remove from the heat, cover the pan, and leave to stand for around 5 minutes.

3 Strain the coffee through a fine strainer, pour into cups, and serve immediately.

ATOLE

THIS DRINK, WHICH IS MADE FROM WHITE CORN MASA, IS TRADITIONALLY FLAVORED WITH PILONCILLO (MEXICAN UNREFINED BROWN SUGAR) AND GROUND CINNAMON. IT HAS THE CONSISTENCY OF A THICK MILKSHAKE. FRESH FRUIT PUREES ARE OFTEN ADDED BEFORE SERVING, AND SOME RECIPES INTRODUCE GROUND ALMONDS OR MILK.

SERVES SIX

INGREDIENTS
    1¾ cups white *masa harina*
    5 cups water
    1 vanilla bean
    ¼ cup *piloncillo* or soft dark brown
      sugar
    ½ teaspoon ground cinnamon
    1 cup fresh strawberries, chopped
      pineapple, or orange segments
      (optional)

1 Put the *masa harina* in a heavy-based pan, without appying any heat. Gradually stir in the water. Beat it to make a smooth paste.

2 Place the pan over a moderate heat add the vanilla bean, and bring the mixture to the boil, stirring constantly until it thickens. Beat in the sugar and ground cinnamon and continue to beat until the sugar has dissolved. Remove from the heat.

3 If adding the fruit, puree it in a food processor or blender until smooth, then press through a strainer.

4 Stir the puree into the corn mixture and return to the heat until warmed through. Remove the vanilla bean. Serve.

CHAMPURRADA

THIS POPULAR VERSION OF ATOLE *IS MADE WITH* MEXICAN *CHOCOLATE. A SPECIAL WOODEN WHISK CALLED A* MOLINOLLO *IS TRADITIONALLY USED WHEN MAKING THIS FROTHY DRINK.*

SERVES SIX

INGREDIENTS
    4 ounces Mexican chocolate, about
    2 disks
    5 cups water or milk, or a mixture
    7 ounces white *masa harina*
    2 tablespoons soft dark brown sugar

COOK'S TIP
If you can't locate Mexican chocolate, improvise by mixing 4 ounces bittersweet chocolate (minimum 70 percent cocoa solids) with ¼ cup ground almonds, ¼ cup superfine sugar, and 2 teaspoons ground cinnamon in a food processor. Process until a fine powder is obtained.

1 Put the chocolate in a mortar and grind with a pestle until it becomes a fine powder. Alternatively, grind the chocolate in a food processor.

2 Put the liquid in a heavy-based pan and gradually stir in all the *masa harina* until a smooth paste is formed. Use a traditional wooden *molinollo*, if you have one, or a wire whisk for a frothier drink.

3 Place the pan over a moderate heat and bring the mixture to the boil, stirring all the time until the frothy drink thickens.

4 Stir in the ground chocolate, then add the sugar. Serve immediately.

MEXICAN HOT CHOCOLATE

MEXICAN CHOCOLATE IS FLAVORED WITH ALMONDS, CINNAMON, AND VANILLA, AND IS SWEETENED WITH SUGAR. ALL THE INGREDIENTS ARE CRUSHED TOGETHER IN A SPECIAL MORTAR, AND HEATED OVER COALS. THE POWDERED MIXTURE IS THEN SHAPED INTO DISKS. MAKING THE CHOCOLATE IS QUITE A TRICKY BUSINESS, BUT FORTUNATELY THE DISKS CAN BE BOUGHT IN SPECIALIST STORES.

SERVES FOUR

INGREDIENTS
    4 cups milk
    2–4 ounces Mexican chocolate
    (1–2 disks)
    1 vanilla bean

VARIATION
If you prefer, you can use bittersweet chocolate instead of Mexican chocolate. You will need slightly less, as the flavor will be more intense.

1 Pour the milk into a pan and add the chocolate. Precisely how much to use will depend on personal taste. Start with one disk and use more next time if necessary.

2 Split the vanilla bean lengthwise using a sharp knife, and add it to the milk.

3 Heat the chocolate milk, gently stirring until all the chocolate has dissolved, then whisking with a wire whisk or a *molinollo* until the mixture boils. Remove the vanilla bean and divide the drink among four mugs or heatproof glasses. Serve at once.

NUTRITIONAL INFORMATION

The nutritional analysis below is per portion, unless otherwise stated.

p84 Cassava Fries Energy 453Kcal/1,900kJ; Protein 3g; Carbohydrate 56.4g, of which sugars 1.4g; Fat 25.6g, of which saturates 3.8g; Cholesterol 0mg; Calcium 30mg; Fiber 2.6g; Sodium 4mg.

p85 Cheese Tamales Energy 197Kcal/825kJ; Protein 3.3g; Carbohydrate 21.2g, of which sugars 0.3g; Fat 11.6g, of which saturates 5.8g; Cholesterol 21mg; Calcium 80mg; Fiber 0g; Sodium 560mg.

p86 Tortilla Chips Energy 172Kcal/723kJ; Protein 2.9g; Carbohydrate 22.6g, of which sugars 0.5g; Fat 8.5g, of which saturates 1.5g; Cholesterol 0mg; Calcium 56mg; Fiber 2.3g; Sodium 323mg.

p86 Pepitas Energy 193Kcal/800kJ; Protein 6.5g; Carbohydrate 7.1g, of which sugars 1.6g; Fat 15.5g, of which saturates 1.5g; Cholesterol 0mg; Calcium 36mg; Fiber 2g; Sodium 1mg.

p88 Tamales de Picadillo Energy 188Kcal/785kJ; Protein 7.8g; Carbohydrate 14.7g, of which sugars 3.0g; Fat 11.3g, of which saturates 4.4g; Cholesterol 26mg; Calcium 13mg; Fiber 0.4g; Sodium 175mg.

p89 Mixed Tostadas Energy 253Kcal/1,068kJ; Protein 14.7g; Carbohydrate 32.8g, of which sugars 3.4g; Fat 7.9g, of which saturates 2.8g; Cholesterol 25mg; Calcium 192mg; Fiber 3.0g; Sodium 424mg.

p90 Chiles Rellenos Energy 498Kcal/2,072kJ; Protein 14.9g; Carbohydrate 27.8g, of which sugars 3.2g; Fat 36.5g, of which saturates 18.6g; Cholesterol 127mg; Calcium 322mg; Fiber 1.8g; Sodium 374mg.

p92 Tortas Energy 638Kcal/2,683kJ; Protein 48.6g; Carbohydrate 53.4g, of which sugars 5.3g; Fat 25.9g, of which saturates 14.6g; Cholesterol 138mg; Calcium 566mg; Fiber 5.7g; Sodium 1,164mg.

p93 Taquitos with Beef Energy 120Kcal/500kJ; Protein 10.6g; Carbohydrate 9.4g, of which sugars 0.2g; Fat 4.3g, of which saturates 1.6g; Cholesterol 24mg; Calcium 3mg; Fiber 0.3g; Sodium 27mg.

p94 Plantain and Sweet Potato Chips Energy 396Kcal/1,658kJ; Protein 1.7g; Carbohydrate 51.5g, of which sugars 12.6g; Fat 21.7g, of which saturates 2.5g; Cholesterol 0mg; Calcium 11mg; Fiber 2.8g; Sodium 11mg.

p94 Coconut Jumbo Shrimp Energy 186Kcal/774kJ; Protein 11.2g; Carbohydrate 3.1g, of which sugars 2.6g; Fat 14.5g, of which saturates 8.4g; Cholesterol 182mg; Calcium 111mg; Fiber 1.7g; Sodium 443mg.

p96 Butterflied Shrimp in Chili Chocolate Energy 133Kcal/554kJ; Protein 9.5g; Carbohydrate 7.4g, of which sugars 3.6g; Fat 6.9g, of which saturates 1.5g; Cholesterol 98mg; Calcium 49mg; Fiber 0.3g; Sodium 97mg.

p97 Desert Nachos (per batch) Energy 1,534Kcal/6,413kJ; Protein 47g; Carbohydrate 135.6g, of which sugars 3.1g; Fat 90.6g, of which saturates 33.8g; Cholesterol 109mg; Calcium 1,196mg; Fiber 14.2g; Sodium 3,314mg.

p98 Empanadas with Ropas Viejas Energy 208Kcal/867kJ; Protein 3.4g; Carbohydrate 25.6g, of which sugars 2g; Fat 10.2g, of which saturates 1.1g; Cholesterol 0mg; Calcium 16mg; Fiber 1.3g; Sodium 4mg.

p100 Cheesy Eggs Energy 167Kcal/ 693kJ; Protein 9.9g; Carbohydrate 0.1g, of which sugars 0.1g; Fat 14.2g, of which saturates 4.7g; Cholesterol 240mg; Calcium 108mg; Fiber 0g; Sodium 179mg.

p101 Red Enchiladas Energy 283Kcal/1,178kJ; Protein 9.5g; Carbohydrate 18.6g, of which sugars 5.3g; Fat 19.5g, of which saturates 10.3g; Cholesterol 47mg; Calcium 181mg; Fiber 1.5g; Sodium 432mg.

p102 Tostadas with Tomato Salsa Energy 360Kcal/1,511kJ; Protein 11.8g; Carbohydrate 46.6g, of which sugars 7.3g; Fat 15.2g, of which saturates 4.5g; Cholesterol 14mg; Calcium 201mg; Fiber 6.9g; Sodium 481mg.

p103 Enchiladas with Hot Tomato and Green Chili Sauce Energy 774Kcal/3,243kJ; Protein 44.1g; Carbohydrate 68.1g, of which sugars 8.8g; Fat 37g, of which saturates 20.3g; Cholesterol 154mg; Calcium 526mg; Fiber 3.8g; Sodium 716mg.

p104 Chicken Flautas Energy 156Kcal/656kJ; Protein 10.3g; Carbohydrate 16.6g, of which sugars 1.7g; Fat 5.8g, of which saturates 1.6g; Cholesterol 26mg; Calcium 60mg; Fiber 1g; Sodium 198mg.

p106 Black-eyed Pea and Shrimp Fritters Energy 136Kcal/570kJ; Protein 7.7g; Carbohydrate 14.7g, of which sugars 1.6g; Fat 5.5g, of which saturates 0.7g; Cholesterol 10mg; Calcium 33mg; Fiber 2.3g; Sodium 83mg

p107 Beef Empanadas Energy 138Kcal/579kJ; Protein 6.6g; Carbohydrate 12.7g, of which sugars 0.8g; Fat 7.1g, of which saturates 3.1g; Cholesterol 23mg; Calcium 20mg; Fiber 0.7g; Sodium 102mg.

p108 Sopes with Picadillo Energy 299Kcal/1,244kJ; Protein 5.2g; Carbohydrate 35.6g, of which sugars 5g; Fat 13.9g, of which saturates 3.8g; Cholesterol 8mg; Calcium 16mg; Fiber 1.8g; Sodium 5mg.

p109 Panuchos Energy 249Kcal/1,038kJ; Protein 18.6g; Carbohydrate 19.1g, of which sugars 0.8g; Fat 10.7g, of which saturates 1.6g; Cholesterol 104mg; Calcium 15mg; Fiber 0.8g; Sodium 61mg.

p110 Quesadillas Energy 260Kcal/1,091kJ; Protein 12.9g; Carbohydrate 29.9g, of which sugars 0.6g; Fat 10.7g, of which saturates 6.9g; Cholesterol 29mg; Calcium 236mg; Fiber 1.2g; Sodium 338mg.

p111 Mexican Rice Energy 162Kcal/676kJ; Protein 2.8g; Carbohydrate 28.4g, of which sugars 1.6g; Fat 4g, of which saturates 0.5g; Cholesterol 0mg; Calcium 11mg; Fiber 0.5g; Sodium 167mg.

p112 Pan-fried Squid Energy 250Kcal/1,043kJ; Protein 32.8g;

Carbohydrate 2.6g, of which sugars 0.1g; Fat 9.2g, of which saturates 1.5g; Cholesterol 500mg; Calcium 33mg; Fiber 0g; Sodium 475mg.

p112 Fried Whitebait with Cayenne Pepper Energy 328Kcal/1,359kJ; Protein 12.2g; Carbohydrate 3.3g, of which sugars 0.1g; Fat 29.7g, of which saturates 5.9g; Cholesterol 0mg; Calcium 538mg; Fiber 0.1g; Sodium 144mg.

p114 Eggs with Chorizo Energy 402Kcal/1674kJ; Protein 34.3g; Carbohydrate 2.9g, of which sugars 2.5g; Fat 27g, of which saturates 9.5g; Cholesterol 375mg; Calcium 76mg; Fiber 0.5g; Sodium 198mg.

p114 Chiles in Cheese Sauce Energy 774Kcal/3,202kJ; Protein 33.6g; Carbohydrate 3.1g, of which sugars 2.7g; Fat 67g, of which saturates 42g; Cholesterol 181mg; Calcium 960mg; Fiber 0.5g; Sodium 918mg.

p116 Molettes Energy 450Kcal/1,886kJ; Protein 19.2g; Carbohydrate 39.9g, of which sugars 4.2g; Fat 24.1g, of which saturates 15g; Cholesterol 63mg; Calcium 392mg; Fiber 4.5g; Sodium 889mg.

p116 Eggs Motulenos Energy 524Kcal/2,208kJ; Protein 34.7g; Carbohydrate 60.3g, of which sugars 4.6g; Fat 17.8g, of which saturates 5.4g; Cholesterol 225mg; Calcium 239mg; Fiber 12.5g; Sodium 978mg.

p118 Eggs Rancheros Energy 294Kcal/1,227kJ; Protein 16g; Carbohydrate 17.2g, of which sugars 2.6g; Fat 18.7g, of which saturates 7.7g; Cholesterol 401mg; Calcium 125mg; Fiber 1.1g; Sodium 225mg.

p120 Mexican Tortilla Parcels Energy 576Kcal/2,422kJ; Protein 17.3g; Carbohydrate 79.5g, of which sugars 12g; Fat 22.5g, of which saturates 7.8g; Cholesterol 28mg; Calcium 340mg; Fiber 5g; Sodium 639mg.

p121 Caribbean Crab Cakes Energy 70Kcal/290kJ; Protein 3.5g; Carbohydrate 2.9g, of which sugars 0.7g; Fat 5g, of which saturates 1.1g; Cholesterol 26mg; Calcium 24mg; Fiber 0.3g; Sodium 95mg.

p122 Spiced Plantain Chips Energy 232Kcal/962kJ; Protein 0.6g; Carbohydrate 14.7g, of which sugars 2.9g; Fat 19.4g, of which saturates 2.3g; Cholesterol 0mg; Calcium 5mg; Fiber 0.7g; Sodium 2mg.

p123 Popcorn with Lime and Chili (per batch) Energy 1,334Kcal/ 5,553kJ; Protein 13.9g; Carbohydrate 109.6g, of which sugars 2.5g; Fat 96.3g, of which saturates 9.7g; Cholesterol 0mg; Calcium 23mg; Fiber 0g; Sodium 9mg.

p126 Vermicelli Soup Energy 128Kcal/537kJ; Protein 4.4g; Carbohydrate 10.5g, of which sugars 5.7g; Fat 8.0g, of which saturates 2.1g; Cholesterol 6mg; Calcium 86mg; Fiber 1.9g; Sodium 101mg.

p126 Tomato Soup Energy 78Kcal/327kJ; Protein 2.1g; Carbohydrate 10.0g, of which sugars 9.0g; Fat 3.6g, of which saturates 0.6g; Cholesterol 0mg; Calcium 26mg; Fiber 2.8g; Sodium 103mg.

p128 Creamy Heart of Palm Soup Energy 441Kcal/1,824kJ; Protein 4.9g; Carbohydrate 13.1g, of which sugars 7.1g; Fat 41.4g, of which saturates 24.5g; Cholesterol 99mg; Calcium 91mg; Fiber 4.5g; Sodium 219mg.

p129 Peanut and Potato Soup with Coriander Energy 259Kcal/1,076kJ; Protein 8.1g; Carbohydrate 14.5g, of which sugars 6.1g; Fat 19.2g, of which saturates 3.7g; Cholesterol 0mg; Calcium 30mg; Fiber 3.0g; Sodium 141mg.

p130 Tlalpeño-Style Soup Energy 225Kcal/946kJ; Protein 22.7g; Carbohydrate 11.3g, of which sugars 0.6g; Fat 10g, of which saturates 3.8g; Cholesterol 53mg; Calcium 131mg; Fiber 3.4g; Sodium 274mg.

p130 Corn Soup Energy 205Kcal/861kJ; Protein 4g; Carbohydrate 27.2g, of which sugars 12.7g; Fat 9.7g, of which saturates 3.7g; Cholesterol 14mg; Calcium 33mg; Fiber 2.2g; Sodium 235mg.

p132 Chilled Coconut Soup Energy 485Kcal/2,009kJ; Protein 8.5g; Carbohydrate 14.4g, of which saturates 14.4g; Fat 44.2g, of which saturates 33.1g; Cholesterol 56mg; Calcium 245mg; Fiber 5.1g; Sodium 163mg.

p133 Avocado Soup Energy 382Kcal/1,573kJ; Protein 2.9g; Carbohydrate 3g, of which sugars 2.1g; Fat 39.8g, of which saturates 22.4g; Cholesterol 85mg; Calcium 69mg; Fiber 2.2g; Sodium 514mg.

p134 Fish and Sweet Potato Soup Energy 125Kcal/528kJ; Protein 11.6g;

Carbohydrate 16.7g, of which sugars 5.0g; Fat 1.7g, of which saturates 0.3g; Cholesterol 20mg; Calcium 44mg; Fiber 8.4g; Sodium 223mg.

p134 Caribbean Vegetable Soup Energy 195Kcal/820kJ; Protein 3.8g; Carbohydrate 33.7g, of which sugars 16.0g; Fat 5.9g, of which saturates 3.4g; Cholesterol 13mg; Calcium 52mg; Fiber 3.4g; Sodium 62mg

p136 Mexican Bean Chili with Nachos Energy 787Kcal/3,291kJ; Protein 50.4g; Carbohydrate 52.9g, of which sugars 9.5g; Fat 41.7g, of which saturates 17.9g; Cholesterol 105mg; Calcium 606mg; Fiber 14.3g; Sodium 1,476mg.

p137 Roasted Pumpkin Soup with Pumpkin Crisps Energy 212Kcal/877kJ; Protein 2.2g; Carbohydrate 5.5g, of which sugars 4.3g; Fat 20.3g, of which saturates 3.1g; Cholesterol 0mg; Calcium 89mg; Fiber 2.7g; Sodium 1mg.

p138 South American Red Bean Soup Energy 254Kcal/1,064kJ; Protein 10.8g; Carbohydrate 29.2g, of which sugars 9.1g; Fat 11.2g, of which saturates 2.1g; Cholesterol 0mg; Calcium 111mg; Fiber 10.6g; Sodium 535mg.

p139 Corn and Red Chile Chowder Energy 632Kcal/2,632kJ; Protein 9.6g; Carbohydrate 49.1g, of which sugars 21.3g; Fat 45.5g, of which saturates 26.7g; Cholesterol 109mg; Calcium 175mg; Fiber 3.5g; Sodium 332mg.

p140 Tortilla Soup Energy 172Kcal/723kJ; Protein 2.9g; Carbohydrate 22.6g, of which sugars 0.5g; Fat 8.5g, of which saturates 1.5g; Cholesterol 0mg; Calcium 56mg; Fiber 2.3g; Sodium 323mg.

p142 Jamaican Rice and Bean Soup Energy 435Kcal/1,819kJ; Protein 23.7g; Carbohydrate 47.8g, of which sugars 5.1g; Fat 16.8g, of which saturates 8.3g; Cholesterol 64mg; Calcium 101mg; Fiber 3.1g; Sodium 524mg.

p143 Avocado and Lime Soup Energy 282Kcal/1,169kJ; Protein 6.6g; Carbohydrate 10.4g, of which sugars 9.4g; Fat 23.9g, of which saturates 8.9g; Cholesterol 28mg; Calcium 171mg; Fiber 3.5g; Sodium 71mg.

p144 Crab, Coconut and Coriander Soup Energy 232Kcal/972kJ; Protein

23.8g; Carbohydrate 7.4g, of which sugars 6.5g; Fat 12.2g, of which saturates 3.7g; Cholesterol 90mg; Calcium 188mg; Fiber 1.0g; Sodium 937mg.

p145 Chili Clam Broth Energy 141Kcal/595kJ; Protein 8.8g; Carbohydrate 11.0g, of which sugars 4.1g; Fat 4.3g, of which saturates 0.7g; Cholesterol 31mg; Calcium 74mg; Fiber 1.2g; Sodium 403mg.

p146 Chunky Shrimp Chupe Energy 259Kcal/1,089kJ; Protein 23.2g; Carbohydrate 26.8g, of which sugars 7.3g; Fat 7.3g, of which saturates 1.1g; Cholesterol 233mg; Calcium 125mg; Fiber 3.7g; Sodium 1.4g.

p147 Caribbean Salt Cod Soup Energy 323Kcal/1,358kJ; Protein 10.7g; Carbohydrate 37g, of which sugars 5.6g; Fat 12.9g, of which saturates 6.7g; Cholesterol 40mg; Calcium 159mg; Fiber 4.6g; Sodium 138mg.

p148 Spiced Lamb Soup Energy 469Kcal/1,974kJ; Protein 41.1g; Carbohydrate 34.2g, of which sugars 6.9g; Fat 19.7g, of which saturates 9.1g; Cholesterol 128mg; Calcium 66mg; Fiber 4.2g; Sodium 157mg.

p149 Plantain Soup with Corn and Chili Energy 191Kcal/808kJ; Protein 2.5g; Carbohydrate 33.9g, of which sugars 9.8g; Fat 6.1g, of which saturates 3.4g; Cholesterol 13mg; Calcium 15mg; Fiber 2g; Sodium 243mg.

p150 Kale, Chorizo and Potato Soup Energy 414Kcal/1,750kJ; Protein 14g; Carbohydrate 67.9g, of which sugars 4.9g; Fat 11.5g, of which saturates 4.2g; Cholesterol 15mg; Calcium 170mg; Fiber 4.4g; Sodium 825mg.

p151 Corn and Sweet Potato Soup Energy 131Kcal/555kJ; Protein 2.7g; Carbohydrate 25.3g, of which sugars 9.7g; Fat 2.9g, of which saturates 0.5g; Cholesterol 0mg; Calcium 11mg; Fiber 1.9g; Sodium 210mg.

p152 Beef and Cassava Soup Energy 332Kcal/1,400kJ; Protein 27.3g; Carbohydrate 28.6g, of which sugars 8.7g; Fat 7.8g, of which saturates 3.1g; Cholesterol 78mg; Calcium 62mg; Fiber 2.4g; Sodium 295mg.

p153 Lamb and Lentil Soup Energy 530Kcal/2,225kJ; Protein 57.0g; Carbohydrate 35.2g, of which sugars 2.8g; Fat 18.8g, of which saturates 8.0g; Cholesterol 167mg; Calcium 57mg; Fiber 3.0g; Sodium 180mg.

p156 Baked Sea Bass with Coconut Energy 227Kcal/961kJ; Protein 38.2g; Carbohydrate 5.4g, of which sugars 4.6g; Fat 6.1g, of which saturates 0.9g; Cholesterol 95mg; Calcium 125mg; Fiber 0.5g; Sodium 326mg.

p156 Pan-Fried Sea Bream with Lime and Tomato Salsa Energy 208Kcal/870kJ; Protein 28.1g; Carbohydrate 2.5g, of which sugars 2.5g; Fat 9.5g, of which saturates 1.4g; Cholesterol 69mg; Calcium 21mg; Fiber 0.8g; Sodium 97mg.

p158 Halibut with Peppers and Coconut Milk Energy 279Kcal/1,175kJ; Protein 23.8g; Carbohydrate 19.9g, of which sugars 7.5g; Fat 12.3g, of which saturates 5.6g; Cholesterol 41mg; Calcium 48mg; Fiber 2.3g; Sodium 122mg.

p159 Caribbean Fish Steaks Energy 176Kcal/735kJ; Protein 17.1g; Carbohydrate 6.5g, of which sugars 5.8g; Fat 9.2g, of which saturates 1.2g; Cholesterol 40mg; Calcium 23mg; Fiber 1.4g; Sodium 63mg.

p160 Salmon in Mango and Ginger Sauce Energy 718Kcal/2,999kJ; Protein 56.8g; Carbohydrate 32.6g, of which sugars 32.3g; Fat 40.9g, of which saturates 11.9g; Cholesterol 164mg; Calcium 79mg; Fiber 2.5g; Sodium 359mg.

p160 Fried Snapper with Avocado Energy 294Kcal/1,223kJ; Protein 27.0g; Carbohydrate 0.9g, of which sugars 0.3g; Fat 20.2g, of which saturates 3.5g; Cholesterol 90mg; Calcium 31mg; Fiber 1.7g; Sodium 146mg.

p162 Salt Cod for Christmas Eve
Energy 301Kcal/1,249kJ; Protein
17.8g; Carbohydrate 6g, of which
sugars 5.4g; Fat 23g, of which
saturates 2.6g; Cholesterol 35mg;
Calcium 77mg; Fiber 3.4g; Sodium
493mg.

**p164 Ceviche with Red Onion,
Avocado, and Sweet Potato** Energy
309Kcal/1,292kJ; Protein 24.7g;
Carbohydrate 17.9g, of which sugars
5.4g; Fat 15.8g, of which saturates
2.6g; Cholesterol 111mg; Calcium
78mg; Fiber 3.2g; Sodium 155mg.

**p165 Seared Tuna Steaks with Red
Onion Salsa** Energy 405Kcal/1,697kJ;
Protein 49.1g; Carbohydrate 7.7g, of
which sugars 6.9g; Fat 20g, of which
saturates 4.3g; Cholesterol 56mg;
Calcium 70mg; Fiber 2.6g; Sodium
105mg.

**p166 Red Snapper with Cilantro and
Almonds** Energy 482Kcal/2,011kJ;
Protein 35.6g; Carbohydrate 16.3g, of
which sugars 1.5g; Fat 31g, of which
saturates 11.4g; Cholesterol 95mg;
Calcium 160mg; Fiber 2.6g; Sodium
237mg.

p167 Veracruz-style Red Snapper
Energy 468Kcal/1,955kJ; Protein
41.3g; Carbohydrate 11.8g, of which
sugars 10.3g; Fat 28.8g, of which
saturates 4.5g; Cholesterol 74mg;
Calcium 125mg; Fiber 3.3g; Sodium
1,070mg.

p168 Pickled Fish Energy
383Kcal/1,594kJ; Protein 41.4g;
Carbohydrate 1.2g, of which sugars
0.9g; Fat 23.6g, of which saturates
3.4g; Cholesterol 104mg; Calcium
24mg; Fiber 0.2g; Sodium 136mg.

p169 Citrus Fish with Chiles Energy
253Kcal/1,056kJ; Protein 32.5g;
Carbohydrate 3.2g, of which sugars

0.9g; Fat 12.3g, of which saturates
1.8g; Cholesterol 81mg; Calcium
23mg; Fiber 0.3g; Sodium 106mg.

p170 Mexican Spicy Fish Energy
217Kcal/911kJ; Protein 39.5g;
Carbohydrate 2.6g, of which sugars
2.4g; Fat 5.4g, of which saturates
0.8g; Cholesterol 115mg; Calcium
34mg; Fiber 0.7g; Sodium 176mg.

p171 Salt Cod in Mild Chili Sauce
Energy 178Kcal/743kJ; Protein 27.8g;
Carbohydrate 1.6g, of which sugars
1.2g; Fat 6.6g, of which saturates 1g;
Cholesterol 69mg; Calcium 20mg;
Fiber 0.3g; Sodium 91mg.

p172 Red Snapper Burritos Energy
519Kcal/2,177kJ; Protein 30g;
Carbohydrate 54.5g, of which sugars
2.9g; Fat 20.7g, of which saturates
6.7g; Cholesterol 52mg; Calcium
326mg; Fiber 3g; Sodium 430mg.

**p173 Sea Bass with Orange Chili
Salsa** Energy 178Kcal/749kJ; Protein
30.2g; Carbohydrate 5.6g, of which
sugars 5.2g; Fat 4g, of which
saturates 0.6g; Cholesterol 120mg;
Calcium 228mg; Fiber 1.1g; Sodium
108mg.

p174 Fried Sole with Lime Energy
287Kcal/1,205kJ; Protein 27.9g;
Carbohydrate 14.6g, of which sugars
0.3g; Fat 13.5g, of which saturates
1.6g; Cholesterol 90mg; Calcium
52mg; Fiber 0.6g; Sodium 143mg.

p174 Baked Salmon with Guava Sauce
Energy 389Kcal/1,621kJ; Protein
31.7g; Carbohydrate 8.7g, of which
sugars 8.2g; Fat 25.5g, of which
saturates 3.8g; Cholesterol 75mg;
Calcium 55mg; Fiber 5.8g; Sodium
76mg.

**p176 Trout in Wine Sauce with
Plantain** Energy 324Kcal/1,353kJ;
Protein 22.0g; Carbohydrate 17.6g, of
which sugars 6.1g; Fat 16.2g, of
which saturates 5.2g; Cholesterol 83g;
Calcium 28mg; Fiber 0.6g; Sodium
139mg.

p177 Eschovished Fish Energy
210Kcal/879kJ; Protein 28.0g;
Carbohydrate 5.4g, of which sugars
4.7g; Fat 8.5g, of which saturates
1.1g; Cholesterol 69mg; Calcium
28mg; Fiber 0.8g; Sodium 91mg.

**p178 Chargrilled Tuna with Fiery
Pepper Puree** Energy
411Kcal/1,718kJ; Protein 43.1g;
Carbohydrate 10.1g, of which sugars
6.4g; Fat 22.3g, of which saturates
4.2g; Cholesterol 49mg; Calcium
46mg; Fiber 1.7g; Sodium 121mg.

p179 Mackerel Escabeche Energy
576Kcal/2,393kJ; Protein 38.5g;
Carbohydrate 8.4g, of which sugars
1.5g; Fat 43.3g, of which saturates
8.2g; Cholesterol 108mg; Calcium
40mg; Fiber 0.6g; Sodium 127mg

**p180 Salmon with Tequila Cream
Sauce** Energy 490Kcal/2,032kJ;
Protein 32.7g; Carbohydrate 2.6g, of
which sugars 1.9g; Fat 36.9g, of
which saturates 9.6g; Cholesterol
96mg; Calcium 77mg; Fiber 1.1g;
Sodium 82mg.

p181 Yucatan-style Shark Steak
Energy 265Kcal/1,117kJ; Protein
46.1g; Carbohydrate 1.2g, of which
sugars 1.2g; Fat 7.7g, of which
saturates 1.2g; Cholesterol 88mg;
Calcium 38mg; Fiber 0g; Sodium
282mg.

**p182 Broiled Swordfish with Chili and
Lime Sauce** Energy 470Kcal/1,957kJ;
Protein 37.5g; Carbohydrate 3.4g, of
which sugars 3.3g; Fat 34.2g, of
which saturates 14.9g; Cholesterol
131mg; Calcium 39mg; Fiber 0.8g;
Sodium 522mg.

p182 Swordfish Tacos Energy
246Kcal/1,036kJ; Protein 21.1g;
Carbohydrate 22.8g, of which sugars
3.1g; Fat 8.4g, of which saturates
1.4g; Cholesterol 41mg; Calcium
56mg; Fiber 1.7g; Sodium 229mg.

p184 Marinated Red Mullet Energy
338Kcal/1,408kJ; Protein 29.9g;
Carbohydrate 12.3g, of which sugars
7.2g; Fat 19.1g, of which saturates
2.8g; Cholesterol 69mg; Calcium
60mg; Fiber 3.9g; Sodium 636mg.

p185 Cod Caramba Energy
307Kcal/1,286kJ; Protein 20.6g;
Carbohydrate 18.5g, of which sugars
7.1g; Fat 14.1g, of which saturates
6.9g; Cholesterol 78mg; Calcium
119mg; Fiber 2.7g; Sodium 720mg.

p186 Creole Fish Stew Energy
172Kcal/724kJ; Protein 17.8g;
Carbohydrate 5.8g, of which sugars
5.1g; Fat 8.7g, of which saturates
1.9g; Cholesterol 45.8mg; Calcium
59mg; Fiber 1.8g; Sodium 222mg.

p187 Salt Fish and Ackee Energy
292Kcal/1,225kJ; Protein 38.4g;
Carbohydrate 7.7g, of which sugars
6.2g; Fat 12.2g, of which saturates
4.3g; Cholesterol 80mg; Calcium
78mg; Fiber 2.4g; Sodium 494mg.

p188 Escabeche Energy
372Kcal/1,549kJ; Protein 41.7g;
Carbohydrate 1.2g, of which sugars

0.9g; Fat 22.2g, of which saturates
3.2g; Cholesterol 104mg; Calcium
47mg; Fiber 1.3g; Sodium 979mg.

p189 Chilean Squid Casserole Energy
260Kcal/1,089kJ; Protein 19.9g;
Carbohydrate 17.2g, of which sugars
3.5g; Fat 8.1g, of which saturates
1.3g; Cholesterol 267mg; Calcium
42mg; Fiber 1.5g; Sodium 333mg.

p190 Jamaican Fish Curry Energy
695Kcal/2,921kJ; Protein 39.5g;
Carbohydrate 69.7g, of which sugars
11.2g; Fat 30.7g, of which saturates
19.3g; Cholesterol 51mg; Calcium
112mg; Fiber 3.3g; Sodium 216mg.

p192 Pueblo Fish Bake Energy
257Kcal/1,077kJ; Protein 31.1g;
Carbohydrate 1.5g, of which sugars
1.1g; Fat 14.1g, of which saturates
2g; Cholesterol 92mg; Calcium 59mg;
Fiber 0g; Sodium 75mg.

p196 Chilean Seafood Platter Energy
205Kcal/863kJ; Protein 32.7g;
Carbohydrate 3.5g, of which
sugars 0.5g; Fat 6.8g, of which
saturates 1.1g; Cholesterol 267mg;
Calcium 146mg; Fiber 0.4g; Sodium
1.6g.

p197 Shrimp and Scallop Ceviche
Energy 137Kcal/576kJ; Protein 19.6g;
Carbohydrate 4.5g, of which sugars
2.5g; Fat 4.6g, of which saturates 1g;
Cholesterol 156mg; Calcium 49mg;
Fiber 1.2g; Sodium 166mg.

p198 Shrimp with Almond Sauce
Energy 457Kcal/1,903kJ; Protein
39.9g; Carbohydrate 6.1g, of which
sugars 5.2g; Fat 30.4g, of which
saturates 10g; Cholesterol 154mg;
Calcium 304mg; Fiber 2.8g; Sodium
2.4g.

p200 Shrimp in Garlic Butter Energy
223Kcal/924kJ; Protein 13.3g;
Carbohydrate 0.3g, of which sugars
0.3g; Fat 18.8g, of which saturates
10.5g; Cholesterol 87mg; Calcium
103mg; Fiber 0.4g; Sodium 1,034mg.

p201 Shrimp Salad Energy
419Kcal/1,734kJ; Protein 25g;
Carbohydrate 4.8g, of which sugars
4.4g; Fat 33.4g, of which saturates
7.6g; Cholesterol 380mg; Calcium
165mg; Fiber 1.5g; Sodium 1,591mg.

p202 Crab with Green Rice Energy
422Kcal/1,769kJ; Protein 28.6g;
Carbohydrate 52.2g, of which sugars
6.5g; Fat 9.8g, of which saturates
1.5g; Cholesterol 90mg; Calcium
205mg; Fiber 2.7g; Sodium 706mg.

p203 Scallops with Garlic and Cilantro
Energy 291Kcal/1,213kJ; Protein
24.2g; Carbohydrate 4.4g, of which
sugars 1g; Fat 19.8g, of which
saturates 10.6g; Cholesterol 87mg;
Calcium 45mg; Fiber 0.5g; Sodium
294mg.

**p204 Jumbo Shrimp in a Coconut and
Nut Cream** Energy 496Kcal/2,072kJ;
Protein 46.5g; Carbohydrate 18.1g, of
which sugars 6.4g; Fat 26.8g, of
which saturates 12.5g; Cholesterol
448mg; Calcium 254mg; Fiber 2.3g;
Sodium 2.8g.

p205 Stuffed Crab Energy
162Kcal/680kJ; Protein 15.9g;
Carbohydrate 8.7g, of which sugars
3.5g; Fat 7.3g, of which saturates
3.7g; Cholesterol 129mg; Calcium
162mg; Fiber 0.9g; Sodium 475mg.

p206 Crab and Corn Gumbo Energy
274Kcal/1,144kJ; Protein 9.8g;
Carbohydrate 24.2g, of which sugars
6.8g; Fat 11.4g, of which saturates
4.1g; Cholesterol 31mg; Calcium
77mg; Fiber 3.4g; Sodium 349mg.

p208 Cuban Seafood Rice Energy
326Kcal/1,379kJ; Protein 28.4g;
Carbohydrate 40.9g, of which sugars
1.1g; Fat 6.6g, of which saturates
1.2g; Cholesterol 286mg; Calcium
112mg; Fiber 0.5g; Sodium 1.2g.

p210 Pumpkin and Shrimp Energy
210Kcal/877kJ; Protein 17.5g;
Carbohydrate 8.7g, of which sugars
6.9g; Fat 11.9g, of which saturates
4.3g; Cholesterol 187mg; Calcium
147mg; Fiber 3.0g; Sodium 1g.

p211 Spicy Shrimp with Cornmeal
Energy 378Kcal/1,582kJ; Protein
42.5g; Carbohydrate 21.2g, of which
sugars 0.2g; Fat 13.4g, of which
saturates 1.5g; Cholesterol 439mg;
Calcium 194mg; Fiber 1g; Sodium

430mg.

p212 Fisherman's Stew Energy
487Kcal/2,032kJ; Protein 40.9g;
Carbohydrate 17.6g, of which sugars
8.7g; Fat 26.8g, of which saturates
15g; Cholesterol 215mg; Calcium
208mg; Fiber 2.2g; Sodium 393mg.

p216 The Gaucho Barbecue Energy
839Kcal/3,501kJ; Protein 88.1g;
Carbohydrate 3.8g, of which sugars
1.1g; Fat 52.5g, of which saturates
22.5g; Cholesterol 249mg; Calcium
63mg; Fiber 0.4g; Sodium 1.2g.

**p217 Beef Stuffed with Eggs and
Spinach** Energy 318Kcal/1,328kJ;
Protein 39.0g; Carbohydrate 3.4g, of
which sugars 2.8g; Fat 16.7g, of
which saturates 4.6g; Cholesterol
161mg; Calcium 103mg; Fiber 1.6g;
Sodium 299mg.

p218 Carbonada Criolla Energy
505Kcal/2,124kJ; Protein 46.1g;
Carbohydrate 33.6g, of which sugars
11.4g; Fat 18.3g, of which saturates
6.1g; Cholesterol 125mg; Calcium
44mg; Fiber 3.6g; Sodium 175mg.

**p220 Garlic and Chili Marinated Beef
with Corn-Crusted Onion Rings** Energy
428Kcal/1,787kJ; Protein 44.2g;
Carbohydrate 17.4g, of which sugars
3g; Fat 20g, of which saturates 5.4g;
Cholesterol 91mg; Calcium 51mg;
Fiber 0.8g; Sodium 136mg.

p221 Mexican Spicy Beef Tortilla
Energy 595Kcal/2,516kJ; Protein
30.3g; Carbohydrate 91.2g, of which
sugars 11.5g; Fat 14.7g, of which
saturates 4.7g; Cholesterol 53mg;
Calcium 153mg; Fiber 4.0g; Sodium
379mg.

p222 Tacos with Shredded Beef
Energy 222Kcal/930kJ; Protein 19g;
Carbohydrate 19.1g, of which sugars
0.6g; Fat 7.6g, of which saturates
1.8g; Cholesterol 44mg; Calcium
6mg; Fiber 0.7g; Sodium 209mg.

p223 Beef Enchiladas with Red Sauce
Energy 503Kcal/2,121kJ; Protein 43g;
Carbohydrate 51.9g, of which sugars
2.9g; Fat 15.1g, of which saturates
3.7g; Cholesterol 98mg; Calcium
101mg; Fiber 2.5g; Sodium 335mg.

p224 Black Bean Chili con Carne
Energy 374Kcal/1,575kJ; Protein
39.0g; Carbohydrate 27.9g, of which
sugars 7.4g; Fat 12.6g, of which
saturates 4.1g; Cholesterol 83mg;
Calcium 60mg; Fiber 4.7g; Sodium
111mg.

**p225 Spicy Meatballs with Tomato
Sauce** Energy 552Kcal/2,296kJ;
Protein 29.9g; Carbohydrate 21.8g, of
which sugars 6.0g; Fat 39.0g, of
which saturates 11.6g; Cholesterol
132mg; Calcium 75mg; Fiber 2.0g;
Sodium 268mg.

p226 Feijoada Energy
779Kcal/3,262kJ; Protein 58.0g;
Carbohydrate 49.9g, of which sugars
3.8g; Fat 39.9g, of which saturates
13.5g; Cholesterol 142mg; Calcium
135mg; Fiber 7.3g; Sodium 1.5g.

**p228 Stuffed Butterfly of Beef with
Cheese and Chili Sauce** Energy
554Kcal/2,300kJ; Protein 45.6g;
Carbohydrate 1.2g, of which sugars
0.9g; Fat 37.9g, of which saturates
19.9g; Cholesterol 160mg; Calcium
365mg; Fiber 0.2g; Sodium 723mg.

p230 Hearty Beef Stew Energy
515Kcal/2,158kJ; Protein 62.6g;
Carbohydrate 13.0g, of which sugars
6.7g; Fat 22.9g, of which saturates
10.9g; Cholesterol 186mg; Calcium
70mg; Fiber 1.5g; Sodium 245mg.

p231 Oxtail and Lima Beans Energy
773Kcal/3,240kJ; Protein 88.0g;
Carbohydrate 29.6g, of which sugars
6.2g; Fat 34.4g, of which saturates
0.2g; Cholesterol 275mg; Calcium
92mg; Fiber 4.8g; Sodium 522mg.

**p232 "Seasoned-up" Lamb in Spinach
Sauce** Energy 331Kcal/1,380kJ;
Protein 35.6g; Carbohydrate 4.0g, of
which sugars 3.1g; Fat 19.4g, of
which saturates 6.7g; Cholesterol
125mg; Calcium 80mg; Fiber 1.2g;
Sodium 241mg.

p232 Lamb Pelau Energy
652Kcal/2,726kJ; Protein 32.1g;
Carbohydrate 96.3g, of which sugars
5.7g; Fat 15.0g, of which saturates
7.3g; Cholesterol 97mg; Calcium
51mg; Fiber 1.0g; Sodium 231mg.

p234 Lamb Stew with Chili Sauce
Energy 367Kcal/1536kJ; Protein 34g;
Carbohydrate 11.8g, of which sugars
1.9g; Fat 20.8g, of which saturates
9g; Cholesterol 127mg; Calcium
19mg; Fiber 0.9g; Sodium 151mg.

p235 Albondigas Energy
412Kcal/1,717kJ; Protein 26.2g;
Carbohydrate 16g, of which sugars
5.9g; Fat 27.6g, of which saturates
7.7g; Cholesterol 118mg; Calcium
50mg; Fiber 1.9g; Sodium 265mg.

p236 Spiced Roast Leg of Lamb
Energy 470Kcal/1,962kJ; Protein

37.2g; Carbohydrate 22.6g, of which
sugars 6.5g; Fat 24.9g, of which
saturates 9.1g; Cholesterol 117mg;
Calcium 38mg; Fiber 7.4g; Sodium
651mg.

p237 Rabbit in Coconut Milk Energy
301Kcal/1,260kJ; Protein 29.9g;
Carbohydrate 10.8g, of which sugars
9.2g; Fat 15.7g, of which saturates
4.0g; Cholesterol 68mg; Calcium
73mg; Fiber 1.5g; Sodium 236mg.

p238 Caribbean Lamb Curry Energy
338Kcal/1,409kJ; Protein 30.8g;
Carbohydrate 3.2g, of which sugars
2.3g; Fat 22.6g, of which saturates
10.1g; Cholesterol 128mg; Calcium
29mg; Fiber 0.5g; Sodium 229mg.

p239 Pork with Pineapple Energy
492Kcal/2,041kJ; Protein 28.7g;
Carbohydrate 12.9g, of which
sugars 12.2g; Fat 36.4g, of which
saturates 12.6g; Cholesterol 92mg;
Calcium 30mg; Fiber 1.2g; Sodium
136mg.

p240 Stuffed Loin of Pork Energy
554Kcal/2,318kJ; Protein 71.8g;
Carbohydrate 8.2g, of which
sugars 7.7g; Fat 24.7g, of which
saturates 7.1g; Cholesterol 213mg;
Calcium 54mg; Fiber 1.2g; Sodium
240mg.

**p242 Enchiladas with Pork and Green
Sauce** Energy 613Kcal/2,574kJ;
Protein 48.9g; Carbohydrate 53.5g, of
which sugars 6.2g; Fat 23.4g, of
which saturates 8.9g; Cholesterol
129mg; Calcium 299mg; Fiber 3.5g;
Sodium 534mg.

p243 Pork in Green Sauce with Cactus
Energy 225Kcal/943kJ; Protein 27.8g;
Carbohydrate 4.2g, of which sugars
3.9g; Fat 10.9g, of which saturates
2.5g; Cholesterol 79mg; Calcium
49mg; Fiber 1.8g; Sodium 140mg.

p244 Tamales filled with Spiced Pork
Energy 490Kcal/2,050kJ; Protein 27.4g;
Carbohydrate 73.9g, of which sugars
0.6g; Fat 8.5g, of which saturates 1.4g;
Cholesterol 53mg; Calcium 11mg; Fiber
2.3g; Sodium 59mg.

**p246 Pork Roasted with Herbs,
Spices, and Rum** Energy
410Kcal/1,712kJ; Protein 42.4g;
Carbohydrate 3.9g, of which sugars
3.8g; Fat 21.4g, of which saturates
8.2g; Cholesterol 132mg; Calcium
16mg; Fiber 0.1g; Sodium 577mg.

**p247 Tostadas with Shredded Pork
and Spices** Energy 334Kcal/1,397kJ;

Protein 25.5g; Carbohydrate 22.9g, of which sugars 3.8g; Fat 16.1g, of which saturates 6.7g; Cholesterol 75mg; Calcium 152mg; Fiber 3.8g; Sodium 836mg.

p248 Pork in Milk Energy 472Kcal/1,957kJ; Protein 27.2g; Carbohydrate 7.5g, of which sugars 7.5g; Fat 37.1g, of which saturates 15.9g; Cholesterol 103g; Calcium 209mg; Fiber 0g; Sodium 159mg.

p248 Baked Ham with Orange and Lime Energy 348Kcal/1,448kJ; Protein 43.8g; Carbohydrate 0.6g, of which sugars 0.6g; Fat 18.8g, of which saturates 6.3g; Cholesterol 58g; Calcium 18mg; Fiber 0g; Sodium 2.2g.

p250 Carnitas Energy 465Kcal/1,931kJ; Protein 40.5g; Carbohydrate 3g, of which sugars 2.6g; Fat 32.3g, of which saturates 12.7g; Cholesterol 141mg; Calcium 25mg; Fiber 0.5g; Sodium 256mg.

p252 Pork Casserole with Onions, Chile, and Dried Fruit Energy 491Kcal/2,053kJ; Protein 39g; Carbohydrate 18.3g, of which sugars 15.3g; Fat 22.5g, of which saturates 4.3g; Cholesterol 105mg; Calcium 62mg; Fiber 3.1g; Sodium 127mg.

p254 Tortilla Pie with Chorizo Energy 740Kcal/3,070kJ; Protein 34.1g; Carbohydrate 14.4g, of which sugars 4.4g; Fat 59.2g, of which saturates 34.1g; Cholesterol 184mg; Calcium 514mg; Fiber 1.5g; Sodium 644mg.

p255 Scrambled Eggs with Chorizo Energy 322Kcal/1,335kJ; Protein 20.3g; Carbohydrate 5.7g, of which sugars 0.6g; Fat 24.3g, of which saturates 7.6g; Cholesterol 472mg; Calcium 101mg; Fiber 0.3g; Sodium 687mg.

p258 Cuban Chicken Pie Energy 521Kcal/2,814kJ; Protein 39.8g; Carbohydrate 35.2g, of which sugars 20.1g; Fat 25.6g, of which saturates 10.8g; Cholesterol 324g; Calcium 62mg; Fiber 2.5g; Sodium 190mg.

p259 Chicken with Okra Energy 122Kcal/511kJ; Protein 10.8g; Carbohydrate 9.7g, of which sugars 7.9g; Fat 4.8g, of which saturates 1.0g; Cholesterol 32g; Calcium 162mg; Fiber 5.1g; Sodium 40mg.

p260 Burritos with Chicken and Rice Energy 552Kcal/2,318kJ; Protein

35.1g; Carbohydrate 65.5g, of which sugars 3.3g; Fat 16.9g, of which saturates 8.7g; Cholesterol 89mg; Calcium 375mg; Fiber 2.5g; Sodium 531mg.

p262 Chicken and Tomatillo Chimichangas Energy 468Kcal/1,968kJ; Protein 27.5g; Carbohydrate 51.1g, of which sugars 6g; Fat 18.5g, of which saturates 2.3g; Cholesterol 61mg; Calcium 105mg; Fiber 3.3g; Sodium 271mg.

p263 Drunken Chicken Energy 752Kcal/3,148kJ; Protein 25.9g; Carbohydrate 62.4g, of which sugars 33.4g; Fat 27.1g, of which saturates 2.9g; Cholesterol 79mg; Calcium 141mg; Fiber 4.9g; Sodium 346mg.

p264 Colombian Chicken Hot-pot Energy 368Kcal/1,559kJ; Protein 29.2g; Carbohydrate 49.6g, of which sugars 6.5g; Fat 7.2g, of which saturates 1.8g; Cholesterol 107mg; Calcium 29mg; Fiber 3.7g; Sodium 190mg.

p266 Chicken with Chipotle Sauce Energy 229Kcal/963kJ; Protein 36.7g; Carbohydrate 4.5g, of which sugars 3.3g; Fat 7.3g, of which saturates 1.1g; Cholesterol 105mg; Calcium 21mg; Fiber 0.8g; Sodium 92mg.

p268 Spinach and Potato Stuffed Chicken Breasts Energy 212Kcal/888kJ; Protein 26.6g; Carbohydrate 5.7g, of which sugars 2.8g; Fat 9.4g, of which saturates 5g; Cholesterol 119mg; Calcium 60mg; Fiber 1.5g; Sodium 159mg.

p269 Mole Poblano de Guajolote Energy 732Kcal/3,061kJ; Protein 76.4g; Carbohydrate 19.3g, of which sugars 14.7g; Fat 39.3g, of which saturates 8.5g; Cholesterol 252mg;

Calcium 139mg; Fiber 3.6g; Sodium 263mg.

p270 Peanut Chicken Energy 326Kcal/1,374kJ; Protein 55.5g; Carbohydrate 4.2g, of which sugars 3.1g; Fat 9.8g, of which saturates 4.5g; Cholesterol 171mg; Calcium 25mg; Fiber 0.9g; Sodium 190mg.

p270 Breast of Turkey with Mango and Wine Energy 351Kcal/1,476kJ; Protein 49.9g; Carbohydrate 9.0g, of which sugars 6.4g; Fat 10.4g, of which saturates 6.0g; Cholesterol 135mg; Calcium 29mg; Fiber 1.5g; Sodium 190mg.

p272 Chicken Fajitas Energy 398Kcal/1,670kJ; Protein 23g; Carbohydrate 44.3g, of which sugars 11.8g; Fat 15.5g, of which saturates 4.4g; Cholesterol 60mg; Calcium 76mg; Fiber 2.8g; Sodium 51mg.

p274 Barbecued Jerk Chicken Energy 460Kcal/1,924kJ; Protein 59.7g; Carbohydrate 2.2g, of which sugars 2.2g; Fat 23.6g, of which saturates 6.4g; Cholesterol 254g; Calcium 26mg; Fiber 0g; Sodium 210mg.

p275 Thyme and Lime Chicken Energy 495Kcal/2,053kJ; Protein 31.6g; Carbohydrate 0.4g, of which sugars 0.4g; Fat 40.8g, of which saturates 16.7g; Cholesterol 212g; Calcium 24mg; Fiber 0.1g; Sodium 250mg.

p276 Chicken, Pork, and Potatoes in Peanut Sauce Energy 405Kcal/1,697kJ; Protein 41.1g; Carbohydrate 18.2g, of which sugars 4.1g; Fat 19.0g, of which saturates 3.8g; Cholesterol 105mg; Calcium 40mg; Fiber 2.5g; Sodium 440mg.

p278 Spicy Fried Chicken Energy 345Kcal/1,442kJ; Protein 35.5g; Carbohydrate 6.7g, of which sugars 1.0g; Fat 19.8g, of which saturates 4.5g; Cholesterol 177g; Calcium 54mg; Fiber 0.2g; Sodium 170mg.

p279 Sunday Roast Chicken Energy 348Kcal/1,455kJ; Protein 37.5g; Carbohydrate 7.8g, of which sugars 7.8g; Fat 18.8g, of which saturates 8.8g; Cholesterol 155mg; Calcium 18mg; Fiber 0g; Sodium 200mg.

p280 Turkey Mole Energy 700Kcal/2,920kJ; Protein 50.6g; Carbohydrate 27.7g, of which sugars 19.1g; Fat 43.8g, of which saturates 6.9g; Cholesterol 86mg; Calcium 267mg; Fiber 7g; Sodium 178mg.

p282 Peruvian Duck with Rice Energy 527Kcal/2,207kJ; Protein 17.6g;

Carbohydrate 55.2g, of which sugars 2.8g; Fat 24.6g, of which saturates 7.2g; Cholesterol 58mg; Calcium 62mg; Fiber 1.8g; Sodium 100mg.

p282 Drunken Duck Energy 693Kcal/2,895kJ; Protein 24.7g; Carbohydrate 45.5g, of which sugars 14.9g; Fat 41.7g, of which saturates 12.5g; Cholesterol 106mg; Calcium 91mg; Fiber 5.6g; Sodium 220mg.

p286 Corn Soufflé Energy 385Kcal/1,605kJ; Protein 15.2g; Carbohydrate 25.3g, of which sugars 8.7g; Fat 25.5g, of which saturates 13.7g; Cholesterol 246mg; Calcium 246mg; Fiber 2.5g; Sodium 480mg.

p287 Layered Potato Bake with Cheese Energy 442Kcal/1,831kJ; Protein 12.2g; Carbohydrate 16.3g, of which sugars 4.1g; Fat 36.9g, of which saturates 7.2g; Cholesterol 132mg; Calcium 137mg; Fiber 2.4g; Sodium 610mg.

p288 Frijoles Energy 201Kcal/851kJ; Protein 13.4g; Carbohydrate 28.3g, of which sugars 3.6g; Fat 4.6g, of which saturates 0.7g; Cholesterol 0mg; Calcium 66mg; Fiber 9.8g; Sodium 14mg.

p289 Black Bean Burritos Energy 586Kcal/2,460kJ; Protein 29.8g; Carbohydrate 59.8g, of which sugars 7.7g; Fat 25.7g, of which saturates 13.4g; Cholesterol 55mg; Calcium 546mg; Fiber 7.1g; Sodium 1g.

p290 Chili Cheese Tortilla with Fresh Tomato Salsa Energy 375Kcal/1,562kJ; Protein 19.3g; Carbohydrate 13.5g, of which sugars 5.7g; Fat 27.1g, of which saturates 10g; Cholesterol 314mg; Calcium 305mg; Fiber 2.6g; Sodium 589mg.

p291 Potato and Onion Tortilla Energy 512Kcal/2,132kJ; Protein 15g; Carbohydrate 40g, of which sugars 5g; Fat 34g, of which saturates 6g; Cholesterol 285mg; Calcium 73mg; Fiber 3.7g; Sodium 100mg.

p292 Heart of Palm Pie Energy 566Kcal/2,361kJ; Protein 10.8g; Carbohydrate 57.1g, of which sugars 6.3g; Fat 34.2g, of which saturates 18.2g; Cholesterol 139mg; Calcium 164mg; Fiber 4.4g; Sodium 430mg.

p294 Macaroni Cheese Pie Energy 609Kcal/2,553kJ; Protein 25.1g; Carbohydrate 60.0g, of which sugars 9.9g; Fat 31.6g, of which saturates 18.6g; Cholesterol 135mg; Calcium 494mg; Fiber 2.4g; Sodium 560mg.

p295 Red Bean Chili Energy 291Kcal/1,224kJ; Protein 12.7g; Carbohydrate 35.7g, of which sugars 11.0g; Fat 6.5g, of which saturates 0.8g; Cholesterol 0mg; Calcium 86mg; Fiber 6.1g; Sodium 1.2g.

p296 Peppers Stuffed with Beans Energy 528Kcal/2,201kJ; Protein 26.1g; Carbohydrate 32.3g, of which sugars 6.8g; Fat 33.6g, of which saturates 12.1g; Cholesterol 118mg; Calcium 286mg; Fiber 10.1g; Sodium 360mg.

p297 Black-Eyed Pea Stew with Spicy Pumpkin Energy 412Kcal/1,734kJ; Protein 20.8g; Carbohydrate 57.1g, of which sugars 16.2g; Fat 12.7g, of which saturates 6.8g; Cholesterol 18mg; Calcium 156mg; Fiber 11.3g; Sodium 80mg.

p298 Spicy Vegetable Chow Mein Energy 414Kcal/1,740kJ; Protein 12.4g; Carbohydrate 62.5g, of which sugars 8.5g; Fat 14.4g, of which saturates 2.7g; Cholesterol 23mg; Calcium 74mg; Fiber 4.7g; Sodium 266mg.

p298 Eggplants Stuffed with Sweet Potato Energy 249Kcal/1,013kJ; Protein 8.1g; Carbohydrate 24.6g, of which sugars 7.9g; Fat 13.1g, of which saturates 5.1g; Cholesterol 15mg; Calcium 186mg; Fiber 5.0g; Sodium 170mg.

p300 Tomato Rice and Beans with Avocado Salsa Energy 530Kcal/2,236kJ; Protein 12g; Carbohydrate 90.1g, of which sugars 10.2g; Fat 16g, of which saturates 2.8g; Cholesterol 0mg; Calcium 120mg; Fiber 7.9g; Sodium 168mg.

p301 Leek, Squash, and Tomato Gratin Energy 317Kcal/1,316kJ; Protein 6.7g; Carbohydrate 13g, of which sugars 11.6g; Fat 26.8g, of which saturates 11.1g; Cholesterol 41mg; Calcium 168mg; Fiber 6g; Sodium 44mg.

p302 Bean and Tomato Casserole Energy 263Kcal/1,111kJ; Protein 11.7g; Carbohydrate 34.3g, of which sugars 10.3g; Fat 9.8g, of which saturates 1.5g; Cholesterol 0mg; Calcium 91mg; Fiber 10g; Sodium 104mg.

p302 Mixed Vegetable Casserole Energy 573Kcal/2,416kJ; Protein 32.5g; Carbohydrate 81.5g, of which sugars 19.5g; Fat 15.3g, of which saturates 2.5g; Cholesterol 0mg;

Calcium 250mg; Fiber 25.7g; Sodium 60mg.

p304 Spinach Plantain Rounds Energy 266Kcal/1,113kJ; Protein 5.9g; Carbohydrate 30.8g, of which sugars 7.6g; Fat 14.1g, of which saturates 3.6g; Cholesterol 65mg; Calcium 207mg; Fiber 3.6g; Sodium 205mg.

p305 Peppery Bean Salad Energy 248Kcal/1,046kJ; Protein 14.0g; Carbohydrate 35.4g, of which sugars 6.5g; Fat 6.5g, of which saturates 0.9g; Cholesterol 0mg; Calcium 122mg; Fiber 11.0g; Sodium 660mg.

p306 Avocado and Grapefruit Salad Energy 351Kcal/1,448kJ; Protein 2.5g; Carbohydrate 5.4g, of which sugars 4.0g; Fat 35.7g, of which saturates 6.4g; Cholesterol 0mg; Calcium 28mg; Fiber 4.1g; Sodium 80mg.

p307 Quinoa Salad with Citrus Dressing Energy 225Kcal/938kJ; Protein 4.1g; Carbohydrate 22.1g, of which sugars 3.1g; Fat 13.9g, of which saturates 2.1g; Cholesterol 0mg; Calcium 40mg; Fiber 3.0g; Sodium 10mg.

p308 Okra and Tomato Salad Energy 154Kcal/639kJ; Protein 3.7g; Carbohydrate 7.9g, of which sugars 6.6g; Fat 12.3g, of which saturates 1.9g; Cholesterol 0mg; Calcium 174mg; Fiber 5.2g; Sodium 15mg.

p308 Tomato, Heart of Palm, and Onion Salad Energy 152Kcal/632kJ; Protein 2.8g; Carbohydrate 8.7g, of which sugars 7.7g; Fat 12.0g, of which saturates 1.8g; Cholesterol 0mg; Calcium 38mg; Fiber 3.9g; Sodium 16mg.

p310 Chayotes with Corn and Chiles Energy 324Kcal/1,345kJ; Protein 6.6g; Carbohydrate 27.5g, of which sugars 16.2g; Fat 21.6g, of which saturates 9.3g; Cholesterol 28mg; Calcium 159mg; Fiber 4.4g; Sodium 227mg.

p311 Spinach Salad Energy 181Kcal/748kJ; Protein 4.7g; Carbohydrate 4.2g, of which sugars 4.1g; Fat 16.3g, of which saturates 5.7g; Cholesterol 18mg; Calcium 209mg; Fiber 3.4g; Sodium 177mg.

p312 Baked Sweet Potato Energy 263Kcal/1,122kJ; Protein 6g; Carbohydrate 60.6g, of which sugars 21g; Fat 1.5g, of which saturates 0.5g; Cholesterol 1mg; Calcium 170mg; Fiber 7.7g; Sodium 151mg.

p313 Warm Hazelnut and Pistachio

Salad Energy 380Kcal/1,587kJ; Protein 6.9g; Carbohydrate 37.4g, of which sugars 3.8g; Fat 23.6g, of which saturates 2.7g; Cholesterol 0mg; Calcium 36mg; Fiber 3.3g; Sodium 65mg.

p314 Jalapeño and Shrimp Salad Energy 419Kcal/1,734kJ; Protein 25g; Carbohydrate 4.8g, of which sugars 4.4g; Fat 33.4g, of which saturates 7.6g; Cholesterol 380mg; Calcium 165mg; Fiber 1.5g; Sodium 1,591mg.

p315 Fava Bean, Mushroom, and Chorizo Salad Energy 287Kcal/1,192kJ; Protein 10.7g; Carbohydrate 11g, of which sugars 2.1g; Fat 22.6g, of which saturates 5.7g; Cholesterol 26mg; Calcium 80mg; Fiber 4.7g; Sodium 384mg.

p316 Nopalitos Salad Energy 78Kcal/325kJ; Protein 1.4g; Carbohydrate 5g, of which sugars 4.5g; Fat 6g, of which saturates 0.8g; Cholesterol 0mg; Calcium 63mg; Fiber 2.4g; Sodium 51mg.

p317 Jicama, Chile and Lime Salad Energy 24Kcal/100kJ; Protein 0.9g; Carbohydrate 4.8g, of which sugars 4.6g; Fat 0.3g, of which saturates 0g; Cholesterol 0mg; Calcium 49mg; Fiber 2.4g; Sodium 261mg.

p318 Chayote Salad Energy 126Kcal/521kJ; Protein 1.2g; Carbohydrate 4.9g, of which sugars 4.1g; Fat 11.4g, of which saturates 1.7g; Cholesterol 0mg; Calcium 36mg; Fiber 1.7g; Sodium 5mg.

p319 Caesar Salad Energy 279Kcal/1,159kJ; Protein 8.3g; Carbohydrate 14g, of which sugars 1.4g; Fat 21.5g, of which saturates 4.4g; Cholesterol 58mg; Calcium 152mg; Fiber 0.8g; Sodium 418mg.

p320 Green Bean and Chile Pepper Salad Energy 280Kcal/1,153kJ; Protein 3.1g; Carbohydrate 9.4g, of which sugars 8.4g; Fat 25.8g, of which saturates 3.8g; Cholesterol 0mg; Calcium 55mg; Fiber 3.9g; Sodium 5mg.

p321 Mango, Tomato, and Red Onion Salad Energy 93Kcal/390kJ; Protein 1.0g; Carbohydrate 10.1g, of which sugars 9.5g; Fat 5.8g, of which saturates 0.7g; Cholesterol 0mg; Calcium 17mg; Fiber 2.1g; Sodium 6mg.

p322 Peruvian Salad Energy 226Kcal/945kJ; Protein 6.2g; Carbohydrate 23.1g, of which sugars

4.6g; Fat 12.7g, of which saturates 2.6g; Cholesterol 78mg; Calcium 59mg; Fiber 3.3g; Sodium 570mg.

p323 Pumpkin Salad Energy 384Kcal/1,583kJ; Protein 2.2g; Carbohydrate 8.7g, of which sugars 6.5g; Fat 38.1g, of which saturates 5.5g; Cholesterol 0mg; Calcium 84mg; Fiber 3.0g; Sodium 10mg.

p326 Plain Rice Energy 241Kcal/1,018kJ; Protein 3.7g; Carbohydrate 42.9g, of which sugars 0g; Fat 7.3g, of which saturates 1.1g; Cholesterol 0mg; Calcium 26mg; Fiber 0.2g; Sodium 0mg.

p326 Black Beans Energy 319Kcal/1,347kJ; Protein 20.7g; Carbohydrate 40.6g, of which sugars 2.2g; Fat 9.4g, of which saturates 2.4g; Cholesterol 12mg; Calcium 62mg; Fiber 6.2g; Sodium 250mg.

p328 Coconut Rice Energy 337Kcal/1,435kJ; Protein 5.5g; Carbohydrate 69.4g, of which sugars 15.8g; Fat 6.2g, of which saturates 3.1g; Cholesterol 8mg; Calcium 120mg; Fiber 0.3g; Sodium 400mg.

p329 Toasted Cassava Flour with Egg and Bacon Energy 218Kcal/918kJ; Protein 8.4g; Carbohydrate 29.2g, of which sugars 0.6g; Fat 8.3g, of which saturates 3.2g; Cholesterol 93mg; Calcium 67mg; Fiber 1.2g; Sodium 230mg.

p330 Green Rice Energy 255Kcal/1,064kJ; Protein 4.8g; Carbohydrate 44.6g, of which sugars 4.5g; Fat 6.2g, of which saturates 0.7g; Cholesterol 0mg; Calcium 40mg; Fiber 1.7g; Sodium 7mg.

p330 Yellow Rice Energy 159Kcal/662kJ; Protein 2.7g; Carbohydrate 27.9g, of which sugars 1.1g; Fat 3.9g, of which saturates 0.4g; Cholesterol 0mg; Calcium 10mg; Fiber 0.3g; Sodium 1mg.

p332 Rice and Peas Energy 449Kcal/1,903kJ; Protein 13.9g; Carbohydrate 83.3g, of which sugars 4.4g; Fat 9.1g, of which saturates 5.7g; Cholesterol 0mg; Calcium 82mg; Fiber 6.3g; Sodium 10mg.

p333 Cou-Cou Energy 264Kcal/1,115kJ; Protein 1.2g; Carbohydrate 52.7g, of which sugars 0.8g; Fat 6.8g, of which saturates 4.1g; Cholesterol 16mg; Calcium 56mg; Fiber 1.2g; Sodium 80mg.

p334 Buttered Spinach and Rice Energy 520Kcal/2,169kJ; Protein 11.5g; Carbohydrate 95.4g, of which sugars 4.6g; Fat 9.7g, of which saturates 5.3g; Cholesterol 21mg; Calcium 184mg; Fiber 2.7g; Sodium 190mg.

p334 Creamed Sweet Potatoes Energy 313Kcal/1,321kJ; Protein 4.4g; Carbohydrate 51.1g, of which sugars 13.4g; Fat 11.6g, of which saturates 6.8g; Cholesterol 27mg; Calcium 74mg; Fiber 9.6g; Sodium 170mg.

p336 Colombian Cheesy Potatoes Energy 448Kcal/1,882kJ; Protein 11.5g; Carbohydrate 55.8g, of which sugars 6.5g; Fat 21.4g, of which saturates 13g; Cholesterol 52mg; Calcium 166mg; Fiber 3.8g; Sodium 150mg.

p337 Caribbean Potato Salad Energy 167Kcal/705kJ; Protein 3.7g; Carbohydrate 30.2g, of which sugars 7.1g; Fat 4.3g, of which saturates 0.7g; Cholesterol 4mg; Calcium 24mg; Fiber 3.5g; Sodium 90mg.

p338 Potatoes with Chorizo and Green Chiles Energy 542Kcal/2,267kJ; Protein 20.9g; Carbohydrate 45.7g, of which sugars 4.9g; Fat 31.1g, of which saturates 15.9g; Cholesterol 66mg; Calcium 332mg; Fiber 3g; Sodium 905mg.

p339 Red Cauliflower Energy 63Kcal/262kJ; Protein 4.2g; Carbohydrate 4.5g, of which sugars 4g; Fat 3.2g, of which saturates 1.9g; Cholesterol 9mg; Calcium 74mg; Fiber 1.9g; Sodium 192mg.

p340 Green Lima Beans in Tomato Sauce Energy 170Kcal/714kJ; Protein 10.1g; Carbohydrate 18.7g, of which sugars 6.3g; Fat 6.6g, of which saturates 1g; Cholesterol 0mg; Calcium 80mg; Fiber 8.7g; Sodium 19mg.

p340 Green Beans with Eggs Energy 120Kcal/497kJ; Protein 6.3g;

Carbohydrate 2.4g, of which sugars 1.7g; Fat 9.4g, of which saturates 3.1g; Cholesterol 103mg; Calcium 96mg; Fiber 1.2g; Sodium 96mg.

p342 Zucchini with Cheese and Green Chiles Energy 143Kcal/587kJ; Protein 2.7g; Carbohydrate 3.3g, of which sugars 3g; Fat 13.3g, of which saturates 6.2g; Cholesterol 18mg; Calcium 47mg; Fiber 1.2g; Sodium 62mg.

p343 Courgette Torte Energy 421Kcal/1,747kJ; Protein 18.8g; Carbohydrate 13.2g, of which sugars 3.2g; Fat 32g, of which saturates 12.9g; Cholesterol 216mg; Calcium 356mg; Fiber 1.7g; Sodium 359mg.

p344 Pumpkin with Spices Energy 84Kcal/347kJ; Protein 1.2g; Carbohydrate 3.7g, of which sugars 2.9g; Fat 7.2g, of which saturates 4.5g; Cholesterol 18mg; Calcium 50mg; Fiber 1.7g; Sodium 214mg.

p345 Potato Cakes Energy 149Kcal/621kJ; Protein 4.8g; Carbohydrate 9.8g, of which sugars 0.9g; Fat 10.1g, of which saturates 3.4g; Cholesterol 30mg; Calcium 101mg; Fiber 0.8g; Sodium 197mg.

p346 Fried Plantain Energy 205Kcal/861kJ; Protein 1.2g; Carbohydrate 29.5g, of which sugars 5.8g; Fat 10g, of which saturates 5.5g; Cholesterol 21mg; Calcium 11mg; Fiber 1.3g; Sodium 65mg.

p346 Fried Potatoes Energy 186Kcal/775kJ; Protein 2.5g; Carbohydrate 19.4g, of which sugars 2.4g; Fat 11.4g, of which saturates 1.4g; Cholesterol 0mg; Calcium 14mg; Fiber 1.3g; Sodium 14mg.

P348 Potato and Onion Tortilla with Fava Beans Energy 755Kcal/3,151kJ; Protein 41.2g; Carbohydrate 59.2g, of

which sugars 18.2g; Fat 40.7g, of which saturates 9g; Cholesterol 761mg; Calcium 306mg; Fiber 14.4g; Sodium 716mg.

p349 Bean Feast with Tomato and Avocado Salsa Energy 436Kcal/1,837kJ; Protein 22.8g; Carbohydrate 67.6g, of which sugars 23.7g; Fat 10g, of which saturates 1.9g; Cholesterol 0mg; Calcium 236mg; Fiber 21.8g; Sodium 1,181mg.

p350 Corn with Cream Energy 258Kcal/1,077kJ; Protein 6.7g; Carbohydrate 23.1g, of which sugars 8.8g; Fat 16.1g, of which saturates 9.6g; Cholesterol 41mg; Calcium 87mg; Fiber 1.3g; Sodium 394mg.

p351 Frijoles de Olla Energy 259Kcal/1,094kJ; Protein 17.6g; Carbohydrate 34.1g, of which sugars 6.9g; Fat 6.8g, of which saturates 3.8g; Cholesterol 18mg; Calcium 166mg; Fiber 11.7g; Sodium 207mg.

p352 Potatoes with Red Chiles Energy 101Kcal/421kJ; Protein 1.4g; Carbohydrate 11.4g, of which sugars 1.8g; Fat 5.8g, of which saturates 0.7g; Cholesterol 0mg; Calcium 20mg; Fiber 1.2g; Sodium 501mg.

p353 Corn with a Garlic Butter Crust Energy 543Kcal/2,267kJ; Protein 6.4g; Carbohydrate 50.6g, of which sugars 13.6g; Fat 36.5g, of which saturates 20.3g; Cholesterol 80mg; Calcium 42mg; Fiber 2.4g; Sodium 734mg.

p354 Vegetables in Peanut and Chili Sauce Energy 157Kcal/656kJ; Protein 5.5g; Carbohydrate 13g, of which sugars 11.4g; Fat 9.6g, of which saturates 2.1g; Cholesterol 0mg; Calcium 110mg; Fiber 5.5g; Sodium 65mg.

p355 Chili Zucchini Energy 97Kcal/402kJ; Protein 3.2g; Carbohydrate 6.9g, of which sugars 6.4g; Fat 6.4g, of which saturates 1g; Cholesterol 0mg; Calcium 55mg; Fiber 2.7g; Sodium 14mg.

p356 Refried Beans Energy 279Kcal/1,174kJ; Protein 16.9g; Carbohydrate 32.8g, of which sugars 5.4g; Fat 9.9g, of which saturates 4.4g; Cholesterol 15mg; Calcium 148mg; Fiber 11.3g; Sodium 197mg.

p357 Frijoles Charros Energy 504Kcal/2,098kJ; Protein 15g; Carbohydrate 33.9g, of which sugars 14.7g; Fat 34.7g, of which saturates

13.7g; Cholesterol 43mg; Calcium 112mg; Fiber 8.7g; Sodium 976mg.

p358 Okra Fried Rice Energy 305Kcal/1,286kJ; Protein 4.7g; Carbohydrate 50.6g, of which sugars 1.9g; Fat 10.7g, of which saturates 3.1g; Cholesterol 8mg; Calcium 35mg; Fiber 0.5g; Sodium 65mg.

p358 Eggplants with Garlic and Scallions Energy 132Kcal/551kJ; Protein 3.2g; Carbohydrate 9.3g, of which sugars 8.7g; Fat 9.5g, of which saturates 1.3g; Cholesterol 0mg; Calcium 36mg; Fiber 5.7g; Sodium 550mg.

p360 Cassava with a Citrus Salsa Energy 305Kcal/1,294kJ; Protein 3g; Carbohydrate 57.2g, of which saturates 2.2g; Fat 8.9g, of which saturates 1.4g; Cholesterol 0mg; Calcium 31mg; Fiber 2.6g; Sodium 0mg.

p361 Stir-fried Collard Greens Energy 111Kcal/459kJ; Protein 6.3g; Carbohydrate 2.5g, of which sugars 2g; Fat 8.5g, of which saturates 2.3g; Cholesterol 16mg; Calcium 159mg; Fiber 2.6g; Sodium 330mg.

p362 Corn Sticks Energy 64Kcal/272kJ; Protein 1.4g; Carbohydrate 11.7g, of which saturates 0.9g; Fat 1.7g, of which saturates 0.9g; Cholesterol 15mg; Calcium 36mg; Fiber 0.2g; Sodium 160mg.

p363 Mushrooms with Chipotle Chiles Energy 84Kcal/346kJ; Protein 1.7g; Carbohydrate 1.9g, of which sugars 1.4g; Fat 7.8g, of which saturates 1.2g; Cholesterol 0mg; Calcium 9mg; Fiber 1.4g; Sodium 5mg.

p366 Argentinian Barbecue Salsa Energy 132Kcal/543kJ; Protein 0.7g; Carbohydrate 3.2g, of which sugars 2.6g; Fat 13g, of which saturates 1.9g; Cholesterol 0mg; Calcium 10mg; Fiber 0.8g; Sodium 0mg.

p366 Hot Chili Salsa Energy 441Kcal/1,820kJ; Protein 3.8g; Carbohydrate 5.8g, of which sugars 5.8g; Fat 45g, of which saturates 6.4g; Cholesterol 0mg; Calcium 40mg; Fiber 1.5g; Sodium 20mg.

p368 Green Tomatillo Sauce Energy 42Kcal/174kJ; Protein 0.9g; Carbohydrate 2.7g, of which sugars 2.6g; Fat 3.1g, of which saturates 0.4g; Cholesterol 0mg; Calcium 30mg; Fiber 1.4g; Sodium 11mg.

p369 Guacamole Energy 262Kcal/1,083kJ; Protein 3.2g; Carbohydrate 5g, of which sugars 3g;

Fat 25.4g, of which saturates 5.4g; Cholesterol 0mg; Calcium 37mg; Fiber 5.5g; Sodium 15mg.

p370 Pinto Bean Salsa Energy 103Kcal/438kJ; Protein 8.1g; Carbohydrate 17.2g, of which sugars 3.3g; Fat 0.7g, of which saturates 0.1g; Cholesterol 0mg; Calcium 44mg; Fiber 5.8g; Sodium 12mg.

p371 Black Bean Salsa Energy 129Kcal/544kJ; Protein 8g; Carbohydrate 17.6g, of which sugars 3.2g; Fat 3.5g, of which saturates 0.5g; Cholesterol 0mg; Calcium 67mg; Fiber 6.3g; Sodium 11mg.

p372 Chipotle Sauce Energy 63Kcal/265kJ; Protein 1g; Carbohydrate 10.4g, of which sugars 10.4g; Fat 0.3g, of which saturates 0.1g; Cholesterol 0mg; Calcium 12mg; Fiber 0.8g; Sodium 11mg.

p372 Guajillo Chili Sauce Energy 43Kcal/181kJ; Protein 1.6g; Carbohydrate 8.3g, of which sugars 8g; Fat 0.6g, of which saturates 0.2g; Cholesterol 0mg; Calcium 15mg; Fiber 1.9g; Sodium 9mg.

p374 Roasted Tomato Salsa Energy 54Kcal/226kJ; Protein 0.8g; Carbohydrate 4.2g, of which sugars 3.7g; Fat 4g, of which saturates 0.6g; Cholesterol 0mg; Calcium 11mg; Fiber 1.1g; Sodium 8mg.

p376 Tamarillo Sauce Energy 112Kcal/468kJ; Protein 0.7g; Carbohydrate 15.5g, of which sugars 15.2g; Fat 5.7g, of which saturates 0.8g; Cholesterol 0mg; Calcium 9mg; Fiber 2.2g; Sodium 0mg.

p377 Avocado Salsa Energy 190Kcal/786kJ; Protein 1.9g; Carbohydrate 5.6g, of which sugars 4g; Fat 18g, of which saturates 3.2g; Cholesterol 0mg; Calcium 20mg; Fiber 3g; Sodium 10mg.

p378 Jicama Salsa Energy 69Kcal/291kJ; Protein 2.4g; Carbohydrate 14.9g, of which sugars 14.3g; Fat 0.5g, of which saturates 0g; Cholesterol 0mg; Calcium 106mg; Fiber 4.7g; Sodium 23mg.

p379 Sweet Potato Salsa Energy 154Kcal/657kJ; Protein 2.3g; Carbohydrate 37.4g, of which sugars 11g; Fat 0.6g, of which saturates 0.2g; Cholesterol 0mg; Calcium 46mg; Fiber 4.2g; Sodium 70mg.

p380 Nopales Salsa Energy 16Kcal/67kJ; Protein 0.8g; Carbohydrate 2.8g, of which sugars

2.4g; Fat 0.3g, of which saturates 0g; Cholesterol 0mg; Calcium 34mg; Fiber 1.3g; Sodium 286mg.

p382 Chili Bean Dip Energy 240Kcal/1,002kJ; Protein 12.3g; Carbohydrate 20.3g, of which sugars 5.4g; Fat 12.3g, of which saturates 4.8g; Cholesterol 18mg; Calcium 219mg; Fiber 6.6g; Sodium 527mg.

p383 Piquant Pineapple Relish Energy 81Kcal/343kJ; Protein 0.7g; Carbohydrate 20.5g, of which sugars 20.4g; Fat 0.1g, of which saturates 0g; Cholesterol 0mg; Calcium 26mg; Fiber 0.9g; Sodium 4mg.

p384 Mango Salsa Energy 56Kcal/239kJ; Protein 1.2g; Carbohydrate 12.9g, of which sugars 12g; Fat 0.4g, of which saturates 0.1g; Cholesterol 0mg; Calcium 40mg; Fiber 2.9g; Sodium 7mg.

p384 Roasted Tomato and Cilantro Salsa Energy 21Kcal/88kJ; Protein 1g; Carbohydrate 3.6g, of which sugars 3.3g; Fat 0.4g, of which saturates 0.1g; Cholesterol 0mg; Calcium 25mg; Fiber 1.4g; Sodium 11mg.

p386 Chayote Salsa Energy 25Kcal/107kJ; Protein 0.6g; Carbohydrate 5.6g, of which sugars 5.4g; Fat 0.2g, of which saturates 0g; Cholesterol 0mg; Calcium 21mg; Fiber 0.7g; Sodium 188mg.

p387 Pumpkin Seed Sauce Energy 237Kcal/986kJ; Protein 7.6g; Carbohydrate 10g, of which sugars 4.5g; Fat 18.6g, of which saturates 1.9g; Cholesterol 0mg; Calcium 48mg; Fiber 3.2g; Sodium 13mg.

p388 Fiery Citrus Salsa Energy 18Kcal/75kJ; Protein 0.4g; Carbohydrate 4.1g, of which sugars 4.1g; Fat 0.1g, of which saturates 0g;

Cholesterol 0mg; Calcium 18mg; Fiber 0.8g; Sodium 2mg.

p389 Broiled Corn-on-the-Cob Salsa Energy 224Kcal/945kJ; Protein 4.7g; Carbohydrate 37g, of which sugars 15.7g; Fat 7.4g, of which saturates 1.2g; Cholesterol 0mg; Calcium 20mg; Fiber 3.1g; Sodium 348mg.

p390 Orange, Tomato, and Chive Salsa Energy 101Kcal/423kJ; Protein 1.9g; Carbohydrate 10.8g, of which sugars 10.8g; Fat 5.9g, of which saturates 0.8g; Cholesterol 0mg; Calcium 78mg; Fiber 2.9g; Sodium 14mg.

p391 Sour Cream Dip Energy 202Kcal/838kJ; Protein 4.1g; Carbohydrate 11.8g, of which sugars 11.5g; Fat 15.7g, of which saturates 9.6g; Cholesterol 45mg; Calcium 104mg; Fiber 2.9g; Sodium 47mg.

p392 Chile Strips with Lime Energy 45Kcal/189kJ; Protein 3.8g; Carbohydrate 6.2g, of which sugars 4.9g; Fat 0.7g, of which saturates 0g; Cholesterol 0mg; Calcium 49mg; Fiber 0.9g; Sodium 9mg.

p393 Onion Relish Energy 151Kcal/629kJ; Protein 5.8g; Carbohydrate 31.8g, of which sugars 22.6g; Fat 1g, of which saturates 0g; Cholesterol 0mg; Calcium 111mg; Fiber 5.6g; Sodium 14mg.

p394 Habeñero Salsa Energy 62Kcal/259kJ; Protein 5.3g; Carbohydrate 7.4g, of which sugars 7.1g; Fat 1.5g, of which saturates 0g; Cholesterol 0mg; Calcium 147mg; Fiber 3g; Sodium 31mg.

p395 Adobo Seasoning Energy 10Kcal/41kJ; Protein 0.9g; Carbohydrate 1.4g, of which sugars 0.2g; Fat 0.1g, of which saturates 0g; Cholesterol 0mg; Calcium 4mg; Fiber 0.3g; Sodium 165mg.

p396 Red Rub Energy 11Kcal/48kJ; Protein 0.3g; Carbohydrate 2.6g, of which sugars 2.6g; Fat 0g, of which saturates 0g; Cholesterol 0mg; Calcium 14mg; Fiber 0.5g; Sodium 2mg.

p396 Red Salsa Energy 195Kcal/818kJ; Protein 2.6g; Carbohydrate 20.6g, of which sugars 20.6g; Fat 12g, of which saturates 1.9g; Cholesterol 0mg; Calcium 35mg; Fiber 3.3g; Sodium 29mg.

p400 Corn Tortillas Energy 70Kcal/296kJ; Protein 0.1g; Carbohydrate 18.1g, of which sugars 0g; Fat 0.1g, of which saturates 0g;

Cholesterol 0mg; Calcium 3mg; Fiber 0g; Sodium 10mg.

p401 Flour Tortillas Energy 64Kcal/272kJ; Protein 1.5g; Carbohydrate 12.5g, of which sugars 0.2g; Fat 1.3g, of which saturates 0.5g; Cholesterol 1mg; Calcium 23mg; Fiber 0.5g; Sodium 140mg.

p402 Dhal Puri Energy 237Kcal/1,004kJ; Protein 9.2g; Carbohydrate 40.8g, of which sugars 1.1g; Fat 5.2g, of which saturates 0.6g; Cholesterol 0mg; Calcium 120mg; Fiber 2.8g; Sodium 120mg.

p403 Fried Dumplins Energy 205Kcal/868kJ; Protein 5g; Carbohydrate 36.3g, of which sugars 2.8g; Fat 5.4g, of which saturates 0.9g; Cholesterol 2mg; Calcium 194mg; Fiber 1.4g; Sodium 270mg.

p404 Corn Griddle Cakes Energy 87Kcal/366kJ; Protein 2.2g; Carbohydrate 12.5g, of which sugars 0.2g; Fat 3.5g, of which saturates 1.9g; Cholesterol 9mg; Calcium 50mg; Fiber 0g; Sodium 260mg.

p406 Paraguayan Corn Bread Energy 232Kcal/971kJ; Protein 6.0g; Carbohydrate 24.7g, of which sugars 3.4g; Fat 12.8g, of which saturates 7.6g; Cholesterol 80mg; Calcium 128mg; Fiber 0.3g; Sodium 30mg.

p407 Mexican "Bread of the Dead" (per loaf) Energy 4,071Kcal/1,7154kJ; Protein 86.6g; Carbohydrate 660.6g, of which sugars 146.2g; Fat 123.5g, of which saturates 67g; Cholesterol 949mg; Calcium 1,080mg; Fiber 20.9g; Sodium 2.9g

p408 Mango Quickbread (per loaf) Energy 2,109Kcal/8,815kJ; Protein 27.1g; Carbohydrate 227.4g, of which sugars 118.6g; Fat 127.8g, of which saturates 31.7g; Cholesterol 285mg; Calcium 320mg; Fiber 13.3g; Sodium 1,100mg.

p408 Zucchini Quickbread (per loaf) Energy 5,232Kcal/21,854kJ; Protein 68g; Carbohydrate 543.4g, of which sugars 324.5g; Fat 325g, of which saturates 61.5g; Cholesterol 688mg; Calcium 813mg; Fiber 14.7g; Sodium 1,562mg.

p410 Buñuelos Energy 203Kcal/848kJ; Protein 2.8g; Carbohydrate 25.1g, of which sugars 10.8g; Fat 10.8g, of which saturates 3.2g; Cholesterol 29mg; Calcium 47mg; Fiber 0.6g; Sodium 38mg.

p412 Garbanzo Cake Energy

277Kcal/1,172kJ; Protein 9.2g; Carbohydrate 50.7g, of which sugars 40.2g; Fat 5.7g, of which saturates 1.2g; Cholesterol 127mg; Calcium 68mg; Fiber 2.7g; Sodium 197mg.

p413 Pecan Cake Energy 421Kcal/1,755kJ; Protein 5.6g; Carbohydrate 34.7g, of which sugars 27.4g; Fat 29.9g, of which saturates 12.4g; Cholesterol 139mg; Calcium 48mg; Fiber 1g; Sodium 163mg.

p414 Caribbean Fruit and Rum Cake (per cake) Energy 10,871Kcal/45,678kJ; Protein 146.1g; Carbohydrate 1,526.5g, of which sugars 1,192.2g; Fat 448g, of which saturates 254.6g; Cholesterol 3.3g; Calcium 2,987mg; Fiber 49.8g; Sodium 5.92g.

p415 Apple and Cinnamon Crumble Cake (per cake) Energy 7,217Kcal/30,269kJ; Protein 89.9g; Carbohydrate 929.9g, of which sugars 500.3g; Fat 374.7g, of which saturates 233.7g; Cholesterol 1.7g; Calcium 2,062mg; Fiber 34.1g; Sodium 4.22g.

p416 Banana and Pecan Bread (per loaf) Energy 3,277Kcal/13,745kJ; Protein 52.8g; Carbohydrate 413.7g, of which sugars 239.9g; Fat 168.2g, of which saturates 69.2g; Cholesterol 1,263mg; Calcium 1,056mg; Fiber 13.1g; Sodium 1,701mg.

p417 Pumpkin and Walnut Bread (per loaf) Energy 2,663Kcal/11,186kJ; Protein 66.8g; Carbohydrate 364.1g, of which sugars 94.4g; Fat 114.7g, of which saturates 36.1g; Cholesterol 677mg; Calcium 840mg; Fiber 18.5g; Sodium 1,516mg.

p418 Nutty Chocolate Squares Energy 180Kcal/749kJ; Protein 2.6g; Carbohydrate 16.1g, of which sugars 13.3g; Fat 12.1g, of which saturates 3.2g; Cholesterol 31mg; Calcium 30mg; Fiber 0.7g; Sodium 52mg.

p419 Pecan Squares Energy 245Kcal/1,016kJ; Protein 2.1g; Carbohydrate 15.5g, of which sugars 10.5g; Fat 19.8g, of which saturates 7.6g; Cholesterol 33mg; Calcium 26mg; Fiber 0.8g; Sodium 71mg.

p420 Barbadian Coconut Sweet Bread (per cake) Energy 4,078Kcal/17,076kJ; Protein 59.2g; Carbohydrate 473.7g, of which sugars 154.2g; Fat 229.5g, of which saturates 156.9g; Cholesterol 609mg; Calcium 1,373mg; Fiber 28.9g; Sodium 2.06g.

p421 Duckanoo Energy 827Kcal/3,499kJ; Protein 7.3g;

Carbohydrate 161.4g, of which sugars 57.9g; Fat 21.5g, of which saturates 15g; Cholesterol 36mg; Calcium 224mg; Fiber 2.4g; Sodium 220mg.

p422 Cornmeal and Fennel Seed Cake Energy 514Kcal/2,170kJ; Protein 10.4g; Carbohydrate 94.7g, of which sugars 38.2g; Fat 12.9g, of which saturates 6.3g; Cholesterol 179mg; Calcium 163mg; Fiber 1.1g; Sodium 630mg.

p422 Banana Bread (per loaf) Energy 2,444Kcal/10,218kJ; Protein 41.4g; Carbohydrate 259.4g, of which sugars 124.4g; Fat 144.9g, of which saturates 67.1g; Cholesterol 714mg; Calcium 782mg; Fiber 9.4g; Sodium 1.5g.

p424 Kings' Day Bread Energy 444Kcal/1,868kJ; Protein 8.3g; Carbohydrate 65g, of which sugars 38.8g; Fat 18.7g, of which saturates 10g; Cholesterol 178mg; Calcium 122mg; Fiber 2.4g; Sodium 344mg.

p426 Pan Dulce Energy 366Kcal/1,538kJ; Protein 7.3g; Carbohydrate 53.7g, of which sugars 17.8g; Fat 15.1g, of which saturates 8.4g; Cholesterol 112mg; Calcium 100mg; Fiber 1.5g; Sodium 119mg.

p427 Almond Cookies Energy 93Kcal/391kJ; Protein 1g; Carbohydrate 11.5g, of which sugars 7.8g; Fat 5.2g, of which saturates 2.6g; Cholesterol 10mg; Calcium 16mg; Fiber 0.3g; Sodium 30mg.

p430 Fruits of the Tropics Salad Energy 154Kcal/658kJ; Protein 1.3g; Carbohydrate 39.0g, of which saturates 0.1g; Cholesterol 0mg; Calcium 31mg; Fiber 4.1g; Sodium 40mg.

p431 Coconut Ice Cream Energy 253Kcal/1,065kJ; Protein 8.6g; Carbohydrate 34.5g, of which sugars 34.5g; Fat 9.9g, of which saturates 6.2g; Cholesterol 35mg; Calcium

305mg; Fiber 0g; Sodium 220mg.

p432 Mango Sorbet Energy 176Kcal/753kJ; Protein 1g; Carbohydrate 45.6g, of which sugars 45.4g; Fat 0.2g, of which saturates 0.1g; Cholesterol 0mg; Calcium 13mg; Fiber 2g; Sodium 10mg.

p433 Colombian Pineapple Custard Energy 214Kcal/908kJ; Protein 5.3g; Carbohydrate 40.5g, of which sugars 40.5g; Fat 4.6g, of which saturates 1.3g; Cholesterol 156mg; Calcium 38mg; Fiber 0.7g; Sodium 60mg.

p434 Churros Energy 101Kcal/421kJ; Protein 1.6g; Carbohydrate 12.4g, of which sugars 1.3g; Fat 5.3g, of which saturates 0.7g; Cholesterol 17mg; Calcium 23mg; Fiber 0.5g; Sodium 42mg.

p434 Sopaipillas Energy 77Kcal/319kJ; Protein 0.7g; Carbohydrate 5.8g, of which sugars 0.1g; Fat 5.8g, of which saturates 0.6g; Cholesterol 0mg; Calcium 11mg; Fiber 0.2g; Sodium 72mg.

p436 Coconut Cream Tart Energy 420Kcal/1,751kJ; Protein 6.3g; Carbohydrate 37g, of which sugars 23.6g; Fat 28.5g, of which saturates 19.1g; Cholesterol 87mg; Calcium 144mg; Fiber 2.9g; Sodium 101mg.

p437 Lemon Coconut Layer Cake Energy 727Kcal/3,044kJ; Protein 9.7g; Carbohydrate 86.1g, of which sugars 65.9g; Fat 40.7g, of which saturates 27g; Cholesterol 244mg; Calcium 96mg; Fiber 3.7g; Sodium 236mg.

p438 Caramel Custard Energy 341Kcal/1,444kJ; Protein 12.2g; Carbohydrate 58.4g, of which sugars 58.4g; Fat 8.4g, of which saturates 3.3g; Cholesterol 200mg; Calcium 254mg; Fiber 0g; Sodium 145mg.

p440 Cold Mango Soufflé Topped with Toasted Coconut Energy 615Kcal/2,566kJ; Protein 4.9g; Carbohydrate 53.9g, of which sugars 53.4g; Fat 43.8g, of which saturates 26.3g; Cholesterol 205mg; Calcium 118mg; Fiber 3.9g; Sodium 39mg.

p441 Almond Pudding with Custard Energy 407Kcal/1,708kJ; Protein 9.1g; Carbohydrate 49.6g, of which sugars 49.6g; Fat 20.7g, of which saturates 11.2g; Cholesterol 234mg; Calcium 123mg; Fiber 0g; Sodium 96mg.

p442 Tapioca Pudding Energy 190Kcal/799kJ; Protein 6.1g; Carbohydrate 25.2g, of which sugars 13.8g; Fat 7.9g, of which saturates 3.7g; Cholesterol 18mg; Calcium

156mg; Fiber 0.2g; Sodium 70mg.

p443 Fried Bananas with Sugar and Rum Energy 290Kcal/1,213kJ; Protein 1.3g; Carbohydrate 34.1g, of which sugars 34.1g; Fat 13.7g, of which saturates 8.6g; Cholesterol 35mg; Calcium 10mg; Fiber 1.1g; Sodium 100mg.

p444 Coconut and Pumpkin Compote Energy 429Kcal/1,811kJ; Protein 2g; Carbohydrate 82.9g, of which sugars 82.2g; Fat 12.2g, of which saturates 10.4g; Cholesterol 0mg; Calcium 51mg; Fiber 4g; Sodium 100mg.

p444 Dulce de Leche Energy 323Kcal/1,357kJ; Protein 11.3g; Carbohydrate 42.7g, of which sugars 42.7g; Fat 13g, of which saturates 8.1g; Cholesterol 47mg; Calcium 387mg; Fiber 0g; Sodium 210mg.

p446 Pumpkin in Brown Sugar Energy 247Kcal/1,054kJ; Protein 1.2g; Carbohydrate 63.9g, of which sugars 63.2g; Fat 0.3g, of which saturates 0.1g; Cholesterol 0mg; Calcium 70mg; Fiber 1.3g; Sodium 4mg.

p447 Coconut Custard Energy 593Kcal/2,474kJ; Protein 12.6g; Carbohydrate 48.3g, of which sugars 48.1g; Fat 40.3g, of which saturates 25.7g; Cholesterol 165mg; Calcium 233mg; Fiber 4.6g; Sodium 119mg.

p448 Fruit Platter Energy 235Kcal/999kJ; Protein 3.3g; Carbohydrate 47.8g, of which sugars 42.8g; Fat 4.8g, of which saturates 0.2g; Cholesterol 0mg; Calcium 84mg; Fiber 6.5g; Sodium 90mg.

p448 Ice Cream with Mexican Chocolate Energy 823Kcal/3,420kJ; Protein 8.6g; Carbohydrate 52.4g, of which sugars 52.1g; Fat 65.9g, of which saturates 39.7g; Cholesterol 256mg; Calcium 151mg; Fiber 0.7g; Sodium 89mg.

p450 Capirotada Energy 555Kcal/2,332kJ; Protein 12.5g; Carbohydrate 72.6g, of which sugars 45.6g; Fat 24.5g, of which saturates 11.4g; Cholesterol 45mg; Calcium 258mg; Fiber 2.4g; Sodium 534mg.

p450 Drunken Plantain Energy 244Kcal/1,021kJ; Protein 2.6g; Carbohydrate 29.7g, of which sugars 13.6g; Fat 11.7g, of which saturates 4.8g; Cholesterol 18mg; Calcium 33mg; Fiber 1.5g; Sodium 56mg.

p452 Caribbean Spiced Rice Pudding Energy 304Kcal/1,288kJ; Protein 8.6g; Carbohydrate 53.9g, of which sugars 37.4g; Fat 7.6g, of which saturates 4.5g; Cholesterol 20mg; Calcium 266mg; Fiber 0.4g; Sodium 110mg.

p453 Jamaican Fruit Trifle Energy 400Kcal/1,664kJ; Protein 2.2g; Carbohydrate 29.1g, of which sugars 28.9g; Fat 30.4g, of which saturates 19.4g; Cholesterol 80mg; Calcium 70mg; Fiber 3.9g; Sodium 20mg.

p454 Brazilian Coconut Flan Energy 334Kcal/1,398kJ; Protein 5.6g; Carbohydrate 36.6g, of which sugars 36.6g; Fat 19.4g, of which saturates 11.2g; Cholesterol 312mg; Calcium 62mg; Fiber 1.7g; Sodium 50mg.

p456 Mexican Wedding Cookies Energy 147Kcal/615kJ; Protein 1.5g; Carbohydrate 14.2g, of which sugars 6.5g; Fat 9.8g, of which saturates 4.2g; Cholesterol 16mg; Calcium 22mg; Fiber 0.5g; Sodium 46mg.

p456 Almond Orange Cookies Energy 148Kcal/617kJ; Protein 2.3g; Carbohydrate 12.1g, of which sugars 5.6g; Fat 10.4g, of which saturates 3.1g; Cholesterol 17mg; Calcium 29mg; Fiber 0.7g; Sodium 6mg.

p458 Rum and Banana Waffles Energy 826Kcal/3,466kJ; Protein 17.4g; Carbohydrate 106.8g, of which sugars 60.7g; Fat 36.9g, of which saturates 10.6g; Cholesterol 148mg; Calcium 275mg; Fiber 4.4g; Sodium 223mg.

p460 Fruit-filled Empanadas Energy 256Kcal/1,078kJ; Protein 3.3g; Carbohydrate 43.6g, of which sugars 18.2g; Fat 8.8g, of which saturates 5.2g; Cholesterol 37mg; Calcium 49mg; Fiber 1.5g; Sodium 73mg.

P461 Christmas Cookies with Walnuts Energy 148Kcal/617kJ; Protein 2.3g; Carbohydrate 12.1g, of which sugars 5.6g; Fat 10.4g, of which saturates 3.1g; Cholesterol 17mg; Calcium 29mg; Fiber 0.7g; Sodium 6mg.

p462 Nut Brittle Energy 239Kcal/1,005kJ; Protein 6.5g; Carbohydrate 29.3g, of which sugars 27.2g; Fat 11.5g, of which saturates 2.2g; Cholesterol 00mg; Calcium 22mg; Fiber 1.5g; Sodium 2mg.

p462 Coconut Sweets Energy 40Kcal/168kJ; Protein 0.1g; Carbohydrate 7.4g, of which sugars 7.4g; Fat 1.2g, of which saturates 1.1g; Cholesterol 0mg; Calcium 3mg; Fiber 0.3g; Sodium 1mg.

p466 Mango Shake Energy 667Kcal/2,793kJ; Protein 26.9g; Carbohydrate 76.2g, of which sugars 75.3g; Fat 29.9g, of which saturates 19.1g; Cholesterol 105mg; Calcium 922mg; Fiber 7.8g; Sodium 330mg.

p466 Pineapple and Mint Juice Energy 113Kcal/485kJ; Protein 2g; Carbohydrate 26.6g, of which sugars 25.3g; Fat 0.7g, of which saturates 0g; Cholesterol 0mg; Calcium 98mg; Fiber 3g; Sodium 10mg.

p468 Cashew Nut Milk Energy 805Kcal/3,397kJ; Protein 29.4g; Carbohydrate 136.6g, of which sugars 133g; Fat 19.2g, of which saturates 2.4g; Cholesterol 0mg; Calcium 192mg; Fiber 2.4g; Sodium 390mg.

p469 Passion Fruit Batida Energy 151Kcal/631kJ; Protein 0.8g; Carbohydrate 9.6g, of which sugars 9.6g; Fat 0.1g, of which saturates 0g; Cholesterol 0mg; Calcium 4mg; Fiber 1g; Sodium 10mg.

p470 Citrus Agua Fresca Energy 106Kcal/452kJ; Protein 0.6g; Carbohydrate 27.5g, of which sugars 27.5g; Fat 0.1g, of which saturates 0g; Cholesterol 0mg; Calcium 23mg; Fiber 0.1g; Sodium 9mg.

p471 Tamarind Agua Fresca Energy 68Kcal/287kJ; Protein 2.9g; Carbohydrate 14.5g, of which sugars 14.5g; Fat 0.2g, of which saturates 0g; Cholesterol 0mg; Calcium 23mg; Fiber 1.6g; Sodium 136mg.

p472 Pineapple and Lime Agua Fresca Energy 131Kcal/564kJ; Protein 0.7g; Carbohydrate 34.1g, of which sugars 34.1g; Fat 0.2g, of which saturates 0g; Cholesterol 0mg; Calcium 23mg; Fiber 0g; Sodium 17mg.

p473 Lime Agua Fresca Energy 52Kcal/221kJ; Protein 0.2g; Carbohydrate 13.6g, of which sugars 13.6g; Fat 0g, of which saturates 0g; Cholesterol 0mg; Calcium 9mg; Fiber 0g; Sodium 1mg.

p474 Pisco Sour Energy 187Kcal/783kJ; Protein 2.9g; Carbohydrate 15.8g, of which sugars 15.8g; Fat 0g, of which saturates 0g; Cholesterol 0mg; Calcium 3mg; Fiber 0g; Sodium 60mg.

p474 Caipirinha Energy 176Kcal/736kJ; Protein 0g; Carbohydrate 15.8g, of which sugars 15.8g; Fat 0g, of which saturates 0g; Cholesterol 0mg; Calcium 2mg; Fiber 0g; Sodium 0mg.

p476 Tequila Energy 111Kcal/460kJ; Protein 0g; Carbohydrate 2g, of which sugars 1.5g; Fat 0g, of which saturates 0g; Cholesterol 0mg; Calcium 0mg; Fiber 0g; Sodium 0mg.

p477 Tequila Sunrise Energy 90Kcal/377kJ; Protein 0.3g; Carbohydrate 6.9g, of which sugars 6.9g; Fat 0.1g, of which saturates 0g; Cholesterol 0mg; Calcium 6mg; Fiber 0.1g; Sodium 7mg.

p478 Pineapple Tequila Energy 403Kcal/1,672kJ; Protein 0.1g; Carbohydrate 8.7g, of which sugars 8.7g; Fat 0g, of which saturates 0g; Cholesterol 0mg; Calcium 5mg; Fiber 0g; Sodium 1mg.

p479 Margarita Energy 167Kcal/696kJ; Protein 0.1g; Carbohydrate 8.6g, of which sugars 8.6g; Fat 0g, of which saturates 0g; Cholesterol 0mg; Calcium 3mg; Fiber 0g; Sodium 3mg.

p480 Mango and Peach Margarita Energy 167Kcal/704kJ; Protein 1.1g; Carbohydrate 19.7g, of which sugars 19.5g; Fat 0.2g, of which saturates 0.1g; Cholesterol 0mg; Calcium 15mg; Fiber 2.8g; Sodium 4mg.

p481 Licuado de Melon Energy 37Kcal/157kJ; Protein 0.2g; Carbohydrate 9.5g, of which sugars 9.5g; Fat 0.1g, of which saturates 0g; Cholesterol 0mg; Calcium 3mg; Fiber 0g; Sodium 2mg.

p482 Mojito Energy 226Kcal/941kJ; Protein 0g; Carbohydrate 15.8g, of which sugars 15.8g; Fat 0g, of which saturates 0g; Cholesterol 0mg; Calcium 2mg; Fiber 0g; Sodium 0mg.

p482 Cubra Libre Energy 130Kcal/542kJ; Protein 0g; Carbohydrate 8.1g, of which sugars 8.1g; Fat 0g, of which saturates 0g; Cholesterol 0mg; Calcium 4mg; Fiber 0g; Sodium 0mg.

p484 Strawberry and Banana Prepado Energy 341Kcal/1,413kJ; Protein 2.6g; Carbohydrate 14.3g, of which sugars 13.4g; Fat 20g, of which saturates 17.1g; Cholesterol 0mg; Calcium 17mg; Fiber 1g; Sodium 12mg.

p485 Bloody Maria Energy 84Kcal/353kJ; Protein 1g; Carbohydrate 3.8g, of which sugars 3.8g; Fat 0g, of which saturates 0g; Cholesterol 0mg; Calcium 13mg;

Fiber 0.8g; Sodium 288mg.

p486 Sangrita Energy 73Kcal/305kJ; Protein 0.6g; Carbohydrate 3.7g, of which sugars 3.5g; Fat 0.2g, of which saturates 0.1g; Cholesterol 0mg; Calcium 7mg; Fiber 0.7g; Sodium 7mg.

p487 Sangria Energy 170Kcal/708kJ; Protein 0.3g; Carbohydrate 10.7g, of which sugars 10.7g; Fat 0g, of which saturates 0g; Cholesterol 0mg; Calcium 15mg; Fiber 0g; Sodium 11mg.

p488 Raw Sugar Rum Punch Energy 237Kcal/993kJ; Protein 1.4g; Carbohydrate 24.1g, of which sugars 24.1g; Fat 0.3g, of which saturates 0g; Cholesterol 0g: Calcium 20mg; Fiber 0mg; Sodium 10mg.

p489 Caribbean Cream Stout Punch Energy 466Kcal/1,950kJ; Protein 16.8g; Carbohydrate 37.7g, of which sugars 37.7g; Fat 17.9g, of which saturates 11.2g; Cholesterol 65mg; Calcium 556mg; Fiber 0g; Sodium 340mg.

p490 Cafe con Leche Energy 79Kcal/337kJ; Protein 4.1g; Carbohydrate 12.1g, of which sugars 12.1g; Fat 2g, of which saturates 1.3g; Cholesterol 7mg; Calcium 146mg; Fiber 0g; Sodium 52mg.

p490 Horchata Energy 683Kcal/2,850kJ; Protein 16.3g; Carbohydrate 105.4g, of which sugars 14.6g; Fat 21.5g, of which saturates 1.7g; Cholesterol 0mg; Calcium 118mg; Fiber 2.8g; Sodium 6mg.

p492 Cafe de Olla Energy 118Kcal/503kJ; Protein 1.1g; Carbohydrate 30.3g, of which sugars 30.1g; Fat 0g, of which saturates 0g; Cholesterol 0mg; Calcium 24mg; Fiber 0g; Sodium 7mg.

p492 Atole Energy 161Kcal/675kJ; Protein 3.3g; Carbohydrate 34.2g, of which sugars 9.9g; Fat 1.1g, of which saturates 0g; Cholesterol 0mg; Calcium 9mg; Fiber 1g; Sodium 2mg.

p494 Champurrada Energy 240Kcal/1,007kJ; Protein 4.1g; Carbohydrate 41.8g, of which sugars 17.2g; Fat 6.5g, of which saturates 3.2g; Cholesterol 1mg; Calcium 19mg; Fiber 1.2g; Sodium 2mg.

p495 Mexican Hot Chocolate Energy 179Kcal/755kJ; Protein 9.1g; Carbohydrate 19.7g, of which sugars 19.6g; Fat 7.8g, of which saturates 4.8g; Cholesterol 16mg; Calcium 304mg; Fiber 0.3g; Sodium 108mg.

INDEX